Modern Business Administration

Modern Business Administration

SIXTH EDITION

Robert C. Appleby BSc Econ (London), ACIS

Worcester College of Technology

PITMAN PUBLISHING
128 Long Acre, London WC2E 9AN

A Division of Pearson Professional Limited

First published in Great Britain 1969
Sixth edition 1994

© R C Appleby 1969, 1972, 1976, 1981, 1987, 1991, 1994

British Library Cataloguing in Publication Data
Appleby, Robert C.
Modern business administration – 6th ed.
1. Business firms. Management
I. Title
658

ISBN 0-273-60282-9

10 9 8 7 6 5

Typeset by PanTek Arts, Maidstone, Kent
Printed and bound in Singapore

CONTENTS

List of figures   viii
Preface   ix
Acknowledgements   xii

**Part 1
MANAGEMENT PRINCIPLES**

1 Nature of management   3

Objectives   4
Problems of terminology   5
Science or art?   6
Management – a profession?   8
Management – a universal process?   9
Development of management thought   10
Elements of management   24
The manager today   26
Time management   30
Excellence in management   31
Management for the future   32
Summary   34
Review questions   35
Review problems   35
Assignments   36
Bibliography   36

**2 Business and its external
environment**   37

Objectives   38
Nature of business activity   38
Business and the economic structure   42
Economic systems   44
Structure of industry   45
Location of industry   46
Stock Exchange   47
Share capital   48
Sources of finance   50
Other institutions providing finance   54
International management   56

Environmental management   60
External environment of organizations   64
Social responsibilities of management   68
Business ethics   70
Multinational companies   71
The Single European Market   74
Exporting to Central and Eastern Europe   75
Comparative management   77
Small business management   78
Summary   81
Review questions   83
Review problems   83
Assignments   84
Bibliography   84

3 Corporate strategy and planning   85

Objectives   86
Planning   86
Forecasting   87
Objectives   91
Policies   95
Planning in practice   97
Corporate planning   101
Analysis of risk and sensitivity   105
Management in a non-profit-making
   organization   106
Management by Objectives (MBO)   107
Decision making   111
Management Information Systems (MIS)   123
Summary   128
Review questions   129
Review problems   130
Assignments   130
Bibliography   131

4 Organizing   132

Objectives   133
Organizing   133
Organizational structure   133

Bureaucratic organization 135
Levels of organization 136
Principles of organization 138
Departmentation 139
Span of control 142
Types of organizational structure 144
Modifications to structure 148
Authority and responsibility 154
Delegation 157
Decentralization of authority 159
Assignment of activities to departments 160
Aids to organization design 161
Organizational change 166
Conflict in organizations 167
The management of change 168
Organizational development (OD) 170
Other forms of organization structure 175
Organization as a system 177
Summary 179
Review questions 180
Review problems 181
Assignments 182
Bibliography 182

5 Directing   **183**

Objectives 184
Nature of directing 184
Leadership 190
Behavioural theories of leadership 191
Co-ordination 197
Motivation 199
Morale and discipline 203
Communication 204
Summary 210
Review questions 211
Review problems 212
Assignments 212
Bibliography 213

6 Controlling   **214**

Objectives 215
Principles of effective control 216
Types of control 217
Accounting 227
Advanced control techniques 244

Summary 254
Review questions 256
Review problems 256
Assignments 257
Bibliography 257

Part 2
MANAGEMENT IN ACTION

7 Marketing and sales management   **261**

Objectives 262
Marketing 262
Marketing organization and administration 263
Organization of the home trade 270
Distribution 278
Market research, advertising and publicity 283
Sales management 294
Pricing theory 299
International marketing 302
Summary 306
Review questions 307
Review problems 308
Assignments 310
Bibliography 310

8 Production and operations management   **312**

Objectives 313
Production 313
Types of production 314
Factory location and layout 315
Production organization 317
Materials handling 345
Automation 346
Newer developments in production 350
Summary 354
Review questions 355
Review problems 356
Assignments 358
Bibliography 358

9 Human resource management   **359**

Objectives 360
Human resource management (HRM) 360

Position of human resources manager
  in organization   362
Human resources policy   363
Manpower planning   364
Recruitment   367
Selection and employment   372
Induction and training   376
Promotion and transfer   397
Wage and salary administration   397
Job restructuring   403
Termination of contracts   405
Employee services   409
Health and safety at work   409
Industrial relations   413
The nature of goals and goal conflict   416
Work roles   421
Training and Enterprise Councils   424
Investors in People (IIP) – a national
  standard   424
Summary   425
Review questions   427
Review problems   428
Assignments   432
Bibliography   432

10 Administrative management   433
Objectives   434
Responsibility for office work   435
Planning and organizing the office   436
Organization and methods (O and M)   439
Office machinery and equipment   444
The future of the office   466
Human aspects of computer usage   467
Security, data protection and audit   468
Management services   471
Electronic Data Interchange (EDI)   476
Summary   477
Review questions   478
Review problems   480
Assignments   481
Bibliography   481

Further review problems relating to
Chapters 1–10   482

Appendix: Brief hints for examination students   484

Glossary of management terms   485

Index   488

LIST OF FIGURES

1.1 The systems approach provides an integrative framework for modern organizational theory and management practice *20*

1.2 A systems approach showing some inter-relationships required *22*

2.1 Flow of resources, goods and services *43*

2.2 Environmental forces impacting on business *59*

2.3 Influence of central government activities on business organizations in the United Kingdom *64*

2.4 The 'black box' *67*

3.1 Simple cycle of business activity *88*

3.2 Hierarchy of organizational objectives and plans *99*

3.3 Long-range profit gap *104*

3.4 Management by Objectives *109*

3.5 Pie chart *121*

3.6 Decision tree *122*

3.7 Decision tree *123*

3.8 Data sources – internal and external *125*

4.1 Organizational pyramid *137*

4.2 Departments in a manufacturing company *140*

4.3 Spans of control *145*

4.4 Matrix organizational structure *148*

4.5 Clover-leaf organizational structure *153*

4.6 Circular organizational structure *154*

4.7 Types of organization charts *163*

4.8 Organization chart *165*

4.9 Interacting factors which govern the behaviour of organizations *171*

5.1 A continuum of leadership behaviour *192*

5.2 A functional leadership approach *195*

5.3 Hierarchy of needs *199*

5.4 Communication as a pattern of inter-connecting lines or networks *206*

6.1 Planning–control feedback cycle *215*

6.2 Budgetary control procedure *219*

6.3 A break-even chart *224*

6.4 An accounting information system *229*

6.5 Circular flow of funds showing sources and applications *237*

6.6 Constituents of return on investment *238*

6.7 Simple illustration of a network *251*

7.1 Elements of marketing mix *266*

7.2 Total market approach using single marketing mix *267*

7.3 Market segmentation approach *267*

7.4 (a) Organization chart for medium to large company; (b) Organization chart emphasizing products sold *269*

7.5 Main channels for manufactured goods *271*

7.6 Summary of main retail trading outlets *272–3*

7.7 Comparison of main methods of distribution open to manufacturer *279*

7.8 Plan of alternative supply routes *281*

7.9 Life-cycle of a product *291*

7.10 Relative competitive position (market share) *292*

8.1 Organization chart for a medium-sized factory *317*

8.2 Optimum quality design *327*

8.3 Director of supplies *339*

9.1 Functions of a human resources department *361*

9.2 Stages of manpower planning *366*

9.3 Aspects of job design *370*

9.4 Analysis of needs for management development and training *377*

9.5 Improving management performance *385*

9.6 Methods of training managers *388*

9.7 The experiential learning model *390*

9.8 Management training techniques *391–3*

10.1 Office services department. Organization chart *436*

10.2 Standard charting symbols *441*

10.3 Data processing system. Computer installation *453*

10.4 Stages of processing data *454*

10.5 Control by PBX network *461*

10.6 Single work station *461*

10.7 Management services section *474*

PREFACE

The subject of management and administration is so vast that one book alone cannot be sufficient to impart more than an outline. An outline, though, is all this book attempts to present. This book should be regarded as a key, explaining succinctly the important aspects of management.

Management is a process which is constantly changing as the results of continuous research are made available and incorporated in management knowledge.

The treatment is brief, simple, factual and practical; unimportant words have been omitted and the latest ideas and techniques have been incorporated. The book should provide a firm basis for the subject and point the way to further specialist reading, which is indicated in the bibliographies at the end of each chapter. If readers are encouraged and stimulated to read further, then this in itself is a satisfactory result.

The author has been encouraged by comments from students and lecturers and the continued demand for this book. This new edition seeks to take into account the changes that have recently occurred in professional and other examinations and those that will come into force from the examinations in 1994.

The responsibilities and activities of managers are becoming more complex each year due to new techniques and knowledge, the technology of information processing and the uncertainty of the external environment.

This *sixth edition* has incorporated as many of the latest ideas and developments as possible.

The structure of the new edition is still mainly based upon the classical approach as this has proved to be an excellent framework for analysing the subject, although other approaches are included and integrated. The author has made choices about content partly because of the specific examination requirements of certain professional syllabi and partly through personal interest and concern for aspects which are not covered adequately in the many other texts which are available that attempt to cover this very wide and fascinating area of knowledge.

The book covers the changes in the syllabi for the following professional examinations:

- Institute of Chartered Secretaries and Administrators;
- Chartered Association of Certified Accountants;
- Chartered Institute of Management Accountants;
- Institute of Administrative Management;
- Association of Accounting Technicians;
- Society of Commercial Accountants;
- Institute of Business Executives;
- Institute of Bankers in England, Wales and Scotland;

- Certified Diploma in Accounting and Finance;
- Association of International Accountants;
- Institute of Management Services;
- Institute of Industrial Managers;
- Institute of Purchasing and Supply.

The topics in the book cover in many cases more than one examination subject in a number of professional associations.

Changes in the structure of subjects in the Business and Technician Education Council examinations have been noted and the book should continue to be of great assistance to the following examinations:

- senior secretarial courses;
- BTEC National and Higher National levels;
- Certificate and Diploma in Management Studies;
- National Examinations Board in Supervisory Management;
- Institute of Supervisory Management;
- degree and post-experience courses.

Most examination bodies have recommended the book either as a basic textbook or for supplementary reading and it is hoped that this new edition will continue to give a *clear and uncomplicated introduction to the principles and practices of management* and encourage readers to pursue the topics in more detail by the use of the carefully selected bibliography.

The main areas of updating in this sixth edition include:

- small business management;
- business ethics;
- the Single European Market and trade in Eastern Europe;
- environmental legislation;
- management of change;
- managing non-profit organizations;
- electronic trading;
- total quality management.

The number of assignments have been increased and the Glossary expanded.

Pedagogical aids. Chapters in the text are designed to stand on their own so teachers can deal with the topics in any order. A large number of cross-references are made to aid the integration of the subject areas.

Objectives. Each chapter begins with a list of the major learning objectives, which can be used as a study aid.

Summary. Summaries at the end of each chapter repeat and provide a brief response to the chapter learning objectives. The summaries emphasize material that is important for present and future managers to have learned.

Review questions. These follow each chapter and are a study aid.

Review problems. These are based upon typical examination questions, and some could be used as a basis for assignments.

Bibliography. This has been carefully selected to enable in-depth consideration of topics.

Glossary. This defines key words that are often used. Mutual understanding of these words forms the basis of communication of facts and ideas.

Key words and phrases. These have been highlighted.

Assignments. These have been included to enable group work to be undertaken and are now at the end of each chapter.

A *Lecturer's Guide* is available free of charge to lecturers who adopt the main book.

The male pronoun is used throughout the book. However, in all cases the word 'he' or 'she', him or her, etc., are interchangeable.

ACKNOWLEDGEMENTS

Thanks are due to Mrs H Berry for her help in the typing of the manuscript.

P F Drucker, for quotations on pages 10 and 94 from *The Practice of Management* (Heinemann).

E F L Brech, for quotations on pages 5 and 6 from *The Principles and Practice of Management* (Longman).

Sir W Brown, for quotation from page 134 from *Exploration in Management* (Heinemann Educational Books Ltd).

The Chartered Institute of Management Accountants, the Chartered Association of Certified and Corporate Accountants, and the Institute of Chartered Secretaries and Administrators, for permission to use recent examination questions.

Scott Bader Co Ltd, for permission to use extracts from their Objectives and Code of Practice (parts of their memorandum).

J Argenti, for the definition of Corporate Planning, *Corporate Planning*, G Allen & Unwin, 1968.

PART 1

Management principles

This part classifies managerial knowledge under the elements of planning, organizing, directing and controlling. There are other classifications but this one is practical and comprehensive. It attempts to explain and analyse the basic science, theory and principles of management and how they relate to the practice of managing.

Part 2 is concerned with the practical side of management and studies the functional or specialist areas of marketing, production and operations management, human resource management and administrative management.

CHAPTER 1

Nature of management

This chapter introduces the concept of management and the elements of management. It identifies major schools of management thought and describes how they evolved. Modern approaches are emphasized and the role of the manager is closely examined.

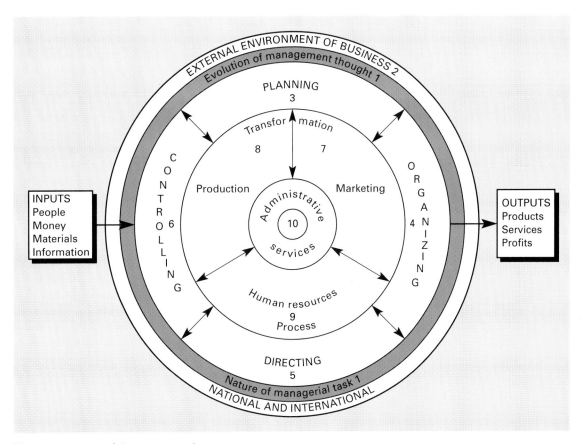

The systems approach to management

OBJECTIVES

Upon completing this chapter you should be able to:

- Describe the concept of management and why it is needed to reach organizational objectives.
- List and describe the basic elements of management.
- Understand the complex nature of the managerial task.
- Identify major schools of management thought and how they have evolved.
- Describe two modern approaches to management that attempt to integrate these various schools.
- State what conclusions can be reached from studies of what managers actually do.

There have been many attempts to describe the contents of the 'job' of management. It has been considered to be a separate activity from the technical functions of production, marketing and finance. Various economists, for example Alfred Marshall, separated it from other factors of production (land, labour and capital). Another economist, J.A. Schumpeter, agreed with the idea that management was a separate entity, being concerned with innovation as well as administration.

In recent years, writers on management have recognized that management deals with a number of variables that are dependent upon each other. These variables will surely increase as companies grow more complex and it will then become more difficult to trace the side-effects of a change in dealing with a specific area of management responsibility.

There are many problems to be solved. Some people try to solve them by considering changes in the *structure* of organizations and the locations of authority and responsibility. Others hope to do it by improving the quality of decisions by new *technological* ideas and the use of modern methods of data processing. Yet another group expects to solve the same problems by concentrating on *human relations*. The vital point to be considered is that the structural, technological and human aspects *cannot be separated* as they all interact. For example, if a firm changes from a functional to a product grouping, problems of interpersonal relations occur. This may in turn affect the techniques of control (i.e. new financial systems may be needed). A knowledge of the above facts should enable a manager to understand that it may not be easy to find a simple answer to a problem but, by acknowledging this fact and using available knowledge wisely, answers can be much more accurate and effective.

This chapter deals with the elements of management, planning, organizing, directing and controlling. Other chapters deal with other activities, including marketing, production, human resource management and administrative organization. The plan of the book which covers diverse areas could vary widely, but the above arrangement is considered to be suitable and helpful for readers who are approaching the subject for the first time.

PROBLEMS OF TERMINOLOGY

The first step in any subject should be to understand the basic terms used, and in many arts and sciences this presents no real problem. In business administration, terms are not precisely defined and some are seen as interchangeable.

The dictionary definition (*Concise Oxford*) of Administration is, 'management', one word being substituted for another. An administrator is a 'manager'; 'one capable of organizing'. Many writers adopt this simple approach and regard the words as interchangeable. This surely should not be allowed to remain the position and indeed cannot in a body of knowledge which people wish to call a science. A precise analysis of theory is possible only when terms are specifically defined.

The words management and administration are defined by writers in accordance with their own needs and purposes. Many other terms used have been in popular use for long periods and have a variety of meanings. A word in country X with *apparently* the same meaning in country Y, may have different *emphasis* owing to the differences in the history of the country's institutions (e.g. president, *président*).

A few of the terms which have varying meanings will be considered here, others will be introduced in the text.

Administration and management

Administration is sometimes used to refer to the activities of the higher level of the management group who determine major aims and policies. This can be called the broader use of the term which is often used in government departments (e.g. the Civil Service). It is also used in the narrower sense, of controlling the day-to-day running of the enterprise.

An administrator can also be a manager; this occurs when the administrator is concerned with implementing policy in dealings with employees to whom responsibilities have been delegated.

Brech defines *administration* as: 'That part of the management process concerned with the institution and carrying out of procedures by which the programme is laid down and communicated, and the progress of activities is regulated and checked against targets and plans.' *Management* has even more meanings than administration. Management can mean:

- a *process* by which scarce resources are combined to achieve given ends. This describes an activity which can be better described by the word *managing;*
- the *management* referring to those people carrying out the activity. This should really be the *managers;*
- the body of knowledge about the *activity of managing,* regarded here as a special field of study, i.e. a *profession.*

Of these three, the first is preferable, management referring to the *process* of management.

A useful approach is to consider management to be a process whereby a suitable environment is created for effort to be organized to accomplish desired goals.

Brech defines *management* as:

. . . a social process entailing responsibility for the effective and economical planning and regulation of the operations of an enterprise, in fulfilment of a given purpose or task, such responsibility involving:

(*a*) judgement and decision in determining plans, and the development of data procedures to assist control of performance and progress against plans; and

(*b*) the guidance, integration, motivation and supervision of the personnel composing the enterprise and carrying out its operations.

It can be seen from the above that the process as a whole is called management – administration being part of it. Students are advised to define the terms in the manner they intend to use them.

The term *top management* usually refers to management above departmental level and is loosely applied to directors.

The word *executive* is correctly used when referring to a person who carries out policy. The phrase *top executive* is used, especially in the USA, for people of a high status, who in fact do no *executive* work at all, as they spend their time formulating policy. (They are of course responsible for executive action done under their jurisdiction.) Where words are associated with status rather than function, precision is impossible.

Organization

There is really no doubt about the present meaning of organizaton. Its purpose is to create an arrangement of positions and responsibilities through and by means of which an enterprise can carry out its work.

Brech's definition is:

. . . the framework of the management process as formed by the definition of:

(*a*) the responsibilities by means of which the activities of the enterprise are dispersed among the (managerial, supervisory and specialist) personnel employed in its service:

(*b*) the formal interrelations established among the personnel by virtue of such responsibilities.

It should be noted that organization should not be regarded as rigid as the term 'framework' implies. Organization structure must be constantly reviewed and note taken of informal relationships which develop.

SCIENCE OR ART?

A great deal of discussion has centred on the question as to whether management is an art or a science. A brief comment is all that need be given on this matter.

The development of any science needs a conceptual framework of theory and principle. Principles of management have existed for a long time, but an acceptable framework to encompass them was needed. A large debt is due to the many writers and researchers who have contributed a great deal to existing principles and accepted practices. It is in the formulation of principles that the science of management can be developed. A management principle distils and organizes knowledge that has been built up through experience and analysis. Management is far from being an exact science at present but, by understanding and applying accepted principles, the quality of management practice can be greatly improved. It is most probable that management will never become wholly an exact science as personal judgement will always be needed to supplement available knowledge; therefore, as a practice, management will always be an art.

In the natural sciences, a theoretical principle is deduced from particular facts which are applicable to a defined group or class and is expressed by a statement that a certain happening *always* occurs if certain conditions are present. Management principles are not fundamental truths, they are *conditional* statements qualified by adverbs, e.g. usually, normally.

It is worthwhile looking briefly at the nature of the two methods of reasoning, deductive and inductive.

Deductive method

The *deductive method* reasons from the general to the particular, i.e. from the attributes of a class it will deduce the attributes of an *individual member* of that class. The following example of deductive reasoning illustrates that if certain facts are admitted as true, then such a thing must be true about the particular case in question, for if it were not so, it would be inconsistent with the fact already admitted as true.

It does mean that premises should be carefully tested before any inference is made from them.

1st premise – All men are mortal
2nd premise – Wilson is a man
Deduction from these premises – Wilson is mortal.

If the deduction is made from false premises, the conclusions are worthless – for example:

All good sailors have beards
Robinson is a good sailor
Therefore he has a beard.

Inductive method

The *inductive* method is the opposite of the deductive.

It starts by *collecting facts* relating to a given point, these facts emerging from observations. Then a statement or *premise* is proposed which is true of all cases observed. For example if, by observation, a number of men – Wilson,

Robinson, Smith, Brown – are discovered to be mortal, we can have confidence in this premise, if a sufficient number of cases have been examined under a variety of circumstances, to see if any conflicting case was noted. A generalization is then built up, or reasoned, regarding the cases in the light of the observed characteristic, e.g. each of the cases examined was a man and therefore all men are mortal. This generalization is no more than a *hypothesis*, the product of inductive thinking, which must now be proved. When the hypothesis is *tested* and no conflicting case found, then a *law* is formulated and this is used to control the present or to predict the future.

Scientific method can be applied to management, for example: the method of inductive thinking can be applied to policy making where work is measurable.

Observation leads to objective examination of present practices; *analysis* breaks them down and studies them; *classification* means comparing them with basic principles and the resultant hypothesis will be an improved new method or practice. A trial run or test will be critically examined and only then accepted and a law formulated.

It can be applied in the management of people, by studying the human factor and observing principles of human relations. This is an important area especially in relation to motivation and co-ordination.

It can also be applied to the manager himself, in developing a scientific attitude of mind towards his problems and the making of his decisions.

MANAGEMENT – A PROFESSION?

In recent years there has been further consideration as to whether management can be regarded as a profession. The conflicting arguments can be considered only if a profession is defined. The following main points seem relevant in the discussion:

- there must exist a body of principles, skills and techniques and specialized knowledge;
- there must be formal methods of acquiring training and experience;
- an organization should be established which forms ethical codes for the guidance and conduct of members.

If the above standards are considered, then management cannot really be called a profession. There are no licences for managers, nor is there an accepted code of ethics, but there are tendencies towards professionalization and these will undoubtedly increase. Mary Parker Follett regarded a profession as connoting a foundation of science and a *motive of service*.

P F Drucker does not agree that it is desirable for management to be a profession. He states: 'management is a practice, rather than a science or profession, though containing elements of both'. He feels that economic performance and achievement are the proper aims of management and that a manager's primary responsibility is to manage a business. A manager should not, therefore, devote time to objectives such as professionalism which lie *outside* the enterprise.

The solution may lie in a balanced approach. At present there are trends towards professionalism, seen in the development of skills and techniques, more formal training facilities and the greater use of management *consultants* and specialized associations.

There have been attempts in a number of countries to specify codes of conduct for managers.

In 1974 The British Institute of Management put forward such a code for individual members of that institute; in addition, there were guides to good practice and a disciplinary structure. Only a few of the points can be mentioned here.

The Institute stressed that managers have to balance their obligations to the undertaking which employs them with the community at large, with other employees, suppliers, consumers, and their own conscience. The Institute believes that because of the growing professionalism of managers there is a need for such a code of conduct. Brief details are noted below:

- to act loyally and honestly in carrying out the policy of the organization and not undermine its image or reputation;
- to accept responsibility for their own work and that of their subordinates;
- not to abuse their authority for personal gain;
- not to injure or attempt to injure the professional reputation, prospects or business of others;
- always to comply strictly with the law and operate within the spirit of the law;
- to order their conduct so as to uphold the dignity, standing and reputation of the Institute.

Other points refer to dealing honestly with the public, promoting the increase in competence and the standing of the profession of management, and recognizing that the organization has obligations to owners, employees, suppliers, customers, users and the general public.

Guides to good practice include:

- establishing objectives for themselves and their subordinates which do not conflict with the organization's overall objectives;
- respecting confidentiality of information and not using it for personal gain;
- making full disclosure of a personal interest to their employer.

Other points refer to helping and training subordinates, ensuring their safety and well-being, honouring contracts to customers and suppliers, ensuring correct information is produced, not tolerating any corrupt practices, and finally to setting up a disciplinary structure to implement the code.

MANAGEMENT – A UNIVERSAL PROCESS?

It was previously noted that a suitable environment is desirable in order to apply the principles of management effectively. Environments differ, and it has to be considered whether management problems vary with the environment and whether management skills can be effectively transferred. A point worth further thought is that in privately owned and capitalistic enterprises, which have reasonable freedom from government control and influence, managers are free to make the basic decisions necessary for profitable operations and where the risk of wrong decisions is accepted by owners and management. The profit motive and free competition make up the system now largely in operation and this book is based upon these assumptions. It can be realized that, where government influence increases, managers are less free to make decisions and many principles may be affected.

If one agrees that management is a universal process, i.e. a fundamental process with universal characteristics and principles, it appears that management skills are transferable, and a manager can successfully apply his knowledge and skill in a wide variety of industries. It implies that general principles are at work and that detailed specialist work in the various businesses can later be absorbed. It then appears to follow that all types of organizations can benefit from such universality, even non-profit-making concerns.

P F Drucker holds the opposite view. He considers that management skill and experience, as such, cannot be applied to the running of different institutions, as the main objective of business is profit, consistent with its security, and stability. This differs from a non-business organization, whose officers do not have the responsibility for producing goods and services or maintaining wealth-producing resources.

Ernest Dale is another who does not agree with this idea of universality – if one considers this to be a theory of universal principles applicable in every field. He does not believe any one person could be a good administrator in academic, business, military or religious concerns, as the underlying philosophy in each constitution is so varied in nature and it is not possible for *one person* to know so much.

It appears to the writer that all resources needed by organizations are scarce and even non-business organizations must allocate men, materials and equipment, time and money to varying needs and aims. This can be done only by managers using their skill and knowledge and to this extent it seems that management skills are transferable.

DEVELOPMENT OF MANAGEMENT THOUGHT

Management is an applied technique and is closely related to many allied fields, e.g. economics. Disciplines devoted to studying people, e.g. psychology, sociology and political science, have grown and generated an expansion of management knowledge.

The development of management thought can, for convenience, be considered to comprise four main periods – early influences, the scientific management movement, the human relations movement, and modern influences, e.g. the revisionist movement.

There are many writers on management subjects and a great volume of interesting material is being published. While many of the ideas may be valid for the particular survey, it does not mean that the idea can be used or introduced in *any* organization.

There are many reasons for this, e.g. the statistical base may be suspect, the organization studied, the nationality, etc., may produce different results in a different environment. So findings in one area or country may not necessarily be valid for other areas or countries. Points to consider are:

- the *age of those in the survey* – older persons have different ideas, e.g. on job security;
- the *age of the survey* – many important writings, e.g. those of Fayol, were published many years ago; are they therefore still relevant today?
- changes in the *law* since the date of the original research may affect conclusions drawn, e.g. attitudes and practices changed after the 1975 Employee Protection Act;
- work done in *one country* may not be the same as in another country with different characteristics;
- surveys based upon *women* may not produce the same results as those based on men.

Other points to note before deciding to introduce new ideas into an organization are: is the period in question a boom or slump; is it a large manufacturing company or a small service company; would Hertzberg's works on accountants and engineers apply equally to other professional areas?

Early influences

Ancient records in China and Greece indicate the importance of organization and administration, but do not give much insight into the principles of management. Outstanding scholars have referred to management activities in the running of city states and empires.

The administration of the Roman Empire was a complex job. The Romans effectively used many basic management ideas, e.g. scalar principle and delegation of authority.

In the period 1400 to 1450, merchants in Venice, Italy, operated various types of business organization, e.g. partnerships, trusts and holding companies. Control emerged in the form of a double-entry book-keeping system and related documentation and records (Lucia Paccioli). In addition there was standardization of material and systems of inventory control.

Concepts of the ideal state were considered by many 16th-century writers. In Sir Thomas More's *Utopia,* for example, his comments upon the reform of the management of Britain were radical. An Italian, Niccolò Machiavelli of Florence, was a good writer and was sent on assignments at home and abroad where he observed governments and men in action. His best known work, *The Prince*, was distilled from his writing of the *The Discourses*. The basic work in *The Prince* was not original, but his approach was forthright and alarming to rulers at that time. Some of his ideas are relevant today, e.g. the need to rely on the consent of the majority of the people. The object of writing *The Prince* was to assist a young prince in acquiring techniques of leadership. He suggested that he should inspire people to greater achievement, offer rewards and incentives and take advantage of *all* opportunities. He stressed that *survival* was the main objective of any organization and no matter what measures were taken to achieve this end, they should be taken. The end justifies the means.

In a much later period, Charles Babbage (1792–1871), who was a professor of mathematics at Cambridge University, recognized that science and mathematics could be applied to the operation of factories and also that more detailed cost measurements were needed. He also developed a calculating machine, but lack of suitable materials made it difficult for him to make many refinements to it.

Scientific management

In the years after 1900 conventional management practices were found to be inadequate to meet demands from the changing economic, social and technological environment. A few pioneers examined causes of inefficiency and experimented to try to find more efficient methods and procedures for control. From these basic experiments a system of management thought developed which came to be known as scientific management.

The method was to investigate every operating problem and try to determine the 'best way' to solve the problems, using scientific methods of research. The concept involved a way of *thinking* about management.

F W Taylor
(1856–1917)

F W Taylor was one of the principal people to be associated with this movement. He was from a middle-class background and worked his way to a high position in an American steel firm; most of his work was involved in experiments to find the 'best method' of doing jobs.

In 1911, he published his book *Principles of Scientific Management*. He spoke on the subject at a conference and stressed that there were mistaken tendencies in uninformed people to grasp at some of the new techniques and then expect these techniques to solve management problems. He warned them against confusing techniques with aims. This comment is surely very relevant today, when many more new techniques are being introduced, e.g. linear programming. The present student of management should consider whether some people are not *again* confusing techniques with aims.

The following principles were suggested by him to guide management:

- each worker should have a large, clearly defined, daily task;
- standard conditions are needed to ensure the task is more easily accomplished;
- high payment should be made for successful completion of tasks. Workers should suffer loss when they fail to meet the standards laid down.

Taylor listed 'new duties' for management. These were:

- the development of a true science;
- the scientific selection, education and development of workmen;
- friendly, close co-operation between management and workers.

A brief summary of the factors he emphasized would cover the need for time and motion study, effective control over performance by the use of the 'exception principle' (*see* p 217), the definition of responsibility and effective selection and training of personnel.

Taylor's work may be overestimated, but he codified and clearly stated practices which had been developing in many well-run factories. He and his contemporaries Gantt, Gilbreth and Emerson stressed the 'engineering approach' and a brief look at their contribution to the subject will now be made.

H L Gantt
(1861–1919)

Gantt worked with Taylor for a time and improved upon Taylor's ideas. He believed management was responsible for creating a favourable environment to obtain worker co-operation. Some of his main contributions were:

- the setting up of a *well-measured task* for a worker, thus giving him a goal to achieve – this made the worker interested in attaining the goal;
- he believed management had a *responsibility to train workers*;
- he advocated proper *methods of planning and control*. He used graphical recording systems, machine and man record charts. His charts showed relationships between 'events' in a production programme and he recognized that total programme goals should be regarded as a series of interrelated plans that people can understand and follow.

F Gilbreth
(1868–1924)

Gilbreth started as an apprentice bricklayer and later managed his own business. He became very interested in the 'best way' of doing a job. This involved doing the job in the most comfortable position, in the fewest motions.

In operating his system of *motion study*, he identified seventeen basic elements in job motions, and any motion can be broken down into all or some of these basic elements. He created a flow process chart, which facilitates the study of complete operations and not just a single task (*see* p 441).

H Emerson
(1853–1931)

Emerson wrote two important books on the subject of efficiency and emphasized the importance of correct organization to achieve higher productivity. He advocated the now popular 'line and staff' organization (*see* p 145), and set out his 'principles of efficiency' which are:

- a clearly defined ideal;
- common sense;
- competent counsel;
- discipline;
- a fair deal;
- reliable, immediate, adequate and permanent records;
- standardized conditions and operations;
- standards and schedules;
- written standard practice instructions;
- reward for efficiency;
- dispatching.

Administrative management

Henri Fayol
(1841–1925)

Fayol was a qualified mining engineer and managing director of a large French company. A year after the death of Taylor he published *General and*

Industrial Management. Fayol, unlike Taylor, started in management and attempted to develop a science of administration for management. He believed that there was a universal science of management applicable to 'commerce, industry, politics, religion, war or philanthropy'. He was one of the first practising managers to draw up a list of management principles.

Fayol thought principles would be useful to all types of managers, but he did not consider that a manager needs anything more than a knowledge of management principles in order manage successfully. At higher levels he said managers depended less upon technical knowledge of what they were managing and more on a knowledge of administration.

Fayol worked independently in France during the period that scientific management was developing in the USA. He trained as an engineer but realized that management of an enterprise required skills other than those he had studied. He emphasized the role of administrative management and concluded that all activities that occur in business organizations could be divided into six main groups.

1 Technical (production, manufacturing).
2 Commercial (buying, selling, exchange).
3 Financial (obtaining and using capital).
4 Security (protection of property and persons).
5 Accounting (balance sheet, stocktaking, statistics, costing).
6 Managerial (planning, organizing, commanding, co-ordinating, controlling).

He concluded that the six groups of activities are interdependent and that it is the role of management to ensure all six activities work smoothly to achieve the goals of an enterprise.

Fayol's 14 principles of management

1 *Division of labour*. Work should be divided to assist specialization.
2 *Authority*. Authority and responsibility should be equal.
3 *Discipline*. Discipline helps workers develop obedience, diligence, energy and respect.
4 *Unity of command*. No subordinate should report to more than one superior.
5 *Unity of direction*. All operations with the same objective should have one manager and one plan.
6 *Subordination of individual interest to general interest*. The interest of one individual or group should not take precedence over the interest of the enterprise as a whole.
7 *Remuneration*. Remuneration and methods of payment should be fair.
8 *Centralization*. Managers must maintain final responsibility but should delegate certain authority to subordinates.
9 *Scalar chain*. A clear line of authority or chain of command should extend from the highest to the lowest level of an enterprise. This helps to ensure an orderly flow of information and supplements the principle of unity of command.

10 *Order.* 'A place for everything and everything in its place.' Proper scheduling of work and timetables to complete work are important. This can ensure materials are in the right place at the right time.

11 *Equity.* Employees should be treated with kindness and justice.

12 *Stability of tenure of personnel.* Management should work towards obtaining long-term commitments from staff. Unnecessary turnover of staff is costly and works against goal accomplishment.

13 *Initiative.* Workers should be allowed to conceive and execute plans in order to develop their capacity to the fullest and feel like an active part of the organization.

14 *Esprit de corps.* Harmony and union help to build the strength of an enterprise. It is an extension of the principle of unity of command, emphasizing the need for teamwork and the importance of communication.

Some of these ideas may seem self-evident today, but they remain important as they continue to have a significant impact on current managerial thinking.

Fayol's main contribution was the idea that management was not an inborn talent but a skill that could be taught. He created a system of ideas that could be applied to all areas of management and laid down basic rules for managing large organizations.

Max Weber
(1864–1920)

Taylor and Fayol directed their attention towards practical problems of managing, while Weber was more concerned with the basic issue of *how enterprises are structured.* Weber was a German sociologist and formulated ideas on the ideal management approach for large organizations. He developed a set of ideas about the structure of an organization that define what we know as *bureaucracy.*

The characteristics of an ideal formalized organization as described in Weber's *Perspective on Administrative Management* are:

- A division of labour. In which authority and responsibility are defined very clearly and set out as official duties.
- Hierarchy of authority. Office or positions are organized in a hierarchy of authority resulting in a chain of command or the scalar principle.
- Formal selection. All employees are selected on the basis of technical qualifications through formal examinations or by education or training.
- Career managers. Managers are professionals who work for fixed salaries and pursue 'careers' within their respective fields. They are not 'owners' of the units they administer.
- Formal rules. Administrators should be subject to strict formal rules and other controls regarding the conduct of their official duties (these rules and controls would be impersonal and uniformly applied). (*See also* p 134 in Chapter 4.)

Human relations movement and behavioural science

Since Taylor, much of the emphasis on scientific management has centred on the worker, and his/her relationship to the company, job and fellow workers.

Advances in the sciences of mankind, and of behaviour as an individual and in groups, e.g. psychology, sociology, etc., have revealed a number of factors which have helped in dealing with business and industrial problems.

Industrial psychology emerged as a specific field about 1913. It was concerned with problems of fatigue and monotony and efficiency in work, as well as in the design of equipment, lighting and other working conditions. It later dealt with problems of selecting and training employees and developed techniques of psychological testing and measurement. Industrial psychology emphasized the study of large and small groups in industry. The basis of the human relations movement was the integration of various disciplines, i.e. industrial psychology and sociology, applied anthropology and social psychology, and was concerned with the human problems which management encountered.

In 1941 the publication of the results of the psychological experiments of Elton Mayo at the Hawthorne (Illinois) plant of the Western Electric Company was a notable landmark. It revolutionized management thinking by focusing attention on the *components of the job and work satisfaction* on the part of employees.

These *Hawthorne Experiments* (as they are referred to) were divided into three phases.

1 Test room studies
These were to assess the effect of *single* variables upon employee performance. A group of women were segregated and variations made in the intensity of illumination, in temperature, hours of work and rest periods, and their performance was noted. The results were surprising, as output rose, even though some changes were made which made working conditions poorer.

It was established that the more important factors were not incentives or working conditions, but the high *esprit de corps* that had developed in the *group* and the more *personal interest* shown by the supervisor and higher management. So, in themselves, conditions of work, lighting, hours, rest periods, etc., could not be viewed as affecting people's work – people subject to the conditions develop attitudes and interpretations which are important factors also.

2 Interviewing studies
This first study led to an interest in the *attitudes* of people at the plant towards their jobs, working conditions and supervision, and a *morale survey*, comprising over 21,000 interviews, was taken. It was not, though, easy to find out objectively the cause of an individual's dissatisfaction.

3 Observational studies
These studies were made to study the normal *group working*. It was found the group developed 'norms' of conduct, output and relations with others *outside* the department. It became obvious that to each individual in the group the relations with his/her fellows were important in his/her motivation and the study showed the importance of *informal organization* in worker motivation.

To summarize, it was obvious a worker was not motivated solely by money. The superior's role was important for morale and productivity. Group spirit and teamwork were vital to accomplish organizational goals and worker satisfaction. Since then, it can be seen how the studies contributed to the growth of human resource management and human relations and pointed the way to the need to study in detail the 'informal group'.

The term 'human relations' is used to indicate the ways in which managers interact with their subordinates. Managers must therefore know *why* employees act in the manner they do, and the psychological, social and other factors which motivate them. After the pioneering attempts of Mayo and his associates, researchers using more sophisticated research methods developed other models to try to explain what motivates people at the workplace (e.g. Maslow, Argyris and McGregor). They became known as 'behavioural scientists' rather than members of the human relations school. It was thought that an understanding of a person's needs would enable a manager to use more accurate methods to motivate subordinates (*see* p 199).

Management science school

The United Kingdom was faced with many complex problems during World War II. *Operational research* teams were set up, composed of mathematicians, physicists and other scientists, who pooled their knowledge to solve problems. After the war these ideas were applied to industrial problems which could not be solved by conventional means. With the development of the electronic computer, these procedures became formalized into a 'management science' school.

The contribution of the quantitative school was greatest in the activities of planning and control. There are many doubts that this school cannot yet deal effectively with 'people'. Some techniques introduced are dealt with in later chapters of this book. They include: capital budgeting, production scheduling, optimum inventory levels and development of product strategies (*see also* p 244 for further discussion on operational research).

The management science school differs from the classical and behavioural schools in the following ways:

- The classical or scientific management approach concentrates on the effiency of the manufacturing process. The management science school places greater weight on the *overall planning and decision-making process* and regards technical efficiency as a tool, rather than an end in itself;
- It *advocates the use of computers and mathematical models in planning*;
- It advocates the *evaluation of effectiveness of models*. Techniques for evaluating the effectiveness of the models emphasize their use in managerial decision making, e.g. the return on investment analysis.

In essence, the management science school, by its use of computers and quantitative analysis, has made it possible to consider the effect of a number of variables in an organization which may otherwise have been overlooked.

It should be noted that statistical evidence by itself may not be sufficient as it may require the more comprehensive techniques of the behavioural school or the administrative management approach. The latter stresses the concern for the welfare of staff and seeks to identify the reasons behind certain behaviour.

Systems approach to management

The approaches already mentioned, scientific, administrative management science and behavioural, are useful in different circumstances, but it is difficult to be sure which one is right in a given situation. In view of this, it is considered that the newer *systems* and *contingency* approaches may provide a more complete integrated approach to the problems of management.

Many activities in an organization were treated in an essentially descriptive fashion before Norbert Weiner published his book on cybernetics in 1948, which encouraged an analytical approach to the activities of management.

'*Cybernetics*' can be traced back to Plato; in his *Republic* he used the Greek term *Kybernetike* (the art of steermanship; a pilot or governor) as an analogy to illustrate piloting the 'ship of state'. Cybernetics is now a branch of applied mathematics used in the study and design of control mechanisms. It is useful to recognize the relationship between control and communication. Norbert Weiner's definition of cybernetics is 'The science of communication and control in the animal and in the machine.'

The basic model used in cybernetics has a number of similarities to the models used in systems – collections of parts that are dynamically combined and interrelated into a purposive whole. The interrelationships occurring through a communications network are self-regulating and *adaptive* to environmental changes in the system.

The essence of cybernetic control is the series of interrelated steps to reach a stage of *homeostasis* (i.e. a stable condition) by means of adjustments made through feeding back into the controlling system information obtained from its interaction with outside environments. A good example is the thermostat, which is sensitive to temperature changes and automatically adjusts the heating mechanism. *Feedback* involves passing information from one point in a system back to an earlier point with a view to modifying behaviour. Cybernetic control is dependant upon the adequacy of feeding back reliable information to a point where action can be taken.

Systems can be divided into two categories:

1 **Deterministic,** where the behaviour can be completely determined, e.g. we know what will happen when we touch the keys of a computer keyboard.
2 **Probabilistic,** where behaviour can only be estimated within degrees of likelihood, e.g. the result of tossing a coin is unpredictable, as it may be a head or a tail.

In a very probabilistic system, we do not know how the machine works, because of its complexity. All we can do is to treat it like a '*black box*'. We cannot see inside the system, or box, and can only make intelligent guesses by manipulating the flows into and out of the box, thus learning about its behaviour by trial and error. We could, for example, institute a sales promotion campaign, but we cannot accurately predict its effect, as the situation is of the probabilistic type.

A system is called *open-loop* when information is fed out from a process so that necessary evaluations and adjustments can be made externally. If the loop is *closed*, a person is not needed to complete the control circuit; it is self-correcting.

Thinking about management with a knowledge of the systems approach can help us to postulate conceptually the interrelationship of apparently separate and even contradictory ideas underlying management theory for the first time. Systems theory tries to synthesize ideas common to several disciplines.

A *system* is an organized combination of parts which form a complex entity, with interrelationships or interactions between the parts and between the system and the environment. Examples of a system are: the schools system, the telephone system, the solar system.

It was not until about the early 1960s that a change in management thought began which reflected the impact of systems thinking, but it was slow to start and it was not until the 1970s that ideas of general systems appeared in formal management theory. Basic systems thinking has become more firmly established and is waiting to be further developed.

A *management system* encourages one to consider the *cutting across* of traditional boundaries of responsibility between departments in order to appreciate the objectives of the whole organization. Distinct demarcation lines between purchasing, manufacturing, engineering, marketing, etc., may become less distinct and a revision of organization may be needed. This is essential in viewing the management process as a system. Russell L. Ackoff in the *General Systems Yearbook* (Vol. 5, 1960, p 6) commented, 'we must stop acting as though nature were organized into disciplines like the Universities are'.

Recent applications of this approach have presented complex systems in the form of *models* for ease of manipulation to simulate a portion of reality. Others have tried to model the life of cities or tried to solve the problems of society with the new tools available. The main problem is that these systems (e.g. cities) are only products of those systems which interact with other more complex systems, which are more difficult to model. A city's problems, for example, derive from its relation to its environment.

The systems approach stresses the need for more understanding in the development of sophisticated problem-solving techniques, e.g. simulation, operations research and computerized information systems. All these aim to improve the *control mechanisms* of organizational systems so that they can plan for, and react more effectively to, changes in the environment (Fig 1.1).

A system may be said to comprise the following elements, which are called sub-systems:

- a *sensing* system or mechanism, to find out the situation and what is going on;
- an *information coding* system, to ensure that data are in usable form;
- a *physical processing* system, requiring two-way communication and feedback of results;
- a *regulating and control* system, based upon actual output and measurement of deviations;
- an *information storage* and *retrieval system*;
- a *goal-getting* or *policy-making* system.

It is inherent in the system that there should be adequate delegation of authority to sub-systems and that effective two-way communication systems are operating (both upwards and downwards).

The systems approach attempts to give managers a way of looking at organizations as a complete whole. It implies that activities in any part of

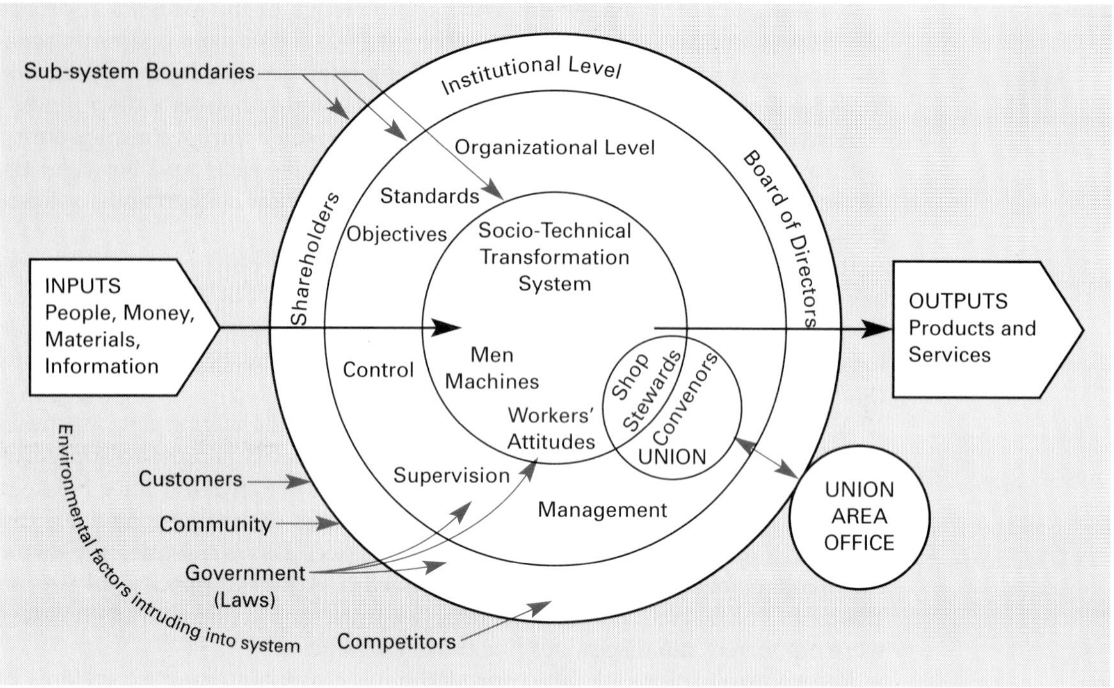

Fig 1.1 The systems approach provides an integrative framework for modern organizational theory and management practice

the organization will affect the activities of every other part. For example, in a *manufacturing* department the ideal arrangement for a production manager would probably be uninterrupted long production runs, operating at 100 per cent efficiency at minimal cost. The *marketing* department would wish to offer delivery of a wider range of products; this implies a more flexible manufacturing schedule which can deal with special orders. Scheduling decisions and their impact on other departments must be taken into account.

In examining a system, a structured methodology is needed. Where objectives are easily defined, the questions opposite indicate what must be considered.

The adoption of a systems approach will involve a marked change in organization, hence the vital need to prepare the organization well in advance for the *need to accept change*.

Whatever classification is given to managerial activities and responsibilities, they are becoming more dynamic and complex because of:

- a greater rate of change and uncertainty in the external environment;
- new techniques and the revolution in knowledge and technology, especially information processing and micro-circuitry);
- problems of co-ordination and integration as more jobs become specialized.

Traditional managerial theory and behavioural science have provided guidelines to cope with uncertainty and change, but the approaches are too fragmented. It is here that a systems approach can help (Fig 1.2).

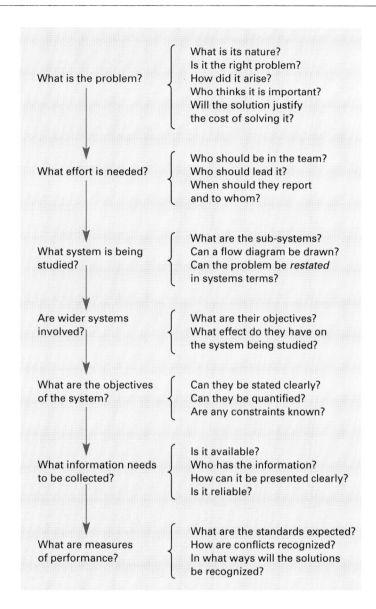

What is the problem?
- What is its nature?
- Is it the right problem?
- How did it arise?
- Who thinks it is important?
- Will the solution justify the cost of solving it?

What effort is needed?
- Who should be in the team?
- Who should lead it?
- When should they report and to whom?

What system is being studied?
- What are the sub-systems?
- Can a flow diagram be drawn?
- Can the problem be *restated* in systems terms?

Are wider systems involved?
- What are their objectives?
- What effect do they have on the system being studied?

What are the objectives of the system?
- Can they be stated clearly?
- Can they be quantified?
- Are any constraints known?

What information needs to be collected?
- Is it available?
- Who has the information?
- How can it be presented clearly?
- Is it reliable?

What are measures of performance?
- What are the standards expected?
- How are conflicts recognized?
- In what ways will the solutions be recognized?

General systems theory provides valuable insights into the structure and process of management and any serious student of management needs to be aware of the ideas of this theory of structure and relationships and to recognize also the impact of systems thinking, arising out of this theory, on management.

The systems approach recognizes variety and offers a way of interrelating differences by reconciling them within the whole. This is an approach which emphasizes theory and conformity.

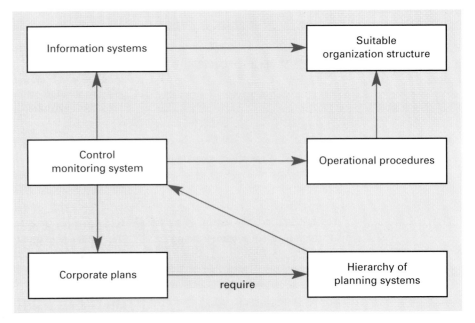

Fig 1.2 A systems approach showing some interrelationships required

Contingency approach to management

This is another modern approach that has attempted to integrate findings of other perspectives. They believe that it is impossible to select one way of managing that works best in all situations. Their approach is to identify the conditions of a task (scientific management school), managerial job (administrative management school) and persons (human relations school) as parts of a complete management situation and attempt to integrate them all into a solution which is most appropriate for a specific circumstance.

Contingency refers to the immediate (contingent or touching) circumstances. One way of expressing the principle is to say that 'it all depends upon this factor and that . . .'.

The manager has to try systematically to identify which technique or approach will, in a particular circumstance or context, best contribute to the attainment of the desired goals.

An example of this is the recurrent problem of *how to increase productivity*. The 'expert' would prescribe as follows:

- Behavioural scientist – create a climate which is psychologically motivating.
- Classical approach – create a new incentive scheme.
- Contingency approach – examine both ideas and see how any answer *fits in* with goals, structure and resources of the organization.

In the above case it may be found that if workers needed money mainly for personal expenses, financial incentive may work well. Skilled workers may prefer job enrichment (*see* p 404) to encourage pride in their work.

The contingency approach may consider, for policy reasons, that an incentive scheme was not relevant. Also the expense of a job enrichment scheme may rule this out. The complexity of each situation should be noted and decisions made in each individual circumstance.

It should be borne in mind that the contingency approach is not really new, as Taylor emphasized the importance of choosing the general type of management *best suited to a particular case*. There was also the point emphasized by Fayol that *there is nothing rigid or absolute in management affairs*.

Similar ideas were expressed in the 1920s by Mary Parker Follett (1865–1933). She was greatly interested in social work and had a gift for relating individual experience to general principles. Her concept of the *Law of the Situation* referred to the necessity of acting in accordance with the specific requirements of a given situation. She noted that these requirements were constantly changing and needed continual efforts to maintain effective working relationships. Her main contributions were on the psychological implications of authority, leadership and control, which are discussed further in Chapter 3.

The *contingency* approach seeks to apply to real life situations ideas drawn from various schools of management thought. Different problems and situations require different approaches and no one approach is universally applicable. Managers must seek to identify the approach that will serve them best in any given situation, so they can achieve their goal.

It is important to note that the contingency approach stresses the need for managers to examine the relationship between the internal and external environment of an organization. (Chapter 2 considers the relationships with the external environment.)

The *systems* approach to management emphasizes that relationships between various parts of an organization are interlocked. The contingency approach has emphasized this idea by focusing on the *nature* of such relationships.

Criticisms of the contingency approach are that it has little theoretical foundation and is basically intuitive. This can be countered by noting that the contingency approach examines each situation to find out its *unique* attributes before management makes a decision. Earlier approaches tended to consider *universal* principles which were not always applicable to specific situations. Managers today are advised to analyse a situation and use ideas from the various schools of thought to find an *appropriate* combination of management techniques to meet the needs of the situation.

A useful summary of this approach can be found in 'The Contingency Theory of Management', *Business Horizons*, June 1973, pp 62–71 (USA).

ELEMENTS OF MANAGEMENT

Whichever way one defines management, a biased approach is of no service to anyone. Too much emphasis on one element does not help to make the subject any easier to understand.

We have seen that the economic system is a complex of activities and these must form the background of management. The goods and services consumers need must be supplied and the means by which they can purchase these must be provided. Management's role must therefore be to promote this in the most efficient manner, by combining factors of production and distribution and directing the efforts of the people concerned to the given purpose.

No matter what type of enterprise (e.g. highly centralized government departments or nationalized industries or commercial concerns) the progress of management is fundamentally the same. Enterprises need plans, direction and control and these will not function without effective organization.

These elements, planning, directing, controlling and organizing, are often called 'functions' by some other writers; the use of this word in this book will be confined to the specialist departmental groupings, e.g. production, marketing, finance, etc. (See the section on Organization for more discussion on this aspect.)

Emphasis on these elements will vary according to the size of the enterprise. Although external environmental conditions affect management policy, these cannot be changed. Internal environmental conditions can be moulded to enable the objectives to be attained and this, the provision of a suitable environment, is part of the job of management. A manager must first of all plan the work for his subordinates, organize them effectively, seeing that they are selected and trained wisely, direct their work and measure results. Later, the ideas of wider responsibility for management, e.g. responsibility to society, which appears to widen management activity, will be considered.

Fayol's classification can be used as a starting point. He listed six spheres of activity – Technical, Commercial, Financial, Security, Accounting, Managerial. It is the last of these, i.e. Managerial, of which he wrote, 'to manage is to forecast and to plan, to organize, to command, to co-ordinate and to control'.

- **Planning.** This referred to forecasting future circumstances and requirements, deciding objectives, making long- and short-term plans, determining policies to be followed and the standards to be set.
- **Organizing.** This activity was concerned with dividing work and allocating it among groups and persons and determining their responsibilities and relations and the extent of their delegation.
- **Commanding.** This was the exercise of centralized authority and leadership.
- **Co-ordinating.** Co-ordinating involved seeing that all groups and persons work efficiently and economically, in harmony, towards the common objective.
- **Controlling.** The activity involved checking to see that plans have been carried out and attending to any deviations.

Modern writers largely accept this classification. Brech sees organization as a function of planning and motivation and leadership is preferred to command. There is no real point in attempting to justify unduly the various classifications of the elements of management, as they are really very closely related. For the purpose of analysis, the following classification has been adopted:

- **Planning** includes the forecasting and selecting of objectives with the policies, programmes and procedures for achieving them. It involves making choices, i.e. decision making.
- **Organizing** involves determining and noting activities needed to achieve the objectives of the undertaking, grouping these and assigning such groups of activities to managers, ensuring effective delegation of authority to enable activities to be carried out and providing co-ordination of authority relationships.

    NB: *Staffing* involves having people in positions needed in the organization structure; this needs the defining of the personnel requirements for each job, appraising and selecting candidates, training and developing them. Some writers consider this a *separate* element of management and, in practice, much of this work is delegated to a Human Resources Manager; but it must be remembered that ultimately top management is responsible for staffing.

- **Direction** involves guiding and supervising subordinates. These subordinates must be orientated into the undertaking's ways, guided towards improved performance and motivated to work effectively towards enterprise goals.
- **Control.** Performance should be measured and deviations from plans corrected or accounted for. It is preferable that someone should be responsible for variations as control of people ensures the control of materials.

    NB: *Co-ordination* is considered by many authorities as a separate element of management; others regard it as the *essence* of management. The reasoning here is that one needs to achieve harmony of effort to accomplish the desired goal and this is itself the purpose of management, and each of the managerial elements can be considered to be an exercise in co-ordination.

    It should be noted that an efficient organization can help towards creating effective co-ordination.

We should note that there are dangers in simplifying and classifying the elements of management as there is a wide range of managerial tasks that do not lend themselves to simple classification. Another danger in attempting to be specific about elements is that each element appears to have equal prominence and emphasis. At each level of management the emphasis changes on the various elements. In other organizations, it can be quite different, e.g. 50 per cent of the time spent may be on control, and in other organizations only 20 per cent. The importance of the elements cannot be assessed by the time spent on them.

THE MANAGER TODAY

The classical approach is adopted in the plan of this book but it may still be of value to examine more closely the approach taken by H Fayol and other writers about the real nature of the manager's task.

Research in the past few years into the nature of the manager's task has produced many ideas. The manager in fact takes on a wider range of roles in pursuing the objectives of the organization.

Many persons have *responsibility* in an organization. But managers also are held *accountable* for the work of others as well as their own. This additional feature can cause concern, in that control of this may not be so easy. A manager may not have time to check everything others do, so there is an element of risk here.

1 A manager assumes responsibility to see that work is done effectively.
2 He must balance competing goals and needs, which require resources which are limited. A balance between the goals and needs of departments and individuals is needed and priorities have to be established.
3 *A manager works with and through other people* at every level in an organization in striving towards goals.
4 He is also:
   - a *mediator* of disputes which may affect morale and productivity;
   - a *politician*, using persuasion and compromise to promote organizational goals;
   - a *diplomat*, representing the company at meetings within and outside the firm.

There are many other roles of a manager. A manager must be flexible to *change roles appropriately* to be truly *effective.*

A manager's responsibilities require performance to be both efficient and effective.

P Drucker (in *Managing for Results*, 1964) stresses the important point that although efficiency is important, effectiveness is vital (i.e. the ability to choose *appropriate* objectives or *means* to achieve an objective). Efficient production of large cars may not be *effective* when the market needs are for small cars, a *situation* which prevails today. A comment from Peter Drucker is relevant: 'The pertinent question is not how to do things right, but how to find the right things to do, and to concentrate resources and efforts on them.'

There are limitations inevitably placed on a manager's ability to perform efficiently or effectively – e.g. a firm may *limit* a manager in his handling of subordinates or what he can do in hiring or motivating them, or his leadership style (*see* p 193) may be in conflict with the current style in the organization.

Research by Robert Katz, who classified three basic types of management skills, suggests that all three are essential to effective management, but their importance depends upon a manager's rank in the organization:

- Technical skill – ability to use tools, procedures and techniques in a specialized area.

- **Human skill** – ability to work with and understand and motivate people as individuals or groups.
- **Conceptual skill** – mental ability to co-ordinate and integrate all of an organization's activities, especially in the long-term decisions affecting the organization. In addition, conceptual skills are needed to see the organization as a whole and recognize how the various factors in a situation are interrelated so actions taken are in the best interests of the organization. Human skills and technical skills are more important at a lower level, where more manager–subordinate interactions occur. Conceptual skills are needed at all levels of management, but the nearer to top management positions, the more time is needed to devote to conceptual skills.

Henry Mintzberg made extensive surveys of existing research and integrated those findings with his own studies of five chief executive officers in his attempts to find *how managers spend their time* and perform their work. The results were interesting and help the understanding of the nature of the managerial task (H Mintzberg, 'The Manager's Job – Folklore and Fact', *Harvard Business Review*, July–August 1975, pp 49–61).

A manager's *interpersonal* roles include that of a *figurehead,* performing ceremonial duties, e.g. receiving visitors. He/she also has a *leader* role, e.g. hiring, training, motivating staff, and a *liaison* role dealing with others outside the organization, e.g. clients and suppliers.

A *manager's informational roles* include *monitoring* and *disseminating* information obtained in numerous ways. As a company *representative* he/she transmits some information to others outside his/her area or organization. An important part of this work is to keep superiors well informed. Mintzberg thought that this was possibly the most important and classified this aspect into three roles – role of *disseminator,* company representative or *spokesman* role, and *monitor* role.

A manager's *decisional* roles can be of four types:

- as an *entrepreneur* – to launch a new idea;
- as a *disturbance handler,* e.g. of strikes;
- as a *resource allocator* – choosing from among competing demands for money, equipment, personnel and management time;
- as a *negotiator,* e.g. drawing up contracts with suppliers. Managers have information and *authority,* therefore they may be heavily engaged in negotiation.

The real effect of Mintzberg's research is to highlight the changing, uncertain environment in which the manager operates. Many things occur which cannot be predicted or controlled. The manager has little time to reflect and must cope with numerous challenges each day.

So although the functions of planning, organizing, decision making and controlling are useful in analysing the work of the manager, the work is more involved than this. In two British studies, managers spent 66 to 80 per cent of their time in *oral* communication. This was similar to Mintzberg's research findings in the USA and is very difficult to classify using classical management analysis.

Managers' jobs are complicated and difficult. They cannot easily delegate, as they keep most of the important information in their heads because it comes to them mainly in verbal form. Brevity, fragmentation of work and verbal communication are features of their work.

Today pressures are becoming greater and they now need to respond not just to owners and directors, but to *subordinates* (who no longer tend to accept unexplained orders), to *consumer groups* and *outside agencies.*

In the future, a manager may need to consider the following questions:

- How can I deal more ably with change and conflict? Changes must be confronted and flexibility practised.
- How can I make better judgements in uncertainty?
- How can I improve my diagnostic and analytical skills and broaden my education?
- How can I manage within a more open environment and become more socially responsible?
- How can I become aware of changing human social values, especially higher-level human needs?

Women in management

Women now account for 45 per cent of the labour force of the United States and the United Kingdom. Women managers are faced with the same basic challenges as men in management. They must, however, also deal with other issues.

The role of women in business was traditionally confined to teaching, nursing and secretarial positions. Many women selected these areas because of family or social pressure or poor career advice. Today, women work in most career or industrial occupations and many have moved into management areas. It is likely that this will greatly increase in the future. Approximately half of business graduates are female.

Women's expectations even now appear to be relatively low. Research has shown that women graduates have lower ultimate salary hopes and expectations than male graduates ('Corporate Women', *Business Week*, USA, June 22 1987, pp 72–7).

An important point to consider is that having lower expectations may function as a self-fulfilling prophecy. The resultant outcome is that women are discouraged from progressing as far as they could in their chosen career. There are still obstacles to women reaching higher levels on merit, including the following:

1 There are not as many role models of career development for women as there are for men.
2 Married and unmarried women have to contend with the career aspirations of their partner and may be directly involved in family responsibilities.
3 Male co-workers may discriminate against women.
4 The policies and procedures of an organization may be very unsupportive.

The greater the number of professional contacts, both male and female, available to women, the more assistance they could receive. Also the use of a mentor (a senior person) to advise and guide a lower-level female employee could be very helpful.

The obstacles mentioned previously – discrimination, sexual stereotyping, conflicting demands of marriage – are more likely to affect women in management than men. They may prevent women from entering management or make it harder for them to do their best work when they become managers.

Legislation advocating equal opportunity has had a marked effect but women have to devote time and energy in dealing with problems, barriers and issues that most men never encounter. Larger numbers of women are obtaining senior managerial positions and there are now more female success models for young people to emulate.

Measures adopted by employers include help with children, special training for women staff and flexible working.

In 1992 a survey was made of the views of 1500 men and 500 of their female counterparts in management. The results give the first detailed breakdown of different attitudes to women in management. The aim of the report is to go *beyond* the debate about the *means* to enable women to combine caring and career and to explore some of the continuing psychological and attitudinal barriers to the progress of women in management. Recommendations are also made to help senior managers counter the damaging effect which such barriers have on the prosperity of their organizations and the development of their managers. (*See* Trudy Coe, *The Key to the Men's Club*, Institute of Management, London, 1992.)

Entrepreneurship and intrapreneurship

Entrepreneurship is enjoying a great deal of attention in many countries today. It can be described as the process of bringing together creative and innovative ideas and coupling these with management and organizational skills in order to combine people, money and resources to meet an identified need and thereby create wealth.

The process may be undertaken by one person or a group. Inventors are innovative and creative but not all are able to use management and organizational skills to produce and market goods or services successfully. Creativity and management strengths do not usually reside in one person, so entrepreneurship is often found in groups which combine their strengths.

Self-employment is encouraged by governments and is very popular at present as it creates jobs and aids the economy of a country. Entrepreneurship is often thought to apply mainly to the management of small businesses, but this idea has been extended to also apply to larger organizations and to managers who carry out entrepreneurial roles. Such managers are aware of opportunities and they initiate changes to take full advantage of them.

The term given to someone who has innovative ideas and transforms them to profitable activities within an organizational environment is called an *intrapreneur*. The *entrepreneur*, in contrast, does the same *outside* the organization.

The world intrapreneurship is attributed to Gordon Pinchott, an American, who founded a school for intrapreneurs to help managers from large corporations to take responsibility for creating innovations and turning ideas into a 'profitable reality'.

Not everyone agrees with this approach to entrepreneurship, the reasons being that an entrepreneur is deemed to be in business for themself and takes risks in initiating change and needs freedom to pursue ideas. None of these can usually be achieved in a large organization. A number of entrepreneurs leave larger companies and set up in business on their own.

In his book, *Intrapreneuring*, Pinchott suggests that a number of factors are needed to be present for intrapreneurship to flourish in a larger organization. These include giving innovators the opportunity to develop ideas and the freedom and resources to see ideas through. There must also be a tolerance of risk-taking and mistakes.

TIME MANAGEMENT

Organizational efficiency is impaired if managers are poorly organized. A major aspect of efficiency is the effective *management of time*. A well organized manager who makes good use of the time available can ensure objectives are successfully achieved.

In the age of scientific management, methods were used to quantify the relationship between time spent and output achieved. This was usually concerned with manual workers and not managerial graded staff. *Managerial time is so expensive* that every organization must benefit by examining issues of time management.

Important issues in time management

Nature of job

- A person whose job involves *regular* contacts with others is more likely to be interrupted than persons working in a more solitary area.
- Those people working in an *established area* will have relatively fewer unpredictable events to deal with than a person employed in a new and developing area of work.
- *Identifying the key tasks* and responsibilities in a job will show which should be given the greatest amount of a manager's time.
- *A detailed diary of time spent* on activities in a given period of time is an easy way of finding out how time is spent and the nature of interruptions allowed. Time is often lost in unnecessary meetings and in travelling to meetings. It is worth exploring newer methods of communication to overcome the waste of time at meetings (*see* p 460).

Personal attributes of jobholder

The personality and amount of self-confidence someone has can have a marked effect on their efficiency. The more self-assured and assertive individual can deal more effectively with people who encroach on their time. Some people can only deal with one item at a time, others can deal with several simultaneously. Some like to delegate work extensively, others prefer to keep jobs to themselves.

The context of a person's job

The nature of the people working with a manager greatly influence the use of his time. (A person's boss, for example, could constantly interrupt his work.) Some managers adopt an 'open door' policy, which, while generally recommended, can affect personal work efficiency. Others adopt an approach discouraging informal contacts. The extent to which accuracy and quality of work is deemed vital can also have an effect on time taken over the work involved.

The demands and constraints of any job can be examined by considering the following:

- **Demands** – the essential items which cannot be passed on. They come from subordinates, peers, senior staff and people outside the organization.
- **Constraints** – items stopping a person from carrying out a job in the way they would prefer. These are usually the resources available, the limitations of equipment, physical location, the policies and procedures of the organization, legal rules and the attitudes of other people.

When all demands and constraints have been identified, a manager is faced with *choices* which refer to what and how the work is to be done. A detailed analysis of a person's job can identify what choices a manager is making and how the range can be extended to give more positive control over choices.

For more details of this aspect see R Stewart, *Choices for the Manager*.

EXCELLENCE IN MANAGEMENT

In 1982 *In Search of Excellence* by Peters and Waterman was published in the USA. In the book the authors analysed the characteristic factors of excellent enterprises. They named 43 excellent companies, including IBM, Kodak and McDonald's.

Eight characteristics of excellent enterprises were identified by Peters and Waterman. These were from organizations which remained increasingly productive and internationally competitive. These organizations:

- *had a bias for action* – organizations which were keen on experimenting and implementing decisions quickly;
- *learned about the needs of their customers* – many organizations which were deemed innovative obtained ideas for good products from their customers by listening carefully and regularly;
- *promoted entrepreneurship and management autonomy* – these organizations encouraged practical risk-taking and supported good attempts at creativity;
- *obtained productivity by paying close attention to the needs of their staff* – every individual on the staff is regarded as important and a source of quality and productivity gain;
- *were encouraged by the philosophy of their organization's leaders;*
- *concentrated on the business they knew best* – excellent performance seemed to favour organizations which stayed reasonably close to the business they knew how to run best;

● *had an organization structure that was simple with a 'lean' staff* – the structural forms and systems of successful companies were simple with a small number of top-level staff and an absence of matrix structures;

● *were organized in a centralized or decentralized manner, whichever was appropriate* – this involved combining firm central direction with maximum individual autonomy.

It can be seen that all the above attributes are characteristics of management activities, skills and functions which are helpful in managing companies in a competitive environment. Peters and Waterman have been criticized for not including other possible factors contributing to corporate excellence, e.g. technological advantages. Also, their method of collecting and interpreting data was not very scientific and was not conducted over a sufficiently long period of time.

MANAGEMENT FOR THE FUTURE

In the United Kingdom there has been recently a growing interest in management education, training and development. Factors which have led to this include:

● more complex demands on existing and new managers;
● structural and demographic changes in employment;
● greater awareness of market influences on employment;
● threats and opportunities arising from the Single European Market.

A number of reports have been produced on many aspects of management, all with the aim of improving existing methods of training and development. One aspect is relevant in this section and it is to look at the *characteristics that will be needed of managers in the future.*

In the Report *Management for the Future* (Ashridge Management Research Group, 1988) the main conclusions were that organizations in the future will need to be:

● market, driven, closer to customers and suppliers;
● 'flatter' and more fluid in structure and much faster moving;
● increasingly decentralized and fragmented yet integrated by overall strategy, corporate culture and information technology;
● able to manage issues such as quality, service and new technology across *the organization* and this will lead to the growing importance of 'horizontal' management (i.e. the management of lateral not vertical hierarchical relationships).

From the above research it was suggested that the profile of a senior manager will include:

● an awareness of and ability to relate to the economic, social and political environment;
● an ability to manage in a turbulent environment;
● an ability to manage with complex organizational structures;

- an ability to be innovative and initiate change;
- an ability to manage and utilize increasingly sophisticated information systems;
- an ability to manage people with widely different and changing values and expectations.

These changes could have marked implications on skills required by managers. A number of the above terms used will be discussed in more detail in other chapters.

The Institute of Manpower Studies in 1988 published a major study *What Makes a Manager*. The intention was to review how employing organizations describe what makes a good manager. Details of skills criteria were obtained and the research concluded that most of the documents listed *known* management skills, often using only a few main headings. They indicated a warning that although management skills may be classified using generally common expressions it could not be inferred that they have a common meaning. 'Leadership', for example, had many diverse meanings.

Management competencies

The above commentary on two publications leads to a debate on *managerial competencies* which has been considered by the Forum for Management Education and Development, and its operating arm, the Management Charter Initiative (MCI). A classification, or common language of the knowledge, skills and qualities of effective managers (i.e. *managerial competencies*) has been published. These provide the basic standards for the provision of management education training and development appropriate to an individual's needs throughout his career.

The idea was that the new classification would replace traditional definitions framed primarily in terms of knowledge input. Competence-based standards would be developed which pertain to management activities *irrespective of functions*.

Criticisms against this classification come from the Institute of Personnel Management (IPM), which is of the opinion that there is no agreement on such general qualities and their relationship to managerial effectiveness. The Institute believes competence is dependent upon the context in which it is demonstrated.

Another criticism comes from Professor Burgoyne who does not believe that management is the sequential exercise of discrete competencies. He emphasized, in his paper 'Management Development for the Individual' (IPM, June 1988), that a universal mechanism was inappropriate and any effective scheme must recognize the inevitability of a large element of judgement and the variability of management across situations.

The Ashridge Management Research Group in the United Kingdom surveyed over 500 UK organizations to find out how much the management competency idea had been accepted. It was found that more than two-thirds of companies replying to the survey had developed a competency-based approach and ran assessment centres.

Competencies have been identified covering every conceivable aspect of a manager's job. Companies can, with this knowledge, design and operate assessment centres where skills can be evaluated against an agreed competency model.

In the USA some companies have been using this technique for over 20 years as a major database for recruitment, performance appraisal, promotion, training and development, and rewards.

A number of companies, though, have largely rejected the idea. These tend to operate in areas of high technology which are rapidly changing and believe their managers should be creative, innovative and adaptable. They believe that successful managers in such a dynamic environment will involve different sets of measures of performance which should be subject to *continuous review* and negotiation. (*See also* Chapter 9.)

SUMMARY

Objective 1 *Describe the concept of management and why it is needed to reach organizational objectives.*

Management may be defined as a process whereby scarce resources (human, material and financial) are combined to achieve organizational goals.

Without management, people would pursue their own objectives independently and this would lead to waste and inefficiency. Management is therefore needed to reach objectives, maintain a balance between conflicting goals, and achieve efficiency and effectiveness.

Objective 2 *List and describe the basic elements of management.*

The basic elements of management may be defined as planning, organizing, directing and controlling. There are many other ways of organizing managerial knowledge, for example by examining what managers do, or what skills they need. In this book the concepts, principles, theory and techniques are organized around the above elements.

Objective 3 *Understand the complex nature of the managerial task.*

Management is both an art and a science. Applying knowledge of the management process effectively requires good judgement. Managers must serve many groups, including owners, employees, customers, governments, the community and society in general. These groups make the managerial task more complex.

Objective 4 *Identify major schools of management thought and how they have evolved.*

Management thought has evolved through various approaches. Pre-scientific management (1775–1885), scientific management (1898 to present), administrative management (1916 to present), human relations (1927 to present), modern management, i.e. systems and contingency (present). It can be seen that today's concepts of management are the product of a long and involved process of evolution. The human relations approach that developed from the Hawthorne Experiments tried to fill the gaps in the mechanistic approach of scientific management. Today's managers must be aware of all approaches, particularly the use of modern approaches which advocate the need to adapt to varied and changing conditions.

Objective 5 *Describe two modern approaches to management that attempt to integrate these various schools.*

Managers who adopt the systems approach view the organization as a single, integrated network of sub-systems. Rather than dealing separately with the various parts of an organization, the systems approach tries to give managers a way of looking at organizations as a whole. Systems theory emphasizes the fact that activity in any part of an organization affects the activity in every other part. The emphasis in the contingency approach is on dealing with problems and situations with an appreciation for their uniqueness. In the contingency approach the task of managers is to try to identify which technique will, in a particular situation, under particular circumstances, at a particular time, best contribute to the achievement of management objectives. These two approaches incorporate many of the major factors in the early schools of management thought.

Objective 6 *State what conclusions can be reached from studies of what managers actually do.*

The major studies in this chapter about a manager's behaviour give some indication of the extent of the managerial problem. The classification of skills (Katz) and roles (Mintzberg) and knowledge of the elements of management are all valuable.

The changing, uncertain environment makes a manager's job complicated and difficult. What can be stated with reasonable certainty is that the higher a manager's position in an organization, the more *likely* he or she will emphasize planning activities and be more concerned with external aspects rather than concentrate on daily operations and activities.

REVIEW QUESTIONS

1 Distinguish between the words administration and management.

2 Is management an art or a science?

3 To what extent can management be regarded as a profession?

4 What is meant by 'scientific management'?

5 What did the following persons contribute to management thought: F W Taylor; H L Gantt; F Gilbreth; H Emerson; H Fayol; Mary Parker Follett?

6 Is there any point in considering the elements of which management is composed?

7 What is meant by 'a management system'?

8 Explain the term 'cybernetics'.

9 Review the systems and contingency approaches to management.

10 What steps do you think should be taken to increase the numbers of women managers?

REVIEW
PROBLEMS

1 It has been said that an effective manager is one who can change roles appropriately. What are the roles of a manager today?

2 Explain the systems approach to management and the advantages of using this approach in discussing management.

3 What are the potential benefits to be derived by managers and administrators from a systematic study of the behavioural sciences? Illustrate your answer with examples showing how organizations have utilized the insights and techniques of the behavioural sciences.

4 Why do you think the Hawthorne Experiments had such an influence on management thinking?

ASSIGNMENTS

1 Look at a selection of recent advertisements showing managerial vacancies in a good quality newspaper. Try to identify from the advertisements a picture of the common characteristics required in a manager.

2 Assume you are a major employer in the public sector (Local Authority) and you are faced with the task of cutting back the numbers of employees to meet budget restrictions. As your organization employs a large number of women on a part-time basis, your Chief Executive is of the opinion that women only work for 'pin money' and should be the main candidates for redundancy, before the full-time male employees of the business. Set up a meeting between the two sides to consider the matter, comprising representatives of the women part-time workers and the male full-time workers.

BIBLIOGRAPHY

Ackoff, R, *The Systems Age* (New York, Wiley, 1974).
Adams, R *et al*, *Changing Corporate Values* (London, Kogan Page, 1992).
Barnard, C I, *The Functions of the Executive* (Cambridge, Mass, Harvard University Press, 1938). Chapters 15–17
Bigelow, J D (Ed), *Management Skills* (London, Sage, 1991).
Burgoyne, J, 'Management Development for the Individual and the Organization' (IPM Conference Paper, June 1988).
Cannon, T, *Corporate Responsibility* (London, *Financial Times*/Pitman Publishing, 1993).
Coe, T, *The Key to the Men's Club* (London, Institute of Management, 1992).
Drucker, P F, *The Practice of Management* (London, Pan, 1977). Conclusion.
Drucker, P F, *The New Realities* (Oxford, Heinemann, 1990).
Handy, C, *The Age of Unreason* (London, Hutchinson, 1989).
Kroeber, D W, *Management Information Systems* (New York, The Free Press, 1982).
Mintzberg, H, *The Nature of Managerial Work* (New York, Harper & Row, 1973).
Peters, T and Waterman, R, *In Search of Excellence* (New York, Harper & Row, 1982).
Pinchott, C, *Intrapreneuring* (New York, Harper & Row, 1985).
Stewart, R, *The Reality of Management* (London, Pan, 1986), Chapters 6 and 8.
Stewart, R, *Choices of the Manager* (London, McGraw-Hill, 1982).
Stewart, R, *Managers and Their Jobs* (Basingstoke, Macmillan, 1988).

CHAPTER 2

Business and its external environment

This chapter seeks to set the scene for the analysis of the organization and commences with a brief introduction of the various types of business activity and the different types of business organization. It then examines different types of economic systems.

Managers, whether in business or government or elsewhere, must take into account the influence of their external environment. They must have sufficient knowledge to be able to identify and evaluate forces that may affect an organization's operations. As discussed in the previous chapter, the company is part of a system open to the environment – the domestic and also the international environment.

Included in the chapter is an introduction to the financial institutions that are an integral part of business operations together with their role in the financial structure. The main sources of finance are also summarized.

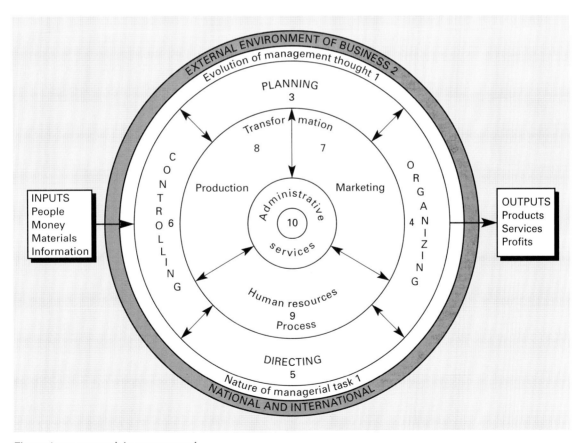

The systems approach to management

OBJECTIVES

Upon completing this chapter, you should be able to:

- Understand the role of business and the economic structure.
- Describe the role of the Stock Exchange and the new issue market.
- Describe briefly the information required before deciding whether or not to become involved in international business.
- Appreciate why managers should be concerned about the relationship between an enterprise and its environment.
- Briefly compare Japanese and Western European management practices.
- Discuss the impact of the Single Market on business in Europe.
- Explain the nature and features of small business management.
- Describe factors involved in exporting to Central and Eastern Europe.

NATURE OF BUSINESS ACTIVITY

Business as an *activity* can be divided into:

- people demanding goods and services. These are the *consumers* (involved in consumption);
- people involved in obtaining, arranging and transforming basic materials into finished products. These are the *producers* (involved in production);
- people who are not in the above categories are those involved in *distributing* (distribution) the products to consumers and others. They also can include those involved in providing financial services (e.g. financial institutions).

Business organizations can be classified by the level of activity, by sector, or by legal structure.

Classification by level of activity

- Primary – firms involved in the *first* stages of production. These are the *extractive* industries (e.g. quarrying, mining, agriculture).
- Secondary – this second stage of production is manufacturing. All manufactured goods are included, e.g. capital or investment goods (plant, buildings, machine tools), durable consumer goods (e.g. cars, washing machines) or non-durable goods (e.g. food, clothing).
- Tertiary – firms providing services, e.g. police, education and other services such as banking, insurance and catering.

Classification by sector

This is quite simply grouping business into private or public areas.

- The *private sector* includes all firms whose ownership is by private enterprise (e.g. IBM or the corner shop).

- The *public* sector includes business which are controlled by government, e.g. British Rail. It is worth noting that examples of the public sector may change with different political parties in power.

The government has a part shareholding in some firms and there has been constant changes in those that are under public ownership in the United Kingdom.

It is obvious that primary, secondary and tertiary activities are all needed. Efficient production and exchange is needed at both national and international levels in order to raise the standard of living of all in society. There are various types of organization, ownership and control and these may change from time to time as society tries to find the 'best' or 'optimum' way of fulfilling its needs.

Classification by legal structure

The term *legal person* can refer to any person who can enjoy certain legal rights and who has certain legal duties. Some do not enjoy *full* legal capacity, e.g. children. The term can also refer to a group of people acting collectively, so the *group* becomes a person in its own right. It can therefore *exist separately* from the individuals that make up the group.

When a company is formed, this is an example of a group of people becoming a 'legal person' which can enjoy all legal rights that an individual has, e.g. it can own property. This concept is very important for business organizations. A company formed in this way becomes 'incorporated' and the people who formed it have separate rights and responsibilities from the firm itself.

Individuals who enter business as a legal person, in their own right, have no rights or responsibilities other than those of an ordinary individual – these businesses have no legal identity and are termed *unincorporated* associations (e.g. sole traders, partnerships).

Unincorporated associations

- **A sole trader** is the most prevalent and simplest form of organization. The owner has complete control and alone is responsible for any debt incurred and has *unlimited liability* for the business.
- **Partnerships** are formed by individuals combining and each person becomes a partner. This may be to bring in new capital or expertise. These are usually a small business unit, e.g. builders or professional services such as solicitors.

The Partnership Act 1890 defines a partnership as 'the relationship which subsists between persons carrying on a business in common with a view to profit'. Membership is generally restricted to not more than 20 persons, although this restriction does not apply to solicitors, accountants or members of a recognized Stock Exchange. Any other profit-making association with greater numbers must form and be registered as a company.

The *personal liability of partners is unlimited*, just like sole traders *unless* the partnership is registered under the Limited Partnership Act of 1907. In these cases, liability is limited to the amount of their subscribed capital. In most cases, though, a partner is liable for the debts and obligations of the firm which were incurred while he was a partner.

A partnership is formed by agreement, which is usually included in a written statement in the form of a deed called Articles of Partnership. The rights, powers and duties of partners are clearly set out in these Articles.

The 1890 Partnership Act includes a model set of Articles that are held to apply if a question is not covered. So, *in the absence of agreement to the contrary*, all partners are entitled to a *share in the running* of the business and an *equal share of profits* and equally contribute to any losses. In practice, profits are shared in proportion to capital or effort contributed. In addition, some partners take a major part in the managing of the partnership, e.g. senior partner in an accountancy firm.

In limited partnerships there must be one partner with *unlimited* liability, and those with limited liability are *not* allowed to take part in the management of the firm nor withdraw their financial contribution while the partnership exists. As this type of firm has no legal identity, the death or departure of one partner will dissolve the partnership.

Registered companies

The Companies Act 1980 (now replaced by the Companies Act 1985, amended by the Companies Act 1989) amended the 1948 Companies Act and redefined the distinction between public and private companies to meet European Community standards. The 1980 Act required a *public* company to have a minimum authorized share capital of £50 000 and to obtain a certificate from the Registrar to enable it to do business and exercise borrowing powers. Public companies were to include the designation 'public limited company' in their names instead of the word 'limited'. The other important change was that the minimum number needed to form a public limited company was changed to only *two*.

The main distinguishing characteristic between public and private companies is that a public company can *offer shares and debentures to the public* and a private company cannot. Any company that does not satisfy the requirements of a public company is deemed a *private* company.

The average size of the private company is small because the maximum number of shareholders is limited to 50. Public companies have no limitation.

The sole trader and the partnership forms of organization are not suitable for larger enterprises that have large capital needs. Shareholders and creditors needed assurances that their money was safe and so the joint-stock company developed from the partnership to allow shareholders to invest money without involving themselves in the running of the business, or having unlimited liability for losses if the business did not prosper.

The types of company operating today are:

- registered companies – these are the most popular and are registered under the Companies Act;
- chartered companies – these are charitable bodies and other institutions that are incorporated by Royal Charter;
- statutory companies – these are formed under a specific Act of Parliment.

Some public companies are very large and operate in several countries. There are other groups of organizations who try to link members in a group which is capable of exerting influence, providing advice and training and other benefits to members. Examples are the *Confederation of British Industry* (CBI) which is an employers' organization and the *Trades Union Congress* (TUC) representing a large number of trade unions (*see* p 413).

Co-operative societies draw their legal personality from the Industrial and Provident Societies Act and register with the Registrar General of Friendly Societies. They were originally self-help organizations working on the basis of *worker* ownership and control. They are successsful more in distribution (wholesaling and retailing) than production. Members (shareholders) have limited liability and one vote per person. Profits are distributed to members in proportion to their purchases from the co-operative, usually in the form of dividend stamps issued at the time of purchase. Larger societies are controlled by full-time management committees.

Public sector organizations

We have already seen that the *private sector* covers firms controlled by any form of private enterprise. Comparisons between companies can be made by turnover (sales), by share of the market or net profit (*see* Chapter 6). *Public sector* organizations are controlled by the government. The number controlled depends upon the ideas of the government in power. After 1945, many industries were nationalized; since 1980, most have been denationalized. Reasons for such changes are a mixture of economic, political and social factors prevailing at different times.

Public organizations trade and supply goods and services at prices which cover their costs. Non-trading sectors supply goods and services freely or at subsidized prices. Others are engaged in purely administrative activities. The government formulates and proposes policy which is approved by Parliment. The agreed policy is implemented by:

● **central government departments,** e.g. Department of Social Services;
● **local government authorities,** e.g. county councils;
● **government agencies;**
● **nationalized industries;**
● **national service organizations,** e.g. Health.

The nationalized industries account for about 10 per cent of the national income and obtain the bulk of their revenue from the sale of their products at commercial prices. The state has a major stake in industrial activity, as these industries employ about 12 per cent of the total workforce and 20 per cent of fixed investment. Management of larger nationalized industries have additional problems as there is a mixture of commercial and non-commercial objectives, and pricing policy is also subject to government control, which may make it more difficult to plan ahead than in private organizations.

Other government agencies as mentioned above include the Training Employment and Education Directorate and the British Broadcasting Authority. These are known as quangos (quasi-autonomous non-governmental organizations). Such organizations (quangos) are a feature of the bureaucratic process and at the present time there are over 1500 of them. The European Union, for example, has a vast number of quangos employed in assisting it.

BUSINESS AND THE ECONOMIC STRUCTURE

In most Western industrial countries, a small number of large enterprises is responsible for the majority of *manufacturing* sales and profits. Similarly, there are large concentrations in transport and public utilities (some of which have been nationalized). In other areas such as retailing, agriculture and construction, smaller firms account for larger proportions of output and sales. Such large-scale organizations have a great effect upon the development of national economies. Their decisions on output, employment prices, investment and research and development have a pronounced effect upon the pattern and direction of the economy. The way in which larger corporations use the resources at their disposal is of major importance in an analysis of Western industrial systems. Some companies, e.g. General Motors of the USA, have subsidiary companies abroad. Their investment decisions, for example in locating, expanding or contracting their plants abroad, may have important consequences for the growth of the economy or the maintenance of full employment. On a similar basis, the international movement of capital can affect the balance-of-payments position in the economy.

The modern business enterprise is also a political as well as an economic entity. It is involved in government processes, by involvement in pressure groups trying to influence economic decision making.

A company's *operational* costs and benefits may have unforeseen consequences as its *social* costs and benefits may produce side-effects which are not wanted, such as pollution of the environment. The business community comprises a *network* of interdependent groups – firms, the government, consumers, employers and investors – all with interacting relationships.

Consumers

Consumers provide the market for goods and services produced by firms. Statistical data is available from the Central Statistical Office showing the number of persons in the community. They can be classified by age, and this knowledge is valuable for those producing goods which appeal to certain age groups. It is important to note that economists are interested in *'effective demand'*, i.e. the number of people who can *pay* for the goods and services.

Another factor to note is the amount of money persons have available for spending in the various age groups. This needs to be analysed carefully to determine effective demand for products which can vary markedly between age groups. An analysis of the distribution of total expenditure among food, drink, tobacco, entertainment, etc., is available. Analysis in detail of each heading is also possible and will be of great value to a firm in deciding their marketing strategy. Car manufacturers will know the sales for each model and their share of the market at home and abroad. Constant research of the consumer market is needed as *consumer preferences* can change quickly. Companies use many methods to encourage consumers to buy their products. Consumers pay for goods and services, and these are called 'expenditure flows'.

Firms and the government

Firms and the government play a vital part in the business and economic structure as previously mentioned. Resources are drawn together and transformed into goods and services, by private or public enterprises. We have briefly considered the consumers who buy the products and must also consider the other factors in the total system. These are the workers or *employees* who produce the goods and services – and the *investors* who provide the money to *finance* the operations of the firm.

Employees

Employees produce the goods and services and can be classified as manual, non-manual and agricultural. In addition to the 'active' population, there are those available for work between 16 and 65 who are unemployed. The total of the two groups plus those in the armed forces give the total available working population.

The management in companies are employees, although they carry out different functions (*see* p 187).

Those who work for themselves or are 'self-employed' constitute about 5 per cent of the total working population.

Investors

Money is needed to finance the operation of firms. Small savers contribute by saving through life assurance policies, commercial banks, building societies, etc. The money saved is invested in a wide range of commercial, industrial and government securities on behalf of individual savers. This is *indirect* investment. Other organizations also place money saved *direct* with firms and the government. The types of investment will be dealt with later. The returns available vary with the type of security and the period invested.

Firms obtain resources from owners of resources and transform them into goods and services. Investors provide the funds to do this and employees provide the workforce. The consumers provide the market for the goods and services (*see* Fig 2.1).

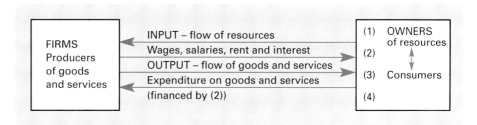

Fig 2.1 Flow of resources, goods and services

ECONOMIC SYSTEMS

Organizations have to take decisions which are affected by the type of economic system in which they exist. So a brief consideration of the main types of economic systems is valuable.

The fundamental economic problem is to allocate scarce resources, which are capable of alternative uses, with many consumer wants. Economics attempts to analyse ways of allocating these limited resources so as to maximize our economic well-being.

There are two main systems that link consumers with resources, a planned economy and a market economy.

Planned economy

Economic resources in this system are in public ownership and *political* choices determine priorities in their allocation. In these countries the *government* decides the *variety* of the goods to be produced, the *quality* produced, the *methods* of production to be used, *who produces* and the ways in which the goods will be *distributed* and *sold*. The planning problems are formidable: various plans are made from 10–15 year plans to plans of one year. Decisions involve many people, resulting in a bureaucratic system which can lead to delayed decision making and problems of co-ordination on a vast scale. If problems are *not solved* there will be shortages of key materials, queues for consumer goods in short supply, or overproduction of other goods, as targets unrelated to demand are being attempted.

Free market economy

A free market economy is the main alternative to a planned economy. The decisions about the allocation of resources are given to all the consumers and business firms whose transactions are guided by free competition and self-interest. It is *market forces* which determine what is produced, how it is produced and in what manner. The private enterprise or capitalist system involves *private* ownership of the means of the production, e.g. land, factories, etc. The central feature in the determination of exchange transactions and the *terms* upon which transactions take place is 'the market'. A *market* may be said to be where exchange transactions are negotiated and where the *terms* are determined. A market can be in a fixed place, e.g. fruit market; in a wider sense, it can be any arrangement that brings consumers and producers or buyers and sellers into contact. In all communities, exchange takes place and in most economies today goods are exchanged through the *medium of money;* this value in exchange is expressed in terms of money or 'price'. The concept of *price* is therefore a key feature in determining what is produced and in what quantity, and who uses the product. There are thousands of markets for the various goods and services with market prices providing the essential link between supply and demand for them. Market prices change in response to changes in the conditions under which demand and supply take place. If demand for a product rises relative to the amounts supplied, price will tend to rise; a fall in demand relative to supply will mean a tendency for price to fall (*see* p 299 for further discussion). These changes in price are indications to producers and consumers to change their behaviour, and *alter their allocation of their* limited *resources.*

We have seen that there are two extreme positions, the planned economy and the 'free' economy. In practice, some modification takes place, whereby the wishes of individuals and government interact. In the United Kingdom, for example, the government plays a role in *exerting pressure on producers and consumers*. The extent of this role will depend upon the political philosophy of the party in power.

The government may feel that the welfare of the nation or its security must be safeguarded and will try to control certain aspects and can control prices or production, thus interfering with the decisions of producers and consumers. Prices charged by nationalized industries are altered to ensure one group is not exploited, which might occur if left to the free interplay of market forces.

In the management of a *mixed economy* as in the United Kingdom, the aim is to achieve a set of outcomes which are different from that resulting from the free interplay of market forces. This implies that the unregulated forces of the market which operate through the price mechanism would not produce satisfactory outcomes.

STRUCTURE OF INDUSTRY

Basic economic theory indicates the economies that may arise when a firm grows. These internal economies are classified as:

- technical economies – referring to actual savings made within the production process;
- financial economies – referring to the fact that larger firms can usually raise capital more easily and cheaply than smaller firms. This is because they can offer better security and appear more stable, particularly if they are quoted on the Stock Exchange;
- managerial economies – are those savings arising from division of labour and the benefits from mechanized administration;
- marketing economies – refer to savings by buying and selling in bulk, as large purchasing or sales orders can result in lower costs;
- risk-bearing economies – possible losses due to changes in *demand* are less for larger firms which can diversify output or markets more easily. Changes in *supply* can be avoided by diversifying sources of supply and methods of production. The activities of a larger firm are usually more diverse than those of a small firm, so a loss or failure in one area of activity may not so easily affect the liability of the whole enterprise.

There are also *economies of scale* which arise as a firm grows. The cost of production per unit of output can fall as output increases, because there is more scope for division of labour and specialization of machines.

LOCATION OF INDUSTRY

The main factors determining the location of industry were historically the easy access to raw materials, availability of suitable power supplies and skilled labour, the proximity to major markets and transport advantages (e.g. nearness to ports).

Businesses which located in these areas obtained economies of scale which resulted in savings in unit costs of production.

Economies that may arise through the *growth of an industry* are called *external economies of scale*. They arise from:

- increased *specialization* of commodities or process;
- availability of *related services*, e.g. research establishments, trade journals, etc.;
- better *quality labour* supply available;
- availability of *subsidiary industries* providing for the main industry (i.e. components or materials);
- development of good transport and communication services;
- availability of specialist local education and training.

All of these advantages make it unlikely that new entrants to an industry would consider locating their business in other places.

Regional policy

Regional policy attempts to change the wide disparities existing between regions. This may have occurred because of the decline of staple industries, which tended to be located on or near coalfields and were very labour intensive. A report in 1983 by the British Institute of Management on the 'Importance of Regional Policy' stressed the difficulties in assessing the effectivness of such policies. The costs and benefits are also difficult to calculate (*see* report in *Management Today*, November 1983, p 145, published by The British Institute of Management).

The following methods are used to influence location of industry at present.

Enterprise Zones

Enterprise Zones are an attempt by the government to encourage companies to locate in areas which were often derelict inner-city and other areas where industrial development would not otherwise take place. The idea is to remove fiscal and administrative barriers which may prevent a company's expansion.

Firms located outside these zones are not happy with this arrangement, which they regard as unfair competition. Existing firms in the zone and new firms all benefit from:

- simplified administrative procedures (e.g. planning);
- financial assistance, e.g. exemption from payment of rates for 10 years.

Assisted Areas

Assisted Areas consist of Development Areas, Special Development Areas and Intermediate Areas in which regional development grants and other assistance is given to firms to encourage them to locate or expand.

Urban aid	Co-operation between local authorities and private enterprise may result in aid being given to urban investment projects.
Office Development Permits	Office Development Permits were introduced in the 1960s to restrict office development in congested large city centres, e.g. London and Birmingham, the aim being to disperse such building to less congested provincial city centres.
Freeports	Freeports are places where goods can be imported, stored and processed and *exported* without having to pay customs duty, which would be payable only if the goods were moved within the United Kingdom.

Many companies consider relocation in a new area or rationalizing dispersed sites by concentrating in a central position. These will be considered in Chapter 3, Corporate Strategy and Planning.

The various regions have differing economic characteristics which result in regional inequalities. These inequalities have been reduced by the regional polices of the government, but have not been eliminated.

STOCK EXCHANGE

The International Stock Exchange in London is a highly organized market for the purchase and sale of *second-hand* quoted securities (these are securities which the Stock Exchange Council has approved). This organized market enables investors to exchange their shares for cash. The advantages for a public limited company in having its shares traded on the Stock Exchange is that it conveys liquidity and marketability on the shares. They are then more attractive to institutional and private investors, making it *easier* and *cheaper* for the company to raise new capital.

The Stock Exchange plays an important part in the economic and commercial life of the country. The following are a few of its benefits:

- it enables *long-term capital to be raised*. Investors may not want to lend their money permanently to a company but the company needs the money permanently – the Stock Exchange allows investors to exchange their shares when they wish for cash;
- members of the Stock Exchange are expected to set high standards of behaviour and *investors are protected* by their careful examination of companies before allowing a quotation;
- it provides a *market* for 'gilt-edged' securities thus assisting government monetary policy which depends upon the sale and purchase of government securities;
- Stock Exchange prices are an important *economic indicator*. Taxation administration is also assisted by valuations of stocks and shares.

SHARE CAPITAL

A limited company can raise capital in a number of ways in order to attract contributions from various kinds of people and institutions, by offering them *shares* in the company. Some shares carry a rate of interest which is *fixed* and also a guarantee of repayment, others do not have a fixed return nor an offer of repayment. A person who buys a share becomes a part-owner of the company, entitled to a share of the profits of the company.

- *Nominal* or *authorized* capital is the maximum amount of money the company is allowed to raise by issuing shares to the public.
- If they issue *part* of the total authorized, this amount is called the *issued* capital.
- When only a *proportion* of the issued capital is required, that part which is paid for is called the *paid-up capital* of the company.

A company's share capital is capital authorized by its Memorandum of Association and is usually divided into shares of different classes with different rights. This is done to appeal to different types of investors so that the market for shares will be broader. Many companies are formed with limited liability and shareholders, as has been mentioned before, are not liable to lose more than they have paid or promised to pay into the business. Limiting the liability of shareholders attracts savings from many persons. The two main types of shares available are ordinary and preference.

Ordinary shares

Ordinary shares represent the risk capital of a business. The holders of these shares are *not* guaranteed any dividend or return on their capital at the end of a trading year as this usually depends on whether or not a company has made a profit. Since each ordinary share provides an *equal* share of the profits available, they are called *equities* and capital raised from issuing them is called *equity capital*. Most ordinary shares carry voting rights which to holders confer control over the company's affairs by voting at general meetings. They share in the profits, *after interest* has been paid to debenture and other *debt* holders and *after dividends* have been paid to preference shareholders. When profits are high, ordinary shares may expect a high dividend, and conversely a low dividend when profits are low.

Preference shares

Preference shares carry a right, a preferential right, in the distribution of profits and in the repayment of capital if a company is wound up. They usually are given a right to a fixed percentage dividend before other classes receive any at all. This *prior claim on profits* makes them less risky than ordinary shares.

Loan capital

A company may acquire funds to finance long-term investments by borrowing for long periods over 10 years. The security given to the lender is usually the assets of the company and interest is payable to the lender at agreed rates.

Debentures

Debentures can be issued to raise money over long periods. They are simply *loans* to the company over which an agreed rate of interest is paid *before* preference or ordinary shareholders receive anything. They are normally *secured* against the property of the company, so in case of the company becoming bankrupt, debenture holders will be assured of reclaiming money lent. Debenture holders do *not share in the ownership* of the company. The debentures may be bought and sold in the capital markets. In recent years, borrowing by debentures offering fixed interest rates has not been popular because of high inflation and volatile interest rates. When the rate of inflation is higher than the rate of interest, borrowers benefit at the expense of the lenders. Measures to safeguard borrowers have been devised to offer an acceptable compromise between borrowers and lenders. One example is the *convertible* debenture, which is a fixed-interest security which carries an *option* that the holder may convert it into ordinary shares at an agreed future time. So this provides a fixed-interest security offering a 'hedge' against inflation.

New issue market finance

Sources of finance from the banking system are mainly designed to meet short-and medium-term needs. Companies which cannot meet their financial needs from retained profits or the banks can raise *long-term* money on the stock market by the issue of equity or loan capital.

In most cases, companies will employ the services of an *issuing house* (see below). The company's accounts and prospects will be closely examined and, if satisfactory, the issuing house will give advice on the most appropriate type and class of security and the terms of the proposed issue to ensure a successful take-up of the offer. If the return (dividend) offered is not satisfactory and shares issued are not taken up, then the issue may not be successful. The issuing house may have agreed, as a form of insurance to the company, to take up any shares not taken up by the public. This is an important function of the issuing house, which is said to have 'underwritten' the issue of the shares.

A new issue of shares may be placed before the public in the following ways:

- **An issue by prospectus to the public.** The offer is usually made in the press and an issuing house usually deals with the often large number of applications. The Companies Acts require certain information to be disclosed in the prospectus which would be of interest to a prospective investor.
- **An offer for sale** is where the whole issue is sold to issuing houses, or other institutions, which then re-sell the shares to the public at a higher price.

- **A private placing** is when a *company* arranges for an institution to buy a block of its shares. They are not then available through a Stock Exchange to a wider market. The issuing house places the shares with other institutions, e.g. insurance companies.
- **A Stock Exchange placing** is where a stockholder, usually with the assistance of an issuing house, arranges for a large number of investors to purchase the shares issued. Placing may be used when an issue is relatively small or unlikely to attract much public interest. This tends to be a cheaper method than an issue by prospectus or an offer for sale and may be attractive to smaller companies.
- **Issues by tender** are made when the price or demand for the issue cannot be determined very accurately. A price is fixed and *tenders* or offers above this price are invited. Shares are then allotted at the highest price that will ensure the issue is fully taken up.
- **A rights issue** may be made by public companies. New shares are offered to *existing* shareholders, who are given the opportunity to subscribe for the new shares in a given proportion to those already held. Or, a shareholder's rights to shares can be *assigned* to someone else. These equity shares can be sold on the Stock Exchange if desired.

The external capital market can be by-passed by this method and whatever the proportion offered (e.g. one new share for five existing shares), it is usually on favourable terms. This represents a *less costly* method of issue for companies.

It is interesting to note that as the price to be paid for new shares offered is *below the market price of existing shares*, the price per share of the enlarged issue tends to fall. Thus a person who does not take up the allocation offered to him, nor assigns his right to it, will suffer a loss on the shares he already holds.

SOURCES OF FINANCE

The function of finance may be defined as the provision of the *amount* of money required at a specific *time* and at an acceptable *cost*. It is not easy to ensure that income will always be available to pay for expenditure at any specific time, as expenditure on expensive equipment or sales of seasonal goods provide peaks that need special provision.

A company needs cash for everyday (i.e. current) working expenses, e.g. wages, rent and stocks of goods. These can be termed short-term investments as they can be recouped by the profit from the sale of products within a relatively short space of time. When investment is made in *fixed* items, e.g. plant or buildings (fixed assets), money is locked away for a long period before any return on the investment is available. *Time* therefore can be seen to be a crucial element in financial planning. The period of finance obtained should match the period of maturity of an investment. These are important factors in the analysis of the solvency of an organization.

Finance is also needed to replace old plant and equipment and it is also important to note that in times of *inflation,* additional money is needed to pay for goods and services.

The factors influencing choice of finance are:

- physical risks – fire, theft;
- technical risks – inferior technical expertise or equipment;
- economic factors – downturn in trade;
- political factors– change in government, civil disturbance or taxation changes;
- management – inadequate management decisions.

Capital must be raised on acceptable terms and firms which have a sound profit record and prospects normally have no problem in raising finance. The problem in obtaining finance for the relatively new small firm is continually being discussed and government measures to assist are partially solving the problem.

Main internal sources of finance

1 **Retained profits.** These give a steady source of finance. The retaining or 'ploughing back' of profits is encouraged by taxation legislation allowing undistributed profits to remain free of income tax. If they are paid as dividends, they would suffer tax.
2 **Provision for depreciation.** Setting aside money for depreciation of assets results in reducing stated profit without actually paying out any cash. Such provisions represent cash retained by an enterprise over and above normal undistributed profit.
3 **Provision for taxation.** Amounts set aside to pay tax when due at a future date are similar to the provision for depreciation.
4 **Reduction in current assets.** If stocks and debtors are reduced, cash funds will be released into the business.

The advantages of internal financing are:

- no interest payments have to be met;
- no repayment is necessary;
- no costs are involved – as would be the case if a financing operation was involved (e.g. in the issue of shares there is the cost of a manager's time locating sources and arranging terms).

Main external sources of finance

The main types of finance and sources of finance in the UK are as follows.

Clearing banks

The five major high street banks are members of the London Clearing House (where most cheques are cleared). They provide a wide network of regional and local offices, providing money in the form of *overdrafts* or *loans.* An *overdraft* allows a firm to overdraw its account, up to an agreed amount. This is a short-term form of borrowing as the bank may not wish to renew this facility and may 'call in' the overdraft; it is flexible and relatively cheap. *Loans* can be granted and are repayable at a specified future date. They are not normally made for large sums or long periods, but policies have been modified in the last few years and banks can lend up to twenty years (e.g. for housing, finance), but most are for short-term periods, say up to five years. Most loans are granted for a specific purpose, e.g. purchase of a car or computer. Repayment of capital and interest is in equal instalments over the period of the loan.

Sources of finance	Period of finance			
	Short-term up to 3 years	Medium-term 3 to 10 years	Long-term over 10 years	Share capital (equity)
Clearing banks	✔	✔	✔	–
Other British and foreign banks	✔	✔	✔	–
Merchant banks	✔	✔	✔	✔
Finance houses	✔	✔	–	–
Discount houses	✔	–	–	–
Factoring companies	✔	–	–	–
Leasing companies	✔	–	–	–
Public sector agencies	–	✔	✔	✔
Insurance companies	–	–	✔	✔
Pension funds	–	–	✔	✔
Stock Exchange	–	–	–	✔
	(A)	(B)	(C)	(D)

Key
A – Temporary working capital, for short-lived assets, e.g. stocks
B – Medium-term finance, e.g. plant and machinery
C – Long-term finance, e.g. buildings
D – Permanent capital for expansion and re-financing of borrowings.

The above table shows the sources of finance available for the more usual purposes of investment in fixed assets and other working capital. These examples of *external* finance are either in share capital or in borrowing – the period of the loan determines the sources available. It is interesting to note that *retained profits* is the most important source of company finance. Such 'internal' finance provides over two-thirds of companies' requirements.

The clearing banks in other countries (e.g. Germany and Japan) play a much larger part in financing business. This has been said to be one of the main reasons why their economies have grown quickly.

Banks also assist in many ways in helping businesses exporting goods and services.

Merchant banks	The term merchant banks refers specifically to the members of the Accepting Houses Committee.

These banks have a more limited range of customers and branch networks as compared with clearing banks. Small firms generally have limited access to their services. They provide help and assistance in many ways, one of their most important being to guarantee the value of paper securities (e.g. bills of exchange) which enables the money market to run smoothly. They also act as financial advisers, guiding businesses in the issuing of shares and new long-term capital. They also make fixed-interest loans to their clients, mainly for medium or long terms (e.g. for capital equipment).

Finance houses

Finance houses compete with banks in many ways. They lend to companies as well as individuals who buy goods on hire purchase. A loan is made for goods which normally have a life expectation longer than the period of the loan. The firm becomes the owner immediately and generally can offset the interest paid to the finance company against tax. Their charges tend to be higher than those of the clearing banks, but for many borrowers they are 'lenders of the last resort'. Short- and medium-term loans may therefore be obtained from these organizations which may also be the subsidiaries of major clearing banks.

Discount houses

A discount house is a financial institution and a member of the Accepting Houses Committee. It is a company which specializes in discounting bills of exchange and borrows for short periods and lends for longer periods. Their role is often questioned as to whether they are really required now. It is generally agreed that they do assist in the gathering of short term or idle money, which is lent to industry and commerce and the government. It also provides a rather sensitive mechanism by which short-term interest rates may be regulated. Discount houses accept money on deposit from individuals and firms, but their main sources are banks.

Firms or banks with large sums of money may leave it with a discount house for short periods. The discount house then uses this money to make a profit. It buys Treasury Bills from the government which issues them to raise money on a short-term basis. These bills are very secure, being guaranteed by the government, and are sold by the government to the highest bidder at a discount (i.e. below their nominal value). Discount houses purchase most of these bills and can either keep them until they mature, when they are paid for by the Treasury at the higher nominal value, or sell them to clearing banks at a profit.

They also purchase British government stocks issued by the government which wishes to borrow for long periods. Local authorities also wish to borrow, and discount houses buy securities issued by them which are for one year. These are usually issued at very favourable rates of interest.

Factoring companies

Factoring is a method whereby finance is raised when a 'factor' buys from an enterprise the invoiced debts which have been accumulated by it. Persons who purchase goods for payment at a later date are the debtors of the company. These debts will generally be paid in the future. The money which is represented by these debts can be obtained quickly by selling a company's 'right' to them. The factor company charges for this service. Debtors then deal directly with the factor, thus relieving the business firm of the costs of debt collection and bad debts.

Leasing companies

Leasing companies are a growing area of industrial finance. A leasing company, usually a bank or other finance house, buys plant, vehicles, equipment, buildings or whatever an organization requires. The leasing company then leases the asset to the company at an agreed rental payable over a period of up to 10 years. The leasing company claims any tax or investment incentives granted by the government and grants the lessee the use of the asset at a relatively low cash outlay while still retaining ownership.

Insurance companies

Insurance companies provide finance to assist the property market. Businesses wishing to develop property are assisted by negotiating mortgage loans for 20 years or more with insurance companies. They may also *purchase the freehold* of a firm's site, and lease or rent it back to the firm for an agreed period. This provides cash for expansion. Insurance companies have made an impact upon the financial markets by obtaining shares in industrial concerns.

Public sector agencies

Organizations in the public sector include nationalized industries, central government departments, local authorities and the Health Service. Central government has always had little difficulty in raising finance. The government controls major sources of finance for its various departments. It does this by limiting each organization's borrowing limits.

Pension funds

These are an important source of funds. They are part of the 'institutional' investors which include insurance companies (see above) and unit trusts. Some of the largest funds are in the public sector. The employee and the employer place an agreed sum on a regular basis into a separate fund (if the scheme is contributory) or paid by the employer alone if non-contributory. The funds are held and invested by trustees and ultimately pensions are paid from the fund to employees who retire, or their dependents.

The amounts invested by pension funds are very large and some politicians argue that the funds should be directed to be invested in particular securities and businesses. Investment decisions made by a few senior pension fund managers can have a marked effect upon industry and the market for capital.

OTHER INSTITUTIONS PROVIDING FINANCE

A *definition of capital* would include goods, physical assets or equipment which were created but not consumed and remain available for use. An individual can spend all his/her income on goods and services or reserve some for future use (savings). This portion saved is called *capital,* and can be kept in a number of forms. It may be in the form of *fixed* assets, i.e. buildings or machinery to be used to produce goods, or may refer to *money* which has been saved to buy these fixed assets.

This section deals with the *sources of funds* that producers use for investing in machinery or buildings etc. It is useful to note at this stage the link between the savings of individuals and the capital of firms. An individual who *saves* some of his income places it, for example, with a bank or building society to hold safely. The bank or building society can lend this money to industry which wants to *invest* it in capital equipment. The *capital market*, which consists of a large number of organizations, exists to bring together the savers and the borrowers.

Banks now provide different types of loans and have widened their traditional role to include taking over leasing companies and subscribing to other organizations which were formed to assist small and medium-sized companies. Some of these organizations are:

- **Investors in Industry.** The funds of this organization are provided by banks and the Bank of England and lent to industry for medium-term periods.
- **Export Finance.** The government runs a programme to assist UK exporters with insurance against political and commercial risks in export contracts. It can also provide for the granting of credit to overseas buyers of UK capital goods and services.
- **The Exports Credits Guarantee Department** (ECGD) can make finance available in several different forms. The greatest providers of export credit finance are the UK clearing banks. The Export Credits Guarantee Department operates as an autonomous unit responsible to the Secretary of State for Trade and Industry and is run as a commercial enterprise.

There are a number of institutions which specialize in the provision of *venture capital* which carries a high risk element. Capital may be provided to help businesses start up as well as to give assistance to existing ones. Funds from £15 000 to £1 million can be provided, but an equity stake and a seat on the board of directors of the company is generally required. There are over ten specialist venture capital institutions in the UK and the general term of loans is between five and ten years.

There are also other specialist institutions providing finance to smaller firms as well as to individual industries, e.g. National Research Development Corporation.

Factors to consider when planning choice of finance

Planning finance involves selecting a mixture of short- or long-term debt, e.g. bank overdraft, debentures or equity; that is, retained profits or capital issues. The following are factors to note:

1 Cost of finance
- *Trade creditors* are virtually costless, unless a cash discount is ordered for prompt payment.
- *Bank overdraft*. The cost is the rate of interest charged, which is on the *daily* balance and not on any fixed sum.
- *Leasing* costs are the rent, plus any hidden cost if restrictions are placed on the use of assets.

2 Control. When issuing new capital, new shareholders may obtain full or partial control of the enterprise. This could be overcome by issuing non-voting shares.

3 Risk. If a project is risky, then it may be better to finance it out of equity. The obligation to pay *regular* interest to a lender may become a *burden* if the project fails, and the riskier the investment the *higher will be the interest rate* demanded by lenders of finance. If equity is reduced because of the gamble failing, this may be preferred to retaining a debt which stops the firm progressing.

4 Payment dates. Interest on debt must be paid on *specific* dates, while dividends on equity need only be paid when it is deemed possible to pay.

5 Claim on assets. Some types of financing may result in a charge being placed on assets which may restrict their use.

6 Availability of finance is an essential feature.

7 Date of repayment. Repayment must not be arranged to be made *before* the time needed for the finance to be used to its maximum advantage. Short-term loans may be difficult or very expensive to obtain.

8 Loan or share capital. The choice between raising equity or loan capital depends partly upon the capital structure of the company and partly upon what is regarded as an acceptable ratio between the sources of funds.

A lot will depend upon the market's assessment of the risk involved, and the relationship between loan capital and the shareholders' funds is an indicator of financial risk. The ratio of debt to equity capital is called *gearing*. High capital gearing means a large amount of debt capital relative to equity. Too high a gearing means a company is borrowing too much in relation to its equity base.

The *advantage* of high capital gearing means that when profits are good, shareholders obtain a very high return as debt capital is rewarded by *fixed* interest payments, leaving all the remaining profit in the hands of a smaller number of shareholders.

The *disadvantage* of high capital gearing is that when profits are low, the payment of *fixed* interest on a high debt capital may leave little remaining as profit for the shareholders. Each of the types of debt will vary in its risk characteristics as interest rates and tax rates and other considerations vary. The final result will be a mixture of debt that can be accepted, considering risk and cost.

The Bank of England suggests as a guide that *equity* should be twice the level of company borrowing, i.e. a capital gearing of 1:2, the *maximum* ratio not exceeding 1:1.

INTERNATIONAL MANAGEMENT

Managerial practices differ from one country to another. Real differences emerge when a comparison is made between the practices in the United States of America and the United Kingdom as against Japan.

Japanese management

A great deal of consideration has been given in the last ten years to the reasons why Japanese practices are so successful. There have been many discussions as to whether aspects of their style of management can be effectively instituted in Western capitalist countries.

Success can be measured in various ways. It appears from research that Japan places more emphasis on *market growth and penetration* and in these aspects they were *definite* leaders (*see* K Bhaskar, *Future of the World Motor Industry* (London, Kogan Page, 1980)); but when measurement was made by *accounting ratios* (on profit margins and return on capital) the Japanese were *not* leaders. Japan has the benefit of a large domestic market but it appears that they also benefit from their emphasis on improvement in product quality and productivity.

From this brief review, we can look at the possible reasons for the success of Japanese enterprise. They have great concern for individual employees, who tend to be employed for their whole life in a single enterprise. When looked at closely, it appears that it is only the *larger* companies who have such a system of job security. Older employees have privileges because of their seniority, but this aspect also appears to be changing. A third aspect is that their unions are organized on a corporate rather than an industry or occupational basis.

Proposals tend to be discussed carefully by various levels of employee. Such consultation takes time, but produces greater commitment and greatly assists the problems of communication.

If the best of Japanese practices are to be adapted by other countries, a close analysis is needed. W G Ouchi (1981) analysed the Japanese management practices which are adapted to the American environment and practised by IBM and other companies. Theory Z is the name that has been given to organizations adopting this approach.

Finally, in this short introduction the work should be noted of the employees of McKinsey & Co (American management consultants) and of Pascale and Athos in *The Art of Japanese Management*. One aspect is emphasized: the seven elements used to compare the approaches of two companies, Matsushita and ITT – strategy, structure, systems, staff, style, skills and superordinate goals (*see* Bibliography).

Planning for international operations

In a wider market place, strategic decisions are more complex and are multi-dimensional. Large multinational corporations have to decide where functional activities, e.g. purchasing, research and development, marketing and sales, can be performed. Each activity may be carried out in *every* country or it may wish to concentrate an activity in a *particular* location to serve the organization on a world-wide basis. *Research and development* may be centralized in one area to serve the whole organization, e.g. the Coca-Cola Company. In this company *manufacturing* is decentralized and tailored to each country as the amount of sweeteners and the type of packaging varies in different countries.

Accurate information is essential to enable an organization to determine whether it can hope to operate in a safe and profitable manner in another country. The following information is the minimum that is required:

- the main factors affecting a country's *business operations* (e.g. labour available, market size);
- an analysis of the *business structure* of a country;
- the strengths and weaknesses of its *economy*;
- a knowledge of current and future *legislation* and the climate for investment;
- a knowledge of possible *political* change.

Effective management in a wide range of environments depends upon managers in each country being able to *answer any immediate need*, without referring each time to management in the parent country. Central control is important but subsidiaries need operational flexibility so they can exploit their own market more effectively.

The extent of the activities of international business operations can be seen by the wide variety of products in the average household, for example Japanese televisions and radios, French wines, German cars, clothes from Hong Kong. The growth of world-wide business operations has meant that the management of an enterprise can have competitors from outside as well as inside their own country to a far greater extent than before. This can be viewed as a threat to enterprises within the UK, but there is also a greater opportunity to sell goods and services in a *world market* for UK firms.

A manager should *be aware of the issues* posed by being involved with business on an international scale. Management in an international setting seeks to achieve the *global objectives* of the enterprise through the efficient utilization of resources.

Problems involved

The problems involved are quite different from those affecting domestic firms. Managers have to interact with staff who have different *cultural and educational* backgrounds and deal with different *legal, economic* and *political* factors.

In order to effectively manage foreign operations, managers need to:

- *develop a greater level of awareness* and knowledge;
- *learn new skills* (e.g. foreign languages) and techniques, as incentives and values that motivate people differ widely;
- *evaluate and adjust* the way they use feedback and control methods to manage employees in different cultures.

The external environment

All enterprises must consider carefully the elements that comprise their environment, whether they are public or private, large or small. All managers should *seek to understand* the *relationship between an enterprise and its environment*, whether they operate a business, government agency, charitable organization or university.

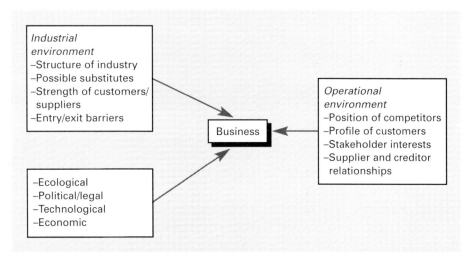

Fig 2.2 Environmental forces impacting on business

One method for understanding the relationship between an enterprise and the environment is to consider the various groups, both internal and external, that can affect or be affected by the accomplishment of its objectives. Each of these groups has a 'stake' in the survival of an enterprise.

Where international management activities are concerned, the constraining influences of external factors on an enterprise are even more crucial.

The various stakeholder groups that affect a business can be seen in Fig 2.2. The importance of each group to the success of an enterprise will vary. For example, in the fashion business, the most critical factor is sensitivity to *customer preferences*. In another business, such as nuclear power generation, *government regulations* may be the key factor affecting the industry's prosperity.

Stakeholders interested in enterprises may include the local community, government, employees, unions, protest groups, owners, competitors, suppliers, customers. They may not, however, always be separate entities; for example, employees of a public utility company may also be customers or shareholders.

The stakeholder approach broadens the scope of social responsibility and managers must be responsible, according to this philosophy, to certain groups that are affected by, or can affect, the interest and objectives of a company.

There are a number of examples of this philosophy (*see* overleaf). In each case the product sold contained material harmful to customers and products were recalled as a precautionary measure, at great expense to the companies involved.

By protecting customers who were an important group of stakeholders the companies concerned protected their corporate image and economic interests. Short-term losses were made with the aim of ensuring long-term profitability. Self-imposed controls reduce the possibility of government intervention. The stakeholder philosophy acknowledges groups to which business should be socially responsible.

The Kellogg Company (USA) in 1986 recalled many thousands of boxes of cereal after metal shavings had been found in three boxes. In 1990 bottles of Perrier water were recalled because traces of benzene had been found in bottles of Perrier water sold in the USA. Stocks all over the world were examined and *all* stocks were withdrawn as a precaution. It was later found that a faulty filter system at the company's plant in Vergeze had probably caused the contamination. The company suffered a drop in share prices as investors sold their shares, while competitors enjoyed increased sales. Perrier pledged to re-cycle the 40 million bottles rejected following the scare.

A methodical approach to obtaining information is vital. Studies have demonstrated that there is a close relationship between the performance of an enterprise and the quality and extent of environmental information obtained. Enterprises that ignore or discount the influence of these factors often fail.

Larger companies continually scan or monitor publications and reports about potential environmental changes (these are potential threats or opportunities). Smaller companies may purchase specialist reports or subscribe to a newspaper-clipping service. Such activities are linked to long-range strategic plans. Effective managers recognize the need for carefully controlled environmental scanning activities so the various stakeholder groups can be monitored.

ENVIRONMENTAL MANAGEMENT

There is a current growing interest in environmental issues which companies must address. A company must take account of consumer pressure groups, legislation, ethical considerations and also potential cost savings. All of these considerations should convince companies that strategic decisions must be made regarding environmental management. These may necessitate marked changes in business practices.

Questions a company must consider include:

- Are we adhering to existing environmental legislation?
- What will be the impact of possible future environmental legislation?
- Are staff encouraged to see environmental improvement as an important goal?
- Are there any constraints in the financial and organizational aspects that may limit environmental improvements?
- Are there any new product opportunities which could be exploited that would have a favourable environmental impact on the market?

When a strategic plan for the environment has been agreed, detailed policies can be set and communicated to staff and the public. There is a need to select staff and give them special environmental responsibilities, preferably including a director with a seat on the main board. Such a person would have to take a strategic view and raise the profile of the environment with all stake-holders and establish systems and methods of monitoring environmental performance.

Environmental auditing

Environmental auditing is an independent objective evaluation of how all aspects of an organization are performing. The aim is to assist management in the control of environmental practice to meet company policies and external regulations.

Such an audit is often carried out by a group of specialists, e.g. engineers, economists, lawyers. The aim of the audit is to minimize risks to human health, safeguard the environment and advise the company on environmental improvements that should be made.

The benefits of periodic auditing are that the company is assured of its conformity to legislation, an improved public image and a possible reduction in costs (e.g. through energy conservation and efficient waste disposal).

The European Community has recently issued discussion papers on environmental auditing. In the United Kingdom the Confederation of British Industry has published procedures for environmental auditing. An increase in interest will result in standardization of practice.

It is likely that environmental concern will become a normal part of business activity. Competitive advantages can be obtained by initiating change within an organization and responding with new environmentally friendly products. As increased competition is to be found because of European integration, it seems likely that careful environmental management will provide firms with a clear competitive edge.

Environmental impact studies

An environmental impact study is an analysis of the impact of a proposed plant location on the quality of life in an area. The study analyses the impact of a proposed plant on facilities for transport and requirements for energy, water and sewage treatment. It also notes the effect on natural plant life and wildlife, on air, water and noise pollution. A number of American States have issued Acts which prohibit the construction of oil refineries or heavy manufacturing industry within a specified radius from the State's coastline.

Forward looking product design managers are examining ways in which all company products are developed to produce the minimum environmental damage. This 'product stewardship':

- considers all raw materials, components and energy sources used in the product and how substitutes can be used which may be more environmentally friendly;
- considers which production processes are more energy efficient and produce less pollution;
- considers ways in which the disposal of the product and production waste can be more effectively recycled.

The increase in environmental legislation, particularly in Europe, may stimulate research to develop environmentally compatible products.

Some European countries, e.g. Germany and Norway, have stringent regulations for companies producing toxic wastes, e.g. nuclear processing plants. Britain is not so particular, despite protests from environmental pressure groups.

Management in practice

> An American multinational chemical company, Union Carbide, had a waste-processing plant in Bhopal, India. A serious accident occurred in the plant in the early 1980s. This was given world-wide publicity and was an example of lax environmental policies. The company was later not allowed to set up a new plant in the United States, by the US Environmental Protection Agency.

The environment and European integration

The Single Europe Act has stated that there is need for legislation on environmental policies for companies. Laws should meet the following objectives:

- to preserve, protect and improve the quality of the environment;
- to protect human health;
- to ensure prudent and rational use of natural resources.

Four principles are advocated to meet these objectives:

- to prevent harm to the environment;
- to control pollution at source;
- to get the polluter to pay;
- to integrate environmental considerations into Community policies.

Denmark's objections that its own standards were higher than those of the EC were met by a clause stating that the Act need not prevent member states taking 'more stringent measures' than the EC standard.

The Single European Market (SEM) means that firms will be exposed to greater competition and can no longer rely on their existing market to provide them with the profits they require. As competition increases it is the most efficient firms that will survive and this can be assisted by, for example, developing responsibility lower down the line and instituting Total Quality Methods (see Chapter 8).

Ecological forces

Ecological forces have made a big impact on managerial decision making. Concern for protecting and preserving the natural environment led to legislation in America and Europe during the 1970s and 1980s, e.g. the US Clean Air and Water Acts and the Resource Conservation and Recovery Act.

The concern that managers must show for ecological balance is far wider than just complying with government legislation. Finite renewable sources such as coal and oil must be carefully used, while some resources can be replenished and even expanded, for example forests.

In the United Kingdom the majority of people are concerned with most environmental issues, e.g. nuclear and chemical waste disposal and oil pollution. As far as companies are concerned a social conscience and sound environmental management is highly rated.

The Brundtland report, *Our Common Future*, by the World Commission on Environment and Development in 1987 highlighted the need for industries to manage renewable and non-renewable resources on a global scale, for the benefit of present and future generations. A number of large industrial manufacturers have been working for years to put their environmental policy and practice in good order. These companies include IBM, 3M, Shell, Glaxo and ICI.

Management in practice

In 1975, the 3M Company initiated a programme called 'Pollution Prevention Pays'. It is the policy of 3M to recognize its responsibility to:

- solve its own environmental pollution and conservation problems;
- prevent pollution at source wherever possible;
- conserve natural resources through the use of reclamation and other methods;
- ensure that facilities and products meet and sustain the regulations of all local environmental agencies.

A key feature is the total commitment of senior management and the involvement of all staff in making it happen.

IBM operates to high environmental standards. *Environment audits* are regularly held and a master review takes place every year. These entail an investigation of all factors that might affect the relationship between the company and the local environment.

Another large company's attitude to community work and public awareness can be seen in Shell UK's 'Better Britain Campaign', which has been running for 20 years and has been very successful.

Today, a demonstrable social conscience is valued and sound environmental management is necessary. *Sustainable development* is a term used to mean the management of renewable and non-renewable resources on a global scale, for the benefit of future generations. '*Green growth*' is another, simpler, term used for the process.

Environmental excellence is an investment for the future and good practice involves building standards into *every* aspect of operation, finding ways to measure them and making people responsible for the results.

EXTERNAL ENVIRONMENT OF ORGANIZATIONS

The various schools of management thought, classical, behavioural and the management science school, tended to pay little attention to the external environment and concentrated on the internal aspects which they could control. This was mainly because the external environment was generally stable and predictable so there was less need for them to be concerned. At present, rapid changes are occurring in the external environment which have marked effects on organizations and their management.

The systems and contingency approaches take account of elements in the environment that affect and are affected by the operations of the organization. Figure 1.1 on p 20 shows environmental factors which affect an organization. Figure 2.3 below shows in more detail the influence of *government* activities on organizations.

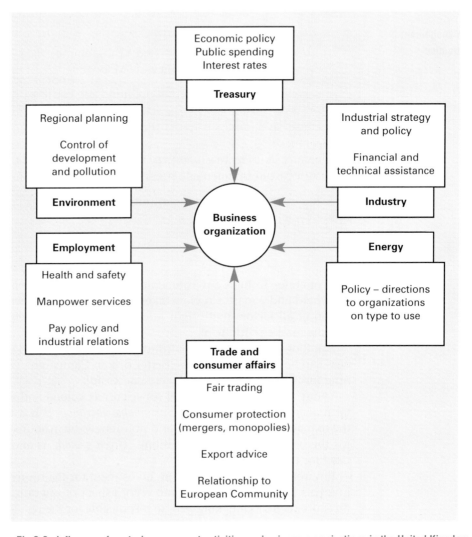

Fig 2.3 Influence of central government activities on business organizations in the United Kingdom

Changing role of business in society

Before we examine the objectives of a business in detail, it is worth while considering the changing role of business in society. A knowledge of basic economics is important in looking at the classical economic approach and seeing how it has since been modified.

The ideas of Adam Smith in his book *The Wealth of Nations* (1776) heralded the beginning of the *'laissez-faire'* approach in economics. He saw human conduct as motivated by: love of self, the habit of labour, the need to be independent and the need to exchange.

The consideration of self-interest was deemed beneficial as *competition* would ensure that companies pursuing their own self-interest had to produce goods and services that people wanted to buy. Any overcharging would lead to sales going to competitors. Even paying staff poor wages would mean workers would go to competitors who paid higher wages. So it was in the interest of companies to produce at competitive prices. This 'invisible' hand of the market guided the way in which individual and community needs were affected. This mechanism could respond automatically to changing needs of customers, and meant that government intervention was unnecessary.

Today the industrial structure is different and the value system upon which it was originally based has changed. Business units have increased in size, securing economies of scale. The increase in market concentration has meant larger concerns are *insulated* from competitive pressure. Larger companies have resources to overcome temporary setbacks and they have the power to influence the allocation of resources. They can, for example, diversify and institute internal transfer pricing. They also have more financial security so they can adopt a longer-term planning approach – *strategic* planning rather than day-to-day *tactical* planning (*see* p 99). Another important feature is that the separation of ownership from control has left more companies in the charge of professional salaried managers, who, as they do not own large numbers of shares, may therefore take a *broader* view than an owner-manager, and hence be more concerned with the *survival* and growth of the company in the long term, rather than short-run profits.

Changing values and attitudes

Where standards of living rise above a certain minimum or subsistence level and people become better educated, their needs and priorities change (their hierarchy of needs). They often become less interested in material possessions and instead aspire to an improved quality of life, job satisfaction, security, a cleaner environment, etc.

Industrialized nations may give lower priority to the pursuit of economic growth, and become concerned with social costs associated with their growth (e.g. air and water pollution) and this will affect plans. In many countries, there exist pressure groups whose aim is to bring about a reduction in pollution. Other groups may express concern about the weak and underprivileged, the fairness of equity or income distribution and industrial democracy or worker participation.

So with public opinion focused upon these areas of company activities, any failures to meet an acceptable standard are widely publicized. The implication is also that a business cannot now confine itself *only* to its traditional economic role of aiming for a profit within existing legal rules, an approach which may imply that the business is being irresponsible in the exercise of its power. So there is now a broadening of the original economic motive to include a wider range of responsibilities. These responsibilities can be illustrated by the following views of the firm:

- **shareholder** – viewing a company as a business existing *solely* to make profits for its *shareholders*. The claims of other interested persons, i.e. employees, customers and the community, operate as a *constraint* upon profit goals;
- **stakeholder** – viewing the company as owing a responsibility to *all* the above groups.

Businesses do not therefore operate in a vacuum; if they are to ensure their long-term survival, they need to respond to growing public criticism of their activities and be seen to be making a positive contribution to meeting the changing needs of society.

There is therefore a move well away from the profit-orientated, *laissez-faire* philosophy which has existed for over 150 years.

Government influence on business purposes

The government has intervened in almost every sphere of human activity during the 20th century. The importance of the role of the state can be seen from the fact that public expenditure accounts for over 40 per cent of the Gross National Product in some Western countries. Such has been the extent of state control and intervention in the United Kingdom that management today has conceded to trade unions and the state rights which would not have even been contemplated in the early 20th century.

It does not appear that the amount of government intervention has been determined by political philosophy; intervention has occurred frequently under left- and right-wing administrations. Private industry has relied upon government aid in many countries, whether from subsidy or protection or the receipt of direct aid.

In most Western industrial countries a small number of large enterprises are responsible for the majority of sales and profits in manufacturing industry. In a survey in the United Kingdom, firms employing less than 200 persons were responsible for only 21 per cent of production in that area. Large firms therefore have a marked effect on the development and operation of national economies, especially their decisions on investment, research and development, prices, employment and output. Such significant effects are not limited to national boundaries. *Multinational* organizations affect the economies of countries other than their own.

The tendency for large organizations to become more impersonal in their employee relationships increases the sense of *alienation* of their employees. This was illustrated by R Blaunder in *Alienation and Freedom* (University of

Chicago Press, 1964). There have been suggestions that this may lead to an increase in industrial relations conflict.

The business enterprise in most countries today is so large and complex that it needs an *inter-disciplinary* approach rather than one which creates disciplines (economics, law, politics, sociology) in isolation.

The *laissez-faire* model assumed that organizations would always act to maximize profits. If they did not act consistently in this way, competitors would force them to make losses at some stage, by controlling the limited factors of raw materials, production and market share. The consequence would be that they were soon out of business.

Black box concept

This can be illustrated in systems terminology. The organization may be thought of as a 'black box' (*see* Fig 2.4). Inputs are fed in – outputs emerge. Economists were not too concerned with actions within the 'black box' (i.e. the organization). They were more concerned with the relationships between inputs and outputs, between prices and amounts of factors of production and products. Problems within the organization of organizational structure and decision making were not of interest.

H Leibenstein in the 1966 *American Economic Review* suggested that in practice organizations do not purchase and use all their inputs in the most efficient way, so it is necessary to look inside the 'black box' and see *how* decisions are made and why some organizations are more efficient. In the 1960s the development of managerial economics and behavioural theories of the organization provided analytical tools with which the *internal* functioning of a business enterprise could be analysed.

Again, the achievement of maximizing growth of profits in an organization may be difficult because of the *different interests* of shareholders and managers, and between managers themselves, who also have departmental interests. Cyert and Marsh in *A Behavioural Theory of the Firm* (Prentice-Hall, 1963) suggest policies may reflect in these cases a balance of interests and agreements that bargaining takes place within the firm to balance a number of different objectives at a satisfactory level. There is not therefore maximizing behaviour, but *satisficing* behaviour, as a result of what Cyert and Marsh call the 'quasi resolution of conflict'.

The above differences of attitude and approach briefly indicate the dangers and limitations of untested or unreal assumptions in economic analysis.

A final word is to stress the need to consider the interdependancy of all parts of the system or organization, not just between parts within the system but also between the system and the environment (*see* Fig 1.1, p 20).

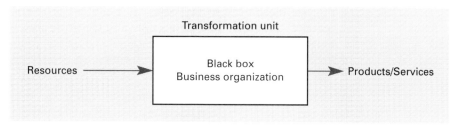

Fig 2.4 The 'black box'

SOCIAL RESPONSIBILITIES OF MANAGEMENT

This topic is frequently discussed and it would take many pages to deal with it adequately. The following brief points may serve to illustrate what is meant by the term.

Managers have a responsibility to their shareholders – this is accepted. Do they have a responsibility to others, particularly the community as a whole?

- *An organization cannot exist in isolation* from the society in which it has its being. An organization provides goods and services for the community and uses raw material and labour and also makes use of other facilities of civilization, e.g. laws, which protect it. No management can ignore the environment in which it operates and the success of organizations may depend to a large extent upon their public image. The attitude of the organization to its employees forms part of this image. Throughout history, management has been influenced by social concepts.
- *The attitude of management to labour* is at the core of the social responsibility of management. Workers have become better protected, e.g. collective bargaining has given more security to workers, Staff Status schemes and the Redundancy Payments Act are for the benefit of the workers. Management must give a lead in these matters and the government periodically 'exhorts' industry to do things which would aid the country socially, for example the location of new companies in development areas.
- *Subscribers of capital*, e.g. shareholders and debenture holders, have allowed their money to be used by a company, and the company is responsible to them as they are entitled to a fair reward for the use of their capital and the risk involved. If such obligations are not honoured, future capital would be harder to obtain and unemployment may result.
- *Consumers* have a right not to be exploited by an organization which depends upon the community in many ways. The question then arises – should an organization *share* its property with its customers, e.g. by lowering prices, because of reduced costs through mass production and increases in sales? Legislation, e.g. on resale price maintenance and monopolies, has shown that the government adopts the attitude that companies must act in the public interest. Management therefore cannot avoid the fact that its responsibility for industrial and commercial direction is mainly its responsibility to society.

Other social issues managers face upon which they have to decide policies (see the example opposite) are:

- marketing policies – should they avoid manufacturing products detrimental to health, e.g. cigarettes, weapons;
- policies that imply social costs, e.g. pollution of rivers – the organization reduces its costs by pumping waste into rivers and this involves social costs in clearing the rivers;
- the relations which an organization should have with political parties;
- whether or not to export to particular countries.

As was previously mentioned, when organizations formulate a strategic plan, not many appear to be considering possible social and political change. This is more important now than ever before. There are action groups of many kinds challenging management's authority, e.g. consumer groups, unions and government legislative activities. Some attempt therefore is needed to assess these challenges and plans formulated to ensure that the organization's goals are achieved.

Management in practice

The Code of Practice of Scott Bader Co Ltd is an example of the modern approach.

> We recognize that we have a responsibility to society in which we live and believe that where we have some special talent or interest we should offer it to the wider community. We are agreed that our social responsibility extends to:
> (a) Limiting the products of our labour to those beneficial to the community, in particular excluding any products for the specific purpose of manufacturing weapons of war.
> (b) Reducing any harmful effect of our work on the natural environment by rigorously avoiding the negligent discharge of pollutants.
> (c) Questioning constantly whether any of our activities are unnecessarily wasteful of the earth's resources.

Methods of assessing social policies and priorities

Social responsibility audit

The suggestion is made by John Humble and others who advocate that organizations should maintain a *social responsibility audit*. This is a checklist of about 14 specific areas of social responsibility against which management action can be reviewed with regard to the effect of policies on the external and internal environment of the organization.

- *External areas* to consider are consumer and community relations, investment and shareholder relations, packaging and pollution, plus the consideration of possible new business opportunities that may reduce social difficulties. This includes ensuring effective communication of information to shareholders and editors of papers, open-dating and full description of goods which are advertised to high standards. Organizations are required to consider social issues in making investment decisions, and this goes so far as to consider *not investing* in other organizations which are deemed to be 'socially irresponsible'.
- *Internal areas* to consider are physical environment factors (e.g. lighting and noise), working conditions, communications, organization structure and management style, industrial relations and the employment and treatment of minority groups, as well as education and training.

All of these areas should be periodically reviewed to see that the organization is pursuing socially responsible policies.

Attitude studies	This involves monitoring changes in the attitude of organizations, employees, shareholders, customers, opinions of leaders in society and government officials to see if possible changes in attitudes can be forecast. Attitudes and events in other countries should always be noted, especially between countries of a similar economic background and philosophy (e.g. the USA and United Kingdom), as events in one country may become evident in the other country.
Social priority analysis	This has been used by a few organizations, in particular the General Electric Company in the USA. The areas of concern that could not be quantified are inserted on a business planning grid. Demands of pressure groups (e.g. conservation, race) are listed and rated as to *intensity* of emphasis of each group. Long-term social trends, e.g. quality of life and education, which may affect pressure groups, are listed and weighted, resulting in a highlighting of important public issues which should be noted in strategic planning. Final decisions are made by the Corporate Policy Committee of General Electric Company. In Europe larger companies are developing political policies and preparing proposals for legislation with the aim of obtaining political and social support for a company's ideas.
Social responsibility and business ethics	In recent years society has called upon organizations, public and private, to take a broader view of the impact their decisions will have on society and communities as a whole. An organization's approach to social responsibility is usually determined by its senior managers and their decisions. Increasingly they seem to be closely in tune with the expectations of society in general.

BUSINESS ETHICS

Ethics can be described as a set of moral principles that govern the action of an individual or group. Business ethics are concerned with truth and justice and include aspects which society expects, e.g. fair competition, social responsibilities, and corporate behaviour.

A *code* is a statement of policies and principles that guides behaviour. *A code of ethics* should guide the behaviour of all persons. Stating a code of ethics is not enough. By appointing an ethics committee, holding regular meetings, checking and enforcing violations to the ethics code and reviewing and updating the code, it can be seen that an enterprise is committed to the principle.

Ethical standards are rarely discussed in management development programmes. Ethical standards differ, particularly among nations and societies. This can cause great concern when managers are working in a foreign country. For example, in some countries it is normal to make payments to expedite business transactions, which may be considered a bribe in other countries. This emphasizes the fact that *managers operate in a complex environment,* where ideas of social responsibility and ethical standards are continually being modified and refined.

The factors affecting a manager involved in making decisions on ethical problems include the law, regulations of government, ethical codes of the organization or industry, social pressures and any tension existing between a manager's personal standards and the needs of the organization.

Corporate social responsiveness

Managers are interested mainly in practical guidelines and specific results and are not too interested in philosophical discussions. Therefore the more precise term, *corporate social responsiveness* is given to studying the ways in which companies become aware and respond to social issues.

An excellent analysis of corporate social responsiveness is to be found in theoretical models advocated by Robert Ackerman in the *Harvard Business Review*, vol 51, no 4 (July–August 1973). He was among the first to advocate that responsiveness not responsibility should be the goal of corporate social activity.

Phase 1 – Senior managers are made aware of a social problem. They are not asked by anyone to deal with it. The problem is merely acknowledged by the company stating its policy on it.

Phase 2 – Specialists, internal or external, are hired to suggest ways of dealing with it.

Phase 3 – The implementation stage does not come quickly, perhaps only after government or public opinion forces action. By this time it may be too late as the company has lost the initiative. Ackerman advises companies to act early in the life-cycle of any social issue so that they can enjoy the largest amount of managerial discretion over the result.

This is a difficulty with the models of Ackerman and others, as they do not provide much advice on *how* to solve disputes that concern fundamentally different ideas of the world or ways of managing conflicts in values.

There are constant changes in the concepts of responsibility and performance in business. Stockbrokers on Wall Street, the financial centre in the USA, the International Stock Exchange in London and the insurers Lloyd's of London have all been involved in accusations of fraud and insider trading, which have shaken public trust and confidence, and the situation has been called a 'crisis of ethics' in business.

Businesses have difficulty in self-regulation but the question to be considered is that if business cannot effectively regulate its activities should government regulation be the answer to the problem?

MULTINATIONAL COMPANIES

This is a comparatively recent development whereby a company has its headquarters in one country and exercises some or all of the functions of a company in other countries.

Management in practice

> In 1988 environmental groups campaigned against the large amounts of rubbish produced by fast-food outlets. McDonald's attracted most of the pressure.
>
> The plastic foam (polystyrene) container (called a clamshell) was carried out of the shop and thrown away. This would have taken centuries to rot. Letters about this environmental threat were sent to the company by thousands of young persons. The company decided to work with a major environmental group (EDF) to reduce its solid waste.
>
> The company experimented with recycling the containers and tried to find uses for recycled materials. Eventually a new wrapping was produced, which was made of quilted paper, made from a layer of tissue pressed between a sheet of paper and a sheet of polyethylene. This cannot be recycled but is far less bulky, taking up barely one-tenth of the space in a rubbish dump.
>
> The result today is that complaints have been greatly reduced, the quilted wrap is cheaper than the clamshell, and everyone in the industry is much more environmentally conscious than before. The environmental organization (EDF) was pleased, as the publicity given to the activities of the giant fast-food chain had been a powerful influence in changing behaviour.

Foreign interests are not large for most British companies but 10 out of the top 40 companies (in size) *produce abroad* over 25 per cent as much as they produce at home. The impetus for this development probably came from improved communication and transportation systems, the growth of larger regional markets through the European Common Market and freer trade agreements.

Some companies are bi-national, where their ownership and control are shared with another country, e.g. British and Dutch companies share Shell and Unilever. It is worth noting that the European Community's company legislation will greatly encourage this type of development in the future.

Many foreign companies own subsidiaries in the home country. In the United Kingdom over 3000 companies are now owned and controlled from abroad. Over 10 per cent of the total United Kingdom output is in the hands of American companies.

There are points for and against these companies from a national point of view. It is usually agreed that foreign investment can be helpful, especially in the creation of jobs. In many cases, lack of capital would have meant the company would have to close down. The Trades Union Congress (*see* p 413) in their Economic Review of 1975 reinforced their uncertainty regarding the increase in multinational corporations. They stressed that government and unions were liable to be threatened because:

- manufacturing operations could be transferred out of the home country to foreign countries;

- capital investment in the home country may lead to practices of blackmail. In order to avoid strikes it may be stated that capital and labour may be transferred elsewhere;
- profits could be transferred out of the home country, thus affecting the balance of payments;
- lack of control by British planning authorities over key sectors of the economy.

Transfer pricing

In transfer pricing, prices are charged by one subsidiary to another subsidiary of the same company in a different country. The prices are decided by the head office of the multinational company in accordance with *its* need. By raising or lowering prices charged, profits can be transferred out of countries with high taxes and moved to those with low taxes.

Multinational decisions

The main company may not be so concerned to increase the export potential of subsidiary firms in a country and can switch markets and sources of supply to enable profits to be made more easily and products to be made more cheaply.

Decisions of the multinational company are made with a view to maximizing profits of the company as a whole and not of its individual subsidiaries. There are, therefore, a number of important problems which may never be satisfactorily agreed. The recent trend towards giving more information to employees and unions may produce a situation where the figures for home subsidiaries may not be sufficient. Questions which will be asked are:

1 To what extent should, or can, the company be asked for a global breakdown?
2 Will trade union co-operation extend across frontiers, especially as union structures vary greatly between countries?

From the point of view of the home country where the parent company is registered, there are points for and against such an operation.

Advantages

- Access to wider markets and the ability to deal in larger investments through organized capital markets.
- Law of comparative advantage could be applied in allowing movement to low-cost areas of production.
- Ability to affect decisions or ideas of government because of their size and effect on the economy of countries.

Disadvantages

- Foreign policies of countries vary and *disputes* between countries who each have within them subsidiaries of the parent company can cause problems (e.g. possible nationalization).
- *Laws* of countries vary, especially taxation laws.
- Uncertainty of *loyalty* of citizens abroad to the parent company.
- Difficulty of *co-ordinating* policies over numerous countries.
- *Local management* may not be too proficient.

THE SINGLE EUROPEAN MARKET

In 1958 the Treaty of Rome established a regional alliance whose general objective was to integrate the economies of the original member countries (Belgium, France, West Germany, Italy, Luxembourg and the Netherlands). The United Kingdom, Eire and Denmark joined in 1973. Spain, Portugal and Greece have now joined. The alliance is known as the European Community (EC) and it is now a major force in world trade.

On 31st December 1992 the heads of government of the member countries committed themselves to the single or 'common' market. The aim of the single market was to eliminate trade restrictions by action in the following areas:

- progressive opening up of government and public body contracts to all Community contractors on an equal basis;
- European regulations and standards so that products approved in any one Community country can be marketed throughout the Community without being subject to import tariffs and taxes;
- more competitive and efficient European-wide services in telecommunications and information technology;
- reduction in administration in road haulage's shipping services between member states should be the same for all member states;
- competition on air routes should increase and airfares should be lower;
- protection of ideas would become easier through consensus of laws on patents and trade marks;
- professional qualifications obtained in all member states would be acceptable in all other member states;
- banks and security houses authorized in their own country should be free to provide banking and investment services anywhere in the Community, and all restrictions on the movement of capital would end.

On 1 January 1993 the Treaty on European Union (Maastricht) was signed, with the objectives of implementing common economic, monetary and foreign policies for all member states. Problems arise because of the different vested national (political and economic) interests of member countries. This has already been seen with the problems caused by membership of the Exchange Rate Mechanism (ERM) (*see* Bibliography).

United Kingdom companies will not only have to consider whether to expand into European markets but also be subject to the effects of European companies expanding into the UK. The question of who will emerge successfully depends upon management and its response.

A feature in European business in recent years has been the great rise in the number of companies that have been *taken over* by companies from abroad. Mergers and acquisitions are increasing because of:

- the end of protected European markets;
- deregulation of European financial markets;
- non-European countries wishing to prepare for greater competition, e.g. Japan and the United States.

Problems generated by the Single European Market

UK companies will have to be aware of, and ready to deal with, the following:

- Changes in company law and standards and the emergence of non-tariff barriers.
- Competitors will enter the market to establish or enhance their share, or will join with others to obtain a greater market share.
- Differential pricing may no longer be sustainable as buyers can more easily seek out the cheapest source.
- Existing distributors may be acquired by competitors and distribution arrangements may need to be completely changed as Europe-wide competition may severely cut rates charged.
- Organizational structures may become more complicated and expensive than those of competitors who are working on a global basis and who have already simplified their structures.
- Every part of the business system needs to be *re-examined*.
- Staff may need to be retrained or changed, and demand for experienced European executives will rise.
- Existing customers could change their behaviour, and may, for example, experiment with new suppliers, or change to new products if they are a customer.

Factors to note in exporting

Factors which should be noted by companies which are considering exporting:

- the *product range* should be modified and adapted to the new market;
- *objectives* should be carefully formulated, communicated and understood by everyone in the organization;
- a clear idea is needed of the *cost* of an operation as well as the reward;
- the need for a *quick response in decision making;*
- centralization should only be considered as a result of carefully determined strategic needs;
- *an organization and control system* must be designed to ensure there is minimum need for referral to the centre;
- the use of *maximum spans of control* (*see* p 142) so that staff will concentrate on essentials.

EXPORTING TO CENTRAL AND EASTERN EUROPE

Changes in Central and Eastern Europe during 1989 and reforms in the Soviet Union have opened up large markets in Europe. Russia has a population of under 300 million, Central and Eastern Europe has a population of 100 million. The European Community has increased aid to Eastern Europe by projects such as TEMPUS and the British Know-How Fund.

Transition from centrally planned to market economies will take time. Factors that need to be dealt with before transition to a market economy takes place include:

- creation of rights for individuals to own property;
- the establishment of a network of legal and financial services;
- safeguards to be in force on ownership and property.

The *privatizing* of state-owned organizations varies from country to country. The process will take a long time and many strategies have been adopted. These include:

- issuing vouchers to workers giving them an entitlement to free shares in their company in return for changes in working practices and the structure of management;
- selling companies to foreign firms;
- breaking up large organizations and selling shares in their individual parts.

Joint venture agreements

Joint venture agreements are a popular method of doing business in Europe. They are usually limited to Western companies having no more than 49 per cent of shareholdings. Western contributions include cash, production knowledge and modern machinery. Eastern partners contribute land, buildings and labour. The biggest problem is deciding upon the right partner.

Co-operation in technical areas

Co-production agreements are becoming popular. Raw materials and components can be exchanged and there may be agreements for the joint assembly or the supply of semi-finished products which are finished in another country. This enables Western manufacturers to have lower costs of production (wages are lower in Eastern Europe) and benefit from economies of scale. A good example of co-operation agreements is in automobile production, where semi-finished parts are brought in for assembly.

The sale of Western knowledge

Licences to use a production or branded product are a popular method of transferring knowledge. Payment could be by a lump sum or by payment of royalties.

International competition

Goods supplied by Western companies may be partly paid for by reciprocal supply of Eastern goods.

The European Union (EU) has increased competition greatly and there is a need for United Kingdom businesses to develop a management system that can improve decision making and improve quality. The internal organization may need to be changed, devolving responsibility further down the management chain. There is also a need to ensure that a comprehensive system is in place to manage total quality management (TQM). This will include developing quality circles and just-in-time management systems (*see* Chapter 8). It is vital that TQM systems should be extended to incorporate environmentally friendly systems.

Organizations and managers today face an international business environment which is characterized by very rapid and complex change. There have been far-reaching changes in political and economic boundaries and companies are having to organize themselves to manage their international operations in ways which will have major implications for the skills and competencies required by an international manager.

A recent report by the Ashridge Management Research Group called *Management Across Frontiers* examined the competencies needed by an international manager and certain key features which would assist the development of managers.

Companies must be able to exploit knowledge and experience gained in one part of the world and apply it in other parts. The ability to compete globally can be assisted by mergers and acquisitions. This will provide economies of scale and size and the formation of partnerships can give them the benefit of their combined experience.

Managers in these environments must be able to create links and relationships between people of diverse cultures, languages and systems. It is considered important for managers to build cultural empathy by becoming fluent in the language of the host country.

COMPARATIVE MANAGEMENT

This can be defined as the study of management in different types of environment and the identification of reasons why enterprises in various countries show different results. The reasons for studying other managerial practices are to see what can be learned in order to improve management, improve productivity and improve economic growth.

Until recently the USA was regarded as a leader in developing modern management practices. Lately there has been great interest in looking at the reasons why Japan and other East Asian countries have greatly improved their productivity.

Specific management techniques and approaches will vary throughout the world in their application because of economic, political, cultural and sociological factors, levels of education, knowledge and skills. One approach by H Koontz analyses enterprise activities into two types, those due to managerial factors and those due to non-managerial factors. He attempts to draw up a model so that universal elements of management can be determined and enable a greater understanding of comparative management to be achieved.

Within the space of this book it is possible only to make a brief comment on differences in managerial practices. Charles Handy *et al*'s book, *Making Managers* (London, Pitman Publishing, 1988), compared and contrasted the education, training and development of managers in the UK, USA, Germany, France and Japan. It was obvious that there was no common generally accepted procedure for learning to be a manager. Each country had its own historical and educational traditions, but similarities were observed in priorities, principle and emphasis. Only 25 per cent of top managers in the United Kingdom were found to have degrees, in comparison with the USA (85 per cent), West Germany (62 per cent), France (65 per cent), and Japan (85 per cent). The analysis concluded that whatever pathway to competent management was taken it should:

- be *appropriate* to the tradition of the culture and educational infrastructure;
- *give early responsibility* and have high expectations and standards;
- give every facility and *encouragement to study* and learn from others.

In conclusion to this introduction to comparative management, a few points of guidance were offered by Peter Drucker in the *Harvard Business Review* (October 1988). He stressed that because management deals with the integration of people in a common venture it is deeply embedded in culture. Managers in Germany, the UK, the USA or Japan do similar things, but the manner in which they do them may be quite different. Managers in a developing country should identify those parts of their own tradition, history and culture that can be used as building blocks. Japan, for example, has imported management concepts into their *own* cultural soil and made them grow.

SMALL BUSINESS MANAGEMENT

There are various definitions of a small business. Comparisons can be made with other businesses, by sales figures, asset values, market share or number of employees. A small business:

- is independently owned and operated;
- has a capital contribution from a limited number of individuals;
- would operate in a local area;
- would probably not be dominant in its field of operation.

The number of employees varies; it may be lower than 100 and most small businesses in the United Kingdom come under this category. In the USA they would regard a small business as under 400 employees.

Examples of a small business include farming, retailing of shoes, jewellery, and flowers. Service firms include restaurants, insurance agents, dentists and accountants.

Differentiating organizations by size can be quite misleading, but this factor can be used to examine the organizational and management issues associated with small business enterprises.

Ownership and management

The manager of a small business is usually the founder and owner, who will usually take a detailed interest in most management decisions. This centralized control could eventually impose a constraint upon the growth of the organization as there is a limit to the ability of an individual to manage larger enterprises.

Planning and control

Jobs are not so rigidly defined as in a large organization and there is more flexibility between jobs. There will be less formality than in larger organizations. Decision making will be quicker and rules and procedures less rigid.

Motivation

Individuals will closely identify themselves with the organization and pay and reward systems may be more personalized than in larger organizations.

There may be a wider range of duties for individuals and this could give greater satisfaction than the narrower range which is more likely in larger organizations. The training and development of managers tend to be less well organized in smaller companies.

Advantages of a small business

- The owner is independent and has freedom to act, although the owner must be concerned about customers, employees, creditors, suppliers and government regulations.
- They can be easily set up and dissolved.
- The profits do not have to be shared, as with partnership or large corporations.
- There is greater flexibility to act as there is no one else to give approval.
- There are fewer overhead costs than in larger firms, so they may be able to earn a profit on a lower price than a large company.
- The organizations are usually lean and have small permanent staffs.
- Specialists (e.g. accountants) are hired when required. Staff in smaller organizations tend to work longer hours without extra pay.

Disadvantages of a small business

- *Poor management.* Management has difficulty in recruiting good employees as they cannot pay adequate salaries. Poor management includes inadequate training in running a business, especially inadequate knowledge of marketing and finance.
- *Finance* may not be easily available when required for expansion. Banks are not so keen to lend to small businesses because of their high failure rate and there are not many other organizations that can help. Banks may lend more if the owner has a reasonable investment in the business.
- Another reason for banks not lending money is insufficient collateral security and a poor record of earning.

Sources of finance for small businesses

The failure rate of small businesses is very high. It is around 60 per cent and one of the main problems is lack of capital particularly in the early years. Sources of finance for small businesses include:.

- commercial banks and building societies;
- Local Enterprise Boards;
- venture or personal capital;
- government agencies, e.g. British Overseas Trade Board or Rural Development Commission;
- local authority business or economic development units;
- retained profits;
- issue of shares in business.

Venture capital

An important source of funds is the *venture capitalist*, private individuals that invest in promising new businesses. Apart from lending money, they may wish to become part-owners of the business. About 50 per cent of the financing of capital for a typical small firm comes from the owner's personal resources.

- Extra funds can be made available by using *retained profits*, which can only be available if the business is profitable.
- If existing shareholders will allow other shareholders into the business it may be possible to issue new shares in order to raise more finance.

Franchises

One method of overcoming the disadvantages of a sole proprietor is to buy a franchise. In a franchise a person pays a national organization a fee for the right to sell its products or services. For these benefits the franchisee must give up some freedom. In many cases the parent firm will:

- fix the price of the product;
- decide upon the physical layout of premises;
- determine standardized accounting procedures;
- require a percentage of profits to be paid back to the parent firm;
- provide assistance in organizing the business, the training of staff and in merchandising.

The more general use of the term 'franchise' relates to businesses where the franchisee purchases a licence to operate an activity. Most features are standardized, e.g. product image, promotional material, style. Strict conditions are imposed on operating methods.

The franchisee often has to invest a substantial sum of money to cover premises, fittings, equipment and stock. The franchisor provides a 'support' package to assist in the running of the business.

Examples of franchises are Body Shop (cosmetics and toilet goods), McDonald's (fast food) and Prontaprint (printing).

Benefits of franchising

- Product or business format has been tested in the market.
- Better prospects of obtaining finance.
- Public are aware of name and standard of quality.
- Help is given in starting up, site selection and training.

- Beneficial terms for bulk buying.
- Standard procedure manual.
- Excellent chance of success (over 85 per cent of new franchises succeed).

Problems of franchising

- High licence fees or royalties.
- Limited use of individual initiative.
- Franchisor may fail and support will not then be available.

It is important to note that purchasing a good franchise requires a careful study of the advantages and disadvantages. It is no different to buying any other business. The franchising concept does not eliminate the risks of investment in a small business; it is merely an alternative.

Management in practice

McDonald's name has worldwide recognition and the company regards franchising as a key factor in the growth of its restaurant system. A McDonald's franchise requires an investment of about £300 000. Franchisees benefit from wide name recognition, advertising and research. Franchisees are expected to be owner-operators to ensure consistent delivery of 'Quality, Service, Cleanliness and Value to Customers' – the company's motto. There are about 8000 franchises worldwide; most of the restaurants are locally owned and operated by independent entrepreneurs.

Over 1 million McDonald's hamburgers are eaten in the United Kingdom every day. The busiest shop in the world is in the Strand, London, where in peak summer periods over 1300 customers are served in an hour.

SUMMARY

Objective 1 *Understand the role of business and the economic structure.*
An explanation of economics is briefly needed before describing business. Economics is the study of how societies use their resources to produce and distribute commodities among their members; it also involves the exchange of things that seem valuable to their owners. Business can be described as the gainful activity through which the various elements of society conduct such exchanges. Modern business is therefore a complex system of production, distribution, consumption, services and regulations.

Objective 2 *Describe the role of the Stock Exchange and the new issue market.*
The Stock Exchange plays an important part in the economic and commercial life of the country. It is a highly organized market for the purchase and sale of 'second-hand' securities. This organized market enables investors to exchange their shares for cash.

Sources of finance from the banking system are mainly designed to meet short- and medium-term needs. Companies which cannot meet their financial needs from retained profits or the commercial banks can raise long-term money by the issue of (new) equity or loan capital.

Objective 3 *Describe briefly the information required before deciding whether or not to become involved in international business.*

The information required to enable a decision to be made whether or not to become involved in international business is varied. Information will include details of a country's structure of business, the economy, legislation, the climate for investment, the political background, the nature of competition, the cultural and educational background of the country's workforce and the potential market size.

Objective 4 *Appreciate why managers should be concerned about the relationship between an enterprise and its environment.*

An enterprise and its immediate environment are closely interdependent. The local community may be a source of labour, capital, materials and customers. The corporate image and economic interests of an enterprise can be enhanced by maintaining a close and harmonious relationship with its immediate environment.

Objective 5 *Briefly compare Japanese and Western European management practices.*

The philosophy of management in Japan and Western European countries seems to be different. Japanese practices show different emphasis as evidenced by these examples: longer term planning, the involvement of many people in making a decision, loyalty to the company, a paternalistic style of leading and control by peers. Western countries tend to show opposite characteristics. A number of Western European companies are using Japanese practices, but tailored to fit in with Western environments (the term Theory Z is applied to companies adopting Japanese practices).

Objective 6 *Discuss the impact of the Single Market on business in Europe.*

There has a been a freer movement of goods and services by opening up country borders. There is wider competition and more freedom now that physical, fiscal and technical barriers have fallen. An environment has been created which encourages business co-operation, especially with the harmonization of company law and safety and environmental standards.

Objective 7 *Explain the nature and features of small business management.*

Small businesses play an important part in the private enterprise system. They are independently owned and do not dominate the market. They account for the majority of commercial enterprises and tend to be concentrated in the retailing and service sectors of the economy.

Objective 8 *Describe factors involved in exporting to Central and Eastern Europe.*

The potential market in Eastern Europe is vast. There is an advantage in entering the market early to build up infrastructures of suppliers and customers, although the markets will take time to mature as the move from a centrally planned to a market economy is not an easy transition. Joint venture, co-production agreements and barter arrangements all form a part of exporting practice.

1 What are likely to be the differences between the operation of a domestic firm and that of a multinational corporation? Select four differences and discuss their importance.

2 How far do you consider the operations of multinational companies to be dangerous to the countries in which they operate? In what respects do you think their activities should be subject to control?

3 The Stock Exchange is said to be a market for second-hand securities. Do you think that this is an adequate description of the functions of the Stock Exchange?

4 What do you understand by 'internally generated funds'? Describe why these are prime sources of finance for investment in the United Kingdom.

5 Explain what you understand by long-term, medium-term and short-term capital and outline the normal methods by which a business would raise each of these categories of finance.

6 Assume you are the managing director of an electronics company and you have been asked by the chairman of your board of directors to prepare a report stating the arguments in favour of moving part of the production into a new factory in a government Development Area. Indicate also, in your report, some of the difficulties that may arise.

7 Outline the problems that a small firm might have in competing with a large company. Indicate in your answer any advantages that may be available for the small firm.

8 Consider the implications for a British business of the Single European Market.

1 In almost all private enterprise economies the state plays a significant role, both directly and indirectly, in the economic life of the nation. Why should the state become so directly involved in industry and commerce?

2 Examine the factors that a company should consider in deciding on the amount of debt to employ in its capital structure.

3 Describe the economic function of the Stock Exchange. To what extent does the Stock Exchange offer protection to investors?

4 Describe the methods used by the government to influence the location of industry.

5 To what extent do you think that the existence of multinational corporations in a country has any harmful effects on the home country?

6 Decribe the main external sources of finance available to a very small company.

7 Consider the reasons why managers should be aware of the concept of social responsibility.

8 Which set of factors do you consider to be the most influential in the general environment of your organization. Consider (a) the present time; (b) four years' time.

9 In the growth of a small business, what aspects need to be paid particular attention and why?

10 Is social responsibility a choice or a necessity for organizations? Use examples from your own experience or issues with which you are familiar to illustrate your answer.

ASSIGNMENTS

1 Assume you are left with £200 000 with a proviso that you set up your own business.

What type of business would you choose?
What organizational structure would be required?
What are the main problems you would initially face?

2 Form groups of six persons and assume each group is a committee of a charitable organization which has to award each year a cash payment of £10 000 to a business organization that has best satisfied its social responsibilities in the year.

You are asked to develop criteria for choosing organizations for the award and research the activities of a number of chosen organizations. Make a choice and be prepared to defend the selection in a class meeting.

What do you think is the motivation behind the organization's activities? Do you agree with this motivation?

BIBLIOGRAPHY

Bennett, R, *Small Business Survival* (London, Pitman Publishing, 1989).

Gowlands, D, *The UK Monetary System* (Oxford, Basil Blackwell, 1985).

Jewell, B R, *The UK Economy and Europe* (London, Pitman Publishing, 1993).

Ledgerwood, G *et al*, *The Environmental Audit and Business Strategy* (London, Pitman Publishing, 1992).

Morris, D, *The Economic System in the UK* (Oxford, Oxford University Press, 3rd edition, 1985).

Ouchi, W G, *Theory Z, How American Business can meet the Japanese Challenge* (Reading, Mass, Addison-Wesley, 1981).

Pascale, R T and Athos, A G, *The Art of Japanese Management* (Harmondsworth, Penguin, 1988).

Smythe-Wood, I (Ed), *The European Companion 1992* (London, Dods Publishing and Research Ltd, 1991).

Swann, D, *The Single European Market and Beyond* (London, Routledge, 1993).

Templeton, P (Ed), *The European Currency Crisis* (London, Probus Europe, 1993).

Trevor, M, *Japan's Reluctant Multinationals* (London, Pinter, 1983).

CHAPTER 3

Corporate strategy and planning

This chapter examines the methods used in forecasting and planning enterprise goals and department objectives and then finding ways of achieving them. It examines the nature of decisions and methods of statistical analysis used in making decisions. The benefits of an integrated management information system are considered.

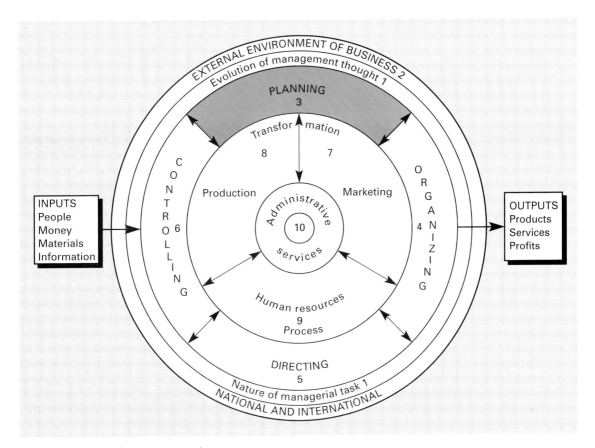

The systems approach to management

OBJECTIVES

Upon completing this chapter you should be able to:

- Explain the concept of management by objectives (MBO).
- Name the key result areas in which all enterprises should establish objectives.
- Describe the phases of the planning process.
- Identify the different types of decisions made by managers.
- Define corporate planning and briefly state why it differs from long-range planning.
- Describe methods of forecasting in a business and limitations to forecasts.
- Define the term 'management information system' and give examples of its practical uses.
- Explain why the formulation of strategy may be different in a non-profit organization.

PLANNING

Planning is one of the four managerial functions; the others are organizing, directing and controlling. Planning is the most basic of managerial functions. It determines organization objectives and purposes, so that everyone understands what they have to accomplish.

All managers are involved in planning but the nature of policies and plans set out by superiors will vary with each manager's authority. While senior executives plan the direction of the organization, managers at various levels prepare plans for their own section which are part of the overall aims of the organization.

Planning involves selecting enterprise goals and department objectives, then finding ways of achieving them. Plans depend upon the existence of alternatives, and then decisions have to be made regarding *what* to do, *how* to do it, *when* to do it and by *whom* it is to be done. A plan is a pre-determined course of action which helps to provide purpose and direction for members of an enterprise. The planning process can be aided by working in an environment which is conducive to it. This is important, as plans develop from the lower levels of administration whose reaction and responses may change and help to form plans.

The most important way management can contribute to growth is by systematic planning. Probabilities are forecast and programmes developed to take advantage of them. Constant attention must be given to changing circumstances and many revisions of plans may be needed. Economists use the terms *ex ante* and *ex post* for this approach, that is revision is continually made of the *basic assumptions* on which the plans were based as circumstances change and thus new plans have to be developed.

FORECASTING

Economic forecasting is basic to planning. Forecasting precedes the preparation of a budget and is concerned with probable events. The future is uncertain and numerous techniques have been evolved to try and limit the amount of uncertainty (*see* section on control). Probability theory is one statistical method used widely. A newer development is *econometric* forecasting. This is done through the construction of mathematical models in which various factors of the economy are given mathematical values and their effect upon each other ascertained through the solution of equations. The level of a country's economy is of course a vital factor upon which a company's sales and revenue plans are based.

Such a forecast enables a *premise* to be made from which plans can be developed and enables the right objectives to be selected. It is in effect a special tool of planning and Fayol considered it so important as to state it was the *essence* of management. He used the word *prévoyance,* or foresight, and referred to plans as syntheses of forecasts and recommended annual forecasts and ten-yearly projections, which were revised every five years or less, depending upon trends.

Sales forecasts are affected by many factors which include trends relating to the general economy, political, international and industrial trends, the strength of competitors and manufacturing cost trends.

Forecasts make management think ahead and give a singleness of purpose to planning by concentrating attention on the future.

Items affecting forecasts

- Political stability.
- Population trends.
- Price levels.
- Government controls and fiscal policy.
- Employment, productivity and national income.
- Technical environment – some areas have shown great changes, e.g. computers, and the impact of the speed of developments must be especially noted.

A simple cycle of business activity can be seen in Fig 3.1. This figure shows that production is distributed via an intermediary to customers. A more accurate cycle would be more involved and refinements will be mentioned in later chapters.

Forecasts of sales are used to determine the scale of activity needed to satisfy the expected market and to indicate the necessary financial resources. Such forecasts are a necessary preliminary to the construction of budgets which can be used to set targets to achieve the objectives which become effective when they are set out in policies.

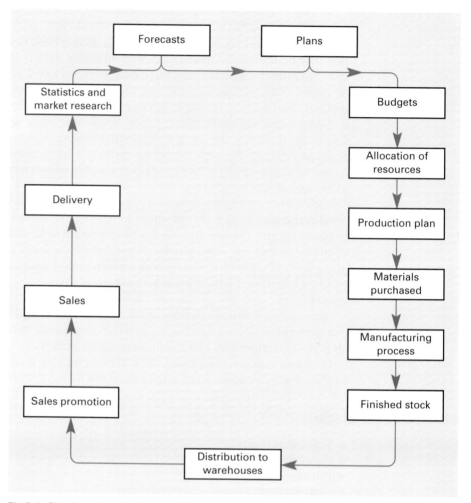

Fig 3.1 Simple cycle of business activity

The sales forecast

The sales forecast, which shows the number of units to be sold and the price expected, will enable the budget of revenue to be calculated. Then the budgeted production costs for this level of sales, plus expected administration costs, can be deducted from the expected revenue to give a budgeted profit figure, which will then show the amounts available for appropriation. Budgets for total resources needed to finance the level of expected production can be drawn up.

Other chapters will show the place of the other activities in more detail, i.e. production, sales, distribution, and how control is effected over the entire cycle of business activity.

In forecasting it is important to stress the need to examine the economic environment and possible fluctuations in company profits and relationships to possible cycles of business activity.

In planning for longer periods, a forecast of technological changes is vital, especially for those companies which are in areas of rapidly advancing technology, e.g. electronic machinery. From an organizational point of view, some companies have separated the basic day-to-day marketing activity from strategic planning for the future. Most organizations today, though, use the sales forecast as the starting point in the planning exercise.

Limitations to forecasting

- Reliability of past data. Although past events are analysed as a guide to the future, a question is raised as to the accuracy of these recorded events.
- Accurate judgement is needed to identify key factors *entering* the forecast, *interpreting* data and *selecting* methods of analysis and *applying* them to problems.
- Measurement of forecasts must have a consistent base and single figure forecasts may be unsatisfactory, as there is a need for *probability* to be attached, thereby evaluating the likelihood of the event occurring.

Forecasting methods

There are a number of approaches available. These range from extrapolation of trends of technology to more advanced methods such as Delphi Time-Scaling.

Time series analysis

Time series analysis is a procedure which identifies information which forms patterns over a period of time. A projection is made by extrapolating from past experience. Trends for the past years are noted and projected into the future.

Qualitative methods

Qualitative methods may be used when past data are not reliable, or perhaps non-existent. If, for example, a new product is introduced, then past data may not be relevant. In these cases *opinions* are noted from senior executives from functional areas, or this may be confined to sales forecasts by the complete sales force. The expectations of customers may also be of assistance. A knowledge of the needs of customers is found by survey, or by asking them personally. Some averaging, weighting or rounding may be needed.

Qualitative methods used to forecast technology are:

- Delphi technique is a procedure for arriving at a consensus of opinion among a group of experts, who are given a detailed questionnaire about a problem. They give written opinions. Everyone reads the opinions of others and can revise their own ideas. Direct contact and debate is avoided purposely as this may produce hasty attachment to some ideas. There is the problem of possible ambiguous questions and the difficulty of taking unexpected events into consideration.
- Brainstorming usually involves conducting a group meeting on a problem, and any idea is welcomed, however strange. The hope is that many ideas may be generated as there is freedom to let ideas flow, and from these, positive solutions may emerge. (This technique is used more frequently in

developing creative ideas for new products and solutions to complex problems.) Studies have shown (Taylor, Berry and Block, *Administrative Science Quarterly* (June 1958) USA) that in some cases, group members did *inhibit* one another's creativity, and individuals working on their own could produce equally good ideas.

● **Scenario construction** is a method used to make long-range forecasts. It is a logical description of events. The committee or 'think-tank' examines details of alternative events. An example is that a company may wish for a 15 per cent increase in its share of the market for computers. So many factors are involved that decisions could not be made with any degree of confidence. A well-constructed scenario exploring each adjustment or re-adjustment may produce a reasonably accurate forecast.

The relationship between critical variables can be shown by using matrices. In Chapter 7 the *Boston Matrix* is described. This is a technique for monitoring product ranges and can be used to form a policy for new product development.

Position or situation analysis

It is important to have a system for regularly analysing the external environment in order to develop the firm's strategic position. Such a system could comprise the following approach:

1 Examine the environment to see what influences are affecting the organization, then assess the nature of these influences.
2 Analyse the key environmental influences and their degree of relevance. This would include examining:

● the entry barriers for new firms in the industry;
● the extent of competition in the industry;
● the nature and strength of substitute products;
● the extent of power possessed by buyers;
● the extent of power possessed by suppliers.

A good analysis of the above factors can be found in M E Porter, *Competitive Strategy Techniques for Analysing Industries and Competitors* (New York, Free Press, 1980).

3 Identify the competitive position of the organization. This can be done by looking at the life-cycle model to identify the stage of development of its markets (*see* Chapter 7). Another way is to map out the power of competitors according to the shares that they hold in specific segments of the markets.
4 The stage after assessing the external environment is to assess the firm's resources based upon a knowledge of its strengths and weaknesses. The main activities and resources of a firm are analysed and assessed and this forms a background for judging the firm as a whole and assessing its efficiency and effectiveness. This will include its planning and control systems, operating procedures and the effectiveness of its organization structure.
5 The strengths and weaknesses of the organization can be examined by considering whether of not the firm's present strategy can deal with all the changes in the business environment. Methods used include:

(a) SWOT analysis – 'Strengths, Weaknesses, Opportunities and Threats'. This aims to relate the strengths and weaknesses of the *internal organization* against the opportunities and threats shown up by an analysis of the *external environment*.

(b) A method advocated by G Johnson and K Scholes, *Exploring Corporate Strategy* (2nd edn, New York, Prentice-Hall, 1988) is popular. This is a simple procedure which attempts to match identified opportunities and threats against the strengths and weaknesses of the organization. Benefits or adverse effects are rated plus or minus and the statements are examined against each other. It is only a crude analysis, providing some rating of opportunities and threats and the degree to which current strategies address the issue of a changing environment.

TOWS Matrix

Another matrix called *TOWS Matrix* is a framework for an analysis that helps to match *external* threats and opportunities with an organization's internal weakness and strengths. There are four alternative strategies possible based on the above and the position deemed most desirable is the one where a company uses its internal strengths to take advantage of external opportunities. (For a fuller discussion see Heinz Weihrich's 'The TOWS Matrix – A Tool for Situational Analysis', *Long Range Planning*, Vol 15, No 2 (1982).

It must be noted that matrix analyses are only relevant at a particular point in time and ideally various matrices will be needed for various time periods.

OBJECTIVES

Nature of objectives

Authorities differ as to the exact nature of objectives for business enterprises. Perhaps the better approach is to consider first what is the objective of our economic system. This is, broadly, to provide goods and services to customers. Industrial and commercial concerns, which comprise the greater part of the economic system, must therefore have the same objective. The objects clause, which is part of the Memorandum of Association of a limited company, invariably states the objective is to manufacture a commodity or provide a service (*see* overleaf). Nationalized industries have the predominant objective of providing an efficient and economical service to customers.

The stakeholder theory

A newer approach to the consideration of objectives is the *'stakeholder' theory* which suggests that a firm has responsibility to maintain an equitable and working balance among the claims of the interested groups, i.e. stockholders, employees, customers, suppliers, vendors and the public.

The following extract from the Memorandum and Articles of Association of the Scott Bader Co Ltd shows a wider definition of goals and objectives.

Company objectives

The basic purpose of the company is to render the best possible service as a corporate body to our fellow men. Towards this end we strive particularly:

(a) To develop the strengths of the company, its efficiency and means of production.
(b) To provide economic security to members and to relieve them of material anxiety or striving for personal advancement at the cost of others.
(c) To produce goods not only beneficial to customers of the company at a fair price and as high a quality as possible, but also for the peaceful purposes and general good of mankind.
(d) To conduct research and provide technical education mainly in synthetic resins and their application in the paint, plastics and allied industries.
(e) To contribute towards the general welfare of society, internationally, nationally and in the company's immediate neighbourhood.

The theory maintains that the objectives of the firm should be derived by balancing the *conflicting claims* of the various 'stakeholders'. The firm has a responsibility to all these and must structure its objectives to give each a measure of satisfaction. In this context the ideas of Maslow seem relevant, that is, that managers have a hierarchy of goals or motives, and once managers have achieved one goal, e.g x per cent profits, then they will turn to satisfy other goals, e.g. improved working conditions for employees.

Another related approach to the 'stakeholder' theory is suggested by Cyert and March who state, 'organizations do not have objectives, only people have objectives'. They suggest a firm's objectives are in reality a consensus of objectives of the participants which have been *negotiated.* (A good discussion on their ideas is in *Management and the Social Science* by Tom Lupton (Chapter 4).)

They suggest that in large firms the task of decision making is distributed throughout the firm, and that companies have five main goals: sales, production, inventory, market share and profit.

These are target areas for managers who are aiming to achieve their particular goal. Managers therefore *bargain* among themselves and eventually this 'conflict' will be resolved by compromise and the goals achieved by the organization may only then be *satisfactory.* This theory may be said to bring into the decision-making process social as well as economic variables.

Profit as objective

The position of 'profits' must now be considered (there are many definitions of profit). Profitability is, to many people, the main objective of a business. They stress that, if a concern had no profits, a business could not exist for very long, and therefore consider profits to be the main objective.

The real answer may be to recognize that the supply of a particular commodity is the *object* of a trading concern, but the *motive* is profit, which is also used as a criterion of success.

Profits, as *an* objective, or as a motive, are becoming increasingly qualified by questions of public importance. It was seen in the previous chapter that business is deemed to have a *social responsibility*.

A brief consideration of the recent views of other writers in the United Kingdom and America may throw more light on this disagreement over the real object of a business.

Brech refers to the overall objectives as prosperity, growth and the continued life of the business. Some firms may have as their main object the provision of the finest car in the world. Others may consider it to be giving the public a service which provides the maximum value for money. Again, *satisfactory,* rather than maximum, profits may be the object, and prosperity may be measured by the annual profit which gives a satisfactory return on capital employed.

Professor Galbraith has stated that, in the USA, businesses are now more interested in growth and stability rather than profit making. Growth can be measured by the actual turnover increase, or an increase in the share of the market. This appears to be an important objective and in this connection a lower return may be accepted now if future prospects appear good. *Continued* life of a business is related to growth and stability and this will suffer a great deal if no provision is made for innovation, research and development and management succession.

It is important to realize that objectives may change in *emphasis* over a period of time. At certain periods one or another objective may be dominant. For example, at present the objective may be to stimulate sales to retain maximum profit; later it may be to maintain a satisfactory profit, while selling a better quality product or giving better quality service to customers.

General and specific objectives

Objectives can be general or specific and may range in time from months to years, they may apply to the whole company or to units or persons. General objectives are determined by the board of directors, who approve other objectives.

It is preferable for objectives to be specific and expressed in quantitative terms. The first question to be answered is, what is the *nature* of the present business? This as we saw previously may change, but it must be understood in order for adaptation to changing customer needs to be possible. For example, a firm selling typewriters and accounting machines can expand with technology and move on to computers. If it decides it is in the 'information processing' business, rather than the 'office machine' business, then expansion will be easier.

Specific objectives usually have time limits, e.g. to open a new spare-parts section in six months' time; or it could be to diversify in certain fields in order to avoid relying on the fortunes of a single market or industry. It can be mentioned here that the big problem in such a venture is whether staff of the right calibre are available effectively to operate these *newer* types of business.

The ideal is for a company to formulate specific objectives and develop policies, within the framework of general objectives, which together result in co-ordinated, and controlled, decision making. Careful planning of objectives helps management to give members a sense of direction and purpose. This is essential to achieve effective results.

To be able to survive, a firm must earn sufficient profits to sell services or products, of a certain quality, at a competitive price. Drucker stresses that survival depends upon the ability to cover the costs of staying in business. These costs include providing for replacement and obsolescence as well as market risk and uncertainty. But it is rare to see survival stated as an objective.

Drucker considers objectives are important in every area where performance and results directly affect the survival and prosperity of a business. These *key areas* must be carefully selected and he distinguishes them by considering:

> 'in what areas would excellence really have an extraordinary impact on the economic results of our business, to the point where it might transform the economic performance of the entire business? . . . in what area would poor performance threaten to damage economic performance greatly, or at least significantly?'

Knowledge of these 'key areas' should enable management to:

> 'organize and plan the whole range of business phenomena in a small number of general statements; to test these statements in actual experience; to predict behaviour; to appraise the soundness of decisions when they are still being made; and to enable practising business men to analyse their own experiences and, as a result, improve their importance.'

He then goes on to mention eight specific areas in which objectives have to be set, in terms of performance and results. These are: market standing; innovation; productivity; physical and financial resources; profitability; manager performance and development; worker performance and attitude; and public responsibility.

It should be noted that the eight key result areas are relevant for public sector and non-profit ventures, even though they were directed at profit orientated enterprises.

Whatever areas are deemed important, it is preferable that any standards desired should be capable of being expressed in quantitative terms (e.g. number of items to be produced monthly).

It is also important to note that if the *organization structure* is not well designed, managers will find it difficult to achieve really high performance.

Some advantages of objectives

- They embody basic ideas and theories concerning what the enterprise is trying to accomplish.
- They provide a basis for directing and guiding the enterprise and provide targets which enable efforts to be observed and aided.
- They help to motivate people and they provide a sense of unity to the various groups in the organization, as an individual unit's contribution can be seen to be integrated with total enterprise goals.

POLICIES

In the administration of business one of the most important tasks is to formulate policy; the work of planning and the determination of company objectives become effective when expressed in policy form.

A policy is a guide to the action or decisions of people. Policies are directives, issued from a higher authority, and provide a continuous framework for the conduct of individuals in a business – they are in effect a type of planning. Policies are expressions of a company's official attitude towards types of behaviour within which it will permit, or desire, employees to act. They express the means by which the company's agreed objectives are to be achieved and usually take the form of statements, telling members how they should act in specific circumstances. Policies reflect management thinking on basic matters and inform those interested in the activities of the company about the company's intentions regarding them.

Formulation of policy

Policy formulation may begin at any level of management and may flow upwards or downwards along the levels of organization. Policy usually is formed by:

- the board of directors and senior management, who determine the main policies;
- being passed up the chain of command until someone takes responsibility for making a decision;
- external influences, e.g. government legislation, may force a policy change.

Policy formulated by executives is usually on broad lines and subordinates have scope in applying it. Any policy should be as specific as possible.

Specific policies

It is not always easy to be specific; words must be carefully chosen and policies must be basically sound and well administered. It may be difficult to state policies that will cover all eventualities, and this therefore may tend to limit the range of the policies and therefore be unduly restrictive.

Advantages of specific policies

- They are easy to refer to and absorb.
- Misunderstandings are fewer.
- New employees can easily be made aware of them in their induction.
- They are a good exercise for management, who must have thought about them seriously before writing them down.

Media for communicating policy, i.e. manuals, letters, conferences, etc., will be discussed later in the chapter on Directing.

Policies should be *flexible* and allow executives discretion in their application. They are more likely to be accepted if they are applied consistently and fairly.

Implied policies

If too much is implied in policies it can be dangerous. For example, if an organization does not employ union labour, it may be implied that this is the policy of the organization and this could cause it to suffer loss at a future date. Or, if all promotions were made in the past from within the organization, this would appear to be implied organizational policy. There would be great concern, therefore, if a new appointment were made from outside, as a 'change of policy' would be assumed.

Examples of policy

Policies regarding functional areas will be shown in more detail in the following chapters, but a brief indication will be given now of some of the major types of policy.

- Product policy involves deciding upon the products to make and depends upon many factors, particularly upon market conditions. Such a policy in turn generates other policies, e.g. marketing, finance and research.
- Production policy deals with, for example: What proportions of plant should be devoted to flow or job or batch production? What items to make or to buy? What use should be made of by-products?
- Market policy involves determining distribution channels, pricing structure of products, volume and type of advertising, credit policy, method of subdividing territory and remuneration of salesmen.
- Purchasing policy involves what organizations buy and to what extent, and what are alternative sources of supply.
- Human resources policy involves methods of training, education, pension schemes, incentive plans, management succession and development, benefits, union relations.

All other functions need policies, but the above will serve to indicate the necessity for clear-cut policies in all sections of an enterprise.

Rules and procedures are often confused with policies.

Rules are more specific than policies and they usually entail penalties for misuse. Policy establishes a guiding framework for rules. Policies are broader than rules and are usually stated in more general language.

Procedures reflect policy and provide a standard method by which work is performed and provide a *check* when events do not occur. They are subordinate to policy and are a useful aid to training.

PLANNING IN PRACTICE

Terminology in the area of planning can be a little confusing as numerous terms are used loosely and have similar meanings.

All managers plan, no matter at what level. Risk and uncertainty is minimized by planning and this is needed more today than before as social and economic conditions alter very quickly and careful planning enables an organization to prepare for change.

Planning helps the organization to define its purposes and activities. It enables performance standards to be set and results can therefore be compared with the standard to enable managers to see how the organization is proceeding towards its goals.

Planning must be *flexible* to deal with a changing environment. When plans are made, for example, for additions to the fleet of lorries of a transport firm, they must take into account possible increases in fuel prices.

The higher up the hierarchy of management, the more attention is paid to planning, particularly in setting out goals and strategies for a long period ahead. Managers lower in the hierarchy usually deal with sections of the total plan, and are concerned with shorter periods of time.

Many persons may be involved in planning activities, which must be a continuous process, but the main point is that these activities must produce a specific *plan*; without plans, planning *activities* have no real effect. One main feature of planning is to make a *decision*. This will involve assumptions about the future and about many variable factors. This is dealt with elsewhere in this book (p 111).

Planning is essential for the long-term survival of any business enterprise as it helps to determine the most profitable way to allocate limited resources among competing ends.

Principles of planning

- Plans should be based upon clearly defined *objectives* and make use of all available information.
- Plans should consider factors in the *environment* which will help or hinder the organization in reaching its goal.
- They should take account of the *existing organization* and provide for control, so performance can be checked with established standards.
- They should be *precise*, practicable and simple to understand and operate.
- They should be *flexible*, to ensure that if circumstances necessitate change, this can be effected without disrupting the plan.

Problems of planning

Time span

The greater the time span, the greater the number of mistakes. *Present conditions* are usually dominant in the planner's mind when he initiates a plan and these may be overstressed. For example, a new building for a computer based upon present ideas (i.e. for use by the finance function only) may be found to be too small; if, in fact, all functions make use of the computer, a larger computer building may be needed. A good illustration of the effect of time on planning can be seen by comparing long- and short-term weather forecasts.

Unforeseen events and lack of communication

Many events are obviously unforeseen, but planning can be aided by techniques giving suggested probabilities of events taking place. Wider consultation with workers is needed, to enable them to understand the nature of obstacles and the reason why management is taking a certain course of action to overcome them.

Size of organization

The larger the scope of the plan, the more complex the planning (e.g. plans for a department and plans for a group of departments).

Strategic and tactical plans

One way of classifying plans is to distinguish between strategic and tactical plans.

Strategic planning involves deciding upon the major goals of an organization and what policies will be used to achieve them. It involves a longer time period and relies on more unreliable long-term forecasts and occurs at more senior levels in an organization (e.g. political and technological changes).

Tactical planning involves deciding upon how resources will be used to help the organization achieve its strategic goals. It relies more on past records and involves shorter time periods.

Hierarchy of plans

Plans are made at various levels in an organization, and may be stated in the form of a hierarchy (Fig 3.2).

It is important to decide what is the purpose and mission of a business. This is usually a very difficult decision, but so essential, as it makes it much easier to state clear and realistic objectives, strategies and plans. (See *Management Tasks, Responsibilities, Practices*, P Drucker, Pan, 1979 (Chapter 5, pp 68–85).)

Goals give a sense of direction for the activities of an organization. They give *broad* guidelines towards which more detailed and specific plans are directed. They consist of the purpose, mission and objectives. Some writers ignore purpose and mission or use goals or objectives interchangeably. A note on their meaning follows.

A **purpose** is the main role society defines for a business organization and applies to *all* types of such organizations, e.g. in Western society, to earn a profit by the production of goods and services.

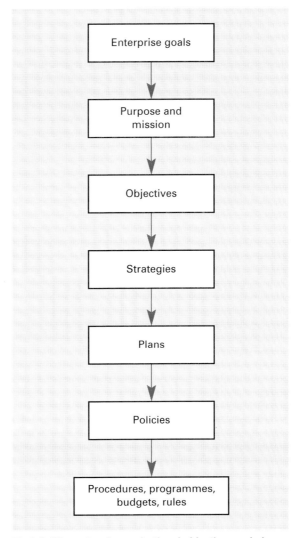

Fig 3.2 Hierarchy of organizational objectives and plans

A **mission** is a narrower form of purpose, which is *unique* to a particular organization, e.g. to produce certain types of goods and services. P Drucker has written about these concepts in *Management Tasks, Responsibilities, Practices* (Pan, 1979). He considers that the way an organization defines its *mission* is crucial to its prosperity and possible survival.

The *mission of an organization* is the broad objective that sets a business apart from others of its type and identifies the extent of its operations in product and market terms. A mission statement clearly states the objective of the organization's management in structuring its basic business activity.

Managers usually concentrate on three elements in stating an organization's mission; these are the primary market, the basic product or service and the main technology. Some companies communicate organizational values as part of their statements of purpose and mission. These *statements of organization values:*

In *People and Performance* (Heinemann, London, 1977) P Drucker refers to four brothers-in-law who formed the organization Marks & Spencer. The firm up to 1924 had built up a good business as a variety chain store. They re-thought the purpose and mission of their business after a visit to America to study Sears Roebuck in 1924. They redefined their business as 'the subversion of the class structure of 19th-century England by making available to the working and lower-middle classes, upper-class goods of better than upper-class quality at prices the working and lower-middle classes could well afford'. They then converted this purpose and mission of 'what our business should be' into clearly defined specific objectives.

- direct the behaviour of staff employed in the business;
- reflect management perceptions about the way society will respond to the business;
- are determined in part by the responses of others to the business.

Organizational values are the philosophical and ethical standards adhered to by personnel in the pursuit of an organization's purpose and mission. Statements of organizational purpose usually include references to owners, customers, employees, profit, growth and survival considerations.

Examples of objectives relating to survival and growth could include

- reducing dependence on certain suppliers;
- closing unprofitable lines.

Productivity objectives usually refer to the number of items sold or service rendered for a unit of input, e.g. the occupancy rate for hotels.

It is increasingly the case that objectives refer to improvements in the quality of a product or service. An increase in market share is a common objective. Another area for objectives is to decide whether a company wishes to be a leader in technology or a follower. Objectives *of public responsibility* are quite common, and refer to customers as well as society in general.

Objectives are those ends that must be achieved in order to carry out a mission. (In the following pages and for the rest of this book, the term 'objectives' will be considered to be interchangeable with 'purpose' and 'mission' for the sake of simplicity of explanation.)

Strategies are broad programmes of activity to achieve organization objectives. They are a guide as to how resources are to be deployed to achieve the objectives. Strategies are carried out by plans, which can be used for one purpose – a *single-use plan* (e.g. to construct a bridge), or by *standard plans* for repeated actions (e.g. credit policy). Plans for a *single use* are of the following types:

1 **Programmes** – cover a larger set of activities (e.g. to develop *management* skills in all supervisors).
2 **Projects** – cover a *smaller* range of activities than a programme, and are specifically defined (e.g. to develop *financial* skills in supervisors).

3 **Budgets** – are statements of financial resources needed and are used to control most activities. The process of budgeting is a key planning activity. They can be regarded as single-use plans (*see* p 217).

Plans for *standard* situations form a guide to enable consistency of action in similar situations.

CORPORATE PLANNING

Corporate planning is a term denoting a line of approach or a style of management, an attitude of mind, which uses a systematic and integrated approach to all aspects of a firm's activities. The idea is to treat the company as a corporate whole, rather than a collection of departments, and on a long-term basis, rather than a short-term one. The company is studied within its environment, past, present and future, and with a precise definition of objectives.

A well-known writer on the subject, John Argenti, defines corporate planning as: 'A systematic and disciplined study designed to help identify the objective of any organization or corporate body, determine an appropriate target, decide upon suitable constraints and devise a practical plan by which the objectives may be achieved' (*Corporate Planning*, G Allen & Unwin Ltd, 1968). This approach is similar to management by objectives (MBO) (*see* p 107). The most interesting and important feature of the MBO approach is the emphasis on the joint establishment of objectives between manager and superior.

Corporate planning is defined by Drucker as 'a continuous process of making entrepreneurial decisions systematically and with the best possible knowledge of their futurity, organizing systematically the effort needed to carry out these decisions and measuring the results against expectations through organized systematic feedback'.

In a study of United Kingdom companies, the reasons stated for the introduction of corporate planning were:

- effective diversification;
- rational allocation of resources;
- improved co-ordination and anticipation of technological change;
- increased profitability and the rate of growth.

It is really more of a style of management working in an atmosphere of change. Yearly profits, although important, are a short-term factor in corporate plans. Manpower and new product development are examples of longer term areas of concern for the survival of the organization. In most of the evidence to date, better results are obtained by companies adopting corporate planning methods.

Management systems and practices in all types of enterprise, e.g. banks, local government and industry, need to be revised to give more weight to strategic considerations. Competition may not be so much in products or markets, but through conflict with government and pressure groups in society, e.g. on matters such as pollution, safety and welfare.

Corporate plans are therefore needed to cope with social and political change. This needs equally careful thought in setting social objectives, policies and plans to ensure the gain of social and political acceptance of the company's ideas. The idea behind this is the strategic problem of *adapting the organization* to its environment, and this will usually mean fundamental changes in management and the organizational structure.

The approach taken in this book is that corporate planning involves more than long-range planning and should adopt a more systematic and integrated approach to all the organization's activities. In this approach, the economy of the country, the position of the organization in its markets and the corporate structure are analysed.

The *whole of the industry* of which the organization is part should be examined, noting the nature of the supply and demand factors, possible future trends and new opportunities, threats or problems. A *comparison* should be made between the organization's performance and that of its competitors. *Trends* in economic and political areas should be noted, e.g. government controls on mergers and economic groupings of countries, such as the European Union. Certain key factors should then be identified which appear likely to improve the organization's position.

The final assessment would cover specific areas and their problems and opportunities. A brief summary follows:

- **research and development** – the need for new products and product improvements;
- **human resources** – the need to ensure staff are available of the desired quantity and quality;
- **sales and marketing** – the relevance of sales policies, share of market, suitability of quality, design and price of products, marketing mix;
- **production** – to ensure production capacity is adequate and other facilities and costs of production are acceptable.

From the above analysis the possibility of reorganization, merger, diversification, etc., can be considered.

The essential need is for the plans from the various areas of a business to be *integrated*, so that functional plans are interlinked to form an overall corporate plan.

A corporate plan, though, is more than just an interlinking of functional plans; it can be considered as a systems approach to achieve the aims of the business over a period of time. Ansoff states this clearly in *Corporate Strategy* (pp 18–19):

> A very important feature of the overall business decision process becomes accentuated in the strategic problem. This is the fact that a large majority of decisions must be made within the framework of a limited total resource. Regardless of how large or small the firm, strategic decisions deal with a choice of resource commitments among alternatives; emphasis on current business will preclude diversification, over-emphasis on diversification will lead to neglect of present products. The object is to produce a resource allocation pattern which will offer the best potential for meeting the firm's objectives.

An interesting account of the various strategies which can be adopted and classifications of opportunities and risks is given in *Managing for Results* by P F Drucker (Chapters 12 and 13).

He points out two important strategies which have to be decided:

(a) One is to decide what *opportunities* or wants the company wishes to pursue and what *risks* it is willing and able to accept.
(b) The other is to decide on the scope and structure and the right balance between specialization, diversification and integration.

His classification of opportunities (additive, complementary and break-through) and of risks are interesting and practical guides to help the formulation of strategies.

A *capability profile* of company strengths and weaknesses can be drawn up; one method is a points scale related to a desired level of performance.

One large company found out for the first time in such an analysis that 75 per cent of its profits came from one product and this market was slowly declining. Many other important factors can come from such an analysis, e.g. under-utilization of financial assets.

A final point regarding this aspect is mentioned by Ansoff (Chapter 5, *Corporate Planning*), where he considers that the measurement of 'synergy' is similar to what is frequently called 'evaluation of strengths and weaknesses'.

> 'In synergy, *joint* effects are measured between two product markets; in strength and weakness evaluation, the firm's competences are rated relative to some desired performance level.
>
> *Synergy* is concerned with the desired characteristics of fit between the firm and its new product-market entries. In business literature it is frequently described as the 2 + 2 = 5 effect, to denote that the firm seeks a product-market posture with a combined performance that is greater than the sum of its parts.'

If a company adds to its existing activities, the extent to which the new activity makes use of existing resources will determine the extent of the synergy. If, for example, the return on investment of the company as a whole is just the return on the existing activities plus that of the new activity, there is no synergy (2 + 2 = 4). But where the new activity *makes use of* existing resources, the return for the company as a whole will be *greater than* the average of the new and existing activities (2 + 2 = 5).

Plans range from those of a broad scope concerned with a long time span, which are the concern of top executives, to short-run, day-to-day operating plans which are the concern of managers at lower levels in the organization.

As the amount of innovation increases in a given period, the time available for new product *exploitation* diminishes. But it still takes the same time to develop and test new products; money has still to be spent on promotion and selling activities and, as the life span of a product falls, profitability will be reduced.

Long-range planning (LRP) enables management to anticipate difficulties and take steps to eliminate them before they arise and can help to bring about a more unified approach to the various factors in a problem. Plans, though, must clearly state which manager is accountable and for what results, i.e. it must be management by specific objectives.

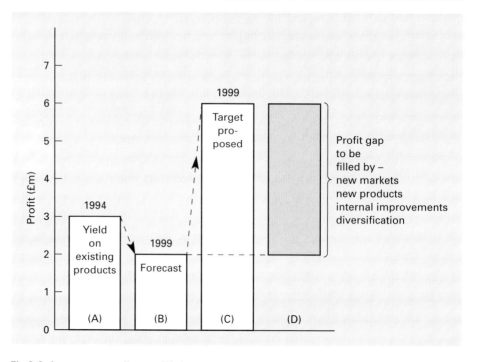

Fig 3.3 Long-range profit gap. (A) If the company continues as it is, the profit in five years will be £2m. (B) The proposed target in five years' time is £6m. (C) And this can only be obtained by a marked change in the factors shown beside the 'profit gap' (D)

The length of plans varies from industry to industry. The more fortunate can plan a few years ahead, e.g. the motor-car industry. Others may plan only six months ahead, e.g. the fashion industry. Often, different aspects of the plan will cover different periods of time, e.g. money needed on loan can be planned a year ahead, whereas plans for a new car cover at least four years ahead. The LRP will of course contain the short-range plan (SRP) which for convenience will be assumed to cover one year. Freedom to change the SRP is limited and may be broken down into monthly commitments, major variances being closely noted. It is imperative to note that assumptions made in LRP must be specified and any change in them examined carefully. (Consider Fig 3.3, showing the long-range profit gap.)

Corporate planning is simply a formal, logical method of running a business, which is comprehensive, embracing all activities of an organization. Individuals are responsible for planned results. Corporate planning is a tool of management to guide the business towards its agreed goals. Corporate planning can be said to incorporate long-range planning and management by objectives and has developed in status since its beginning in the USA in the 1950s.

The position of the corporate planner in an organization can indicate the status of the activity. The person usually has a staff role, to advise management; he generally reports to a senior person, sometimes the chief executive.

Responsible to: Chief executive.

Responsible for:

- organizing the section;
- preparing an agreed planning system;
- ensuring all roles are known and everyone is fulfilling standards agreed;
- acting on behalf of chief executive in preparing, co-ordinating and controlling the corporate plan;
- preparing reports on progress.

Special responsibilities:

- considering opportunities for growth and devising objectives and strategies to exploit growth;
- keeping abreast of business trends and developments in management techniques.

Limitations to authority:

- only responsible for members of own staff;
- advises chief executive of events affecting corporate plan.

There are many advertisements for corporate planners and qualifications required usually include: a degree with a good knowledge of mathematics, statistics and management techniques; at least eight years' experience in companies, or more than one industry; a personality that is acceptable to most people.

Their role is to install and maintain a system: corporate planners do not plan the system; if they do, this will lead to many problems. (A good discussion on these problems is contained in J Argenti, *Corporate Planning* (Allen & Unwin, 1968, Chapter 18, p 231).)

ANALYSIS OF RISK AND SENSITIVITY

Forecasters make assumptions from past data. Some of the dependent variable data, e.g. sales, in the forecast may be *significant* and may be *sensitive* to variations in forecasted values of other independent variables. A forecast for sales may be 10 per cent, but variations in independent variables may suggest growth rates of 5 per cent or 15 per cent. It is valuable to know, therefore, the *probability* that each of these three forecasts will occur.

There are techniques that may help to reduce uncertainty of the future and hence are valuable.

The idea of *sensitivity analysis* is to vary each piece of input data in turn while holding the remaining data fixed and each time evaluate a scheme's profitability. The uses of this method are:

- it can be seen whether more *exact* information would be useful in arriving at a decision;

- whether specific items should be rigorously *controlled* after a decision has been taken.

In the area of investment decisions, probability forecasts are very important, e.g. variable estimates of future sales costs and prices will affect the estimated rates of return on capital invested in projects.

A *single-figure* estimate of the return on an investment is not so valuable as a number of figures in the form of a distribution of the probability of the happening of various returns on investment.

Probability distributions are obviously more informative than single figures of returns, as managers can take *risk* into account when selecting projects. The return chosen will depend upon a manager's attitude towards risk.

Estimates are taken of the *worst* and the *best* likely conditions and re-estimates of the value of items. Probability distributions for the values of each of the different items are then made and evaluated by random selection methods weighted by probabilities. Risk *analysis* can highlight schemes where the profitability is subject to greater than normal uncertainty, so that management's attention can be directed to schemes requiring closer control.

Both sensitivity and risk analysis *complement one another* in their approach to the ever-present aim to reduce uncertainty in strategy and tactics.

More sophisticated techniques are also used to assess future possibilities, e.g. morphological analysis, the Delphi technique, scenarios, cross-impact analysis, value profiles and priority analysis and probability diffusion indices (see end of chapter for references).

MANAGEMENT IN A NON-PROFIT-MAKING ORGANIZATION

The formulation of strategy is often different depending upon the type of organization involved.

Large businesses often use a planning department structured on formal lines. Specialized planning staff are needed to deal with all the factors which must be noted in making strategic decisions. In other large businesses, planning staff may work with line managers in strategic planning and not work in isolation in a formal planning team.

Small businesses differ from large businesses, as we have seen in Chapter 2. So different methods of formulating strategy are used in small businesses. They are less formal or systematic than in larger organizations.

The above brief review indicates the general ways in which *profit-making* organizations tend to use strategic planning.

Organizations that *do not try to make a profit* differ greatly from each other, as they all have different reasons for existing. They also differ from profit-making firms in the following ways:

- The influence of the 'customer' may not be strong.
- The service provided may not be easily measurable.
- There may be very strict rules and guidelines regarding the payment of rewards to employees.

- Resolution of conflicts may be achieved mainly by the strength of character of the 'leader'.

There are other differences and they all affect the way the organization responds to the determination of strategy. The organization may have no strategies at all. It could be managed for short-term budget cycles, rather than long-term cycles. Alternatively, it may be managed for personal goals, rather than considering changes in its mission because of changing external circumstances.

Examples of non-profit-making organizations include schools and colleges, which now have greater independence in the United Kingdom and may be incorporated charities. The Red Cross, the Spastics Society and political parties are other examples.

There is no doubt that there is a trend towards a more professional approach in these organizations as more people from industry join them. This is highlighted in their more positive approach to marketing. They need to do this because of:

- increased competition from other organizations;
- cutbacks in government or local funding.

Marketing these organizations is becoming more professional and could, for example, be aimed at:

- a *person* who would be the focus of attention, such as a political candidate;
- a *place*, such as a city or country. There are numerous promotions each year, e.g. fly-drive holidays in the USA;
- an *idea*, such as child abuse or overeating.

No matter whether the organization is profit-making or not, a marketing strategy is needed to reach customers effectively (*see* Chapter 7).

MANAGEMENT BY OBJECTIVES (MBO)

This system must not be looked at as 'just another management technique' and given little consideration. It can be considered to be an approach to practical management. In essence it embraces a clear-cut strategic plan and its translation into departmental and personal goals, which are reviewed when results are obtained.

Although a great deal has been written on MBO since Drucker's first references in *Practice of Management* in 1954, especially by J Humble (UK) and D McGregor (USA), less than 10 per cent of firms in a recent survey regard its effect as 'very successful'; *some* applications, though, have been successful.

MBO systems vary greatly. Some are used for the organization as a whole, others are prepared for sub-units of an organization. Methods and approaches used by managers differ greatly. In the UK, MBO is used mainly for corporate strategy and planning, while in the USA the emphasis appears to be more on human needs and motivation and increasing subordinates' participation in setting objectives.

Effective planning using the approach of MBO depends upon every manager having very clearly defined objectives for his function in the company. These objectives must also be part of the contribution to other objectives of the company. If objectives are set which do not require any assistance from managers, there is much less chance of them being effected. Drucker goes a stage further by suggesting that managers at every level should participate in devising objectives for the *next higher* level of management. The important thing is to ensure that the individuals' objectives are related to the common goal.

Douglas McGregor (*Human Side of Enterprise*) stresses the value of MBO, especially the aspect of performance appraisal (*see* p 383). McGregor's approach suggests that we look at two sets of assumptions about individuals and their reaction to work. Theory X assumes that people work to survive and need therefore a strict, authoritarian approach to dealing with subordinates. Theory Y assumes people do *not* dislike work, and derive satisfaction from it. The manager's task under the assumptions of Theory Y is to *help* subordinates to achieve their fullest capabilities and not to control them. It is these assumptions which are the basis of the MBO system.

The stages in management by objectives are:

- the *desired results* (objectives) set by management are clarified and defined;
- *performance standards* are set, which must of course not conflict with the main objectives of the business;
- the *organization structure* must be provided, within which the manager has the maximum freedom and flexibility to perform;
- *control information* must be supplied at suitable times so the manager can take corrective action quickly;
- *appraisal of performance* identifies areas where a manager needs help and provision with guidance;
- employees are *motivated* by relating results achieved to rewards and promotion opportunities.

Other points to note are that each functional objective and target is tied to the *overall* objectives. It may mean reorganization is needed as quite often many organization schemes are either very elementary and leave out vital functions, or so complicated that they are very difficult to understand. (The next chapter will discuss organizing.)

Another important point is that *new techniques are no better than the people who use them* and proper attention must therefore be given to the training and development of management at all levels. Also, advanced methods of performance appraisal are needed to identify areas where managers need help and guidance.

Figure 3.4 attempts to show the relationship between the Long Range Plan and the Annual Profit Plan and how the manager's standards and priorities can be integrated and put into perspective. Further consideration of this approach will be made in Chapter 9 on Human Resource Management.

Participation in the setting of objectives can vary widely. Subordinates may only be involved by being present when being *told* what management has

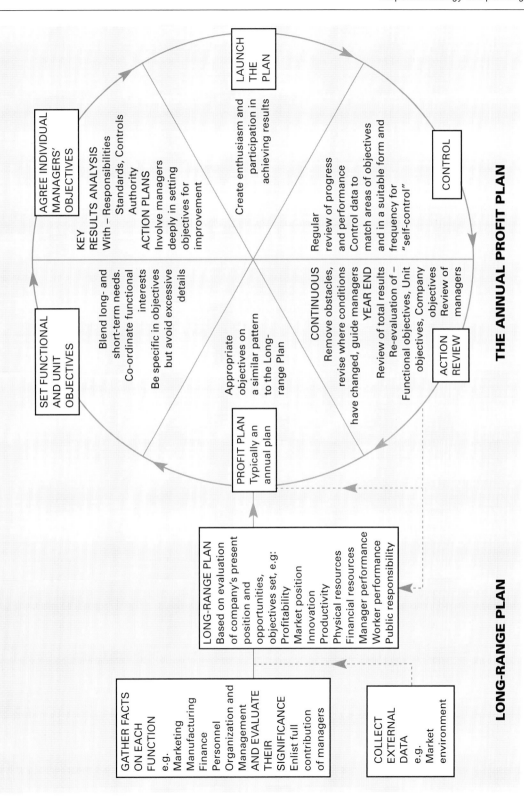

Fig 3.4 Management by Objectives. (Reproduced by permission of Urwick, Orr and Partners Ltd)

decided. Or, they may *set the objectives* and *decide the methods* by which they are to be achieved. In practice, methods adopted lie between these two extremes and the greater participation of both managers and subordinates in the setting of objectives, the more likely they are to be achieved.

To implement an effective MBO programme needs complete support throughout the organization as well as time and effort. It can be a highly motivating exercise as it enables both managers and subordinates to see their role more clearly.

Research has shown that participation of employees will lead to *greater employee acceptance of performance goals and management decisions* and improvements in communication and understanding, among both managers and their subordinates (H L Tosi and S J Carroll, 'Managerial Reaction to MBO', *Academy of Management Journal*, Dec 1968, USA).

Advantages of MBO

- The need to clarify objectives is stressed and suggestions for improvement are obtained from all management levels.
- All managers have a clear idea of the important areas of their work and of the standards required.
- The performance of staff can be assumed and their needs for improvement highlighted.
- Greater participation may improve morale and communication.
- Managers have to plan to achieve *results,* which are a means of achieving growth and profits.
- It makes individuals more aware of organizational goals.

Disadvantages of MBO

- It takes a few years to be effective.
- Too much paperwork and difficulty in measuring key operations.
- Achieving objectives may be at the expense of organizational goals, e.g. cost reduction programmes achieved by deferring maintenance. Sacrificing everything to meet goals may lead to poor managerial judgement.
- Some companies tend always to raise targets; if these are too high, staff become frustrated.
- Appraisals are sometimes made on personality traits rather than on performance.
- Some companies have geared their salary administration to appraisal by results (easy targets may be set to allow a promotion).
- It is not easy to set measurable objectives for staff groups who only exist to help the 'line' achieve its ends.
- Review and counselling of managers may be ineffective.
- Some employees do not want to be held responsible and goals forced upon them may lead to ill-feeling.

● Some of those giving appraisals may not be properly trained, may not be motivated to make the system work and may tend to treat it in a mechanical manner.

Another development of this approach is discussed by W J Reddin in *Effective MBO* (1971, Management Publications Ltd). He seeks to define MBO concepts by new interpretations stressing achievement and output results rather than 'input behaviour'. Planning is emphasized, so is the need for relevant correct information providing checks against standards.

DECISION MAKING

Definition

A decision is a choice whereby a person forms a conclusion about a situation. This represents a course of behaviour about what must or what must not be done. It is the point at which plans, policies and objectives are translated into concrete actions. Planning leads to decisions guided by company policy and objectives and implies the *selection from alternative* objectives, policies, procedures and programmes. The purpose of decision making is to direct human behaviour towards a future goal. If there were no alternatives, there would be no need for a decision.

Types of decisions

A brief comment on some of the ways decisions can be distinguished is all that is needed at this stage. Drucker distinguishes between 'tactical' and 'strategic' decisions.

Strategy can be defined as the behaviour of management in trying to achieve success for company goals in an environment of competition. It is based upon the action, or possible action, of others. Strategies are solely calculated to implement plans and objectives, bearing in mind all manner of uncertainties, so that an advantageous position is attained over an opponent.

'Tactical' decisions are routine, usually contain few alternatives and relate to the economic use of resources.

'Strategic' decisions are made by management and involve 'either finding out what the situation is, or changing it; either finding out what the resources are, or what they should be'. These include decisions upon basic objectives and may affect the productivity, organization or operation of the business.

Other classifications include a division between *organizational* and *personal* decisions:

1 **Organizational** decisions are those made in the role of an official of the company and reflect company policy.
2 **Personal** decisions refer to those made by a manager as an individual and cannot be delegated.

Another classification is between *basic* and *routine* decisions:

1 **Basic** decisions are long-range in scope, e.g. the location of factory in a Development Area, or deciding what product to make. Wrong decisions on these matters can be costly.

2 **Routine** decisions are those which are made repetitively and need little thought.

A final, similar, classification by H A Simon distinguishes between *programmed* and *unprogrammed* decisions:

1 **Programmed** decisions are those which are routine and repetitive and have procedures set up to deal with them. Risks involved are not high and they therefore can be more easily delegated. Assessment can often be made in quantitative terms and can therefore more easily be *programmed* into a computer.

2 **Unprogrammed** decisions are new and non-repetitive, where risks involved are high and they cannot easily be assessed in quantitative terms. There are many courses of action possible and decisions made will mean a greater expenditure of resources.

The process of decision making

A little earlier on in the chapter, it was stated that knowledge of objectives and policies is needed before decisions can be taken. Such decisions may be said to consist of the following steps:

- define the problem to be solved;
- find alternative solutions;
- analyse and compare these alternatives;
- select the plan to be followed noting relevant factors;
- make the decision effective – by taking action to put the decision into effect.

Decision making really involves removing doubt. It involves having an objective to achieve and the tests of whether that objective is being achieved or not form the control criteria. Decisions involve the future and involve choice, therefore they can be wrong. The point to consider is, who makes decisions in an organization, and what are the criteria in delegating some decisions to subordinates? These questions can be answered by finding out those decisions where the chances of being wrong are high and the cost of correction is large; these can then be *reserved for top management*. Lower ranks would be allowed to decide where there was more certainty of being correct and the cost of correction is low.

One important point to consider is that no course should be taken that would create the need for a *new* decision after a short period of time.

Research into how decisions are made has greatly increased in recent years; the results show that decision behaviour is very complex and variable.

Many decisions are made by managers from a certain number of factors they have considered. The reality of the situation is that there may in fact be many more factors unknown to them that they should have considered.

Analysis of alternatives and their possible consequences can be assisted by techniques, particularly by mathematical models and the use of probability theory (e.g. decision tree, *see* p Fig 3.7 later).

A premise is made, e.g. if A then B (*see* p 7). Factual premises can be observed and measured and any value judgements involved must be recognized in any decision.

Once a decision is made it needs to be accepted by staff, who must first of all have the decision *communicated* to them and then they must be *motivated* to implement the decision.

A few of the *rules* used today in making decisions are:

1 Minimax Rule – this is said to guarantee a minimum gain, or avoidance of maximum loss. This is often used when risks are high, or when a possible loss could be serious. If a stock controller observed this rule, he could hold too much stock which may be uneconomic, but he cannot be criticized for being out of stock.
2 Maximax Rule – is the opposite of the above, where the aim is the highest possible value of an outcome regardless of risks involved.
3 The Average Rule – is simply mid-way between the other two rules.

It should be noted that, whatever decision criteria are chosen, decisions are affected by:

- the importance of the decision;
- characteristics of the organization;
- the personality of the decision maker;
- his/her state of mind when making the decision.

It may be useful to look at decisions in terms of systems theory. Any choice that induces *flow*, or changes in the flow rate, is a decision. Rates are where the action *is*, i.e. what takes place between levels in a system. An example of this is when a person withdraws money from a bank; the level of money in the bank has been reduced – thus the action (decision) has caused a change from the previous state.

Another example is that if an accountant decides to stop credit to a customer (this action changes the flow rate), this is a decision in systems terminology. This can be further considered. If the flow rate continues (i.e. of credit) it can be said that a decision has been made to *let it continue*.

Decisions result from a comparison of actual with standard. Some decisions are made without being influenced by man. For example, if the temperature outside a person's body changes, then without any effort by man, his body temperature changes. The aim of the human system is to maintain standards; therefore any decision taken aims to effect changes in flow rates to *move existing states* in the desired direction.

Improving the quality of decisions

In order to improve the quality of decisions it is important to evaluate them at the time of deciding. One approach, advocated by Norman Maier in *Problem-solving, Discussions and Conferences; Leadership Methods and Skills* (New York, McGraw-Hill, 1963), is to decide:

1 What is the *objective quality* of the decision? Was the *full* process of decision making adopted, i.e. diagnosing all facts, evaluating them, developing alternatives; if so, the decision should be *high-quality*. The more technical the problem, the more a quality decision will solve it.

2 What is the *amount of acceptance* of the decision by subordinates? Difficulty would ensue if *quality* considerations conflicted with *acceptance*. Subordinates may resist a decision they thought was made with insufficient facts or inaccurate logic. A manager can, of course, compel or persuade subordinates to accept the decision. The more *people* are involved in a problem, the less likely a decision based on 'quality' would be sufficient.

Maier suggested managers should evaluate each problem to see how they can increase the effectiveness of decisions by seeing how important it was to have *quality* and/or *acceptance*:

- where high quality is important, not high acceptance (in financial areas, for example, acceptance is not so important);
- where acceptance is more important than quality (*group* decisions help here to ensure a solution is made to work, e.g. holiday rota);
- where both high quality and acceptance is needed (e.g. a change in the wage payment system – this could be solved by management stating its views, but a better (more acceptable) way would be to lead group discussions to come to an acceptable answer).

Statistical information for decision making

Information is collected by everybody through the media and people pick out those items that interest them. In business, certain information is needed and it is important that it is known where to find it and how to collect it.

Statistics is that part of mathematics that deals with collecting and analysing data. *Data* are items known or assumed as a basis for inference. Statistics is concerned with the systematic collection and interpretation of numerical data.

Business statistics therefore provides quantitative bases for arriving at decisions with respect to selected matters connected with the operation of a business. *Business statistics includes also* the methods and inferences needed to:

- *provide* an adequate flow of quality raw material;
- *select* and evaluate the performance of both machines and human resources;
- *design* products and maintain their quality;
- *evaluate* new methods of production, advertising and selling the goods and services of industry at the present time and in the future.

Many people do not find statistical statements easy to read and there is a tendency to translate statistics into a verbal form.

Any survey or investigation must be planned and designed carefully in order to reach a valid conclusion. Statistical treatment of a problem is more than examination of data, making calculations and coming to a conclusion. Questions that are also important are:

- How was the data collected?
- How was the survey planned?

Numerical data by itself is meaningless unless it is related in some way. For example, if inflation is said to be 5 per cent, this can have a number of meanings. Does it relate to the last year or the last six months, or is it the average inflation over a period of years? Statistics are used at times to exaggerate, inflate or oversimplify, and careful attention needs to be placed on the method used to collect and summarize the data.

Descriptive statistics is a term used to denote tabular or graphical presentation of data including the calculation of percentages and averages and the measurement of correlation and dispersion – in other words, any treatment of numerical data which does not involve generalizations.

Inductive statistics involves making generalizations, estimations or predictions. Many of the methods used are based directly on probability theory.

Primary and secondary data

- **Primary data** is collected by or on behalf of persons who hope to make use of it.
- **Secondary data** is derived from the processing or publicizing of primary data. In other words, if data is used by persons other than those for whom it was collected, it is secondary data. This is why it is important to know *how data has been collected* and processed, *how far it is a summary* and *how accurate* it is, before one can appreciate its reliability and full meaning.

Statistics compiled from secondary data are termed secondary statistics. For example, the government publish tables of unemployment figures (these are secondary data): when this *data* is used for calculations, they are termed secondary *statistics*.

Sources of information

Before data is collected, careful planning is needed of the study and the precise formulation of its purpose, scope and objectives. Data taken from a company's *internal* records, e.g. production, marketing and finance data, is specific to the business itself.

External data is that obtained from outside the organization, e.g. public sector and government. This could be information on population, unemployment or finance. Both types of data may be required for some studies.

Government statistics

These are widely available and are produced to measure the effects of their policies and the effect external factors have on them. Trends can also be noted and this assists future planning. The Central Statistical Office co-ordinates the government's statistical services.

Main statistical publications

- *Guide to Official Statistics* – contains a description of all official statistics.
- *Monthly Digest of Statistics* – this is a collection from all government departments.
- *Financial Statistics* – a monthly summary of important financial statistics.
- *Economic Trends* – a monthly bulletin on trends in the UK economy with a useful selection of tables and charts.
- *Municipal Year Book* – provides details of local authority areas.
- *Employment Gazette* – a monthly publication from the Department of Employment.

Other monthly or weekly publications deal with details of economic and business areas. Also published is a range of *Indexes* on prices, production, sales, etc. There are also various census results, e.g. Census of Production, Distribution and Population. The Bank of England and commercial banks also publish monthly or quarterly bulletins and reports. It is important to note that figures collected for one purpose may not be entirely suitable for another. This is especially relevant to official statistics which are a by-product of administrative processes to meet needs at a particular time. Firms can compare their own statistics with other firms in their industry.

Accuracy of information

Statistical information is rarely perfectly accurate and *approximations* have to be made quite often. The accountant can be very precise in the collection and paying out of cash. Government statistics of the trade figures are rounded to thousands or hundreds of thousands of units. High levels of accuracy may not always be needed. There is always the consideration of the high cost of very accurate measurements. The *degree* of accuracy required in statistics will depend upon the type of data being measured and also its proposed uses.

Formal arithmetic is concerned with manipulating *exact* quantities; statisticians are generally concerned with the manipulation of quantities which are only known *approximately*. The real measurements of a continuous variable can only be given to a number of decimal places, depending upon the accuracy of the measuring instrument. For example, the length of a page of a book may be measured at 20.6 cm but could be between 20.55 and 20.65 cm: if the answer is made correct to *three significant figures*, then the answer is 20.6 cm.

An accountant usually records cash to the last penny in the accounts. For other summaries of accounting data, he may only consider pounds and ignore pence. He will then round off to the nearest pound. The convention is to round fractions or decimals to the nearest whole number by rounding 0.5 and above to the next highest whole number and 0.4999 (recurring) to the next lowest whole number. It is important to use rounding methods carefully in order that biased errors do not occur. If the figures are very large, rounding makes them more comprehensible, giving sufficiently accurate figures.

Types of error

An *absolute* error is the difference between an estimate and the true figure. For example, an estimate of money to be spent on stationery may be £20. If the actual money spent was £25, the absolute error is £5. Someone else may expect to spend £40 on stationery and actually spend £45. The absolute error is £5 as before.

The error in the first example was 25 per cent of the original estimate. The other example produced an error of 12q-Σ per cent.

A *relative error* gives more precise information and is the absolute error divided by the estimate, and is often expressed as a percentage. For example:

$$(1) \ \frac{£5}{£20} \times 100 = 25\% \qquad\qquad (2) \ \frac{5}{40} \times 100 = 12\frac{1}{2}\%$$

Collection of information

Some problems can only be solved by collecting primary data and this involves carrying out an inquiry or survey. A *survey* which is brief and not systematic may not give accurate enough results. The larger the number of observations and the more detailed the survey will mean more credibility will be given to its results.

Surveys

Businesses are particularly interested in *market research* surveys. The ideal survey will cover 100 per cent of the items to be surveyed. In practice, a *sample* of this total may be used. The Census of Population in the UK is based on 100 per cent of the population. Other surveys must decide upon a suitable *size of the sample* to be used and also upon the *methods of collection* of the information.

Often a *preliminary or pilot* survey is carried out on a small scale to ensure the survey is designed correctly and the right methods are being used to give the information required.

Primary data are mainly collected through observation, questionnaire and interview. Questions are often coded so that answers can be classified and made easier for tabulation, whether by computer or manually. The final step is usually to prepare a report using suitable graphs and charts.

1 **Direct observation** used in a survey may not always be suitable as this may result in untypical results. For example, if workers know they are being observed they may either increase *or* restrict their output.
   The problems of observation include:

   ● observers may interpret meanings to the actions of persons which were not intentional;
   ● observers can select features for reporting upon which they may be unintentionally biased.

   One method used to overcome human 'errors' is the use of *mechanical methods,* such as is used for measuring the number of cars on roads, which is very accurate.

2 **Interviews** are used widely and, if conducted carefully, can give good results in the collection of information. The training of interviewers also helps a consistent unbiased approach. Street interviews are usually conducted by experienced interviewers and are widely used in consumer surveys (*see* p 284). The interview tends to be more structured than in general conversation. Each question will be set out to achieve a particular objective and additional questions may elicit further desired objectives.

Formal interviews use set questions. *Informal* interviews use similar questions but vary in response to answers received.

Interviews may be successful, but there are a number of problems that could occur, for example:

- interviewers have different skills and abilities;
- the way the question is asked may influence answers;
- interviewees may give answers they think are expected of them or they may not be very motivated and give inaccurate answers.

3 **Questionnaires.** Devising a set of questions to elicit information is not easy. Questions must be free from bias, set out in logical order, be relevant and unambiguous and be clearly and simply worded. Ease of completing the questionnaire is important, so the correct design of the form is vital. A questionnaire will only produce the desired information if it is organized and designed carefully.

Sampling

There are many investigations for which a full survey of the population is not possible, so a limited number of items must be selected: the group selected is known as a *sample.* The act of investigating the group is sampling. The *population* is the total group of people or items about which information is required. A sample can be of any size, and will be needed if it is very costly in time or money to have a 100 per cent examination of the total population. Sometimes investigations may lead to the destruction of the items tested, e.g. finding out the life span of motorcar components.

Advantages of sampling

- **Cheaper** to collect from a sample than total population.
- **Time** is saved which may be important as decisions can be taken sooner than if a full survey is made.
- **Tests** made may be destructive of items tested, so the fewer destroyed the lower the costs incurred.
- **Reliability** – a high level of reliability is possible if care is taken in selecting the sample and the staff operating the investigation. *Sufficient accuracy* may be obtained for a decision to be made from a sample, thus saving resources.

The *objectives* of sample surveys are to estimate certain statistics from the selected sample and this is used as an estimate of the total population. In all cases it is important that the statistics should be accompanied by a statement of the accuracy of the results. Any variability of the statistic sampled is indicated by a method called *standard error.* Sampling may be carried out by selecting the required number of items at *random,* or by a *purposive* method, or a mixture of the two methods. If the total population (or universe) is divided into 'strata', or sections, it is called *stratified* sampling.

Random sampling occurs when each member of the population has the *same chance* of being selected. It is not easy to select items at random; anything influencing one side is said to have *bias*. The method selected for random sampling will depend upon the size and nature of the population. Tables of random numbers are used to ensure there is no bias. *The law of statistical regularity* states that a reasonably large sample which is selected from a large population at random will on average be *representative* of the characteristics of the population.

Another law is worth noting. This is the law of the *inertia of large numbers*, which states that *large groups* of data show a higher degree of stability than small ones. Any variations in the data have a tendency to cancel each other out.

It is important to stress that errors due to *bias* can make the results of an investigation useless. The errors will increase, the greater size of the sample, and cannot be calculated. In these cases, bias will occur if there is any form of deliberate selection or part of the sample selected is omitted.

Sampling errors are the difference between the *estimate* of a value obtained from a sample and the *actual* value. For example, if the average weekly sales of a sample group of sales representatives is £6000 and the actual value of their sales shows an average of £6500, the sampling error is £500. Providing the sampling method used is based upon random selection, the *probability of errors* may be measured.

The *design of a sample* is important and can include random, systematic, stratified random, or quota sampling.

Visual and graphical presentation of information

The *arrangement and presentation* of primary and secondary data is needed before information in the data can be interpreted. The aim is to communicate information to other persons, so their needs and interests must determine the method of presentation used.

The bringing together of items with a common characteristic is known as *classification* and there are four methods: by geography (e.g. where people live), by a qualitative basis (e.g. by sex or colour), by a quantitative basis (e.g. height or weight) or by a time basis (e.g. months).

Any characteristic that varies from one member to another is known as a *variable,* which can be either discrete or continuous. The number of rooms in an office building is a *discrete* variable and is measured in single units. *Continuous* variables are units of measurement which can be broken down into definite gradations, such as the temperature of an office in decimals of a degree (e.g. 68.4°C).

In practice, continuous variables are converted to a discrete form by using the nearest appropriate unit of measurement.

After material has been collected and classified, it has to be arranged in such a manner that the important aspects can be noted easily. This can be achieved by *tabulation.*

Tabulation plays a large part in statistical publications (e.g. *Monthly Extract of Government Statistics*). A great amount of practice is needed to collect and classify items in a table so it can be easily interpreted.

Tables are used to present original figures in an orderly fashion, providing information in order to solve problems, or to show a distinct pattern or a concise summary of the figures.

Points to note in the construction of tables

- A title should be given to the table.
- Column and row headings should be brief and clearly named.
- Units of measurement should be stated.
- Material should be classified.
- Source of data must be stated.
- Vertical arrangement of figures is generally preferred to horizontal.
- Thin and thick lines can be used to make a large table easier to read.
- Data which has to be compared should be close together.
- Symbols should be used to draw attention to items needing further clarification (e.g. approximations or omissions).

Where a large number of variables and combinations are involved, a computer program can produce tables quickly.

Closer inspection of published tables is of great assistance in helping a person to become competent at drawing up successful tables of statistics.

A manager should be able to read data in geographical form; understand how quality control charts are adjusted, for example; and also what is meant by probability in an operational research problem. The following brief summary of methods of pictorial and graphical representation will introduce the use of statistical method as an important management aid.

Charts and graphs

Charts and graphs are a pictorial way of presenting data. Computer software packages enable these to be produced very easily. They can be grouped under four headings:

1 pictorial charts, e.g. pie charts and pictograms;
2 block charts, e.g. bar charts, histograms or Gantt charts;
3 graphs, e.g. line graphs and cumulative percentage frequency curves;
4 distribution graphs, e.g. those plotted with the frequency of occurrence of data on the vertical axis.

Pictorial charts

These are helpful in presenting technical data to managers and others.

Pictograms

These show information in a picture form by representing fixed groups of units by a symbol. Symbols of the same size represent specific amounts. They can be an attractive method of representing data but should only be used for showing relatively simple information.

Pie charts

These show the breakdown of a total into its component parts. The components are shown as percentage 'parts' or 'slices' of a circle. This is a very effective method of dealing with information concerned with one period of time. Each area of a sector is shown proportionate to the magnitude of the class it represents. The area of a sector of a circle is proportionate to the angle of the sector. For example, if the quantity of a variable is 30 units out of a total of 90, the variable must occupy 30/90ths of the area of the circle. There are 360° in a circle, so the variable must occupy $30/90 \times 360° = 120°$.

The finances of a business are often simplified by the use of pie charts. Assume profit was £30 000, taxes £20 000 and costs £40 000.

$$\text{Taxes} = \frac{20}{90} \times 360° = 80°$$

$$\text{Costs} = \frac{40}{90} \times 360° = 160°$$

The pie chart would look like that shown in Fig 3.5.

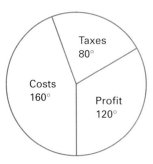

Fig 3.5 Pie chart

Colour shading can improve the figure, as can arranging the sectors in order of magnitude. *Pie charts are useful* when there are not many items and where proportions are more important than numerical values. They do not always provide details of absolute values and can involve long calculations unless they are generated by using a computer program.

Decision trees

By means of a diagram a number of future chance events which may affect a decision can be shown. A set of values is arrived at for predicted outcomes of each possible decision. The highest value indicates the course most likely to produce the greatest return.

This is a procedure for ensuring that alternatives are considered at every stage of an operation, as they may otherwise be overlooked.

The tree is usually horizontal and its base is the *present* decision point (usually shown as a square); it is here where alternative courses of action present themselves. Branches begin at the *first chance event* (shown as a circle); each chance event produces two or more possible effects, some of which may lead to other chance events and subsequent decision points. The values of the tree are based upon research which provides *probabilities* that certain chance events will occur, showing predicted payout or cash-flow estimates for each possible outcome as affected by possible chance events.

The statistical probability is based upon knowledge and experience. Subjective probabilities can range from complete certainty (probability of 1.0) through situations giving an even chance (0.5) to completely impossible situations (probability of 0.0).

It is basically a simple graphic method for analysing potential outcomes of a complex decision. It provides a way of showing the interplay among present decisions, chance events and possible future decisions, so enabling the manager to evaluate the various opportunities available at a given decision point.

More precise figures can be obtained, by *discounting* values assigned to *future* stages of the tree.

1st decision – to take car or bus.
2nd decision – to drive all the way, or stop and use public transport.
3rd decision – to use meter or drive to free parking area.

Each action can be given a financial or convenience value. Problems are more easily defined, and risks, costs and opportunities quantified by the use of decision trees (Figs 3.6 and 3.7).

In Fig 3.7, A and B are chance events affecting the decision either to continue with regional distribution or have national distribution of a product. Assume national distribution is considered and research has shown that if there is a large national demand it will realize £5.0m and the probability of this is 70 per cent (i.e. 0.7). There is a 30 per cent chance demand will be limited; this may realize £0.5m.

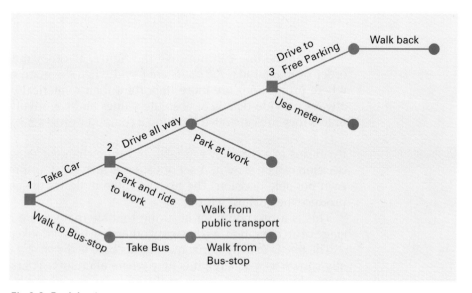

Fig 3.6 Decision tree

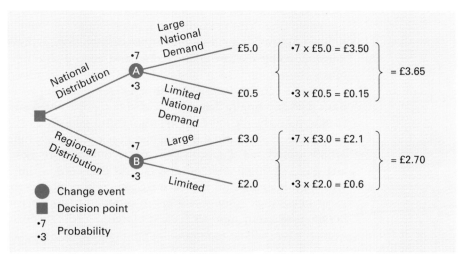

Fig 3.7 Decision tree

Assume regional distribution is considered – if national demand is limited the firm could realize £2m.

Payout amounts are then multiplied by the figure for probability, e.g.

$$0.7 \times £5 = £3.5\text{m}.$$

Each two amounts from the same 'branch', i.e. national or regional, are added together and the amounts compared – the highest result is to be taken and this is to *expand nationally*.

Catastrophe theory

A French mathematician, René Thom, used a branch of mathematics to prove a theorem which would be useful in studying the behaviour of human activity systems. This is that *gradual* changes in control can cause *sudden catastrophic* changes in *behaviour*, and if these changes could be predicted, this would be very beneficial. Nature is itself full of discontinuities; for example, a gradual rise in the temperature of water eventually causes a marked change – it boils. In economics, when controls are steadily relaxed after an economic 'squeeze', a sudden inflation explosion may occur. The protagonists of this *catastrophe theory* hope that it may become a useful tool in the study of the behaviour observed in human activity systems.

MANAGEMENT INFORMATION SYSTEMS (MIS)

There are three ways to organize the leadership of planning effort:

1 A *senior* executive adopts the responsibility for planning.
2 An *existing* function is responsible, e.g. finance, marketing.
3 A *separate* planning department is set up.

A decision is needed early as to whether or not an MIS will be useful in setting up plans. If an MIS is feasible, the information requirements of the organization should be determined, the processing system and program specifications decided, computer programs coded and procedures and instructions developed. The system is then modified, maintained and audited continuously.

Systems can be designed with a *bottom-to-top* approach, i.e. starting with basic data and finally determining corporate objectives, strategies and policies.

Alternatively, the *top-down approach* formulates first of all the objectives and constraints under which the business operates. Then functions and activities are identified, e.g. finance (e.g. cost accounting), market research; these are analysed, and then strategic and tactical decisions within which the activities will operate are specified. The next step is important – to determine *what the major information requirements are* in order to make decisions. These are then broken down into subsystems and placed in order, to ensure relevant data are available for each sub-system.

Information needed in an MIS

- A starting point in planning is to gather information from both internal and external sources and develop assumptions and scenarios (Fig 3.8). Before any information is placed in a computer, the *value* of the information to the future of the organization must be found. If little impact is calculated, it may be decided it is *too expensive* to adopt. (NB: Time is needed to collect data and put it in the machine in readable form; space is needed to store the data.) Possible non-use of data should be noted. Another point to determine is whether the *presence* or *absence* of data has a significant impact on decision making, as it may cost more money than it is worth to eliminate uncertainty.
- Given that information required is useful, it should then be put in the machine in readable form so files can be created, updated and manipulated by the computer.

An *MIS* is an integrated manual/computer system that provides information to support the operations, management and decision-making functions in an organization.

All the above functions are unlikely to be fully integrated into an MIS as the planning model becomes too complex. When a system is too general, it is costly to operate and difficult to use.

What can be done is to prepare separate planning models for each functional area and see that each separate model uses a common database wherever possible.

Regular updating of the MIS files is essential. A survey of systems in the USA confirmed that financial applications dominate the usage of MIS, for example:

- cash flow analysis – financial forecasting;
- balance sheet projections – profit planning;
- long-term forecasts – budgeting;
- sales forecasts – investment analysis;
- financial analysis.

The use of an MIS in *planning* allows us to obtain:

- evaluation of alternatives, long- and short-term planning;
- financial projections, decision making;
- preparation of reports, analysis.

Mathematical models manipulate the data using techniques such as linear programming, econometrics, game theory, cost-benefit analysis.

The planning model attempts to eliminate as much risk as possible by developing scenarios; these are complete sets of data and assumptions about the future. The MIS can give descriptions of the conditions under which a particular set of scenarios is possible. Alternatives are evaluated to find the cost and effects of a specified set of scenarios on each functional area.

Interrelations between various factors can be highlighted, e.g. the effect of price changes on production, cash flow and profit and loss statement.

Very few firms in the USA and the UK have fully integrated and co-ordinated all the functions shown in Fig 3.8 into a corporate model.

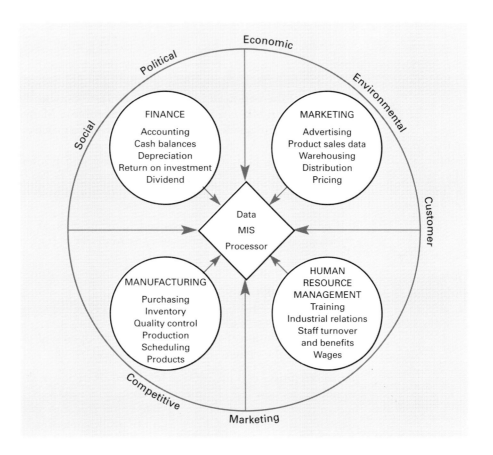

Fig 3.8 Data sources – internal and external

An MIS, whether computerized or manual, is a system for obtaining timely and relevant information on which to base management decisions. An effective MIS invariably employs computers and related technologies to process data of a business so that the decision-making process is facilitated.

Database

The centre of any information system is its *database,* which is a collection of the data resources of an organization designed to meet the requirements of the company for processing and retrieving information by decision makers. One important use of databases is to target more precisely marketing efforts. In the USA the latest trend in management information systems is the *executive information system* which is used by senior managers. Quality software produces full colour displays on large high quality monitors.

Figure 3.8 shows that both internal and external factors affect the organization. Information is drawn from all functional areas, e.g. production, marketing, finance, and this is integrated with information from the external environment and results in the creation of an information system.

An effective MIS should be:

- accurate;
- up to date;
- concise;
- relevant;
- complete.

Managers at the various levels of the organization make demands on the MIS. The *design* of an MIS is a long-term complex project. Many kinds of specialists and managers are needed to design and implement such a system.

Problems in implementing an MIS

1 Departmental boundaries may be affected which alters existing working relationships.
2 Established practices may need to be altered and any change may be resisted.
3 If only a few persons are involved with the change, there will be greater resistance than if most employees are involved.

Ways of overcoming resistance to installing an MIS

1 Encourage full participation in the scheme and ensure users become competent in its use.
2 Everyone should understand that giving routine tasks to a computer, releases managers to be more productive.
3 Finally, communication systems should be open and the aims and characteristics of the system should be understood by all.

Managers must keep themselves informed of trends in computer design and capability, as new developments in computer hardware and software occur frequently. Failure to keep up to date could threaten an organization's competitive position. Examples of current trends are telecommuting, videotext (*see* Chapter 10), database management, artificial intelligence and expert systems (*see* below).

There are various sub-systems in management information. These are accounting, manufacturing, human resources, marketing and office management. There is always the possibility of duplication. The purpose of database management is to reduce duplication wherever possible and the term is used to mean the *integration* of the various sub-systems of information so that duplication is reduced. Names and other details of employees may, for example, be held by the accounting system as well as in personnel files.

Artificial intelligence refers to the field of information technology that tries to simulate human processes, for example reasoning, problem solving, learning and communication by language. Whether computers will ever 'think for themselves' is debatable but is a constant aim for researchers.

An effective MIS integrates all the sub-systems so that managers are provided with better information for decision making.

Expert systems

The majority of computers follow *algorithms* which are precise sets of instructions or rules for solving a specific type of problem. The aim now is to replace algorithms by *heuristics,* which are programs which attempt to *improve* their own performance as a result of learning from previous actions within the program. When this goal is reached computers will be able to carry out tasks in a more human way. This means, for example, that they could react to natural language and appear to reason. To do this, computers must be programmed with heuristics and must be able to draw on an expandable database of facts and relationships.

An artificially intelligent computer with a knowledge database is an *expert system*. An expert system, therefore, can be defined as a database of facts and relationships from which the software makes deductions in the same manner as a human would. An expert system could approach the standards of a *human expert*. In expert systems, the knowledge of human experts is captured in a 'bank' of knowledge and this is made available to unskilled workers, who, when they interact with the system, become experts in their own right.

Expert systems are currently used in engineering, medicine, law and business. If the database is set up correctly and problems are stated correctly the expert system could give a *better* solution than a human being. There is great interest in expert systems in the USA, Japan and the United Kingdom.

Management in practice – expert systems

- A company in Luton, BIS Mackintosh, is working on an assembly line balancing project for the food industry. Savings will be made by freeing expert engineers from routine scheduling tasks, allowing them to work on other important areas.
- IBM has a system for the diagnostic testing of disk drives which saved over $59 million in the first year of its use.

SUMMARY

Objective 1 *Explain the concept of Management by Objectives.*

Management by Objectives is one approach to planning that enables all managers to participate fully in planning activities. Subordinates and managers meet to establish objectives and periodically review progress. It is based upon a set of assumptions (Theory Y) that under proper conditions, people will find satisfaction at work and will accept responsibility for their results. The basic elements include:

- goals set by managers;
- participation by subordinates in setting objectives;
- periodic review of performance and commitment of all to the programme.

Objective 2 *Name the key result areas in which all enterprises should establish objectives.*

Drucker identified these areas as:

- market standing;
- innovation;
- productivity;
- physical and financial resources;
- profitability;
- manager performance and development;
- worker performance and attitude;
- social responsibility.

Objective 3 *Describe the phases of the planning process.*

The five phases of the planning process are:

- establishing objectives;
- developing premises;
- decision making;
- implementing a course of action;
- evaluating results.

During the examination of each phase the organization should look ahead and back to see how other phases may affect implementation at any particular point in time.

Objective 4 *Identify the different types of decisions made by managers.*

The purpose of decision making is to direct human behaviour towards a future goal. A decision is a choice whereby a person forms a conclusion about a situation. Decisions can be strategic or tactical, organizational or personal, basic or routine, programmed or unprogrammed. The decisions managers make, and the conditions under which they make them, will vary and they must therefore tailor their decision-making approach to their particular problems and circumstances.

Objective 5 *Define corporate planning and briefly state why it differs from long-range planning.*

Corporate planning denotes a style of management which uses a systematic and integrated approach to all aspects of a firm's activities. The company is considered as a corporate whole and not a collection of departments. Activities are viewed on a long-term basis, rather than a short-term one. It is this wider approach which distinguishes it from long-range planning which focuses on parts of an organization in a selective manner. Corporate planning adopts a more comprehensive approach than long-term planning.

Objective 6 *Describe methods of forecasting in a business and limitations to forecasts.*

A forecast enables a premise to be made, from which plans can be developed and enables the right objectives to be selected. Methods of forecasting include:

- econometric forecasting;
- time series analysis;
- Delphi technique;
- scenario construction;
- sales forecasts and surveys.

Limitations to forecasting are the inability to keep a consistent base for measurement, poor interpretation and analysis of data, and the uncertain reliability of past data.

Objective 7 *Define the term 'management information system' and give examples of its practical uses.*

A management information system is an integrated reporting system specifically designed to help managers plan, execute and control the activities of an organization. It generates reports from various transaction processing systems. Examples of its practical uses are in financial forecasting, budgeting, investment analysis, balance sheet projections and various other reports.

Objective 8 *Explain why the formulation of strategy may be different in a non-profit organization.*

Non-profit organizations tend to be managed more from a short-term point of view than in a strategic sense. They differ greatly from profit-seeking firms and the service they provide is difficult to measure and often intangible. The tendency now is for a more methodical approach to planning in some organizations, e.g. schools, because of demands for greater accountability.

REVIEW QUESTIONS

1 Briefly review the place of forecasting in business and the techniques which are used in forecasting.

2 What factors must be considered in forecasting?

3 What do you understand by the objectives of a business?

4 Distinguish between specific and implied policies.

5 What are the obstacles to accurate planning?

6 Define decision making and comment on types of decisions.

7 What steps are involved in making a decision?

8 What is meant by the word 'synergy'?

9 Comment on the benefits in considering management as a system.

10 Explain the purpose of a 'decision tree'.

**REVIEW
PROBLEMS**

1 One of the *basic principles of planning* is that policies establish the framework upon which planning procedures and programmes are constructed. Discuss what is meant by policies and show how they are formulated and developed. One broad classification of policies deals with functions of the business – sales, production, finance, etc. Take any one of these functions and give the majority policy questions in this area, showing the factors to be considered in making policy decisions thereon.

2 Many businesses are now engaging in *long-range planning* of their production and marketing effort. Why have they become conscious of the need for long-range planning? What benefits can be anticipated from such planning? In the planning process definite goals must be set in five fields. What are these fields?

3 What would be the major factors you would wish to consider if you were drawing up a five-year corporate plan for *one* of the following organizations:

(*a*) hospital
(*b*) car manufacturing company
(*c*) bank
(*d*) nationalized industry.

4 Outline the process of *decision making* in industrial management. Show the stages of the process which will be assisted by the use of an electronic computer. Illustrate with an application to a specific problem in the top management field. What difficulties might arise in practice from dependence on computers?

5 Herbert Simon has argued that decision making is a matter of compromise. The alternative that is selected never permits complete achievement of objectives, but is the best solution available in the circumstances. Discuss.

6 State the case for and against employee participation in decision making in an organization. In your answer you should take account of the various levels of decision making within an organization. Specify the type of organization you are considering.

7 'The great advantage of taking profit maximization as the objective of a business firm is that this single target is so much simpler and more readily understood than a complex set of economic, ethical and social goals.' Discuss.

8 Describe what you understand by the phrase 'Management Information System'. In particular you should explain how the effective provision of information can assist management decision making.

9 Do you accept the view that the ultimate test of an organization's strategy is financial performance?

ASSIGNMENTS

1 From the following list of industries choose one and list the changes in technological, economic, social and political areas you think are likely to affect them over the next seven years. State briefly, giving examples, how organizations within that industry could begin to plan to meet the identified effects of these changes.

- Leisure and tourism
- Banking
- Public transport

2 You are asked to undertake a SWOT analysis of you own organization's position. Consider the main opportunities facing your organization and whether current strategies are appropriate to take advantage of them.

Comment also on the main weaknesses of your business and suggest possible ways of remedying them.

BIBLIOGRAPHY

Albert, K J, *The Strategic Management Handbook* (New York, McGraw-Hill, 1983).

Ansoff, H I (Ed), *Business Strategy* (London, Penguin, 1969).

Argenti, J, *Practical Corporate Planning* (London, Allen & Unwin, 1980).

Bendell, T, Kelly, J and Boulter, L, *Benchmarking for Competitive Advantage* (London, *Financial Times*/Pitman Publishing, 1993).

Drucker, P F, *The Practice of Management* (London, Heinemann, 1989). Chapters 5, 6, 7, 8 and 28.

Drucker, P F, *Managing for Results* (London, Heinemann, 1994).

Ellis, J and Williams, D, *Corporate Strategy and Financial Analysis* (London, Pitman Publishing, 1993).

Grundy, T, *Corporate Strategy and Financial Decisions* (London, Kogan Page, 1992).

Humble, J W, *Improving Business Results* (Maidenhead, McGraw-Hill, 1982).

Johnson, G and Scholes, K, *Exploring Corporate Strateg*y, (New York, Prentice-Hall, 2nd edition, 1988).

Kotler, J P and Heskett, J L, *Corporate Culture and Performance* (New York, Free Press, 1992).

Lumby, S, *Investment Appraisal* (London, Van Nostrand Reinhold, 2nd edition, 1981).

Smith, J G, *Business Strategy* (Oxford, Basil Blackwell Ltd, 1985).

Stacey, R, *Strategic Management and Organizational Dynamics* (London, Pitman Publishing, 1993).

Thomas, J J, *An Introduction to Statistical Analysis for Economics* (London, Weidenfeld & Nicolson, 2nd edition, 1983).

Weihrich, H, *Management Excellence, Productivity through MBO* (New York, McGraw-Hill, 1985).

CHAPTER 4

Organizing

An organization exists where two or more people agree to get together and co-ordinate their activities so as to achieve common goals. Organization theories developed from the early part of the 20th century and seek to understand, explain and attempt to predict human behaviour in organizations. Organization structures are examined in detail, especially the impact of bureaucracy on the development of some structures. The importance of authority and responsibility and delegation are highlighted and the importance of groups is discussed.

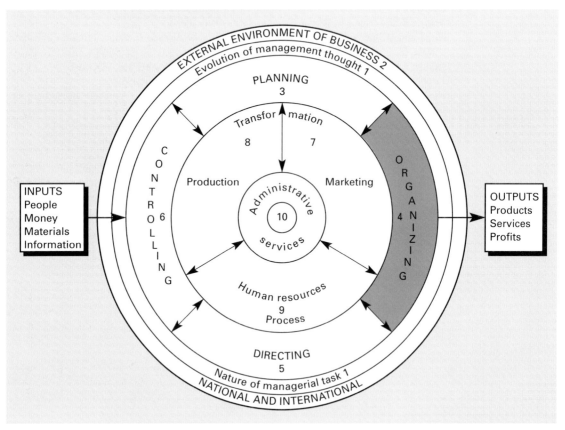

The systems approach to management

OBJECTIVES

Upon completing this chapter you should be able to:

- Describe the organizing process and explain why it is important to effective management.
- Define the formal structure of an organization and identify the various ways an organization can be structured.
- Define the term delegation and explain the differences between responsibility, accountability and authority.
- Explain the difference between decentralization and delegation, and discuss the factors that affect an organization's degree of decentralization.
- Describe the organizational development approach to change and the assumptions and values upon which this approach is based.

ORGANIZING

Organizing is defined in a number of ways. In the study of management it can refer to the structure of relationships among individuals. A less static approach regards organizing as a process or an element of management concerned with *change* or *growth* of the structure. The traditional approach will be considered first.

Organizations are primarily complex goal-seeking units which in order to survive must accomplish secondary tasks, e.g. they must maintain their internal system to co-ordinate the *human side of enterprise* and must adapt to and shape the external environment.

One area of conflict is the difference between the goals of management and the goals of individual workers. To overcome this conflict, a number of theories have been propounded to allow for mediation of interests. Motivation theories will be considered in more detail later (*see* p 199). Elton Mayo and his associates (*see* p 16) saw that the human affiliation of man could be a motivating force and viewed the industrial organization as a *social* as well as an economic–technical system. They considered managers should be judged by their ability to sustain co-operation. The interesting point which can be considered is that, once a *primary* group is seen as a motivating force, it may be said that a managerial elite will become obsolete, as the work group itself becomes the decision maker! Decisions are then made at the point in the organization where they are most relevant, i.e. where data are available.

Whether or not this is possible, it does appear that a change is needed in interpersonal relations, and it is here that management can help by instilling *values* which permit the expression of feeling and trust and *concern for the individual* (for further consideration of the ideas of R R Blake, *see* p 390).

ORGANIZATIONAL STRUCTURE

The organizational structure is the basic framework within which the executive's decision-making behaviour occurs. The quality and nature of the decisions made are influenced by the nature of the structure. Organization, as an element of management, is concerned with the *grouping* of activities in such a manner that enterprise objectives are attained, the *assignment* of these activities to appropriate departments and the *provision* for authority, delegation and co-ordination. It is important to note that, in order to accomplish any goal, activities must be grouped logically and authority should be granted so that conflicts do not occur.

Organization can be divided into two parts, formal and informal.

Formal

This can be simply defined as the network of communications in an enterprise; it is the *official* channel through which information passes. Barnard referred to an organization as formal, when the activities of two or more persons are *consciously* co-ordinated towards a given objective. He stated that formal organization comes into being when persons are:

- willing to communicate with one another;
- willing to act and share a common purpose.

This appears to be too broad and is not generally accepted. W Brown in *Exploration in Management* said: 'I personally believe that the more formalization that exists, the more clearly we will know the bounds of discretion which we are authorized to use and will be held responsible for; and prescribed policies make clear to people the area in which they had freedom to act.' There is concern that formal organizations are inflexible, but there should always be room for individual discretion in a well-organized enterprise.

One means of *controlling the behaviour of the employees* of an organization is *to establish written policies and procedures* which prescribe expected action. This is then followed up with systems of recording to ensure effective communication of action taken. Such formalization is central to bureaucracy and is often called 'red tape'. There are many times when predictability of actions that must be taken are essential to an organization, but too much conformity may result in a loss of initiative in non-standard situations.

There is a *reason why formalization extends* as an organization grows. It *assists control and co-ordination* and helps to establish a framework of rules which enables decision making to be delegated with results which are fairly well *predictable*. Research by J Child in 1975 found that large organizations which combine delegation and formalization in their control strategy tended to perform better on financial criteria than similar-sized companies which were more centralized and less formalized. It is of course true that large firms operating in a dynamic environment may find it *difficult to be innovative and adaptive* if they adopt systems of high formalization.

However, it should be possible for formal organization to have a reasonable amount of flexibility if there is good organizational practice. For example, there should be *room for individual discretion and creativity* and the organizational structure should be such as to produce an environment whereby individual performance most effectively contributes towards group goals. One principle that has been mentioned to enable an effective formal organization to be developed was advocated by L Urwick and C Barnard.

This is the *principle of unity of objective*. If an organizational structure helps individuals to meet company objectives, then it may be said to be effective.

It must also be noted that the cost of attaining those enterprise objectives must be the lowest cost that gives workers maximum work satisfaction and appropriate participation, while providing them with security, status and a reasonable remuneration. This is not easy to measure in a financial sense; many of the items are discussed in detail in Chapter 9.

Informal

The formal structure theory has been modified by the research of the social scientists who stress informal organization, which cannot be represented on an organization chart. Small groups, working together, form ideas and attitudes, as the Hawthorne Experiments showed. The attitude of the groups could help or hinder the company goals, to the extent that these attitudes are subordinated to the purpose of the enterprise.

Management determines the formal structure and the social desires of persons find their expression in the informal structure, which should not be disregarded by management. It is far better if informal relations are put on as formal a footing as possible in order to ensure that they do not go against formal relations. For example, informal meetings of union members may undermine the authority of the union and management.

BUREAUCRATIC ORGANIZATION

As previously mentioned on page 15, Max Weber studied organizational structures and he considered that they could be divided into three types:

- *traditional* – based upon the *head*, or chief's, *authority*;
- *rational-legal* – based upon *power*, which people recognized and accepted in a given situation;
- *charismatic* – based upon the *exceptional ability* or personality of someone who has 'charisma'.

Bureaucracy may be defined as a type of organization designed to accomplish large-scale administrative tasks by co-ordinating the work of a large number of persons in a systematic manner.

Warren Bennis regards bureaucracy as a social invention perfected during the Industrial Revolution to organize and direct the activities of a business firm. It may be useful to summarize briefly *some* of the advantages and disadvantages of bureaucracy.

Advantages	*Disadvantages*
Impartial application of rules.	Confusion and conflict among roles.
Clearly defined system of authority.	Arbitrary rules.
System of procedures for processing work.	No room for personal growth.
Division of labour based upon functional specialization.	Poor communications and numerous informal organizations.
	Slow to adapt to new technology.

Weber's ideas on bureaucracy which stemmed from his studies of formalized bureaucratic structures were developed at a time (early 20th century) when organizations approaching a bureaucratic model were considered efficient and modern. He never fully explored inefficient features but his ideas have a marked influence in any discussion on this topic.

Criticisms of the classical bureaucratic model:

- Merton (1960) was concerned about the fact that as individuals became more specialized they would be devoted to *means* rather than ends whenever situations changed. The goals of these specialists were regarded as 'ends in themselves' and not as a means towards reaching the broader goals of the organization.
- Thompson (1961) was concerned with the very competitive nature of life in bureaucracies where managers must meet high standards of performance and the subordinates of managers may have *more technical* knowledge than themselves. This feeling of insecurity was often 'protected' by managers behaving in an aloof and cold manner. Thompson believed such personal insecurities were part of a bureaucratic structure and tended to weaken communication between managers and subordinates.
- Gouldner (1955). This American sociologist studied a company which had adopted an informal style of organization. When a more formal style was introduced, these changes were disliked by the workers, resulting in a *reduction* in efficiency. The opinions and feelings of the workforce were important factors in the success or failure of the organization. He argued that rules were followed because *both* management *and* employees agreed on their value. This *representative* bureaucracy regarded rules as being necessary and in their *own* interest. These differed from *punishment-centred* bureaucracies, in which compliance was reluctant on both sides, but disregard of the rules would form grounds for the imposition of sanctions by either side.

Current research in work organization is still concerned with the complexity and rigidity of bureaucracy, the subversion of bureaucratic goals and employee disenchantment. Weber's statements on bureaucracy will still exert an influence in the future.

LEVELS OF ORGANIZATION

Small businesses have a simple organizational structure. There is specialization of jobs, but it is flexible. Often jobs were made to *fit the person available*, e.g. the sales manager may have an aptitude for figures and so be placed in charge of Accounts. Relations are informal and the lower ranks can talk direct to the managing director about their problems. Rules are few, and decisions are based largely upon experience.

As the business expands, more specialists and managers are employed. The organization becomes more complex as management levels are more numerous, and therefore need to be more closely defined. Duties, also, may have to be more specific and the qualities and qualifications needed by the personnel for each job are also more closely defined; this tends to lead to appointments becoming less personal. Detailed rules governing all aspects are formulated to guide managers in the running of their departments.

Levels of authority

Levels of authority can vary greatly from two or ten or more. The number of levels depends, among other things, upon the number and type of employees. For example, a company with a large number of manual workers will usually have fewer tiers than a similar-sized company with more clerical workers, because the supervisory ratio tends to be greater on the shop floor.

The growing firm, therefore, hires more men, subordinates are given more authority and work is grouped into sections and a manager placed in charge. Thus two levels are made, which will be further increased as the number of subordinates increases.

Figure 4.1 shows the vertical and horizontal dimensions of the structure of the organization. The broad base indicates that lower down there is a greater number of operating employees. Towards the top, fewer operating workers are needed where more managerial and administrative work is done.

In a complex organization the number of levels may be many and each succeeding lower level represents decreasing authority and status. The practice

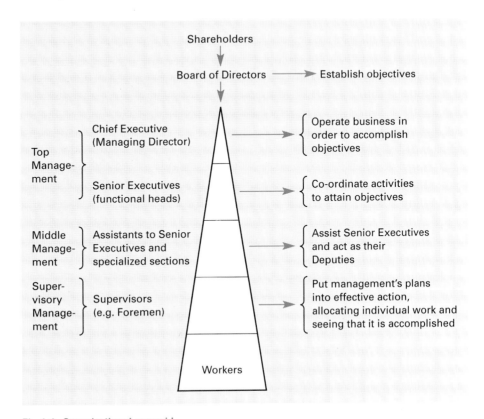

Fig 4.1 Organizational pyramid

of delegation creates a 'chain of command' (scalar principle). These scalar levels are important as they provide a framework for transmitting authority and aid communication.

Each of the above levels is responsible to the level immediately above.

Logical steps in forming an organization are:

- establish enterprise *objectives,* policies and plans;
- find out the *activities* needed to execute these plans;
- *classify* and group these activities in the best way;
- *assign* to these groups the authority needed to perform these activities;
- endeavour to *integrate* these groupings through authority relationships, horizontally, vertically and laterally.

PRINCIPLES OF ORGANIZATION

Many authorities have published principles and many of these principles are common; any list can be regarded as inadequate, but they do serve as *a guide* and many are of universal application. The following are some of the main principles:

- *unity of objective* – every part of the organization must contribute to the attainment of the objective of the enterprise;
- *span of control* – consideration is needed to find the number of persons an individual can effectively manage. The number varies for many reasons, but a figure often quoted is that six subordinates is the largest number a person should supervise;
- *delegation* – authority should be delegated as far down the levels as possible;
- *unity of command* – instructions from two or more superiors may conflict. This is why each subordinate should have only one superior (*see* Chapter 5);
- *scalar principle* – someone must have ultimate authority and a clear line of authority should be in existence to all parts of the enterprise;
- *responsibility* – the responsibility of a subordinate to a superior for delegated authority is absolute and responsibility should be on a par with the amount of authority given.

It is unlikely that a body of principles will ever be obtained to apply to all organizational problems. Brech considers the primary purpose of principles: 'is to serve as a guide to the correct formulation of a sound framework of integrated executive action'.

H A Simon considers principles are essentially useless, but that his study provides: '. . . a framework for the analysis and description of administrative situations, and with a set of factors that must be weighed in arriving at any valid proposal for administrative organization.' There are a number of principles set out by many authorities, e.g. the American Management Association, Fayol; they all have items in common and many people regard them to be of universal application; others say they are too general and are therefore of limited use. A modern approach is to find out how organizations *work in practice* and then try to generalize about the nature of organization. (*see* later in this chapter.)

Organization culture

Very rarely do you find two organizations which are similar in methods of working and have similar working atmospheres. In fact, there is so little in common. These different values, norms and beliefs are reflected in the way their structures and systems are organized. They have *different cultures*. C B Handy in *Understanding Organisations* regards *culture* in organizations as 'deep set beliefs about the way work should be organised, the way authority should be exercised, people rewarded and people controlled'.

This notion of *culture* has been used recently in developing a more comprehensive perspective. Earlier management theory tried to find universal formulae and put forward the idea of a common organizational structure. Organizational variety recognizes ways in which attitudes and habits change in new circumstances. Different countries have different economic and political priorities which have a marked effect upon education and training systems.

The approach of the culturist indicates that any attempt to structure rationally the execution of tasks on the basis of theory may not work. The modern approach, therefore, is concerned with the matching of people to systems, task and environment. The interrelations between these four aspects is part of the systems approach to management theory. Custom, tradition and rituals (e.g. company songs in Japanese and some American organizations) all are part of the value and traditions of a group, that is part of its culture. Handy indicates that in any organization there will be a mix of cultures which may vary according to an organization's history and ownership, goals and objectives, size, technological base, the state of the environment (i.e. stable or unstable) and the members of the organization.

DEPARTMENTATION

In order to decide upon the method of grouping or division of work, the main objectives of the business must be considered. The grouping of functions or tasks is referred to as departmentation. The main methods are:

Functional

This is the most widely used basis. Three main categories occur in most enterprises, i.e. production (the creation of, or addition to utility of, a good or service), selling (finding customers for goods and services at a price), and finance (obtaining and expending funds). As types of enterprise vary, department names vary, e.g. a wholesaler does not produce, he buys, therefore his departments may be buying, selling and finance. Often the amount of money spent may determine the department and the chief business activity is usually made a separate unit, e.g. the auditing department in an accountancy firm. Figure 4.2 shows this type of classification.

Fig 4.2 Departments in a manufacturing company

Advantages

- This method is easy and logical to decide and usually effective in practice.
- It follows the principle of specialization and economies result.

Disadvantages

- Functions may not be so important as the *area* covered by the organization, e.g. the territory may be widespread and another grouping (geographical) may be better.
- Such specialization may invoke *narrowness of outlook*, i.e. inability to see the business *as a whole*.
- Management positions need men of wide experience and this is not readily available in a rigid department system which affords poor training grounds for managers.

Geographical

As companies grow and are widely spread over the country, it may be found desirable to divide some activities among branches away from the main centre of operations. A manager is put in charge of the area and is given responsibility for all aspects of the unit's activities. Local factors are not now neglected in decision making. Plants for manufacture and assembly can be so located as to reduce transport costs. Manufacturers of bulky products tend to divide their work on a territorial basis, with a separate plant to serve each area or district.

Advantages

- Lower cost of operating.
- Knowledge of local circumstances helps decision making and aids the creation of customer goodwill.
- Provides a good training ground for managers.

Disadvantages

Loss of control and co-ordination by head office.

It is possible to envisage each area being completely responsible for all functions. These are independent units with no headquarters services. Usually some activity is centralized; the most common one is finance, as local factors do not appear to have any merit and the economies of centralizing finance appear overwhelming.

Product or service

In departmentation by product, a production unit is set up for each good and service. It is mainly adopted by large organizations, but can work effectively in smaller ones. Top management can delegate wide authority to a division or plant which manufactures and sells a product.

Advantages
- Aids specialization of men and machines.
- Co-ordination is facilitated and customers given better service.
- Responsibility for profit can be introduced, by setting a standard for a product department with the manager responsible for most of the functions involved.
- Management is given a wider responsibility. For example, responsibility for a section of a retail store could be given, where all aspects are controlled by one person (i.e. buying, selling, human resources, etc.). It is not usual for *all* functions to form part of product grouping. Usually finance and industrial relations are centralized, central control being deemed imperative.

Disadvantages
- Difficulty of maintaining co-ordination among product areas.
- Duplicates services in each division.

Customer

This may be found in sales departments which have various types of customer, e.g. large and small customers, or wholesalers and industrial buyers. One could envisage, in the extreme case, a bank's having departments specializing in commercial loans to, say, the fruit industry, and dividing each customer group so that each, e.g. apple growers or orange growers, was represented by one department.

The advantage of this method is mainly that it caters for customers of different needs and brings benefit of specialization.

The *disadvantages* arise in co-ordinating departments.

Process or equipment

The purpose here is to achieve economies by grouping activities around a process, or type of equipment which cannot be made in economical small units and must therefore be costly and specialized. The boot and shoe industry is divided into six main divisions of the process of production, e.g. checking, closing, press cutting, lasting, finishing, glossing and cleaning.

Advantages
- Similar types of equipment and labour are brought together.
- Departments are separated by *clear-cut* technical considerations.

Any separation of activities creates problems of co-ordination and each of the above methods of departmentation has advantages and disadvantages. A rigid structure is not the answer and *more than one* basis for grouping activities may have to be employed in order to achieve the objectives of the enterprise.

SPAN OF CONTROL

The previous paragraphs mentioned that a department was a specific area or branch over which a manager has authority for the performance of specified variables. Departmentation was necessary as a single person was unable to manage 'too many' subordinates, i.e. his span of control was too wide. This span of control, or, preferably, span of management responsibility is simply the *number of subordinates that an executive supervises*. It is important to note that the phrase refers to executive or supervisory subordinates over whom an individual has authority, and not to subordinate *operating* personnel. There are of course other factors than the *number* of subordinates to consider, e.g. the abilities of supervisors and subordinates.

V A Graicunas published a paper in 1933 emphasizing the complexity of managing more than a few subordinates. The more individuals that are added to the span of reporting executives, the greater the increase in the number of relationships. He put his theory in mathematical terms for emphasis and calculated that with six subordinates there were 222 relationships, with seven over 490 relationships. The maximum number of relationships is shown by a formula, but this will never be attained in reality. The actual number of relationships is not so important as the demands made upon a manager's time, and how frequently they occur.

The number of subordinates that a superior can manage must be determined by every organization. L Urwick considered the ideal number to be four 'for all superior authorities' and between eight to twelve 'at the lowest level of organization'. There are many other suggestions which tend to concentrate on the span near the top of an enterprise, but the fact is that many companies which are considered well managed have varying spans of control.

The greater the number of levels can result in:

- *communication* problems, particularly due to misinterpretation of decisions when passed from one level to another;
- *planning and control* becomes more difficult;
- *costs* of maintaining staff at the various levels may be high.

In view of the numerous variables that affect the management situation, it is unlikely that there will be an agreed limit to the number of subordinates that can be effectively supervised by a manager.

The following list of factors tend to influence the number and frequency of relationships, but an overriding factor is *how effectively a manager makes use of time spent* in dealing with subordinates. (*See* p 30 on time management.)

- **The nature of the work**, e.g. the more repetitive the work, the greater the number that can be controlled.
- **The ability and training of subordinates** and supervisors.
- **Degree of delegation** exercised, in particular the clarity of delegation. If there is a poor organization structure making it difficult to delegate authority to a specific task, more time will be needed to make such delegation effective.

- **The degree of change** in the organization's environment. If work changes fast, e.g. as in financial markets, then narrow spans of control will enable action to be communicated more efficiently.
- **Effectiveness of communication** and the amount of personal contact. The greater the number of face-to-face encounters, the less time there is to plan and organize. The question which is relevant here is whether so much time be spent at meetings. (*See* p 460 for the use of new technology to aid communication.)

Management in practice

If it is agreed that the exact number of subordinates cannot be determined, but that it depends upon certain variables, then a brief comment on the research study undertaken by the former Lockheed Missiles and Space Company is worthwhile. The company adopted a contingency approach in selecting an appropriate management span by identifying seven factors that most affect the choice of span. They then tried to determine which factors were more critical than others. The more complex the functions for which managers were responsible, the more difficult their job became and the span was therefore narrow. A ranking by points value was given and each managerial position was analysed so that for each total points position *a suggested span of management* was established. The result was an increase in efficiency in each sub-unit and the reduction from seven levels to five, making a great improvement in co-ordination and communication; payroll and other administrative costs were also reduced.

Lists of factors selected by Lockheed Company:

- *similarity of functions* – the degree to which the functions or subordinate tasks for which the manager is responsible are alike or different;
- *geographic contiguity* – how closely located are the functions or subordinates to the manager;
- *complexity of functions supervised* – the nature of the task done and the department managed;
- *direction and control needed by subordinates* – the degree of supervision that subordinates require;
- *co-ordination* – the degree to which the manager must integrate functions between a sub-unit and other divisional or company activities;
- *planning* – the degree to which a manager has to programme and review the activities of his or her unit;
- *organizational assistance received* – the more assistance a manager had, the more his or her score was reduced by this factor.

Narrow spans of control result in *tall* organizational structures, having many levels of supervision. *Tall* structures (narrow spans) have *advantages* of close supervision and control and fast communication between subordinates and superiors. *Disadvantages* are high costs due to the numerous levels, superiors may get too involved in the work of subordinates and undue delay may be caused because information has to be carried through several levels, upwards and downwards. *Flat* structures (wide spans) have the *advantage* of supervisors having to delegate and ensure clear policies are laid down (*see* Fig 4.3 for an example of a flat structure). *Disadvantages* include the possible loss of control by the supervisor and the need for high-quality managers as their work load tends to be so high that bottlenecks may occur. Numerous research studies have not produced definitive conclusions as to whether tall or flat structures are best. Extremely tall or flat structures are the exceptions and usually growth is directed so that the dimensions are kept in reasonable balance. An important objective of organizational planning should be *simplicity* which helps communications and can reduce overhead costs.

TYPES OF ORGANIZATIONAL STRUCTURE

Four types can be considered for analysis – line, staff, functional and committee. It must be noted that the idea of types of organization serves little useful purpose. Terminology in this area is very confused – functional, for example, has come to mean the same as line and staff in some areas. Modern scholars are critical of formal organizational structure and believe it creates a feeling of dependency on the part of subordinates, and stifles initiative.

Line organization

This is a type of structure consisting of direct vertical relationships connecting the positions at each level with those above and below. These line relationships are the channels through which authority flows from its source to points of action.

This structure forms a basic framework for the whole organization. The other types of structure are, in effect, modifications of it and must rely on it for authoritative action. It is usually depicted on charts by solid lines connecting the positions.

Line relations or direct or executive relations are those existing between a senior and his subordinates at all levels of command. The senior's instructions are to be complied with as authority is direct.

Staff organization

When organization is small, so leaders can effectively direct and control, line structure is usually adopted. All major functions therefore must be performed or supervised by the owner.

As business grows, time must be allocated among many functions and those which the owner prefers are more efficiently performed. The others will sooner or later be given to specialists and their abilities can be included in the organization by applying concepts of (*a*) staff or (*b*) functional structures.

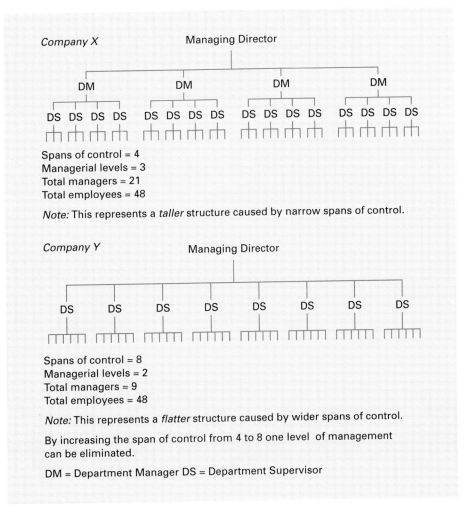

Fig 4.3 Spans of control

Staff structure occurs in two forms, staff assistant and specialist. Staff assistants perform their work subject to the approval of their superior; they have no formal authority to command the actions of others and act in the *name of their superior.*

For example, an assistant to the general manager takes over functions the general manager can do least well. The scalar chain is not lengthened, and assistants perform work which is subject to the approval and support of their chief.

Staff specialists are a modification of line structure. The structure consists of departments manned by staff specialists, who assist the line manager, e.g. industrial relations.

It is worth noting that a line manager cannot ignore a superior's staff officer, as the staff officer's suggestion will usually result in formal orders being issued by the line manager's superior. The human resources function has often been regarded as staff. In practice, industrial relations departments have often taken over responsibility for hiring, firing, union negotiations and grievance settlements.

Staff relations arise from such appointments. Staff assistants assist the executive to whom they are allocated, but have no executive authority of their own and act on behalf of their superior. Often they represent their chief, when they may assume 'representative' authority and responsibility.

Functional organization

This type of structure is a method of relating specialists to the line organization. It is necessary to preserve the coherence of specialized sections through the various levels in the organization without subjecting them to control by line managers at the various levels. For example, a human resources manager, in a branch, reports direct to the plant manager, but in human resource matters is also supervised by the head office human resources officer. Divided loyalties may arise on some questions and it is essential that clear-cut distinctions be made about the roles and scope of the two supervisors.

Functional organization is often applied to systems where functional managers are responsible for certain activities and are given *substantial executive authority*. Functional departments may, with the authority of general management, set programmes and standards with which operative departments must comply.

Functional relations arise when a specialist contributes a service to the line managers, who are the organization executives. This specialist is often called a 'functional' officer, and has responsibility to see that his or her special activities are effectively carried out throughout the organization. The specialist advises 'line' colleagues and is responsible for assisting line managers.

If specialists have a staff of their own, the relationship is then 'direct'. Service, advice and direction are given, but the functional post must not interfere with the application of the operating manager's authority along the line of command.

Lateral (horizontal) relations are those existing between executives or supervisors at the *same level* of responsibility and holding equal authority. Such co-operation is necessary to aid efforts to reach organization goals and when this relationship operates between executives or supervisors they should act with the knowledge of their line supervisors. This is known as Fayol's 'bridge theory'. There are two types: (*a*) *colleague* relationships, which are those between managers in the *same* department who work together under one superior; and (*b*) *collateral* relationships, which exist between managers in *different* departments and serve to discharge responsibility more effectively.

Neither line nor functional types exist separately in their pure form in most organizations. A third type exists, whereby the main operational activities are in a 'line' pattern, but there are specialized activities of a non-operational nature for which a senior executive is responsible and staff will have relationships of a line nature to the executive.

Committee organization

Committees are a controversial device of organization. They consist of a group of persons to which some matter is committed. Some undertake management functions, e.g policy making; others do not, e.g. operating committees. Some make decisions, others deliberate but do not decide, some have authority to make recommendations to a superior, others are formed purely to receive information without recommending or deciding.

Ad hoc committees are usually temporary, as they are created for a specific purpose, or to solve short-range problems, rather than for administrative purposes. If they are established as part of the organizational structure, with specifically delegated duties and authority, they are called *formal*.

Advantages

- Actions and ideas of related company units are co-ordinated.
- Communications are improved.
- Judgement and executive talents are pooled and full use is made of specialization.
- Responsibilities for decisions are shared, rather than borne by a person.

Disadvantages

- They are often a waste of time or resources, especially if there are unsatisfactory compromises, or delays by a few members.
- Executives may hide behind committee decisions and avoid responsibility for their individual actions.

Confusion as to the nature of committees has arisen because of the variation of authority assigned to them. They therefore should have a clear purpose and be effectively led.

Types of committee

- Board of directors – *see* section on Directing.
- Works committees – e.g. joint productivity, accident prevention.
- Cost reduction – usually having representatives from various sections.
- Joint consultation – *see* p 420 in Chapter 9 on Human Resource Management.
- Budget committee – for use where budgetary control is operating.

The growing emphasis on group management and group participation may mean that there will be an increase in the use of committees. They will only be effective if they overcome the disadvantages mentioned above. The *authority* of a committee and the *scope* of the subjects to be considered should be made very clear. Committees should also be reviewed from time to time to ensure they are *still needed*. The size of a committee is important. Too large a committee may not give individuals time to give their point of view but if everyone did speak it would waste valuable time. Too small a group may mean a lack of breadth of expertise, or decisions may be made with insufficient deliberation. The ideal number is difficult to fix. Research in the USA indicates that five members are an ideal number.

A *successful committee should*:

- be *representative* of all interests;
- have a chairman (usually now called the chair or chairperson) *respected* by the group, who can integrate committee deliberation and handle the group firmly and fairly;

- choose *suitable subjects* for group action and make precise proposals by agenda; any reports should be circulated prior to the meeting;
- have clear-cut *terms of reference;*
- have *minutes* circulated and approved;
- be *worth the cost* of its operation.

MODIFICATIONS TO STRUCTURE

Matrix structure

The idea originated from the aerospace industry where this type of structure was used for specific projects. Examples of projects where it is used today are in the development of a new product or in building a factory.

A more flexible and adaptable system was needed to achieve project objectives. The matrix organization attempts to merge traditional line authority for decision making with a project-orientated, multi-disciplinary, team-based approach.

Personnel from functional departments are assigned for the duration of the project. *Project* managers define *what* has to be done. *Functional* managers determine *how* to do it. The project manager must integrate the work of functional departments and the project teams. Members of the project team agree to accept the authority of the project manager for the duration of the project. It is interesting to note that more 'senior' persons than the project manager may be in the team. Conventional vertical authority relationships are now changed and day-to-day working problems may have to be agreed or *negotiated* (Fig 4.4).

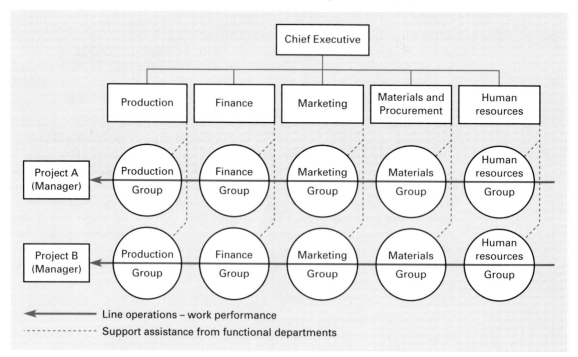

Fig 4.4   **Matrix organizational structure**

Project management aims to achieve specified performance within an agreed time scale and budget. The work of the project manager starts at the *procurement and specification stage* where details of performance, time and cost are needed describing ways of meeting the specifications. Every aspect of the project is defined, e.g. quality and reliability, weight, power, etc. Other points to consider are design, tendering, manufacture, construction, etc., right up to post-sales services.

Knowledge required by an engineer for the post of project manager includes a knowledge of the legal bases of contracts as well as professional experience.

After procurement and specification stages, there is the *tender* for the contract, which states how performance and achievement is to be demonstrated. Then a *programme* needs to be compiled (network analysis is used – *see* p 250); activities are planned in the right order and departments receive orders in minute detail. Finally there is the *progressing* aspect which needs fast and accurate reporting back of forecasted and actual stage activities.

Advantages

- Better control of project; greater security.
- Better customer relations, and higher morale of staff.
- Lower programme costs, and higher profit margins.
- Shorter project development time.
- Aids the development of managers, as the work includes wider responsibilities.

Disadvantages

- More complex internal operations.
- Lower staff utilization.
- More difficult to manage and possible inconsistent application of company policy.
- Functional groups may neglect their job and let the project organization do everything.
- Too much shifting of staff from project to project may hinder training of new employees.

The degree of the project manager's authority and relationships to functional departments must be specified.

The degree of authority given to the project manager may vary from company to company and therefore it is very important for the project manager to have the backing of top management. It is also wise to ensure that the project manager reports to at least the same level of management as the functional heads.

Requirements of a good project manager

- Ability to select and organize a team of persons with a variety of skills.
- Ability to smooth out difficulties between specialist groups and present facts clearly to management.
- Ability to understand the nature of technical details.
- Ability to run meetings and communicate effectively.
- Ability to deal with contract documents and negotiate with customers.

Project management can be considered an outcome of applying systems thinking to organization.

Working groups

There are various types of group working; some are fairly similar in nature, others have quite distinct features. Matrix or project groups have already been discussed and boards of directors and committees are considered elsewhere in the book. Other types of group working are dealt with below.

An important aspect of the study of organizations is the *study of people's behaviour in groups*. This can give indications of why certain groups are effective and others are not. Research studies have been many in this area, one of the first being the Hawthorne Experiments.

Where two or more persons who interact with and influence each other join together, they can be said to form a *group*. They need a common aim or purpose which may be permanent or temporary.

Distinctions have been made between formal and informal groupings. A *formal* group consists of carefully selected members who have skills and attributes that can assist the reaching of a desired goal. It will have a leader, subordinates, a location and a task to accomplish – for example, a planning committee.

There can also be rather informal groupings with participative leaders and few rules, but as long as they are officially set up, they are considered formal. *True informal groupings* are those which have been developed in accordance with the needs of members, whether or not managers desire or encourage them. Some informal groups may have objectives that go against organizational goals. Members of informal groups tend to subordinate some of their individual needs to group needs as a whole. Some of these groupings may *assist* an organization (e.g. company football clubs); others may *oppose* organizational objectives which they think will harm the group (e.g. higher efficiency standards).

Group members in an organization will have one or more goals in common, such as to produce or market a product. Communication is essential within each group and members of a group have *roles* to play in order to achieve the group task. Expected behaviour patterns are developed within each group and these are referred to as *norms.* Any deviation from norms will bring group pressure to force a return to the 'norm'. Too low or too high an output as compared with the 'norm' may mean admonishment by group members.

Managers cannot prevent group pressures. What they should do is to try to channel them into constructive activities that are in the interests of the organization. One answer has been to *obtain more employee participation* in decisions that affect their interests so that group members will not be so much against management.

The *solidarity* of some groups or their *cohesiveness* is an indication of how much influence the group has over individual members. Members are not so likely to violate group norms if they are strongly attached.

Managers must be aware of certain aspects of group performance. One is that in groups which are highly cohesive, norms can be very influential in encouraging high or low productivity of members of the group. One method of increasing the cohesiveness of a group is to give members more say in the *selection of persons they will be working with.* This is part of the general conclusion that the *involvement of workers more and more in the decision-making process can reduce antagonism and enable group members to see themselves as part of the whole organization.*

Groups provide security, social satisfaction for members, support individual needs and promote communication, formally or informally (e.g. through the grapevine). They also are liable to show all the problems found in our consideration of committees. So it can be seen that a study of group concepts is important for studying aspects of communication, motivation and leadership.

Group technology

This is a method of organizing small-batch or multi-product production processes so that specialist machines on the shop floor and their operators are grouped into cells, each cell containing various machines which perform *all* of the operations on a 'family' of products (e.g. drilling, turning, and grinding). This compares with the more usual arrangement where machines are grouped into large shops, each shop containing only *one type* of machine.

Advantages include:

- reduction of delivery times and delays and reduction of stock and work in progress;
- easier progress chasing and control of quality;
- social benefits from group working.

Disadvantages include organizational problems, e.g. adapting payment systems, the structure of management and control of stocks.

Autonomous work groups

A great deal of attention has been given to experiments in group working on *assembly line* production. These groups can also be formed in continuous process industries. It is often said that workers on production lines have such a monotonous, boring job that they are dissatisfied, even though other benefits are satisfactory, e.g. wages, welfare, etc. Sometimes it is forgotten that some workers may *not* want to work in groups, obtain recognition or exercise autonomy. Surveys among workers on flow-line production rarely show that more than 25 per cent are dissatisfied with their job. This does not mean that changes to group working may not prove beneficial to most workers as well as management.

Motor-car producers, Volvo and Saab, have not entirely abandoned flow-line working; what they have done is provide for job enrichment (*see* p 404) through the addition of certain changes in the work organization.

In Chapter 1 it was stated that one must be careful when considering implementing ideas found to be successful in other countries as cultural differences may be so great. Bearing this in mind, some of the *factors to be considered* before going ahead with this idea are shown below.

- There must be a strong desire for participation by workers, and a positive co-operative attitude.
- Management must be forward looking and believe in worker participation.
- There must be a suitable industrial relations mechanism to ensure effective negotiation and consultation.

Benefits from group working include:

For management
- group can accommodate labour absenteeism, and turnover of labour is reduced;
- the more flexible system can deal with frequent changes in production requirements and helps to ensure effective working interrelationships;
- easier to set standards and targets because fewer units are involved;
- aid to training newcomers to group;
- more effective communication and less supervision.

For members of group
- more variety for individual through job rotation;
- possible 'social' satisfaction because of belonging to group;
- more autonomy in planning is allowed than if an individual;
- sharing of responsibility means it is not so easy to blame an individual.

General disadvantages are:

- as added responsibilities are given to workers, if work is transferred from supervisors it may mean the supervisors are no longer needed!
- some workers *resist* changes to the structure of jobs;
- workers may ask for *increased wages*, to compensate for their utilization of further skills and their flexibility and their assumption of greater responsibility;
- some unions consider that the power of collective shop floor action may be lessened.

A number of *implications for managers* can be noted if group working becomes more widespread at *supervisory and management levels*. Specialists form part of a team on a project and they may often make decisions and advise their group without reference to their superior; also if the group agrees on a course of action advocated (by say the accountant in the group), it may be very difficult for a senior accountant to alter that course of action. The implication is that specialists in lower levels of the organization may have more autonomy.

Another implication is that specialists in groups will have to have a wider knowledge of other functions and this needs consideration by those responsible for training.

Clover-leaf structure

This is a further type of organization structure advocated by B C J Lievegood in *The Developing Organisation* (Tavistock, 1973). It has been described as a project management approach applied to the *whole* organization, making use of the ideas of systems thinking and the need to consider worker satisfaction.

In Fig 4.5 the board of directors can be seen at the centre co-ordinating and linking with four main areas of organizational management.

The board of directors is not at the *apex* of a pyramid. Directors have interests in all areas and identify overall objectives and policies to carry them out. The importance and practical effort of this new approach will be looked upon with interest.

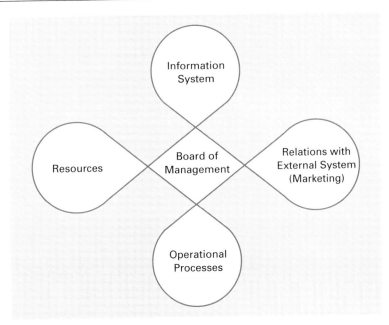

Fig 4.5 Clover-leaf organizational structure

Circular organizational structure

In the book *The Systems Age* (Wiley, 1974) Ackoff advocated a structure based upon the hierarchical system, whereby managers at each level work with an *associated board*. This board would be responsible for policy and evaluation of the managers' performance. The composition of each board was the immediate senior manager, who would be chairman, the immediate subordinate managers and the manager himself. It can be seen in Fig 4.6 that every level would have representation on the board of the immediate superior.

A further suggestion was that the top board should contain representatives of stakeholders, i.e. in addition to shareholders customers and suppliers, investors, the public and employees. Ackoff claimed this would enable employees to have wider opportunities for participation and allow the organization, to a greater extent, to serve the purposes of its members and its own purposes.

'Linking-pin' structure

Rensis Likert, in *New Patterns of Management* (McGraw-Hill, 1961), recommended an overlapping form of organizational structure in which a 'linking-pin' function is performed to integrate the activities of the various sub-systems in the organization. Each supervisor or manager is a member of two groups at the same time, e.g. directors who are also heads of their own departments. They are members of the *higher level* group and also members of their *own group*. They are a linking pin, joining groups together, and serve as channels of communication and influence.

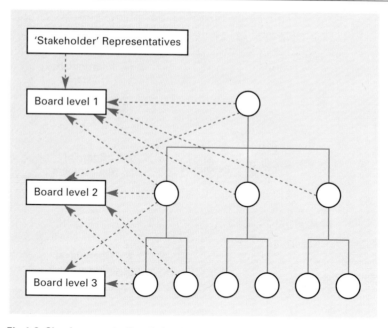

Fig 4.6 Circular organizational structure

AUTHORITY AND RESPONSIBILITY

Authority in the context of organization and administration of a business enterprise has been defined in a number of ways. H Fayol regarded it as 'the right to give orders and the power to exact obedience'.

H A Simon regarded it as 'the power to make decisions which guide the actions of another'.

Research findings in this area of power and authority are limited. It is obvious that authority over people can be effective only when they *accept* it. Many instructions are obeyed because of custom, but acceptance of authority may in some cases be ensured only by resorting to the use of power.

Authority is not power. Power is the product of personality in a specific situation. Sir Frederic Hooper in his book *Management Survey* states:

'Authority can be delegated; power cannot. Either it exists or it does not. One may invest a person with authority and with responsibility, but one can no more invest him with power, than one can provide him with imagination and understanding.'

Authority can be regarded as the right or power to delegate responsibility and it emanates in a company from shareholders to the board of directors, and down the scalar chain.

Responsibility is an *obligation* to use authority to see duties are performed. It is an obligation to perform owed to a person's superior.

Accountability is concerned with the fact that each person who is given authority and responsibility must recognize that the executive above him or her will judge the quality of his/her performance.

By accepting authority, a person denotes the acceptance of responsibility and accountability. The person who is delegating requires subordinates to allow their performance to be reviewed and evaluated and holds them accountable for results.

Power

Every organization tries to define the power of its various members. *Power* is the ability of individuals (or groups) to induce or influence the beliefs or actions of others. This ability may derive from various sources and a manager must understand these and further develop them in order to gain and maintain the support of followers and understand the social relationships among them.

The works of John French and Bertram Raven (the 'Bases of Social Power' in *Group Dynamics, Research and Theory*, eds D Cartwright and A Zander (New York, Harper & Row, 1960)) and Paul Hersey and W Natemeyer (a report from the Centre for Creative Leadership, Greensboro, North Carolina) give useful insights into the various aspects of power.

Positional powers

- **Legitimate power** – is based upon the cultural system of rights, obligations and duties where a 'position' is accepted by subordinates as 'legitimate'. The higher a manager's position in an organization, the greater the legitimate power.
- **Reward power** – is based upon the ability of a leader to provide rewards, such as pay, promotion and recognition, to those followers who comply with his wishes.
- **Coercive power** – is based on the subordinate's fear of the manager. It is the manager's ability to punish, whether by firing a subordinate, withholding a merit increase, or giving undesirable work assignments.
- **Information power** – is based upon a manager's knowledge of, or privileged access to, information that is believed to be valuable to others.

Personal powers

- **Expert power** – is based upon a manager's possession of expertise, knowledge or skills that makes people respect him, for example the skill of a surgeon or lawyer. Leaders who rely on expert power use their perceived ability to improve the job performance of others as their means of controlling decision making.
- **Connection power** – is based upon a manager's close social relationships with influential people inside and outside the organization. The preferences of the manager who has high connection power are followed for the possible favours such connections may bring.
- **Referent power** – is the influence that people or groups may exercise because people believe in them and their ideas. It is based upon the personal attributes or charisma of the leader. People accede to the leader's influence in order to increase identification with him. Examples of such power can be found in well-known military or religious people.

Recent research has shown that the most effective managers rely more on the use of personal powers than on positional powers.

Kinds of authority

- **Formal** authority is conferred by law or delegated within an organization.
- **Functional** authority is based upon specialized knowledge.
- **Personal** authority is based upon seniority or leadership.

Another method of analysis is to show the kinds of authority which correspond to the structure types, i.e. line, function and staff.

Line authority

This authority can be regarded as the main authority in an organization; it is the ultimate authority to decide upon matters affecting others and is the main feature of the superior–subordinate relationship. Line authority is not absolute; it must be applied with discretion, within the limits of delegated authority, and must relate to the performance of jobs which lead to the attainment of the objectives of the organization.

Staff authority

Staff authority is not easy to describe. Its scope is very limited as there is no right to command. It is concerned with assisting and advising and is used where line authority becomes inadequate and occurs in all but the smallest companies. Specialized skills are used to direct or perform those activities which the line manager cannot so effectively perform. Staff authority is subordinate to line authority and its purpose is to aid the activities which are directed and controlled by the line organization. A human resources officer, for example, has line authority over his own staff, but he cannot control production workers, even on human resource matters. Examples of staff departments are legal, public relations and human resources; the heads are staff executives who exercise staff authority. It is worth noting that, if these departments did not exist, or were abolished, their functions would have to be performed in the line, where they originally existed.

Functional authority

This type of authority is subordinate to line authority but, in comparison with staff authority, it confers upon the holder the *right to command* in matters relating to the function. It therefore has a limited right to command and helps the superior to delegate authority to command to specialists, without bestowing full line authority. Where organizations have a central head office and branches or divisions, functional authority is often used. For example, a head office human resources director renders staff functions for the whole company, but he usually exercises functional authority on human resource matters in his relationships with branch human resources officers. This of course ensures uniform policy.

It was mentioned previously that the staff specialist gives advice to his line superior. One modification of this occurs where the superior delegates authority to the staff specialist to deal directly with line personnel. For example, where the staff specialist is showing how to deal with labour problems, he may also *consult* with line executives and aid in putting the recommendations into effect.

True functional authority occurs when the staff assistant is delegated *specific authority* to prescribe procedures and processes or policy to be followed by operating departments, for example where a finance director is given authority to prescribe procedures and the nature of the accounting records to be kept by the production sales departments. Such authority should be restricted authority. It is possible for some line managers to exercise functional authority over some process in *another line* department; a sales manager may exercise functional authority over aspects of manufacturing, e.g. packaging.

It is often said that most organizations have *line and staff* structures. This denotes the interrelation of operational and functional responsibilities. But it is not always easy to determine which department is line or which is staff, as some operations do not conform to specific boundaries and probably only by examining the intentions and actions of the person who is delegating can it really be known. Confusion may occur if a staff executive is given implied authority to act in the name of the delegating executive and it may then appear that the staff executive is exercising line authority. Perhaps *the degree of closeness to the primary objectives* of a company can be used to distinguish between line and staff functions. For example, the closer to basic activities, e.g. production and selling, the more activities are line; assisting activities may be deemed staff.

In view of the difficulty surrounding the definition and operation of *line and staff* it is better not to use such confusing terms.

In considering the limits of authority, an obvious limitation is that action must conform with the policies and programmes of the company. In many cases, specific limitations are made (e.g. not to take on more staff without the approval of a superior). The reason *why* a subordinate accepts a superior's decision has been considered by many authorities. One line of thought is that there is an 'area of acceptance' wherein the subordinate is willing to accept the superior's instructions.

DELEGATION

In a previous section authority was seen to reside with the board of directors and to be delegated to the chief executive and down to all those in the company, until they are given the requisite amount of authority to carry out their allotted work.

The main purpose of delegation is to make organization possible. As we have seen earlier in this chapter, one person cannot exercise all authority in making decisions as a firm grows. There is a limit to the number of persons that a manager can personally supervise. After this limit, the manager must delegate authority to subordinates to make decisions.

Delegation is the *process* whereby an individual or group transfers to some other individual or group the duty of carrying out some particular action and, at the same time, taking some particular decision. It means, in effect, entrusting some part of the work of management to subordinates. Responsibility is not, though, surrendered, as no manager avoids *ultimate* responsibility by delegating. The work is delegated and the superior holds the subordinate *accountable*. The subordinate is responsible for *doing* the job; it is the superior's responsibility to *see* the job is done.

When authority is delegated, all it means is that someone has been granted *permission* to do something; the superior must ensure that the subordinate has *sufficient authority* to do the job and that the subordinate has been told *how* the authority is to be used. Delegation can therefore be briefly stated to be a process whereby a manager:

- *assigns* duties to subordinates;
- grants them *authority* to make commitments to the extent thought necessary to enable those duties to be carried out;
- creates an *obligation* on the part of each subordinate for the satisfactory performance of the job.

Responsibilities should be clearly defined at all levels before work can be delegated.

Reasons for delegation

- Lack of time or energy.
- Complexity of rules and new techniques means specialists are needed.
- Need for training for management succession.

It is noteworthy that superiors cannot delegate *all* their authority, otherwise they pass their position to their subordinates. When a superior delegates, a calculated risk is being taken on the abilities of a subordinate. Supervision is needed but should not be too close as this tends to stifle initiative. Many managers fear to delegate because of the possible incompetence of subordinates.

Delegation is therefore an art and the following points should be noted:

- a manager should ensure that the subordinate accepts and understands what is involved;
- after giving an outline of the job, the control limits and the desired standards, a manager should leave the subordinate to do the job;
- checking should be done periodically, and the superior should be willing to listen to the ideas of subordinates;
- authority must be given to subordinates, as a manager cannot make all the decisions personally. The manager must trust subordinates to do their job, and delegate to them those matters which the subordinates are most competent to deal with, even though the manager may make better decisions than the subordinate.

Degree of delegation

This is an illustration of the principle of comparative costs as applied to delegation. This principle will be understood by readers who have studied economics.

- Cost of decision. The more costly the action to be decided upon, the more probable it is that the decision will be made higher up. For example, a decision to purchase a computer will be made higher up the scale of authority than a decision to buy a storage box for computer disks.

- Need for uniformity of policy. The greater the need for uniformity, the greater the amount of centralizatioin. For example, there often is a need to treat all customers alike. But too much uniformity means local knowledge is not used and initiative is stifled.
- History of the organization. This could be an important factor as there is a tendency to retain decentralized authority, particularly at first when a business amalgamates and consolidates with other businesses, whereas if an organization has grown up from a small group there is a tendency to centralize. The philosophy of management is also important. For example, Henry Ford senior, the American motor-car manufacturer, was very keen on centralization and, wherever possible, made every major decision himself.
- Availability of capable managers. If there are few managers of quality there will be less decentralization of authority. The solution here lies in efficient training and decentralization is a good method of obtaining management experience.
- Size of organization. The larger the organization, the more complex it is, and the greater the difficulty in co-ordination. Decisions are more slowly reached and therefore more costly; decentralization can reduce this problem.
- Controls available. If control techniques are good, management will be keener to delegate authority. If subordinates can be controlled easily, a manager is more likely to delegate authority to them.

DECENTRALIZATION OF AUTHORITY

This is a situation where ultimate authority to command and ultimate responsibility for results is localized as far down the organization as efficiency permits.

If authority is not delegated, it is centralized. The two extremes, centralization and decentralization, have disadvantages and in practice a combination of the two occurs.

Centralization refers to the withholding of delegated authority. Decentralization is closely related to delegation of authority and is concerned with what should be transferred down, what policies are needed to guide actions and the need to train and select people and control their actions.

Centralization is sometimes used to refer to centralizing performance where the operation is under one roof or one location. It often refers to department activities, e.g. *centralization* of office services. But, where centralization is discussed as an *aspect of management,* it refers to the withholding of delegation of authority and the way authority and decisions are dispersed. Decentralization is closely related to delegation, but it includes all areas of management and requires a great deal more than handing authority to subordinates.

Drucker refers to *federal decentralization*, where activities are organized into separate product businesses, each having its own market and responsible for its own profit or loss. They are, in effect, independent operating units. The other type is *functional decentralization* whereby units are set up with total responsibility for distinct stages of the business. This type is generally applied to management organization, but has certain weaknesses, as the narrowness of outlook inherent in functions and standards set cannot easily be linked to objectives of the business.

Federal decentralization has many advantages, particularly the ease of managing by objectives, whereby the efforts and results of managers and units are easily assessed.

Production and sales are often the first functions to be decentralized and finance and human resources the last.

The degree of centralization to be adopted is not easy to determine. Some decisions must be taken locally and management must decide what are vital decisions and keep these, then delegate the rest (e.g. a price change is a vital decision).

The *degree of decentralization* may be said to be greater where:

• the greater the number and the more important are the decisions made lower down the hierarchy;
• less checking is needed on a decision, especially if few people need be consulted on a decision;
• the greater the number of functions affected by decisions made at lower levels, e.g. a company which allows financial decisions to be made by branches is invariably greatly decentralized.

Decentralization should not be blindly applied as the size of operations and their complexity may not warrant it. Dangers arise from non-uniform policy and the difficulty of control the more a unit becomes independent. The whole of specialized headquarters services such as accounting and statistics may becoming duplicated, resulting in high costs and less efficiency.

A final comment on this question is that the best balance between centralization and decentralization may *vary in various periods in the organization's history*. The newer it is, the more the need for centralization at first to establish common policies. Once managers know the tradition of the organization, they are more likely to think and act in that way when they are in charge of decentralized units.

ASSIGNMENT OF ACTIVITIES TO DEPARTMENTS

Guides to assignment of activities

Earlier in the chapter it was noted that activities could be grouped in various ways. Another problem is which activities should be assigned to each functional department or to a customer, territory or product department. Activities have to be assigned or moved, and some activities may not be so easy to classify, e.g. should transport be assigned to the production or marketing department?

- Some managers who have a special talent and interest for certain activities may be assigned these activities, especially in the early stages of a company's growth.
- Those activities which are mostly used by one department may be put under that department's control. This is a simple, logical method, whereby, for example, a production manager, who uses transport for handling raw materials in the factory and for transferring finished goods to a warehouse, may be given charge of transport.
- Activities may be assigned to those departments which will best ensure the attainment of the objectives of the company. For example, the credit control section may be considered best allocated to the accounting department as it may apply company policies better than if control were given to the sales manager who may adopt too liberal a policy.

    NB: Some activities overlap department boundaries and often the same equipment is used by more than one department, but divided control does not work effectively so a choice has to be made.
- Co-ordination of activities is essential and the *point of co-ordination* may be a guide as to the method of departmental integration. For example, if sales, advertising and warehouse sections all report to the marketing manager, these sections may comprise one group.

Organization structure, therefore, greatly aids co-ordination of activities. It is important to note that the *reasons* for co-ordination may vary from executive to executive. The converse to the above must also be considered: where an inspection department is under the control of the production department this may put pressure on inspection not to be too rigid in the interpretation of standards in case production output suffers from too many rejects. By making inspection reports to the design department manager, who sets the standards, one may overcome this problem while maintaining quality. The principle here is that an activity must not be assigned to a department whose activities it checks (often called the separation principle).

The above are only guides. Good judgement is required to select from alternatives. The *stage of growth* of a firm is important, as small firms may find the guides difficult to implement in some cases, as economies of specialization may be difficult to achieve. As firms grow, emphasis changes on activities and organization structures need to be altered. The final guide should be the assignment of activities in such a manner that the objective is achieved in the most effective way.

AIDS TO ORGANIZATION DESIGN

Many tools, methods and techniques are available and it is essential to place them in their proper perspective. Their value depends upon the skill used by the executive in their selection and application. Relationships can be formalized and communicated to the members of an enterprise in the following ways.

Records

If these are kept over a period of time, they give the background picture which can help organizational change. Similarly, human resource records enable an accurate evaluation of human resources to aid determination of job selection. In addition, *reports* can be used to see if there are any defects in organizational structure.

Organization charts

No diagram can effectively convey the reality of executive responsibilities or functional interrelationships. Organization charts are an *endeavour* to record the formal relationships in an organization, showing some of the relationships, the main lines of communication and the downward flow of authority and responsibility through all the levels of the management hierarchy.

Advantages

- *Thought* is needed in constructing charts, as this exercise forces executives to think more specifically about organizational relationships.
- Records and charts provide *information* to people who wish to know about the enterprise and are useful in instructing new personnel on company organization.
- They form a basis for organizational change and by projection into the future can aid the evaluation of organizational planning as strengths and weaknesses can be observed.

Disadvantages

- They soon become *out of date*.
- *Human relationships* cannot be shown on paper, even when they can be defined and described.
- They introduce *rigidity* into relationships, as people tend to keep within their charted area and become too conscious of boundary lines. (This is one reason why the American Chrysler Corporation deferred using organization charts for a long time. They wished to encourage the crossing of lines of authority and to retain flexibility.)
- *Costs* of preparation, storing and studying charts may be more than their benefits are worth.
- They introduce *status* problems. People may not wish comparisons to be made between themselves and others. (The writer recently asked a human resources manager why his company had no organization chart. He replied in one word, 'Politics'.)

If the above disadvantages are considered carefully most of them can be overcome and, if the charts are carefully compiled, kept up to date and regarded purely as an *aid*, they can be of assistance to management.

There are certain conventions which are generally in use in the compilation of charts. Line relationships are shown by a continuous line. A position, function or unit is often enclosed by a 'box'. Sometimes names of personnel occupying positions are also included in the box. Broken or dotted lines are used to denote functional relationships and vertical and horizontal lines link boxes. Figure 4.7 shows three types of chart.

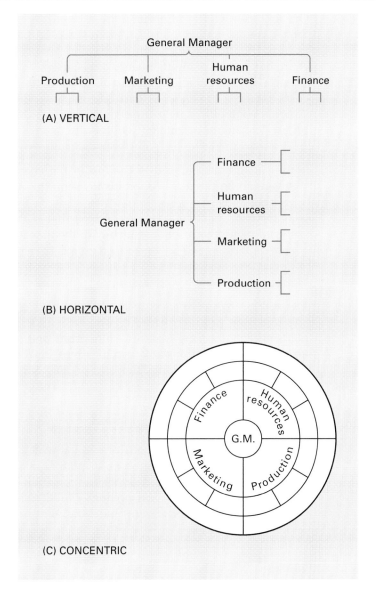

Fig 4.7 Types of organization charts

Vertical charts (A) are a traditional method.

Horizontal charts (B) make use of the normal method of reading from left to right and minimize the idea of levels and superior–subordinate relationships.

Concentric charts (C) consist of circles which indicate echelon levels with the chief executive in the centre. These charts show the dynamic nature of personal relationships and eliminate the status implications of 'above' and 'below'. The distance from the centre indicates the degree of closeness to the chief executive. Sectors show different divisions and no appendages to organization are included.

Organization charts attempt to be a two-dimensional representation of a three-dimensional relationship, and a few recent attempts have been made to portray this third dimension pictorially. This cannot be done on a normal chart, but special planning boards can be used.

An adaptation of all these charts is given in the chart shown in Fig 4.8. This chart depicts a consumer-orientated company which sells consumer goods in a highly competitive field through the normal channels of distribution. (The phrase 'consumer-orientated' will be discussed in Chapter 7 on Marketing.)

The chart in Fig 4.8 has some unusual features:

- the consumer is placed at the top of the chart, as a reminder that he is sovereign and that it is upon his decision (to buy) that the company's success depends;
- as the chart is circular, it can be seen that each main department, headed by a director, is closely in touch with the managing director and with adjacent departments. The impression given is of a closely-knit, balanced team;
- departments shown are in sequence, showing the flow of information, thought, decision and action.

Market Research feeds facts to the Marketing Department, creating strategy and initiating product planning. The *Design* Department translates product plans into engineering realities – blueprints and specifications. The *Manufacturing* Department translates specifications into finished products. The *Sales* Department then persuades shops to display and stock hoping then that the *Customer* buys.

Organization manuals

Some organizations have a book or manual which sets out in more detail each position and often includes job descriptions, salaries, relationships, detailed descriptions of activities and duties, responsibilities and functions. It is often compiled by first getting each job holder to fill in a questionnaire. A loose-leaf system is desirable and careful indexing is needed. The manual should be reviewed periodically.

Schedules of responsibility

A job title is usually descriptive of the work involved but is inadequate as a *definition* of duties and responsibilities. Schedules are therefore used and the following information is recommended to be noted:

- title of job;
- date;
- code or reference number;
- grade of job;
- department concerned;
- an account of duties and an assessment of responsibility carried;
- number and nature of employees supervised;

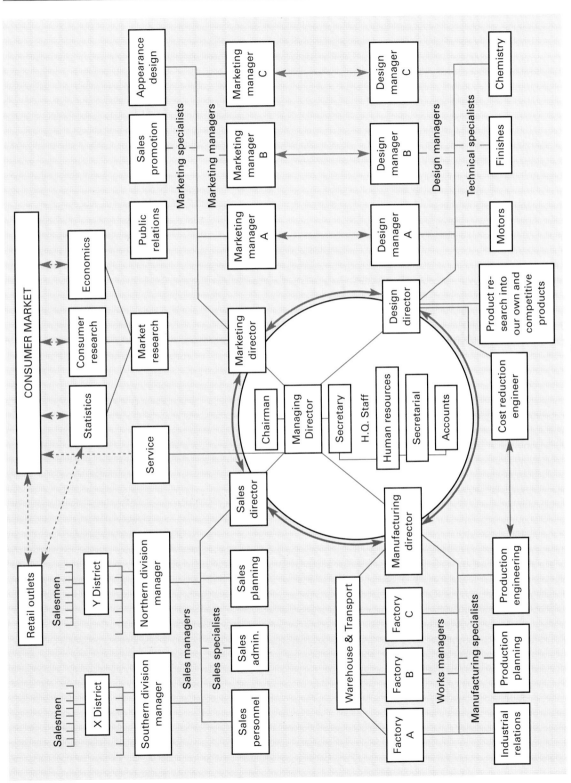

Fig 4.8 Organization chart. (Reproduced by permission of the British Productivity Council)

- nature of liaison with colleagues;
- person to whom responsible;
- any special responsibilities.

It should be clear for what activities an employee has executive responsibility and those for which he acts in an advisory capacity. A person should know the limits of his authority, which may be stated specifically, e.g. no authority to purchase equipment over £1000 without reference to a superior.

If the following plan is used to set out such schedules, they will be found to be more easily compiled.

Position title	Date of issue ......
Responsible to......	Schedule reviewed......
Responsible for	
Subordinates	
Special responsibilities	
Limitations	
Code reference	

ORGANIZATIONAL CHANGE

Changes have occurred gradually, from the methods used by Taylor, to the mechanization and automatic production lines of modern industry. Changes occurred in technology, marketing, and numerous management techniques, some of which were concerned with human problems. Most of the changes were made in a rather disjointed or *piecemeal* manner. The approach emerging today is to use the growing body of ideas and systematic thought to consider innovatory ideas on organization and to adopt a more *systematic* comprehensive look at problems, so that we look at the *whole* instead of looking at *separate parts*.

Individuals have a lot of freedom, apart from certain laws of society, but when they join an organization their freedom is restricted and their effort must be joined with those of others to achieve organizational goals. There can therefore be *friction* between individual and business goals. Some administrative apparatus is needed through which managerial authority is exercised. Therefore a hierarchy is formed which issues policy statements to ensure any discretion that individuals may have in their work is exercised in the spirit or attitude of the organization.

The *economic environment* has an effect upon the structure of the organization. The Industrial Revolution brought forth a very competitive, stable environment, and a pyramid structure of authority, whereby a few persons with resources controlled enterprises. This seemed a suitable arrangement for tasks which were basically *routine*. Since then the environment has become less stable and structures are not mechanistic. As science research and technology have grown, there is greater *interdependence* between the economic and other sectors of society and particularly between countries (e.g. European Community). All this has resulted in more complicated legal and public regulation and greater competition between firms leading to a merging of resources.

These changes will continue as rapidly as technology changes and organizations diversify to an even greater extent. *Other factors* in the change in organizations are:

'The trend of *population growth*, whereby education increases and for example more graduates are employed. The skills in *human interaction* (interpersonal relations) will become more important, because of the need to collaborate in larger projects or concerns.'

Further changes in the structure of organization are noted by Alvin Tofler in his book *Future Shock* (1970, Random House). He thinks bureaucracy will be supplemented by a new structure called '*ad-hocracy*' (*ad-hoc* meaning: for a particular purpose). He stresses the need for organizations to respond and adapt to changes in the environment. The concept of the project team (*see* p 148) is considered in depth by two other well-known writers on change in organizations:

E Trist: In *Matrix Organization*, Ed D L Kingdom (1973, Tavistock).
W G Bennis: *Changing Organisations* (1966, McGraw-Hill).

CONFLICT IN ORGANIZATIONS

In the past conflict had been overlooked by behavioural scientists partly because it was felt that conflict was damaging to an organization and efforts should be concentrated on measures to create harmony. Conflict is now treated seriously as an important aspect in the proper understanding of organizational behaviour. It has been realized that not all conflict is harmful and that perhaps a certain level of conflict is inevitable. The need, therefore, is to understand the causes of conflict and to develop constructive measures to control and use the energies released by conflict. Modern management practice emphasizes the need for free expression and encourages open communications, especially between superiors and subordinates, and methods of continuing consultation and negotiation. The task for managers is therefore not just to resolve or suppress all conflict, but to manage it so as to reduce its harmful effects and benefit from its good effects.

A simple definition of conflict is that it is any personal divergence of interests between groups or individuals. Another definition is that conflict is behaviour intended to obstruct the achievement of the goals of other persons. The types of conflict which are possible in organizations are:

- within an individual;
- between individuals;
- between individuals and groups;
- between groups in the same organization;
- between organizations.

The sources of organizational conflict that will be considered here are more related to intergroup conflict, but apply to some extent to conflict between invididuals, and between individuals and groups. The major sources of conflict arise from:

- the need to share scarce resources;
- differences in goals between organizational units;
- interdependence of work activities in the organization;
- differences in values, attitudes or perceptions among members of different units;
- ambiguously defined work responsibilities and communication problems.

Work group conflict may not always be detrimental. Conflict can bring these benefits:

- bring hidden issues to the surface;
- increase cohesion of a group when directed at an external agent;
- encourage creativity and innovation;
- enhance communication and make change more acceptable.

Methods for managing conflict

These can be briefly summarized and include methods of conflict stimulation, reduction and resolution:

- restructuring the organization – the authority–responsibility relationships should be clarified when the structure is changed;
- rearrangements of task and work locations;
- human resource policies and procedures can be made more equitable and attention paid to the possibility of non-monetary rewards;
- development of staff interpersonal/group process skills;
- bringing in 'outsiders' to an organization who have different values and styles;
- encouraging a more participative and supportive style of leadership with the aim of creating greater employee commitment and co-operation.

THE MANAGEMENT OF CHANGE

Change in any organization can never be easy, particularly when there are restraints on unilateral management actions. Managers cannot so easily fire a person who does not conform to change. Union grievance procedures and a need to ensure staff continue to be motivated are restraining factors.

Managers must understand change and be ready to implement it. Effective managers should expect constant change and regard it as necessary and generally beneficial. Thre is a need to effect planned change and one important way of doing this is by organizational development (*see* p 170)

The process of change

Kurt Lewin introduced a model which helps to describe the change process in *Field Theory in Social Science* (New York, Harper & Bros, 1951). It was suggested that change occurs in three phases:

Phase 1 – occurs where an individual or group *senses the need* to do work in a different way. Problems encountered indicate the need for change. Discussions occur on changes that *might* be made to solve the problems.

Phase 2 – of the change process begins while changes are *being made* in the behaviour of individuals or in the organizational process. A simple example is where training is given to staff to use a computer and change from keeping manual records to recording on a computer is required. Such changes are made subject to the staff being convinced of potential better results by the new system.

Phase 3 – of the change process is called *re-freezing,* and is when the changes are *accepted* as the new position by the persons most affected by the change.

Managers need to spend time dealing with situations arising from resistance to change and they are more effective if they *understand* why people resist change. They can then develop methods to overcome any resistance.

Sources of resistance to change

1 *Lack of understanding of the need for change.* People may not trust those initiating change, or they feel they have not been told the *real* reasons for the change.
2 *Uncertainty* of the effect the change will have on their lives. People may wonder if they are able to cope with the new method or worry about how secure their job really is.
3 *Self-interest.* Staff may resist change because it may, in their opinion, take away from them something they value. This could take the form of a loss of prestige or financial benefits.

Ways of overcoming resistance to change

The following ways are reasonably straightforward and are based upon approaches indicated by J P Kotter and L A Schlesinger, *Harvard Business Review*, March–April 1979.

1 **Communication and education.** Resistance to change can be overcome if it is anticipated sufficiently far ahead. Staff can then be educated and prepared for the change.
2 **Participation.** Ensure the persons involved in the change take part in the planning and designing of the change. They are then more likely to feel a part of the change as the element of uncertainty about its impact will have been removed.
3 **Negotiation.** Managers may need to negotiate with staff directly affected by a change in order to reduce their resistance to it. A key department, for example, may agree to a change after guarantees or concessions are made. Changes may, for example, be made in work practices in return for monetary reward.
4 **Coercion.** This is more of a last resort to force change when time is short, or where other approaches have failed or where managers involved hold senior positions. This could take the form of dismissal, monetary compensation, re-assignment of jobs, or a threat of no promotion.
5 **Support from top management.** Changes affecting more than one department are more likely to be accepted if top management give their approval to the change.

ORGANIZATIONAL DEVELOPMENT (OD)

Behavioural scientists have recently learned how to help organizations to cope with a changing internal and external environment. Research into industrial psychology has changed to the examination of *organization* psychology, with emphasis on groups and relations between groups. The emphasis was on *individual* training and development, but it appeared that a broader outlook was needed to consider the complete *organization,* concentrating on organizational, group and interpersonal processes, and develop plans to improve the whole system.

Organizational development (OD) can be considered as an approach to the introduction of planned change, concentrating on the *process* of change rather than the content. It involves a number of behavioural science techniques which are designed to build a more effective organization. The concept aims to help the organization gain an insight into its own processes. The emphasis is on creating a more flexible open-minded organization, which is more receptive to change and where people can recognize the *need* for change and implement action themselves.

The increasing need for change leading to the development of OD was created by changes in:

- technology and labour skills;
- attitudes of employees;
- size of organization;
- need to improve performance.

Traditional training methods did not appear to be adequate to cope with the need to bring about changes in social system behaviour. Ideas from social psychology of attitude change, group dynamics techniques, 'change agent' skill and counselling are all part of OD.

The reasons why conventional training methods do not appear to produce satisfactory long-term benefits may be because:

1 Persons who have been on training courses are often disillusioned as their newly acquired skills have little chance of being used when they return to work.
2 The attitude of senior managers to training is often on a short-term basis; they look for certain results soon after the course and tend to lose interest if they are not forthcoming.

Aspects of OD

Agent of change

An *'agent of change'* is needed to act as a catalyst. He may be from inside or outside the organization. The aim is to help the company solve its own problems and the focus is on organizational, group and interpersonal *processes* (process consultancy).

Many aspects of the organization are examined and activities are largely group based. Members are encouraged to speak more openly about problems and inter-group activities are encouraged.

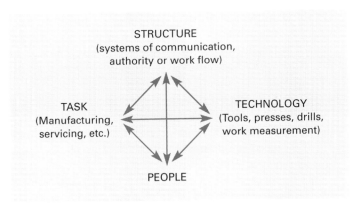

Fig 4.9 Interacting factors which govern the behaviour of organizations

Interacting factors which govern the behaviour of organizations are clearly set out by H J Leavitt in *A Handbook of Organizations* (1965, Rand McNally). Figure 4.9 summarizes the points involved.

The above factors are all interdependent as a change in one, for example *technology* (the introduction of a computer), will influence *tasks* (nature of work changes, i.e. output is greater and quicker); organization *structure* (fewer staff needed); *people* (by their accepting or not accepting the need for a computer). It is often the case that there is too much rigidity in the organization and this does not allow creative ideas to be introduced. Some methods used to overcome this are:

- **diversification** – businesses with too narrow a product base may buy interests in other industries;
- **decentralization** – the parent company has overall control, but units are given authority to make major decisions and the unit managers are held accountable for the results to the parent company;
- **venture groups** – a group is given the resources to develop a new idea, which may have come from a group member.

One major problem is that usually people do not like to change. Change is a threat to routine and their role in the organization. It is also true that many persons do *not* know what their role is, and in recent years attempts have been made to clarify individual roles or objectives (key result areas) by management by objectives. MBO involves the management of organizational change. (*See* p 107 and note the stereotyped attitude to MBO by some companies.) The *task* can be boring, because of specialization; remedies include job rotation, job enlargement and enrichment (*see* p 404). Only in job enrichment does an operative get the chance to discuss with management ways of re-organizing the work.

Advantages and objectives of organizational development programmes

- Creates a working environment in which formal authority is supplemented by authority based upon knowledge and skill.
- Increases the job satisfaction and enthusiasm of employees and encourages open communication.

- Increases the responsibility of individuals and groups in planning and implementing activities.
- Encourages confronting the problems of an enterprise rather than keeping them 'hidden'.

Disadvantages

- Difficult to convince staff of the *need* to change.
- May be costly to implement.
- Needs continual support by top management and their *conviction* of the need for change. Methods for introducing change

Methods for introducing change

Method	Illustration
Task	Job enrichment, job enlargement, redesign of jobs.
Structure	Change basis of departmentation, spans of control, authority delegation.
Technology	New equipment, computer based systems.
People	Team building, activity analysis, training in group activities and interpersonal skills.

Suggested stages of the process of OD are:

- the 'change agent' and senior executives *discuss* the *aims* of the programme and the ideas behind it, bearing in mind future needs;
- the *main problems* and objectives are set out clearly;
- an *'audit' of the organization* is effected, e.g. state of morale, existing relationships between persons (this can be done by interview, questionnaire, etc.);
- targets for *improvement* can then be set and agreed;
- a *check on effect* of plans is needed to ensure that the new methods are maintained.

Experience has shown that managers would be more effective if they:

- did not rely *too much* on their experience;
- adopted a more flexible role in discussions;
- encouraged the definition of problems in many varied ways;
- helped others to methodically talk through points involved;
- are skilled in questioning persons and working *with* them in making decisions;
- have a management 'style' conducive to change.

It can be seen that the work of a manager in a changing environment is more complex; there are various pressures he has to integrate, e.g. from colleagues, subordinates, superiors, in addition to external agents, such as suppliers, customers and the government, who form around him certain *boundaries* which produce relationships he has to manage to ensure his territory remains intact. It is therefore important to examine briefly the preferred 'styles' of managers who have to implement changes and consider the need for good 'integrators'.

Paul R Laurence and Jay W Lorsch pointed out (*Harvard Business Review*, December 1967) the difficulties that managers have in reconciling the need for specialization with the need for integration of effort. Inter-departmental conflicts need to be resolved and decisions made more quickly and smoothly. So in order to co-ordinate and integrate more effectively the person appointed should have certain attributes and adopt suitable behaviour characteristics in the resolution of conflict. Preferred styles were found to be from managers who:

- prefer to take the initiative and are confident and persuasive;
- seek status and are forceful and effective in communication;
- have wide scope and breadth of personal interests and social poise;
- are enthusiastic, imaginative, spontaneous, adventurous, humorous, flexible and assertive.

This is an area where research into the effectiveness of OD is sparse but will become increasingly more important, perhaps to the extent that the status of the *integrative function* will reach senior management, or at least departmental level. Organizations in a dynamic environment wishing to achieve a competitive advantage must pay special attention to the planning and integration of jobs and to the selection and development of persons to fill them.

It has already been stated that the organizational structure of large organizations often changes as their goals and their environment change. A change would be needed from existing centralized control which served the purpose when producing, for example, a small variety of products with limited demand, to the need for a diversified range to cope with increases in personal income and population. This often needs a more diversified organizational structure to maintain effective control.

If the design of an organization is inappropriate, this can be costly and inefficient. Mergers may appear to make economic sense but may involve problems inbuilt at the design stage which may never be overcome.

Review of approaches to OD

Classical approach

The classical approach to OD was mainly by earlier writers, Max Weber, Frederick Taylor and Henry Fayol. They stressed (see earlier chapters) the need for a hierarchical structure based on formal authority and sets of rules and regulations and a sense of duty to the organization. It is important to note that they developed their theories in a period of industrial revolution when large organizations seemed to offer a modern and efficient model.

The main problems of the classical approach were that it neglected the human aspects of members of the organization who were deemed to be motivated solely by economic considerations. There was also no way in which necessary changes could be made quickly to cope with uncertain environments caused by technological changes. So as new workers joined the organization with greater technical skills and education, senior managers became out of touch with the views of those on a lower level of the organization.

Human relations

Human relations researchers (McGregor, Argyris and Likert) tried to improve on the classical model; they stressed that a new set of values (Theory Y) would increase productivity and staff satisfaction, i.e.:

● a more informal organizational design (Argyris) to give staff greater power and independence;
● greater group participation in decision making (Likert's System 4).

The above approaches enriched the work of the classical writers who tried to find the one best way of designing an organization. But they seemed to over-look other variables that can affect the organization, e.g. technological and environmental factors. They tended to *simplify* the complex nature of human motivation.

Contingency approach

The contingency approach to organizational design stressed the need to fit an organization's structure to its strategy, technology, environment and people. *Structure* is affected by:

● **organization strategy**, which determines the *type* of tasks employees will perform;
● **technology** and task (some structures are more appropriate for some tasks and some technologies than others) (Joan Woodward's South-East Essex Studies, 1965);
● **external environment** – the more stable, the more mechanistic; the more volatile, the more organic the design (Burns and Stalker (1961), *The Management of Innovation*). This was supported by and added to by R Lawrence and J Lorsch (*Organization and the Environment*, 1967).

People in an organization will affect OD. Their work involvement, level of education and attitudes and values can directly influence structure – particularly as managers are responsible for designing the organization. Employees' attitudes can also affect structure, e.g. their demands for greater participation and need for job satisfaction.
OD is a continuous process as the variables change.

Creativity as an aid to OD

Creativity can help to *anticipate* change and works best in a dynamic, tolerant atmosphere. New ideas are *created*, developed and translated into a new product. Creativity implies the formation of a new idea, innovation implies bringing this new idea into effective use. *Creativity can be stimulated by*:

● brainstorming (*see* p 89) which attempts to prevent criticism from stopping the free flow of ideas so that many ideas are encouraged;
● synectics which aims for only *one* new idea to be considered in an area. Here only the group leader knows the problem (he tries to direct discussion towards the problem) by starting with a related topic.

For the innovation of new ideas to be successful a high degree of *integration* is needed between all concerned (e.g. engineering, production management, marketing). Organizations that are too rigidly structured may find integration of all necessary activities very difficult. Current thinking is that the type of organization suitable for innovation is the matrix structure (p 148) which encourages interdepartmental communication and integration.

A suitable climate to encourage creativity may not be so easy to obtain. It would need to be permissive; but many would fear such a climate may lead to lack of discipline. The following points may help to create a suitable climate and encourage creativity:

- there should be a clear statement from management to encourage new ideas and allow them to be conveyed upwards;
- try to overcome resistance to change by allowing staff to participate in making decisions to change the existing situation;
- allow opportunity to interact with others. Foster a creative climate by encouraging interchange of ideas;
- give a clear statement of objectives and tolerate failure of some ideas;
- recognize and reward creativity in a practical way (e.g. financial reward).

OTHER FORMS OF ORGANIZATION STRUCTURE

Wilfred Brown argues for retaining the pyramid or hierarchical structure of organization because some persons are better than others at making decisions and as work becomes more complex there are fewer persons able to deal with more involved problems.

Three main features of authority are noted by Brown – managerial authority can: (a) veto appointments of subordinates; (b) assess their work; (c) or transfer them.

Brown advocates a *representative* system of manager and shop floor workers, in the form of a Works Council for each area (W Brown: *Organization* (1971, Heinemann)).

These councils must *unanimously* agree on matters relating to duties and entitlements of members of the company. *No action* is therefore taken if one person disagrees. The management and workers *both* agree not to force any changes, thus strikes are breaches of the constitution and full representation in formulating policies, etc., is allowed together with all information the company can provide.

This structure aims at reducing conflict. There are very clear role definitions, a strong managerial line of command and a separate sub-system of consultation and participation.

There are criticisms of this approach to management and although the company's procedures and record of industrial action is good this is no indication that this type of organization could be used with *similar* success elsewhere.

Further, consideration must be given to a series of investigations at the Glacier Metal Company. Continuous analytical observations were made by a team led by Elliott Jacques. They hoped to find the real nature of managerial relationships. *Kinds of work* were distinguished, i.e. managing an operational or primary activity, or specialist or advisory work, and managerial work was claimed to be either partly 'prescribed' or 'discretionary'.

The *prescribed* content contained those elements in which the worker has no authorized choice. This is always specific, e.g. check all documents before posting them.

The *discretionary* content consists of those elements in which the choice is left to the operator's judgement, e.g. adopt the best method of control.

This distinction makes possible a more critical appreciation of managers' tasks and can help to improve their work.

It is upon this discretionary content that people feel the weight of responsibility and this is deemed measurable by finding the maximum period during which a person is relied upon to use his own judgement. The term 'time-span of discretion' therefore refers to the longest period that can pass before a superior makes an effective check on a person's work. This theory has two important implications, one regarding *delegation,* the other regarding a realistic *wage basis* for all workers. As far as delegation is concerned, if a superior has a clear idea of a subordinate's time-span of discretion and his level of responsibility, he may feel he can delegate *more freely.* The subordinates will be more ready to accept their assignments knowing the differentials are fair and reasonable and that they are remunerated accordingly.

Management in practice

> *Scott Bader Ltd*
>
> This company has been owned collectively by the employees since 1951. The company in Northamptonshire was a market leader in polyester resins.
>
> Any employee over 18 who has worked in the company for over one year can join Scott Bader Commonwealth Ltd; this is a company limited by guarantee and owns all shares in Scott Bader Company Ltd.
>
> Employees can participate in policy making through the Community Council which can make recommendations to the Board of Management on company policy.
>
> Points to note are that there is increased opportunity of participation in policy making, common ownership, more autonomy for work groups, and, by introducing more project groups, a weakening of line management structure.
>
> Whether this company has been 'successful' or not is not easy to say, but the absenteeism and strike records are very good.
>
> The company's Code of Practice makes interesting reading. A question to consider is – could the company exist if it was not commercially successful, even though they have agreed to share available work in a downturn of trade?

Finally, it is worth considering two interesting research studies on organizational analysis. In 1958 Joan Woodward (in her book *Industrial Organization: Theory and Practice*) supported Drucker's analysis of the different organization needs of *different types of production processes*. Her investigations of 100 firms showed that, when grouped into types of production, i.e. flow, batch and single units, and process, the successful firms each had a *similar* pattern of organization which was *related to the technical methods* employed.

Burns and Stalker published, in 1961, a study of companies, *The Management of Innovation*. The electronics industry, which was in a period of rapid change, was compared with a routine producer of rayon filament yarn. The comparison suggested that the *amount* of change affecting the organization influenced its flexibility. Two types of management system were described, 'mechanistic', which is suitable for stable conditions, and 'organic', suitable for changing conditions.

Briefly, in the *'mechanistic'* type of management, everyone knew his job and its limits, little consultation was needed and work flowed through clearly-defined channels. Management in such stable conditions can be treated as a mechanical structure.

The *'organic'* type of management had flexible work boundaries and there was more consultation and interaction with others and less command. There was a greater sense of freedom and a great deal of later communication compared with the 'mechanistic' type.

This report, and others, make it clear that there is *no one ideal form of organization*. Burns and Stalker noted that most structures lie *between* the two extreme types; some companies contain elements of both and may change from one type to another, depending upon their stability. Furthermore, it was management's responsibility constantly to review their objectives and aims and adapt the organization structure suitably.

ORGANIZATION AS A SYSTEM

Traditional theorists attempted to devise an organization which would allocate and co-ordinate resources efficiently. Various positions were given authority and responsibility to accomplish tasks. Stable structures, e.g. military or public bureaucracies, were taken as guides. Certain principles of organization were considered which were aimed at establishing clearly lines of authority and relationships:

- Specialization of tasks led to departmentation and the division of labour.
- The scalar principle established a hierarchical structure, referring to the vertical division of authority and responsibility with duties assigned along the 'scalar chain'. This emphasized the supervisory–subordinate relationship with authority and responsibility flowing vertically from the highest to lowest levels. Organization charts today still illustrate this principle.
- Authority, responsibility, accountability, unity of command and span of control complete the main ideas of traditionalists.

Line and staff functions as we have seen are traditionally the basis of differentiating managerial activities. This enabled activities of specialists to be integrated. As organizations became more complex, *staff roles* have become more important. The idea of line having command authority and staff only advising is not always true, as the expertise of *some* staff roles may be considered a source of authority in organizations. This occurs when staff have functional authority, e.g. the industrial relations department has functional authority over aspects of human resource practice in *all* departments. An interesting point is made by Etzioni in *Modern Organisations* (1964, Prentice-Hall) where he mentions that the roles of staff and line may be reversed in certain areas, for example in hospitals, research laboratories and universities. A main factor in the change in staff and line form relates to companies which are in changing or dynamic environments and which find it more difficult to accept the traditional approach. The more stable the environment, the more acceptable is the traditional approach.

An organization can be considered as a single *system.* It is an open system, i.e. open and in interaction with its environment. Traditional theories were closed-system views, because they considered the system concerned was self-contained, concentrating upon the internal operation of the organization and believing it could be suitably analysed *without* reference to the external environment.

An open-system view recognizes that the social system is in a *dynamic* relationship with its environment, whereby inputs are received, transformed and *outputs* are passed on. This is a continuous cycle. (Fig 1.1 on p 20 can be referred to again here.)

E L Trist and his associates at the Tavistock Institute hold the view that the organization can be viewed as a *socio-technical system.* Organization is the structuring and integrating of human activities around various technologies, but the effectiveness and efficiency in using the technologies is determined by the *social system.* The various approaches to organization and management tended to emphasize parts of the system (i.e. sub-systems), for example the technological sub-system or the social sub-system. The importance of other sub-systems was not considered in the old approaches. The modern approach views the organization as a structured socio-technical (open) system which considers *all* of the sub-systems and their interactions between each other and the environment.

The older approach has *rigid* boundaries defining the areas and these are a barrier to interaction between people within the boundary and those outside. Management must link the various sub-systems together to ensure integration and co-operation, acting as a boundary agent between the organization and the environment. The area of contact between one system and another is called an *interface.*

Emery and Trist in *Management Sciences* (1960, Rerga Press) suggest that the idea is for an organization to reach a state where the system remains in dynamic equilibrium and can adapt to changes in its environment; this is called *steady state.* In social organizations, managers are working at the boundary of the system (interface), trying to maintain a state of *dynamic* equilibrium between the system and the environment which is constantly changing.

SUMMARY

Objective 1 *Describe the organizing process and explain why it is important to effective management.*

Organizing is the process of defining the essential relationships among people and tasks and activities, so that all the resources of the organization are integrated and co-ordinated to accomplish its objectives effectively.

The steps required in forming an organization are:

- establish enterprise objectives, policies and plans;
- find out the activities needed to execute these plans;
- classify and group these activities into meaningful units so that group members can work together effectively;
- decide who should be responsible for managing each of the groups of activities and assign to each group the authority needed to perform those activities;
- endeavour to integrate these groupings through authority relationships, horizontally, vertically and laterally.

Objective 2 *Define the formal structure of an organization and identify the various ways an organization can be structured.*

The formal structure of an organization is usually shown on an organization chart which defines the division of work, managers and subordinates, the type of work being performed, the grouping of work segments and the levels of management. Organization by *function* brings together in one department all those engaged in one activity or several related activities. For example, a sales manager could be responsible for *all* products manufactured by the company. Organization by *division* brings together in one department all those involved in the production and marketing of a product or related group of products, all in a geographical area, or those dealing with a certain type of customer, product, process or equipment. A divisional head, for example, would be responsible for the manufacturing, marketing, and sales activities of a complete unit.

Objective 3 *Define the term delegation and explain the differences between responsibility, accountability and authority.*

Delegation is the process whereby a manager assigns tasks and authority to subordinates who accept responsibility for those jobs. Responsibility, accountability and authority are three interrelated elements of the process of delegation. Responsibility results from the assignment of tasks to immediate subordinates. Accountability is the obligation of the subordinate to the manager to perform the duties assigned in a satisfactory manner. Authority, commensurate with assigned duties, must then be granted so that the accepted responsibility can be fulfilled.

Objective 4 *Explain the difference between decentralization and delegation, and discuss the factors that affect an organization's degree of decentralization.*

Delegation is the process of assigning tasks and granting sufficient authority for their accomplishment. Decentralization refers to the degree to which that authority is distributed throughout the organization. The amount of decentralization may vary during the history of a firm, but the following factors have a significant influence in decentralization:

● company size;
● attitude towards cost control;
● desire for uniform policy;
● homogeneity of product line;
● management philosophy.

Objective 5 *Describe the organizational development approach to change and the assumptions and values upon which this approach is based.*

Organizational development is an approach to the introduction of planned change. It concentrates on the process of change and involves a number of behavioural science techniques designed to build a more effective organization. The emphasis is on creating a more flexible and open-minded organization which is more receptive to change and where people can recognize the need for change and implement action themselves. Successful change involves two key factors:

● a redistribution of power so that decision-making practices move towards the greater use of shared power;
● the redistribution of power through a process of development change which can involve changes in task, structure, technology and people.

REVIEW QUESTIONS

1 What is meant by formal and informal organization?

2 Are there any accepted principles of organization?

3 Outline the findings of studies on the different patterns of organization to be found in the UK.

4 Consider the advantages and disadvantages of grouping functions and tasks.

5 'The span of control principle is unimportant.' Discuss.

6 Describe the types of organization structure.

7 What factors determine the delegation of authority?

8 Are there any guides to the assignment of activities to departments?

9 'Organization charts serve no useful purpose.' Discuss.

10 What do you understand by the term 'working groups'?

11 What benefit is it to study the systems approach to organization?

12 Explain the term 'Organizational Development'.

13 In what sense is the matrix structure a compromise?

14 What steps should be taken to prepare subordinates for the performance of delegated tasks?

15 How might further advances in computerization affect problems of centralization or decentralization?

REVIEW PROBLEMS

1 You have been selected to be the first manager of a new department which will commence operations in two months' time. The managing director has now asked you for a report indicating how you mean to set up this new department, especially stating (*a*) the departmental organizational structure and (*b*) the objectives of the department.

The new department can be any *one* of the following:

(i)   Production
(ii) Human resources
(iii) Accounts

(iv) R & D
(v) Marketing
(vi) Data processing

Draft your report accordingly.

2 How would you apply the principles of organizational structure when examining an enterprise? What common weaknesses in organization are found in business? Classify these weaknesses under:

(a) definition of responsibilities;
(b) span of supervision;
(c) general management;
(d) functional specialists;
(e) co-ordination.

3 Evaluate the impact of the informal organization on the operation of the formal structure (preferably using illustrative examples from your own experience). Indicate whether, in your view, it is desirable for management to try to strengthen (or weaken) the informal organization, and why.

4 'The manager's relationship to his superior and his relationship to his subordinate are two-way relationships. Both are formal and informal relationships of authority as well as of information. Both are relationships of mutual dependence.' (Peter Drucker, *Management*, 1974). Discuss.

5 A large organization in road transport operates nationwide in general haulage. This field has become very competitive and recently has become only marginally profitable. It has been suggested that the strategic structure of the company should be widened to include other aspects of physical distribution, so that the maximum synergy would be obtained from that type of diversification.

(a) Name three activities which might fit into the suggested new strategic structure, explaining each one briefly.

(b) Explain how each of these activities could be incorporated into the existing structure.

(c) State the advantages and disadvantages of such diversification.

ASSIGNMENTS

1 Take an organization which you know well and consider what would happen if, in a short space of time, it increased threefold in size and had started to export to Europe. You can choose any organization you wish to answer the following questions:

Would the organization have been able to continue without any changes in structure?

What type of structure would you advocate for the greatly enlarged organization?

2 Find out how a professional accountancy firm organizes its auditing activities and how it tries to motivate and control its staff. Can you identify any theories of organization and motivation that you think lie behind its operations?

BIBLIOGRAPHY

Adam-Smith, D and Peacock, A (eds), *Cases in Organisational Behaviour* (London, Pitman Publishing, 1994).

Barnard, C I, *The Functions of the Executive* (Cambridge, Mass, Harvard University Press, 1982).

Beishon, R J, and Peters, G (eds), *Systems Behaviour* (The Open University Press, Harper & Row, 3rd edition, 1982).

Bennett, R, *Organisational Behaviour* (London, M+E Handbooks, Pitman Publishing, 2nd edition, 1994).

Burnes, B, *Managing Change* (London, Pitman Publishing, 1992).

Child, J, *A Guide to Problems and Practice* (London, Harper & Row, 1984).

Drucker, P F, *The Practice of Management* (London, Heinemann, 1989). Chapters 16–18.

Handy, C B, *Understanding Organizations* (London, Penguin, 4th edition, 1993).

Handy, C B, *Inside Organizations* (London, BBC Books, 1990).

Holloway, W, *Work Psychology and Organizational Behaviour* (London, Sage, 1991).

Knight, K (ed), *Matrix Management* (Farnborough, Gower, 1977).

Luthans, F, *Organizational Behavior,* (New York, McGraw-Hill, 4th edition, 1985).

Mintzberg, H, *The Structuring of Organizations* (Englewood Cliffs, NJ, Prentice-Hall, 1979).

Mullins, L, *Management and Organisational Behaviour* (London, Pitman Publishing, 3rd edition, 1993).

Pugh, D S, *Writers on Organizations* (London, Penguin, 1990).

Stewart, R, *The Reality of Organizations* (London, Pan, 1986).

CHAPTER 5

Directing

The previous chapter showed the various ways of structuring an organization so that resources were effectively used. The effectiveness also depends upon the leadership provided by managers and some of the theories regarding the relationship between managers and employees are considered. In order to motivate people, managers must understand their needs and hence discussion on theories of motivation follows. Other important aspects of morale and discipline are considered together with communication systems and channels.

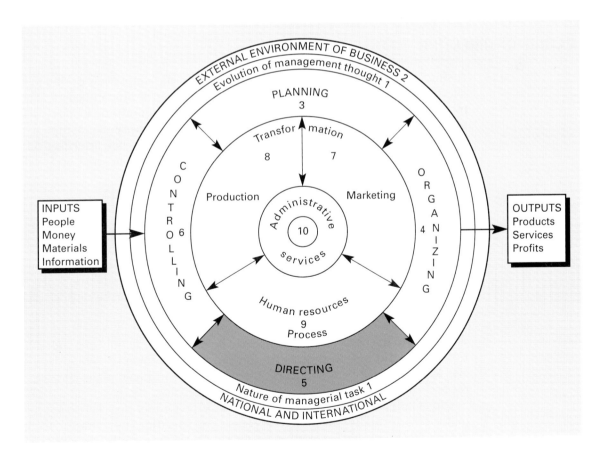

The systems approach to management

OBJECTIVES

Upon completing this chapter you should be able to:

- Explain why an understanding of leadership is important, and how a manager's underlying assumptions about human behaviour will influence his behaviour as a leader.
- Explain the importance of communication and identify some barriers to communication.
- Explain the various ways motivation plays a role in most enterprises.
- Explain why co-ordination of the activities and objectives of an organization is necessary and the co-ordinating mechanisms that managers can use.
- Describe the contributions of the various theorists on motivation and state how their work is related to motivation in organizations.

In order to direct subordinates, a manager must lead, motivate, communicate and ensure co-ordination of activities so that enterprise objectives are achieved.

NATURE OF DIRECTING

A simple definition is that directing entails ensuring employees do the jobs allotted to them. All firms use the combined services of human beings, who must be directed, through communication and orientation, to carry out assignments with the utmost co-operation. Working relationships are involved at all levels and these must be governed to see they are effectively executed. Proper motivation is needed to encourage them to work and various techniques may be used to this end.

Principles

Harmony of objectives

There must be harmony between the objectives of a subordinate and those of the firm. This may not be easy to attain, as goals may not be *identical*, but, if individual motives can be directed to achieve group goals, the work is easier. The aim should be to see if the subordinate's needs can be satisfied and at the same time contribute to enterprise objectives.

Unity of command

This refers to the need for subordinates to be responsible to only one superior. F W Taylor did not do this, as he allowed eight foremen to give orders to one worker. If one person directs, it is easier to co-ordinate plans and select the best techniques to be used to achieve group goals.

Direction is aided by delegation of authority. Orders may be issued formally or informally, and may be general or specific. They should all be enforceable by the employment of sanctions. Delegation can be regarded as a more general form of direction than issuing orders. In some cases *detailed* authority may be granted (e.g. to do a specific job); in others it may be *broad* (e.g. to discipline subordinates). It will of course be broader at the top of the pyramid of organization and more detailed towards the bottom.

The human resources function (see Chapter 9) usually deals with the methods of introducing and informing newcomers in the ways of the firm. The supervision of this orientation should be done by management. The subordinate should know his own job, its scope, purpose and position in the organization, the methods of control used, how jobs interrelate and what facilities are available to help him (e.g. service departments). This is a constant job using all methods of communication to aid co-ordination of activities. Managers, as well as subordinates, must come under this plan of orientation.

Board of directors

The directing authority is a person, or a group of persons, who represent the owners and who bear final responsibility for the formulation of basic policy and the direction of enterprise. In a public company the board of directors is a committee elected by shareholders and responsible to them.

Duties of a board
of directors

These duties comprise:

- laying down strategy, general policy and broad sectional policies;
- seeing legal requirements are met and the company is operating in accordance with its Memorandum and Articles of Association;
- sanctioning capital expenditure and the method of disposal of profits;
- ensuring sufficient capital is available and maintaining an efficient system to control the affairs of the company;
- appointing a managing director and seeing he creates a sound structure, maintains co-ordination among senior management and develops good morale.

The board is vitally interested in the appointment of the senior managers, and determines their salary structure and the nature of their 'fringe benefits'. (*See* Chapter 9 on Human Resources Management.)

The board should also be interested in management succession and in this connection training schemes for managers should receive their close attention.

Chairman of the
board of directors

The chairman is usually elected from full-time members. Often the managing director is also chairman. This term is used to denote a person in charge of functional executives and who is also on the board.

The position of the general manager is not the same, as this term strictly means he is only an executive and has no seat on the board. In practice, most general managers are also managing directors and, for convenience, will be treated hereafter in this way.

It is not considered entirely satisfactory for a managing director to be chairman of the board as he acts as an executive (a manager) on the one hand, and when appearing on the board acts as a director and this may lead to a conflict of interest. If a director is divorced from the duties of managing director he can take a more detached view. The German system shows this 'separation of powers' by having a separate supervisory board, which appoints the actual management.

NB: The duties of the chairman were set out in the previous chapter on Organizing, and apply to all chairmen.

The managing director

The managing director is appointed by and responsible to the board of directors and often is also chairman of the board. He is the link between the formation of policy and its execution by managers and is responsible to the board for the effective management of the enterprise, within the framework of policy laid down.

Duties of the managing director. The duties of the managing director can be summarized as follows:

- to represent the board of directors, interpret policy and ensure it is carried out by all members of the company;
- to formulate programmes to attain objectives and establish a structure of delegated responsibility to ensure effective control of operations;
- to submit statements to the board and keeps all activities (e.g. design, sales, production, quality, new techniques) of the company under periodical review;
- to see that staff are content as regards salaries, promotions, etc., and ensure that morale is high.

Appointment of directors

Articles of Association often recommend that directors shall be appointed only if they hold a specified number of shares in the company. This may be a nominal holding or a substantial one: such a share qualification varies widely. The Companies Act provides that a Register of Shareholdings be kept and remain open for inspection. Articles often provide for one third of directors to retire yearly, but shall be eligible for re-election. Upper age limits are often set (e.g. 67 years), as this is some guarantee that persons with new ideas will be obtained.

Functional executives, e.g. production and manufacturing section heads, are often appointed directors. Directors are also appointed who have no executive function; these may be full-time or part-time.

Size and composition of boards

Boardroom organization varies greatly in the United Kingdom, from management by committee to virtually one-person rule. If one person is in command, authority is centralized and unity of command upheld, but problems arise, particularly of succession.

In some companies part-time directors are employed and these can bring specialized skill and experience and a more objective approach to deliberations. If too many executive directors are appointed, they may tend to have too narrow a viewpoint. In addition, they may not be able to accomplish the two jobs of managing and directing. As the jobs are of a different character, one person will find it very difficult.

Difference between direction and management

Directing is concerned more with the long-term affairs of the company and the *obtaining* of resources. It is concerned with deciding the *broad* course of action to be followed and then decisions made are operative over a number of years.

Management, by a full-time executive, is concerned with the day-to-day affairs and the *detailed allocation* of resources obtained. Procedures adopted are more specific than general and decisions made are effected immediately.

A recent survey of the top 120 companies in the UK (i.e. top by market capitalization) showed:

- 63 per cent have chairmen, who are also chief executives;
- 21 per cent have part-time chairmen;
- 11 per cent have three or more managing directors.

Another feature brought out was that compared with many USA companies there generally was not a clear-cut position as deputy, i.e. someone who would take over in succession to the chairman. General Motors of USA had a person who moved to chairman automatically; but Imperial Chemical Industries had to choose from their four deputy chairmen plus outsiders. It is preferable for succession to be certain in most cases.

There are companies where most of the directors also hold full-time executive posts and situations may occur when an individual director may feel that he is entitled to formulate policy and give rulings on policy, or to interpret a policy decision in his own way that has been made by the board as a corporate decision. This practice could lead to directors in different sections of the company carrying out their own ideas which may vary from the corporate decisions.

Boards of directors therefore need to *examine* periodically their own *composition*, as well as the ways they conduct their affairs. This is pointed out very clearly in *Managing for Revival* (1972, Management Publications Ltd). E F L Brech suggests that boards should reassure themselves of two factors:

1 that the board is so composed that objectives of performance, productivity and profitability can be correctly and firmly set, and policies formulated that can be expected to achieve successful outcome;
2 that the board has a managing director knowledgeable and competent to undertake the programme of action and improvement that will attain the new objectives.

Surveys constantly show that in many companies there are more executive directors than outside directors and the majority of time spent in board meetings is devoted to matters of functional (executive) practice, with little time for strategy and other important considerations.

This distinction between direction and management can take the form of organizing the board as a two-tier or two-part board. To show which board is senior it is often called a 'supervisory' or 'management' board. This senior board is concerned with devising policies, setting objectives and evaluating results, whereas the second board is responsible for translating objectives into tangible plans.

It is possible for some members to serve on both boards but they may work more effectively if such an overlap in membership is limited. The Fifth Directive of the Council of European Communities (CEC) (1972) recommended a new form of company, for countries in the European Community (EC). This emphasizes the authority of the supervisory board and goes as far as to recommend that the members of the management 'organ' may be *dismissed* by the supervisory organ.

The majority of directors on boards, especially full-time directors, have a dual role which tends to generate *conflicts of interest*. A head of a division, for example, who has to ensure operations keep up to schedule and keep staff happy, may then attend a meeting of the board which is discussing changes in output and staffing. This could mean harsh decisions are required. The two-board structure would at least give the two roles to separate persons – the policy board for long-term considerations, the executive board for everyday operations.

The policy board would probably consist of a chairman, non-executive directors and the managing director who would be co-opted to give all relevant information to enable the policy board to make major decisions, e.g. mergers, or large amounts of capital expenditure. Membership of the executive board could consist of the managing director as chairman, and all the heads of functions and divisions, but *no* outside directors.

One major point to consider carefully is the question of whether the information received by the policy board is sufficiently adequate and *unbiased* for them to make decisions. In the above example, only the managing director is the common member. This could presumably be overcome by holding meetings of the two boards and periodically co-opting executive members to the policy board. As long as the boards (however they are organized) trust each other and operate in an environment where information is freely exchanged, their chances of success will be higher.

Worker participation

A starting point in considering to what extent (if any) worker representatives should be on boards of directors is to note the Fifth Directive of the CEC, which states that 'at least *one-third* of the members of the supervisory organ shall be appointed by the workers or their representatives'.

There are, though, many ideas as to what is meant by the words *worker participation*, so that the comments made by D McGregor (*Human Side of Enterprise*) are worth quoting:

> 'Participation is one of the most misunderstood ideas that have emerged from the field of human relations. It is praised by some, condemned by others, and used with considerable success by still others.
>
> Some proponents of participation give the impression that it is a magic formula which will eliminate conflict and disagreement and come pretty close to solving all of management's problems. These enthusiasts appear to believe that people yearn to participate . . . that it is a formula which can be applied by any manager regardless of his skill, that virtually no preparation is necessary for its use, and that it can spring full-blown into existence and transform industrial relationships overnight.

Some critics of participation, on the other hand, see it as a form of managerial abdication. It is a dangerous idea that will undermine managerial prerogatives and almost certainly get out of control . . . It wastes time, lowers efficiency and weakens management's effectiveness.

A third group of managers view participation as a useful item in their bag of managerial tricks. It is for them a manipulative device for getting people to do what they want, under conditions that delude the "participators" into thinking they have had a voice in decision making.

A fourth group of managers make successful use of participation, but they don't think of it a panacea or magic formula. They do not share either the unrestrained enthusiasm of the faddists or the fears of the critics.'

It is therefore very important to specify exactly what is the main object of any scheme for participation. It is concerned with *sharing* power to allow employees to influence decisions. This may be *specific* (i.e. relating to an *individual* – his career, promotion, remuneration, etc.) or *general* (i.e. representing *groups* of employees who are involved in decisions affecting sections of the workpeople) and may refer to participation in profit sharing, ownership of assets and decisions that affect the career or remuneration of employees.

There are, therefore, many possible levels of involvement in participation. A wide or a narrow approach to participation could range from, on the one hand, little information being given to employees and, where some suggestions are allowed, to decisions being decentralized and employees participating in setting company objectives, worker representation on the board and perhaps eventual transfer of ownership.

There are many ways of devising schemes of participation where management and employees commit themselves to voluntary or legal agreements. The main point to consider is 'what is participation designed to achieve?' It could be considered to be either:

- to improve the material well-being of employees (e.g. profit sharing and bonus schemes);
- to improve the efficiency of the company (e.g. to set up works councils, planning and consultative committees);
- to own the enterprise (e.g. worker representatives on board and transfer of ownership schemes);
- to safeguard position of individuals.

(It is important to ensure that group decisions do not unduly affect the individual worker's own position to determine his own well-being.)

It was mentioned earlier that *mutual confidence* between management and worker is of paramount importance. If this is not present it is very doubtful if this can be installed by legislation. It requires *employees* to look at the needs of the enterprise as a whole and not to pursue sectional interests, and *management* to believe participation is beneficial to the enterprise, and the employees have a *right* to be consulted and kept informed.

The Fifth Directive of the CEC lays down certain rules regarding the percentage of employee representatives on the two boards (supervisory and management). In the German system, one-third of the board must be appointed by workers or their representatives, or on the proportion of workers or representatives. The Dutch system aims at a balance of representatives from both sides and co-option for the whole supervisory board including any worker representatives.

A final comment on this important area which has evolved more quickly in recent years is that there is a real problem in considering the reason why an individual should be appointed as a director. Is the appointment because of personal qualities, experience and professional abilities, *or* should they be elected to act as *delegates* who represent certain sectional interests? There is a strong feeling that there is a conflict of interests, *gains to employees* may occur at the *expense of customers, shareholders and suppliers*, because the workers representative would have to give priority to the interests of the employees.

LEADERSHIP

Leadership is a means of directing. A leader's actions are devoted to helping a group to attain its objectives. *Leadership* is the ability of management to induce subordinates to work towards group goals with confidence and keenness. Leadership also implies that the leader accepts responsibility for the achievement of the group objective and it is therefore essential for trust and co-operation from both sides to be in evidence all the time.

It must be noted that leadership is not synonymous with administrative ability and that numerous attempts have been made to analyse the nature of leadership. One is to contrast authoritarian and democratic leadership.

Types of leader

The authoritarian leader gets others to do things by giving them little scope to influence decisions. He uses fear, threats, and his authority and personality to get his way.

The democratic leader seeks to persuade and considers the feelings of persons and encourages their participation in decision making.

Studies have shown that the democratic method gives followers greater job satisfaction and enables them to co-operate better, but there is doubt as to whether decisions taken under this sort of leadership are better. Recent studies are more doubtful about democratic leadership because outside influences, e.g. government, consumers, exert pressure and, if a leader becomes *too* employee-centred, production may suffer and morale fall.

Leadership can be *formal*, i.e. having delegated authority, and can exert great influence. *Informal* leaders can initiate action, but do not have the same authority. The choice of leader, therefore, should be based on an accurate diagnosis of the environment, i.e. its reality, noting that effective leadership depends upon *many* conditions.

Qualities of leader

No two persons would ever agree on the desired qualities, as almost every human strength or virtue will be quoted. The elements of persuasion, compulsion and example may be considered to be essential to effect leadership. It has also been said that a leader should make it his job to be *known to all* and that it is more important to be *recognized* than to be popular.

Lord Montgomery, in his book *Path to Leadership*, described a leader as:

'. . . one who can be looked up to, whose personal judgement is trusted, who can inspire and warm the hearts of those he leads, gaining their trust and confidence and explaining what is needed in language which can be understood.'

Chester Barnard in *Functions of an Executive* considers a leader should have the following attributes – skill, technology, perception, knowledge, physique, memory, imagination, determination, endurance and courage.

It must be carefully noted that the leadership qualities that are needed in a particular situation are not usually found in any one individual. From this it can be seen that, if a particular vacancy has to be filled, the strengths and weaknesses of the person who is being appointed should be considered, along with those of the people he will be working with.

The successful leader therefore can be considered to be perceptible and flexible and able to act *appropriately*, i.e. in one situation he is strong, in another he is permissive. It is worth noting also that the *formal status* of an individual does not indicate the ability he has to influence others, as such ability is rather a combination of his *position* and his *personality*.

BEHAVIOURAL THEORIES OF LEADERSHIP

These theories began when the ideas of unique leader traits were questioned in the 1940s. It was considered that the qualities of leaders could be analysed better by looking at their *behaviour* or their behavioural *style* that causes others to follow them.

Trait theory

A *trait* is a physical or psychological characteristic that accounts for the behaviour of a person. *Trait theories* grew out of qualities found in great or well-known natural leaders, whom it was thought were born with leadership qualities.

It was later considered that if traits of natural leaders were identified it would be possible for others to acquire them through *learning* and *experience*.

Social psychologists were interested in leadership as an aspect of behaviour in the workplace and not just in personal characteristics. Two studies on leadership, which are important, occurred at the Universities of Ohio and Michigan in the USA. These studies were led by R Stogdill and R Likert and both concluded that there were two principal aspects of leader behaviour:

- a concern for people;
- a concern for production.

These studies led to the development of a matrix to depict managerial leadership styles. This was created by R Blake and J Mouton and called 'The Managerial Grid' (*see* p 390 on other training techniques).

R Tannenbaum and W Schmidt found that managers were often uncertain how to handle specific types of problem. In particular, how to distinguish between the types of problem they should handle themselves and those that should be resolved with their subordinates.

They concluded that in making an appropriate choice of how autocratic or democratic to be, a manager needed to consider three sets of issues:

1 **Personal concerns** – managers had to consider their own values, their inclinations towards leadership, and the level of confidence they had in their subordinates.

2 **Subordinate concerns** – managers had to consider their subordinates' needs for responsibility and independence, their knowledge and interest of the problem, and the amount they desired to be involved in solving problems.

3 **Concern for the situation** – this included concern for the nature of the problem, the competence of the group in handling the problem, the time available and the type and history of the organization.

They suggested a continuum of possible leadership behaviour which is available to a manager, along which may be placed various styles of leadership. At one extreme, leadership was boss-centred (or authoritarian) and at the other extreme, leadership was subordinate-centred (or democratic). The continuum, therefore, represents a range of action which relates to the degree of authority used by a manager and the area of freedom available to subordinates in arriving at decisions.

There is a relationship, therefore, to McGregor's Theory X and Y. Boss-centred leadership relates towards Theory X and subordinate-centred leadership, towards Theory Y.

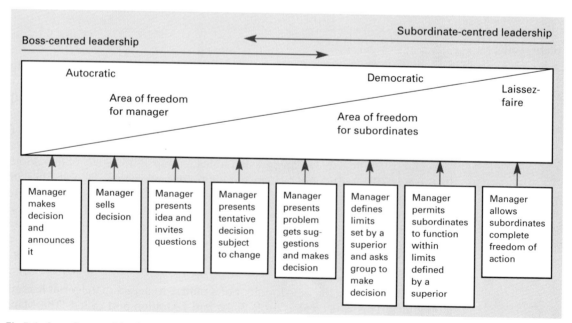

Fig 5.1 A continuum of leadership behaviour
Source: R Tannenbaum and W H Schmidt (Harvard, 1973)

Leadership styles

A well-known approach to leadership styles by D McGregor in the *Human Side of Enterprise* (1960, McGraw-Hill) has been discussed and criticized a great deal. His assumptions of human nature and behaviour were expressed in an analysis of two theories of leadership, called Theory X and Theory Y.

He considered people were being treated to a Theory X approach, which he considered wrong. This approach assumes:

- the average person dislikes work and will avoid it if possible;
- people therefore must be coerced, controlled and directed and threatened with punishment in order to get them to work towards organizational goals;
- the average person prefers to be directed and wants to avoid responsibility, he has little ambition and desires security above all.

McGregor considered this approach was based upon wrong assumptions about motivation and Theory Y was preferred, i.e.:

- expenditure of physical and mental effort in work is as natural as play or rest. Work can be a source of satisfaction;
- people can exercise self-direction and control to achieve objectives to which they are committed;
- commitment to objectives is a function of the rewards associated with their achievement;
- under proper conditions people can learn to accept and seek responsibility;
- ability to use imagination and creative thinking is widely distributed in the population;
- the intellectual potential of the average person in industrial life is only partially realized.

The practical manager can be helped by analysing various approaches to leadership styles, but he must come to his own conclusions and adapt to the actual situation.

Contingency or situational theories of leadership

The most recent approach to the understanding of leadership builds on the previous behavioural theories. The theories state that the appropriativeness of the actions of a leader depend upon the actual *situation* in which actions are taken. An autocratic leadership approach may, for example, be suitable for managers in a factory but not for managers of development and design staff.

This is called the *contingency or situational approach*, and attempts to explain leadership within the context of the larger situation in which it occurs. This is in contrast to earlier theories which concentrated on the behaviour of leaders.

Research into leadership by F Fiedler in Ohio, USA, has been summarized in his book *A Theory of Leadership Effectiveness* (1970, McGraw-Hill). Leaders are placed on a scale depending upon whether they are *task-orientated* or *people-orientated*. R Likert was involved in these investigations and the findings appear to confirm research by others. These are, when foremen created an atmosphere which contributed to discussion of work problems in a relaxed, natural way, when they had time to discuss personal problems and stand up and support their men, the result showed the workers had a higher satisfaction and low absenteeism.

Research by Fiedler can be of practical advantage to managers. He gave advice on what should be the *appropriate* leadership style or behaviour in various situations. He suggested that the extent to which a manager should be democratic or authoritarian in his leadership style related to:

- the *authority and power* he had in his position as manager (i.e. right to hire, dismiss, reward);
- the extent and nature of the *interpersonal relations* between the leader and members of the group (i.e. high – as on a conveyor assembly; low or unstructured – as on an investigation, needing wide discretion).

In this *contingency theory of leadership* he suggests that where relations between members and leader are good and the task basically unstructured and the power of the leader weak, his style should be more democratic and considerate. If the converse was the case, then a more authoritarian style would appear to be appropriate.

A brief comment must be made on the work of Robert Tannenbaum and Warren Schmidt called 'How to Choose a Leadership Pattern' in the *Harvard Business Review*, 1973. They argued that the appropriateness of a leader's actions depend upon the actual situation in which actions are taken. They tried to distinguish between the types of problems managers should handle themselves and those handled jointly with their subordinates. Their conclusions sought to guide a manager in making the appropriate choice of how autocratic or democratic to be in making a decision.

For many years writers have considered the qualities or traits needed for a leader and brief summaries of these are on p 191. Research into these areas has become more specific, and is not just a listing of personal abilities. Modern trait research is more scientific. These tests have shown that:

- leaders show better judgement, they are better adjusted psychologically, they interact more socially than non-leaders;
- leaders tend to ask for and give more information and take the lead in summing up or interpreting a situation.

This approach is still not considered really satisfactory. One objection is that the degree to which a person exhibits leadership depends not only on *his or her characteristics*, but on the characteristics of the *situation* in which he or she finds him or herself. A person, therefore, may show better leadership in a hostile situation than in a group which is friendly and co-operative.

Peter Principle

There are people who arrive at a senior position through their abilities, but these abilities may *not* act to their advantage when they are there. This seems to reflect the approach taken by Lawrence J Peter in his book *The Peter Princi-*

ple . . . which states 'in a hierarchy, each employee tends to rise to his level of incompetence: Every post tends to be occupied by an employee incompetent to execute his duties.' He illustrates this by suggesting that usually competent workers became incompetent supervisors, and competent junior executives became incompetent senior executives. The fact is, that there *are* competent persons at the top of each hierarchy, but only because there are not enough ranks for them to have reached *their level of incompetence*. This idea has wide implications, particularly for management training, but must not be considered a universal statement applying to all organizations or persons.

Leadership training

Some abilities as a leader may take a person to the top but may not be to his or her advantage when he or she is there. From this approach there is a point of view which suggests that in a group almost *any* member may become a better leader if there are circumstances that enable him or her to perform the needed functions of leadership, and *different* persons may contribute in different ways to the leadership of the group. This implies that leadership is an 'organizational function' rather than a personal quality.

A fairly successful model of leadership training used on some management courses in the United Kingdom is by J Adair (*Effective Leadership*, 1983). The model is based upon three overlapping circles that form part of any leadership situation (*see* Fig 5.2). It is a functional leadership approach, which identifies functions of a leader in relation to the basic needs which are common in all leadership situations. Individual needs are distinguished from *group* needs and the needs of the *task* to be done. There will never really be a perfect match between the three elements and the job of the leader is to be aware of these aspects and manage each situation by giving suitable priority to the variables. Adair considers that the *skills of leadership can be recognized and developed* to be sufficiently sensitive to these leadership variables.

Training is organized around the eight elements of: defining objectives (tasks), planning, controlling, evaluating, motivating, organizing, briefing and setting an example. The idea of the model is to encourage a *flexible* approach to leadership and he considers leadership to be more in the adopting of *appropriate* behaviour than of personal traits.

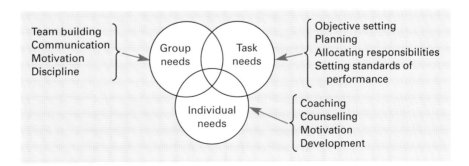

Fig 5.2 A functional leadership approach

Each situation is different and affects the priority given to each area of need. An effective leader will note these priorities and give certain needs preference in any situation.

This concept of leadership proposed by Adair is really a *contingency* approach whereby the leader's action is determined by the overall situation and therefore needs to be adaptive.

A final comment is that of the analysis by C B Handy in this book *Understanding Organizations* (1985, 3rd edition). He suggests a 'best-fit' approach to leadership and that a leader must take four sets of influencing factors into consideration in any situation.

- the leader – his preferred style of operating and his personal characteristics;
- the subordinates – their preferred style of leadership in the light of circumstances;
- the task – the job, its objectives and its technology.

All of the above factors and their 'fit' will depend upon:

- the environment – the organizational setting of the leader, his group and the importance of the task.

He emphasizes that 'there is no such thing as the "right" style of leadership, but that leadership will be most effective when the requirements of the leader, the subordinates and the task fit together'.

Systems approach

A *systems* approach to leadership would regard the leader, the follower and situation as inter-dependent units, all engaged in the production of desired outputs, and would consider – what are the relationships involved and to what extent are they aimed at mutual goals? Several key factors interact in a leadership-group situation and a modern approach is to consider that the leader and the group adjust their behaviour dynamically to each other.

It is not easy to summarize briefly the various approaches, but it appears that no one type of person, or set of personality characteristics, can be associated with successful leaders. Factors which were considered important were found by examining the *type of task* personality, whether the leader is elected or appointed, and any *special* competence of the leader.

The last few years have seen a great deal of uncertainty confronting managers in their role as leaders. Many factors which were usually considered fixed are now unpredictable.

Tom Peters in his book *Thriving on Chaos* (Pan Books, London, 1987) emphasized the necessity of re-appraising traditional ideas of managing. He advocated new forms of organization and new forms of evaluating management. Every process, procedure and relationship should be re-examined constantly to adapt to a constantly changing environment.

Companies which are among the fastest growing in the USA (3M and Pepsi Cola) keep their positions because they are constantly adapting and re-organizing. Constant change is consistent with the aim of pursuing perfection in quality and service. This concept is in direct contrast to traditional ideas of stable organization structures. The theme from these ideas is that leaders at every level must be obsessed with change and managers should accept that change is normal and not a cause for alarm.

CO-ORDINATION

Co-ordination and leadership are intimately bound, as each affects the other. One cannot achieve co-ordination without effective leadership: together they ensure that all efforts are channelled effectively towards the right goal.

Some authorities, e.g. Mooney and Reiley, regard co-ordination as the first principle of organization. Others – Koontz and O'Donnell – prefer to regard it as the *essence* of management and regard *each* of the managerial functions as an exercise in co-ordination.

No matter how a firm is organized, its functions must be effectively co-ordinated.

Definition

Co-ordination is the process whereby the effort of a group is synchronized so that the desired goal is obtained. Responsibility for co-ordination rests mainly with the board of directors and chief executive. The need for a common purpose or goal is imperative as, if there is more than one purpose in people's minds, co-ordination of effort is not possible.

As people cannot be compelled to co-operate, the right environment for the exchange of information is required. There are many conflicts which can arise between management and workers. These must be smoothed out and, if, to use Fayol's phrase, *esprit de corps* can be attained, problems can be more easily overcome. Often departmental interests and goals are regarded as ends in themselves, e.g. deliveries required to be made by the marketing department may be considered secondary to the production manager's production programme.

Problems

As concerns expand, many functions and activities have to be delegated to many people. In addition, larger concerns tend to have a greater number of specialists.

Co-ordination problems are essentially those of communication which will be dealt with at the end of this section. Difficulties lie in horrizontal and vertical communications and a big problem is that when the elements to be co-ordinated are *human* the variables emerging are numerous.

In many firms, *routine* questions are presented to a far higher authority than necessary for the decision. This is not co-ordination and may often be due to the desire of the individual to be noticed.

Ways of achieving co-ordination

In order to be successful, co-ordination must not be directed in an autocratic manner, but rather encouraged in a democratic manner, everyone participating in a unified way. It operates vertically as well as horizontally and should be effected at the most appropriate time. In addition to these points, Mary Parker Follett suggested three more factors of effective co-ordination:

- by *direct contact* between the persons immediately concerned;
- it must commence at the *earliest stages* of planning and policy-making;
- it must be a *continuous* process.

It is apparent that everyone is influenced by their colleagues and by the total environment; co-ordination will be easier to achieve if they understand each other's jobs and they will compromise more if information is exchanged. The ideal is for arrangements for *co-ordination* to be such that problems can be *anticipated* and therefore more easily prevented.

As previously stated, co-ordination exists horizontally and vertically, and it is essential for authority and responsibility to be *clearly delegated* so that department heads know the limits of permissible behaviour. It can be appreciated that as more functions are self-contained the number of organizational relationships will be reduced and less co-operation will be required.

If authority *overlaps*, co-ordination generally will be more difficult; but this may be permissible in some cases especially if the objectives of each department concerned were different.

Techniques

Committees aid co-ordination in that they:

- pool resources to solve problems;
- co-ordinate overlapping or conflicting functions;
- ensure prior consultation and lead to greater acceptance of decisions;
- enable executives to be trained.

Staff meetings are useful, particularly if they are informal. An agenda is preferable and these meetings should:

- give a sense of unity to the work of the organization;
- provide an opportunity for subordinates to question superiors and provide a forum for discussion;
- inform staff of new developments and problems.

Conferences. These are another method of making a group decision. They aid free discussion and help to improve understanding of company matters and this 'face to face' communication is an important factor in effective co-ordination.

Programmes are instruments of co-ordination, i.e. a timetable or a production programme enable results to be compared with standards and actions to be taken where necessary. These programmes register and communicate decisions, and hence allow them to be delegated.

Co-ordination outside industry

There are other areas in which co-ordination is achieved. In the government of the United Kingdom the Cabinet has various devices to aid co-ordination, e.g. the use of committees (*ad hoc* and standing) and the civil service hierarchy. Some departments are co-ordinating departments, e.g. the Treasury; the town clerk in local government acted as a co-ordinator between specialist departments and chief officers. Under the present system the numerous council activities are effectively co-ordinated by a professional manager who may have a greater effectiveness to co-ordinate successfully than the town clerk; he is called 'chief executive'.

MOTIVATION

A large part of a manager's task is getting things done through people; he must therefore try to understand people's motivation.

This aspect of the management element of direction is concerned with inducing people to work to the best of their ability. All aspects of motivation of employees cannot be provided by management as other influences occur *outside* the working environment, e.g. community and family pressures.

Motivation refers to the way urges, aspirations, drives and needs of human beings direct or control or explain their behaviour. It may simply be described as keenness for a particular pattern of behaviour.

Why people work

It is worthwhile taking a closer look at theories of motivation and one approach which is widely known by managers is clearly set out by Abraham H Maslow in his book *Motivation and Personality* (1970 edn, Harper & Row).

Maslow's theory of motivation claims that human motives develop in sequence according to five levels of need (Fig 5.3). This theory assumes needs

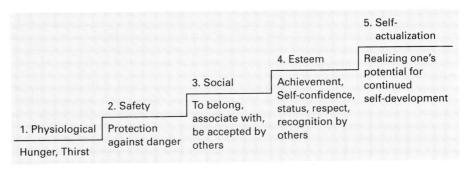

Fig 5.3 Hierarchy of needs

follow in sequence and when one need is satisfied it decreases in strength and the higher need then dominates behaviour. This leads to the statement that a satisfied need is not a motivator. There is a doubt whether this really applies in practice to the higher needs as it is likely that self-esteem requires *continual* stimulation and renewal.

Few attempts have been made to test the validity of Maslow's ideas. A big problem is that people do not necessarily satisfy higher-order needs through their *jobs* or occupations, and this cannot really be tested. Another point is that he viewed *satisfaction* as a major motivator and this is not *directly* related to production. He also does not mention the time period between various needs – does a person *immediately* turn to a higher need or is it after a few years?

In 1968 Hall and Nougaim studied a company in America and used four of Maslow's needs categories (2 to 5 above). The survey of 49 young managers in an organizational setting only provided modest support to his theory, but stressed the importance of environmental factors in the development of a person's needs towards the top of the hierarchy.

Hertzberg's theory of motivation

It was not until F V Hertzberg in his book *Work and the Nature of Man* (1968, Staples Press) presented his two-factor theory of motivation that differences between higher and lower needs were elaborated. Here again the outcomes related to satisfaction rather than productivity. He stated that factors which create satisfaction (satisfiers or motivators) are those stemming from the *intrinsic* content of a job (e.g. recognition and responsibility, meaning and challenge) – these satisfy higher needs; factors which create dissatisfaction (dissatisfiers or hygiene factors) stem from the *extrinsic* job context (e.g. working conditions, pay, supervision) – these satisfy lower needs. An important point in the theory is that as dissatisfaction stems from lower needs not being satisfied, when these are satisfied, this only *removes dissatisfaction*, and does not increase motivation. If hygiene factors did not reach a certain standard (e.g. salary, working conditions, job security, poor supervision) they felt *bad* about their jobs, and were unhappy. Positive motivation and a feeling of well-being could only be achieved, *not* by just improving these hygiene factors, but by improving *genuine motivators* such as recognition, achievement, responsibility, advancement and the work itself.

The theory has been critized by other researchers; one criticism is that Hertzberg omitted other behavioural criteria, such as performance, absenteeism and labour turnover; another is that he only concentrated upon satisfaction and dissatisfaction. Researchers since Hertzberg's studies have generally agreed that extrinsic and intrinsic factors do separately contribute to satisfaction.

Another approach recognizes that people will act *only* when they have a reasonable expectation that their actions will lead to desired goals. They will perform better if they believe that money will follow effective performance, so if money has a positive value for an individual, higher performance will follow. This is called *Expectancy Theory*, which places emphasis on performance noting that there must be a clearly recognized goal and relationship between performance and outcome. Motivation (M) is a function of the Expectancy (E) of attaining a certain outcome in performing a certain act multiplied by the Value (V) of the outcome for the performer.

$$M \propto E \times V$$

Outcomes that are highly valued and having higher expectations of being realized will direct a person to make a greater effort in his task. Outcomes with high expectations which are less highly valued (or even disliked) will reduce effort expended.

Other studies on expectations and job performance emphasize the greater importance of intrinsic motivation factors, e.g. Hackman and Porter (1968) and Lawler and Porter (1967), *Managerial Attitudes and Performance* (1968, Irwin). All of these studies show that money, if properly used and tied to performance, can help to increase *motivation* – whether or not or to what extent it increases *performance* can only be surmised.

In looking at the *job* of work, studies agreeing with Hertzberg indicate that to improve the job, it must be enlarged, that is, made more interesting, giving more responsibility and discretion for decision making. But Hulin and Blood (*Psychological Bulletin*, 1968) point to the mixed reaction to job enlargement. They find that many persons *prefer* working on routine jobs and wish to avoid responsibilities, and also that there are great differences between those who respond to job enlargement and those who do not. Workers who accept middle-class values (e.g. hard work and achievement) and come from small non-industrial areas are favourable to job enlargement, whereas those from large, urban, industrialized communities are alienated from middle-class work values and are not so favourable to job enlargement. (For further consideration of job enlargement see Human Resource Management, Chapter 9.)

It is not easy to summarize all the research evidence, but it appears that people desire a variety of outcomes, a *combination* of extrinsic and intrinsic. They will respond to a greater degree to jobs which optimize the outcomes, and will try and combine favourable characteristics of each. On balance, job behaviour and satisfaction depend more on the *content* of work than on the conditions surrounding it.

Rensis Likert: systems of management

The work of *Rensis Likert* was mentioned in the chapter on Organizing and one aspect of his book *New Patterns of Management* relates to motivation and the most effective way to lead a group. Likert considered four systems of management:

System 1 Exploitive–authoritative: managers make all work-related decisions and order subordinates to carry them out. Management do not trust employees and set rigid standards where failure means punishment. Subordinates fear management. Productivity tends to be poor.

System 2 Benevolent–authoritative: orders are still issued by management but subordinates can comment on the orders and have some flexibility to carry out their work. Rewards are available and both sides are cautious of the other. Production is satisfactory.

System 3 Consultative: goals are set and orders given after discussion with subordinates. Teamwork is encouraged and subordinates are generally trusted to carry out their work. Rewards rather than threats are used to motivate.

System 4 Participative: this is his most favoured style of management. Goals are set and work-related decisions are made by the group. There is full participation in reaching a decision which leads to commitment to the organization's goals. Managers motivate by economic reward and try to give subordinates feelings of importance and need. There is good communication with excellent productivity and low absenteeism and labour turnover.

There are some criticisms of System 4. They are generally based upon the fact that the research was done with *small* groups, so that results may not be the same for the *whole* organization. Also the System 4 approaches are often implemented in more profitable times and may not have such an effect if conditions were less economically favourable. In any case, managers should be careful when applying the principles and in particular take account of local circumstances.

Requirements of a good system of motivation

Some requirements of a good system are as follows:

- subordinates must be *induced to work* and produce more;
- a good system must be *comprehensive* in providing for the satisfaction of all needs;
- the system must be *flexible* in order to account for varying requirements of people who need different stimuli, e.g. some would work harder for more pay; others for status only;
- provision must be made for financial *opportunities* particularly those giving more personal freedom, e.g. shares in the company;
- *security* is a vital element. It means more than the promise of a job and a wage. A recent survey showed that if people knew the situation in their industry, i.e. where they stood in relation to the firm, and if more information were made available by managers, *morale* would be higher.

The confidence of workers must be won by management and one important factor is the right environment to create the right physiological climate, e.g. equitable arrangement of work flow, rest periods, heating, lighting and ventilating, etc.

Government regulations have helped in this respect (e.g. Factory and Offices, Shops and Railway Premises Acts), and have also, to a large extent, ensured that the primary needs are catered for (e.g. contracts of employment and redundancy payments). The working environment is now safer and a person's livelihood is safeguarded to some extent. People now are more interested in secondary needs (e.g. a worthwhile job, good conditions and promotion) and this may be seen in trade union negotiations.

The desire for social relationships is often a neglected consideration. The need of a job which gives a person a respected position in society and enables social relationships to develop is very important and must be recognized by managers.

Basic needs can be attained only if the job is secure; this coupled with a good level of wages is needed. Other needs, e.g. self-respect, group participation, can then be developed. In this context, job descriptions (reflecting status), e.g. rodent inspector not rat catcher, all have a part to play. Self-esteem is helped by letting subordinates participate in the work and decisions of the superior. Status can be shown by extra holidays, job title, method of payment (monthly or weekly) (*Note* – there is a trend towards staff status for manual workers), provision of a company car, parking and travel facilities.

MORALE AND DISCIPLINE

Morale

Morale can be a combination of many factors. A simple definition is that it is the state of a person's (or a group's) feelings and attitudes. In a more military sense, it is the *quality* that exists in a group of people, which arises from faith in their efficiency and discipline, and in the competent and fair way with which they are led. A rather broader meaning is given when it is used in business management – it is the collective attitude of workers towards each other, their work and management.

When morale is high, work is done willingly, and with less supervision; when it is low, work is of poor quality and problems arise, e.g. with a high labour turnover and absenteeism. When groups emerge in industry, each person must sacrifice some part of his individuality, as he in effect joins the group to serve the group purpose, thereby (impliedly or otherwise) *agreeing to obey* those who are in charge. Each group has a particular kind of acceptable behaviour, which is implanted in the member's thoughts, and this participation tends to give the members a feeling of superiority over non-group members. Craftsmen often adopt this attitude over non-craftsmen.

Team spirit

If a group can constantly work towards the common purpose, morale can be maintained. The purpose of the *group*, e.g. to win a race, or to produce an article, becomes accepted as the purpose of the *individual*. Individual interests, though, must be subordinated to the group interest and, if this can be done, morale will be high. If morale is good, team spirit should be good as this arises where all members of the group know every member is working to achieve the group goal and obeys internal authority. But, if some members are aware that others are more interested in *personal* success, morale will be low and team spirit will be low.

In industry, for example, the manufacturing department may not achieve its target because of lack of material, and the planning department may be blamed. Many similar cases occur daily, in business – morale may be high (as everyone is trying to achieve the desired goal), but team spirit may be low because people (rightly or wrongly) are aware that some members are not pulling their weight.

The remedy for lack of team spirit is to give staff better education and knowledge of the other person's or section's problems and to make them aware of the fundamental interrelations between departments.

Discipline

A basis for effective discipline is good motivation and sound, clearly-given instructions. It is essential for good communications to be used in order to let staff know what they are required to do.

Ideally, discipline should be based upon co-operation and a high morale, which will ensure rules and conditions are obeyed willingly. By virtue of his position, a superior has the right to command and enforce obedience, if necessary. This gives him the right to punish, because of the harm which may be done to the group's purpose.

Discipline can be obtained by rewards as well as by punishment, but usually punishment is expected if accepted norms of behaviour are not upheld.

Disciplinary action should contribute towards improved behaviour, but certain matters must be noted:

- behaviour expected must be *made known* and this is best done in the period of induction;
- discipline should be exercised *fairly*, with no favouritism or excessive penalties, and as *soon after* the breach as possible. (Some methods of disciplining are by reprimand, downgrading, suspension, refusing a wage increase, transfer or dismissal);
- management should *not break rules itself*. A good example is essential;
- the quality of discipline can vary with the type of leadership and the understanding of the common purpose of the organization.

COMMUNICATION

It has been said that management is concerned with the way jobs are done *through other people*. Communication therefore is the means whereby people in an organization exchange information regarding the operations of an enterprise. It is the interchange of ideas, facts, and emotions by two or more persons by the use of words, letters and symbols.

Every aspect of management requires good communication but it is particularly important in directing and will be treated in this section for convenience.

It is widely considered that the organizing element of management should concern itself with the system and environment within which communication functions. Management of the communications process requires not only attention to the media of communications, but to the *personal interrelationships of people in the organization*.

Chester Barnard stressed the need for communication to occupy a central place in organization theory 'because the structure, extensiveness and scope of organization are almost entirely determined by communication techniques'. Communication can be regarded as the foundation upon which organization and administration must be built. Barnard again stressed that 'the first executive function is to develop and maintain a system of communication'.

Communication is a process which links various parts of a system and problems of communication have been divided into three aspects:

1 **the technical problems** of how accurately the symbols can be transmitted;
2 **the semantic problem** of how precisely the symbols convey the desired meaning;
3 **the effectiveness problem** of how effectively the received meaning affects conduct in the desired way.

Cybernetics (*see* p 18) has helped to answer problems in group 1 above. Information, in *information theory*, is the quantitative measure of the amount of order in a system. If the properties of a system are known, the maximum rate at which a communication system can transmit information can be calculated. The more probable a message is, the less information it gives and the more uncertain a situation is, then the more information is needed to describe it completely. (See Shannon and Weaver, *The Mathematical Theory of Communication*; 1949, University of Illinois Press.)

As far as group 2 above is concerned – that is the meaning a message has to the receiver – a person may *say* one thing but may hear something different, even though the same words were sent and received. A manager must try and check whether the *meaning* of the communication has been understood.

In group 3 above, it is usually found that the more *direct* the communication, the more effective it is. The more levels of the organization it passes through affects the action that is eventually taken. So the problem is really to consider how the receiver actually *accepts* the communication. It depends upon his needs, past experience, the complexity of phrases used, the distinction between facts and opinions and the environment in which the communication takes place.

Formal communications are planned to meet the specific requirements of an organization, but informal communications are very important. One informal channel is the 'grapevine', where rumour passes quickly around. It is not an accurate method, but can be used to the advantage of management at times. It can be considered to serve the social needs of individuals in the organization.

Another approach is to view communications as a pattern of interconnecting lines or *networks*. Examples are as shown in Fig 5.4.

Problems and barriers to effective communication

The following cover most of the elements in a faulty system of communication:

- lack of sound *objectives*, words which are vague, imprecise, omitting necessary information;
- faulty *organization*, such as lack of definition of responsibilities, too long chains of command and too wide spans of control;
- too many *assumptions* made by a receiver, who may be too quick in evaluating the meaning because of his inability to listen carefully;
- *use of technical jargon*, particularly in new specialist fields, e.g. computers. In addition, the *different* educational and social *backgrounds* of recipients do not aid effective understanding;
- *the atmosphere* or environment may not be normal, and innocent remarks may be given wrong interpretations;

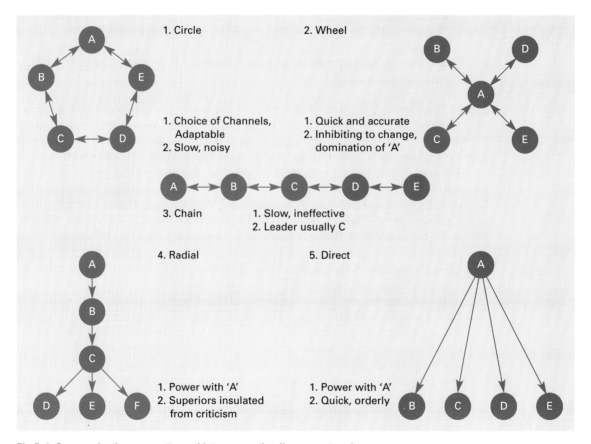

Fig 5.4 Communication as a pattern of interconnecting lines or networks

- failure by subordinates to *judge accurately* what should be in *reports* to superiors or failure to communicate at all;
- if every *instruction* is not *written* down, people may use this absence of any written instruction and do nothing, using it as an excuse for not using their initiative;
- *lack of informal or formal opportunities* is a barrier to upward communication, and feelings are not made known. Management has more ways to communicate than workers, who often have only their union, which generally confines its activities to wages and grievances.

NB: Appraisal and development interviews are a good means of two-way communication. (*See* Human Resource Management, Chapter 9.)

Barriers to communication can be classified in another way:

- **transmission** problems, distorted messages because of imprecise or inadequate words due to narrow interpretation of specialists. Remedy is to widen understanding of managers (e.g. by job rotation);

- **filtering** or sifting data so only parts are transmitted to a superior. Good relationships with subordinates, encouragement for them to report problems and a more efficient control system all help to overcome this;
- **irrelevant data** tend to block communication systems. Too much data, too long reports, slow the actions of managers. The remedy is to ensure efficient passing of only relevant, good quality data, by careful sifting.

Communications are aided by good morale. Other points which help are to try to ensure the goals of individuals and the company are similar, and to recognize the benefit to the company of the work of the employees. One of the best ways of removing conflict is by good communications. For example, a change to a computer system from a manual one should be explained clearly to employees, well before the implementation. If this is delayed and rumours go round, the issue may be distorted. Good communications can help to minimize conflicts and prevent unnecessary misunderstandings.

Principles of communication

The following points should be considered carefully:

1 Clarity. The language used should be clear and concise, the user should bear in mind the objectives of the communication.
2 Attention should be paid by the recipient of the communication – lack of careful attention is a human failing.
3 Integrity and sincerity. The more workers are told of the company and its future, the more they will respect the integrity of management and morale will be raised and harmony of working encouraged. Any changes should be carefully explained at an early stage. Communications should wherever possible also be sent down the accepted line of authority, because if people are by-passed they lose status and resent the action.
4 Choice of media. It is important to choose the most appropriate media:

- *face to face* – for interviews, meetings and conferences;
- *oral* – telephone, radio, inter-communicating systems;
- *written* – letters, books, periodicals, circulars, manuals, newspapers, advertisements, suggestion schemes.

Correct timing is also essential and the use of the right language is vital. In this connection the use of financial terms is helpful as they form a type of common denominator.

In his book, *Changing Culture of a Factory*, Elliott Jacques considered that the effectiveness of communication does not depend alone upon the executive's skill with language, but rather on:

- a known and comprehensive *communication structure*;
- a *code*, governing relations among people occupying various roles;
- a *quality of relationship* among people immediately connected with each other.

As stated before, in downward communication, management has access to numerous methods; there are fewer methods for upward communication. Horizontal communication among specialized departments is essential, but can cause difficulty as barriers are set up. Strictly, communication should be via the line of authority, but use of Fayol's bridge theory is time-saving and more accurate than using the chain of command. But, there must be an understanding that these relationships are encouraged by superiors, that subordinates refrain from making any policy commitments beyond their authority and that they keep their superiors fully informed of all these interdepartmental activities.

Written communications are more accurate and more carefully formulated and are used for legal records, minutes, contracts, etc. But they may be poorly phrased and are expensive.

Oral communications are quick and allow questions to be asked if incorrectly understood. Some are a waste of time, e.g. some conferences, and are not suited to lengthy communications. *Note* also that oral transmission is decreasingly accurate; it has been calculated that at the most only 50 per cent of information is retained.

Accurate information is essential and organizations should have access to a good abstracting service, e.g. Anbar. The need for a good library service should be considered.

Good techniques are not enough, because communication is a co-operative, or two-way process; the attitude of the recipient and his skill in listening and ability are as important as the skill, clarity and accuracy of the manager's words.

Reports

There are numerous types of reports. These can be from executives to their seniors, from committees to their appointing bodies, from directors to shareholders.

The function of a report is to present facts and perhaps make a recommendation. The object is to give the person to whom it is presented, sufficient information to enable him to take suitable action, if necessary. Facts must be stated fairly and accurately, be set out in logical order and in a concise manner. Sufficient detail must be given and this may be presented in an attached schedule; what must be avoided is obscuring the main facts by too much detail. Those reports that require a recommendation, as in some organization and methods reports, should show the reasoning leading up to the recommendation. The terms of reference for a report must of course be observed.

One type of report is in a similar form to a business letter. It is addressed to the person asking for the report (e.g. the board of directors). The salutation may be, 'Gentlemen', and end 'yours faithfully' and be signed; the report should be in the first person.

Other reports may not be addressed to a specific person; these may be written impersonally, as in the case of a committee report, e.g. 'the committee found'.

The salutation and end must not be shown. This is sent with a covering letter to the person requiring the report. This is appropriate where these reports are submitted to a higher authority.

A report consists of the following stages:

1 Collection of data.
2 Collection of particulars.
3 Writing the report.

As far as writing the report is concerned, the custom of the body concerned must be followed, otherwise, the following are good rules.

- The title should be clear and brief.
- The opening paragraph should state any terms of reference.
- Some reports, e.g. an organization and methods report, may give a summary of any recommendations at the beginning.
- The body of the report should be set out in clear numbered paragraphs and side headings may be shown.
- Recommendations, if required, may be given at the end of each section, or at the end.
- The report must be signed and dated.
- Appendices, references and an index may be required.

A company report takes the form of the annual report to be submitted with the accounts; it is usually signed by the chairman of the board. The Stock Exchange has asked quoted companies to prepare interim reports on their progress. The report must include information as to the state of the company's affairs, the amount, if any, which the directors recommend should be paid by way of dividend, and the amount, if any, which they propose to carry to reserve.

The report and accounts may be the only information shareholders receive as to the company's activities and results; therefore, careful attention is needed to ensure the presentation of facts so that the average reader can understand. Statements of accounts should be easy to read and may be illustrated by showing a breakdown of information detailed in the accounts, e.g. though bar charts or 'pie' diagrams.

Finally, a periodic review of all reports is needed in order to see whether they are still required, or whether they have to be modified, continued or scrapped. This is similar to forms control and can effectively be done at the same time.

Communications audit

This term has been used for a number of years to mean a systematic approach to check procedures, policies, networks and all aspects of communication in an organization. The approach is that communication is examined in a methodical way to see to what extent it is achieving the goals of the organization. The audit may include, interviews, questionnaires, and an analysis of documents.

A communications system links the managerial functions of planning, organizing, directing and controlling and it also links the enterprise to the external environment.

SUMMARY

Objective 1 *Explain why an understanding of leadership is important, and how a manager's underlying assumptions about human behaviour will influence his behaviour as a leader.*

An understanding of leadership is important for various reasons:

- leadership binds a working group together and assists employee motivation, enabling an enterprise to perform successfully;
- good leadership sets the tone of an enterprise's culture and creates a climate in which personal growth is encouraged;
- an understanding of theories of leadership can assist managers in developing their leadership skills;
- if managers assume their subordinates are lazy, uncooperative and need to be controlled, they will treat them accordingly (Theory X). But if they assume subordinates are hard-working, friendly and cooperative they will treat them quite differently (Theory Y).

Objective 2 *Explain the importance of communication and identify some barriers to communication.*

Communication is important for a number of reasons:

- the success of enterprises depends upon it in formulating and implementing plans and achieving enterprise objectives;
- it forms the basis of successfully introducing change;
- an understanding of the process and barriers to communication should lead to more effective management;
- it is a vital element in external enterprise relations.

Explanations of barriers to communication are:

- problems of transmission – where messages become distorted because of imprecise or inadequate wording due to incorrect interpretation;
- problems in filtering or sifting data so that only parts are transmitted to a superior;
- irrelevant data blocks communication systems.

Objective 3 *Explain the various ways motivation plays a role in most enterprises.*

People must be attracted or motivated (a) to join an enterprise and remain with it, (b) to exert sufficient energy and effort at an acceptable rate, and (c) to maintain and develop the human resources of the enterprise.

For managers to motivate subordinates, they must create a working environment in which their employees can understand how the achievement of organizational goals will simultaneously satisfy a range of their own personal needs.

Objective 4 *Explain why co-ordination of the activities and objectives of an organization is necessary and the co-ordinating mechanisms that managers can use.*

Co-ordination enables the activities and objectives of all sections of an organization to be integrated harmoniously so that the goals of the organization can be efficiently achieved.

There are a number of co-ordinating mechanisms that can be used:

- the managerial hierarchy allows managers to exercise their authority, establish procedures and resolve disagreements to ensure efficient operation of an enterprise;
- interdepartmental communication allows managers from different sections to integrate activities;
- organizational committees provide formal occasions where staff can meet and make joint decisions;
- another aid to communication is people with interdepartmental liaison responsibilities, such as project managers.

Objective 5 *Describe the contributions of the various theorists on motivation and state how their work is related to motivation in organizations.*

Motivation is a complex area of study and there are many competing theories, all of which have their critics, or have been subject to alternative findings. It is evident that there are many motives which influence people's behaviour at work. The work of the theorists directs attention to the problem of how staff can be motivated to work willingly and effectively and provide a basis for study and discussion and to consider the best motivational style to be applied in particular work situations.

Content theories stress the importance of individual needs or drives as motives for the action of individuals. Such theories include Maslow's hierarchy of needs model, and Hertzberg's two factor theory.

Process theories emphasize how and by what goals individuals are motivated; they place emphasis on the actual process of motivation and the relationships among the variables which make up motivation. One approach under this category is the expectancy-based model of Lawler and Porter.

REVIEW QUESTIONS

1 What are the main duties of the board of directors?

2 Consider the types of leaders and the qualities a leader should have.

3 Define co-ordination, and consider the ways in which it may be achieved.

4 What are the requirements of a good system of motivation?

5 'Discipline should be based upon co-operation and high morale.' Discuss.

6 Consider the methods and media used in communication.

7 What is meant by 'leadership style'?

8 Consider the various theories on leadership.

9 Is the hierarchy of needs exactly the same for all employees within one organization?

10 What light does Maslow throw on the significance of (a) promotion policies (b) status symbols (c) job enrichment?

11 'Wherever possible discipline within an organization should be imposed quietly and impersonally.' Discuss.

1 Motivation of subordinates is an important aspect of a manager's job.

   (a) What do you think motivates a person to work well?

   (b) What steps can a manager take to motivate his subordinates?

2 Explain whether or not you would expect the work motivation of salaried staff in an organization to differ from that of wage-earning 'shop-floor' workers.

3 What are the functions and responsibilities of a company director? State the particular contributions the board should expect from a non-executive director. What action may a director take if he is dissatisfied with:

   (a) the policy, and

   (b) the performance of this company?

4 'There is little or no evidence to support the hypothesis that man has needs or that these needs are arranged in a hierarchy.' Evaluate this view, and discuss its implications for an analysis of the behaviour of people at work.

5 Discuss, in depth, the composition of *boards of directors*. Cover the following points in your study:

   (a) The number of directors on the boards of companies of different sizes, histories and trades.

   (b) The frequency with which directors are appointed.

   (c) The considerations to be weighed in making each appointment to the board, and the relative importance of each.

   (d) The proportions on different boards as between executive and non-executive directors.

   (e) The extent of the shareholdings of the directors.

   (f) The number of directorships held by individual directors.

6 You are the manager of a department where morale is high and the work is well done. However, you have a young section-leader who, although technically brilliant, seems to constantly irritate people and 'get their backs up' . What action would you take to improve the situation?

7 Chester Barnard said: 'the first executive function is to develop and maintain a system of *communications*'. Discuss this view, dealing in particular with:

   (a) The common sins of communication.

   (b) The guiding principles for a manager wishing to improve his communication skills.

   (c) The nature of communication in a business environment.

8 Set out in detail the role of chairman of the board of directors.

ASSIGNMENTS

1 Exercise in communication. Take a current issue which is contentious and try to convince someone with opposite views to yourself of the merits of your point of view.

Use a variety of communications media to illustrate your case. This exercise can be operated on a 'one-to-one' student basis or in small groups.

2 Discuss in small groups the idea of the 'Peter Principle'. Do you think it could ever apply to you? Does it imply that all chief executives are incompetent?

BIBLIOGRAPHY

Brown, J A C, *Social Psychology of Industry* (Business Library, Harmondsworth, Penguin, 1974).

Drucker, P F, *The Practice of Management* (London, Pan, 1968), Chapters 21–23.

Hertzberg, F, *Work and the Nature of Man* (London, Crosby Lockwood, 1961).

Jefkins, F, *Public Relations* (London, Heinemann, 1988).

Kendall, N and Sheridan, T, *Corporate Governance* (London, Financial Times/Pitman Publishing, 1992).

Likert, R, *New Patterns of Management* (New York, McGraw-Hill, 1961).

Locke, M, *How to Run Committees and Meetings* (London, Macmillan, 1980).

Peters, T, *Thriving on Chaos* (London, Pan, 1987)

Simon, H A, *Administrative Behavior* (Free Press, US, 3rd edition, 1976).

Tannenbaum, R and Schmidt, W, *How to Choose a Leadership Pattern* (Harvard Business Review, 1973).

CHAPTER 6

Controlling

Controlling is an important function of management and has as its aim the measurement of performance against standards so that corrective action can be taken to keep plans on course. This chapter considers principles of effective control, budgetary and non-budgetary, and examines advanced control techniques. Financial accounting conventions are considered as they form the basis of information which enables management to make decisions.

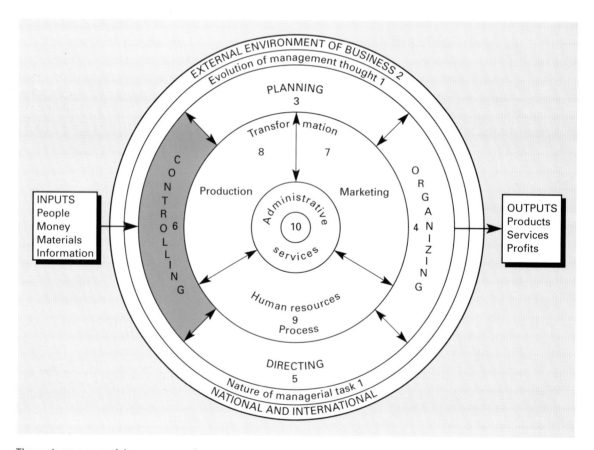

The systems approach to management

OBJECTIVES

Upon completing this chapter you should be able to:

- Explain the steps in the control process and why control is necessary.
- Summarize the issues managers have to deal with in designing a control system and the principles of effective control.
- Describe the budgeting process and identify the various types of budgets an organization can use.
- Describe various types of financial control methods and why they are used by managers.
- Describe the main types of auditing methods.

Controlling is an element of managerial tasks and involves the measurement and correction of the performance of subordinates to make sure that the objectives of the enterprise and the plans devised to attain them are accomplished efficiently and economically. Controlling involves:

- setting standards;
- measuring performance against standards;
- feedback of results;
- correcting deviations from standards.

Figure 6.1 shows the planning–control feedback cycle and the connection between planning, with its determination of instructions to be used as directives for activity, and standards for comparison. Control comes from the comparison with standards showing the need for corrective action, and analysis of deviations so future plans can be readjusted. There are many types of control,

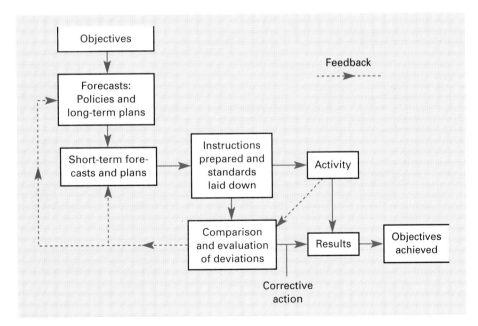

Fig 6.1 Planning–control feedback cycle

for example, control of quality of products, morale, etc. There must be, in all cases, clear and unambiguous plans to enable managers to carry them out efficiently and effectively.

Standards are an expression of planning goals and may be of many kinds, e.g. physical (numbers produced) or monetary. Some goals cannot easily be expressed in quantitative form, e.g. morale of a group, and may be measured only in a qualitative manner.

The more jobs move away from the assembly line, the more difficult, and the more important, becomes the control of them.

Planning and controlling are closely related and both are equally important, as objectives and plans are needed in order that control is possible. Every manager at all levels is responsible for the exercise of control which is an essential function of management.

There have been criticisms of the use of feedback from the output of a system being used as a means of control. Such data is *historical and out of date* and too late to allow for corrective action. The more effective systems use the most up-to-date information for forecasting and so programmes can be changed quickly; even this could result in action being taken too late.

The ideal answer would seem to be to devise a system that can tell management the problems that *will occur* if action is not taken now. This idea of *future-directed control,* or *feed-forward control* systems, is that they *monitor inputs* into a process to see if they are as planned. So if they are not as planned, either the inputs or the process can be changed to enable the desired results to be obtained. An illustration often used is that of a driver of a car aiming to maintain a constant speed, who depresses the accelerator before going up a hill. This is *before* he is warned by the speedometer of a drop in speed.

Management, therefore, should decide on those input variables that *materially influence key inputs.*

PRINCIPLES OF EFFECTIVE CONTROL

To maintain effective control, certain principles must be adhered to:

1 **Controls must be set according to the nature of the job to be performed.** Small firms need different systems of control from large firms. It is important to note that although the same techniques are universally used, e.g. budgets, break-even charts, financial ratios and standard costs, one must never assume any of the techniques can be used in a given situation.
2 **Deviations should be reported immediately.** In an 'ideal' situation, notification is made before deviations occur. In practice, such information is usually supplied too late to be of immediate use, and can be used only for future planning. Electronic accounting machines have speeded up data processing; this will mean more recent data will be available.
3 **Controls must conform to the pattern of the organization.** If the organization pattern is clear and responsibility for work done is well defined, control becomes more effective and it is simpler to isolate persons responsible for deviations. It should be noted here that the correct choice of cost control centres is vital.

4 **Controls should show exceptions at selected points.** The 'exception' principle, whereby only exceptions to the standard are notified, should be adopted. Note must be taken of the varying nature of exceptions, as small exceptions in certain areas may be of greater significance than larger exceptions elsewhere.

5 **Controls should be flexible and economical in operation.** A system should be sufficiently flexible to allow or provide for alternative remedies where failures occur. (*See* p 220, flexible budget.) A system of control should not cost more than it is worth. For example, a complete system of standard costing may be installed, where in fact a simpler system would have been cheaper and more suitable.

6 **Controls should be simple to understand and should indicate corrective action.**

Presentation of control information in a way management can understand is vital. Some controls, e.g. of a mathematical nature, such as complex breakeven charts, are not understood by many managers. In this connection, management training schemes are important, to familiarize management with these techniques. If deviations are detected, this is not very useful in itself. It is essential that the results point the way to causes, e.g. *where* the failures are occurring, *who is* responsible for them, and *what* shall be done about them.

TYPES OF CONTROL

Budgets

Budgeting is the word given to the formulation of plans for a given future period, expressed in quantitative terms. Budgets can be stated in financial terms, e.g. capital and revenue expenditure budgets, or in non-financial terms, e.g. units of production.

Purpose of budgeting

Taking the structure of the organization into consideration, one then breaks down the numerical statements of plans into constituent parts; this enables the budgets to correlate planning and allows authority to be delegated without loss of control.

Plans reduced to specific figures show where money is going or where physical input and output have taken place. With this knowledge, a manager can delegate authority more easily in order to make plans effective, within the budget limits.

Methods of budgeting

In order to locate responsibility it is necessary to divide a business into areas which coincide with functional responsibility. Examples of normal divisions are: production or manufacturing, selling and distribution, administration, research and development. In addition to functional budgets there must be departmental budgets. The areas selected here should comply with the normal responsibilities of supervisors and are known as budget or cost centres. Department budgets are an integral part of the functional budget. All the functional budgets are then co-ordinated in a master budget.

Co-ordination is essential, and means viewing the system as a whole and harmoniously fitting the various budgets together so that all restraining factors are noted and the policy of the company is followed. A restraining or key factor, for example, may be the fact that finance is in short supply.

The budgets are also used as checks on the actual results of a business. Deviations from predetermined plans are seen by comparing actual and budgeted performances and costs. The subsequent analysis of the differences or variances and the action taken are a vital part of the control mechanism.

An integral part of the budgetary control is the recognition that performances and costs can be traced to the people concerned, e.g. manager or foreman. In variance analysis an attempt is made to isolate any controllable variances from the budgeted costs; they are controllable if they can be traced to a person or group and if they are influenced by factors internal to the organization.

A system of budgetary control enables members of the management team to work together according to a clearly-defined financial policy and to authorize specific expenditure to executives. Requirements more than the budget would necessitate special authority and would have to be carefully examined. In this way control can be centralized and responsibility and authority delegated.

Where budgeted and actual figures agree, no action is normally required. Only exceptions are reported, thus enabling corrective action to be taken.

The procedures to be followed in designing and operating a budgetary control system vary from business to business, but a brief summary of the usual forecasts which would be made is as follows:

- sales;
- production;
- stocks;
- costs – broken down into production, administration, selling and distribution;
- capital expenditure, including research and development;
- cash;
- credit – debtors and creditors;
- purchasing;
- master forecast, incorporating forecast of profit and loss and balance sheet.

In building up the master budget, alternative combinations of forecasts are considered and note of the restraining factors is taken. These forecasts are possible plans and when they are co-ordinated in the master plan, they become budgets.

The period covered by a budget can vary from months to many years. Obviously the longer the period, the less reliable will be the figures in the budget.

Budgetary control

Standards of performance need to be set to act as guidelines in order to reach successfully the budget plan. The annual plan is divided into shorter periods, months or weeks, for control purposes. For each period, the budget is compared with the actual and reasons for any deviations are noted. Any corrective action needed is thereby taken. The aim of monitoring *shorter period plans* is to see what steps must be taken so that long-term objectives are still possible. Similarly, budgetary control is geared towards the achievement of the long-range plan.

Budgetary control concerns itself with the total costs for each department. If the plan is to be fulfiled, the responsibility for doing this must be assigned to persons responsible, e.g. supervisors and managers of sections. Each manager must feel that the budget for his section is realistic and relevant, and not imposed upon him from above (*see* p 199 on behavioural aspects).

Figure 6.2 shows a diagram of the budgetary control procedure.

Managerial use of budget information

There is nothing too difficult technically in the preparation of a budget. Overall budgets are built up from budgets for centres of individual responsibility which depend upon the structure of an organization.

There is much evidence of the *incorporation of bias into budget estimates* (e.g. Lowe and Shaw, 1968) by managers and this means that the aggregation of estimates may mean inaccurate forecasts. If this is the case, there is a danger in using them in other decision-making processes, e.g. evaluating capital investment proposals or pricing policy.

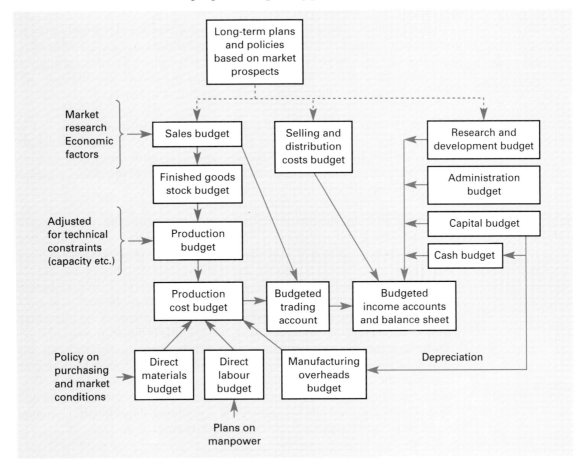

Fig 6.2 Budgetary control procedure

One role of a budget is to set a motivational target for a manager and there is more likelihood of the desired motivational effect occurring if the manager *accepts* the target. This is more likely to be achieved by allowing a manager to participate in the budget-setting process.

It is important to note that participation is not a universal panacea. Research has shown that participation has a *positive* motivational effect only with managers who feel confident of their ability to *cope with and control* the various factors that can influence their performance. If they lack this confidence, participation may only increase their feelings of stress and tension due to uncertainty.

Budgets are also used as standards to evaluate the performance of managers. The *rewards given* (salary, enhanced promotion etc.) for achieving performance standards (and enhanced status) are major motivational factors.

Standard costing

This is a method of predetermining the cost of each product, by breaking down the product into each element of cost, i.e. labour, material and overheads. These costs are the standard costs representing what they *should be* under stated conditions and volume of output. The use of a flexible budget allows standard costs to be set for different levels of output.

As the work proceeds, actual costs are compared with the standard and the variances (if any) are analysed.

Under suitable conditions, budgetary control and standard costs may be used in conjunction with one another. Planning and control can be more effective if this can be done; one helps to strengthen the other. The *detailed* analysis and control provided by standard costing and the *overall* co-ordination and control of budgetary control can be most effective, if wisely used.

Variable or flexible budgets

These are designed to vary usually with sales or production volume and so are largely limited in application to expense budgets. Expense items are analysed to see how individual costs *should* vary with volume of output. Alternative budgets may be prepared for varying levels of operation, e.g. high or low, each department being told which budget to use.

Points to consider on budgeting

1 *Too much detail* in budgetary control renders it meaningless and is expensive. Too rigid and too detailed control may mean the cost of budgeting exceeds the cost controlled. Some flexibility of action must be given to managers.
2 Budgets may hide *inefficiencies.* If an expense is allowed in one budget, it may always be provided for in the future, whether it is essential or not. As budget requests are usually scaled down, managers often ask for more than they need. A constant re-examination of standards is therefore needed.
3 Budgetary controls must not supersede company goals. Department goals may take precedence, as the department budget limits appear very important, but they must not override the main objectives of the company, e.g. sales department should not be refused information because the cost of getting it would exceed the budget of the accounting department. Common sense must not be replaced by strict budgetary rules.

4 Too much dependence may be placed upon the budget by management; the scope and limitations must be noted.

5 *Inflexibility* is a danger, as numerical terms appear very definite. Sometimes certain expenses must be incurred, in excess of the budget, in order to increase profits.

Marginal or direct costing

This is a recognition by accountants of basic economic principles – that is, many costs vary in whole, or in part, with volume of output.

A marginal cost is the amount by which aggregate costs are changed if the volume of output is increased or decreased by one unit. It includes direct wages, materials, expenses and variable overheads. Fixed costs are disregarded when considering product cost; these are met by the difference between sales revenue and marginal costs, which difference is called the 'contribution'.

A problem is that some costs are semi-variable and the ascertainment of the fixed and variable elements is not usually easy. The marginal cost approach can help price-fixing, but the difficulty lies in knowing if the estimated changes in revenue expected from a course of action are correct.

Planning, programming and budgeting systems (PPBS)

This is a system which analyses and classifies expenditure according to the policy ends the expenditure is to achieve. Government and public authorities do not find it as easy to formulate such precise objectives as industrial and commercial organizations. The output of various government activities is not easily measured or evaluated as no market is involved. Choices have to be made in planning public expenditure and allocating money among various parts of the public sector. The purpose of PPBS is to provide an improved framework of information analysis to enable decisions to be reached about the allocation of resources and establishing just what a department is trying to achieve.

A sequence of stages begins with:

1 Identification of *strategic problems.*
2 The definition of *objectives* (e.g. the *reason* for services for the aged).
3 Each major objective is broken down into groups of activities or *programmes,* which are identified as closely as possible with policy objectives. Proposed, as well as current, activities are to be shown and they should not be constrained by departmental boundaries. An analysis of the programme may involve calculation of financial costs and revenues and possible cost-benefit analysis. These are aids to decision taking.
4 A budget so formed is called a *programme budget* and may be prepared for a few years ahead. Benefits expected are shown and expenditure on different policy objectives can be compared.
5 The programme plan provides a guide to check against actual performance by *periodical reviews* (usually annual reviews).

PPBS strengthens decision making by:

● Emphasizing *outputs* of programmes rather than inputs and helps to encourage consideration of effective performances.

- As programmes are grouped together to achieve an objective, relationships between departments and also between the authority and outside bodies are highlighted.
- The full cost implications of current and past policy decisions are known and information obtained helps to re-define objectives.

This emphasizes the need for an inter-departmental approach to planning, programming and budgeting.

Non-budgetary controls

There are many devices for control which are not directly connected with budgets. Brief consideration will be given to ratio analysis, break-even charts and statistical data and reports, and use of audit, in a wider sense than accountants generally use.

Ratio analysis

This term is used to describe significant relationships which exist between various figures shown in the accounts. Ratio analyses can serve many purposes:

- they provide a means of showing interrelationships between groups of figures and can be used as a measure of efficiency;
- they enable a large volume of data to be conveniently summarized;
- they can be used in forecasting and planning;
- they can serve as an aid to communication, as people can more easily see changes in a business;
- they can be used to assess solvency, overtrading and profitability.

Ratios must be carefully compiled, presented quickly, bearing in mind the department head who is to receive them, e.g. sales managers will not usually be interested in ratios other than those relating to sales.

Many ratios can be used, and a single ratio by itself may often mislead. Another point is that one cannot assume that standard ratios can be established for all types of business.

There are three main categories of ratios:

- *financial,* or balance sheet, ratios, showing the relationship between items in the balance sheet, e.g. liquid ratio, current and stock ratios;
- *operating* ratios, derived from the profit and loss account (e.g. turnover and expense ratios);
- *interrelated* ratios show relationship between the financial and operating ratios, e.g. capital or earnings ratios.

A full description of *all* possible ratios is outside the scope of this book, but the following ratios are in common use.

1 **Return on capital employed (or primary ratio).** This compares net profit with assets employed and is a reflection of the overall efficiency of the business. 'Capital employed' can have different meanings, but is generally taken to mean the fixed assets and working capital of the unit. Care must

be taken in comparisons to note changes in money values over time. A low return may indicate capital is under-employed or that capital is fully, but inefficiently, employed.

2 **Liquid (or quick) ratio.** This ratio is calculated by dividing liquid assets by current liabilities. *Liquid* assets comprise cash in hand and debts realizable easily; current liabilities are amounts due for payment in the near future. This ratio should be at least 1:1 in most cases.

3 **Current ratio.** This ratio is often called 2 to 1 ratio. It is calculated by dividing current assets by current liabilities. This shows how much working capital is available. As stated above, the ratio should usually be 2:1, but again this depends upon the nature of the firm (e.g. seasonal trades will have a great variation in liquid resources).

4 **Sales ratios.**
- Sales/Debtors – showing the rate cash is received from credit sales, e.g. if payment is made monthly, ratio would be 12:1.
- Sales/Fixed Assets – showing efficiency achieved in using fixed assets.
- Sales/Working Capital – showing efficiency achieved in using working capital.

5 **Stock ratios.** These may help to indicate efficiency of stock control. Stock problems vary from company to company, e.g. some firms have little work in progress, and in job production there should be no stock of finished goods. Ratios can be only a guide in controlling stocks and some useful guides are:
- Raw Material/Total Sales Turnover – shows stockholding in relation to amount sold.
- Work in Progress/Total Turnover – shows stockholding in relation to amount sold.
- Raw Material/Purchases – shows number of times stock is 'turned over'. The average stock of raw material is divided into total purchases for the year.

6 **Cost ratios.** There are many cost or expense ratios. They must therefore be used intelligently and are a useful tool with which to measure relative efficiency. They show the trend of costs in relation to important factors, e.g. sales. Some cost/sales ratios are:
- factory cost/sales;
- administration cost/sales;
- selling cost/sales;
- distribution cost/sales;
- research and development cost/sales.

7 **Other ratios.** Ratios need not be limited to financial figures as above. Physical quantities may be the basis for calculations. These are used often in standard costing (e.g. Standard Hours of Actual Output divided by Standard Hours for Budgeted Output × 100 – this is Activity Ratio). Many others are used.

Published accounts now show some of these ratios in the annual report and this trend will surely increase. Trends can more easily be seen and company progress observed over periods of years by using ratios wisely.

8 **The Centre for Inter-firm Comparison (CIC).** The CIC is a body established in 1959 to which many organizations contribute financial data, in confidence. The centre prepares a brief report which is sent to the contributing organizations showing data indicating the average, for the type of industry, and the range of performance of contributors. The information enables management to determine the efficiency of the organization as compared with other, similar businesses. An attempt is made to show *why* results vary between organizations in similar categories. Great use is made of financial or cost ratios. The Centre:

- carries out research to enable the best methods of comparison to be made available;
- offers specialist advice to organizations and trade associations;
- arranges seminars on the use of ratios and inter-organization comparison.

Management can draw conclusions from the figures which may enable it to see the areas where efficiency could be raised. Comparability between organizations is not easy to obtain as those contributing may not prepare their returns in the same way. It is therefore important to define carefully what items are to be included, in what categories and particularly ways of valuing and depreciating assets. Some organizations are reluctant to give information in case competitors may use it against them.

The CIC recognizes that too many ratios become confusing, as all ratios do not suit all trades and industries, and therefore a selection of relevant ratios is taken.

The use of a 'pyramid' structure, showing the ratios in order of importance, is in current use; the most important – the return on capital – being at the apex of the pyramid and the detailed breakdown of how this is determined being shown underneath.

Break-even point analysis

The chart in Fig 6.3 shows the relationship of sales and expenses in such a way as to show at what volume revenues exactly cover expenses.

It can be seen that, at a lower volume, a loss would occur and, at a higher volume, a profit.

Break-even analysis is an extension of marginal costing (briefly mentioned on p 221).

The break-even point coincides with the volume of output at which neither profit nor loss appears.

Problems which may be solved by break-even analysis

- The determination of the price which gives the desired break-even point and profit.
- The volume of sales needed to cover return on capital employed, dividends and reserves.
- The calculation of costs and revenues for all possible volumes of output and the calculation of variable cost per unit.

Criticisms of chart

- As costs do not vary directly in proportion to output, the total cost line should not be shown as a straight line (i.e. linear relationship). The same variable cost cannot be attributed to *each* unit sold.

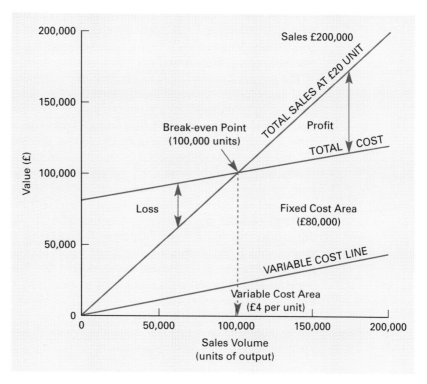

Fig 6.3 A break-even chart

- The sales-revenue line may similarly be incorrect.
- Each *product* should preferably have its own break-even chart.
- The chart usually depicts *past* results, i.e. it is static.

If these criticisms are borne in mind, the chart and the many variations are very useful in planning and control as they emphasize the marginal concept. Ratios tend to overlook the impact of fixed costs. The break-even chart does emphasize the effects of additional sales or profits and shows clearly the effects of additional expenses or changes in volume, bringing to the manager's attention the marginal results of his decisions.

Special and routine reports and analyses

In addition to routine reports and statistical data, special reports are needed.

Data are collected, stored, processed and transmitted and information from all sources is provided for management control. The subject of reports is dealt with in the previous section on Communication. (*See* p 208.) Control reports can be functional, i.e. those on department progress; human resources management, e.g. staff appraisal; investigations, e.g. on a new machine.

In the section on Administrative Management, the need to review forms is considered; similarly there is a need to review any report which is of a routine nature.

Control by audit

1 **External audit**. The role of the external audit is traditionally the independent appraisal of an organization's financial records and statements. Assets and liabilities are verified by qualified accounting personnel employed by external accountancy firms.

The *purpose of the audit* is to verify that the organization, in preparing its own financial statements, has followed acceptable accounting principles and has applied them in a correct manner. The external audit is a check against fraud within the organization and provides people in financial and other institutions (e.g. bankers and potential investors) with evidence that statements have been prepared in an honest and consistent manner.

The external audit is not very helpful in controlling the everyday operations of an organization as it concentrates upon a limited number of statements and transactions. It is, however, a deterrent to fraud.

2 **Internal audit** is an effective tool of managerial control. The term is often limited to the auditing of accounts. It should be considered in a wider aspect, that is involving the appraisal of all operations, e.g. appraisal of policies, procedures, quality of management. The concept of internal auditing could be broadened as there is no reason why the actions of management should not be audited.

3 **Management audit** is the term which has been given to this approach. It can be regarded as a procedure for systematically examining and appraising a management's *overall* performance.

The *object is* to determine the present position of the business by assessing the results of its operations in specified areas, in relation to accepted standards. Imperfections found can be remedied.

Management audit

In the USA the American Institute of Management goes very deeply into audit and lists ten areas of appraisal, and awards points for each area. The results are used to compare the efficiency of various organizations. This goes further than normal ratio analysis. These detailed audits as used in the USA are not accepted by all, but they do attempt to define the nature and components of management ability.

Appraisers must be qualified in various fields, e.g. finance, production, and such a team should preferably be composed of outside persons, who can be more objective in their assessment of management efficiency. The team would of course be responsible to the board of directors. The team has to define the problems and suggest solutions.

Items to be *appraised* usually include questions on capital and organization structure, management policies and practices. They may cover:

Effectiveness of delegation, channels of communication, effectiveness of organization (e.g. Is organization structure appropriate for its purpose?).

Effectiveness of co-ordination, adequacy of planning and control methods, effectiveness of use of management data, executive competence (regarded as the most important), consideration of company's products and markets (e.g. What products contribute most to profits, etc?).

It can be seen that any method used to put management on a more 'correct' or 'effective' path must be considered and new methods must be carefully assessed before being dismissed as unimportant or pointless.

Enterprise audit
It has been noted that the management report goes beyond the standard accounting auditors' report. An enterprise audit differs from a management audit in that it embraces more than an evaluation of the quality of management. An enterprise audit looks at where a company is heading in the future, noting the economic, social and political developments which may affect its operations.

When future objectives have been determined, the need to revise existing plans should be considered. If changes are going to take place in the social, technical or political environment, action must be taken, otherwise the existence of the enterprise may be threatened. The enterprise audit makes managers look ahead and is usually made every three or five years.

Audit committee
The concept of an *audit committee* as a statutory requirement for larger public companies has support to a limited extent in the United Kingdom. These committees have statutory backing in the USA and Canada but their real benefit is not easy to see.

A most useful contribution to the discussion is in the book *The Independent Director* by R I Tricker (Tolley, 1979). Professor Tricker sees the *principal functions* of this type of committee to be:

1 To review, with a company's external auditors, its accounting policies and internal controls, annual financial statements and the audit report.
2 To advise the board of directors on appointment of auditors.
3 To provide auditors with direct access to the board of directors.
4 To consider other matters relating to audit and accounts.

Two of the three members of this committee are recommended to be *non-executive* directors.

Points against this concept appear to be:

• This new sub-committee may indicate to other directors that they are relieved of some of their own responsibilities.
• Non-executive directors may be at a disadvantage in having to rely solely on information supplied and the fact of being co-opted to an audit committee may not ensure they are any better served.
• The difficulty in finding suitably experienced managers who are free to take on the tasks.

ACCOUNTING

A useful definition of accounting can be found in a book by Glautier and Underdown (*Accounting Theory and Practice*, Pitman Publishing, 1991). It is defined as 'the process of identifying, measuring and communicating socioeconomic information to permit informed judgements and decisions by the users of the information'.

Accounting has moved slowly away from its traditional *procedural* base, which included keeping records, preparing budgets and final accounts, towards a role emphasizing its *social* importance. The boundaries of accounting have been extended by the changing environment.

Accounting is concerned with *collecting* data of the activities of an enterprise and the use of its resources. It also *analyses* the data for the purpose of decision making and helps to *control* the use of resources. An accountant must draw upon a range of disciplines, for example:

Economics – concepts of income, capital, pricing, foreign currency fluctuations, inflation.
Law – all operations are within a framework of regulations, e.g. the requirements of company law.
Organizational behaviour – how people in an organization may respond to information and control.
Data processing systems – for the efficient manipulation of data.
Quantitative techniques – to assist analysis of data and in planning.

Accountancy is a subject area with very open boundaries. Some countries in Europe describe a more narrow role for an 'accountant' than the role in the United Kingdom.

The different types or approaches to accounting reflect different social developments.

1 **Stewardship accounting** refers to safeguarding the owners of wealth from theft and this is the basis of financial reporting today. Book-keeping principles were evolved by merchants in Italy in the 13th and 14th centuries and the concept of double-entry book-keeping became popular in Western Europe in the early 19th century.

2 **Financial accounting** evolved later, particularly as larger scale businesses were formed in the period of the industrial expansion in the early 19th century. Methods of financing changed with the advent of public participation in taking 'shares' in a company (*see* p 48). The limitation of liability was thought by many to lend itself to abuse of shareholders' and investors' interest, so companies were granted joint stock status and limited liability on the condition of disclosure of information by the way of income statements and balance sheets. Legislation since then has provided for more and more disclosure by the various Companies Acts. Similarly, the American Securities and Exchange Commission and the European Community have pressed for higher standards of reporting, especially regarding disclosure and consistency of practice. The greater the amount of worker participation in management, the more information is asked for by employees of a company.

3 **Management accounting** – this was developed to assist managers of large industries in using accounting information as an aid to *future* management decisions and the focus was moved from recording and analysis to using information for future planning.

4 **Social responsibility accounting** considers the effects business decisions have on society. There is a trend today towards increasing social awareness of undesirable economic activities. Management may have to show in accounting statements how they have contributed towards overcoming or assisting in social problems, e.g. pollution.

We have seen in Chapter 2 that a business organization is an open-system interacting with its environment.

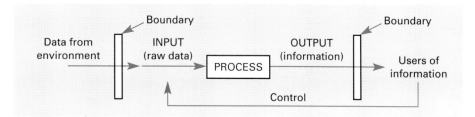

Fig 6.4 An accounting information system

A systems approach to accounting makes it easier to study the interdisciplinary nature of accounting as it is *one* element or sub-system of a business organization.

Uses of accounting as an information system

Raw data is *selected* by the accountant by the *conventions of accounting*. Selected data forms the input to the accounting system; once raw data is selected, it becomes *input* data. After processing, the information (output) is used by management and passed to users. The boundaries to the accounting system can be seen in Fig 6.4.

Persons interested in the output of the accounting information system are:

1 **Equity investor group** – shareholders and investors are concerned with the value of their investment and any income they expect to derive from shareholdings. Financial reports give them an account of how directors have handled resources given to them. The Companies Acts specify directors' emoluments, personal interest in contracts showing shareholders what personal benefits directors have derived from the business. Shareholders may exercise their voting rights on what is shown in the accounts, especially when they vote for the appointment of directors. They also may decide to increase, reduce or maintain their shareholdings.

2 **Loan creditor group** – long-term investors who have committed or may be prepared to commit funds to the company by way of debentures or other loan stock, and providers of short-term secured and unsecured loans and finance. *Short-term* creditors will be interested in assessing the *solvency* of the company (i.e. its ability to meet liabilities when they fall due). *Long-term creditors* will be interested in the profitability and performance of the company. The ability of the company to repay borrowings if it went into liquidation is of interest to *all* creditors.

3 **The employee group.** This *includes trade unions* who act on their behalf. Reports may indicate future prospects of the company and its ability to pay increased wages. Employee participation in management decisions have important implications for supplying information to employees. Wage disputes, profit-sharing between employees, shareholders and management can more easily be settled by full disclosure of information.

4 **Analyst-adviser group.** This includes members of the financial press and others advising on the purchase of company securities.

5 **Business contact group.** This includes trade creditors, suppliers, customers and competitors. Creditors are all those who have supplied materials, goods and services and accepted a delay in payment or repayment. They all want to know if the company is able to meet its financial obligations. Creditors want to know how *liquid* the firm is, i.e. how many cash or near-cash resources are available. If they have any doubt about a company's willingness to pay, they will press for payment immediately. They are interested in solvency and liquidity. Competitors are also likely to be interested in how other companies in the same industry are performing.

6 **The government.** The accounts of an organization are used as a basis for deciding the amount of taxation to be paid, in addition to regulatory aspects on mergers of companies which might create monopolies. The accounts give an indication also of the state of the economy. The government also lends money to individual companies and have similar interests to those of shareholders.

7 **The public.** This includes any member of the community who may interact in some way with the company, e.g. taxpayers, ratepayers, consumers, political parties and environmental protection societies.

An accountant has a responsibility to each of these categories in reporting on past results.

Accounting procedures and methods

The accounting process

Glautier and Underdown define accounting as being concerned with the process of:

- *'identifying* and selecting information which intended users will need;
- *evaluating* the information in the manner which is most useful to intended users;
- *communicating* the information selected and processed in the form most appropriate to the requirements of its users.'

As previously mentioned, the nature and methods of financial accounting are determined to a large extent by accounting conventions. It is important that the rules regarding the selection, measurement and communication of information to external users should all be the same. Conventions provide for uniformity and comparability of information, but it should be noted that the ease of comparability between companies is made more difficult by conventions themselves permitting a *variety* of practices.

Financial accounting conventions

The following list of conventions are constantly being changed and many have been criticized. The term conventions has been used instead of 'principles' or 'concepts' to describe basic points of agreement. The accounting bodies in the UK and the USA have committees to review conventions and practices, i.e. Accounting Standards Board and the Financial Reporting Council Ltd.

General conventions are fundamental to the nature of financial accounting.

Business entity convention

The affairs of the business are distinguished from the owner's personal affairs. If a proprietor places £5000 cash into a firm as capital, the books will show the firm has £5000 additional cash, and his capital has increased by £5000. The capital invested shows the initial assets of the business and the measure of indebtedness to the owner. The accounting records are therefore limited only to the firm and do not extend to the personal resources of the proprietor.

As we saw in Chapter 2, a sole trader is legally liable at law for all debts of the business, although this convention makes a fictional distinction between the trader's private and business affairs whereas in the case of corporations there is a *legal distinction* between the owners or shareholders and the business. Shareholders are only liable up to the amount of capital they have agreed to invest.

Money measurement convention

The communication of information about a business in *terms of money is* the basis of modern accounting theory and practice. Accounting information deals *only* with those facts capable of expression in monetary terms. This therefore sets a *limit* to the type of information which may be selected and measured by accountants and hence limits the information they may communicate about a business.

Items of importance that may be *omitted* include: how good or poor are the staff or the management team; how poor morale is in the firm; how the firm will be affected by a new product of a competitor. The question raised is: should not the reader of a financial report expect that such important facts be disclosed?

The other problems of using money as a standard of measurement in accounting are that it does not remain constant in value through time, nor does the value of specific assets remain the same. The effect of changing price levels is discussed later.

Other conventions

1 **Going concern.** The assumption is made that a firm will continue to operate over an indefinitely long period of time. Many assets derive their value from their employment in the firm and if they were sold when a firm closed down, their sale value would probably be less than their recorded book value.

   This convention enables a method to be used of finding the present value of an asset by reference to the discounted value of future returns which are expected from the use of the asset. The value of assets are therefore related to *future anticipated profits* of a going concern.

2 **The cost convention.** The value of an asset is determined by its *cost of acquisition* and not to any value of future returns. Assets are normally shown at cost price and this is the basis for assessing the future usage of an asset.

   Problems raised by this convention are that *historic cost is not a dependable* guide to current value as it does not reflect *changes in the value of money* or changes in the value of specific assets in relation to money.

In addition, the writing off of certain assets as depreciation against income enables the cost to be completely removed from the accounts. Other assets which can create income, e.g. the skill of staff who are highly organized and managed (*see* p 242 for discussion on Human Asset Accounting) are not included.

3 **Realization convention.** There is no certainty of income until a sale has been made, so increases in value which have not been realized are not recorded. Changes in the value of an asset may only be recognized at the moment the business *realizes or disposes* of that asset. Non-accountants recognize increases in the value of assets as income, even though it may be *unsold.* Accountants will only recognize income increases if a contract of sale has taken place and the customer incurs legal liability for the asset sold.

Gains from increases in value from holding an asset (holding gains) are not recorded. Gains from selling assets (trading or operating gains) are recorded. So, in effect, a business records only *part* of total increases in value accruing to a firm during the period of accounting. It is important to note that cash does not have to be received before a transaction is recorded.

4 **Accrual convention.** This convention requires the accountant to treat as expenses only those sums which are due and payable. A payment made *in advance,* for example, must not be treated as an expense. The recipient is treated as a debtor until his right to receive cash matures. Similarly with cash paid out in error, this is not an expense; the person to whom it was paid is treated as a debtor until it can be recovered. On the other hand, when an expense has been *incurred* and no payment made, this expense must be recorded and the person to whom the payment should have been made is shown as a *creditor.*

5 **Matching convention.** A simple way of calculating net profit for a period would seem to be to *match* the actual payments for items against the revenue in that period. The fact that expenses consist of assets used up in obtaining the revenues of a period and that cash paid out in a period is usually different from the expenses of a period is often misunderstood.

So, in summary, the *realization* convention identifies the *timing* of gains and the *accrual* convention enables the *proper recording* of revenues and expenses. The calculation of *income is* made possible by the *matching convention* which *links* revenues with their related expenses.

6 **Periodicity convention.** The idea of making yearly reports grew out of custom and yearly budgets are also used by governments. Such periodicity is now required by law as regards reports on profit and loss accounts and balance sheets. Some companies produce reports at other times of the year in order to provide more frequent financial information. This convention causes problems in allocating fixed assets as expenses of a particular year. This problem of *depreciation* has produced many arguments from economists about the correct way of measuring income.

7 **Consistency convention.** This is when a firm has fixed a method of treating an item in its accounts, so it will treat all similar items in the same way. Changes in methods would lead to a distortion of profit calculations. Any changes from previous accounting methods should be mentioned, e.g. changes in valuation of stock.

It was mentioned earlier that conventions may produce consistency, but still allow different methods of measurement and treatment which make it difficult for investors in comparing one company with another.

The work of the Accounting Standards Steering Committee endeavours to ensure comparability of information.

8 **Convention of conservatism.** When an accountant chooses a figure he may rather *understate* rather than overstate a profit. All losses though are incorporated in the accounts but profits are not to be anticipated by recording them prematurely. These rules reflect the accountant's view of his social responsibilities in providing information.

There are problems in such caution, for example:

- To understate is *as bad as overstating.* Investment in a business should not be discouraged by restricting statements to their lowest value as investors and shareholders need reliable information.
- Modern approaches to accounting methods can be frustrated by rigid application of conservative conventions.

Reliable information may *not necessarily be useful.* There is also the fact that accounting conventions do not always produce uniformity, e.g. there are many methods of valuing inventory.

Financial control methods

This term refers to financial statements and methods which help to determine business performance. Financial statements record the flow of goods and services to and from the organization. These statements show:

- *Liquidity* – ability to convert assets into cash in order to meet current financial needs and obligations.
- *Profitability* of organization over a period.
- *General financial position* of organization.

These statements are generally prepared in retrospect and refer to a past period and this tends to reduce their usefulness. Quarterly or monthly statements can provide indications of trends and enable corrective action to be made within the current year.

The main types of financial statements are now described.

1 **Balance sheet** shows the financial position at a particular point in time. Assets are described in an agreed manner, and indicate the way in which the funds of the business have been invested, and where these funds have come from. The modern, vertical, method of presentation is shown on p 234.
2 **Income statements** are an attempt to determine the wealth created for the owners of capital in a given period of time. They usually start with a figure of gross receipts for sales, then deduct costs of sales and running the business, the remainder being available for dividends to shareholders or re-investment in the business. The names given to these statements are the Trading Profit and Loss Account or Income Statement (*see* p 235).

Financial Statements
Metallic Metals plc

Balance Sheet as at 31 December 1994

Share capital	Authorized	Issued and fully paid
	£	£
9% Preference shares at £1 each	30,000	20,000
Ordinary shares of £1 each	250,000	100,000
	280,000	120,000

Reserves

Share premium account	7,000	
Retained income	40,860	47,860
Shareholders' funds employed		167,860
Debenture 12% – secured redeemable 1 January 2000		10,000
Funds employed		177,860

Represented by:	Cost	Depreciation	Net
	£	£	£
Fixed assets	130,000	54,500	75,600
Current assets			
Inventory		113,650	
Debtors	56,000		
Less Provision for doubtful debts	2,800	53,200	
Repayments		1,160	
Cash in hand		730	
		168,740	
Less Current liabilities			
Creditors	38,110		
Accrued expenses	2,080		
Dividends	11,800		
Provision for taxation	7,400		
Bank overdraft	7,090	65,480	102,260
			177,860

Income statement for year ended 31 December 1994

	£	£	£
Sales			322,100
Less Cost of Sales –			
Opening inventory		96,450	
Purchases		232,100	
		328,550	
Less Closing inventory		113,650	214,900
			107,200
Less Selling and administration expenses			
Packing	5,680		
Carriage outwards	6,410		
Advertising	11,260	23,350	
Administration expenses			
Wages and salaries	12,550		
General expenses	4,020		
Audit fee	250	16,820	
Establishment expenses			
Rent, rates and insurance	9,160		
Lighting and heating	7,690		
Depreciation	11,500	28,350	
Financial expenses £			
Bad debts 3,410			
Provision for 710			
doubtful debts	4,120		
Bank interest	700		
Debenture interest	1,200	6,020	74,540
Net income before tax			32,660
Less Provision for taxation			7,400
Net income after tax			25,260
Retained income at 1 Jan 1994			
brought forward			27,400
			52,660
Less Dividends 9% Preference		1,080	
Proposed Ordinary at 10%		10,000	11,800
Retained income carried forward			£40,860

Cash flow statements

These statements indicate the new wealth that has become available to a business in the year and how it has been invested in the business. They can be constructed to highlight changes in the firm's cash position. They emphasize different aspects of management of finance.

Surpluses or shortfalls are noted in the reconciliation of opening and closing balances.

Cash budgets are vital in forward planning and it is obligatory for all businesses to publish a cash flow statement showing the source of funds and their use (Financial Report Standard FRS1).

The main *sources* of funds are:

- capital introduced by owner;
- loans to business;
- sale of assets;
- income from operations.

Uses or applications of funds are:

- owner's withdrawals;
- loan repayments;
- purchase of assets;
- losses from operations;
- payments to tax authorities.

Cash flow statements are now required in financial reports because success depends on maximizing the flow of cash throughout each year (*see* Fig 6.5). They are very useful for budget forecasts.

Planning capital expenditure

Planned investment in new assets, often called *capital budgeting*, involves deciding upon capital expenditure required and arranging the finance required. Only a brief reference to this aspect can be made. A capital investment gives returns over a number of future time periods and calculations have to be made to find out the total cash outlay required to obtain the investment and changes in the net cash inflow or outflow which will result from the investment.

No attempt will be made to evaluate the investment proposals here by any of the following most commonly used methods (i.e. pay-back period, accounting rate of return, or discounted cash flow techniques). A good description may be found in *Accounting Theory and Practice*, Glautier and Underdown (Pitman Publishing).

The most useful procedures to evaluate capital investment proposals are the discounted cash flow techniques, which take into account the value of money over periods of time. For example, £1 received now would be preferred to the receipt of £1 in a year's time, unless the year's wait is compensated by interest. This interest factor is shown by a discount rate. In this matter like is compared with like.

People requiring information from an accounting system are: managers, shareholders, customers, employees, creditors, community.

Financial accountancy relies on historical statistics. The financial accountant measures the actual costs of a business and income in units of currency.

The American Institute of Certified Public Accountants in 1971 published a report on the objectives of financial statements – the main one was said to be 'to provide information useful for making economic decisions'.

To provide more information to a wider section of the community, in 1975 the Accounting Standards Committee of the Institute of Chartered Accountants in England and Wales published a Discussion Paper 'The Corporate Report', in which it set out to re-examine the scope and aims of published reports in the light of modern needs and conditions. The paper identified seven groups as having a reasonable right to information and felt provision should be made in corporate reports for:

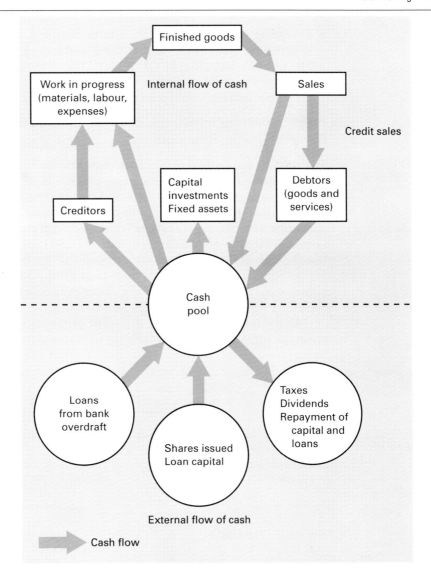

Fig 6.5 Circular flow of funds showing sources and applications

- The **equity investor group**, including existing or potential shareholders.
- The **loan creditor group** – long-term investors who have committed, or might be prepared to commit, funds to the company by way of debentures or other loan stock, and providers of short-term secured and unsecured loans and finance.
- The **employee group** – including existing, potential and past employees.
- The **analyst-adviser group** – including members of the financial press, analysts and anyone advising on the purchase of company securities.
- The **business contact group** – including trade creditors and suppliers, customers and competitors.

- The government – including tax authorities and those concerned with the supervision of commerce and industry and local authorities.
- The public – including any member of the community who may interact in some way with the company, e.g. taxpayers, ratepayers, consumers, political parties and environmental protection societies.

An accountant has a responsibility to each of these categories in reporting on past results.

Comparability of financial reports

The need to use reports to compare one concern with another has expanded greatly. Standardization of accounting practice is essential for the assessment of the relative economic situations of different companies. It was recognized, however, that it was not practicable to establish a code to cater for all business situations. The two organizations concerned with reporting standards are the Financial Accountancy Standards Board (USA) and Accounting Standards Board (ASB) in the UK. The ASB is responsible for drafting the new Financial Report Standards (FRSs) and its predecessor, the Accounting Standards Committee, was responsible for drafting Statements of Standard Accounting Practice (SSAPs).

One method of comparing different organizations is to examine their return on capital invested (Fig 6.6).

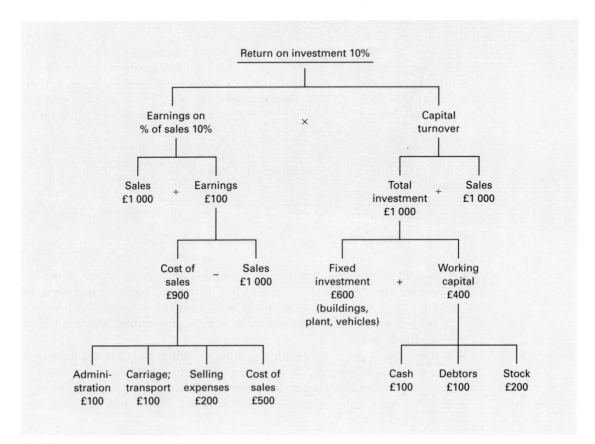

Fig 6.6 Constituents of return on investment

Financial accountancy as a reporting technique has adapted to the changing business and social environment. The financial accountant measures the cost of a business in monetary terms, setting them against income. Resources consumed measurable in monetary terms are called expenditure, and offset against revenue to estimate profits.

The work of an accountant today involves a much broader knowledge than ever before, e.g. the use of mathematically-based techniques (linear programming) (p 249) and of discounted cash flow (p 236). Broader economic knowledge and the extended role of government policy all have marked effects on financial policy.

When inflation rates are high, the preparation of accounts on a 'true and fair' basis is not possible, and profit determination becomes very difficult. The 'correction' of accounts for inflation enables more meaningful comparisons to be made, although there are two schools of thought on this matter in the United Kingdom. Two alternative methods are the *current cost accounting* (CCA) method and the *current purchasing power* (CPP) method (for further details *see Accounting Theory and Practice*, Glautier and Underdown, Pitman Publishing, 1991).

Role of accounting information

Earlier in this chapter accounting conventions were considered. It was seen that accounting information can serve different accounting purposes, which may conflict to some extent.

If an organization has a clearly defined responsibility structure where managers are in charge of aspects which are mainly independent of each other, then conflict may be small. In organizations with less defined responsibility structures operating in non-routine ways in an uncertain market, then accounting information becomes more difficult to produce and interpret. There could be conflicts between managers who need to understand in more depth the nature of accounting information.

Accounting information is only one part of a management information system, but it does require to be carefully used by managers who must understand what it is, or is not, capable of doing. Accounting can be regarded as a 'language' where the performance of various parts of the business can be collated to give an overall picture. The only quantitative measure available to an organization is *money*.

Two of the main problem areas in a management accounting system are:

1 when data is initially entered in the system. Materials can be charged to incorrect accounts or allocated to incorrect time periods in order to manipulate accounts;
2 when cost or revenue is allocated between several centres of responsibility or time periods.

The allocation may be useful for one purpose but not for another for which the information is used. For example, old assets may be fully depreciated and may *continue to be used*, rather than replacing them with new, because a better profit figure is shown.

Accounting information has limitations, and if it is used in performance evaluation it directly affects line managers who may be in a position to influence both the information gathered and actions that are taken as a result. Therefore senior management and designers of systems need to be fully aware of the limitations of accounting measurement procedures and the possible effects of ways in which managers use accounting information.

Accounting
differences
between countries

This seems a suitable time to look at the different methods of preparing financial statements, since the United Kingdom is part of the European Community (EC).

There are so many differences in accounting practices that it is very difficult to attempt to interpret and compare the information contained in company financial statements.

Land and buildings may be shown at historic cost in the balance sheet of a United Kingdom company, *but may be revalued*. Asset revaluations seldom occur in Germany, Spain, France and Italy, so comparisons are difficult.

Legal and taxation systems differ and these are other factors which may significantly affect comparisons.

In most European countries, the accounting profession provides financial statements which are 'legally' correct, but this does not require auditors to concern themselves with reports regarding the 'fairness' or commercial significance of the accounts. The auditors are more concerned with certifying that the accounts are correct legally and mathematically.

Auditors in the UK must report on 'truth and fairness' of financial statements, and are open to being criticized if they do not comment in sufficient depth on the financial reports of companies.

The Eighth Accounting Directive of the Economic Community now asks for 'truth and fairness' in financial statements. The interpretation, however, is still slanted towards complying with the statutory laws of the country.

Management
accounting and
behavioural
science

The impact of behavioural sciences and research into individual and small group behaviour in large-scale organizations has greatly influenced ideas about management theory and practice. Accounting to management has also had to change as a result of the influence of behavioural sciences.

It has been seen (p 199) that human beings are complex, motivated by many drives as noted by Maslow. Because people vary in training, environment and goals, they can react differently to the same stimuli, and they appear to work harder when they have personal commitment to any task. Traditional ideas of motivation assumed that economic rewards were given for good performance and sanctions for inadequate performance, and that people are naturally lazy, uninterested in organized goals and hostile to authority. These ideas are not now favoured.

The outcome of this change suggests that if controls are made rigid and authoritarian, there is no firm indication that these controls will ensure satisfactory performance. Research suggests that tight controls discourage innovation and create indifferent, often hostile attitudes to the organization.

Management accounting plays an important part in influencing behaviour, for example, in the setting of goals, evaluating performance and suggesting corrective actions to be taken. Accountants have wide discretion in the selection, processing and reporting of data. So if the information produced by accountants is used as a basis to evaluate the performance of other members of an organization, the other members may become frustrated and irritated by standards set which they either do not understand, or do not agree with; the seeds of conflict may have been sown!

Behavioural considerations are very important for the designer of a management information system. The effectiveness of accounting information is evidenced in the manner in which it affects behaviour.

> The budget process alone is not sufficient to maintain adequate management control. Too often, organizations tend to expect results from budgetary control and fail to recognize its behavioural implications. As a result, pressures are created leading to mistrust, hostility and actions detrimental to the long term prospects of an organization. It follows that accountants should work more closely with behavioural scientists and that they should learn more about the behavioural implications of organizational control. (Glautier and Underdown, *Accounting Theory and Practice.*)

A knowledge of organization theory is therefore very useful to an accountant, especially in understanding internal and external influences affecting the nature of organizational activities and the environment in which decisions are made.

'An information system can only function effectively where there exists a satisfactory organizational structure, within which managerial roles are properly defined, and where the style of management favours the free flow of information' (Glautier and Underdown, above).

When budgets are being developed the following reactions may occur to influence the allocation of resources:

- information *withheld* until very late to highlight its importance;
- *delay* and unhelpfulness in giving information to those compiling budgets because of discontent with previous allocations;
- *overstatement* of requirements to compensate for expected cuts. 'Slack' is built into budgets and this makes accurate budgeting impossible.

It is very important that everyone should if possible participate in budget preparation, as this make them more likely to accept allocations and reduce rivalry and tension between departments.

Budgets as motivational devices

It is widely assumed that budget standards create pressure on employees to achieve the agreed standard. One attempt to analyse the motivational impact of budgets was developed by Kurt Lewin in *Group Decision & Social Change – Readings in Social Psychology* (New York, Holt, Rinehart Winston, 1958). He suggested using *force field analysis*. The budget process often creates driving forces that increase pressure on employees who cannot easily escape censure if their results do not reach the standard when goals are stated precisely. On the one hand managers try to motivate by increasing *driving* forces (e.g. more rewards or reprimands). While this may raise performance, there may be counteracting restraining forces preventing permanent improvement. Workers may raise their performance and work harder, *but* they may not work *efficiently* and may obtain less enjoyment from their work.

So the answer according to his theory appears to be, *not to increase* driving forces, but to *reduce restraining* forces – these are, for example, fear of loss of job if standards not achieved, or union agreements against speeding up output. Lewin suggested that behaviour is the result of an equilibrium between the opposing forces of driving and restraining.

Human asset accounting

It has already been stated that accounting information is prepared and presented to interested persons with a view to influencing their behaviour and decisions. A good system of providing information for management to control future activities of an organization should record *every* financial or economic fact in a manner which is understood by everyone; this information is usually presented in monetary terms.

Management must control and utilize resources effectively; this includes physical resources, e.g. patent rights and human resources.

One simple definition of management is 'getting things done through people,' and yet it is strange that the value of *human* resources does not appear in reports and statements of organizations. Some personnel are very valuable and they may leave or join another company. Normal accounting information does not give any indication of the value of personnel in the firm. Points which should be known are: has a change occurred in human assets during the year? Is the value of the company significantly affected? Decision making may be said to be inaccurate if information on the effects on human assets of alternative courses of action are not made available to managers.

Accounting procedures usually treat expenditure on building up human assets as expenditure of a revenue nature. Expenditure on recruiting, induction, training and developing personnel is charged against the income of the period in which the expenditure was incurred. Other assets deemed 'capital' are shown in the accounts, some at a reduced value (because of depreciation), some perhaps at an increased value. The main point is that they are shown as being part of the company's present asset value. If human assets were treated in the same way, the statement of income of an organization, and also the *attitude* of management to such expenditure, would be greatly affected, that is if the expenditure were not regarded as costs to be borne out of current income, but contributing to the building of assets which would bring benefits for future years. A number of writers have pointed out this need to evaluate human assets, but only recently has serious thought been given to this problem.

The need for such a measurement of human assets and the difficulties were mentioned by W A Paton in his book *Accounting Theory*, published in 1922. He referred to a well-organized and loyal personnel being of greater importance as an asset than a stock of merchandise: this of course leads to one of the limitations of the conventional balance sheet.

There are, of course, many difficulties in isolating and measuring the cost of human assets, for example:

- what period should be used to calculate the benefit to be received?
- accounting conventions were influenced by social and economic influences which were quite different from those existing at the present time;
- management does not think of people as assets, or owning people as other assets are considered to be owned, in a legal sense;
- people may feel degraded in being given a monetary value.

It is only when other assets are combined with human assets that the full potential of an organization can be realized, so it ideally should be possible and preferable to find a system which includes all assets. Any such information system would show the investments made in human assets and the financial effects of any changes.

Professor Rensis Likert of Michigan University has recommended that human assets should be accounted for in an accounting system. The system could isolate expenditure on recruitment and training of employees and the cost written off over the expected working lives of employees.

A British working party was set up in 1973 by the Institute of Cost and Management Accountants (Chartered Institute of Management Accountants) and the Institute of Personnel Management. A system was advocated which differed from the American one. Briefly, this method produces human asset values by using multipliers. The staff is divided into four categories: senior and middle management, supervisors and clerical and operative grades. Multipliers are then applied to the salaries of each of these groups and an asset value obtained.

The behavioural impact of this method must be considered. Most accounting information reflects the results of the activity of successful and unsuccessful efforts of human beings, and influences their decisions in an attempt to control the future. Unless the system is carefully explained to staff and their participation encouraged, adverse reactions could occur. All managers involved should examine carefully the behavioural problems and ensure that the systems of communication are working well in order that the system can be effected.

Benefits are numerous. Management will be stimulated to take appropriate action to reduce the cost, when they become aware of the true cost of labour turnover. Industrial relations may improve as conventional accounting tends to encourage management to underestimate the importance of employees. The fact that a company is making an effort to record and report investments in the human resources has developed an interest among managers in the economic importance of people. Managers are now provided with information regarding human assets which will help them to budget more effectively and ensure a more satisfactory allocation of human resources.

Finally, it is important to note that human asset accounting systems can be developed to become an important element in information systems. The main aim of the systems will not be to value the individual employee, but rather to evaluate the investment in the human assets of the organization. Can industry afford to ignore such valuable assets when making decisions affecting the future of the firm, its employees and society?

Management in
practice

> The R G Barry Corporation of Colombus, Ohio, USA, on 1 January 1968, started the first human asset accounting system. The corporation had over 2000 staff. It had low capital assets and the management recognized that success depended largely upon the organization's human assets, especially employee and customer loyalty. The corporation contacted Professor Likert and a team of Michigan University staff and they helped the corporation staff to develop a system. The system specified seven functional accounts: recruiting, acquisition, formal training and induction costs, also informal training, familiarization, investment building experience and development costs.
>
> Investments in human resources are regarded as being of two types:
>
> 1 Direct expenditures on, for example, recruiting and training people.
> 2 Allocations of salary for periods of training and development when the corporation is not fully benefiting from a person's efforts.
>
> Managers received quarterly reports showing how actual performance compared with the plan – 'The Human Resource Capital Plan.' It was operated independently of the accounting system.

ADVANCED CONTROL TECHNIQUES

Operational research (OR)

Management action must be quick and flexible to take advantage of changes in environment which could be economic, political or social. Newer techniques are available to give a more scientific approach to the control of problems. As only a brief outline of these new techniques is possible, readers are referred to the bibliography at the end of this chapter for further books on the subject.

The use of electronic equipment and more accurate programming enables information to be classified so that management can have sufficient information to act quickly. It is, though, necessary to ensure that management knows *how to use* the information and this means that management training must be sufficiently thorough (*see* chapter on Human Resource Management).

Background

Operational research has a military origin. Mathematical theory was applied to army problems, and military applications, such as the optimum convoy size, were the main areas of development at first. Later, it was applied to industrial problems.

A feature which distinguishes operational research from other research and engineering investigations is that it analyses operations *as a whole* and employs people of *various specialities*, e.g. chemistry, logic, mathematics, physics, psychology. It usually uses an inter-disciplinary approach, although most of the present business applications are concerned with mathematical and statistical analyses of the results of possible alternative actions in specific areas.

Approach

Trained researchers, using tools of various sciences, often construct a conceptual or mathematical model to represent the system to be studied. There are usually equations or formulae developed to relate important factors of the operations studied. These factors can be mathematically operated upon to determine the effects of changing the value of the variables. One main factor is the *optimization* (i.e. best, highest or lowest) of some criterion. This is a measure by which results can be evaluated, for example, the ultimate object may be net profit, cost, or return on investment.

Techniques and tools used include statistical methods and computers and, in particular, the following have been developed – linear programming, game theory, simulation, sequencing and replacement theory.

The procedure in *applying* OR is similar to the steps involved in planning, i.e. formulate the problem, construct a model, derive a solution, test the solution, provide controls for the model and solution; then put the solution into effect.

Definition

A simple definition of OR is that it is a scientific method which assesses alternative courses of action in a system providing an improved basis for management decision making.

The definition used by the Operational Research Society is more specific:

The attack of modern science on complex problems arising in the direction and management of large systems of men, machines, materials and money in industry, business, government and defence.

The distinctive approach is to develop a scientific model of the system, incorporate measurements of factors such as chance and risk, in order to predict and compare the outcomes of alternative decisions, strategies and controls. The purpose is to help management determine its policy and actions scientifically.

Position in
organization

Existing staff could be trained to operate an OR section which when formed, it must be noted, usually acts in an *advisory* capacity. The position in the organization varies and often it is placed as part of the function of production. This may cause friction and a better place is probably to require the section to report direct to a senior executive, preferably the managing director. If there is a management services department, responsibility to the head of the department is usually satisfactory.

Like the organization and methods section (*see* Chapter 10) the OR section must be accepted by the staff of the other sections and usually the work it is first given is of a minor nature, with a high probability of success. For example, the congestion at a small unit store, or production scheduling for a single product. This enables confidence to be gained so that wider-ranging, more important problems can be considered.

Personnel in the team must have a knowledge of OR techniques and an understanding of the theory of probability. In addition to knowledge of a specialist nature they must have an interest in management problems and be able to communicate well.

Uses of OR

When OR was applied to industry, the first problems tackled were mainly in the field of production where measurement was comparatively easy and objectives reasonably clear. It is now carried out in all functional areas, marketing, finance, human resources management, research and development, purchasing and overall planning.

The following are brief details of the fields in which OR has been used.

- Production
  Sequences of jobs, machine loading and work scheduling.
  The best 'mix' of products and the correct amounts to produce to maximize profit.
- Marketing
  Location of warehouses and factories and retail outlets.
  Scheduling of vehicles, minimizing transport costs.
  Problems of excessive queues at arrival and departure points.
  Stock or inventory control.
  Optimum size and best allocation of a sales force.
- Purchasing
  Economic purchasing quantities.
  Decisions to make or buy.
- Research and development
  Priorities of projects.
  The life and reliability of projects.
- Overall planning
  Systems of communication.
  Policies of diversification.

One important point is that particular assignments usually cover one small part of the organization and that any scheme to 'optimize' this small area may not be optimum when taking into account the whole of a firm's operations. This *concept of 'sub-optimization'* is clearly dangerous as the consequences on departmental interrelations cannot always be fully explored. The recognition of inter-dependence of the activities of an organization is called the *systems* approach which was described in Chapter 1.

Limitations of OR
- Lack of mathematical knowledge among managers and lack of managerial knowledge among OR men.
- Can be very expensive to have detailed OR analyses and computer usage.
- Many decisions involve intangible and unmeasurable factors which, there-fore, cannot form part of a model. Judgements must therefore be non-quantitative and more likely to be wrong.

The study of OR often follows similar lines and the following areas are chosen for consideration.

Stock or inventory control; replacement policies; queuing or waiting – line problems; competitive strategies (game theory); sequencing problems; linear programming; critical path analysis.

Most of these will be discussed further after the next section on Simulation.

Simulation

Before discussing in more detail the various applications of OR it is worth considering first the nature of simulation, which people have used for a long time in one form or another. Simulation is now thought of as a branch of OR but the origins are closely connected with probability theory.

Nature

If we abstract from reality in order to create an image this will aid us in thinking about something. If these abstractions are in quantitative form or can be mechanically manipulated, they are called *models*. These are widely used in the physical sciences. Simulation models are used to investigate the facts about a system or compare systems, or examine the relationships within a system and to understand the effect of change.

A *management system* comprises many systems of activities and functions. A knowledge is needed of possible changes on the existing system and such an assessment is not easy as many factors interact. Uncertainty and risk are basic elements in our environment and the ability to detect changes and adapt an organization to minimize adverse consequences and maximize opportunities is particularly valuable. In this connection, models facilitate effective planning.

A road map is an abstraction for a physical road network; the conditions of roads and the distances between points are shown. Such an abstraction can be of use to some people, but not to others. A motorist would find it interesting, but not a sociologist, who would prefer a *different* type of map, showing, for example, population density. An abstraction is not very detailed and is small, but is more flexible than reality, and enables relationships to be more easily understood. To simulate is to manipulate a model to help us to find out things about the complex systems in reality.

Abstraction is not a new idea. Accountancy systems record results of operations; these are synthesized into financial reports and create an abstraction of one element – the financial structure of an organization.

NB: An abstraction becomes a model only when it can be manipulated in quantitative terms.

It is worthwhile noting that a group of techniques exist called analytical models, e.g. linear programming. These are not simulation models because:

- these systems often contain decisions for which there are not yet mathematically precise rules;
- information about the system is not *sufficiently* complete;
- as optimization is a main object there is a tendency to over-simplify the *complex* goals in a large management system.

Examples

1 **Game simulation.** This is part of a competitive model (*see* 3 below). This is rather a tool of exploration giving an insight into *broad aspects* of problems, and its purpose is rather to produce ideas than quantitative solutions.

2 **Training simulation.** The flight trainer, or simulator, has been a great success for training pilots as it reproduces in great detail the conditions and environment of an aircraft flight.

3 **Computer simulation.** The availability of computers and the application of mathematics have increased the scope of simulation. Economic models for a country can be built whereby small elements in an economy can be changed and the effect analysed.

Problems   Training and judgement are required in developing systems.

Models may be over-simplified or even over-simulated, i.e. *too many* factors included resulting in loss of flexibility and greater expense.

As the simulation is an abstraction from the real world, the results have then got to be *interpreted back* into the existing real system.

Competitive strategies (game theory)

This is a branch of mathematical analysis and simulation techniques are used. It is an extension of decision theory where one's choice of action is determined by the possible alternative actions of an opponent who is playing the same game. Usually action is taken by one person after the opponent has made his move, and various rules have been formulated. The *minimax rule,* for example, gives the maximum assurance of a loss not greater than a certain minimum.

Usually in a given situation one can choose a certain mixture of strategies so that, whatever the opponent does, he cannot do better than attain a result which is *calculable beforehand,* and this foreknowledge is very important in such competitive situations.

This theory can be applied where firms are in direct opposition, where any extra customers must come from the competing firm. One example of its use is in the correct timing of an advertising campaign.

Sequencing

Briefly, these problems involve deciding what is the best order for tasks in a process to be performed. The order must bear in mind technological feasibility, e.g. plant limitation, regarding the number of machines available, or to optimize from a particular criterion, e.g. lowest amount of production time per article.

The use of a computer in selecting the 'best' order of sales representative's routes can be seen in Chapter 7.

Stock or inventory problems

The problem of holding the minimum amount of stock necessary to satisfy production requirements and yet not be too high is a typical problem. Stock control is concerned with the relationship between:

- cost of holding stock, i.e. capital tied up, deterioration and obsolescence and cost of warehouse space;
- loss of profit in being unable to meet demand through shortage of materials;
- amount and variability of demand;
- cost of placing order;
- discounts obtainable by ordering large quantities.

Models have been developed for different combinations of the above conditions.

Many organizations, though, have given insufficient thought to solving this problem and many stocks are far too high. They tend to play safe by keeping high stocks. One reason for this might be that decisions about what are safe stock quantities are *made too low* in the level of the organization, such personnel being afraid to be out of stock.

Statistical methods can be used to evaluate the level of stock needed, while providing an acceptable level of protection. If the delivery period for replacement is short, the percentage of possible out-of-stock items may be calculated and a decision to risk being out of stock may be made, if there is a low probability of the events occurring.

Advanced stock control systems need good sales forecasting techniques to be successful. Research in this field has produced techniques for evaluating errors between forecast values of sale and actual values; these errors are 'fedback' to adjust the original equations which determined the original forecast value. This is the cybernetic approach, where mistakes made are noted and the system is adjusted automatically.

An example of this is *exponential-smoothing* where the estimated value of a time series is modified by a proportion of the amount by which it was most recently in error, thus giving a new forecast.

A method called *Box-Jenkins* has been developed, whereby the forecast adjusts the last observed value by an amount which is the sum of proportional, first difference and cumulative terms. Again, the deviations operated upon are the past errors of prediction; in essence, the forecast controls itself.

Queuing theory

Queues form everywhere. Members of a queue may arrive in a random manner or a prescribed manner, in groups or individually; they may be served individually (as in a dentist's surgery) or in groups (as passengers in a train).

A manager may have a number of people waiting to see him or a storekeeper a number awaiting him to be served. If, therefore, the causes of queue formation can be discovered, a remedy may be forthcoming to save the time wasted.

Queuing theory is a branch of probability theory and has been used regarding serving customers in retail stores, loading and unloading ships in port, setting up a balanced assembly line, where output rates of machines vary.

It is of interest to find the average length of waiting time of the queue and then try to reduce it. Simple queues are solved by many simultaneous equations; more difficult queues by statistical probability and simulation.

Monte-Carlo methods (a branch of simulation) can be used to find the time spent in a queue, by setting up a *model* of the real situation. Variables are selected at random, from tables of random numbers.

Linear programming

Programming is concerned with the determination of optimum allocation of resources in complex situations. The use of a mathematical model is to set out the necessary computations, so that the optimum is reached without any limitations being exceeded. For example, one limit in transporting goods is the size of the lorry.

Definition

Linear programming is a technique for determining the optimum combination of resources to obtain a desired goal. It is based upon the assumption that there is a linear, or straight line, relationship between variables and that the limits of the variations can be easily determined.

Examples of
problems solved

It is used in all parts of the transport industry and the fuel industry, where a solution is designed to minimize distance travelled and costs incurred or to maximize profit. (This is a typical resource allocation problem.)

- **Transport example.** Assume six warehouses supply four shops. A specific number of barrels are known to be in the warehouses. Orders from two shops are made and road haulage charges are known. The problem is, how should managers of the business satisfy the wants of the two shops while minimizing transport costs?
- **Product mix example.** If the problem is to make a type of food of lowest cost, with a protein content of say 40–45 units per tonne, the many ingredients that could be used and their cost have to be considered. Calculations can be done by computers to determine the lowest cost for a mix of the required protein content. There are similar problems in the petroleum industry to give petrol blendings of the required ingredients.

  NB: There could be more constraints of course than protein content and cost.

Network analysis

In the early part of the 20th century, H L Gantt used a chart system which showed time-relationships between 'events' in a production programme. He recognized that total programme goals should be regarded as a series of inter-related plans (or events) that could be followed easily. This simple theme has been developed and some of the new methods show which elements of a plan are the most important or the most urgent.

Many projects of a complex nature, e.g. building a motorway, can be more effectively planned, co-ordinated and controlled by using network techniques. Two common methods are critical path method (CPM) and programme evaluation and review technique (PERT).

They evolved from two different sources almost simultaneously. CPM was developed about 1957 by an American company which wished to improve the planning, scheduling and co-ordination of its new plant construction programme. In 1958 PERT was used to aid the United States missile development programme. Their common factor is that they both use a planning network; they are different in that they include different combinations of facilities. In a simple exposition there is little to gain by differentiating between the two: the term PERT will be used to embrace both methods.

Basic terms

An *activity* is an operation requiring time or resources which has a definite beginning and end. It is portrayed by an arrow and represents the smallest unit over which control is desired.

An *event* is a significant point of time within the project. It is portrayed by a circle and represents the beginning or end of an activity. No expenditure of resources is associated with an event.

Construction of a network

The first stage in a PERT control system is to define the project in terms of a network model; this will illustrate the dependencies existing between the activities in the project. Each of these activities has certain constraints regarding its starting time – either they can begin as soon as the project begins, or their start is dependent upon the completion of another activity or group of activities. Clearly, most activities will be of this latter nature (for example, parts cannot be assembled unless they have been ordered and received).

In the construction of a network it is usually best to begin with the final activity in the project and work backwards, determining which activities must be completed before a given activity can begin. Normal PERT and CPM systems require events to be numbered. This facilitates computer processing by making it possible to refer to an activity in terms of its beginning and end events.

Estimating time

The network, therefore, forms a framework relating important characteristics of activities contained in it. Total project time is very important and in PERT three estimates of the time required for an activity are needed:

'optimistic' – which assumes everything goes well;
'pessimistic' – assuming every possible hindrance;
'normal' – the most likely time.

In the CPM approach only a single time estimate is required. Where there is a high degree of uncertainty, numerous time estimates are needed (as in research and development for which PERT was originally designed). PERT can also be applied to maintenance and training programmes and sales campaigns. Network methods are best applied to the development and achievement of specific tasks, not repetitive work (e.g. flow production).

Procedure in PERT analysis

1 List all jobs or activities in a project noting their interrelationship.
2 Estimate the time for each activity.
3 Draw the network diagram.
4 Analyse the network.

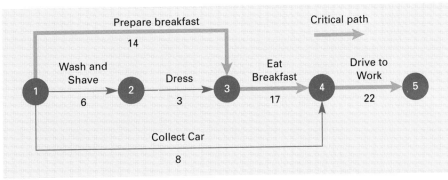

Fig 6.7 Simple illustration of network. (Reproduced by permission of the British Broadcasting Corporation.)

Assume that person, A, is helped to go to work by his mother, who prepares breakfast, and his sister, who collects A's car from a nearby garage, and that their duties commence when the alarm bell rings in the morning. The ringing of this bell is the starting event and allows the initial activities to begin – i.e. prepare breakfast, wash and shave, collect car.

To ensure that the end result (arrival at work) is reached on time, A must wash and shave, dress, eat breakfast, and drive to work – and we shall assume that he always performs the tasks in that order. Thus he can start dressing only when 'wash and shave' is finished; 'eat breakfast' depends upon *two* activities being completed, preparation of breakfast and dressing. 'Drive to work' is dependent upon eating breakfast and collection of car.

Minimum project time. Time durations can be obtained for the activities and these are:

wash and shave	– 6 minutes
dress	– 3 minutes
prepare breakfast	– 14 minutes
eat breakfast	– 17 minutes
collect car	– 8 minutes
drive to work	– 22 minutes.

These are inserted on the network.

There are three routes through the network and the times of these routes can be calculated. These are:

1–3, 3–4, 4–5	– 53 minutes
1–2, 2–3, 3–4, 4–5	– 48 minutes
1–4, 4–5	– 30 minutes.

The greatest time, 53 minutes, is the *minimum project time* and the corresponding route is the *critical path,* i.e. 1–3, 3–4, 4–5. (NB: Event 3 is reached in 14 minutes; add duration time for activity 3–4, making a total of 31 minutes; and the 22 minutes for driving to work brings the total to 53 minutes, when the last event is reached.)

All activities on this path are *critical* and must be completed on time if the whole project is not to be delayed.

Any *spare time* available in performing other activities is called float. Fetching the car, for example, requires 8 minutes and may be performed at any time within a period of 31 minutes (i.e. 14 + 17). The difference between 31 and 8 is 23 minutes and represents *float.* Also, washing, shaving and dressing takes 6 + 3 = 9 minutes and there is a float of 5 minutes between this total and the 14 minutes needed to prepare breakfast. A could stay in bed 5 minutes more and still be ready when breakfast was; the time along the critical path would not be affected.

This *knowledge of float values* is therefore very important where resources are limited. For example, if the car could not be collected because the sister was ill, the mother could, after preparing breakfast, collect the car herself and still the car would be ready for A by the time he had eaten breakfast (14 + 8 = 22 minutes; there are 9 minutes to spare before the 31 minutes to event 4 elapse).

These principles can be applied to thousands of activities and, usually, when more than about 100 activities are involved, a computer is used. Finding the critical path will identify those activities which must be completed on time to avoid project delay. Progress can be *reviewed* by comparing achieved figures with original estimates of durations, and a systematic use of float values ensures that resources are allocated to the best advantage.

In the case of a contract containing penalty clauses the contractor, faced with delay on the critical path, can make an objective choice between paying the penalty and incurring additional costs (e.g. by working overtime). Vital activities can be seen, and so can those activities which may safely be delayed.

Management action

As typical PERT analyses run into tens of thousands of events, computers are used and vast amounts of data are obtained. Discrimination is therefore essential and a useful method is to pre-define certain events of particular management interest, and give a *summary network* to the managers concerned. The information can also be portrayed in a graphic form by the computer. A good reporting system attracts management's attention to areas which threaten scheduled progress.

If the schedule cannot be met, a new plan is needed, which may require answers to the following questions:

- Can sequential activities be performed in parallel?
- Can manpower or resources be diverted from activities with larger float?

NB: If the critical path is now shortened, there may appear another critical path; contemplated changes may be processed on a computer and this network is not, in effect, a *simulation model*.

By focusing management attention on activities lying on the critical path, management by exception is facilitated.

Advantages of PERT

- Managers are forced to plan in making up a network.
- All departments must co-operate in planning.
- Attention is concentrated on critical elements.
- Control can be immediate and enables corrective action to be taken.
- Management is given the ability to plan the best possible use of resources to achieve a goal, within the limitations of cost and time.
- Interdependencies and problem areas are revealed which are either not obvious or not well defined.

Disadvantages of PERT

- The project must not be nebulous, i.e. it must be specific enough to time accurately.
- It is not practicable for routine planning, e.g. flow production.
- If emphasis is purely on time and not cost, its value diminishes. Certain adaptations of PERT are rectifying this matter. (See PERT/Cost.)

Applications

Network analysis can be used in the office, e.g. in completing a balance sheet by a certain date and noting the numerous interdependent activities, or in the installation of a new accounting system. It can be used for planning and controlling auditing programmes, and on the marketing side it is being applied increasingly to the launching of new products. Some kinds of administrative project – an office move, for example – are well suited to critical path methods.

PERT/Cost

The construction and process industries have successfully used a *cost extension of CPM* to determine the optimum combination of manpower and costs to meet a directed project completion date. PERT originally had time as the only relevant factor and the importance of cost was such that it had to be included and this was introduced in 1962 by the American government.

Estimated costs are collected for small groups of related activities. Labour, material and overhead costs are noted and, as the project continues, actual accrued costs for each cost collection point are gathered and revised estimates submitted if needed. Time and cost data are available, enabling management to identify activity groups contributing to over-runs of time or cost. A projection of *manpower needs* for each category of job can be obtained by computer and the number of man-hours needed can be broken down over the months in each category and, if demand for a skill exceeds supply, overtime can be worked, or more personnel hired, or activities can be *re-scheduled.*

Resource allocation and multi-project scheduling (RAMPS)

PERT and CPM do not take complete account of resources and often, when a number of projects are being carried out simultaneously, there will be fairly severe restrictions on available resources. RAMPS was developed to tackle such problems. Based on the network model, it allows various restrictions to be placed on resources and copes with the *planning of a number of projects* that need to be carried out *simultaneously.* The aim is to minimize the total cost, by allocating resources where alternatives exist.

SUMMARY

Objective 1 *Explain the steps in the control process and why control is necessary.*
Control is the process through which managers assure that actual activities conform to planned activities. It involves establishing standards and measures, the measurement of results, the comparison of results with standards, and taking corrective action where necessary.

The changing environment, the increasing complexity of organizations, the fact that members of organizations make mistakes and that managers must delegate authority, are the main factors that make control necessary.

Objective 2 *Summarize the issues managers have to deal with in designing a control system and the principles of effective control.*
In designing a system of control managers must decide on the types and number of measurements required, who will set the standards, how flexible the standards will be, the frequency of measurement and the direction that feedback will take.

Principles of effective control include:

- setting controls according to the nature of the job to be performed;
- reporting deviations immediately;
- ensuring controls conform to the pattern of the organization;
- showing exceptions at key points;
- being flexible and economic in operation; and
- being simple to understand and indicating corrective action.

Objective 3 *Describe the budgeting process and identify the various types of budgets an organization can use.*

The budgeting process begins when top management sets the strategies and goals for the organization. Usually lower level managers devise budgets for their sections. These will be reviewed by their superiors and this will be passed up the chain of command so that they are all integrated in a final budget. It is important to ensure wide participation in the preparation of budgets to overcome some of the anxiety managers may develop in the resource allocations they receive.

Budgets may be classified in many ways. One method is to look at operating budgets, i.e. the goods and services an organization expects to consume in the period. They are usually expressed in physical quantities (e.g. machines produced) and cost figures. Financial budgets detail the money the organization intends to spend in the same period and where that money will come from. Budgets may also be classified as fixed, variable or semi-variable.

Objective 4 *Describe various types of financial control methods and why they are used by managers.*

Financial control methods include financial statements, ratio analysis, and break-even analysis. Commonly used methods are after the event financial statements such as balance sheets, profit and loss accounts and cash flow statements. These are used by managers to control the activities of the organization and by individuals outside the organization to evaluate its effectiveness. Common types of ratio analysis include liquidity, debt and return on investment ratios, which may be used to compare the performance of the organization against its own performance in the past or the performance of competitors. Break-even analysis is designed to illustrate the relationship between costs, sales volume and profits and can be used as a control device or as a decision-making aid.

Objective 5 *Describe the main types of auditing methods.*

There are three types of auditing methods:

- external auditing, which involves an independent appraisal of an organization's financial accounts and statements;
- internal auditing, which is performed by members of the organization and appraises the financial statements of an organization, also its operational efficiency;
- management auditing which is a comprehensive systematic appraisal of the management and organizational performance of an enterprise.

1 What are the principles of effective control?

2 Distinguish carefully between budgetary and non-budgetary controls.

3 What can operational research contribute to effective management?

4 Give examples of the use of simulation techniques.

5 What are the main factors to consider in stock control?

6 What do you understand by queuing theory?

7 Give examples of the problems solved by linear programming.

8 How can network analysis aid the optimum allocation of resources?

9 What is meant by planning, programming and budgeting systems?

10 What is meant by human asset accounting?

11 List the main persons requiring information from an accounting system.

12 Why is feedback an essential ingredient of an effective control system?

13 How might budgetary control produce organizational conflict?

14 'A management audit picks up where a financial audit leaves off.' Discuss.

1 Discuss the proposition that budgetary control is of limited use to managers in that it:

   (a) indicates the existence of some problems rather than suggesting their solution;
   (b) may concentrate on expenditure whilst tending to neglect income; and
   (c) may direct their energies to activities which do not improve the efficiency of the company.

2 Discuss the practical value to organizations of human resource (or human asset) accounting as a means of measuring the value of the people employed. What are the problems associated with the application of this technique, and how might they be overcome?

3 Your company is reconsidering its organizational structure and is concerned that in the future some means of measuring departmental efficiency should be available.
   As management accountant you are requested to prepare a discussion paper for circulation to other members of the management team, clearly setting out the problems of selecting appropriate measures of efficiency for departments of your company.

4 What is meant in a company balance sheet by:

   (a) the equity of the company;
   (b) debenture stock;
   (c) preference shares?

5 A number of accounting ratios are used to measure the efficiency with which the resources of a company are being managed. Describe any four of these ratios and indicate how they may be applied.

ASSIGNMENTS

1 In many universities and colleges student performance in a course is evaluated by regularly submitted course work and a final examination. Assume that during a year you submit course work regularly and participate in classes, but your marks are always below what you expect. What do you do?

Then compare and contrast your reactions with those of a manager of a division of a company whose annual bonus is determined solely on the basis of comparing budgeted and actual financial performance. What modifications or changes would you recommend in both cases?

2 Divide into two groups and discuss the following proposition – 'One of the main problems of industry these days is that accountants have taken over. Their main concern is how financial targets will be met rather than producing the right product for the market'.

BIBLIOGRAPHY

Armstrong, M, *Handbook of Management Techniques* (London, Kogan Page, 1993).
Buyers and Holmes, *Principles of Cost Accountancy (UK*, Holt Saunders, 5th edition, 1986).
Glautier, M W E and Underdown, B, *Accounting Theory and Practice* (London, Pitman Publishing, 4th edition, 1991).
Higson, C J, *Business Finance*, 2nd edition (London, Butterworth, 1992).
McLaney, E J, *Business Finance for Decision-Makers* (London, Pitman Publishing, 1991).
Morris, C, *Quantitative Approaches in Business Studies* (London, Pitman Publishing, 1993).
Owen, F and Jones, R, *Statistics* (London, Pitman Publishing, 4th edition, 1994).
Peters, T J and Waterman, R H, *In Search of Excellence* (New York, Harper & Row, 1983).
Watts, B K R, *Business and Financial Management* (London, M+E Handbooks, Pitman Publishing, 1991).
Whitehead, P and Whitehead, G, *Statistics for Business* (Pitman Publishing, 1992).
Wisniewski, M, *Quantitative Methods for Decision Makers* (London, Pitman Publishing, 1994).

PART 2

Management in action

Part 1 sought to explain and analyse the basic science, theory and principles of management and how they relate to the practice of managing. It emphasized the need for a systems approach and that practice must take into account actual situations and contingencies. This part is concerned with the practical side of management and studies the issues of marketing, production, human resource management and office organization. Marketing seeks to widen public understanding and confidence in the goods and services of an organization and a main aim is to keep the customer satisfied.

Part 2 then describes the production function of an enterprise, studies issues of the production process, production planning and control, research and development, design, purchasing, materials handling, automation and Flexible Manufacturing Systems.

Human resource management is then considered; it is that part of the process of management that is concerned with the maintenance of human relationships and ensuring the physical well-being of employees, so that they give maximum contribution to efficient working. The final chapter considers the importance of the role of management of the modern office and the impact of electronic equipment which is affecting all parts of the office environment. Companies ignoring this great increase in automation in the office will not be able to match the efficiency of competitors.

CHAPTER 7

Marketing and sales management

Marketing has been defined in many different ways. It is the set of activities that directs the flow of goods and services from the producer to satisfy consumers and accomplish the objectives of the organization. Marketing can consist of many activities: selling, transportation, storage, risk taking, gathering market information etc.

The marketing sub-system has a major objective in getting the products of a firm into the hands of consumers. This can include sending out information through advertising and personal selling, pricing the products, transporting and storing products to meet consumers' needs.

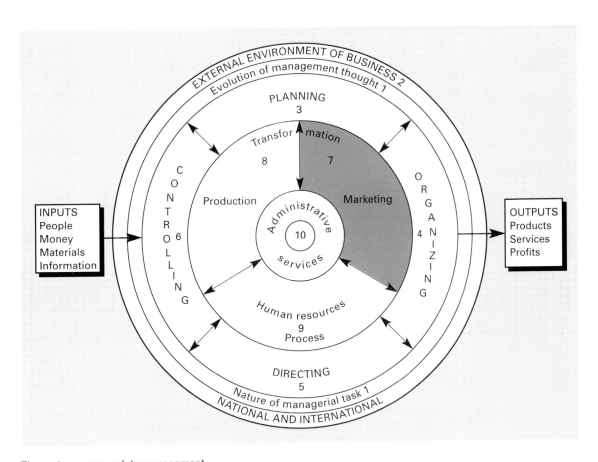

The systems approach to management

Marketing provides the match between the organization's human, financial and physical resources and the wants of customers. This includes gathering data about direct and indirect competition, economic uncertainties, legal and political and other constraints. All this must be done against an environmental background of change and uncertainty. An organization communicates with target markets by a combination of personal selling, advertising, sales promotion and publicity. Personal selling is communication between a salesperson and a customer regarding the firm and its products.

The main channels of distribution are considered together with the various types of retail trading outlets.

The many problems in determining prices are considered. It is noted that even though the product may be at the right place at the right time, it will not sell adequately if the price is not right.

The final section of the chapter considers the problems of exporting goods and the assistance that can be given.

OBJECTIVES

Upon completing this chapter you should be able to:

- Understand how the marketing sub-system of a business contributes to the whole business.
- Define the process of market segmentation and its purposes.
- Describe briefly the importance of pricing decisions in marketing strategy and the procedures and methods adopted to meet agreed goals.
- Explain why enterprise might enter the international business field.
- Describe briefly the minimum amount of information required by an enterprise to enable it to determine whether it should operate in another country.

MARKETING

In small organizations the person in charge of marketing may also be responsible for one or more of the other functions, for example, finance. As the business grows, delegation of certain duties is needed and usually one person is given the responsibility of marketing.

This term should be correctly used. It may be simply defined as bringing the right goods and services to the customer in the most efficient and profitable manner.

The Institute of Marketing uses the following definition:

Marketing is the creative management function which promotes trade and employment by assessing consumer needs and initiating research and development to meet them. It co-ordinates the resources of production and distribution of the goods and services; determines the nature of the total effort required to sell profitably the maximum production to the ultimate user.

Effective marketing is the means whereby all the activities of a business are drawn together to a common goal, with the full co-operation of other departments – production, research and finance.

The term 'sales manager' is often used in place of 'marketing manager'. To be more specific the term 'sales manager' should be confined to the organization and control of the selling and distribution activities. The wider duties of the marketing manager can be seen from the following schedule.

MARKETING ORGANIZATION AND ADMINISTRATION

Schedule of responsibilities of marketing manager

The schedule might include:

- advising board of directors on marketing policy;
- within the limits of policy laid down, the marketing manager will plan and execute all the activities for assessing and creating consumer demand and for the sale, storage and distribution of the company's goods;
- as concerns market research, the marketing manager will keep the market under review, noting the extent of the market, the company's share and the share of the market held by competitors, and all aspects of changing demand;
- sales promotion – advertising and display, pricing policy, discounts and credit terms;
- budget preparation – preparation of sales budgets in liaison with production and finance departments;
- control of distribution – this involves selection of channels of distribution, warehousing and transport facilities;
- control of personnel – in collaboration with human resources manager, selection and training of selling, clerical and warehouse staff.

A more detailed schedule of responsibilities would include an indication of any special duties and possible limitations in his authority, for example: 'the authority of the managing director is required if credit is to be allowed.'

Marketing objectives

In selling, most emphasis is on actual sales: in marketing, the needs of the buyer are considered and a product to satisfy these needs should be the aim.

The ideal position could be said to be where the planned volume of goods is produced, which is then sold to give the planned profit.

Marketing policy

This involves the appraisal of many factors in order to decide the broad principles which the company is to follow. Correct answers to the following important questions are needed:

- What is the nature of competition and the present position in the 'life' of existing products? (*See* Fig 7.9, p 291).
- What are the most effective methods of distribution and advertising?
- What methods of transport, wholesaling, allocation of sales quotas, sales training and control of human resources should be adopted?

NB: It is sometimes preferable for a committee comprising heads of production, finance and marketing to determine policy, to ensure complete co-ordination.

Marketing plans
Whatever plans are made to direct and control the marketing operation, they must be flexible, as there are many outside factors which can easily affect the plans, e.g. government legislation. These plans can be set up for each aspect of marketing, e.g. media strategy, sales promotion, budget appropriation.

Marketing policy should be known by all the staff; this enables them to act in a unified manner with wholesalers, retailers and customers. An organization's reputation is largely built up on its selling policy, e.g. Marks and Spencer – the lowest price consistent with product quality and reliability.

It is worthwhile considering an example of the need for careful forecasting. There is a current trend to build hypermarkets on the outskirts of urban developments, where land is low in price and the site is convenient for consumers who are more mobile than in the past. Some of the points that will need to be considered include the estimates of:

- the growth of the country's economy (Gross National Product);
- availability of suitable sites and their cost;
- changes in spending habits of consumers;
- attitude to self-service;
- population trends and the rate of urban development;
- local plans for road building;
- availability of motor transport, especially for housewives.

The preparation of the marketing plan can be assisted by an analysis of the true position of the business in the market place. One method used in completing a marketing audit is the preparation of a *SWOT analysis.*

Internal factors are the basic strengths and weaknesses of a company, e.g. managerial, financial, technical. *External factors* are the opportunities and threats outside a company's direct control, e.g. technology, competitors, government legislation.

A SWOT analysis seeks to identify the *s*trengths, *w*eaknesses, *o*pportunities and *t*hreats and presents such information clearly to enable a company to state its position on key issues. For example, what do our customers need? What are our competitors doing?

A *marketing audit* covers a wide area. In the *business and economic* environment, there is a *wide range of areas to be examined,* in order to isolate those factors considered critical to the performance of a company, e.g. economic, social, political, business, legal, technological, international. In the *competitive* and company environment, the product range, market share, pricing, promotion and distribution need to be examined. The nature of supply and demand for the products and the market size and trends are also part of the total audit checklist.

If a marketing audit is properly completed it will provide the basis for setting realistic marketing objectives and strategies.

It is important to note that customers are attracted to the *benefits* that a product will bring and not the product itself. So a *customer-* or market-orientated approach is required to product development, rather than a product-orientated approach. The needs and wants of the customer are of paramount importance.

Public image

It is important that a company should decide, as an important matter of policy, what type of *public image* is required. To this end, all policies – marketing, manufacturing and human resources – should reflect this overall policy of image. Then a basic public relations policy can be put forward to ensure that the public are influenced to react to the company in the desired way. There are a number of publics, e.g. shareholders, customers, employees (potential and present), suppliers and government. The various 'publics' can be influenced by good public relations to regard the organization as:

- public spirited with a civic responsibility;
- a good organization to work for, or invest in;
- a company whose products can be purchased with confidence and reliability.

It is also important to increase morale both inside and outside the company. If employees are proud of the organization, its achievements and service to the community, this will be reflected in their daily work. This can, for example, help salespeople to be more confident in their approach to selling.

Effective public relations can also be of help in the promotion of products (*see* p 287), the purpose being to back up advertising and to ensure the customers are more favourably disposed towards the products of the company which are to be advertised. So in effect, public relations promotes a company and its products to a wider range of public than normal advertising and sales promotion. There is a problem in trying to measure the effectiveness of public relations as its results may not be too evident or capable of measurement.

Management must ask itself a basic question about the present business of the company and its future plans. A close watch is needed on existing product stages, to consider whether they need to be revitalized, dropped, or new products introduced. The answers obtained will form the basis for product planning decisions for the future profitability of the company. The various elements of product planning have to be modified or changed during the various phases of the cycle, for example, policies for pricing, research and development, market research, packaging, advertising, sales promotion schemes. The right mix of the marketing ingredients is vital.

The marketing mix

This refers to the combination of policies and procedures adopted from time to time by a company in its marketing programme. It involves the integration of the elements of a marketing programme that will best achieve the objects of a company in a given time period. Success can be measured by a company producing most profit from a mix of the following variables: product planning, pricing, branding and channels of distribution, selling, advertising and promotion, packaging and display, servicing, physical handling, fact-finding and analysis. There are other forces beyond the control of the marketing manager in the short term, e.g. buyer and trade behaviour, the position and behaviour of competitors, and also government action. Each variable intercuts

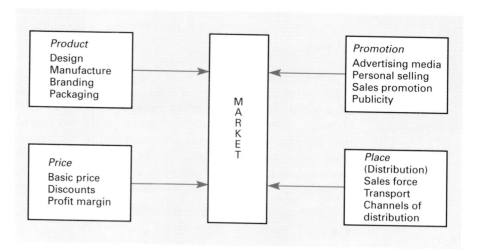

Fig 7.1 Elements of marketing mix

with another, and they can be broken down further; for example, distribution may be direct, or through intermediaries, exclusive dealers, part-owned dealers or franchises.

The position of the product life-cycle has an important bearing on the marketing mix. It is therefore important not to ignore the change in marketing strategy when phases 2, 3, and 4 are reached (*see* Fig 7.9, p 291).

The four Ps of the marketing mix must all be examined separately, but must be all considered when they interact. The solution for one year may be unrelated to the next.

Products or services may be introduced, improved upon, then made obsolete. *Prices may be undercut and promotions* affected by competitive campaigns. The *place* where customers purchase can also change because of the changing alternative retail shopping and distribution activities.

The concept of marketing mix was first presented by Neil Borden of Harvard University ('The Concept of Marketing Mix', *Journal of Advertising Research,* June 1964, USA).

At any *one point in time* there is a combination of elements giving the right mix, for a specific product, for a specific company, for a specific market, for specific customers (*see* Fig 7.1).

Market segmentation

1 An organization may use a total market approach and develop a marketing mix that tries to satisfy *everyone* in a specific market with that *one mix* (*see* Fig 7.2). People in the market may have *varying* needs and to this extent a total market approach is not suitable.

2 For some products, consumers' wants and needs may *vary*, so a single marketing mix would not satisfy everyone.

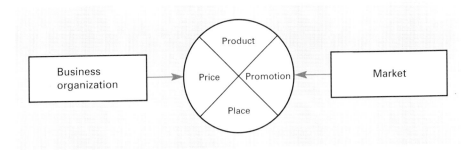

Fig 7.2 Total market approach using single marketing mix

There are numerous products for which consumers' wants and needs are not the same, so for a product of this type the organization should not aim to produce one marketing mix for all consumers, as not many would be satisfied.

Marketing segmentation is a process whereby persons in a market are divided into groups or segments according to one or more characteristics that affect the ability and willingness to buy a product. *The purpose* is to single out from a total market a group of persons who appear to have relatively *similar tastes* in order to create a marketing mix that meets their particular wants and needs. For example, the automobile market is divided by *age,* as this strongly affects buyers' wants and needs for cars. Some cars are designed for young adults, others for the age group 25–45 years who need more carrying capacity and space. By dividing the market this way, the sales potential of each major segment can be evaluated and it can be determined if other firms are already meeting the demand.

The example in Fig 7.3 shows that efforts are being directed at two of the four market segments. It may well be that an analysis could tell the firm that it should not concentrate on *any* segment.

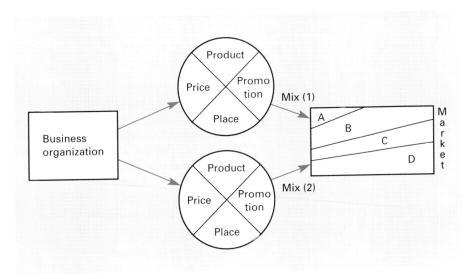

Fig 7.3 Market segmentation approach

Segmentation strategy involves:

- *defining market* segment boundaries;
- *selecting target market* by matching products of the firm to the wants of certain segments;
- *developing a marketing programme* to serve target market;
- *implementing and controlling* the programme.

The economic theory of pure competition (*see* p 44) assumes that homogeneous products of suppliers will be matched with the homogeneous desires and wants of consumers by price adjustments. In reality, the situation is more complex. From the *demand* side, consumers' desires and wants are *diverse*. From the *supply* side, *products* may differ for a number of reasons, e.g. manufacturing techniques, raw material composition, advertising campaigns. Markets are really heterogeneous, where consumer demands are *different*.

Characteristics
of market
segmentation

There are many characteristics that can be used to segment a market and they are very important in consumer markets.

1 **Geographical characteristics.** These include climate, city size, county size, population density, region. Climate influences sporting goods and clothing. Rainwear products, for example, will sell more in the wetter parts of a country. Retail chains locate stores in areas of high population density.

2 **Demographic (or socio-economic) characteristics.** These include age, sex, income, size of family, level of education, occupation, social class. These correspond with human wants and needs for products and they are quite easily measured. Periodicals are aimed at segmented readership, which could be by age of reader or sex. Similarly, advertising within each magazine also reflects such segmentation. Income also segments a market for items such as cameras, cars, housing.

3 **Personality (or psychographic) characteristics.** These include personality characteristics of independence, introverts, extroverts, status seekers. Social class also comes under this heading as the home background influences tastes, values and attitudes. Newspapers, for example, advertise that their readers come from a range of social class backgrounds, ranging from A (upper middle class) to D/E (working class and subsistence levels).

The above approaches are more usually applied to consumer goods and markets.
Industrial segmentation is mainly by type of buyer (government or private firm); size of organization (large or small); trade group (using the Standard Industrial Classification); type of use (plant and equipment); location of company (home or overseas). Generally speaking, industrial and commercial buyers are *more rational* in their buying decisions. In some cases the whole market may consist of only a few customers.

A final point to consider in any strategy of segmentation is that markets require not only to be identified, but should be *responsive* and *significant*. A segment is *responsive* if it *demonstrates effective demand*, that is:

- money (income, assets, credit worthiness);
- authority to buy;
- desire to buy.

Significance refers to the market potential of the segment, i.e. will demand be great enough to be worthwhile?

Marketing organization

It has already been stated that policy must be formulated in conjunction with finance and production. Proper co-ordination is essential and techniques such as budgetary control are most useful. The actual composition of the sales organization varies greatly between firms. Current trends in marketing organization reflect the following points:

- many functions, formerly considered non-marketing, are being assigned to or co-ordinated with marketing, e.g. product development;
- market research has assumed greater importance.

Companies which manufacture electronic equipment will have different marketing problems from motor-car manufacturers. If a company is part of a group, individual company policy may be subordinated to group policy. Some firms buy goods for the market, others manufacture goods and then pass them to separate marketing bodies.

Figure 7.4(a) shows a grouping of various specialist managers, under a marketing manager. In large organizations, it may be advisable to appoint product managers, who would co-ordinate marketing activities relating to single products or groups of products.

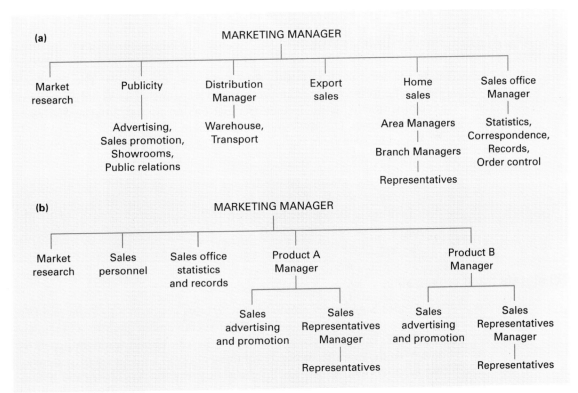

Fig 7.4 (a) Organization chart for medium to large company; (b) Organization chart – emphasizing products sold

Figure 7.4(b) shows such a grouping under products. Other groupings can be chosen depending upon, for example:

(a) The market – electricity is sold to home and industrial users. Two sales managers may be needed, for home and industrial.
(b) Applications of products – similarly, where oil, for example, is used for heating and also for cars, etc., two managers, one for each use, may be required.

Marketing philosophy

A principle of the utmost importance is that a firm should be consumer-orientated.

Many firms were, and many still are, production-orientated. After the Second World War, many products were sold in large numbers because of the high demand and little regard was paid to the real needs of the consumer. Later, more firms competed for the customer's money and firms found they had to take heed of the customer's requirements in order to keep, or increase, their hold on the market.

Firms that treat their customers as being of the utmost importance, so that products are made with the needs of the customer in mind, are said to be consumer-orientated.

The application of this principle can be seen in the organization chart in Fig 4.8 (*see* p 165).

ORGANIZATION OF THE HOME TRADE

Goods are produced and most find their way to a buyer. The ideal may appear to be to sell direct from producer to consumer. This is not always possible or profitable, as many factors must be considered. Intermediaries are used in most cases, i.e. wholesalers and retailers.

As can be seen from Fig 7.5, the main channels of distribution for manufactured goods are:

● direct sales, e.g. sale of a computer to a firm;
● distribution to retailer direct;
● distribution via wholesaler to retailer;
● via agent, wholesaler to retailer;
● via agent to retailer.

Wholesale trade organization

A wholesaler is generally a merchant who buys goods in bulk from manufacturers in his particular trade, selling them in convenient quantities to retailers. By buying in bulk and paying promptly, he can obtain trade and cash discounts from the manufacturers. From these allowances he must provide warehouse accommodation and a selling and delivery service. He tries to obtain a quicker turnover to minimize loss through deterioration or obsolescence. If he

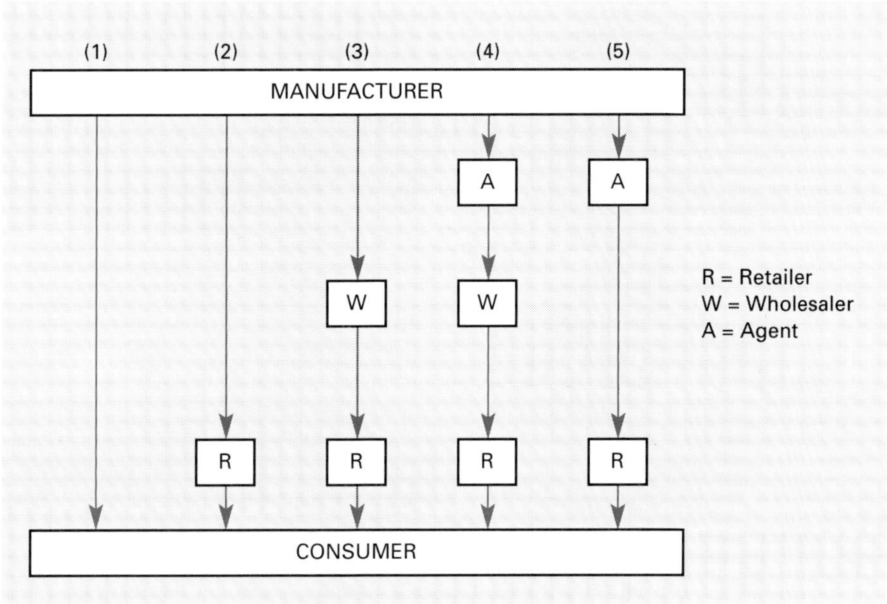

```
        (1)         (2)         (3)         (4)         (5)
    ┌──────────────────────────────────────────────────────┐
    │                      MANUFACTURER                      │
    └──────────────────────────────────────────────────────┘
     │           │           │        ┌───┐       ┌───┐
     │           │           │        │ A │       │ A │
     │           │           │        └───┘       └───┘
     │           │        ┌───┐     ┌───┐
     │           │        │ W │     │ W │            R = Retailer
     │           │        └───┘     └───┘            W = Wholesaler
     │           │           │        │              A = Agent
     │        ┌───┐       ┌───┐    ┌───┐          ┌───┐
     │        │ R │       │ R │    │ R │          │ R │
     │        └───┘       └───┘    └───┘          └───┘
    ┌──────────────────────────────────────────────────────┐
    │                       CONSUMER                         │
    └──────────────────────────────────────────────────────┘
```

Fig 7.5 **Main channels for manufactured goods**

keeps too narrow a range, some customers may go elsewhere, so he may stock slow-moving lines to retain their custom.

He delivers at varying times; in some trades he expects cash on delivery, in others he extends credit to his customers. Some manufacturers act as wholesalers and may also buy other firms' goods. There are also large retailers who act as wholesalers for smaller shops in an area, and make a profit by receiving quantity discounts.

Any manufacturer who decides to *omit the wholesaler* must take over his functions. This will mean opening warehouses in suitable areas and engaging more staff. Deliveries may be later than before and only his lines will be sold. It has been found that in many cases the cost to the manufacturers is rarely less than when the original wholesaler was used.

'Cash and Carry' wholesalers

The main features are:

- retailers collect from wholesaler's warehouse and provide their own transport;
- few credit facilities or delivery services are given;
- the wholesaler has lower occupancy costs as the warehouse is outside the city centre;
- retailers pay less for their purchases.

Retail trade organization

Figure 7.6 shows the main retail trading outlets in the UK. It is important to note that there is a tendency for these to merge and overlap, e.g. department stores combine to form groups in the fashion of multiple stores.

Type	Description	Trading pattern	Other features
Department store (e.g. Selfridges)	Large shop (annual sales £100 000) carrying great variety of merchandise under one roof. There are many departments each specializing in one type of good.	They give good personal service – credit accounts and delivery services. They have reputation for good window displays and special offers.	Good quality personnel. They are flexible and benefit from specialized buying, office staff and centralized management.
Multiple shop (e.g. Burton)	Group of shops, each dealing with similar product, e.g. shoes, under central control.	They deal in small range of goods and offer standard quality and price. Control is strong and flexible. They react quickly to consumer demand.	Benefit from centralized administration and decentralized selling. Large-scale operation justifies use of special equipment, e.g. computers. Bulk-buying and use of ware-houses enable them to integrate wholesaling with retailing. Standardization and restricted stock range ensure good stock control.
Variety chain store (e.g. British Home Stores)	Similar features to multiple shop. Each shop in group sells a larger range of products, usually of lower value.	Minimum service is given. Large range of cheaper goods offered which are in strong consumer demand. Stock turn is high.	Benefit from centralizing buying and central control. Wage costs are lower, because young assistants are employed, who have restricted range of duties. Close control of manufacturers. Marks and Spencer benefit from good quality produce, which is rigidly inspected.
Co-operative stores	Association of individuals organized on voluntary basis to supply goods and services to members.	Pattern varies. Could be any of above types. Slow tendency to modernize, now including more self-service shops.	Restricted range of goods has been a handicap. Over 50 per cent of goods are supplied by Co-operative Wholesale Society. Management committees are elected by lay members (part-time), centralized buying to produce greater economies. Recently, concentrating on thorough reorganization.
Hypermarket	Minimum sales area of 50 000 sq.ft. Situated near large towns	Self service. Wide range of food and non-food items.	Low wage costs. Large car park.
Superstore	Over 25 000 sq.ft. A large supermarket carrying a wide range of food and non-food items.	Usually trades on one floor. Low prices.	Large car park. Meeting all routine needs of customers.
Supermarkets (e.g. Safeway)	Selling space over 2000 sq.ft. with at least 3 check-out points. Mainly self-service, with wide range of merchandise, particularly food and household requirements.	Shop arranged to encourage high turnover and easy flow. Cut-prices and special offers are main techniques to encourage trade. Little service is given.	Impulse buying encouraged by self-service. Fixed costs are high and high turnover is expected. Low labour cost to sales ratio, and low profit margins per item. Problems are pilfering and marking of over 6000 items.

Fig 7.6 Summary of main retail trading outlets

Mail order (e.g. Freemans)	A method of retailing whereby goods are sold by description and illustrations – they are advertised in magazines, catalogues and press. Goods are delivered by post.	Credit or hire-purchase terms are usually offered and a guarantee of satisfaction or money back is given. Many agents are used; they receive a percentage commission (about 10 per cent of cash recieved). Fairly wide range of goods, not so many as department store.	Bulk-buying, centralized delivery and payment, and close co-operation with suppliers give worthwhile economies. Very convenient to public. Costs of catalogues are high and so is expenditure on transport. Steady growth in volume of trade in recent years.
Discount houses	Self-service stores dealing in non-food items at reduced prices. Usually having area of 10 000 to 18 000 sq.ft. Similar to supermarket.	Situated on outskirts of city centres, easily accessible large open building. Little service is given; customers take goods away. Low cost because of low overhead charges and very low rent. Goods mainly consumer durables.	Goods mainly non-price-fixed goods. High rate of stock turn, low capital investment cost, minimum expenditure on fittings. (NB Not same success as in USA probably because of fewer cars per head, and general suspicion of retail trade).
Auto-vending	Sale by machine.	Mainly in populated central areas. Often additional facility given by shops.	Growing steadily. High cost, so must be justified by high sales. Mainly liquids, cigarettes and chocolates sold, but extended to clothing and other commodities as technology develops.
Independent retailers	Single units, or small group of shops under private ownership. Generally only one owner.	Very personal service. Some may have numerous small departments.	Trend is to groups of retailers, to get more efficiency, in all aspects of management.

Fig 7.6 Continued

Other trading outlets

- House-to-house selling and travelling shops;
- Voluntary groups, e.g. retailers' co-operatives, such as Spar.

Other trading outlets are independent retail shops, participating in a reciprocal arrangement with a wholesaler to obtain economies of purchasing. Each retailer agrees to take a percentage of the goods from the wholesaler. The tendency is for groups to develop their own lines and brand names. Group advertising is possible, e.g. on television, which would not be practicable for an individual retailer. In addition, services such as shop conversion and help in display are given to retailers.

Trading stamps

Trading stamps are a method used by retailers to attract customers. Stamps are given in accordance with the value of purchases made. The stamps can be exchanged later for gifts by a trading stamp company. The retailer buys the stamps in bulk from the stamp company and distributes them. They can be regarded as retail sales promotion on a long-term basis. The *cost to the retailer* is approximately 2 per cent of his turnover, plus time spent in distributing them. It is expected that increased turnover will more than pay for the cost of the stamps.

The peak period was between 1960 and the early 1970s. After inflation caused real living standards to fall a small price difference seemed important and many preferred to pay less rather than obtain stamps. Slowly by the mid-1970s trading stamps lost ground, particularly in large distribution chains. Co-operative societies still maintain stamps as an alternative to their payment of dividend on purchases.

The Trading Stamps Act of 1964 allowed the holder to convert stamps to cash and the cash value of the stamp had to be stated.

Resale price maintenance

Resale price maintenance is the practice whereby a manufacturer fixes the price the retailer is to charge the customer. The passing of the Resale Prices Act 1964 was intended to restore competition in the distributive trades and keep prices down. The Act:

- rendered *void* any condition imposed by a supplier for the maintenance of a minimum resale price, unless the supplier has claimed exemption for the class of goods concerned;
- rendered *unlawful* any withholding of supplies from a dealer on the ground that he has sold or is likely to sell the supplier's goods at less than his fixed or recommended resale price, unless he has sold them as 'loss leaders'.

It was recognized by the Act that, for some goods, price-cutting may be to the detriment of the consumer, e.g. making it difficult for the retailer to provide an efficient service. So a supplier could register a class of goods with the Office of Fair Trading and, until the Restrictive Practices Court examined the applications and ordered otherwise, the goods would be exempted from the provisions of the Act. Exemption would only be granted if the supplier could show:

(a) public detriment would otherwise result;

(b) there would be a reduction in the number of varieties or quality of goods, or number of retail establishments, or in necessary sales or after-sales service, or increase in danger to public health, or an eventual price increase, outweighing the detriment arising from a continuance of Resale Price Maintenance.

NB: The Act did *not prohibit* the fixing of maximum prices or of recommended minimum prices.

Where a supplier is entitled to maintain prices, he makes it a condition in his agreement with wholesalers and retailers. Compliance can be enforced by withholding similar goods, or suing the retailer for damages for breach of contract.

Consumer protection

Not every organization places customer's needs and desires before everything else. In most environments the customers will sometimes be treated badly. This may be just an error of judgement rather than deliberate.

A number of organizations have been set up to protect the consumer. Some of these are government sponsored as well as private. Pressure groups, or consumer protection groups, attempt to ensure rules and codes are provided for conducting relations between organizations and their customers.

Complaints from customers tend to express dissatisfaction with the ways in which organizations match their resources with the needs of customers. So any customer protest (consumerism) must act as a spur to encourage an organization to pay attention to what customers need. Marketing should not therefore make exaggerated claims about products or services offered. The *caveat emptor* 'let the buyer beware' was a doctrine widely accepted. However, since the end of the 19th century the responsibility for the quality of a service or a product has moved more and more on to the vendor's shoulders. This in effect could change the phrase to '*caveat vendor*'.

There are many countries within the European Union (EU) which have agreed to strengthen laws in favour of the customer, because of consumer pressure groups. Examples of regulation in Europe to inform the buyer of the true facts include showing clearly:

- the true cost of an item under 'unit pricing';
- the full cost of credit or loans given;
- the constituent elements of products to be shown on labels;
- the freshness of foods, shown by date-marking.

In the United Kingdom consumer interests are protected by the common law, statutory rights, codes of practice and various consumer groups. *Common law rights* are general rules of custom and practice which can apply to the rights of consumers, although they may have to be strengthened by statutory regulation. For example, a radio repair business has a common law 'duty of care' for radios left for repair. *Statutory rights* protect consumers in the United Kingdom and are provided by parliamentary legislation. These are shown on p 277–8 together with examples of Codes of Practice. Examples of *independent pressure groups* are:

- **Consumers' Association** who carries out tests on consumer goods and services which are recorded in a monthly magazine called *Which?*.
- **Citizens Advice Bureaux** provide a wide range of advice free to consumers.

Examples of *consumer groups publicly appointed* to monitor privatised companies are:

- OFTEL (Office of Telecommunications)
- OFGAS (Office of Gas Supply)

The argument of consumerists is that manufacturers should assume liability for *all* malfunctioning products. Safety standards and quality of medicines are protected by legislative controls and more products are coming under such protection.

A final comment on consumerism is that it opens up *opportunities* for those organizations who take it up and is not a threat. Examples of the *disadvantages* some products have brought to society and how they have been overcome by consumer pressure on companies include:

- reduced lead content in petrol;
- degradable plastic containers;
- phosphate-free detergents;
- low-polluting manufacturing plants.

The above examples show that social responsibility must be considered carefully and companies must be prepared to change and adapt to meet the evolving requirements of society.

Brief notes on the legislation affecting marketing and the consumer

Restrictive Trade Practices Acts 1976 and 1977. Certain restrictive trading agreements between persons carrying on business in the production, supply or processing of goods are made illegal by these Acts. These include agreements restricting the prices to be charged, the quantities to be produced, and the persons to whom goods are to be supplied. These Acts also apply to restrictive agreements made between suppliers of services. It is possible to apply to the Restrictive Practices Court, which may allow an agreement to be enforced if it feels that this would be beneficial to the public interest.

Resale Prices Act 1976. This makes it illegal for a manufacturer or other supplier, when supplying goods to a dealer, to impose a term in the contract laying down a minimum price at which the dealer can re-sell those goods. The Restrictive Practices Court may exempt a particular class of goods from the Act if, for instance, it is proved that, if there was no minimum price agreement, the number of shops selling those goods would be substantially reduced and the resulting detriment to the public would outweigh the detriment resulting from the resale price agreement.

Prices Acts 1974/1975. These relate to the showing of prices and the display of price tariffs.

The Consumer Credit Act 1974 regulates the whole of the credit industry. Thus, hire-purchase, credit-sales and moneylending contracts, among others, are covered. One of the main objects is to safeguard anyone buying on credit, although the Act normally only applies to credit agreements where the amount lent is under £15,000.

Theft Act 1968. Under this Act, a trader who cheats may commit the criminal offence of obtaining property by deception.

Trade Description Acts (1968/1972). These make it a criminal offence for a trader to give a false or misleading description of what is being sold. They apply to sales of goods and services.

The Fair Trading Act 1973 provides for the appointment of a Director-General of Fair Trading, who is to keep under review any commercial activities which may adversely affect the interests of consumers. The Director is empowered to take action against persons who, in the course of business, persist in a course of conduct which is detrimental to consumers' interests and unfair. This can be conduct involving breaches of the civil or criminal law. The Act also contains detailed provisions relating to monopolies and mergers and many regulations have been made under the Act relating to various aspects of consumer protection.

Consumer Safety Act 1978. This gives the government wide powers to make regulations regarding goods which are considered to be risks to their users.

Unsolicited Goods and Services Acts 1971 and 1975. These make it an offence for traders to demand payment for goods not ordered.

Sale of Goods Act 1979. This states that when goods are bought from a trader, it is automatically implied that the goods correspond to their description and are of 'merchantable quality' and reasonably fit for the purpose for which they were sold.

The Supply of Goods (Implied Terms) Act 1973. This provides that traders cannot use exclusion clauses to deprive consumers of the above rights under the Sale of Goods Act. In addition it is a criminal offence to exhibit such exclusion clauses.

The Unfair Contract Terms Act 1977 deals with clauses which exclude liability where services are supplied; for instance, notices in car parks, hotels, and laundries. Clauses excluding liability for death or personal injury have no effect, and other exclusion clauses are subject to a test of reasonableness.

Some statutes affecting consumer law	Main Acts which apply
Statement of and Control of Prices	Trade Descriptions Act 1968 Resale Prices Act 1976 Consumer Protection Act 1987
Food Quality and Hygiene	Food and Drugs Act 1955 Food and Drugs (Control of Premises) Act 1976
Short Measure	Sale of Goods Act 1979 Weights and Measures Act 1985 Theft Act 1968 Trade Descriptions Act 1968

False or Misleading Description	Sale of Goods Act 1979
	Food and Drugs Act 1955
	Misrepresentation Act 1967
	Theft Act 1968
	Trade Description Act 1968
Credit	Consumer Credit Act 1974
Consumer Safety	Sale of Goods Act 1979
(Dangerous Goods)	Consumer Protection Act 1987
Faulty Goods	Sale of Goods Act 1979
	Supply of Goods Act 1982
	Consumer Protection Act 1987

DISTRIBUTION

This word is used in a different sense from the economic meaning of the word, which deals with the rewards to factors of production. In the marketing context, it means the transfer of goods from producer to consumer.

Selection of channels of distribution

Five main channels of distribution are shown on the chart in Fig 7.5 on p 271, but the problem of selecting the most satisfactory channel for each product is complex, and should involve consideration of the following:

1 **Nature of product.** In this connection, the distinction between industrial and consumer goods should be considered:

(a) Industrial goods include capital equipment and raw material for further processing. These are usually sold direct to firms. Distribution policy for such goods is usually simpler, as outlets are fewer and average values per sale are greater; there is less need for a large sales force and average overhead marketing cost to sales is lower.
(b) Consumer goods are mainly purchased by the public and are goods in constant demand, e.g. food, clothing, cars. They are sold through many dispersed retail outlets (Fig 7.6).

2 **Financial position of manufacturer.** The fewer the number of organizations in the chain, the smaller the financial burden on the manufacturer. Expenditure on distribution through alternative channels must be noted.

3 **Variety of products to be sold.** A wide variety may necessitate numerous channels. Some producers may run their own retail outlets if the volume is sufficient, e.g. Boots. They may also sell other organizations' products.

Method	Advantages	Disadvantages	Remarks
Indirect 1 Wholesaler to retailer to customer.	(a) Large orders dealt with resulting in lower delivery and packaging costs. (b) Fewer representatives needed. (c) Fewer accounts required, hence reduction in bad debts.	(a) Lower profit margin on goods sold. (b) Producers must rely on wholesalers to promote goods. No guarantee wholesaler will promote his lines.	Nature of product must be considered. If goods are in regular demand at low price the low profit margins will not allow expensive selling campaign; so wholesaler may be used for staple goods, e.g. soap and clothes.
2 Retailer to consumer.	(a) Profit margin larger. (b) Shorter chain to consumer enables producer to have more say on sales promotion. (c) Closer link aids knowledge of consumer attitudes.	(a) Needs large sales force. (b) Greater costs of packing and delivery and bad debts. (c) Extra costs if retailer is assisted, e.g. by displays.	Similar goods to above method. Particularly perishables, e.g. bread.
Direct 3 Producer to consumer. (a) Canvassing.	Direct control selling methods, by using own salespeople.	Higher selling costs.	Useful for specialized goods, e.g. accounting machines.
(b) Mail order.	Saving salespeople's salaries. Great convenience to customers especially if away from shops.	No personal contact by salespeople. High cost of printing catalogues, packaging and advertising.	All non-perishable goods.
(c) Manufacturer's own shops.	Good control over sales methods.	High cost of delivery and purchase of sites.	Examples, shoes, confectionery.
(d) Direct services (nationalized industries)	Centralized control.	Great volume of work may lead to some inefficiency in distribution.	Examples, British Coal, British Rail.

Fig 7.7 Comparison of main methods of distribution open to manufacturer

The actual selection may fall into the established pattern for the trade, which has proved satisfactory. Manufacturers who introduce a new product will usually adopt the customary method; they should, of course, consider changes.

For a comparison of the main methods of distribution *see* Fig 7.7 above.

Warehousing

Whatever efforts marketing managers make to regulate consumer demand, it is very difficult to equate demand to manufacturing programmes. Warehousing is therefore needed to store the finished products.

Transport is costly, so a decision has to be made as to whether warehouses are to be centrally situated or decentralized.

Function of
warehouses

- They act as a buffer for holding goods between the production process and the user, as many goods are not made directly against customer orders.
- They can be used to break bulk and reduce transport costs.
- If located in a suitable position, they can provide a source for quick supply to customers, e.g. spare-part warehouses.

The 'best' number of warehouses for a particular organization depends upon a number of factors. The right balance between the factors depends more upon the optimum loading of transport units than the actual distance from production point to user.

Factors in
warehouse
planning and
organization

Design and layout. This is of great importance. Ideally, a single floor allows for better movement of goods. A stock rotation system is needed to avoid possible deterioration of goods. Goods which are moved most frequently should be in a conveniently accessible place.

Warehouse space can be allocated according to the earning capacity of the goods. This principle is used in retail stores for counter space allocation.

Mechanical handling. This can mean a vital saving in costs, but consideration should be given to future needs before buying equipment. The maximum use should be made of height.

Choice of
sites

The following points should be considered:

- study past records of shipments and future marketing plans;
- consider the possibility of a shift in population and industry;
- examine size and type of existing and future orders, availability and cost of transport, cost and time in obtaining stock replacements;
- speed and efficiency in processing customer orders.

Transport

One can own or hire transport, or use public transport; it is not easy to compare costs, but a decision has to be taken. Figure 7.8 shows a plan of alternative supply routes open to a manufacturer.

Transport is closely linked to location policy. A manager is usually placed in charge of this section and he may come under the sales or production manager's authority.

Time, size and weight are important factors. Fast transport is more costly and it should preferably be used for light and perishable goods.

Methods of
transport

Some factors to consider in deciding upon a method of transport include:

1 **Own transport.** A firm which sells on a large scale direct to other industrial users, or direct to its own retailers or independent retailers who are widely spread, may prefer its own transport system. In such a case the following factors need consideration:

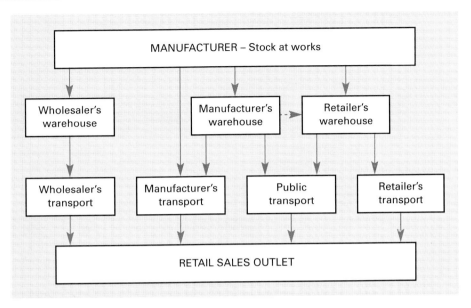

Fig 7.8 Plan of alternative supply routes

- Control of cost of vehicles is essential. Standard costing may be used.
- Work must be *planned,* so that vehicles are effectively employed.

It may be good policy to employ a smaller fleet than necessary and to use outside contractors for extra work. Waste from half-empty lorries and empty return journeys must be avoided.

2 **Outside transport.**
- *Relative costs* of different types of transport are important.
- Goods which deteriorate rapidly, or which are required promptly will need *fast transport,* e.g. air or road.
- The *nature of the product* may require a special type of transport.

Close co-operation between all departments concerned is needed to minimize transport costs and the following two examples illustrate this point:

- Links with purchasing department may lead to vehicles picking up material to use in the factory, instead of returning empty after deliveries to customers.
- Design of packaging may enable greater amounts to be handled by making sizes easier to handle.

3 **Operational research** is valuable in improving aspects of distribution procedure. The following problems can be solved by simulation techniques, i.e. by the mathematical representation of the whole distribution system, noting transport rates, warehouse operating costs, customer's demand and buying patterns, factory locations, production capacity, etc.

- How many warehouses should there be, and where should they be located?
- What customers should each warehouse service?
- What volume should each warehouse handle?

4 Stock levels. Records must be up to date and quickly accessible, particularly where demand fluctuates rapidly because of weather, fashion, etc. The right levels of stock must be fixed. Most firms carry too high levels of stock and any firm which is attempting to reduce stocks must note the factor dealt with in Chapter 6 under stock or inventory problems.

Logistics and physical distribution management

For many years, production inefficiencies have been criticized and scrutinized in order to increase productivity. There has been little close examination of possible savings in the area of physical distribution, now known as logistics. There is a movement towards a closer analysis of all aspects of logistics. This is particularly important where selling and distribution costs are high (e.g. 35–40 per cent of total costs spent on salespeople, transport, warehousing, insurance, packaging, deterioration and obsolescence of stocks, order processing and handling, size of customer's orders and delivery). All factors referring to the above can be considered as cogs, which in the past were treated separately, rather than the present emphasis in which they are joined and affect each other in a unified system.

Whatever savings are considered, it is important to note that the *total* cost of distribution is the relevant figure. Cost reductions in some areas may mean a higher overall cost in a subsequent activity. Actions taken, for example in selecting one method of distribution, may only show cost reductions in the long term, and may show cost *increases* in the short term.

Distribution costs are important, but it should be noted that they are only one element (a sub-system) of the marketing function.

The process of physically distributing products has been called various names, for example, *physical distribution management* or *materials management* or *marketing logistics*. Not many companies have paid attention to the importance of the distribution effort as being a positive factor in contributing to profitability through its impact on customer service.

The idea behind the logistics concept concerns systems, and it *rejects the traditional ideas* that each activity (marketing, production, purchasing, and distribution) should try to optimize their *own* set of logistic activities, while disregarding the involvement of others in the flow of materials.

Looking at the concept from a *total* viewpoint, may indicate that some parts of the system can operate at less that the optimum in order to make the whole system more effective. For example the production manager may need to schedule shorter runs, or the transport manager more frequent deliveries, if it benefits the total logistics system. Acceptance of the logistics concept implies a recognition of the fact that an action affecting one part may affect all others. So a united approach is needed in order to maximize overall effectiveness.

Logistics mix

Customers want products available in the right sizes, at the right time and in perfect condition. This is possible if five key decisions are co-ordinated, that is facility, inventory, communication, utilization and transport. These five areas comprise the total costs of physical distribution and a decision in one area may affect the other four areas. Closing a warehouse, for example, will affect costs of transport and inventory allocation. Correct management of the logistics function has as its aim to obtain a reduction in *total* costs by changing the cost structure in some areas. It must be noted that transport costs are only *one element* among others and may account for only a small part of the total logistics costs. The five key elements are:

- facility decisions are concerned with problems such as the number of warehouses to have and their location;
- inventory decisions refer to the holding of stock, how much should be held, where, in what quantities, and the frequency of replenishment;
- transport decisions include the mode of transport, the leasing or use of own vehicles, transporting overseas by air or sea and scheduling delivery;
- communication decisions include the order processing and invoicing systems;
- utilization decisions include the way goods are packaged and incorporated into larger unit sizes, such as a pallet or container load, which saves handling and warehousing costs.

It is important to remember that physical distribution management refers to the flow of materials from the end of the production line to the customer. Logistics incorporates the total flow of information and materials into, through and out of the system.

MARKET RESEARCH, ADVERTISING AND PUBLICITY

Market research

The assessment of the nature and level of demand for products and services must be accurate, if economic resources are not to be misused. It is the purpose of market research to find out, as accurately as possible, present and future market requirements.

More complex manufacturing techniques involve larger capital investment, and planning has to be made farther ahead. Personal incomes have levelled-up and this affects consumer requirements, so information must be up to date in order that correct decisions are made.

Ideally, market research should provide information to enable a manufacturer to design a product in accordance with customers' preferences, to manufacture it in quantities that can be sold, to pack it suitably, making appropriate arrangements for effective advertising and distribution. In this ideal case, overproduction and losses in tying up unsaleable stocks will not occur.

Types of research The finished product of a firm usually passes through two phases before reaching the consumer. The first is from producer to distributor, the second is from distributor to consumer.

1 **Distributor research.** It is important to know the reason why goods are 'slow movers', or why dealers are not keen to distribute them. Research can vary from a few questions to a complete investigation. These retail or shop audits should preferably be continuous, using trained investigators. Such investigation should show, among other items, the answers to the following:

What is the popularity of competing brands?
What proportion of each brand is stocked?
From which channels are supplies received?

A useful information service is run by Nielsen. This organization prepares reports at regular intervals and sends them to subscribers periodically. A representative sample of grocers and chemists is taken. Subscribers can be given an analysis, covering sales of one's own brand and competing brands, broken up into area, type of shop, etc.

2 **Consumer research.** As in distributor research, surveys can be continuous or *ad hoc*.

An *ad hoc* survey is designed for a specific purpose and the questionnaire is designed around main issues, and may try to find:

Which class of person buys the product, what sex, age group, how often, how many, etc.

By continuous survey the questions try to find information to assess the movement of demand of goods. A well-known survey by independent organizations is called the Brand Barometer. It is designed to measure the movement of branded goods.

Regular figures are provided to manufacturers who subscribe. These figures show, for example, details of total purchases of all brands in various groups in regions, etc. Trends can be seen and suitable action taken.

A *Consumer Panel* consists of a large number of persons who agree to record carefully their purchases, preferences, actions and to answer periodic questionnaires. The constitution of the panel must be carefully drawn up to avoid bias. This method is expensive, but gives continuous detailed information about consumers' buying actions to price changes, advertising changes, etc. (e.g. BBC Listeners' Panel).

3 **Product research.** Product research or product testing is designed mainly to test the acceptability of a product and to check features of a product already marketed, if sales fall below the required standard. Briefly, various types of an article are given to the co-operator to use. These products look the same, but are specially marked. The reports of these persons are analysed. Again, care must be taken in drafting questions or inferences may be incorrect.

4 **Advertising research.** This can take many forms – it covers all the media used in advertising. It is invaluable to know what the impact is of advertisements. A good method is the continuous research available from readership surveys, e.g. those published by Hulton Press and IPA. The popularity of various newspapers, magazines, details of readers, their social classification, etc., is given.

5 **Motivation research.** Strictly, this should form part of consumer research, but it is so important that a separate heading has been given to it. The term is used to embrace techniques or methods used in the field of social psychology, in order to try to determine *why* people buy one brand rather than another. Many answers in surveys have been found to be false or incorrect. Often a socially acceptable answer is given, e.g. the number of cigarettes smoked is far greater than the number ascertained by consumer research.

Motivation research is founded upon the assumption that consumer behaviour *may* be influenced by factors, the existence of which an individual may not suspect or may be unwilling to reveal. These facts must be studied and examined to obtain an accurate understanding of consumer behaviour. The information obtained helps in designing the product, packaging, pricing and advertising. This knowledge is very important, particularly from the advertising point of view, as all advertising 'copy' is based upon certain assumptions, as to *why* people purchase products. In the past, intuition and inspired guesses were used: today, systematic surveys form the basis of decisions.

Techniques used in motivation research may briefly be considered:

Group discussion is based upon the theory that, if rapport can be established between a small group of persons, then individual members of that group may be encouraged to express themselves more freely and fully than they might do if questioned alone.

Depth interview is an attempt to find a way beneath the more superficial levels of consciousness, by asking questions in such a way as to encourage the maximum amount of free expression.

Some attitudes cannot be uncovered by direct questioning, so subtler techniques are needed. These are most valuable where the respondent will not supply information on matters where social stigma or prestige are connected, e.g. frequency of cleaning one's teeth, or washing one's hands. Methods used are the completion of pictures or cartoons; or the interpretation of an indefinite picture. In these cases the results of the tests are analysed and interpreted by an experienced psychologist.

Advertising and publicity

These terms are often used synonymously. Strictly, publicity has a wider significance. It includes all forms of advertising and all activities which attempt to inform the public about a firm; this includes public relations.

The role played by advertising in the marketing activities of firms varies greatly. Advertising can be direct or indirect. The object of most advertising is to present information about a product, arouse interest, build desire and get customers in a favourable frame of mind to buy the product. Firms may have their own advertising department, but usually they ask an advertising agency to help.

An *advertising agency* is an independent business organization, staffed by specialists, which develops and places advertisements in advertising media and assists in overall planning. The agency obtains facts, plans campaign strategy and the media to be used. The final plans are presented for approval by the firm. The agency acts as a middleman between the advertising firm and the suppliers of the advertising media, e.g. television companies, and they are paid by the owner of the media employed and not by their client.

An *advertising consultant* offers a different service. This is normally a one-person business who, for an agreed fee, prepares the advertising plan and dictates its general direction. The consultant continues to watch over the operation and give further advice.

There are a number of points to consider in communicating to the public by an advertisement. This should be *specific*, expressing ideas clearly, and having *authority* and *impact*. It must be so *distinctive* as to impinge itself on the memory. It must be *believable* and *acceptable* and related to the *needs of the recipient* and must be presented at the right *time*. A person should be made aware of the product or service and understand its advantages, be *convinced* of its value – this should then, ideally, bring a *response* or action to look at or to take steps to purchase.

It may be worthwhile now to consider briefly beliefs which are often quoted. One is that any price reduction which is made possible by using the amount of money spent on advertising would induce the consumer to buy more. The price reduction, if spread over a wide range of products, would be rather small and hardly noticeable to consumers.

Another belief is that advertising is done to avoid direct price competition. This, though, does not take into consideration that a lot of advertising is made to *support* price reductions. Advertising makes price promotions much more effective by making customers aware of reductions.

A third example of wrong beliefs is that price by itself is the determining factor in sales. This ignores the fact that they may buy for the brand image, distinction, e.g. Rolls-Royce cars, and the fact that an article is *expensive*, rather than for a lower price.

Principal forms of advertising

Below are the principal forms of advertising:

1 Direct mail. Information is sent direct to prospective customers. It can be used as the main advertising method. Mailing lists can be compiled from certain directories and year books; or the aid of certain professional organizations, which provide lists of firms in particular trades, graded in size and status, can be obtained.

2 Press. This includes all newspapers and journals and specialized magazines. Payment is made by the vertical column inch and varies according to circulation or net sales, position in the paper, status of the paper, use of colour, etc. It is important to note that readership is more important than circulation figures, e.g. newspapers may be read by a few people, magazines may be read by many in a family.

3 Posters. Sites are mainly in the hands of bill-posting contractors who grade their sites according to position. A bill-posting contract is on a rental basis – this includes fixing, inspecting and renewing if necessary. This method is useful to *supplement* a press, television, or radio campaign, as the effects last over a period. It also allows concentration of advertising in a particular area, e.g. on transport vehicles.

4 **Cinema and television.** Costs are heavy, particularly on television, but displays are 'live' and seen by many in a favourable environment. Consideration is needed for declining cinema audiences and their more youthful nature.

5 **Other methods.** Special displays and exhibitions, e.g. motor shows, local radio, trade journals.

Sales promotion

This term is often used to describe a wide range of marketing activities. In this book, it refers to the provision of special buying incentives for a limited period of time. They are more often used in consumer goods advertising than in industrial advertising.

They are supplementary to normal advertising and encourage dealers to open accounts or increase stock levels and, if used judiciously, are an invaluable aid to marketing.

Co-operation from distributors is vital and timing is very important. In addition, the period of the offer must not be too long. Problems could arise; for example, if the special offer is very attractive the regular stock will move at a slower rate. It is convenient to divide promotions into dealer and consumer.

Dealer promotions. These are designed to encourage dealers to participate. They are offered some of the following: *cash discounts*, which are either in cash or deducted from invoices on orders over specified amounts; or *gifts and prizes*, awarded on basis of sales or display.

Consumer promotions. These may be divided into the following:

- **Temporary price reductions**, e.g. '20 pence off' the usual price; these will be prominently displayed on special packs. Distributors obtain the same gross margin as on the regular pack and sales usually increase. Success is usually judged by the number of new customers who are persuaded to buy.
- **Coupons are given to consumers,** who then can obtain a reduced price when they are handed over to a dealer. The costs incurred are in the printing, mailing, or delivering by hand, of the coupons. The allowance to the dealer is a fraction of a penny per coupon. The effect of this method is reduced if competitors offer similar coupons.
- **Premium offers** – there are various types of such offers –

  Self-liquidating: if a box top plus cash is sent, an article well below market price is obtained. As the company buys in bulk, no loss is made. Such articles must be widely desired and consumers must be able to check market price – this aids the success of the offer.

Box top premiums: cut-out tops are sent for a gift – this helps to retain consumer loyalty to the product.
Container premiums: here the jar container itself is useful.
Enclosed premiums: within the packets of the product are gifts, e.g. toys.

- **Bargain packs** – often two products are banded together, the products being usually produced by the same company, e.g. soap and toothpaste. It may be, though, a product from another source, e.g. soap powder and clothes pegs. The problems here are mainly in packaging, transport and stacking on retailers' shelves.
- **Contests** – an example of this method is the completion of a coupon which shows ten features of a car in order of importance. It is policy to add a further contest, e.g. involving coining a slogan, in case more than one person is correct. It is essential that the main prizes be attractive if sales are to be increased. The manufacturers of the prizes obtain good indirect publicity and usually offer good buying terms. Contests can offer smaller value prizes of greater number, which are often aimed at children.

One successful offer gave away a pair of earrings to customers purchasing Babycham, a soft drink. For an example of a badly-planned offer, *see* p 289. It must be noted that all such offers need to be backed up by excellent distribution and display and an adequate stock build-up. Such co-ordination is essential to success.

Branding

Many goods originally sold in bulk are now sold with a 'brand' or distinctive name, e.g. Typhoo tea. This also occurs in manufactured articles, e.g. Black and Decker drills.

This practice was introduced by manufacturers who wished to distribute products nationally, using national advertising. Such a product establishes its individuality and gives the manufacturer a good control over prices. A manufacturer can then advertise his particular brand of cigarettes, not cigarettes in general. Brand names are also used by department and multiple stores; as rival brands are advertised wholesalers and retailers have to stock more in order to meet consumer demand. Such goods usually carry a smaller profit margin than unbranded goods as they are deemed easier to sell.

Branding is a *grading device*. A purchaser will assume the quality will also be the same if he buys a brand. Branding may also be said to give a *sense of security*, e.g. a wholesaler may have a large business with a manufacturer, who may suddenly sell direct to retailers. If the wholesaler has his own brand, he is secure.

Today, the growing tendency to ask for a brand makes it difficult for a new manufacturer to enter a market; existing manufacturers therefore have a monopoly.

Effective advertising

Some principles of effective advertising are:

- **selection of correct media** – money spent will be wasted if a product is advertised in inappropriate media. For example, a new animal food would be advertised in magazines devoted to animals and not in general magazines;

Management in
practice

> Hoover is a well known company manufacturing domestic appliances and in 1992 commenced a campaign to promote its products in the United Kingdom and Ireland. The aim was to tempt consumers to purchase in a very depressed market. Cash would be raised in a short period from extra sales and costs of the promotion would not have to be met until later.
>
> The offer was to give two free return flights to America or Europe if they purchased any of its vacuum cleaners, washing machines or other household appliances worth more than £100 ($150).
>
> The campaign was *too perfect*. There was a great increase in sales but most people were more interested in free flights than household appliances. Over 200 000 applications for flights were made which was far more than the company expected.
>
> Most people purchased cheap vacuum cleaners which sold for £120. (The cheapest return air tickets to New York for two people cost about £500.) People were not deterred from claiming their flights by restriction on hotels, flights and times of travel offered.
>
> The *outcome* was that every national newspaper ridiculed the offer. Hoover's American parent company – Maytag – sacked the top three executives. Since its takeover, Maytag had given Hoover a great deal of independence but required a better financial performance. Hoover had restructured, moved work from France to Scotland (a controversial decision), and tried to improve its financial performance.
>
> Maytag had intended to use Hoover's name and large market share in the United Kingdom to build up its sales outside America.
>
> The result of this ill-fated promotion was that Hoover's name was tarnished, because of the complete failure of the promotion and unfavourable allegations made by consumer groups, who had many complaints from dissatisfied customers.

- sufficient concentration – the weight of advertising must be sufficient to impress the public. For example, it may be better to advertise locally for a long period, rather than nationally for a short time;
- repetition – it is important to observe continuity of style and phrases when varying media are used; this makes impressions more permanent;
- timing – a time must be chosen when the public are more receptive to the advertisements.

Example of a
timetable for
an advertising
campaign

In this illustration, assume a manufacturer has produced a small amount of a new product which he intends to market.

1 The product is taken to an *advertising agency,* after having been checked for quality, etc., and to see that there are no harmful effects no matter how the product is misused. It is better to do this before the public or the government find out; e.g. inflammable material should not be used in the product.

2 *Samples* may then be distributed in certain areas to find out the comments of people using them (test-marketing). These tests will show the advantages and disadvantages of the product and will suggest the lines upon which eventual advertising will be based.

3 If the product is *worth promoting,* the market research department will then find out the market for the product, the best method of advertising, etc.

4 Whether a *national or local campaign* should be instituted must be decided upon. It may be policy to try in one area first. Before a national campaign is tried, the manufacturer must be sure he is able to produce sufficient quantities to meet national sales.

5 The agency then *plans the campaign;* all staff are used, e.g. artists, photographers, copywriters, etc.

6 The *interest of the retailers,* who will sell the product, should be obtained, in order to obtain their help in promoting sales. They could receive discounts, special leaflets, and display material.

7 *Following up the progress* of the campaign is essential.

Public relations (PR)

The function of PR is to promote public understanding and acceptance of a company, its products and services. The purpose is to ensure that the 'image' or impression which the public carry of the company is a favourable one, so that ultimately there will be greater sales of the products of the company.

The Institute of Public Relations defined PR as: *'a planned and sustained effort to establish and maintain mutual understanding between an organization and its public.'*

PR is a function of management, it is more than just press relations, and the PR officer is often responsible to the board of directors.

PR uses a variety of methods and, if reliable and interesting information is given to the press on a new product, or method of working, good, free publicity may materialize.

A company may set up its own PR department or utilize the PR department of an advertising agency, or engage an outside PR agency.

The qualities needed in a Public Relations Officer. The qualities needed include:

● integrity, discretion and ability to make the right contacts;
● a sense of timing and good journalistic ability;
● good knowledge of media, e.g. television, exhibitions, press.

Duties of a Public Relations Officer. The duties of a PRO may comprise:

● providing information, e.g. on new models of cars; dealing with all enquiries on matters affecting the firm, e.g. intention to raise prices;
● dealing with all relations with press and other advertising organizations, other than normal advertising matters:
● organization of visits abroad and exhibitions;
● responsibility for house journal, i.e. internal company magazine.

Concept of life-cycle in marketing

New products are introduced after being developed; they grow, reach maturity and then eventually decline. The duration of such phases varies with different types of products; goods affected by fashion have short life-cycles.

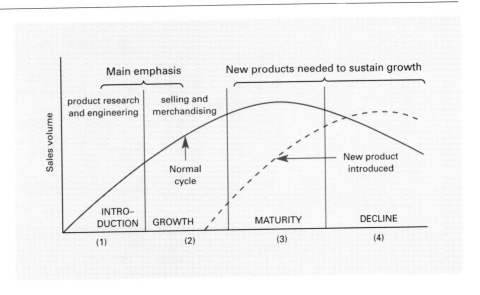

Fig 7.9 Life-cycle of a product

A correct knowledge of the phase the product is at is helpful, and often vital, in planning accurately for the future. Questions to be answered are:

Which products are now in decline?
When should new products be introduced?

Figure 7.9 shows the life-cycle of a product. Often, after the first stages of decline in sales, a manufacturer tries to make his product more attractive, or introduce a new product. It is then usually *too late* and customers may be lost to competitors.

Ideally, a knowledge of consumer attitudes is needed; improvements and new products should be available before Stage 3 ends. In the growth and maturity stages, new uses, or new products must be found for the product, e.g. model changes in cars.

Promotion and distribution strategies are related to a product's position in the cycle. A well-balanced product programme should balance a certain number of products in each stage of the life-cycle.

In Fig 7.9, the dotted line shows when a product is required to maintain or increase a firm's share of the market. In most cases the life-cycle is quite long (e.g. the Volkswagen small car, the Golf replacing the Beetle).

Analysis of product range

There are a number of techniques to help organizations to analyse the effectiveness of their business. One method is to look at the life-cycle stages of a product (*see* Fig 7.9). Such examination of the product range can ensure the firm has the required mix of products. That is, some aiming for long-term growth, some for increase in cash flow where high initial sales are expected but the life is short. This 'portfolio' of products must be analysed and monitored.

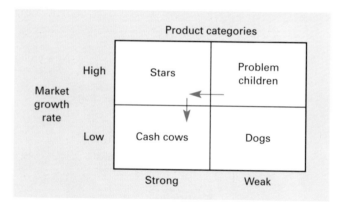

Fig 7.10 Relative competitive position (market share)

A popular technique for monitoring product range is the 'Boston Portfolio Matrix'. This concept was initiated by the Boston Consulting Group in 1972. The matrix is based on the fact that different types of products will generate different levels of cash flow for the company. So cash flow, and not profitability (which is affected by other influences), is a key factor in the ability of a company to develop its management of the range or portfolio of its products.

Products are classified by their positions on two dimensions, relative market share and market growth rate. *Market share* indicates how well a product can generate cash and is measured against its competitors. It therefore shows *how dominant* the product is in the market place. Market growth shows the cash requirements of the product. Figure 7.10 shows the linkages between the growth rate of the business and the relative competitive position of the firm, identified by the market share. Each quadrant gives a label to the product provided.

Problem child. This is a product with a weak market share and a high growth rate and requires a *cash investment* so it can become a star.

The star is a product with a strong competing position; it has a high share in a high growth market and is still growing. It needs cash input but almost generates sufficient cash itself.

Cash cow is a product which was the 'star' of yesterday and has a strong competitive position with a low growth cost. These products are usually well established and are made at a low cost. They can help to develop other products by producing a good cash flow.

The dog is a product with a low relative share in a low growth market which can drain cash from the organization. As the product is in decline, it is usually not profitable and should be disposed of.

The original matrix was developed for large corporations with several divisions. It has been considered *too simplistic* an approach and the yardsticks of growth rate and market share rather inadequate or insufficient.

The Boston matrix can be used to form a policy on new product development and help decisions on how to manage existing products. The matrix could *help to develop a corporate plan* if the implications of different product – market strategies are understood and any potential weaknesses of present strategies clearly identified.

Packaging

The packaging of goods has become extremely important – partly because of the role it is thought to play in attracting the consumer – and there have been revolutionary changes in styles and materials. In addition, containers have been improved functionally and the often conflicting needs of the packer, distributor and consumer have to be met. Packaging can be regarded as the vehicle from which a product is to be sold and it must therefore protect and attract. Packaging is part of the 'marketing mix' and involves production, protection, transportation, distribution, advertising, merchandising and the selling of the product.

Use of outside specialist companies

The use of outside specialist companies gives a comprehensive service to a manufacturer and accounts for a large part of the total amount spent on packaging. A manufacturer must consider the additional cost of transport to and from the packaging company and must be certain of a reliable delivery service. These specialist companies provide experience and have the capital equipment which manufacturers must have themselves if they do not avail themselves of these services.

An organization's own packaging department

The organization's own packaging department may be under the control of a committee, consisting of persons drawn from various departments. The trend, though, is towards specialization under one person (sometimes called a packaging manager). This department may come under marketing or production and this depends upon the type of business activity. For example, if the business is food, drugs or cosmetics, it will be more market research-orientated and the section will come under the marketing manager. If packaging is for an industrial product, it may come under the production manager.

Factors to be considered in packaging

Briefly, packages must be designed on a drawing board, tools obtained, packages tested for compatibility with the product under conditions of use and sale. Blocks for graphics have to be made and machines for filling, erecting and closing obtained. Research and development must be planned and co-ordinated, use of colour carefully selected and controlled, together with the careful checking of the quality components. Information is needed on all aspects of the product. Attention should be paid to the following:

- special protection in packing, shelf-life, uses of product, conditions of use, type of user, type of market;
- predicted volume, special processing needed, e.g. vacuum packing, channels of distribution, needs of storage, e.g. for shipping, method of handling;

- promotional needs, e.g. consumer articles may be attached to the package of a good as a gift, as part of sales promotion;
- legal requirements, e.g. Trade Description Acts 1968–72.

Merchandising

Merchandising means assisting the retailer with publicity at the point of display, to help in maximizing retail sales. This involves instructing the retailer in the best use of shelf space, the provision of display material and advice on its use.

Merchandising, by means of improved packaging and display, has been a notable feature in the sales of many products. Packaging should be attractive, convenient for the customer, and protect the product.

Pre-packaging is greatly increasing, especially in the greengrocery business.

It is worth noting that manufacturers of branded consumer goods obtain many orders from the head office of supermarkets and large retail groups, so the job of the manufacturer's traveller now, when calling on retail groups, is mainly to advise on displays and on merchandising problems.

Role of computers in marketing

Traditional departmental boundaries have been weakened by the increase in electronic data processing systems coupled with the emphasis on the consumer orientated 'marketing concept' – that a firm should satisfy the needs of consumers, at a profit.

An illustration of the role of a computer in implementing a 'systems' approach follows:

Assume a customer places an order for 1000 items, for immediate delivery. The telephone call can be made to a local sales office and during the phone call the answer can be given within 6 seconds as to whether the order can be met on time.

1 Computer makes a credit check on the customer (to see if the customer is creditworthy).
2 It checks to see if items are in stock and if situated conveniently.
3 If these conditions are satisfied, the computer prepares the order and the invoice to the customer, alters stock records; and prepares a list so new stock can be ordered when the minimum level is reached.
4 Information is then received back from the computer by the salesperson to say the order can be taken.

In this integrated system traditional departmental boundaries are of minor importance.

SALES MANAGEMENT

Unless managers have their own retail outlets, they need sales representatives who will mainly be responsible for disposing of the company's products.

Sales administration

This assists the representatives and co-operates with those responsible for marketing policy and production programmes, in order that intelligent forecasting and accurate budgetary control be applied. The sales force must be used efficiently. This depends upon a number of factors and includes initial selection and training in co-operation with the human resources officer, good organization and accurate reporting of results, satisfactory salaries and conditions of employment.

A good administrator should possess the following qualities:

- ability to control salespeople and assess performance, set targets and keep enthusiasm high;
- knowledge of modern techniques is needed, so that they can be used in relevant cases. In addition, the administrator must possess flair and imagination.

Selection and training of salespeople

General selection and training techniques are dealt with in Chapter 9. A brief programme for a training scheme might include:

1 basic principles of salesmanship, e.g. approach, courtesy, self-control, closing techniques;
2 product knowledge – characteristics of the product, materials used in manufacture and assembly, possible defects through misuse;
3 procedures of company – company policy, routines for orders, complaints, reports, etc.

Planning of territories

The size of the outdoor staff depends upon many factors, particularly the method of sales (i.e. to wholesalers or retailers, or consumers). Geographical size of territory usually depends upon the physical nature of the product or service. For example:

- the sale of office equipment in London may need one representative per square mile. In East Anglia, only one representative may be needed and a large part of the time will be spent in travelling;
- a person selling specialized products to industry needs less area than one who sells staple products to dealers;
- if a product is sold to wholesalers first, the territory will be larger and fewer representatives will be needed than if sold direct to retailers;
- competition and habits of buyers must be noted;
- the final allocation must give the salesperson a territory which produces sufficient orders to give a satisfactory remuneration and standard of living.

Quota setting

Sales forecasting and budgetary procedures were dealt with in Chapter 3. Brief mention is made here of the setting of quotas.

A sales forecast is normally prepared and allocated to territories on the basis of the potential of the territory – this becomes the salesperson's target for a period (e.g. a year). It is preferable to break this down into monthly quotas, noting any seasonal trends. A comparison of actual sales with this standard can easily be made. If quotas are adhered to, production can continue in an orderly manner; they can also be used as a basis for competition among sales staff and a basis for bonus payments.

Remuneration of sales representatives

Incentives must be given to obtain best results: they must be fair and reasonably easy to attain. The rewards of speciality salespeople may be higher than those to salespeople of staple goods, as they constantly have to break new ground and have few repeat orders. The speciality salesperson's personal efforts are more responsible for sales than those of a salesperson of staple goods who has the benefits of a secure market. Any of the following methods, or combination of methods, of remuneration may be used.

Salary

This method may be used where seasonal fluctuations occur. It also applies where the product is well known and established. The salesperson's function is primarily to maintain personal contact with customers and collect orders. The salesperson has security, but no incentive, especially where selling is against competition of other travellers.

Commission

Commission is often used when a company is being built up; there is no financial risk to the employer, but there is little direct control over sales staff. The security of salespeople is small and therefore they should receive guarantees, e.g. commission on *all* orders from their territory whether they collected them or not.

Salary and commission

Under the salary and commission system the salary gives the salespeople security while the commission acts as an incentive. A change in commission on various lines can be a useful method of pushing poor selling lines.

The more often after-sales service, or investigating, is needed, the greater should be the salary element.

Bonuses and special incentives

Bonus and special incentives can be used for special efforts, for example, to sell excess stocks at the end of the season, or they may be given to a group which achieves more than their sales quota. It is worth noting that, if made annually, the reward is too far removed from the actual effort to give much incentive value.

Organization of sales office

Office practices are dealt with in Chapter 10. Only the special points relating to the sales office are noted here. The situation of the sales office will vary according to the needs of the business. There are advantages in having it near the factory but, as excellent communication systems are available, e.g. fax, it is not so necessary. Customer accessibility, or a central position for control of salespeople may be more important.

Duties of the office manager

The manager in charge of the sales office usually has responsibility for order control, statistics, correspondence and records. An efficient sales office makes the salesperson's job much easier. The manager must have a good knowledge of systems and must be able to prepare reports and statistics for control purposes.

Correspondence and report

Correspondence with customers and salespeople. All enquiries must be dealt with promptly. The use of standard forms for quotations and orders is essential. Complaints from customers must be especially noted and dealt with by a senior in the office. Enquiries from customers must be sent direct to the salespeople concerned, in addition to all quotations and letters sent to customers.

Salespeople's reports. These must be designed to secure economy of time in preparing them as well as to give sufficient information for control. The nature of the business will determine the particular form of report:

- Unit reports, separate for each call made, are needed by speciality companies. The contents may show – person seen, position held, goods discussed, special problems, stage of negotiations reached, etc.;
- Omnibus reports are daily reports which show orders taken, orders analysed into customers called upon, etc. They are often used for staple goods.

Statistics and salesperson's records

Basic personal information will be in the hands of the human resources office, but the following records are most useful to the sales office manager.

- Personal record card, showing monthly totals of salary, commission, expenses, etc.
- Monthly record of sales analysed over lines, cumulatively, giving comparison over years.

Other statistical records will show a customer index, often kept on computer, and either arranged alphabetically under towns, or under each salesperson's area of duty, giving: name of organization, chief buyer, credit rating, discounts given, normal order, special preferences, etc. Records of old customers should be kept and also of prospective customers, tenders submitted and results, costs of distribution, condition of salesperson's cars, etc.

Control of credit

This is an important function of sales management. The degree of control varies widely, but procedures must be laid down and observed. The following factors must be considered:

- What procedures must be followed to find the security of new customers?
- What amount of initial orders must pass before a check is completed?
- How long can credit be extended; what discounts are to be allowed?

A *credit rating* can be given to each account. The initial rating can be made by the salesperson, but the final rating is the responsibility of the credit manager. This is based upon salesperson's reports, trade references and special enquiries from trade protection societies.

The following is an example of the use of modern methods in aiding some problems of sales management.

To obtain the greatest efficiency the following questions must be answered in the affirmative:

- Are salespeople distributed properly around the country?
- Do they know, or are they going on calls in, the 'best' order?

By the use of a computer, programmed to take account of the variable factors, these points can be answered. It has already been mentioned how these techniques can aid warehouse location and loading of vehicles. Now an answer to the above questions must take into account all the variable characteristics in a salesperson's journey. A basic computer program must cover the following characteristics:

- maximum daily distance, maximum time, noting average possible speed, distance and time per call;
- maximum number of visits, order of calls to be made, i.e. first or last, or morning or afternoon.

The procedure is as follows:

1 Examine all outlets in the country and find the total amount of 'face to face' selling.
2 Are the prospects evenly scattered or grouped in certain localities?
3 Certain basic facts must be noted, e.g. most firms have a London representative.
4 The numerous possible conclusions are then fed to the computer.

Each case is different and the computer arrives at the 'optimum' result in terms of numbers of men, territories defined and sequence of calls.

A knowledge of National Grid References is needed and details are given to the computer. Allowances are to be made for natural barriers, e.g. rivers and mountains; common sense is essential.

Most vehicle touring and fleet-planning problems can all be catered for by programming a computer to find good routes in a very short time and a saving in vehicles of between 5 per cent and 30 per cent may be possible. It is also possible to compare the routes produced for a given load schedule, using a *simulated* fleet, with those used by the actual fleet and thereby a more effective fleet structure can be evolved.

PRICING THEORY

A brief revision of elementary economic concepts must first be made. Briefly economic theory states that price is determined by the interaction of supply and demand. Cost is the main ingredient of supply and price the main ingredient of demand; they work together and continually adjust to each other.

An organization, it is said, should charge such a price and produce such an output as will enable it to equate marginal cost and marginal revenue. *Marginal cost* represents the change in total cost when another unit of output is produced; *marginal revenue* is the revenue obtained from selling this marginal unit of output. When an organization equates marginal cost and marginal revenue, the highest profit is obtained, as the difference between total cost and total revenue is at its greatest. This principle provides a key to the understanding of the factors that determine maximization of profits.

The two extreme economic conditions of perfect competition and pure monopoly do not really exist, and business is conducted in the intermediary conditions of imperfect or monopolistic competition.

In practice, business people rarely consciously set prices in this manner, for the following reasons:

- information available is usually limited; e.g. details of price elasticity of demand (needed to get marginal revenue) cannot be easily obtained;
- price elasticity is hardly ever constant for any length of time, so if prices were changed by applying the marginal principle, the numerous changes needed would not be practicable to operate;
- it is not easy for firms to attempt to equate costs and revenue of marginal units of output, especially if marginal units are very large, e.g. in the shipbuilding industry.

To survive or expand, firms must charge a price covering total costs of production in the long run and produce a normal or reasonable return on capital. The use of break-even analysis can be briefly mentioned here: for a more detailed consideration, *see* Fig 6.3 in Chapter 6.

This simple diagram shows that an output of more than 100 000 units is needed in order to make a profit. Sales below 100 000 units result in a loss. The greatest distance between sales and total cost curves shows the optimum sales or optimum output position.

Costing processes

These often form the basis for price setting. If one considers a firm engaged upon a long production run, first of all production and output capacity is estimated and fixed costs are calculated, to which are added overhead costs. The allocation of overhead costs to each separate commodity usually entails the use of a number of *arbitrary accounting assumptions.* To the total of production costs is added a margin to cover a 'fair' return on capital. This margin or 'mark up' varies widely; often the normal or conventional mark up for an industry is adopted.

This 'cost plus' system of pricing is usually inflexible in the face of demand changes, but is favoured as it is very simple to operate. In the short run, there may be good reasons for keeping prices stable, but profits would tend to be higher if larger 'mark ups' were added when demand was expanding and vice versa.

Pricing decisions

There is no simple formula for management when making pricing decisions, because of the following interacting factors:

The economic framework

The economic framework, e.g. imperfect or monopolistic competition, in which the firm operates is an important factor.

Customer demand

A knowledge of the elasticity of demand for a product is required in order to find the volume of goods that can be sold in a given period of time and within a given price schedule; bearing in mind that consumer responses to prices may be affected by considerations other than economic.

Competitors

Any price decision must anticipate action by competitors, which it can be said sets an *upper limit* on price. A price below market price will produce only a temporary increase in sales. Competitors may then reduce their prices and this may lead to a price-war. Some firms have composite price policies; depending upon the prices of competitors. For example, 10 per cent below prices of nearest competitors, as long as selling price is not below total manufacturing costs.

Costs

Numerous cost concepts are used, e.g. marginal cost, and these usually set a *lower* limit on pricing. The effect of volume on costs and profits should be noted. Many companies find that their average costs per unit fall as volume is increased. Often unit costs do not decline as rapidly as the necessary reduction in prices and, in order to get additional sales volume, profit per unit diminishes. Total profit, therefore, depends upon sales volume, as well as cost per unit.

Objectives of company

If a company, for example, wished to become a quality leader, this policy would be reflected in pricing policy. If product differentiation were present in the market, the company would probably decide to charge a comparable price with its competitors' products and build up sales by superior quality. Other firms may offer other services; free delivery, for example.

In most cases, therefore, the actual choice depends upon consumer reaction, as to how much they will pay for superior quality, how long differentiation exists and how much unit costs would fall if volume, rather than a high price, is sought.

Legal restraints

The possibility of government action must be considered; e.g. on monopolies. Pricing is affected directly by both the Resale Prices Act 1976 and the work of the Office for Fair Trading.

Pricing decisions are very complex and are one of the more difficult tasks for company management. The following are important factors to consider:

1 There is *no universal formula* for arriving at the right price. Price-setting involves a variety of factors and influences both inside and outside the firm and so may be different from theoretical economics.
2 *Costs alone cannot form* the base for pricing decisions, although they form an important part of many firms' pricing decisions. Successful decisions on pricing depends upon the firm's ability to understand and respond to the *needs and conditions of the market* (e.g. buyer's attitudes and motivations and competition).
3 Considerations of pricing are very important in new *product planning*, where market conditions and price ranges have to be anticipated, before product planning and investment take place. Products selected for development must be those standing the best chance of obtaining a good rate of return on investment.
4 *Price is an important element in the marketing mix.* It is a positive tool for obtaining marketing goals and managers must co-ordinate pricing decisions from the point of view of their longer-term (strategic) impact and implications rather than from the short-term (tactical) benefits.

The pricing process was described by Oxenfeldt (1960) as a series of decisions taken over a period of time consisting of six steps: the identification of target markets; choosing an appropriate image; constructing the marketing mix; selecting a pricing policy; determining price strategy; determining a specific price.

Pricing discrimination

Price discrimination can be used to obtain more revenue. Markets exist for every grade of prices and consumers spend their money in accordance with their scale of preferences. If markets can be divided into sections, it may be possible to charge a different price in each market, the object being to increase total revenue from any given level of production. This is done when the marginal revenue in each market is the same. This will happen only if production is in the hands of a monopolist or group of firms acting in this way and if the price elasticity of demand in each section is different. It must, of course, either be impossible to transfer goods from one section of the market to another, or the cost of transporting the goods between the markets must exceed the difference in price between the two markets.

Example

Tea may be sold for a high price in a branded pack, or sold loose, with no label, at a lower price.

Many other factors can be considered in pricing theory and these can be studied in the more detailed books mentioned in the bibliography at the end of the chapter.

Examples of pricing strategy

Penetration pricing. A company may set price levels that will only be profitable at specified high sales levels. In this case low initial prices are set to keep out competition and when volume expands and the company leads the market, prices can then be raised.

Skimming price strategy. This is a method which starts with high prices (as can be asked for a new invention or technology). Then when demand increases, and competitors start to enter, price is lowered. A large part of the initial investment can then be recovered before any real competitors emerge.

Diversionary pricing. This occurs where one product is sold cheaply so that an associated product which has a high profit margin is automatically sold. For example, low-cost photocopying machines are sold with high-priced photocopy paper. In this case there is often one company who takes over as price-leader and others follow its lead. The outcome could lead to a price war with the winner carrying losses on some product lines by making sufficient profit from the rest.

A marketing approach to pricing considers the ability to give the customer *value*. Companies should evaluate what areas are their strength. Is it their:

● Unique knowledge (such as a technological breakthrough)?
● Unique marketing techniques or service to customers?
● Effective research and development?
● Effective control of manufacture and distribution channels?
● Protection by patents?

INTERNATIONAL MARKETING

Successive governments have stressed the necessity for expanding exports and the need for small firms as well as medium-sized firms to enter the export field. Sixty per cent of British exports are at present achieved by only 300 companies. The potential is therefore enormous.

Objections to exporting usually follow these lines:

● too much effort is needed to find out how to sell abroad;
● risks are too great, especially if the home market is safe and produces a good return on capital;
● lack of expert knowledge in packaging, transport, insurance, etc.;
● exports may rely on one or two overseas markets which may be cut off by changes in legislation, e.g. licensing laws or quotas.

The marketing of goods across national boundaries, often called global marketing, can bring many problems to the marketing manager. A number of organizations that can assist are briefly mentioned on p 304–5.

Two common mistakes made by companies who are successful in domestic-orientated business who consider exporting are:

1 They consider long-range planning on a *regional* rather than an individual country basis (i.e. Europe, rather than France). This means that they tend to ignore the subtle differences which may be significant between the political and social environment of each country.

2 They are unaware of local trends which can be vital to the success of the venture. For example the United States Department of Commerce has specified 27 non-tariff barriers which exist in overseas trade, including special labels, packaging and safety standards.

To solve these problems the formation of a subsidiary company for selling a product is one answer. Other ways are to buy an existing company, to acquire shares in one, start a completely new company, or consider some form of joint venture with a local firm.

A brief consideration of the major points to consider will include:

- total population of country, wealth (gross domestic product per head of population);
- demographic structure, rate of inflation;
- assessment of risk and finance needed, availability of loan capital and stability of local currency;
- taxes, government incentives to exporters, regulations on foreign investment and transfer of profits to main country;
- data regarding local markets (state of local industry and competitors, nature of protection given to home industry);
- existing and potential market growth;
- availability of raw materials, storage facilities, climate;
- legal constraints (pollution, patent laws), costs of labour;
- political constraints, possibility of nationalization and assessment of stability of government;
- labour availability, trade union organization.

The above factors may cause problems in marketing products abroad. However, as attitudes converge the easier it is to market multinational brands. Hence when political conflicts subside people from various countries can collaborate on multinational brands to make them successful, e.g. Marlboro, Ford and Coca-Cola.

It is also important to research the market carefully using, for example, the services of the International Research Institute for Social Change. Their annual surveys in twelve European countries, North America, Brazil, Argentina and Japan, produce data which can be highly beneficial to companies marketing their products internationally.

Advantages of global marketing

- Larger volume of production – this may justify investment in more mechanized methods of production and would increase efficiency.
- Greater opportunities to counter falling orders from one area, by increases from other areas.

- Increasing marketing knowledge from contact with a wider range of markets and competitors.
- Opportunities to gain experience of design, development and production of goods and services which are not needed in home country.
- Company is better placed to compete with foreign enterprises in home market.

First steps in exporting

Assuming a manufacturer has a good product and feels this would sell abroad, the steps should be:

1 Pick a market, preferably not one which is experiencing economic difficulties, or where home competition is strong, or where political overtones exist.

2 Notify the regional officer of the Department of Trade and Industry and the British Overseas Trade Board, and give the Board full descriptions and samples of goods.

3 The British Overseas Trade Board will contact its representative in the market (Commercial Officer of the Diplomatic Service) and obtain a market report, which will say what competition exists, noting any special local regulations and if prospects seem reasonable.

4 Further information may be obtained from banks, chambers of commerce and trade associations. Each country has its own peculiarities and customs. Research is essential to see if the design, packing, name and colour satisfy local requirements and the price charged leaves sufficient profit. The Export Marketing Research Scheme provides exporters with consultancy advice on planning marketing research.

5 Extra costs may include.

- costs of packing and transport to docks, shipping agent's charges, marine and freight insurance and overseas delivery charges;
- costs of setting up an export department;
- customs duties, port dues, agent's commission;
- insurance of credit risk.

Organizations which assist exporting firms

Department of Trade and Industry

The regional offices each has an export officer to deal with enquiries. Their services include:

- provision of basic market information and suggested promising markets, and advice on market research through the Export Marketing Research Scheme;
- giving information about tariffs, licensing and special duties, regulations, local customs and methods of business;
- helping businesses to solve problems of how to exploit the chosen market;
- providing status information on potential business contacts;
- guaranteeing credit given to foreign businesses. Suppliers of capital goods and contractors for large projects have to offer, in most cases, credit over a

number of years. The *Export Credits Guarantee Department* of the Department of Trade and Industry *offers guarantees* to the commercial banks, which can provide exporters with finance at a reasonable rate of interest.

There is also a risk that payment for goods exported may not be made by a foreign buyer. Normal insurance companies do not insure for such a risk, but the Export Credits Guarantee Department has a scheme whereby it will provide complete cover for most risks up to 85–90 per cent of the value of the goods concerned, for a period of up to 50 years.

British Overseas Trade Board
: This body gives directions for the development of export activities and operates an Overseas Visitors' Bureau, which organizes and funds the visits of overseas buyers to the United Kingdom.

Confederation of British Industries
: This has a permanent staff overseas who carry out similar work to the Department of Trade and Industry. A special feature is that they can arrange for the small new entrant to the export market to obtain help from a larger, well-established company in the export field, which makes its services available without charge and gives the small business the benefit of its experience.

Methods of exporting

A manufacturer can sell to:

1 **A buying agent**. Buying agents are based in the UK and may also be known as confirming or indent houses. They act as commission agents for overseas buyers, by whom they are remunerated by commission, and from whom they receive their orders, specifying the goods they wish the agent to purchase on their behalf. The agent obtains quotations, places orders in the principal's name and arranges shipping.

2 **Export merchant houses**. Export merchant houses based in the UK may be employed. They buy goods on their own account and sell them overseas in markets in which they have specialized knowledge and where they have warehousing and selling facilities.

3 **An export agent**. A manufacturer may employ an export agent based in the UK. The agent will sell goods abroad and may act for a number of manufacturers of non-competitive lines. The agency carries out research and promotes sales overseas and can provide a complete service to a manufacturer.

4 **Import merchants**. Import merchants, based overseas, purchase at a large discount and make their profit on the resale. They may be given exclusive rights to handle a manufacturer's products in a country or area.

5 **A commission agent**. Such an agent, based in the importing country, may be given sole selling rights. This is a very popular method, but careful selection is essential in obtaining an agent and in drawing up the agency agreement.

6 **Direct to overseas buyer**. This method may be used for large capital projects, e.g. nuclear reactors.

All detailed arrangements in 1 – 6 above must be done by the organization's own exporting department, unless a company of forwarding agents is used. These agents can take over when the goods leave the factory and arrange for all transport and documentation to the destination.

SUMMARY

Objective 1 *Understand how the marketing sub-system of a business contributes to the whole business.*
Marketing activities include the various procedures that direct the flow of goods and services from producer to the ultimate users in order to satisfy consumers and accomplish the firm's objectives. A business takes in inputs, processes them and places outputs back into the environment. The marketing sub-system acquires information and helps to process this and other inputs into outputs. A major task is to get desirable outputs into the hands of consumers.

Information about consumers' wants is studied to determine what types of product they want in the future. Other activities include sending out information through advertising and personal selling, pricing products and using methods of transportation and storage of products, so they are available when consumers want them.

Objective 2 *Define the process of market segmentation and its purposes.*
Market segmentation is a process in which the individuals in a market are divided into segments according to a characteristic that influences their probable purchase of the product. Socio-economic examples of characteristics used to segment a market include age, income, race, sex, family size, occupation and level of education. Geographical characteristics include climate, size of area and population density. Personality characteristics are also used to segment a market.

The purposes of market segmentation are to single out a group of people who are believed to have similar wants and needs for a product owing to one or more common characteristics, and to design a marketing mix that best satisfies the individuals in this segment.

Objective 3 *Describe briefly the importance of pricing decisions in marketing strategy and the procedures and methods adopted to meet agreed goals.*
The price of a product should be related to the achievement of marketing and corporate goals. The role of price must therefore be established in relation to such factors as the product life-cycle, the requirements of the total product portfolio, and the sales and market share objectives.

The procedures and methods adopted to meet agreed goals will depend as much upon market and competitive circumstances as on costs. Costs can be considered as a constraint which may determine a lower limit to price, rather than as a basis on which price is determined. It is also important to note that pricing should be planned across the whole product line and not just for single products separately.

Objective 4 *Explain why an enterprise might enter the international business field.*
The decision is often stimulated by the desire to get ahead of competitors.

One way may be to expand abroad where the costs of labour are lower or raw materials are less expensive. Or, in order to achieve maximum economies of scale it must sell more than the home market can absorb. In addition, enterprises may enter the international business field when certain impediments are removed, such as trade barriers or high transportation costs.

Objective 5 *Describe briefly the minimum amount of information required by an enterprise to enable it to determine whether it should operate in another country.*
The main information required is an analysis of a country's business structure, the market size and labour availability, the strengths and weaknesses of the economy, knowledge of current and future legislation, the climate for investment and knowledge of possible political change.

REVIEW QUESTIONS

Marketing organization and administration

1 Outline a Schedule of Responsibilities for a marketing manager.

2 Consider the position of the wholesaler in modern marketing and outline any new trends.

3 What are the advantages and disadvantages of trading stamps?

Distribution

1 What factors should be considered in selecting a channel of distribution?

2 What are the main factors to consider in choosing the site, design and layout of a warehouse?

3 How can operational research improve aspects of distribution procedure?

4 What do you understand by the term 'physical distribution management'?

Market research, advertising and publicity

1 Differentiate carefully between consumer and distributor research.

2 What other types of research are there in distribution?

3 What are the principal forms of advertising?

4 What forms of special buying incentives are there?

5 Consider the principles of effective advertising.

6 Draw up a timetable for an advertising campaign.

7 Show how packaging has an important part to play in marketing.

Sales management

1 What methods are there of remunerating salespeople?

2 Consider the types of records and statistics which would be of use to a sales office manager.

3 Suggest a method to control credit.

4 Describe a method of vehicle routing with the help of a computer.

Pricing theory

1 Show how prices are formed in economic theory and how in practice the theory is modified.

2 What are the factors that must be considered when making pricing decisions?

Export marketing

1 What steps should a manufacturer take in considering exporting for the first time?

2 Name and briefly describe the work of organizations that can help the exporter.

3 What are the various methods of exporting?

REVIEW PROBLEMS

1 The chairman of a company which manufactures a proprietary brand of firelighters asks you to report on:

(a) A method of operating a national campaign whereby members of the public are allowed to make postal purchases of motoring rugs at two-thirds of the normal retail selling price on the condition that the top flaps from three firelighter cartons shall be attached to the remittance for each rug.

(b) The possible benefits to the company of conducting such a campaign.

2 Explain the connection between branding and advertising and state why it is necessary to spend large sums in advertising goods that are already well known by their brand name. Does the consumer pay for the advertising and does he really benefit from it?

3 A small retail trader is considering whether to join other retailers and wholesalers in a voluntary organization which will purchase goods from manufacturers and distribute them to participating members of the organization. Outline the advantages that could accrue to the retail traders as a result of joining this organization.

4 The board of a raincoat manufacturing company, with capital employed of about £250 000 has discussed the possibility of increasing the company sales by entering the export field. You are required to advise the board about the information necessary to a decision on whether to export or not and to state the sources from which advisory information for exporters may be obtained.

5 List the factors which affect long-range *planning for marketing*. Long-range planning requires the backing of senior management and their willingness to organize properly for such planning. Describe the characteristics of a climate propitious for long-range planning.

6 Specialization in particular products is frequently one of the ingredients in a successful business.

(a) What are the reasons for this?
(b) What constraints does this impose on managers?
(c) What are the problems that may arise out of a salesperson's request to undertake a special order for a non-standard product and how should a manager deal with those problems?

7 What are the points to be observed when designing and marketing products which are intended mainly for export?

8 The sales staff of a company is bringing in a steadily decreasing flow of orders. As sales manager, what investigations would you make and what action would you take to remedy the situation?

9 Set out in sequence the steps to be taken to develop a product from its first concept to the time when it is ready to be put on the production line.

10 For what activities is the marketing director of a group of companies likely to be responsible?
  What specialist services may be utilized?
  How may the marketing director 'keep a finger on the pulse' of the business?

11 What factors would you take into consideration when setting the price of a new product?

12 You are asked to examine a system for the despatch and delivery of goods to customers. What aspects would you consider to be important to ensure an efficient and economic service?

13 Explain the function of a public relations officer and compare this work with that of an advertising manager.

14 Give examples of statistical information which may be required by a sales manager. Each example should include a brief outline of how it would assist in decisions on sales strategy.

15 What does the marketing function of management comprise? Illustrate your answer with a chart which shows the organization of the marketing division of a manufacturing company which sells its products direct to the retailer.

16 Comment briefly on each of the major elements normally included in the term 'marketing mix'.

17 Explain fully how pricing policies are likely to be determined in a company manufacturing and marketing specialized components. How may the management accountant contribute to pricing decisions?

(*See* p 482 for further problems on Marketing and Sales Management.)

18 In what stage of the life cycle would you consider your own organization's product/service to be?

Consider the possible courses of action your organization could reasonably take when the end of the cycle is reached.

ASSIGNMENTS

1 Form groups of 4–6 persons. Assume each group are marketing executives who hope to produce plans to produce and sell a series of games. Each group should choose *four characteristics for segmenting the market* for games, and for each characteristic they should break down each classification in detail. (For example, if geographical areas are chosen as a characteristic, the country should be divided into specific regions.)

After short group discussions, a group representative should report group's decision regarding the characteristics of segmentation.

Questions which can be discussed also are:

(a) What were the main factors affecting the group's selection of market segmentation?

(b) If you used only *one* characteristic to segment the games market, which would you choose and why?

2 Consider the last major purchase you made for your household. When your household was considering alternatives, how did you receive notification of the product from the manufacturers? Which of the communications used had a major influence on the final choice?

3 Compare a selection of your own recent purchases, such as a car, a newspaper, a tube of toothpaste and an insurance policy. In each decision, what was the relative importance of the product itself, its price, the place where it was available and the way in which it was promoted?

BIBLIOGRAPHY   Adcock, D, *et al*, *Marketing: Principles and Practice* (London, Pitman Publishing, 1993).

Ansoff, H L, *Corporate Strategy* (London, Penguin, 1969).

Bolt, G J, *Market and Sales Forecasting* (London, Kogan Page, 1993).

Christopher, M, *Logistics and Supply Chain Management* (London, Pitman Publishing, 1992).

Gattorna, J, *Handbook of Physical Distribution Management* (London, Gower, 2nd edition, 1990).

Inwood, D and Hammond, J, *Product Development* (London, Kogan Page, 1993).

Jobber, D and Lancaster, G, *Selling and Sales Management* (London, Pitman Publishing, 3rd edition, 1994).

Kotler, P, *Principles of Marketing* (New York, Prentice-Hall, 1989).

Peattie, K, *Green Marketing* (London, Pitman Publishing, 1992).

CHAPTER 8

Production and operations management

This chapter examines the production function and the place of product design and development, the location of plant, the layout of equipment and the importance of planning and control. The need for quality is emphasized, the efficient control of purchasing and stores and the need for good maintenance of plant, equipment and buildings. The use of automation in the handling of materials is also emphasized.

Production and operations management is used not only to describe factory environments, but applies to all organizations including, for example, banks and schools. It is the application of techniques to the design and operation of any system that transforms inputs into finished goods and services. Many of the techniques are applicable to service industries as well as manufacturing.

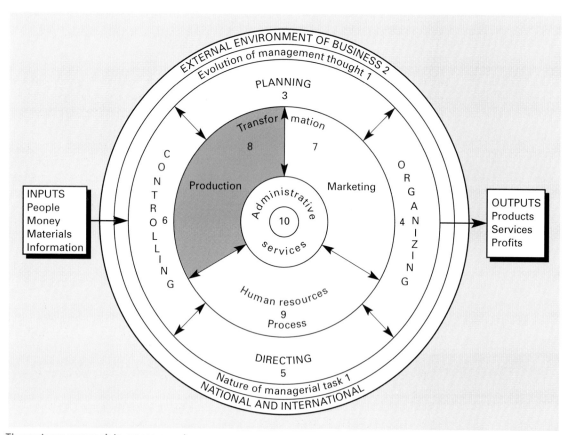

The systems approach to management

OBJECTIVES

Upon completing this chapter you should be able to:

- Discuss the various roles production management may play in supporting the strategic plan of an enterprise.
- Explain the importance of materials management in production operations and describe newer methods used to ensure efficient use of materials.
- Identify situations in which repetitive production and batch production would be appropriate.
- Appreciate the importance of quality control and describe the new emphasis that is being used to improve product quality.
- Describe the basis of a Total Quality Management System.

PRODUCTION

Production can simply be defined as the activity of transforming raw materials or components into finished products. *Production management* is the process of the effective planning and control of the operations of that section of an enterprise devoted to transforming materials into finished products.

Industries vary a great deal and even within an industry companies vary in organization and methods of work. Terminology also has not been standardized to a large extent, but there are basic principles which can be *used* and *adapted* to the varying types of production.

In this chapter, a great deal of detail will of necessity be omitted, but the reader is referred to more specialized books at the end of the chapter. The terminology used is generally accepted but there are some areas where authorities differ; here an attempt has been made to indicate the nature of these other terms and meanings.

Research is made into the market to see if there is a demand for a new product. Further research is needed to give information for the design of a prototype or model. Designers then produce a specification for a product which is developed and this prototype is carefully tested. Sample products are made and these may be given to consumers for their use and they are asked to inform the company of the advantages and particularly the disadvantages they have noticed. Only then, when the disadvantages have been considered and rectified, does actual full-scale manufacture take place.

Production strategy

Production strategy is concerned with guiding investment decisions. Decisions made today provide guidelines for future production operations. The following points need to be considered in developing a strategy:

- should resources be placed in production rather than in other areas of a business?
- decide capacity needed to meet agreed production and corporate objectives and when production should commence;
- decide where plant should be located and the type of technology to use.

Some items may be more economically purchased from a sub-contractor. This may release space which can be used for other activities, e.g. research and development. The size of production should be considered carefully, bearing in mind the uncertainty of long-term forecasts. If maximum expected demand is catered for, this may lead to surplus capacity, which may or may not be able to be utilized; under-utilized plant is not economical. If a smaller capacity is provided for and orders increase, they may be met by sub-contracting, or possibly by importing. Some organizations deliberately keep their organization small and hence keep order books very long, e.g. 3–5 years ahead.

Factors critical to decisions on location should be noted. Conventional location reasons are: raw materials, skilled labour availability, financial incentives and transport; these may *not* be so important now. Innovation and new technological processes render plant obsolete quickly, so technological forecasting must be given high priority, in addition to noting carefully the impact of social, political and economic factors.

TYPES OF PRODUCTION

Before production commences, forecasting and planning are needed and the actual procedure adopted depends upon a number of items, e.g. whether a standard range of goods is required or whether designing is to follow special orders from customers.

Production policy therefore must be known and then the processes of manufacture, machine requirements, factory layout, storage and handling systems, skills required in the workforce and the method of training can be determined. This policy is largely determined by the nature of the work being carried out. Factors to consider are the following.

Amount of repetition

Amount of repetition is a dominating factor and there are three reasonably definite types:

1 Job production (or unit production). This occurs when a customer requires a single product made to his specifications, e.g. a ship or a suit. Demand can be only broadly forecasted and generally production schedules can be prepared only when the customer's order arrives. There is no production for stock and there are only limited stocks of materials kept. There must be a wider variety of machines and equipment available to do all types of work and labour must have varied skills; this may not be too easy to achieve.

In practice, a firm specializing in job production may be able to produce more of a particular article and the organization may be similar to that of small batch production.

2 Batch production. This occurs where a quantity of products or components are made at the same time. There is repetition, but not continuous produc-

tion. Production often is for stock, but if a batch is required to fulfil a special order the items are usually completed in one run. Small batches are virtually unit production and the choice of an economic batch size is very important. The numerous factors determining this size are considered in various formulae.

3 **Flow production.** This occurs where there is a continuous production of products of a more or less identical nature. There is very little waiting between the execution of one operation and another and each machine is continually used for one product and these are often specialized single-purpose machines. There can also be greater expenditure on equipment because of the high rate of breakdown. It is vital that maintenance be planned to prevent breakdowns, as the breakdown of one machine can stop the production line.

There should be reliability of machines and in the supply of raw material. There must of course be a continuous demand for the products and the work must be arranged so that the best use is made of machinery.

The newer forms of flow production are automated, whereby the product is automatically transferred from one machine to another.

NB: The term 'mass production' should be avoided as it simply means a large quantity of production, and this can be achieved *without* using the flow technique.

Range of products

This will vary greatly from job production on the one hand to flow production on the other. Some organizations are widely diversified and produce a large mixture of products.

Quality

The material used must be appropriate and strict observance of uniformity of quality can mean high purchase and inspection costs.

Workmanship can vary and if permitted tolerances are finely set it could mean greater accuracy is achieved than is necessary; this increases cost and is therefore wasteful.

FACTORY LOCATION AND LAYOUT

The following are among the many factors to be considered.

Selection of site

The selection of a site may be dependent upon:

- **Availability of land.** Land of the right nature and price must be available. There must be provision for expansion. In this connection there are government aids, e.g. in Development Areas, which provide facilities for easy land purchase, and give other benefits.

- **Availability of labour.** The availability of labour of the right type is a strong locational factor.
- **Availability of raw material.** This is closely linked up with *transport facilities*, with regard to obtaining the raw material and later in disposing of the product. Proximity to sea, river, road or rail is usually important and essential; for example, the disposal of waste from electricity power stations usually necessitates a site near a river or the sea.
- **Climate.** For some industries climate may be a very important consideration in the choice of a site.
- **Local regulations or by-laws.** These may be an important consideration as they may place restrictions on the industry.
- **Social facilities.** Availability of cultural and recreational activities, for example, and the suitability of housing accommodation may be important.

Selection of type of building

Brief consideration will be paid here to some factors, particularly to the height of the building and to the use of single- or multi-storey construction.

Single-storey buildings

Single-storey buildings can make better use of natural lighting. Heavy machinery can be placed with fewer restrictions compared with multi-storey buildings. Transport and movement of materials is quicker and easier and there is a lower cost of building and maintenance.

Multi-storey buildings

These buildings make better use of scarce land. Gravity can be used for moving materials and there is economy of cabling and heating.

There are of course many other factors to be considered by the architect, e.g. position of workshops, canteen, offices, etc. Whatever type of building is considered, Factory Act regulations must be noted, especially regarding heating, lighting, ventilation and safety.

Layout

There are two main types of layout which can be adopted:

1 **Product layout.** Where machines are laid out in accordance with sequences of operations to be carried out on the product. Material should move from stores through the factory to distribution areas with a minimum of movement. Design changes will greatly increase the costs of production as plant layout and re-tooling are very costly, for example, in the car industry.

2 **Process layout.** With this layout machines are grouped in sections, which depend upon the type of operation performed, e.g. welding. These specialized sections are more suitable for job and batch production and are adaptable, but involve greater materials handling.

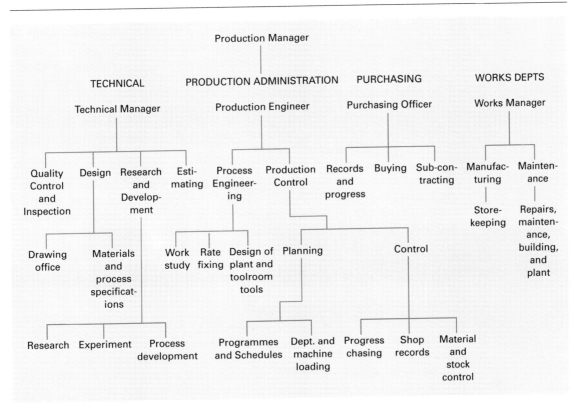

Fig 8.1 Organization chart for a medium-sized factory

PRODUCTION ORGANIZATION

Organization varies widely between firms and industries. This is partly accounted for by the varying sizes and the nature of goods produced and the manufacturing processes involved. The chart of an organization shown in Fig 8.1 will be used as a guide to consider each department in turn and briefly describe the nature of work carried out therein.

In smaller concerns one person may be in charge of the technical and administration section and many other variations may occur.

The technical activity is headed by a technical manager and comprises the following sections.

Research and development

The nature of this activity varies from industry to industry and from the different sizes and types of organization.

Research

Research can be considered to consist of the following types:

● **Pure or fundamental research.** This is concerned with obtaining new scientific principles such as the basic properties of a new element.

- **Applied research.** This involves creating a practical proposition from an idea. The knowledge obtained by basic research is used to solve industrial problems. It involves improving existing methods, organization, processes or equipment, or reducing the cost of products, or finding new uses for existing products or by-products.

It will have been noted from Fig 7.9 on p 291 that innovation is essential in order to arrest the decline of profits which will eventually occur if existing products are not altered or changed.

Development

Development involves the design and engineering work necessary to enable a project to reach production stage. It involves models, prototypes and pilot plants. Development is therefore associated with research and with design and there is really no specific division between these three activities.

A survey by the Confederation of British Industry showed that firms with the highest rate of internal research per 100 employees had a rate of growth of total net assets half as high again as those with the lowest expenditure on research.

The *stages of research* follow these lines:

(a) *the initial concept* is formed; this is the ideas stage;
(b) *a feasibility study* then takes place, whereby problems are defined, terms of reference drawn up and the possible sales are estimated and consideration is given to the economic justification of the project;
(c) the actual project is then *agreed upon* or rejected;
(d) if accepted, a *prototype* is developed, or pilot plant built;
(e) a *full-scale model* is then constructed with full co-operation between research and the production staff who will have responsibility for its commercial operation.

There are of course many problems, for example, the project may soon be made obsolete by technical developments, or a change in taste by consumers or a competitor's new ideas; the policy of the company could also change. (The aircraft industry is a good illustration of a case where vast amounts of money may be spent on research and development, the projects being later cancelled.)

Organization of research

There are many types of research work, and in all cases the organization of a company should enable all ideas to be co-ordinated. This sometimes is done by a research committee responsible to a research director. Many companies though will not be able to afford their own research and consequently they can take one of the following courses of action:

(a) Employ outside *consultants,* or consult independent research organizations, e.g. Science Research Council. The Council maintains a number of specialized research establishments such as the National Physical Laboratory and the Building and Chemical Research Laboratories.

(b) Join *Trade Research Associations* (e.g. Machine-Tool Research Association) which are supported by firms in those industries concerned and, by combining resources, can afford to hire top quality researchers. Member firms can obtain their help, as research information is supplied to all members.

(c) Contract with *University or Technical College* Research Departments to undertake research for them.

(d) The *National Research Development Corporation* is financed by the Department of Trade and Industry and aids ideas which it appears industry is not going to back, but which are presumed to be in the public interest. The Hovercraft is an illustration of a project it backed.

The head of a research department (R/D) may be responsible to the technical manager or direct to the production manager. In some of the more recent industries, e.g. electronics, R/D reports direct to general management.

The question, whether R/D should be represented at board level, is sometimes asked. There can be no set answer, and the same applies to any of the other activities: it all depends whether the *person* concerned can make an effective contribution to management problems of the *business*. 'Representation' as such cannot really be a criterion of appointment to the board.

There is, though, no reason why such specialists cannot be co-opted to the board to give special research advice.

The *qualities of a research worker* can be summarized: 'technical qualifications and creative and analytical ability, enthusiasm and single-mindedness of purpose, appreciation of the commercial aspects of the firm and ability to mix with people'. Some of these qualities will need to be stressed more than others, depending upon the type of research upon which engaged.

As values are different in scientific fields, a knowledge of sociology can help to manage personnel in R/D. Scientific achievement and the discovery of new knowledge and the resultant status from professional reputation is often a reward in itself.

Monetary reward is of course important, and a *suitable environment* may include such factors as:

- *opportunity* for research and appreciation of work done;
- allowing individuals *latitude* in following their own ideas;
- giving *incentives* to creative work, by sympathetic management action and freedom in professional dealings.

Relationships with other departments, especially with the marketing department, are necessary. Close liaison is essential and it is here that the research programme budget can help. An interchange of personnel can be most beneficial.

Financial control of research

Management must establish objectives and policies for research and then a programme is required to attain these objectives. The main restriction is money and the allocation of money can vary enormously as there are few guidelines.

The board must consider many factors, such as the future economic position of the firm and the country, the rate of obsolescence of existing products and the amount needed (at least) to replace these, whether human resources and equipment are available, whether competitors are strong and forward-looking.

The main costs are salaries, equipment provided and the upkeep of the laboratory: these are mainly fixed costs. One graduate scientist, for example, with attendant staff and services, would cost at least £40 000.

Control over research expenditure can be exercised by:

- overall financial policy;
- actual research programme;
- control over each individual step from initial to commercial exploitation.

Method suggested

1 A long-term and annual plan must be drawn up and then broken down into quarter years.
2 This gives a basis for manpower needs.
3 This programme, which is concerned with broad allocation of resources, can first of all be divided between different types of research, e.g. basic, applied, etc.
4 Within these types of research, a further breakdown into stages is made, e.g. initial ideas, feasibility, etc.
5 A further breakdown of each stage of work into, for example, division of a company, or subsidiaries, improvement of materials or reduction of costs, or customers' sponsored R/D work, etc., will enable resources to be spread so that a balanced R/D programme can be built up.
6 Individual projects can now be considered within this overall framework. A list of priorities and estimated man hours and total costs required are calculated and expenditure budgets prepared.
7 Periodic review and analysis of actual expenditure with the budget is essential, preferably by a policy committee composed of sales, production, finance and research personnel. Projects not considered worthwhile must be cancelled.
8 Future quarters' budgets can be put into a better perspective by noting the present quarter's results.
9 Ratios may be used to analyse research spending and show the factors having important effects on profitability, e.g. research costs to capital investment, total sales, or new product sales, or number of employees.

Ratios must of course be analysed carefully and, if comparisons are made with other companies in the same industry, great care is needed.

Design

The purpose of design is more than to improve the appearance of a product: it must also satisfy the customer in its performance, durability, simplicity of operation and cheapness. A new or changed design can be costly, as it may need new tools, or new layout of works and employees may have to be retrained.

Design *policy* must be formulated in terms a designer can understand and act upon. For example, a car firm requires low cost and high performance, while incorporating as many features as possible from higher priced models.

Producer selection, simplification and standardization are also closely linked in discussing design policy. Variety reduction, for example, cuts out wasteful practices, and standard components may be used instead of special ones. (This point will be discussed later in the chapter.)

Product design indicates the formulation of articles to be made so as to specify shape and dimensions, materials and parts required and the type of finish. The product is given a complete specification to enable everyone concerned to be aware of all requirements. Design can have several aspects:

- Design for production – this is to ensure component parts are made easily and economically, so that they can be assembled and transported easily and sold at an attractive price.

  The designer must therefore be aware of the production processes, the alternative methods available and their cost.
- Design for function – value in use implies quality and reliability: the product must satisfy the customer in its purpose and give long service.
- Design for appearance – to please the eye and attract customers.
- Design for distribution – to enable easy packing, reduction of storage space and packing costs.

A designer's ideas must be merged with those of the production engineer and the marketing side, who give market research information of customers' requirements and enable decisions to be made as to whether full-scale production should be authorized. A development committee, which was mentioned before, would contain representatives from all interested departments.

Organization of the design department

A design director may be in charge of designers in a large organization, and may also be in charge of research and drawing office staff. Small organization's may have one designer or give the work to a consultant.

NB: The Council of Industrial Design offers services to manufacturers, e.g. free advice on problems of design policy and organization, and will assist in the selection of designers.

A *design and development engineer* may be appointed to be in charge of the technical department and the following job specification shows the range of the work.

Responsible to:
Production Manager.

Responsible for:
- Interpretation of company trading policy regarding new product formulation and the modification of existing products.
- Determination of the design and specification of the product to be manufactured.
- Establishing and maintaining the necessary facilities for drawing office and research and development work.

- Preparing estimates of the cost of producing a job to customer's requirements – the estimates to be sent via the marketing department to the customer.
- Providing facilities and staff, under a chief inspector, for the objective
  inspection of manufacturing components and assemblies.
- Preparation of programme for R/D projects.
- Improving existing products or extending the range.
- Maintaining records of progress of projects and submission of reports and
  statements of expenditure incurred.

Limitations: No responsibility or authority for:
- Choice of product to be manufactured.
- Manufacturing programmes or delivery dates.
- Purchase of plant or equipment.

Special relationships:
(a) with *Production Manager* for the maintenance of scheme for classification
    and coding; review of manufacturing methods and investigation into
    components proving difficult to manufacture, establishing routines for
    inspection of parts produced by factory.
(b) with *Marketing Manager* for standards of finish and consideration of tech-
    nical aspects of customers' requests for product improvements.

The duties are numerous and this key position calls for a person of wide
knowledge. A designer must therefore identify the many factors influencing
design and any solution must cover the demands of competing requirements
(e.g. function, ergonomics, economics, brand presentation, aesthetics, motivation and production).

The drawing office

The drawing office is in many firms responsible for designing all products
manufactured. In the case of stock items, the office has responsibility for keeping the product up to date in design and appearance. The head should therefore be fully aware of the use of the product and the methods of manufacture.

The customers' specifications are often broad in outline and the drawing
office prepares detailed drawings or decides which of the standard drawings
shall be used.

It is important that work is not duplicated and that blueprints can be found
quickly. A code number is given to each *drawing*. Each *part* also has a number.
If a part can be used elsewhere all that needs to be done is to state the original
drawing and part number. Drawings can be classified according to product or
type of part. Standard drawings of all parts in frequent use are convenient
and are issued to operatives. (*See* also p 352, computer-aided design.) Old and
new drawings must be *withdrawn immediately* to obviate their being used in
error.

A satisfactory method in use today is to let the drawing office, rather than
the work's foreman, prepare specification lists or bills of materials, and copies
are sent to production and stores. The materials required will be automati-

cally issued before a job commences. The use of master specifications for standard lines saves time.

Estimating

Particulars of the final design are given to the planner who must have guidance as to the estimated cost. If a product is to be made to customer specifications a quotation will have been given, such details of cost being supplied by the estimating section. In smaller concerns the estimator is also the planner. If a product is internally designed, the estimate can be discussed with the marketing department which may suggest a lower price and this may mean an alteration in design. The estimator has less work to do when products are more standard. The activity is usually concerned with producing costs for making or repairing equipment for other companies rather than the general public.

The prices of standard articles are easily found, but a quotation requires careful consideration of numerous factors. Data are available from past records and a good knowledge of customer needs is essential. A cost chart can be prepared; this enables future varying requirements to be readily calculated. A knowledge of limiting or special factors of the machines and equipment is needed, e.g. the size of doorways or lifting capacity of cranes. Special arrangements may then have to be made with a corresponding cost increase.

Full co-operation between departments is needed, i.e. financial, production engineering, drawing office, marketing. The final estimate involves considering material content and expected prices, labour hours and rates, overhead costs and profit margin. The use of marginal costing for estimating is advocated by many accountants and this may be appropriate in certain circumstances.

Standardization, simplification and specialization

We will examine each of these terms separately.

Standardization

The word standardization is used in many ways, but a precise definition is that it is the process of obtaining agreement on:

- a standard for a product, range of products or procedure. (This may be a standard of performance, testing, method of manufacture, composition or dimension);
- the application of that standard.

The object is to facilitate interchangeability between parts and reduce costs, e.g. the use of the same instruments in all ranges of cars. The design department can play a large part. There are often small differences existing between parts, and with little effort a slight change in design could mean one part only could be used in place of a number of parts.

The British Standards Institution have now issued over 5000 standards; these are based upon the best present practice and provide a suitable standard and equitable basis for tenders.

Advantages to
producer

- *Reduction in variety,* offering long production runs, and lowering tooling and setting up costs.
- Greater use can be made of *special-purpose machines* as output is greater – this will mean lower operating costs.
- Reduction in stocks, materials, components and finished products, tools, idle time and overhead costs.
- *Quality* can be more consistent and there will be less maintenance and service costs.
- *Purchasing costs* would fall because of the smaller range of materials.
- *Training costs* would fall as training became shorter and simpler.

Advantages to
consumer

- Lower prices.
- Interchangeability.
- Better supplies, service and maintenance available.

Disadvantages

The disadvantages of standardization must be noted:

- slowness in bringing out new inventions and fewer beneficial design changes, which can have a marked effect on any sales of some products, e.g. cars;
- customers have fewer choices of product and there is less chance of special orders being produced;
- cost of standardization involves possible redundant stocks;
- parts or materials may be used which are not really suitable to get maximum standardization.

The procedure to install standardization involves examining the existing or proposed range and selecting items which are similar in material, shape or purpose. Then they are examined to see if standardization is possible in initial design or existing designs and changes can then be considered by a departmental committee.

Simplification

This is the process of reducing the number of types and varieties made. In practice simplification and standardization are closely linked, as for example when considering reduction in variety it may be seen that standard components may be introduced. The problems of variety reduction vary, but the objective, to cut out *wasteful* variety, is necessary (e.g. two engine sizes were used instead of the previous five in a motor car manufacturer's). An efficient costing system can aid the identification of products absorbing an undue proportion of manufacturing resources.

Advantages

- Longer runs which allow increased batch size and may lead to more production and greater mechanization.
- Tooling and setting up times can be reduced.
- Simpler and cheaper inspection – more use can be made of specialized inspection equipment.
- Stock control and storekeeping will be cheaper, as less capital is tied up in raw materials, components and finished products.

- Fewer drawings will be needed.
- Marketing policy could be made simpler, as prices could be lower, especially as a reduction in advertising and other costs is possible.
- Administration in general will be more efficient as there will be economies in all functions. There will also be less time spent on training staff.

The *consumer* benefits by better value, better service in delivery and repairs and product quality.

Specialization   This occurs where resources are exclusively used to make a narrow range of products. This basic economic principle (so clearly illustrated by the example of pin-making in Adam Smith's book *Wealth of Nations*, 1796) can take many forms, e.g. product or worker specialization.

The advantages are that the skills are enhanced because of concentrating on a limited range of work. Costs of maintenance and stocks fall because variety is reduced and this enables a greater concentration to be made in marketing.

The *disadvantages* include the fact that too much specialization may lead to loss as technology changes rapidly. Diversification is needed and many companies today are realizing this. There is also less flexibility and too narrow an outlook.

Quality control (QC)

Quality control is of vital importance to British industry especially as competition is intense and consumers become more discriminating. A survey showed that larger organizations are more likely to have QC departments: 92 per cent of organizations employing over 2000 have QC departments, compared with 62 per cent of organizations with under 300 staff. The food and chemical industries are strongly devoted to QC, largely because health inspectors enforce food and drug laws.

It has been stated that QC is an attitude of mind, and there is a great deal of truth in this statement. Some qualities cannot be directly measured, these are called 'attributes'; measurable qualities are called 'variables'.

Quality determines the direction or objective: control is the statistical element which measures product quality. Statistical quality control is a method of measuring deviations from standard quality by recording sample tests on charts. If limits are known, they can be easily seen. The theory of probability is applied to samples, enabling trends to be seen and corrective action to be taken, to avoid unnecessary scrap.

Quality begins and ends with marketing; once customer requirements are defined, a quick reporting process is needed, which should be maintained throughout design, specification, manufacture and inspection.

It is the primary concern of management to find and maintain the right quality which forms the basis of a product's profitability. For example, in 1992 thousands of new cars were called in by manufacturers to replace one defective part – this was a costly operation.

Management in
practice

> A grain-sized speck of paint was responsible for crippling the £800 million Hubble Space telescope, researchers discovered in 1990.
>
> After four months of investigation into one of America's most embarrassing space flops, scientists found that a single fragment of non-reflective film which fell from a lens-testing device was to blame for blurring the vision of the world's most expensive astronomical instrument.
>
> 'A total of 100 000 people worked on Hubble', said Dr Ed Weiler, NASA's Hubble programme manager. 'Of these, 99 997 did their job perfectly. The other three made the error.' Now space officials are struggling to find a way to restore Hubble's vision to its intended clarity.

Organization
for quality

The position of the QC department shows how seriously an organization regards it. In the previously mentioned survey 44 per cent of organizations said the head of QC was responsible to the board of directors, 25 per cent said he was responsible to the works manager and 11 per cent to the production manager.

The question arises, should the head of QC be independent of production and free to report direct to top management, or is QC a function and responsibility of production? Most authorities would prefer QC to be in a position where production could not over-ride its decisions. The *purposes of quality control* organization are:

- to establish standards of quality;
- to assess conformity to them;
- to take corrective action;
- to prepare improved standards.

Controls are required for design, supplier appraisal, incoming inspection of materials, process control, research and testing. The sources of quality lie in the *decisions and actions of people in many departments,* hence there should be good internal communications and reliable feedback of information from all departments and from consumers and preferably an after-sales service.

A designer has a problem as greater quality usually means greater cost and a proper balance must be obtained. He soon comes up against financial or technical barriers, and he must try to find the *optimum quality of design.*

The most profitable quality level is achieved by a balance between cost of quality to the manufacturers and value of quality to the consumer. (*See Fig 8.2.*)

Quality and reliability are two different but closely related aspects of the provision of a better service to customers.

A customer buys a product largely on the probability that it will continue to function satisfactorily throughout its planned working life, provided that it is used and maintained as intended. Reliability is proof of quality. In many cars there are over 600 critical components so it needs a reliability level per individual component of over 99 per cent for a high proportion of vehicles to operate satisfactorily.

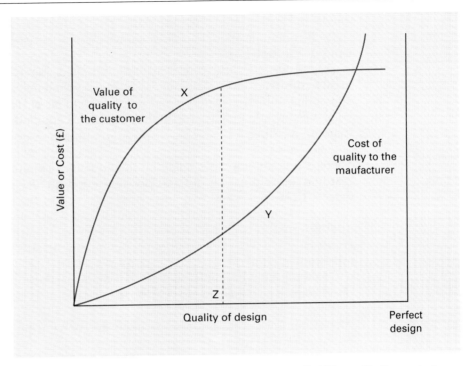

Fig 8.2 Optimum quality design. Z is a point of optimum profitability, and is the greatest distance between X and Y. Above the optimum, the cost of achieving greater quality of design more than outweighs any increase in market value

The investigations of Dr J M Juran, the American consultant, show about 80 per cent of quality failures are *management-controllable.* Quick action is needed to secure quality and reliability and that is why any QC organization must have top management backing and control.

In quality control, the taking of samples of raw materials, finished goods, etc., is known as *acceptance sampling.* Inspection of parts of a process as they are produced to detect variations is known as *process control.*

In acceptance sampling, quality levels are agreed with the supplier for sampling the materials and if rejects in a sample exceed the agreed percentage the batch is rejected.

Quality circles

The concept of Quality Circles, which is in widespread use in Japan, is being used more and more in the United Kingdom and the USA. The idea evolved from worker suggestion programmes and the training of employees in analysing problems relating to product quality. Problems are considered by a team of workers and sometimes supervisors. There are voluntary regular meetings of about 6–10 employees with a shared area of responsibility. They meet in company time, on company premises to discuss quality problems, with the object of:

- suggesting improvements;
- arranging their implementation.

The learning programme required for effective use of these Circles includes skills in communication, measurement techniques and how to develop problem solving strategies.

The benefits of Quality Circles include improved quality and productivity, greater motivation and awareness of work problems, and confidence in attempting to devise solutions and put them into effect. Topics discussed are wide and include quality, cost reduction, use of equipment, safety and efficiency in working.

Quality at the source

There is a great emphasis today on total quality planning. This means that manufacturers must try for 100 per cent good quality products, with no defects. Costs associated with inspection and costs of the failure of the product to meet customer requirements should ideally be *eliminated*. This view of quality must be strived for and fits in very well with the Just-in-Time approach (*see* p 351). A system of perfect quality must be designed to minimize human error.

Quality-at-source training will enable employees to work in small group – improvement activities, such as Quality Circles.

Inspection

Any system of appraisal depends upon decisions of the inspector, who is often responsible for:

- organizing the work of other inspectors to see that they are instructed and trained;
- seeing that the company's policy regarding quality and standards of finish is upheld;
- inspecting work and raw materials, recording results, notifying foremen of rejects and passing acceptable goods;
- seeing that gauges and tools are properly maintained;
- keeping up to date with new developments in methods of inspection.

Requirements of an inspector

Impartiality and strength of character to abide by a decision, skill in inspection and ability to decide quickly from various facts, are required of an inspector. He has to please (a) the works department which requires greater output at lower cost; (b) the sales and design departments which require high quality; thus he must be tactful and diplomatic.

The first requirement is to prevent faulty work going on to the next stage or process and preferably to stop it being made.

In some industries 100 per cent inspection is necessary, e.g. in the making of submarines. This is very costly, and often the first item produced is inspected in each batch. Reports of rejects are sent periodically to the department head and only inspectors are allowed to scrap work and arrange for re-processing or rectification of faulty work.

Centralized inspection

Under this system all work is sent to the inspection department before passing to the next operation.

The *advantages* of centralized inspection are:

- division of labour is possible and more expensive machines may be purchased, allowing less-skilled labour to be employed;
- work is more easily supervised;
- the shop floor is cleaner and losses from scrap, etc., more easily observed.

The *disadvantages* arise from the greater amount of handling, transport and work in progress.

Floor inspection

Here inspectors go to the machine or work bench and inspect on the shop floor. This type of inspection has the following advantages:

- less handling and delay in transfer to and from the central inspection department;
- work in progress is reduced and faults can be remedied immediately;
- advice can be given to the operator immediately.

BS 5750

British Standard 5750 lays down the standards for a quality system. It can be applied to any organization and includes setting standards for the assurance of quality of material and/or services.

To gain certification for BS 5750 qualification an organization:

- Prepares a 'quality' manual in consultation with the organization who will make the award. This manual sets out the company's policy and procedures on quality assurance (using standards of performance which the company may choose for itself).
- An assessor will then visit the client company to check that the procedures in the quality manual are being followed. Corrective action is taken where necessary.
- The Certificate is then issued if approval is given and many companies widely advertise their success in achieving the Standard.
- Thereafter, there is continuing assessment to see standards set are being maintained. These could involve two or more yearly visits.

Criticisms have been levied at the standard and often include the following:

- costs may be higher than expected and an annual fee will also be payable;
- organizations making the award vary in quality, as control by the Department of Trade is not complete. Anyone can set themselves up in business to make the award at present;
- Certification is concerned with monitoring the *procedures* by which the attainment of standards is assured. It is not concerned with establishing the standards themselves. A *low* standard could be set by some companies – BS 5750 does not necessarily denote high quality.

BS 5750 originated in industries, such as defence where quality procedures were monitored against well-established standards. It has now spread to industries where standards are not so fully developed or understood.

In 1992 a survey was carried out by the Small Business Research Trust on the effect of BS 5750 on small firms. The results were published in the

National Westminster Bank's *Quarterly Survey of Small Businesses in Britain.* Firms were aware of the shortcomings of the standard but felt they had to adopt it in case they lost contracts from Government bodies.

Value engineering (VE) or value analysis

This is another discipline which originated in the USA and was brought to the UK in the early 1950s. In 1964 full details of savings made were published and centres were set up giving instructions in this technique.

VE is a technique which endeavours to discover the most economical way of performing the function of each part of a manufactured product.

It is more a psychological discipline, an attitude of mind rather than a scientific formula. Management must play a large part in developing a VE programme and impress upon everyone that their co-operation is essential.

The analysis is brought right back to the *design stage,* instead of beginning with design and examining the methods used from that point forward.

Summary of method

1 *Define* the function of each item or part.
2 Consider *alternative* ways of performing the same function.
3 Find the *cost* of these alternatives.
4 If, at this stage, no alternative is significantly cheaper, either find more alternatives or abandon analysis.
5 A more *detailed cost analysis* is then made of acceptable alternatives.
6 *Selection* is made of the more acceptable alternatives and after careful examination, if it enables the *same function* to be performed as the original part, and if it is *less costly,* it will be approved.

It is simply a *discipline* used to examine each component in a design, logically and systematically, to see if a part, or an alternative part, can be made to perform the same function more cheaply. Conventional cost reducing techniques begin with cost and seek to reduce it. VE starts with the function, then considers the cost.

Place in organization

As a staff function VE may form part of a quality control section or, in a few large organizations, a separate function reporting to production management.

In *purchasing,* the value analyst has prime responsibility for value in material and services procured. He serves as a consultant to buyers.

A basic engineering training is usually essential plus training in value analysis. The value analyst must have a high degree of initiative and creativity, be able to sell his ideas and be *cost-conscious.*

When costs are reduced by this technique, often the quality and reliability of the product are improved, because the thinking was directed to improving the function of the part in the best possible way.

Total quality management (TQM) system

A TQM system is based on the theory that as quality improves, costs fall through lower failure rates and less waste. TQM involves more than assurance of quality of products or services. It is a system which looks at quality in *every stage* of the process of production, both internally and externally.

All senior executives must be committed to a TQM programme as it requires *full commitment* and *effective teamwork* and *leadership*. Every part of the organization must be integrated and form part of a complete system.

If the system is not complete, organizational gaps could lead to wastage or failure to meet the requirements of another part of the organization. TQM is an organizational strategy which aims at improving a business's effectiveness and flexibility, by eliminating waste so that results can be achieved quicker and more cheaply. Quality is seen as the responsibility of *all* employees. It is pursed through various methods that are intended to ensure consumer satisfaction. TQM involves building in quality, from product planning to design, to pre-production, to purchasing, production, sales and service. The strategy seeks to place quality, as top priority, rather than short-term profits.

Traditional quality control as we have seen, refers mainly to inspection of the product during and at the end of the production process. The focus is more on corrective controls which correct mistakes when they have occurred rather than making the product 'right first time'.

Production administration

This consists of process engineering, production planning and production control.

Process engineering

This is a branch of production administration responsible for deciding how work is to be done, the measurement of work and the establishment of standard times and practices, the preparation and revision of process specifications and the design of tools and equipment.

The work of the head of process engineering may briefly comprise:

(a) Investigations into processes and operations to establish the correct way to carry them out, to reduce fatigue and to eliminate unnecessary operations.
(b) Preparation of drawings for jigs and tools and inspection equipment.
(c) Establishing standard times after collecting data and operation times.
(d) Reporting and investigating excess costs and being aware of modem trends in manufacturing methods and machines.
(e) Maintaining company's human resources policy, training staff effectively.

Work study

Work study is a management tool comprising those techniques, particularly method study and work measurement, which are used in the examination of human work in all its contexts and which lead systematically to the investigation of all the factors which affect the efficiency and economy of the situation being reviewed, in order to effect improvement. This definition is an extract from British Standard 3138.

The performance of a firm can be increased by either improving the processes of manufacture or by developing new and more suitable machines and equipment. This usually takes a long time for research and is called *process study*. It often requires considerable expenditure and is really part of research and development. It is linked with work study and in practice there is no clear line of demarcation between them.

Work study can bring quick improvements for the outlay of little capital expenditure.

Work study is needed because it:

- leads to saving in production costs and makes more effective use of human effort;
- provides information and reveals inefficiency;
- improves conditions, methods and layout;
- ensures a steady flow of material and an equal reward for the same skill and effort;
- establishes a standard rate or time for a job.

There are two techniques comprising work study, these are method study and work measurement.

Method study

Method study is the detailed analysis of an existing or proposed method as a basis for improvements. It is the first part of work study, and its objectives are to improve methods, or establish a correct method for job or process; this will economize in human effort and make more efficient use of men, materials and machines.

It can be applied in the office or factory and should be considered in the design stages of new jobs, as important economies can be made at this stage. The basic procedure is to:

- Select work to be studied.
- Report relevant facts of method used.
- Examine facts logically.
- Develop a more effective method.
- Install and maintain this method as standard practice.

Recording is made easier by using video-cameras, but basic recording techniques comprise:

1 Process charting, which shows in a diagrammatic form the sequence of events in manufacture. Symbols are used which enable information to be set down logically and can be used to visualize the problem more easily. (*See* section on Organization and Methods in Chapter 10.)
2 Flow diagrams are scale diagrams showing in detail the progress of the material or component through various departments. Multiple activity charts, motion charts and films may be used.

Work measurement

Work measurement is the application of techniques designed to establish the time for a qualified worker to carry out a specified job at a defined level of performance (British Standard definition). The unit of measurement which is common to most jobs is time. Time study is generally based upon noting the time for each element of a job. Allowances are made for personal needs, and the speed and effort of the worker and a work standard can be built up and the 'time allowed', which is a standard, may be used as a basis for accurate costing, planning or incentive schemes. It is best suited to repetitive work.

Predetermined motion time systems (PMTS)

PMTS establish times for basic human motions and are used to build up the time for a job at a defined level of performance. Operations are divided into a limited number of basic manual motions, for each of which a time has been established, this time being determined by the *nature* of the motion and the *conditions* under which it is made. The same principle can now be applied to the office as well as in the factory.

Plant and tool designers play a valuable part in designing new tools, department layouts and special machines. Tool design and making must be integrated with production programmes and this work must be closely linked with that of work study engineers in designing improvements to present methods.

Ergonomics

Ergonomics is called human engineering in the UK or human factors engineering in the USA, and there is a difference in *emphasis* between the terms used in the two countries.

In the past, there have been many studies of the impact of nature and environment on the capacity of people to work. Many of the new words in management describe, in a different way, approaches to subjects which have occurred in the past. Ergonomics is such a word, derived from the Greek *ergon* (work) and *nomos* (law) and has been defined as the scientific study of the relationship between man and his working environment and the application of anatomical, physiological and psychological knowledge to the problems arising therefrom.

The human machine is studied, in order to produce machines and equipment to reduce physical and mental strain. The area of activity covered by ergonomics is large and the following areas are examples:

- Environment in general. Studies are made of the effect of light, temperature, ventilation, noise, etc., on the health of workers, e.g. avoidance of high-pitched sounds which irritate.
- In the workplace – physical problems of work are studied, including layout of equipment. Use of better-designed chairs, better positioning of hand and foot controls, and control panels.
- Mental problems at work would involve studies in fatigue, fault-finding analysis, problems of age. The older workers have problems of hearing and eyesight and have a slower reaction.

Production control

This is one aspect of the control function and there are many definitions of what comprises production control. No ideal system can be stated. Every enterprise is different but no matter what method of organization is adopted, production must be planned and controlled so that products are supplied in the right quantity and quality at the right time, at minimum cost.

In smaller concerns, memory and experience are relied upon to a large extent in planning and control. Larger concerns need an efficient, flexible system to plan and control the mass of information, materials and machines.

Production planning

Production planning may be said to comprise the following purposes:

1 To transform marketing requirements into instructions to the production departments. These take the form of works orders or programmes.
2 To see people and materials are employed on work for which they are most suited and to keep schedules up to date, so that deviations from programmes can easily be seen.
3 To maintain a balance between the various manufacturing processes, to stop work 'bottlenecks' which would mean lower utilization of people and machines.
4 To arrange manufacturing orders in the best sequence, in economic batches.
5 To liaise between marketing and production and to reschedule production if necessary so that delivery requirements can be fulfilled.

Simple example of routines involved

(a) When an enquiry (invitation to quote) is received, the production control section must see if the necessary labour, material and plant capacity are available. A capacity record is needed and also a record of the load on each process or group of machines.
(b) Orders when received are broken down into operations and the time each machine will be occupied is estimated and noted on a *load record.* This record will be reduced by work completed and this loading determines whether or not orders can be accepted, or whether delivery can be on time.
(c) From the drawings (prepared by the drawing office) *parts lists* (or specifications) can be prepared, showing material required, part numbers, numbers required and detailed descriptions.
(d) From the parts lists, *material schedules* can be prepared; these show all material needed for the contract. Then the operation or process planning layout (or sequence schedule or route card) is prepared, showing processing sequences and the time for each process or operation, specifying *jigs and tools* required. It may also show particulars of materials, e.g. size and quality, and the particular machine and operations to be performed. The *full specification* will be shown on the top part of the document.
(e) The *scheduling* section will examine this layout chart and compile hours of work for drilling, milling, etc., breaking details into weekly quantities over the production timetable.
(f) Target dates can now be set for the *master production schedule.* This shows *shop* load programmes enabling foremen to see required weekly output. The use of a *material delivery schedule* enables a check to be made as to whether suppliers are dispatching materials on time.

When schedules have been compiled, the next stage is to authorize the production of an order, called a *works order.* This is an instruction to the foreman to manufacture a specific quantity of products. They should ideally be drawn up in advance of the time required and issued by a central authority in the production control department. Other documents need to be issued to permit the withdrawal of tools and stores. In many firms these documents may comprise material movement forms, inspection tickets and work payment tickets as well as the works orders.

The control part of production planning and control can be said to comprise progress and material control. *Progress control* implies the checking and review of all aspects of the production plan. It is the means by which the production plan is co-ordinated so as to reveal any variations. Information as to the progress of manufacture is 'fed back' to ensure a smooth production flow. Successful progress control requires speed and accuracy and a wide range of visual charting methods can be used to aid progressing.

Expediting

Expediting or the progressing of work needs a type of person who is flexible, friendly and firm in his actions and with a sound knowledge of all the company's products. Co-operation with supervisors is essential as programmes may frequently be changed and this could cause friction.

One aspect of expediting is to see that components and assemblies flow smoothly through the stages of manufacture. Another is to see information is quickly available and disseminated. The follow-up procedure is the function of the progress 'chasers' who may have a status equivalent to that of assistant foreman. They are organized in two ways:

1 By having one progress person responsible for a section or department.
2 A progress person responsible for a production or group of components.

Some organizations may operate both systems.

Examination of periodic lists of jobs overdue, and special checks on items having no 'margin' (i.e. on the critical path) are basic duties of the progress chaser.

Materials control

This section is responsible for ensuring that the right quantity and quality of material is available when and where required. At the same time capital must not be tied up unduly, nor must there be undue loss from deterioration and obsolescence.

A good system of materials control requires:

- centralization of purchasing under a buyer;
- department co-ordination – in purchasing, inspecting, receiving, storing and issuing materials;
- simplifying and standardizing whenever possible;
- efficiency in storing in suitable accommodation, with safeguards against pilfering, deterioration, waste, etc;
- planning and scheduling materials requirements, and preferably control by budget;
- stocktaking procedure to be efficient.

NB: It is pointed out later that material and stock control come under the purchasing officer in some companies.

Stores control

The position of the stores in the organization varies widely. Some companies have the stores under the purchasing officer: others prefer the section to be under the works manager. A satisfactory arrangement is for the recording of the stores to be under production control, while the physical aspect is under the works department. The details of stock should be readily available to production control so that stocks can be replenished when necessary.

Stocks are held to make production possible even though demand fluctuates. Factors aiding stock control are:

- accurate coding and classifying of stores;
- perpetual inventory records and periodic physical checking of stock;
- efficient accounting procedures and a system of preventing obsolete or surplus stock.

Stores may be ledger cards or on computer, showing minimum and maximum stock level, order or re-order level, standard order, the item's catalogue and part number, in addition to opening and closing balances, receipts and issues.

Stock levels

Maximum levels when set must consider price fluctuations and available capital, possible obsolescence, available storage space and whether material can be stored a long time or not, economic ordering quantity and rate of consumption and cost of insurance.

Minimum levels will be fixed after noting the purchasing time cycle. The time between placing an order and its subsequent fulfilment is called *lead* time, made up of time in placing order, time in executing order and time in receiving order. Factors affecting minimum stock are:

- uncertainty of demand – the greater the uncertainty, the greater the stock;
- uncertainty of lead time – if this is great, the higher the stock needs to be;
- the size of the batch – the larger the batch, the less frequently will the stock fall to 'danger' level, and the smaller the minimum stock required;
- the more standard the item, the more easily it will be obtainable. A special item may take longer to obtain.

Re-order levels are important and must note lead time and normal consumption.

Duties of storekeeper

1 Supervise and guide staff in their duties.
2 See records are up to date and all departments are given an efficient service.
3 Co-operate with planning, purchasing and inspection departments.
4 Receive goods from outside, check number, and arrange for inspection, reporting variances from order to purchasing section.
5 Check stock physically at least once a year and ensure it is stored neatly and safely.

6 Issue stock on appropriate instructions and record accurately stock movements on documents involved, e.g. copy order, materials release note, etc.

Types of store

Raw material stores vary with the type of industry. Component stores carry piece parts to be manufactured in the factory or purchased from outside. Raw material and component stores often go together. Finished part stores are used where the company is not using transfer machines, and finished parts have to be stored in readiness for assembly and sub-assembly. Indirect stores are, for example, the tool store, issuing tools in exchange for a tool check bearing operator's name and number.

Other tools are consumable, e.g. files. Indirect materials are stored separately, e.g. oil.

Maintenance stores keep all parts required for routine and preventive maintenance.

Arrangement of stores

The stores must be convenient for the factory. The layout should be convenient to the class of goods handled and bins, etc., should be arranged in a logical order; the following rules are important:

- heavy goods should be kept near the floor;
- goods most frequently required should be easily accessible;
- goods susceptible to dampness should be kept dry and inflammable materials to be kept in fireproof containers;
- valuable or fragile goods should receive special protection.

The maximum use should be made of height, e.g. use of fork-lift trucks and pallets. Metal racks are strong and conveniently easy to erect and dismantle. Materials should flow into stores via the inspection department and then flow to works. Finished goods should move via inspection to despatch. The place and method of storage must, of course, suit the method of handling and gangways should be sufficiently wide for mechanical aids.

Centralized or departmental stores

The advantages of centralized stores are:

- specialized facilities can be installed, e.g. refrigeration;
- similar stocks can be carried, thus reducing risks of deterioration and obsolescence, reducing working capital and storage space and lowering insurance costs;
- physical stock control is easier;
- total staff may be reduced.

The disadvantages are, in effect, the advantages of departmental stores:

- greater convenience to each department in having its own stores, as main stores may be far away;
- saving is made in freight and handling costs by having departmental stores. Some heavy raw materials, e.g. coal, may be easier to keep in a decentralized store.

In practice a main store for raw materials issues materials against requisitions submitted by sub-stores in each manufacturing department and replenishment is on an 'imprest system'.

Pre-production planning

This term is sometimes used and can be considered to be a branch of production administration, which includes those functions that must be carried out before production begins. It is concerned with:

- **Product Design and Development.** The needs of the customer must be known and continuous research is needed into new methods, markets and materials. The physical limitations of production capacity must be known so that orders are not accepted if they cannot be produced on time.
- **Production Engineering.** Standard times and methods of working must be considered both for manufacturing jigs and tools and actual manufacturing operations.
- **Estimating.** Material specifications may be built up and parts lists and operation schedules prepared so the cost can be calculated and a price fixed.
- **Production Planning.** The other information required before production actually commences can be considered under this heading. It includes knowledge of available orders and stocks, etc., to enable an analysis of requirements of materials and components, length of time operations will take, etc. Each order can then be analysed into component factors, e.g. machine and labour hours.

Pre-production planning can be simply defined as follows: the co-ordination of information on manufacturing capacity and material availability so that control of new manufacturing requirements is facilitated. It is also concerned with the possible effect on capacity of research trends, changes in design and methods of manufacture.

Purchasing

The procurement of supplies for any type of enterprise is often not given the importance which the job warrants. In many cases over 50 per cent of money spent is on materials purchased and this may exceed payments for salaries and wages.

Materials may be purchased at too high a price, or of the wrong quality, or too great a quantity, which may lead to obsolescence and loss of interest on capital. Too little purchased means production delays. So incorrect buying can have a marked effect upon profits.

Organization

The position of the purchasing officer or buyer varies widely. Often the total cost of materials purchased may determine whether the buyer is of equal status to the other departmental heads or is a director. He is often responsible to the works manager or another section of the production department, but no specific place can be fixed for his position.

A buyer's responsibilities vary, and in some cases he may be responsible for stores records and stores departments. In order to take advantage of spe-

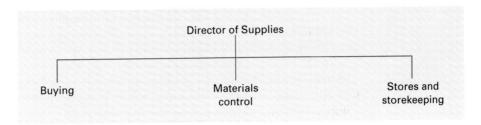

Fig 8.3 Director of supplies

cialization of skills, it may be considered that too many varied sections should not be placed under the purchasing officer. Stores records for example are often placed under the jurisdiction of the planning department and the works departments may have the stores under its care. This arrangement is considered very practical as the planners need stock details, and as storekeeping is a physical job intimately connected with works, which may be dispersed, it can best be controlled by the works department.

Purchasing may be divided among buying staff according to the *types of material:* this makes full use of specialization. Another method is for a buyer to handle all purchases for a *specific section* of the business. The progress section must see all purchases are received on time and records all information in this respect. The *records* aspect deals with invoices, receipts and routine information.

A company with numerous factories may have local buyers in each factory in addition to head office buyers. Other larger companies may have a director of purchasing or supplies in charge of the function, as in Fig 8.3.

Whatever the organization structure, the company objectives on purchasing must be upheld. These may involve:

- buying materials at the lowest cost consistent with the service and quality required;
- avoiding any waste or duplication, while maintaining the lowest possible outlay on stock consistent with making the material needed for production available when required.

The use of a purchasing manual enables responsibilities to be defined and the establishment of uniform policies and procedures. This is essential where buying is decentralized.

Briefly, purchasing *policy* may be concerned with:

(a) Whether to buy on *contract* on a medium- or long-term basis; this can be used where price variations are small. This avoids holding large stocks and such continuity of supply is very important in flow production.

(b) To buy when *required;* this involves limiting purchases to minimum requirements and the buyer has wide discretion. This is likely to be used for non-standard goods and results in less capital tied up in stock and hence less storage is needed. Price fluctuations are not likely to be so important, but there can be little gain if prices fall as quantities purchased are small.

The purchase of small quantities will raise unit cost, as well as increase handling and packing costs.

(c) *Speculative* or *bargain* buying. As with any speculation, profits and losses could be high. Material is purchased with the hope of future price rises, thus saving money or with the expectation of re-sale at a profit later on. This latter system is used in some industries, particularly staple goods, e.g. copper. If adopted it is essential for a senior executive to control such actions.

The advantages of centralizing buying are:

- higher degree of specialization as individuals can concentrate on a limited number of fields;
- control is easier as records are centralized;
- because of increased quantities, advantage can be taken of quantity discounts;
- standardization of specifications is easier to obtain.

If stores are under purchasing control and are situated a distance away, then control can be costly and inflexible. In general, some compromise between local and centralized purchasing may be the solution. This can be done by having a manual of standard procedures, with details of local purchases being sent to head office immediately. Limits to the amounts local buyers can spend would be made. Exceptional purchases over these limits would need head office approval. Efficient two-way communication is essential.

The work of the purchasing department

A purchasing officer studies commodities, sources of supply, systems and procedures, inventory problems and market trends, the most effective method of delivery, whether maximum discounts are being earned, the amount and use of waste material. These are a few of the wide range of activities he may deal with. Very large companies may have a purchasing research department which has to consider world-wide supply and seasonal trends.

If we consider the responsibilities of a 'typical' purchasing officer, the work of the department can be clearly seen. The purchasing officer is responsible for:

- material and equipment purchases while adhering to the company's purchasing policy;
- studying all markets for prices, trends and delivery times and maintaining accurate records of sources of materials, etc;
- developing and maintaining morale of staff, instructing, guiding and training them according to the company's human resources policy;
- seeing the work of the department is efficiently organized, e.g

1 Interviewing suppliers' representatives.
2 Ensuring that requisitions are duly authorized before making out orders or contracts with suppliers.
3 Collating quotations, accepting the most desirable, and advising departments concerned of any change in prices or delivery dates.

4 Processing orders to see if delivery will be on time, vouching invoices when received, authorizing disposal of waste material. He must co-operate with many departments, especially the planning and progress departments for material deliveries and quotations.

Purchasing officer

High ethical standards are needed in a purchasing officer coupled with integrity and breadth of vision. A knowledge of office methods, law and accounting and often some specialized technical knowledge are basic requirements in certain industries. Personal contact is very important, so a courteous manner is essential to cultivate the goodwill of the suppliers.

Sub-contracting

In some industries arrangements are made with other firms for the supply of components instead of the firm making them itself. It is widely used in the motor-car industry and often the components can be supplied at a lower cost than if the firm made them itself. Cost may not be the main factor, as firms may need more components than they can produce in order to meet their customers' requirements and sub-contracting is then the answer.

Reliability of quality and quantity and delivery is a problem and, if a large amount is purchased in this way, a separate section may deal with it.

Resource management is concerned with the management of *all* physical resources from origin to final consumption. It encompasses materials management, purchasing and physical distribution management (*see* p 282). It adopts a systems approach and involves:

- an internally considered appraisal of strengths and weaknesses of all resources required;
- external appraisal of environment, noting threats and opportunities and trends, particularly for essential items;
- planning for a number of years ahead; establishing a material or resources gap and planning how it shall be filled, e.g. by increasing efficiency, diversifying, new materials or new supplies, or even no growth at all.

Availability of resources

Limitations in the supply of resources, e.g. oil and minerals, are making organizations more careful about planning for resources. The need to give purchasing decisions more attention is slowly growing in strength, considering that in manufacturing industry more than half of the amount of sales turnover is the cost of purchasing goods and services.

Long-range planning for purchasing should be given equal strength to plans for marketing. Security of supplies is so important to many concerns that they have integrated backwards, e.g. to ensure availability of tea, tea plantations have been purchased.

Given that survival is an objective, it is obvious that ensuring the availability of supplies is vital and must be considered of high importance. An example of an organization that has paid great attention to ensuring quality suppliers at competitive prices is Marks & Spencer.

Purchasing and quality assurance

The purchasing department operates with other departments in arranging for the supply of goods by outside organizations. Detailed specifications of goods required and tolerances must be prepared. Then when goods are received there must be a system to ensure conformity with the specification. The purchasing department is concerned with the availability of alternative materials and the possibility of obtaining the quality required at an acceptable price.

The *selection of suppliers* is very important. This may involve *approving their system* of quality control and inspection of goods received. An inspection is costly, therefore if suppliers could be relied upon to supply goods which were consistently acceptable, this would mean a great saving in cost. Many companies carry out their own investigations of suppliers or they use other investigators to assist.

Standards of quality and safety must be upheld in addition to setting up procedures to ensure suppliers supply the goods to the correct specification. As mentioned above, the ideal would be to rely *entirely* on the suppliers' checks on quality or allow goods into the company with the very minimum checks being made.

Supplier information is required to ensure that purchases are of a good quality, that there are high standards of service, reliability of delivery and continuity of supply. Information is needed on actual or potential suppliers, i.e. their:

- **production capability** – their capacity, efficiency, planning and control and inspection methods;
- **technical capability** – the quality of their facilities for design and development, production and testing to see if they could ensure quality of output at all stages of production;
- **financial capability** – to see how stable they are financially and the credit-rating of the company;
- **management capability** – to see how efficient are the supplier's administration systems.

Maintenance of plant, equipment, and buildings

Poor maintenance may lead to plant failure and consequent delays in production. Companies with large capital investment must pay great attention to maintenance and it is usually a good plan to have a separate maintenance department responsible to the works manager.

The head of the section is responsible for:

- the maintenance of buildings, plant and machinery to ensure efficient working order;
- regular periodic inspection and attention to all breakdowns and repair work;
- maintaining discipline and the supervision and control of personnel in the department;
- ensuring that tools and equipment are in good order and accurate records of work are kept.

The department may include many skilled trades, e.g. electricians, carpenters and bricklayers. Alternatively, this work may be contracted out to specialist firms.

Before maintenance policy plans can be drawn up the following information must be available, bearing in mind plant replacement policy:

- the relationship between the frequency and extent of inspection and plant breakdowns;
- cost of inspection and the cost in making good the production lost through breakdowns.

Preventive maintenance

There are various types of maintenance, from routine servicing to temporary stoppage of production and yearly complete overhauls.

In setting up a scheme for preventive maintenance it is necessary to:

- prepare an inventory of plant, noting those parts of equipment most likely to wear first or break down;
- draw up schedules, showing the location of plant and noting the frequency of inspection;
- assess standard times for inspection. The inspection card must include maker's name, original cost, special manufacturing instructions and records of breakdowns.

It is important to keep impressing the importance of maintenance to all staff and a constant check on the cost of maintenance is essential.

The use of *mechanical fuses* is common. One part of the machine is made intentionally weak, so that if it is overworked it stops and only the weak or cheaper parts need to be replaced.

Production control and the computer

The amount of clerical work involved in production control is extensive. Attempts have been made to reduce the amount by ensuring a document is used for more than one purpose to reduce movement by integration and reduction of staff. Because of the large number of calculations, sorting and storage of large quantities of data and printing large amounts of information, it can be seen how the production control activities were considered eminently suitable for programming on a computer.

An introduction to the nature of computers is given in Chapter 10 on Administrative Management. The main aim of the computer is to provide management with information so that decisions can be made. A major function of computers in production control is to supply relevant information at the time that it is required.

Examples of the way a computer can assist production control are as follows:

1 **Stock re-ordering.** The computer is programmed to compare recorded stock balances with re-order level; if the stock balance is below this, then the files in the computer can produce the name and address of a supplier and raise an order for replenishment. A more elaborate system would analyse the demand data for an item and calculate re-order parameters.

2 **Capacity loading problem.** Details of operations and bills of quantities can be held on the computer file. When an order is obtained from a customer, the computer can break the product into component parts and load each manufacturing operation into its appropriate cost centre when capacity is available in accordance with a time schedule to ensure production is not delayed.

3 **Operation details and bills of quantities.** Details of raw materials, jigs and tools needed for the finished product and the setting up and taking down times, can be held in the memory for each manufacturing stage. The computer can then determine dates for which purchased materials should be obtained and the stages when manufacturing should commence so that customers' requirements are met on the given date. It could produce a critical path analysis (*see* p 250). Analyses can then be made of actual and standard operating times and produce data to show labour absenteeism and machine breakdowns.

4 **Works order documentation.** Complete documentation for works orders is possible. The benefits of a management information system are mentioned elsewhere in this book. Some of these benefits are obtainable especially in the integration of production control and other functions. Because the computer works so fast one can combine from customers' orders:

- an updating of the order book, and breakdown of parts needed;
- the raising of works documentation (e.g orders raised on suppliers);
- allocation of stock items, loading capacity data and job costing data.

Other departmental activities which could be integrated include invoicing, progressing, stock valuation, standard costing and variance analysis, planned maintenance schedules and analyses of sales representatives' performances.

Advantages of computer-assisted production control
- Reduced clerical costs.
- Minimization of work in progress and setting-up times, etc.
- Maximum machine utilization.
- Reduction in stocks.
- Reduction of delivery times to customers.

Disadvantages
- Cost of installation of computer and data processing personnel outweighs financial savings in clerical staff.
- The greater amount of information from the computer may need *more* persons to analyse data.

It may be difficult to compare the extra cost of the computer system with the benefit of better control and utilization of people, machines and material. Such systems are expensive, but the use of standard programs can reduce this. It has taken a long time to convince management that the computer can play an effective part in production control and help to overcome the inadequacies of most manual production control systems.

Management of energy

In order to remain competitive, every aspect of cost must be examined in order make savings. In the past few years a government policy to encourage the efficient use of energy has emphasized the potential savings in this area.

Often a senior member of the board of directors is given responsibility to conserve energy and statements of energy costs and savings are needed in all proposals for capital investment. *Energy audits* can show for all departments the consumption of energy and its cost. If staff are aware of the need and are given training, savings can be high.

Avoidable losses can be highlighted, e.g. inadequate insulation, lighting which is too bright. Energy savings targets are set and often up to 10 per cent reduction in energy use is obtained by implementing the findings of an energy audit.

Only large organizations could appoint energy managers but small organizations can practise energy conservation by using simple checklists and implementing 'good housekeeping' procedures.

Microprocessor control systems are a great help in the efficient use of energy. They can be applied, for example, to the control of heating, lighting and ventilation. All control units are self-regulating and control sensors lead to quick corrective action to remedy waste detected. Such a comprehensive control system is also an aid to preventive maintenance.

MATERIALS HANDLING

In some basic industries, materials handling represents 85 per cent of all production costs; in others, about 15 per cent. It is therefore obvious that by effective materials handling a marked reduction in costs is possible. The problem is often the limitation of older buildings and the lack of proper planning which makes the use of newer equipment very difficult.

If only warehousing operations are involved, it is easier to modernize, but in complex manufacturing areas integrated handling can be used only if plans are made well before building commences. The more materials handling can be eliminated and the more there is processing 'on the move' the more efficient industry will become. Co-ordinated flow lines are needed from raw materials through receiving, processing, warehousing and shipping to primary centres of distribution.

Reduction in costs is possible by the use of handling equipment and the elimination of unnecessary handling and improved layout. Accidents are reduced and work in progress kept at a minimum.

In general, there are three classes of handling equipment:

1 For moving materials over a line of travel between two *fixed* points. This can be done by the use of conveyor belts, gravity or power rollers and overhead trolleys and cranes.

2 For *vertical* movement in multi-storeyed buildings – elevators, hoists and spiral gravity chutes and conveyors can be used.

3 For movement *between* points not in a fixed line – tractors with trucks, e.g. stillage and fork-lift trucks, can be used.

A *fork-lift truck* is a vehicle with two arms or forks which can be positioned under crates, etc. The forks move up or down the column in front of the truck, thereby raising or lowering the crates and stacking them to the desired height.

The *pallet* is a form of fork-lift truck which lifts its load only a few inches off the ground in order to transport it. The platform or pallet usually remains under the goods from the collection point to delivery point. This conception of a *unit* load is becoming standard practice. Containers can be very large and, as the goods remain intact for the whole journey, handling costs are greatly reduced, as well as costs of pilfering and packing.

Automatic pallet loaders can take as many as ten different packages from production lines, sort and stock them in any desired sequence and forward the loaded pallet by conveyor to the next stage, without human effort.

Standardization is essential, both in pallet sizes and in the loading and heights of lorry-floors; but there is still a long way to go in this field. Materials handling is so highly regarded in the USA that some companies have a director of materials handling.

AUTOMATION

This word is often used to refer to systems not completely automatic. In essence there must be completely automatic transfer between machines and automatic control and recordings. It is best applied in flow production, e.g. flour milling, chemical industry. It is, of course, limited by the extent of the market and cannot be universally adopted.

By a combination of electronic and magnetic trips, machine tools are automatically controlled and thus work can be automatically transferred to the next stage.

Automation is the operation of individual automatic machines or groups of machines integrated by transfer mechanisms. Advances in closed-loop systems which sense what is happening enable errors to be automatically corrected.

The oldest form of automation is found in machine tools that perform certain operations automatically. Later the addition of a computer enabled impulses from the computer to be used to instruct and operate the machine.

As there was a limit to the amount of work which could be done in the one place, transfer to another machine by transfer mechanism was the next stage.

Feedback on information can operate adjustments automatically when errors are sensed – this is automatic control, i.e. where corrections are made with no human intervention.

Robots are being used increasingly in the production process, particularly in the production of motor vehicles. Machine set-up time and costs are being greatly reduced and fewer workers are needed. Machines are being used efficiently, direct labour costs are lower and work in progress inventories are also reduced.

Effects on organization

- Better managers and a higher ratio of managers to operating personnel are needed. Management training is more essential especially in social leadership.
- Need for shift working.
- New trades introduced, especially the maintenance of complex machines.
- Increased dependence on machines makes it difficult to operate financial incentive schemes.
- Smaller labour force and need for redeployment and retraining.
- Better working conditions.
- Increasing capital costs, especially fixed costs.
- More standardization.
- More leisure time, which raises a big problem of how it will be spent.

Warehousing

Order selection is one of the functions of warehousing that is the most intensive uses of labour per unit of throughput. A system of order picking should be efficient so that a fully representative range of stock is presented in as small an area as possible, that is conducive with safe operation. This enables orders to be selected accurately, avoiding excessive movement from reserve to forward location.

Large warehousing systems, especially *mail order*, divide their systems departmentally, according to merchandise or by size and throughput of product. Orders are routed only to the departments concerned with the items required on an order and bypass the rest. The majority of order-picking systems in the United Kingdom are based upon a fixed location system, requiring order-pickers to learn the location of any product. If the picker has to walk long distances to complete an order, this is inefficient. A system which brings the *goods to the picker is* highly cost effective, but is not easy to provide as it is a very complex problem.

Efficient handling of paperwork is important as this can account for 25 per cent of the time of an operative, e.g. looking up stock location and stock cards, listing of products in a different order to the picking run etc. The introduction of a small computer can be a great help.

Automated warehousing

Stocks are required to absorb variations in supply and demand, and to ensure even flow through productive and distributive systems. Storage, including labour, lighting and handling and accounting, only add to the price paid by consumer and can account for an extra 25–50 per cent on original price.

The use of automatic machinery, integrated with data processing by computer, which maintains stock records and accounts, can give the following advantages:

- similar items need not be stored together, since finding and selecting are not done by human labour;
- gangways for automatic machines are narrow and stocks can be stored higher. As people are not involved, warehouse temperature can be reduced and lighting is needed only for maintenance inspections;
- there is a maximum use of space because a whole rack is not allocated to an item in small demand;
- damage by carelessness is reduced and accuracy of order picking and stock records greatly improved;
- issue of advice notes and invoices and reminders is made speedily and encourages quick payment. Accurate calculations of stock are made by computer.

Examples of automated warehousing

Goods are checked on arrival and placed on a pallet. Relevant information, usually on computer, is processed by the stock controller and the pallet is placed by fork-lift truck on the platform of the automatic warehousing machine. The data is input into the computer, and by pressing a button the pallet is transported and stored automatically, usually on special racks. Mechanical handling is controlled pneumatically by contacts of photo-electric cells which feed information to the computer. Goods are stored in the most suitable space according to the computer program and documents and pay cheques prepared for the supplier. Goods are *withdrawn* by inputting the data on the computer. The machine retrieves the pallet and discharges it at the delivery point and stock records are amended immediately and the customer advised.

Management in practice

Yamazaki-Masak has a highly automated machine tool factory at Worcester. Around 80 per cent of output is exported and within two years of starting production sales per employee were around £200 000. The machine tools produced are manufactured using Masak machine tools. The factory is an interesting blend of English and Japanese culture.

The £35 million factory began production in 1987. The company policy had changed to using Flexible Manufacturing Systems (FMS) and had pioneered FMS involving Computer Integrated Manufacture (CIM) in Japan.

The company had decided in 1986 to build the factory in the United Kingdom rather than Germany because the English language was less of a problem than German for the Japanese, and the company president liked the idea of building in the home of the industrial revolution. In addition, Worcester was the base of an existing sales team, skilled labour was available and the local council was very supportive.

The Worcester factory uses a Manufacturing Resource Planning system (MRP II). The system operates at three levels, scheduling, process control and specific machine tools. An IBM mainframe computer processes orders entered in the Sales Department into a sequence of operations involving the purchase of required components and the insertion of the individual order into the master schedule. Information updates are received twice daily from the factory floor and this enables the arrival of the required components to be monitored and the initiation of the machining process. Data on current progress is received and it distributes instructions based upon optimizing the product mix via three DEC computers. One computer is in charge of the automatic warehouse and the movements of four auto-guided vehicles. Another channels instructions towards three computer controlled automatic machining lines. The third computer is dedicated to tool management, the creation and maintenance of a life-cycle for each tool and the scheduling of automatic replacement. Only the *machining areas* run on total CIM systems with the automatic feeding of CNC machines from banks of pallets continuing throughout the unmanned night shifts.

The IBM informs the DEC computer responsible for the machining lines that a particular pallet will soon be arriving at one of three automatic FMS production lines. The DEC then downloads the necessary drawings and requirements to the target machining centre or lathe.

Each Masak CNC machine has its own built-in computerized control system which runs another program prescribing the cutting sequence and effects the necessary tool changes. It also programs and monitors the feed and speed of the cutting tool to ensure a standard repeatable performance.

The machine tool industry experiences sharp cyclical movements and the idea was to limit these by taking advantage of the greater flexibility CIM allows. Another benefit was that a large proportion of value-added was created by the machinery itself, reducing any problems of labour shortages. Machines can be switched on or off without incurring additional costs, and production lead times were cut from an industry average of 25 weeks to eight weeks. The short lead times enable the production to be adjusted accurately every month and also ensure there is no expensive stock-piling of bought-in components.

Worcester-assembled machine tools are now *fully European products*. European suppliers now provide more than 70 per cent of the components going into the finished product.

The key posts of managing director, plant production manager and total quality control manager are held by Japanese. All employees, including the managing director, clock on (using computerized bar-code readers) and have staff status, with monthly paid cheques, life insurance, private pension and health-care plans. Everyone works a 40 hour week.

The *emphasis on total quality control* means *any* aspect of quality, not just machines and mechanical components, but also quality of people. The responsibility of the total quality control manager includes, human resource aspects, such as training and job motivation, customer feedback and physical control systems. The aim is to ensure that the machine purchased by the customer will never break down.

The conventional British approach to quality control is to have inspectors checking components, so the operator only produces a component and has no other responsibilities. The Japanese method is that all components produced by the machine section or fitted in the assembly section are inspected by the individuals themselves. Each person has to sign, so they feel responsible and this encourages self-motivation. The company encourages a good working atmosphere. Brief meetings are held every day by each section leader with the staff in the section to discuss the previous day's problems and the current tasks.

The quality of the Worcester product is as high as in Japan and this is one example of the successful combination of two cultures in a highly automated environment.

NEWER DEVELOPMENTS IN PRODUCTION

Material Requirements Planning (MRP)

This is a procedure used in production and inventory planning to ensure that the necessary parts and materials are available at the right time and place, and in the correct amounts. MRP procedures usually require the use of extensive data processing by computers. MRP is invaluable in systems involving complex production procedures involving outside suppliers of components. The concept has been expanded to include all resources required and is not limited only to material resources. This expanded concept is called MRP II.

Manufacturing Resource Planning (MRP II)

This includes monitoring inventory levels, workforce levels, orders and jobs based upon an agreed priority system. The system can also be used to monitor purchase orders placed with suppliers. This system also integrates production management with marketing, finance and human resources functions.

An integrated system like MRP II requires changes in the attitudes and responses of management and staff. *Management needs to give a strong lead and firmly commit the organization to the change* and try to ensure that the methodologies of MRP II become part of the corporate culture.

The computer systems which support MRP II are an essential component of the system and the evidence from many companies who have implemented the system indicates the need for a great improvement in staff expertise and computer literacy. Apart from improving their own technical skills, managers have to understand the impact computers will have on themselves and on their departments.

MRP II systems are essentially computerized databases of parts, components, finished goods, work in progress and requirements, lead times and relationships between parts. This data is used to calculate the best way to meet the master production schedule. MRP II generates a forecast of demand and a *manufacturing plan* is developed to meet those demands. This *plan* drives the issue of works orders. Requirements are calculated and forecast in terms of quantity and time, and these requirements are 'exploded' into the Bills of Materials files, which break down a product into its constituent parts. Net requirements are calculated by deducting the available inventory from the gross requirements. Work orders are then issued to work centres. Changes are continually 'fed back' into the system.

Implementation of Manufacturing Resource Planning (MRP II)

The selection and implementation of complex manufacturing systems like MRP II is not easy. An enterprise may:

● select a system inappropriate for its needs;
● fail to recognize the place the system takes in its management structure;
● commit too few resources (people or time);
● pay too little attention to the need for education and training of staff;
● fail to introduce the discipline of financial standards which can measure success.

Just-in-Time (JIT)

The Japanese are credited with developing *zero inventory or Just-in-Time*. The concept was conceived to ensure that the inventory has only what is needed, when it is needed. A JIT production system aims to:

● produce finished goods just-in-time to be sold;
● assemble sub-assemblies into finished goods just-in-time;
● buy fabricated goods just-in-time to go into sub-assemblies;
● transform purchased materials into fabricated parts just-in-time.

There is no room in JIT to adopt the practice of buying in additional stock or reordering to overcome the problem of an unreliable raw materials supplier. The Japanese approach is to help the supplier achieve more dependable deliveries and hence reduce the lead time and stock levels. Production is matched perfectly to market demand and all stocks are eliminated. The system requires quick machine set-ups and simple material flows. Multi-skilled workers are usually organized into teams with responsibility and accountability for their 'own' products; specialist functions, e.g. quality control and maintenance, become the responsibility of the team.

The underlying philosophy of JIT is to devise a production system that encourages staff to strive consistently for improvements. This enhances performance. The aim is to identify problems at the outset and it is the *responsibility of staff* to prevent them from recurring.

JIT is often called a philosophy as it goes beyond inventory control to *include* quality planning and control and production scheduling. The system was developed for *repetitive production,* e.g. in a motor-car production line. Repetitive (or mass) production implies large volume production of batches of small numbers of similar products.

It is essential in a JIT system to have high quality materials. Any defect could bring production to a halt. This occurs when faulty parts are produced and no others are available because inventory levels have been reduced. Where little or no inventory is allowed, defects can be found quickly and problems corrected. As a result of this quality gains attention throughout the factory and the organization.

The Japanese approach to quality is often referred to as total quality control or zero defects. It must be noted, however, that a total quality programme is not just a system to obtain zero defects in the production services provided by a company. Total quality is not just a technical system, it deals with people at all levels within an organization, their motivation, awareness and understanding, and buildings.

The definition usually assigned to total quality control is that it is a cost effective system for integrating the continuous efforts of people at all levels in an organization to deliver products and services which ensure customer satisfaction.

It is interesting to note that much of the current training in practices of quality management was developed by W. Edwards Deming, who guided the Japanese in their approach to quality management. The Japanese were found to be more receptive to his ideas than western managers.

In the United Kingdom, many organizations have instituted quality management processes to receive accreditation under the British Standards BS 5750 series, or, under the International Standard, ISO 9000. Both standards lay down the requirements for a cost-effective quality system and how to establish and maintain it, with the aim of demonstrating to customers that their organization is committed to quality. However, this does not necessarily mean that they have a total quality philosophy in their organization.

Effective JIT systems include training each employee to do a variety of different tasks, which eliminates the need for specialists. The theory held is that by training employees to do a variety of tasks it gives them the ability to view problems from many perspectives and problem solving can then be transferred from staff specialists to line employees, giving much greater staff flexibility.

Benefits of JIT/zero inventory systems
- Greater productivity, smaller inventory.
- Better quality/less waste.
- Better motivated employees.
- Better customer service, less administration.
- Fewer stockrooms, less materials handling.
- Less production control staff and inventory accounts.

Computer Aided Design (CAD)

This refers to a computer based system where a designer uses a computer system to develop a detailed product design which can be manipulated, modified and refined on a visual display unit (VDU) screen without drawing it on paper. Design calculations can be inserted and information retained in the computer file and then printed out as a drawing of the detailed product design. Such a system facilitates the design process and increases design productivity.

Computer Aided Manufacture (CAM)

This refers to *any* system of production in which manufacturing equipment is controlled by a computer. It can produce information for computer-controlled manufacturing processes. For example, a computer-controlled machining centre will need data to enable it to make necessary cuts in the material. The required sequence of operations can be produced from the database for transfer to the machining centre, or transferred *directly* through a CAD/CAM system to the machining centre.

A comprehensive design/manufacturing database is needed for the effective use of CAD/CAM and for computer-controlled integrated manufacturing systems.

Computer Integrated Manufacturing (CIM)

This refers to the control of manufacture in a plant by computers and data-driven automation. CIM seeks to achieve the fully integrated control of manufacture from the design stage to the delivery of finished goods. There is an interlinking of previously separate areas of responsibility by computer-controlled systems. For example, the fields of design, process planning, production planning and scheduling, inventory management, production control, quality control and despatch are linked by computers. By integrating the total manufacturing system in this way, greater economies are possible.

CIM is the use of management control and automation technologies to integrate the manufacturing design and business operations of an organization. The use of CIM management at all levels allows management to have access to timely, purpose-directed information for decision making, controlling and reporting.

The use of a comprehensive database with computers that have different memory capacity, and the direct transmission of data between operations, is an important feature of CIM.

Flexible Manufacturing Systems (FMS)

A Flexible Manufacturing System consists of computer-controlled machining centres producing metal parts, robots handling the parts and remote controlled trucks delivering materials. Electronic controls link the various stages of the manufacturing process. FMS enables the manufacturer to produce different versions of a product in small batches at high speeds, similar to mass production methods.

Flexible Manufacturing Systems have developed because of the availability of computer-controlled machine tools with automatic tool-changing facilities, together with automatic transfer of materials between machines, and automatic loading using robotic devices.

The use of FMS in the manufacture of similar items is a very efficient form of manufacture compared with traditional batch working through a function or process layout (*see* p 316). Examples of industries using this system are food industries, pharmaceuticals and clothing.

In batch production (*see* p 314) every time an item is manufactured a batch is produced to build up an *output stock* that will satisfy demand until the item is manufactured again. The most *economic batch size* is a function of:

- the *cost of setting-up* facilities for manufacture of the item; and
- the *cost of holding* completed items in stock.

If setting-up costs increase for a specific stock-holding cost, the economic batch size will increase, and vice versa. If items to be made are similar, the facilities set-up costs will be smaller. In addition, the *more flexible* the facilities to be used (i.e. the more they can be adapted to produce different items) the set-up costs will become smaller. Following on from this, if similar items can be grouped and more flexible manufacturing facilities can be used, a *more efficient method* of batch production can be employed. In this case:

- batch sizes will be small;
- throughput time reduced;
- output stock levels will be smaller.

Robots

An industrial robot is a manipulative device that is programmable and which can be set to perform different tasks, or *recognize* the need to do *different* tasks. This is different from mechanical or electro-mechanical devices which are designed for a specific operation.

Robots can be used, for example, for welding, paint-spraying, assembly, inspection and in situations where it is dangerous to use people. Some robots have improved sensing facilities, e.g. sight and touch and are widely used in the automotive industry.

SUMMARY

Objective 1 *Discuss the various roles production management may play in supporting the strategic plan of an enterprise.*
In the past the role of production management was generally to produce goods/services at the lowest possible cost. This required equipment that could produce high volumes of the same or similar goods. There are other objectives to consider today, such as the variety of the product, high quality, quick response to customer's orders, quick introduction of new products and more flexible handling of different levels or volume of output.

Objective 2 *Explain the importance of materials management in production operations and describe newer methods used to ensure efficient use of materials.*
Materials management, which includes purchasing and storage, is very important as the cost of materials to most manufacturing companies accounts for about 50 per cent of total revenue received from their products. Management often has to consider whether to make or buy materials and this decision may vary according to the level of operations. Methods to reduce inventory costs include Just-in-Time (JIT) scheduling although some inventory is usually needed. Material Requirements Planning (MRP), which usually

requires a computer, keeps records of the exact amounts of materials needed on a given date, so that they may be ordered to arrive just-in-time. An expansion of this concept, is Manufacturing Resource Planning (MRP II) which is a management information system designed to simulate the manufacturing environment of an enterprise.

Objective 3 *Identify situations in which repetitive production and batch production would be appropriate.*
Repetitive production is appropriate for manufacturing items that have a relatively high volume, are reasonably homogeneous and can economically justify the cost of specialized equipment. On the other hand batch production is appropriate for items that are produced in relatively low volumes, and are relatively heterogeneous and can justify the cost of only general purpose equipment.

Objective 4 *Appreciate the importance of quality control and describe the new emphasis that is being used to improve product quality.*
Quality control involves inspecting the product at various stages of processing to ensure that quality standards are met. Inspection can be done either at the production site, or at a testing laboratory. Inspection points should be set up at the beginning and end of the production cyde. Units should also be checked prior to operations that are particularly expensive, that permanently change materials or that hide defects. Inspection may be on a 100 per cent basis or it may be appropriate to sample only a few items in each production lot. Careful production scheduling and quality control help to assure that customers will get quality products on time.

American, Japanese and British producers are moving responsibility for quality from a separate quality assurance department to quality at source, the source being the production department or more precisely the production worker. To accomplish the change employees are being trained in statistical quality control and Quality Circles.

Objective 5 *Describe the basis of a Total Quality Management System.*
Total Quality Management is a system that looks at quality at every stage of the production process. It is a strategic commitment to improving quality by combining statistical quality control methods with a cultural commitment to seeking improvements that improve quality and reduce cost. It requires the integration of all parts of the organization so that waste is eliminated and results are achieved quicker and more cheaply.

REVIEW QUESTIONS

1 What factors must be considered in the determination of production policy?

2 What problems may arise in the consideration of a suitable site for a factory?

3 Distinguish between research and development.

4 What are the main stages in a research project?

5 What facilities for assistance in research exist outside the firm?

6 What principles should determine how much a firm spends on research and develop- ment and how can such expenditure be allocated and controlled?

7 What are the objects of product design and who are interested in it?

8 Outline the Schedule of Responsibility for a design and development engineer.

9 Distinguish between standardization, simplification and specialization.

10 What are the purposes of quality control?

11 Consider the need for inspection and list the qualities required in an inspector.

12 What are the advantages and disadvantages of centralized and floor inspection?

13 Define value engineering and describe how it is applied.

14 What is covered by the term production administration?

15 Explain the need for work study.

16 What is meant by ergonomics and how can its study increase output?

17 Definitions of production control vary; explain what you consider is meant by the term.

18 What is meant by production planning?

19 Briefly list the requirements of a good system of material control.

20 What are the duties of a storekeeper?

21 Examine the reasons for having centralized or departmental stores.

22 What is covered by the term pre-production planning?

23 What should be the position of the purchasing section in an organization?

24 Outline a Schedule of Responsibility for a purchasing officer.

25 What is meant by preventive maintenance?

26 Explain the importance of materials handling in a manufacturing organization.

27 Define automation and give an illustration of its use.

28 Define Flexible Manufacturing Systems.

29 Differentiate between the terms Material Requirements Planning (MRP) and Manu- facturing Resource Planning (MRP II).

30 Explain what you understand by the term Just-in-Time.

31 Define the following: CAD/CAM and FMS.

1 Assume that you are a quality control manager in a large-scale multiple retail business and that you are required to investigate the quality procedure of a large supplier of frozen foods as a preliminary to your company placing a contract for supplies. How would you conduct a survey to ascertain the effectiveness of the quality control in force?

2 There is always the possibility of error in product design. The product may appear correct from one point of view and yet be quite wrong from another. List the possible areas and sources of error, illustrating fully to show your understanding and indicating how such errors can be detected.

3 The internal transport and materials handling costs in a light engineering concern are believed to be unduly high. Suggest how they might be reduced, and indicate in what directions advantages may be gained thereby.

4 Detail the long- and short-term benefits and difficulties brought about by automation in an industry with which you are familiar.

5 Set out the details which an estimator would require in order to build up a quotation.

How would his approach differ if he were:

(a) quoting for a special product for one customer; and
(b) preparing a selling price for a mass produced item?

6 What is meant by batch production?

State the factors which must be taken into consideration to ensure that batches are set at an economic level.

7 What is meant by a product specification and what is its purpose in relation to production, purchasing and selling?

8 (a) Discuss and distinguish between:

(i) stock recording procedures; and
(ii) stock control systems.

(b) How far should the attention of management be directed to the movement of stock and its rates of change rather than to the quantities of stock in hand?
(c) Explain how an analysis of stock value and movement can aid control.

9 State the causes of losses and waste in a materials store. Consider what action should be taken to eliminate them.

10 Describe a procedure for the control of a tool store. To what extent is the inspection function linked with the tool store?

11 Describe the stages of a time study exercise in a production department. To what extent is consultation with the operatives necessary?

12 Why is it essential that all buying must be controlled by the purchasing officer?
    Give three sources of information from which the buyer can obtain details of requirements on which to base an order.

13 (a) Describe the various facets of a purchasing officer's duties and state the principles on which those duties are based.
    (b) In what ways are the functions of the purchasing officer, stock controller and production controller inter-dependent?
    (c) Do you consider that the appointment of an overall materials controller responsible for all materials and supply functions would be an advantage? Give your reasons.
    (*See* p 482 for further problems on Production.)

ASSIGNMENTS

1 Identify a company that has received BS 5750 accreditation. Find out the problems it encountered in obtaining approval and list the benefits it expects to receive from obtaining accreditation.

2 It is often said that mass production techniques may result in jobs which are limited in scope and are unrewarding for the persons doing them. Organizations have become aware of this factor and are trying to introduce methods to improve job satisfaction. Take an organization of your choice and show how changes have occurred to improve job satisfaction on the production line.

BIBLIOGRAPHY

Bailey, P H J, Farmer, D J, Jessop, D and Jones, D *Purchasing Principles and Management* (London, Pitman Publishing, 7th edition, 1994).

Harrison, A, *Just in Time Management in Perspective* (London, Prentice-Hall, 1992).

Jackson, D and Ashton, D, *Implementing Quality Through BS 5750 (ISO 9000)* (London, Kogan Page, 1993).

Jessop, D and Morrison, A, *Storage and Supply of Materials* (London, Pitman Publishing, 6th edition, 1994).

Johnston, R, *et al*, *Cases in Operations Management* (London, Pitman Publishing, 1993).

Lysons, C K, *Purchasing* (London, M+E Handbooks, Pitman Publishing, 3rd edition, 1993).

Muhlemann, A, Oakland, J and Lockyer, K, *Production and Operations Management* (London, Pitman Publishing 6th edition, 1992).

Stranks, J, *A Manager's Guide to Health and Safety at Work* (London, Kogan Page, 1993).

Stranks, J, *The ROSPA Handbook of Health and Safety Practice* (London, Pitman Publishing, 1991).

Wild, R, *Production and Operations Management* (Cassell, 4th edition, 1989.)

CHAPTER 9

Human resource management

Human resource management can be said to be the responsibility of all those who manage people as well as a description of persons who are employed as specialists. It is that part of management that involves planning for human resource needs, including recruitment selection, training and development, promotion and transfer, redundancy and retirement. It also includes welfare and safety, wage and salary administration, collective bargaining and dealing with most aspects of industrial relations.

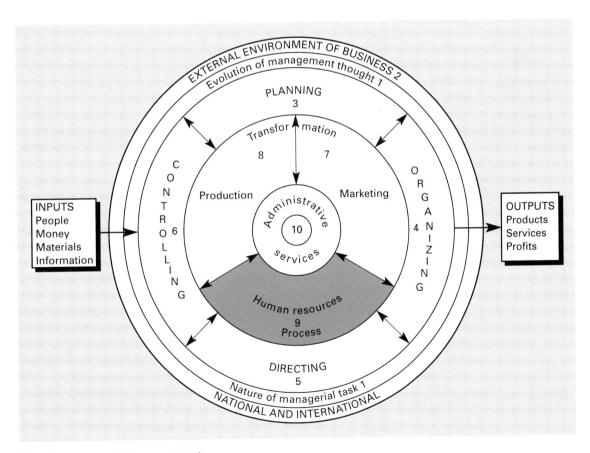

The systems approach to management

OBJECTIVES

Upon completing this chapter you should be able to:

- Explain how effective human resource management contributes to the accomplishment of enterprise objectives.
- Describe the term manpower planning and list the main points to consider in instituting such a system in an enterprise.
- Outline the purposes that can be served by a good system of performance appraisal.
- Describe the sources of the various types of conflicts and methods used to manage conflict.
- Appreciate the importance of an effective system of management education and training and development and indicate how training can be effectively evaluated.

HUMAN RESOURCE MANAGEMENT (HRM)

Human resource management developed gradually during the 19th century as working conditions became intolerable and it was considered that such exploitation was counter-productive. Some owners, e.g. Robert Owen in Britain, introduced principles of welfare and education into profit-orientated business. Production was very different from early methods and enlightened factory owners became more aware of the need to integrate the workforce into the newer production processes which meant a loss of traditional autonomy. The functions of human resource management evolved in line with changes in the cultural and social environment. The human resources function is now highly specialized and perhaps can be said to be at the centre of conflict between labour and capital. They in effect operate on the 'boundary' between the workforce and the organization.

The human resources manager has to seek to achieve the workforce's compliance with organizational goals, and the methods used to achieve this will depend upon whether they regard the workers as purely concerned with 'rewards' or as more 'responsible'.

Internally (within the organization) a human resources manager is concerned with integrating the workforce, motivating and training and extending the skills of the worker.

Externally he is concerned with labour shortages, union policies on strikes, influencing educational institutions and the legal framework.

Human resources departments are vulnerable to a greater extent if their work can be devolved back to other department managers. If their activities cannot easily be substituted and taken over, they are more secure. The more difficult it is to organize the environment the more power, responsibility and resources the human resources department needs.

Human resource management is that part of the process of management that is concerned with the maintenance of human relationships and ensuring the physical well-being of employees so that they give the maximum contribution to efficient working. It is obviously closely related to the management process as a whole and each functional manager and supervisor must apply the principles effectively. Departmental managers, by effective leadership, should ensure human resources policy is adhered to and department activities are successfully carried out. It is essential that every manager and supervisor be aware of the principles of human resource management and a close link with the human resources department should be maintained.

Human resources managers have to advise the managing director on the formulation of policy and see that procedures to carry it out are effected. It is a servicing section to other managers and the department has *functional* responsibility for human resources.

A logical approach to the consideration of this function is to look first of all at the problem of overall company organization and manpower planning, then the operations necessary to implement the plan, that is, recruitment and selection, training and development, and wage and salary administration. Other aspects of human resource management include industrial relations and the law of employment, welfare and safety, and other employee services.

Human resource management is intimately involved with the environment in general and certain trends are noticeable. Government intervention is growing and many new Acts have affected human resource management, e.g. Employment Protection Act.

New terms and techniques have appeared, for example, manpower planning and management by objectives. Manpower planning should not, though, be regarded as a *new* technique as it embraces existing techniques, i.e. work study, job evaluation, and description performance rating, etc. Whatever new ideas appear, the criterion should be more efficient utilization of labour.

Figure 9.1 shows the main functions of a large human resources department.

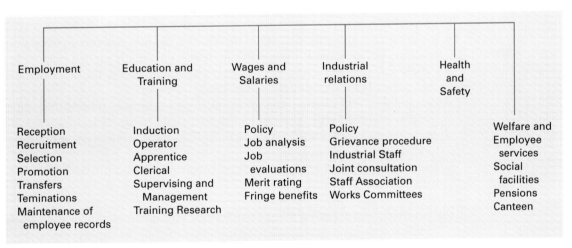

Employment	Education and Training	Wages and Salaries	Industrial relations	Health and Safety
Reception	Induction	Policy	Policy	Welfare and
Recruitment	Operator	Job analysis	Grievance procedure	Employee
Selection	Apprentice	Job	Industrial Staff	services
Promotion	Clerical	evaluations	Joint consultation	Social
Transfers	Supervising and	Merit rating	Staff Association	facilities
Teminations	Management	Fringe benefits	Works Committees	Pensions
Maintenance of	Training Research			Canteen
employee records				

Fig 9.1 Functions of a human resources department. This could be used as an organization chart for a large company. The human resources manager in charge of the six sections may serve on the board and his job would be to interpret and maintain the company policy and advise on the attitude to adopt in trade union negotiations

POSITION OF HUMAN RESOURCES MANAGER IN ORGANIZATION

The human resources manager is a specialist to whom the general manager has entrusted the responsibility for certain work. He may be responsible to the general manager directly or he may report to other functional heads. In smaller concerns the human resources and administrative manager may be the same person. Whatever the size of the organization, someone must perform the function of a human resources manager and titles vary greatly; he may be called labour relations or welfare officer.

His responsibility and status vary with the type of organization and he is often shown on organization charts on a level with other functional managers, e.g. marketing manager. This does not necessarily mean equality of salary and status. He usually has direct access to the chief executive and is responsible to him.

There may be human resources assistants in the branches of some companies who are responsible to the human resources manager for training and other human resource activities in the local branches, but otherwise they are directly responsible to the line manager. The human resources manager exercises *line* authority over the specialized activities which come under his direct jurisdiction, e.g. canteen, education, welfare.

The *qualities* required in a human resources manager vary with the extent of his work. Basic qualities required are a background knowledge of economics and industry and living conditions, an understanding of men and women and knowledge of social and psychological problems – good judge of human nature, friendly, firm, patient and impartial.

Summarized schedule of responsibility for human resources manager

Responsible to: Managing director

Responsible for:
- assisting and advising managing director on human resources policy and ensuring policy is made known to staff and is effectively carried out;
- developing and maintaining procedures in conjunction with other departmental heads for recruitment and training;
- determining and maintaining good relations with trade unions and other bodies concerned with employment and working conditions;
- ensuring adequate safety precautions and welfare services including canteen and health services;
- assisting employees with personal problems, maintaining records and statistics of employment.

Special duties

(a) Advising and assisting managing director on human resources policy formulation and the development of training schemes for supervisory staff.
(b) Representing the company in all negotiations with trade unions and trade associations and maintaining interests in new ideas in human resource management.

Limitations   No right to engage or dismiss staff or determine rates of pay, without referring to relevant senior executive or managing director.

HUMAN RESOURCES POLICY

The co-operation of workers must be obtained if the business is to run smoothly. The workers must have confidence in the firm and this may not be easy when technical advances produce a fear of unemployment and unrest.

Policy must be determined by the board and must be clearly defined, and those employees who have to administer the policy should be given an opportunity to contribute. This may be done in joint consultative committees. In order to have a good policy, a knowledge of those factors an employee regards as important is essential. This involves a knowledge of the industrial application of sociological and psychological theory, and the forces generated should be known and controlled in order to ensure effective collaboration of individuals and groups with that company and individual goals can be reached. 'Harmony of objectives' must be the goal.

Social scientists are being enrolled in industry to examine sociological problems. A recent approach is to examine the organizational environment, the objectives and methods of management, and the forms of company structure. It may be that these conditions limit what the individual can achieve. *Human resource policies*, therefore, are concerned with providing an effective organizational structure, manning it with appropriate personnel and securing optimum working conditions; the object being to create and maintain a level of morale which evokes the full contribution of all employees in ensuring that the company operates at maximum efficiency.

The following factors may be regarded as important and necessary in a human resources policy:

1 **Remuneration**. This must be at least the market rate for the job and give the employee a reasonable standard of living.
2 **Security**. This is vital to the average worker; it is not so important to the young, or where there is full employment, but stability of employment is essential and there must be guarantees against unfair dismissal.
3 **Opportunity**. If this is not available, a worker may look elsewhere. Vacancies should therefore be filled within a firm whenever possible or practicable. This does emphasize the need for good education and training policies so that existing staff can be trained to fill vacancies.
4 **Status**. In Chapter 1 it was stated that the Hawthorne Experiments showed that a person feeling that he 'counted' or 'mattered' and that he was a respected member of a group can influence output and lead to the retention of workers.
5 **Justice**. This can be simply defined as confidence in being treated fairly. The security of the worker must not be threatened and specific rules regarding punishment, judgement and appeals procedure must be invoked. These should include guarantees of confidential access to the human resources manager.

6 **Democracy.** In a capitalist structure it may not be easy to invoke the idea that a man has the right to a voice in the *way* he is governed, and by *whom* he is governed. Attempts along these lines are the formation of joint consultative committees and the establishment of procedures for regular consultation between managers and employees.

7 **General.** To assist employees in developing social, educational and recreational amenities and to maintain policies without discrimination between employees.

MANPOWER PLANNING

Manpower planning seeks to maintain and improve an organization's ability to achieve corporate objectives by developing strategies which are designed to increase the present and future contribution of manpower.

There is great difficulty in forecasting future demand because of the *changes* in the following areas:

- Technological – changes in materials, technical systems and methods of power.
- Economic – marketing, capital formation.
- Social – population trends, social mobility and education.
- Political – industrial legislation (wages and salaries, monetary policy, training, redundancy).

Advantages

- The right number of staff is recruited at each level in the hierarchy.
- Staffing requirements can be better balanced and movement of staff made easier.
- Areas of high labour turnover are highlighted.
- Implications of changes in recruitment, promotion and succession plans are foreseeable.

Limitations

- Detailed records are needed plus expensive clerical staff.
- Problems of forecasting changes, especially technological and government policy areas.
- Forecasts can be uncertain even for a few years ahead.

The traditional attitude to manpower is that it is a *cost*; there is greater consideration now towards the idea that it is an *investment*. Therefore the best use of this investment should be made so as to ensure that manpower achieves personal satisfaction and the company achieves a maximum return on the 'costs' it represents. (*See* p 242 for consideration of accounting for human assets.)

It is important to stress the problem of uncertainty today; changes can occur in the following more detailed analysis:

- production and sales targets and new products;
- plans for diversifying, expanding or contracting production;
- centralization or other organizational change;
- technological changes, e.g. mechanization, improved methods, new management techniques;

- changes in hours of work, holidays, negotiations with trade unions and collective agreements;
- national policies regarding taxation and redundancy;
- changes within company, e.g. retirements, age structure, promotions.

A company must be able to recruit and retain manpower of the type and calibre it requires for efficient operation. Change is a dominant factor today. Processes, products, systems and methods change quickly. The role of the computer is increasing and there is at present a shortage of systems analysts and programmers, and this will continue for a number of years. New techniques, e.g. operational research, influence the organizational structure of companies and alter the pattern of manning. Some jobs need increased skills, others need less. Thus a high standard of planning is needed. The rewards to a company are high as a great reduction in costs is possible; reduction in one area in particular, labour turnover, can save a great deal of money.

Stages of planning

1 **The existing situation** is examined to see if the existing organizational and manning effectiveness can be improved. Procedure involved will include job analysis and grading, performance and potential appraisals.
2 **Planning** to assess and determine future *objectives* for all parts of the business.
3 **Organization** is then planned, breaking down the *objectives* into posts capable of being filled. The method of organization can greatly aid co-ordination of activities.
4 **Precise requirements** for all types of manpower are then identified.
5 **Planning the supply** involves noting present stock and its potential and determining the basis for additional requirements. Organization charts can be projected to the future, noting possible promotion candidates and people earmarked for certain jobs.
6 **Career requirements** of individuals must be noted. The payment of salaries commensurate with worth is an essential part of wages and salary administration.

It was stated in Chapter 1 that organization should be designed to attain the objectives of the company. Functional objectives are set and organization planned to attain them. Each department must be staffed so that the available skills and abilities are equated with tasks to be done.

There may be changes in the external markets, in the supply of local labour skills, changes in comparative earnings for each category of employee. Other relevant information includes output per man hour and total man hours available. The manpower plan can then be prepared and will also include consideration of policies on: recruitment; promotion and career planning; pay and productivity; retirement, redundancy and redeployment; training and development; industrial relations.

Reviews of the progress of plans will take place periodically, with yearly revisions as part of a longer-term planning cycle. Monthly budget statements will be prepared and a comparison of actual and planned targets will be made and variances noted. Information obtained will be then fed back to earlier parts of the cycle which may then indicate the need for changes in the plans.

Manpower planning should be an integral part of corporate planning and top management backing is essential. The skills of individuals must be continually developed in order to meet the needs of technological, economic and social change.

The recruitment and selection processes must be continually *reviewed* and *evaluated,* as the cost of the process is high. Many company reports now contain the average numbers of persons employed over the year and the amount of wages and salaries paid to them. Labour turnover figures may also give valuable information.

Figure 9.2 shows some of the more important aspects of the main stages in manpower planning. The starting point is the overall corporate objectives and plans of which manpower plans are part.

The manpower demand forecast relies on sales forecasts. These are related to forecasted production levels and required manpower is then determined.

The manpower supply forecast requires information on the current labour force, labour turnover and retirement trends, training, skills available, etc.

Man hours available will vary with shift patterns, overtime, sickness, etc.

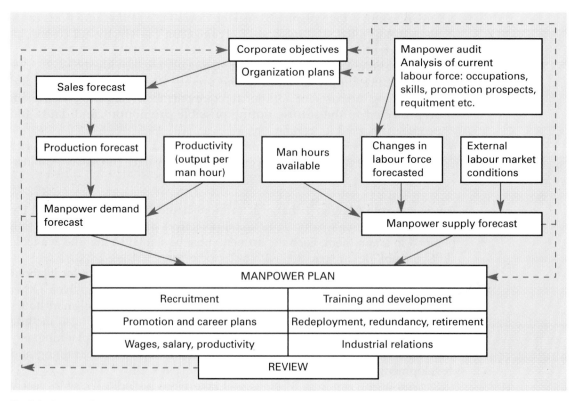

Fig 9.2 Stages of manpower planning

Forecasting

First of all, existing manpower strength and work volume are analysed and detailed forecasts made of future work volume and probable changes in methods used are considered. The future work volume is then related to past ratios to give a forecast. This is called ratio-trend forecasting.

Another method is called *theoretical requirements forecasting* and involves assessing and defining the type and volume of activity needed to attain desired results. Specific objectives are given to management. Existing manpower and work volume are compared with forecasted future work volume and manpower, noting any probable changes in methods. So, for each category of staff, there is a statement of present and future positions, and this enables manpower requirements to be calculated.

Personal records must be adequate and kept up to date. Records containing relevant facts must be easily available: some firms have the details on computer files. Information may include these details:

(a) Identification – name, date of birth and service, nationality, reference number, home address and next of kin.
(b) Education – schools, universities, technical or professional training.
(c) Experience – employment history and details of current job including details of remuneration.
(d) Potential – assessments, a note of career development and training, assignments planned and completed.
(e) General – leisure interests, armed forces, medical history.

Employment inventories are useful, and analysis into male and female job categories, part- and full-time, is needed. The pattern of *ages* should be noted as it may be that many are retiring shortly or many are ready for promotion. Thus the problems which may arise can be dealt with if known in time. Turnover can be analysed into reasons for leaving, length of service, age group and type. The cost of turnover is great.

An ordinary *clerical* job involves these costs – advertising, management time on interviewing, temporary help or overtime paid during staff shortage, reduced output during training time and trainee's time. This could easily add up to £2000 per job vacancy. A reduction in job turnover from 10 per cent to 5 per cent in a firm is an enormous saving.

International Business Machines (IBM) has a five-year forward plan, broken down into about fifteen main occupational groups, showing numbers to be recruited to replace predicted staff turnover and to meet the company's growth plans, which are based upon market research and product development forecasts. The key is a very detailed job classification, which is expressed in a four-digit code for computer processing.

RECRUITMENT

The position of the economy of a country has a marked effect upon the employment of personnel and hence upon recruitment and selection.

Economic uncertainty may cause people to remain in their present job, and discourage them from moving elsewhere, particularly when finance from building societies and banks is difficult to obtain. Married people with children may be less disposed to move and movement will mainly be among younger persons. Growth industries may therefore find it difficult to obtain the experienced persons required.

Selection or appointment consultants

The aim of management development is to get the right person, with the right equipment in the right place at the right time.

The use of consultants to recruit and select supervisory or management positions is becoming increasingly common because:

- advances in science, technology and specialization are making it difficult to obtain the right person. Small to medium firms may not have a properly equipped human resources department scientifically to test and select persons;
- the cost of selection is great;
- consultants are impartial in their assessment of applicants;
- candidates may not wish to disclose their identity, unless they are reasonably certain of being considered and consultants will not disclose candidates' names until they have been short-listed.

Method adopted by consultants

1 They *visit* the firm and appraise job requirements and talk over the qualifications, etc., the employer wants.
2 A job *specification* is then drawn up in detail, plus additional information, e.g. location, living conditions available, place in organization.
3 An *advertisement* is then drawn up and the employer asked to approve. Applicants receive the firm's own application form and copy of the job specification. Applications are sifted and some selected for interview.
4 Members of an *interview panel* are chosen because of their special knowledge of the type of position. A short list is prepared and only then are identities disclosed and references taken up.
5 A *short list* is sent to the employer, with reports of interviewers and their recommendations.
6 *Final interviews* are conducted by the employer, who makes the choice.

Consultants deal in a wide range of appointments, although some do specialize.

The *disadvantages* are that some consultants do not know the requirements of certain jobs and may have little experience in a particular field.

Some consultants have adopted an American approach whereby a list of ideal candidates for a job is drawn up; these candidates are then asked to join the new firm. This is called 'head hunting' and is not generally favoured, although it has been used much more widely in recent years.

Main sources of staff recruitment

- **Employee recommendations.** These have the advantage that applicants will know a lot about the firm when they arrive and employees may have more interest in their work if allowed to recommend workers. They may not, of course, be good judges.
- **Department of Employment Job Centres.** Companies notify job vacancies to centres who display jobs in each centre. Jobs are mainly for manual, clerical and unskilled work.
- **Private employment bureaux.** These charge fees for every employee supplied.
- **Advertisements.** Situations vacant may be advertised in newspapers and journals. The correct journal must be chosen.
- **Staff notice-board.** This should always be used even if there are no likely responses.
- **Professional organizations.** These usually keep registers of vacancies.
- **Universities, technical colleges and schools.** Advertising is perhaps the most popular method of recruitment, but many firms do not make full use of advertising. Firms should bear in mind the following points when planning advertisements:

(a) *Salary* or the salary range should preferably be stated, but it is often omitted; also the duties and responsibilities of the job and nature of the organization should be given.

(b) It is preferable to state the *name of the company* in most cases and the part of the country where the job is situated.

(c) *Prospects* should be mentioned, but not exaggerated.

(d) *Box numbers* should preferably not be used as it is too impersonal and the applicant may not wish certain organizations to know he is applying for jobs. An applicant can overcome this problem by stipulating those organizations he does not wish to see his application.

A poor advertisement may raise doubts about a company's stability and efficiency. As there is usually a large volume of advertising, the right phrasing and the correct choice of media are essential. Factual information is needed and too 'brash' or startling an advertisement may have the opposite effect to that desired. This may be all right for some sales advertisements, but a carefully worded, neatly set out advertisement, stressing the main features, is an economical way of obtaining staff.

Application forms

These need not be sent for unskilled work as they can be filled in on the interview day. Form filling can be used as a selection device, as a person's expressions on paper are a guide to his ability. A standard form makes it easier for the candidate to reply, rather than devise his own plan, and such forms are easier to evaluate.

Details usually shown on the form comprise most of the details listed for the record card on p 367. In addition, office information is shown, e.g. remarks after acceptance of position, date commenced, department, salary, receipt of National Insurance card and income tax card.

Job design

Correct selection of personnel is very important to the success of an enterprise. The manpower plan has to be translated into position and job design requirements which have to be matched with certain characteristics of individuals.

Effective selection of personnel requires an objective analysis of the requirements of each position and the job must be designed to meet the needs of the organization and the needs of the *individual*.

Job design involves specifying the content of a job, the work methods used in its performance and how the job relates to other jobs in the organization. The idea is that jobs should be designed in such a way as to allow employees to control aspects of their work, the reason being that by doing this it enhances the quality of the worklife, makes more effective use of the potential of the worker and thereby improves worker performance.

This should, according to current research, ideally include the following basic principles (*see* Fig 9.3):

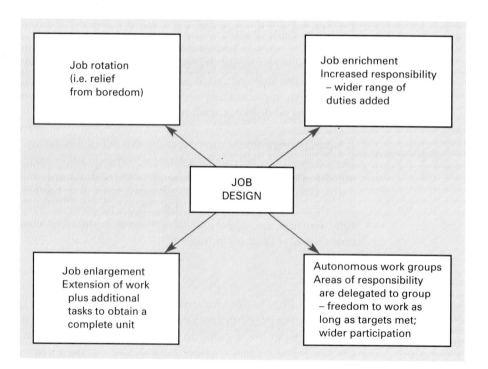

Fig 9.3 Aspects of job design

- a *variety* of tasks sufficient not to lead to boredom;
- tasks which have some *obvious relationship* to the whole task;
- a work *cycle* of just the right *length* bearing in mind physical demands and concentration of an average person;
- some provision to *allow the individual* to set quality and standards (above the minimum required) and feedback by management on personal results to keep motivation strong;
- the need for care, skill and effort so that the work will carry respect *in the community.*

Job description (or analysis or specification)

These are statements of facts describing the work performed, the responsibilities involved, the skill and training required, the conditions under which the job is done, relationships with other jobs and personal requirements of the job.

The three terms have different meanings. *Job analysis* records the facts, i.e. all the elements involved in performing a job; *job description* outlines the facts compiled from the job analysis, concisely identifying and describing the contents of a job; and a *job specification* refers to the personal characteristics required to do a job, e.g. skill, experience, special aptitudes.

The statements of facts of a job guide management in the selection, promotion, or transfer of employees and aid the establishment of comparative wage scales and are used for training schemes.

A job description would show the following.

Job factors

Job factors include:

- title of job, and department and job code number;
- job summary – showing in a few paragraphs the major functions and tools, machinery and special equipment used;
- job content – lists the sequence of operations that constitute the job, noting main levels of difficulty;
- statement showing relation of job to other closely associated jobs;
- training required, working hours and peculiar conditions of employment, e.g. very hot or humid.

Employee factors

These include sex and age and physical characteristics required, e.g. size or strength; mental abilities and emotional qualifications needed; cultural requirements, e.g. speech; experience and skill needed.

In the United States a *Dictionary of Occupational Titles* shows over 30 000 descriptions which aid the use of standard job titles.

Summary of procedure for recruitment and selection of staff

1 A *staff requisition* form is required to be completed by the head of the department where the vacancy arises, noting full details of the vacancy, e.g. job title, date of commencement. This can be checked against the com-

pany's establishment by the human resources department who would arrange to insert the advertisement.

2 *Advertisement* is placed. It is important to word the advertisement correctly so applicants who are not really suitable do not apply. A vaguely worded advertisement will bring in more unsuitable applications. The media used for advertising should be checked periodically to ensure it is effective.

3 *Short-list* drawn up and interviews arranged.

4 *References* can be taken up before the interviews and used to determine the final selection at the interviews.

5 *Interviews* themselves can take many forms. They may be structured using standard procedures and techniques, e.g. five- or seven-point plan.

6 *Tests* for specific skills are usually left to the time of the interview. Professional qualifications claimed should be checked.

7 *Medical* examination may be essential and appointments are often made conditional upon passing. The Health and Safety at Work Act 1974 regulations may mean more consideration needs to be given to this aspect, as employing persons should consider every possible area of uncertainty, and any person who has suffered from an illness which may recur should be examined.

8 *Unsuccessful candidates* are informed of the decision.

9 *Successful* candidates are informed and company records updated.

It is important to note that under the Health and Safety at Work Act, the employer's liability is greater and he must take steps which are 'reasonably practical' to safeguard the health of staff.

SELECTION AND EMPLOYMENT

Selection

When the short list of candidates for interview is drawn up a timetable should be prepared allocating specific periods for each interview so that there is sufficient time to interview each person properly.

The objects of interviews are:

- to assess personality of applicants;
- to obtain further details on certain matters;
- to agree terms of employment;
- to provide candidates with more information about the job.

The reception of candidates is very important as their first impression of the organization is obtained at the interview. The following points should be observed:

(a) The *waiting room* should be comfortable and the room where the interviews are held should be private and preferably the candidate should not be facing strong light.

(b) It is essential to *put candidates at ease* and questions at first should be so directed.
(c) *Methodical assessment* is aided by having a check-list of questions or the use of a rating schedule as suggested by the National Institute of Industrial Psychology's *Seven Point Plan*. This sets out each quality to be assessed, e.g. attainments, general intelligence, special aptitudes, disposition, interests and aims, health and circumstances. It is of course true that individuals cannot readily be divided into neat categories and that judgement is still essential, but a systematic approach is preferable.

Many interviews consist of a panel of persons who question the candidates *individually*. The panel usually comprises the manager of the department concerned and other interested parties; often the human resources manager is in the chair.

Group interviews are those whereby candidates are brought together and observed simultaneously by assessors, who give the group a problem to discuss, which is in the form of a committee exercise. This method can show personal reactions, e.g. those who are tactful, persuasive, or domineering. The Civil Service use this method, but it is considered that the method is probably better used for internal promotions for certain supervisory posts, as candidates may not wish their applications to be known, nor wish to meet applicants who may know them. One variant of the panel interview is where the candidate is asked to go from one interviewer to another: these interviewers meet later to compare appraisals.

Testing supplements direct personal contacts at interviews. The test creates a situation in which the applicant reacts; such reactions being regarded as samples of this behaviour in the work for which he is applying. The following tests may be given:

● achievement tests, which sample and measure the applicant's accomplishments and developed abilities;
● aptitude tests measure a person's capacity and potential. One form is an intelligence test designed to measure the ability to remember or reason;
● interest tests use selected questions or items to identify areas of interest or special concern to the applicant;
● personality tests try to find dominant qualities of a personality, the combination of aptitude, interests, mood and temperament.

Appraisal of test results is vitally important, as tests can be misused and misinterpreted. These points are noteworthy:

● tests should be regarded as a supplement to, rather than a substitute for, other selection techniques;
● most tests emphasize what a candidate can do, rather than what he will do, and are useful in picking out potential failures;
● a test should be *valid*, in that it can be shown to serve the purpose for which it was intended.

Employment

The formal offer of the appointment is made and acknowledged. The offer states certain main terms and conditions. Sometimes a handbook is sent with all conditions of work, etc., explained carefully.

A formal contract may be prepared for senior staff. Such a contract usually states:

- Period of employment, place of employment, capacity.
- Hours, salary, increments payable, illness arrangements, expenses and other benefits.
- Whether inventions belong to employer; provision for arbitration in disputes.

Salespeople may have additional points in their contracts:

- Calculation of salary, e.g. commission on sales plus expenses.
- Agreement to work exclusively for employer.
- Whether to charge commission on bad debts.
- Not to compete within a certain radius after termination of their contract; not to solicit employer's customers.

A *medical examination* may be regarded as essential in some jobs. It ensures a person is physically suited for the job and safeguards the firm from the engagement of anyone who suffers from infectious diseases and strictly forms part of selection procedures.

Equal opportunities and discrimination

Discrimination against various groups in an organization has been made unlawful and legislation designed to avoid discrimination includes:

The Sex Discrimination Act 1975 makes it unlawful to treat a person less favourably than a person of the opposite sex purely on the ground of sex. The Act applies to offers of employment, dismissal, and opportunities for promotion, transfer, training and other benefits. Advertisements of jobs must be sexually neutral. However, the Act does not apply where being a person of one sex is a genuine occupational qualification for a job. The Act does not apply to firms with five or fewer employees but, if it does apply, the employer is liable for acts of discrimination committed by employees unless the employer can show that he has done everything practicable to prevent discrimination.
The Race Relations Act 1976 is similar in its details to the Sex Discrimination Act except that it applies to discrimination on racial grounds (defined as colour, race, or ethnic or national origins) and it applies to all firms. Complaints about discrimination are made to Industrial Tribunals.
Disabled Persons (Employment) Acts states that employers with more than 20 people employed are required to employ a quota of registered disabled people.
Rehabilitation of Offenders Act 1974 states that some convictions become 'spent' after a certain period of time in prison. This means that in recruitment

an employer is not allowed to ask if an applicant has any spent convictions. If he is asked, he may legally reply 'no'.

A national drive to promote equal opportunities for women at work in the United Kingdom began in 1992 with the aim of commiting employers to going through a three-stage process of:

- auditing existing policies
- setting measurable goals
- making a public commitment from top management to achieving them. Organizations achieve their own goals in line with their business objectives.

One practical result of this drive was that Iceland Frozen Foods pledged to increase the proportion of female store managers from under 10 per cent to 15 per cent by the end of the year.

Contracts of employment

The *Employment Protection (Consolidation) Act 1978* imposes the following duties on employers:

1 Within thirteen weeks of commencing employment, an employer must give the employee written particulars stating the parties, date of commencement, remuneration and intervals of payment, the terms and conditions relating to hours of work, holidays and holiday pay, pensions, sick pay, the length of notice the employee is obliged to give and entitled to receive to terminate his employment.
2 The Act applies to all employees, whether their contract is in writing, oral or implied.
3 The obligation does not apply to temporary, seasonal or part-time workers.
4 The minimum period of notice that must be given by an employer is stated.

The Trade Union and Labour Relations (Consolidation) Act 1992 and the Trade Union Reform and Employment Rights Act 1993 (known as TURERA) have enhanced many of the employee rights in the 1978 Act, and should be consulted for full details.

The written statement should not be confused with the contract of employment and it is not required if all the particulars specified are included in a written contract.

There is no compulsion to give a reference for a former employee but, if one is given, care is needed in the phrasing or there may be a case for defamation of character if it can be proved that the employer has acted maliciously.

Equal Pay Act 1970

The Equal Pay Act seeks to eliminate differences between men and women as regards pay and other terms and conditions of employment by:

- Establishing the right of the individual woman to equal treatment when employed on work of the same or similar nature to men, or which has been given an equal value by job evaluation. (The Act also gives men this right.)
- Providing for the Central Arbitration Committee to remove discrimination in collective agreements, statutory wages orders and employers' pay structures, where they contain provisions for men or women only.

Any disagreement with an employer can be referred to an Industrial Tribunal for a decision.

INDUCTION AND TRAINING

Induction

Arrangements should be made for new employees to be introduced to the firm and to the job. A new employee must be shown where his place is in the organization. This service varies greatly among organizations, but a systematic course of induction should cover:

- brief history of company, products, place in industry, present organization, names of department heads and the work of various departments;
- the rules of working and safety and health regulations;
- human resources policy regarding discipline, education and training and promotion, holidays, method of computation, and date of payment of salaries and wages;
- introduction to the new employee's own department and a detailed summary of department's work;

Training

Some form of training is needed for all employees. It may give a wider general knowledge of new techniques or a broader outlook, but can be most beneficial to employee and employer.

An effective training programme can:

- improve efficiency and morale;
- introduce new techniques;
- provide for succession, enabling qualified replacements to be available;
- raise the standard of unskilled personnel, thus helping overcome labour shortages;
- develop supervisors and decrease the amount of supervision needed;
- lead to a reduction in scrap rates and improve machine utilization.

Before discussing methods of training, the concept of the *learning curve* can be considered. The curve seeks to present in diagrammatic form the progress of an individual. It ascends quickly, showing increasing proficiency, then levels out later. There are various plateaux in the curve, where a person is consolidating and developing his knowledge. Where a group of persons is being trained, the group may set 'norms' which may stop individuals from moving ahead, and therefore it is important to ensure that the group norms are the same as the objectives of the trainer, so that individuals can progress.

Many companies do not regard training as a professional activity, and in many cases training officers are not themselves trained. Many courses are held and employees sent to college without any serious thought being given to the *real training needs* of a company.

After identifying the development needs of the individual the choice of course must be made. Some firms have noted the waste of money on external training. Course objectives are often ill defined: these should be determined together with the staff's qualifications and experience. Course literature is more attractive than informative and the training officer needs objective advice on courses. A system of reporting back after each course is essential. The report should go to the training officer as well as to the departmental head. In addition, individuals must be given an *opportunity to use* the knowledge gained. (*See* Fig 9.4.)

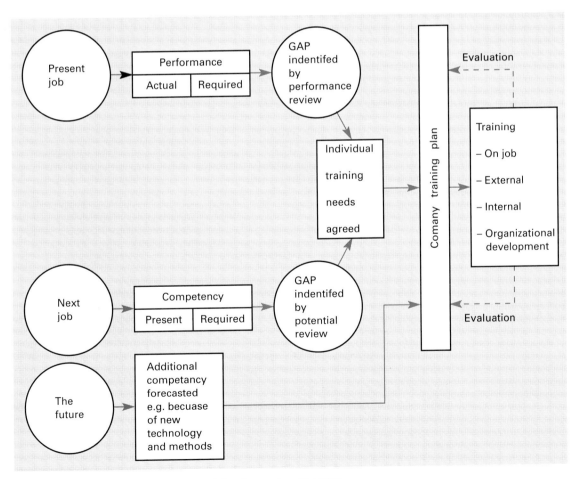

Fig 9.4 **Analysis of needs for management development and training**

Training needs must be assessed to determine:

- the jobs for which planned training is required;
- the number of people who need to be trained annually for these jobs;
- the standards of training required.

When the skills and knowledge required have been noted, a training programme is needed. An essential part of the programme is the need to train instructional staff and design a method of controlling progress. These programmes should be, of course, periodically evaluated. The training officer, therefore, advises management on training policy, basing his advice on training needs. He analyses jobs to identify skills; he plans programmes and follows them up. He must be familiar with the assessment of training needs and job analysis; he must know how to plan programmes and evaluate cost of training; also he must keep abreast with methods of training, including *programmed learning*. A *linear* programme, for example, presents information in very small steps, each step being followed by a question and on the next frame the correct answer appears. If an incorrect answer is given, a person may have to return to the previous frame. In a *branching* programme, each frame contains more information and questions are of the multiple choice type; each question and answer contains a branch of further information. If a correct answer is given, a person moves to the next frame; if incorrect, he is given information of a remedial nature.

Training can be considered as the creation of learning opportunities.

The required needs of managers and supervisors can be said to consist of:

1 **Knowledge.** Basic knowledge for the job; this usually comes from education early in his work, or before employment. Reading assignments, seminar discussions aid the post-experience manager, especially drawing examples from the working environment. A senior colleague could act as tutor, or programmed learning could be used to teach specific techniques.
2 **Skill and experience.** These are related closely to the job content. Preparation for new jobs can be made by giving a person assignments, case studies, decision-making exercises and management games to simulate real conditions. Group projects and role playing can supplement planned work experience to enable a person to increase his effectiveness.
3 **Attitude.** The development and conditioning of attitudes and patterns of behaviour depend more upon *learning experiences.* A person will, for example, benefit more by experiencing co-operation than reading about it, and a person's ability to adapt to change, co-operate with others and be more self-confident, comes partly from the work situation. The development of attitudes can be quickened by organizational development training. These methods, briefly, teach a group to monitor its own performance, identify and agree problems and their resolution. Other business exercises can be operated under conditions of stress to improve the effectiveness of the individual, the group and the company.

Managers learn better when they see the *relevance* of what they are learning in relation to their own jobs. In everyday work, there is no time to conceptualize.

A person should be given an opportunity to try out his ideas in a situation as near as possible to real life conditions and practices. Therefore training that is relevant and provides persons or groups with an opportunity to use the ideas learnt will be preferred.

Effective learning can take place according to Bass and Vaughan (1966) when the following four requirements exist:

- Drive – that is the motivation of the individual who must accept and be committed to the need for training.
- Stimulus – the signal received and interpreted by a trainee.
- Response – the behaviour resulting from a stimulus. This can be developed through training.
- Reinforcement – information that the learner receives giving an indication of progress – ideally as soon as possible to enable more effective learning to occur.

It is important to note that a training officer must work closely with line management in preparing programmes of training which meet the needs of employees and minimize their learning problems.

Education can be considered to be instruction in knowledge and skills to enable people to be prepared for various roles in society. Its focus is mainly broadly based for the needs of the individual and to a lesser extent the needs of society.

Training relates to the acquisition of knowledge and skills for the purposes of an occupation or task. Its focus is much more narrowly based than education or development, and is job- or task-orientated.

Development is concerned more with changes in attitude, behaviour and employee potential than with immediate skill. It relates more to *career* development than *job* development. It is a learning activity concentrating on the future needs of an organization.

Factors influencing the training and development of employees

- *Extent of change* in external and internal environments (e.g. change in technology, new processes, legislation, new markets etc.);
- extent of *suitable skills of existing* workforce and their adaptability and flexibility to use new technology and methods;
- the *interest of senior management* in training and career development;
- *teaching ability* of those responsible for the *actual training*.

Apprentice training

Apprentice training originated in the age of hand craftsmen where the individual craftsman taught the practical skills to the apprentice. Briefly, a systematic scheme for training apprentices involves:

1 Employer taking responsibility for training and assessing the training needs annually to determine the numbers required in each category.
2 The required skills and knowledge are then analysed.
3 With this information a programme can be prepared for:

- Induction training.
- Basic training in skills required.
- Planned experience, to enable skills to be applied on the job. This needs detailed specifications of what should be taught and needs a good system of recording and measurement. Projects are required to meet an apprentice's skill and progress.
- Further education; to provide technical knowledge of a general nature. This can be done at a College of Further Education or at University.

Operative training

The traditional method of training operatives is for them to learn by watching others. This is often inefficient as the others may do the job wrongly or they may be poor teachers. An operative training programme may include the following:

- Selection of the job to be studied.
- Analysis of *what* is done and *how* it is done.
- Recording and analysing common faults.
- Determining the elements of a job to be taught in parts and devising exercises to illustrate the parts.
- Setting target times and standards to see if speeds of experienced workers can be reached.
- Writing syllabus, training staff, preparing timetables, designing record forms.
- Checking results frequently.

Supervisory training

Again, the nature of the work must first be analysed. From an analysis of the job, the skills and knowledge required can be determined and from this an *appraisal* of the performance of existing supervisors is needed in order to identify their training needs. Ideally, appraisal should be based upon target setting and the supervisor should preferably help to set his own targets.

Training programmes may be conducted internally or externally and may take the form of:

- courses in skills and knowledge of a general or specific kind;
- on-the-job development, by planned project work and planned experience under immediate superior.

Internal courses can instruct upon technical subjects and company procedures. It is preferable to use participation techniques rather than lectures.

External courses are of particular use to the smaller company. They can be for the National Examination Board's Certificate in Supervisory Management. It is important to see that such courses meet a *specific* training need and be organized in a practical manner.

Management training and development

The main objective is to improve current performance and provide a suitably trained staff to meet present and future needs. A person's knowledge and skills have to be improved and his attitude and behaviour modified by training and development.

The volume of management training and development has increased greatly in recent years and there is a proliferation of courses available. These courses are not necessarily geared to the needs of the individual and, therefore, before the courses are organized, it is vital to analyse training *needs*.

Once the true needs are known the most effective means of training can be determined. Within the framework of overall manpower needs, supervisory and management succession plans can be drawn up. The needs of each individual manager must be considered and his performance appraised and weakness remedied.

From a recent survey of 30 organizations on the system of appraisals for managers it was found that the more successful schemes showed common characteristics.

- appraisal was a regular activity, with a continuous monitoring of performance by subordinates;
- salary review was a separate activity from appraisal;
- the outcome of appraisal meetings was not predetermined;
- self-appraisal was part of a move towards self-development.

An *individual* benefits from appraisal when he understands his strengths and weaknesses as a manager and his potential for future development is indicated.

An *organization* benefits if information is obtained about total management resources available for planning and deciding on the needs of training and management development.

There are a number of reasons for performance appraisal, some of which are:

- to reduce any element of favouritism;
- to help staff improve their present job performance and indicate possible career development;
- to create a more effective organization where staff know what they are doing and the reason for it.

Further points to note on an appraisal system include:

- all levels of management, unions and employees should accept the scheme and understand its purpose and nature;
- line managers shoulder the final responsibility of appraisal and they should be properly trained to implement the scheme;
- the methods of appraisal should be uniform and the system reviewed periodically and necessary changes made;
- subordinate participation in the setting of performance targets increases the commitment to, and success in, achieving them.

Problems which have arisen from such schemes are:

- quality of appraisal reviews is not of a high average standard, and the time scale often used (one year) may be too long;
- the real reasons for the appraisal may still be unclear and persons receiving a favourable interview may lead them to expect rewards or promotion;
- some managers have inadequate job descriptions of their staff and take no follow-up action after the appraisal. They are reluctant to take adequate time over appraisal and some are reluctant to discuss results with subordinates.

Other *advantages* which have been found are:

- people understand their jobs better because of job descriptions being required;
- managers are appointed usually up to their experience and ability (not beyond, as suggested by the 'Peter Principle' (*see* p 194));
- people are encouraged to develop themselves and take higher qualifications, and some like the opportunity to discuss their problems in performing their jobs with superiors.

A rating system for management staff

This requires the rater to consider certain features and mark according to a scale. For example, *analytical ability* (ability to grasp essentials and make sound conclusions). A number of items are shown on a scale and one of them is to be marked, e.g. A – outstanding; B – very good; C – average; D – fair; E – poor.

This can be continued for other qualities, e.g. co-operativeness, dependability, self-expression, knowledge of job, judgement, leadership and organizing ability. The working of the five points in the above scale may differ a little for each characteristic.

Forced distribution rating scales

These start with a distribution theoretically expected for a given group of workers on similar jobs. Using this basis, a five-point scale may be used to distribute a group of employees between the extremes of good and bad job performances, e.g. 10 per cent – outstanding; 20 per cent – good; 40 per cent – satisfactory; 20 per cent – fair; 10 per cent – unsatisfactory. The assessor is asked to rate the group so that ratings are distributed in the above percentages.

Graphic rating scales

These permit the rater to mark performance at some point on a line from 'excellent' to 'poor' on separate factors, or an overall judgement.

For example, *leadership* – the ratings range from *not acceptable*, poor leader and negative personality, on the one hand, to a fifth rating of *outstanding leader*, good judgement, accepted without question.

Ranking systems

People are compared with *each other* and listed in order of merit and placed in a simple grouping. Few of these schemes are linked with performance and the appraisals are subjective.

Management by objectives

This is a different approach, and has been described briefly on pp 107–11. It uses a *performance-based* approach using, wherever possible, objective standards of measurement. The basis of the system is that every manager is given a clear idea of the results expected. A detailed job description and targets required are agreed *with the superior*. Appraisal is made by comparing results with targets.

Fundamentally, management achieves objectives through people. If therefore the objectives of people could be linked with those of management a *harmony of objectives* would result to benefit all.

Management by objectives (MBO) was an idea expounded by Drucker in the 1950s, it had a participative connotation and required many managers to change their basic dispositions or 'style of management'.

It is based on the assumption that managers will be more effective and will be more committed to objectives if they are themselves involved in establishing them.

It also presupposes that they work in an organization that encourages self-control and self-development.

McGregor and Hertzberg adopt the approach of the need first to change management style or attitudes and behaviour, and then other changes may occur.

MBO is not yet practised on a very wide scale, although it has been widely talked and written about. Larger companies, as may be expected, use it to a greater extent than small companies. A main feature of the idea is the recognition of the importance of company strategy, especially the function of marketing. More details of how to change management style will be mentioned later.

Key results areas for individual managers must reflect the overall strategy, which is reflected in the marketing programme. The main points in the approach have been described on p. 108.

Characteristics of effective appraisal

- Constructive attitudes by superior, and the outcome not predetermined;
- participation in discussion and decision of the subordinate should be of a high level;
- mutual approach to solving problems;
- opportunity for self-appraisal encouraged, so manager can be encouraged to develop himself;
- appraisal must be a regular activity. A year is used to reflect the needs of the organization (e.g. end of budget cycle), rather than to suit the needs of individuals or work groups;
- salary review must be separated. Schemes that try to deal with salary grading have most discussions on this aspect rather than objective appraisal of performance.

The establishment of company objectives was discussed in Chapter 1 and these objectives must be known before divisional or sectional goals can be clarified. They should be known by each person so that he understands how his own goals relate to the broader objectives of the business. The objectives should, of course, be periodically redefined.

- J W Humble in his booklet *Improving Management Performance* advocates stating for each manager the *key results* he should achieve; these key results areas are important areas of objectives.
- Within these areas, a *performance standard* must be set; these standards may be quantitative, e.g. units produced in a week, or qualitative. In any case, they need to be prepared for all subordinates and agreed with them by superiors.
- The organizational structure must provide for freedom to perform them, as badly designed structures affect performance. There may, for example, be no clear line of authority, or badly arranged divisional or functional organization.
- Control information should be in a convenient form, and sufficiently frequent, so that managers can take quick corrective action.
- Then follows a *review of performance* of managers. The superior analyses how far the key results have been achieved and this formal review enables any gaps to be filled by guidance and training.
- At the time the *potential* of a manager is considered, to assess whether for example he is ready for promotion now, or should he be given more varied work.
- The final stage involves *frank discussions* between manager and subordinate.

NB: This review stands or falls on the ability of the appraisers, the way they appraise and how specific are the discussions. There is a great tendency to generalize and, if little attention is paid by the management to appraisal reports, then managers will pay little attention to appraisal.

Figure 9.5 shows in a brief form how to *improve management performance*.

Management training

Once the real needs are known, training can begin. The training should develop knowledge, skills and attitudes, through various methods of instruction, demonstration and experience. The following methods are adopted:

Job rotation

This can be instituted within a department, within a company, or within another company. The purpose is to improve a manager's understanding of jobs other than his own and provide a specific experience which will equip him for promotion. It is, of course, easier to arrange for lower levels of management. Short periods in different departments was at one time widely used for induction training of university graduates, but it was never fully satisfactory and led to a high labour turnover. As the period was so short, it did not enable the trainee to feel a sense of responsibility as he was not answerable for the results of his decisions.

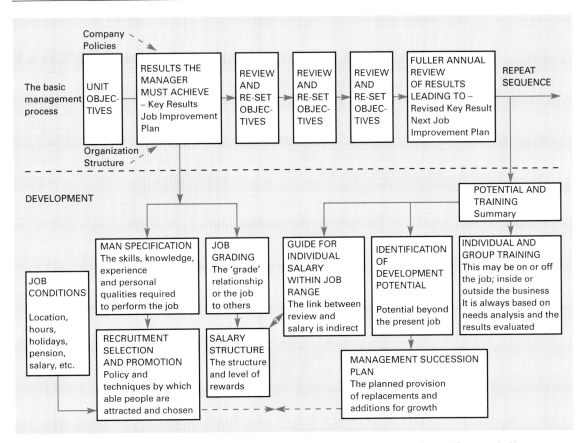

Fig 9.5 Improving management performance. (Reproduced by permission of Urwick, Orr and Partners Ltd.)

| Projects and assignments | A good assignment should involve investigations into a number of departments and can reveal a person's capabilities. Superiors should be interested and carefully examine findings. Assignments given to a group of managers will give good experience in team-working. This approach is adopted on management courses, where members are split into syndicates to work on a problem, and here the problems of other departments become known to all. |

| Junior board | A junior board is a group of young people from different functions, appointed by top management for a limited period. Terms of reference are laid down by the senior board and problems given to them are of a general nature, e.g. problems of staff and public relations. The junior board will investigate and submit recommendations to the senior board. Group assessment is possible and it provides a good experience in general management. |

| Personal assistant | The *assistant to a manager* is a staff role and he/she speaks only in the name of his/her superior and helps him/her in his/her work.

An *assistant manager* has a line role, as he/she shares some responsibility with his/her superior. The position is often the centre of controversy as reporting relationships become uncertain. |

Formal
management
courses

Formal management courses cannot teach anyone to manage, but can accelerate management development, if combined with the right experience. New management tools are occurring frequently and formal courses are efficient and economical. They can modify and widen perspectives and this is needed by functional managers who aspire to general management.

Management courses are often not effective because:

- they accept too wide a spectrum of members (e.g. graduate trainee and senior executive). This can limit discussions;
- they do not allow interaction and participation between course members themselves and the tutors;
- the background knowledge and experience of tutors are not credible;
- the concepts and ideas on the course are not able to be put into practice or are not related to work situations;
- the place of the course and its surroundings may not be conducive to free speaking. Reports made while a person is on a course can inhibit the contribution from that member.

Training needs must be noted carefully. Training is required to make persons behave differently or more efficiently, for example, to improve *performance* of operators or to improve *attitudes* of salespeople. Needs can arise from variations between existing and desired performance which may be due, for example, to present manpower lacking in potential or knowledge to do jobs effectively. Training needs also arise from the recognition of a person's potential for a higher position and the preparation of the person for the position.

A most important factor should be considered. Assuming all the relevant points have been noted, for example, the job has been defined and its function stated, the levels of authority and responsibility determined and the training need; the *attitude* of the person who is to be trained should be considered carefully. One cannot *impose* training, the person to be trained should be motivated or persuaded to be enthusiastic and the *benefits* to the individual should be made clear to him. Course members usually pose themselves these questions:

Will I be able, after training, to: earn more, make my job easier or more interesting, earn promotion and improve my status?
Will I be reported upon? Why have I been chosen? What are the administrative arrangements (food and accommodation)?
Will I be shown up on the course because it is too demanding? Will I be able to practise the new ideas shown to me?

Therefore clear guidelines should be given, showing *how* the course learning can be applied to the work situation. Persons should be selected carefully for training and their individual training needs analysed, and false hopes should not be aroused. There must be effective briefing and de-briefing on return from the course and action programmes prepared within a stated period.

Training programmes should therefore be systematically *planned* and *supported* by relevant human resources policies which are based upon objectives of the company, and should be periodically *reviewed*.

Management training and development can never be fully effective unless the manager himself recognizes a *need*.

This can be simply illustrated as follows by showing various needs and the methods by which they can be effected.

Need	*Method*
Agree what you expect from me.	Key results areas and statement of objectives.
Give me an opportunity to perform.	Job improvement plan and organizational planning.
Let me know how I am getting on.	Control information and performance review.
Give me guidance when I need it.	Management development methods and potential review.
Reward me according to my contribution.	Salary structure and succession plan.

An excellent analysis can be found in *Improving Manager Performance* by John Humble.

Figure 9.6 shows how various methods of training can increase managerial effectiveness.

Internal courses

Internal courses may meet some training needs. Many management courses are residential and companies set up Staff Colleges where courses are held which are concerned with outlook and attitudes; the different atmosphere aids work.

Open learning enables people to learn at a time, place and/or pace which suits them best and also gives them a wide choice of what they study. It may involve self-study at home or work at convenient times, supported by telephone tutorials and practical work. It may also involve tailor-made workshops and groups, or flexible access to equipment, training centres, colleges or other sources of help and advice. It can make use of tapes, video, computer-based learning, and so on. Whatever form it takes, open learning starts with the needs and circumstances of particular groups of people and tries to meet them.

Accreditation of Prior Learning (APL)

APL is a process by which an individual may obtain formal recognition for *achievements of past learning* and experience. The basic premise of APL is that people learn throughout their lives and much of this learning (whether at home, work or during leisure time) is vocationally relevant.

Accreditation refers to the processes of *assessment* and *certification*. The use and application of APL is of particular value to people without formal qualifications who intend to enter or re-enter employment.

APL is important particularly in countries which are experiencing significant changes. These include demographic changes; for example, in the

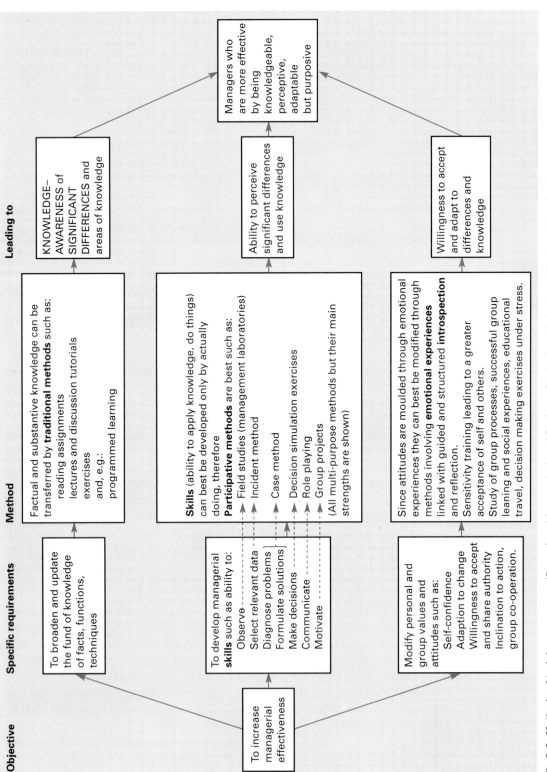

Objective

Specific requirements

Method

Leading to

To increase managerial effectiveness

To broaden and update the fund of knowledge of facts, functions, techniques

Factual and substantive knowledge can be transferred by **traditional methods** such as:
reading assignments
lectures and discussion tutorials
exercises
and, e.g.:
programmed learning

KNOWLEDGE–AWARENESS of SIGNIFICANT DIFFERENCES and areas of knowledge

Managers who are more effective by being knowledgeable, perceptive, adaptable but purposive

To develop managerial **skills** such as ability to:
Observe
Select relevant data
Diagnose problems
Formulate solutions
Make decisions
Communicate
Motivate

Skills (ability to apply knowledge, do things) can best be developed only by actually doing, therefore
Participative methods are best such as:
Field studies (management laboratories)
Incident method
Case method
Decision simulation exercises
Role playing
Group projects
(All multi-purpose methods but their main strengths are shown)

Ability to perceive significant differences and use knowledge

Modify personal and group values and attitudes such as:
Self-confidence
Adaption to change
Willingness to accept and share authority
Inclination to action, group co-operation.

Since attitudes are moulded through emotional experiences they can best be modified through methods involving **emotional experiences** linked with guided and structured **introspection** and reflection.
Sensitivity training leading to a greater acceptance of self and others.
Study of group processes, successful group leaning and social experiences, educational travel, decision making exercises under stress.

Willingness to accept and adapt to differences and knowledge

Fig 9.6 Methods of training managers. (Reproduced by permission of Business Books from H. Buckner, *Business Planning.*)

United Kingdom the number of young people leaving school is significantly declining and employers will have to recruit from an adult market. APL:

- *recognizes skills* which already exist in the current and potential workforce;
- provides a *method of judging* achieved skills;
- *widens access* to education and training and access to nationally recognized vocational qualifications;
- *reduces time involved* in training by assessing and accrediting existing competencies.

This means that individuals only need to be trained in areas of work where they have been unable to demonstrate competence.

APL is not a traditional form of assessment but is being actively considered by many countries. In 1987 the Government Training Agency and the National Council for Vocational Qualifications (NCVQ) launched a study on the feasibility of APL. It is now recognized that APL acts as an *agent for change* and can assist in the motivation and development of the workforce, as well as contributing to more effective and relevant training.

Stages in accreditation of previous work achievement

1 Self-analysis against units of competence.
2 Reflection on and identification of previous work experience.
3 Match prior experience to competency statements.
4 Individual development plans.
5 Collection of prior evidence to support competence.
6 Preparation of portfolio to present for assessment.

The Management Charter Initiative

The Management Charter Initiative (MCI) (which was briefly noted in Chapter 1) was established by employers and supported by many organizations and has shown that experienced managers from all types of organizations can successfully demonstrate their competence through the process called Accreditation of Prior Learning (APL). MCI believe the term 'Crediting Competence' better describes the process, although the term APL will be used in this book.

Management Standards of Competence

The process involves participants collecting examples of their day-to-day activities, e.g. marketing plans, accounts, and documents which demonstrate their competence at their job. These are then assessed against the Management Standards. If components are found to be lacking, advice is given and individuals re-submit evidence until it reaches the desired standard. Once the portfolio of relevent and current work evidence is complete, participants undergo a rigorous assessment and interview eventually leading to a National Vocational Qualification. Competence can be credited at licensed centres in the country.

Reflection on experiences is an instrinsic part of the APL process, where one can reflect and *value* all a person can do and has done in the past. Most people learn by doing; by reflecting upon what we have learned or done we can prepare ourselves for other experiences or learning opportunities. The

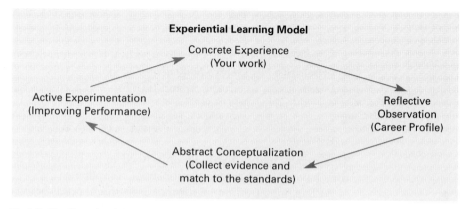

Fig 9.7 **The Experiential Learning Model.**
From D.A. Kolb and R. Fry, 'Towards an Applied Theory of Experiential Learning', in C.L. Cooper (ed.), *Theories of Group Process* (New York, John Wiley, 1975)

Experiential Learning Model (Fig 9.7) was developed by American psychologist David Kolb and is a way of defining learning.

Management training techniques

The main techniques used are shown in Fig 9.8.

Group dynamics can be considered further. Another name is sensitivity training or T Groups.

Students are put in groups, which may be *structured,* i.e. with a set idea and a brief plan, or *unstructured,* with no plan at all. Discussion ensues and students are encouraged to observe the stresses and strains that occur between members, how these shift as the group takes on new tasks and as individuals assume different roles. There is no *agenda,* goal or formal authority, and frustrations, conflicts and collaboration abound. By observing this, group members begin to observe the dynamics of group behaviour. Again, skilled instructors are needed as it is a strain on members, who should be selected carefully.

Other training techniques

The managerial grid

Grid organization development was evolved by R R Blake and J S Mouton, *The Managerial Grid* (1965, Gulf Publishing Co). The model postulates that a manager's two main concerns, for production and people, can be shown on a matrix. Each scale from 1 to 9 expresses either a concern for people or a concern for production. Blake selects five positions (1/1, 1/9, 9/1, 9/9 and 5/5) for consideration. He suggests we accept 9/9 as the preferred management style, showing a maximum concern for people and production. Managers complete a questionnaire and place themselves on the two scales, deficiencies are highlighted the farther they are away from 9; these 'deficiencies' can be acted upon. Managers tend to accept this approach, although the idea does not have much evidence to support the link between managerial style and organizational performance.

Method	What it is	What it will achieve	Points to watch
Lecture	A talk given without much, if any, participation in the form of questions or discussion on the part of the trainees.	Suitable for large audiences where participation of the trainees is not possible because of numbers. The information to be put over can be exactly worked out beforehand – even to the precise word. The timing can be accurately worked out.	The lack of participation on the part of the audience means that, unless the whole of it, from beginning to end, is fully understood and assimilated, the sense will be lost.
Talk	A talk incorporating a variety of techniques, and allowing for participation by the trainees. The participation may be in the form of questions asked of trainees, their questions to the speaker, or brief periods of discussion during the currency of the session.	Suitable for putting across information to groups of not more than 20 trainees. Participation by the trainees keeps their interest and helps them to learn.	The trainees have the opportunity to participate but may not wish to do so. The communication will then be all one way and the session will be little different from a lecture.
Job (skill) instruction	A session during which a job or part of a job is learned in the following formula: 1 The trainee is told how to do the job. 2 The trainee is shown how to do the job. 3 The trainee does the job under supervision. Each of these parts may be a complete session in itself: (a) talk (b) demonstration (c) practice.	1 Suitable for putting across skills. The job is broken down into small stages which are practised. The whole skill is thus built up in easily understood stages. 2 This gives the trainees confidence and helps them to learn. 3 More suitable when the skill to be learned is one which depends on a lot of knowledge first being learned. Many clerical skills are of this sort.	1 The skill to be acquired may best be learned as a 'whole' rather than as parts. 3 It is difficult for trainees to absorb large chunks of information and then to be shown what to do at some length before they get the opportunity to put the learning into practice.
Discussion	Knowledge, ideas and opinions on a particular subject are freely exchanged among the trainees and the instructor.	Suitable where the application of information is a matter of opinion. Also when attitudes need to be induced or changed. Trainees are more likely to change attitudes after discussion than they would if they were told during a talk that their attitude should be changed. Also suitable as a means of obtaining feedback to the instructor about the way in which trainees may apply the knowledge learned.	The trainees may stray from the subject matter or fail to discuss it usefully. The whole session may be blurred and woolly. Trainees may become entrenched about their attitudes rather than be prepared to change them.

Fig 9.8 **Management training techniques**

Method	What it is	What it will achieve	Points to watch
Role-play	Trainees are asked to enact, in the training situation, the role they will be called upon to play in their job of work. Used mainly for the practice of dealing with face to face situations (i.e. where people come together in the work situation).	Suitable where the subject is one where a near-to-life practice in the training situation is helpful to the trainees. The trainees can practise and receive expert advice or criticism and opinions of their colleagues in a 'protected' training situation. This gives confidence as well as offering guidelines. The trainees get the feel of the pressures of the real life situation.	Trainees may be embarrassed and their confidence sapped rather than built up. It can also be regarded as 'a bit of a lark' and not taken seriously.
Case study	A history of some event or set of circumstances, with the relevant details, is examined by the trainees. Case-studies fall into two broad categories: 1 Those in which the trainees diagnose the causes of a particular problem. 2 Those in which the trainees set out to solve a particular problem.	Suitable where a cool look at the problem or set of circumstances, free from the pressures of the actual event, is beneficial. It provides opportunities for exchange of ideas and consideration of possible solutions to problems the trainees will face in the work situation.	Trainees may get the wrong impression of the real work situation. They may fail to realize that decisions taken in the training situation are different from those which have to be made on the spot in a live situation.
Exercise	Trainees are asked to undertake a particular task, leading to a required result, following lines laid down by the trainers. It is usually a practice or a test of knowledge put over prior to the exercise. Exercises may be used to discover trainees' existing knowledge or ideas before further information or new ideas are introduced. Exercises may be posed for individuals or for groups.	Suitable for any situation where the trainees need to practise following a particular pattern or formula to reach a required objective. The trainees are to some extent 'on their own'. This is a highly active form of learning. Exercises are frequently used instead of formal tests to find out how much the trainee has assimilated. There is a lot of scope in this method for the imaginative trainer.	The exercise must be realistic and the expected result reasonably attainable by all trainees or the trainees will lose confidence and experience frustration.

Project	Similar to an exercise but giving the trainee much greater opportunity for the display of initiative and creative ideas.
	    The particular task is laid down by the trainer but the lines to be followed to achieve the objectives are left to the trainee to decide.
	    Like exercises, projects may be set for either individuals or groups.
		Suitable where initiative and creativity need stimulating or testing.
		    Projects provide feedback on a range of personal qualities of trainees as well as their range of knowledge and attitude to the job. Like exercises, projects may be used instead of formal tests.
		    Again there is a lot of scope for the imaginative trainer.
			It is essential that the project is undertaken with the trainee's full interest and co-operation. It must also be seen by the trainee to be directly relevant to his needs. If the trainee fails, or feels he has failed, in the project there will be severe loss of confidence on his part and possible antagonism towards the trainer.
			    Trainees are often hypersensitive to criticism of project work.

Fig 9.8 Continued

Method	What it is	What will it achieve	Points to watch
In-tray	Trainees are given a series of files, papers and letters similar to those they will be required to deal with at the place of work (i.e. the typical content of a desk worker's in-tray). Trainees take action on each piece of work. The results are marked or compared with another.	Suitable for giving trainee desk workers a clear understanding of the real life problems and their solutions. The simulation of the real situation aids the transfer of learning from the training to the work situation. A valuable way of obtaining feedback on the trainees' progress. Also useful for developing attitudes towards the work, e.g. priorities, customers' complaints, superiors, etc.	It is important that the contents of the in-tray are realistic. The aim should be to provide trainees with a typical in-tray. The marking or comparison of results must be done in a way which will not sap the confidence of the weaker trainee.
Business and management games	Trainees are presented with information about a company – financial position, products, markets, etc. They are given different management roles to perform. One group may be concerned with sales, another with production and so on. These groups then 'run' the company. Decisions are made and actions are taken. The probable result of these decisions in terms of profitability is then calculated.	Suitable for giving trainee managers practice in dealing with management problems. The simulation of the real-life situation not only aids the transfer of learning but is necessary because a trainee manager applying only broad theoretical knowledge to the work situation could cause major problems. Also a valuable way of assessing the potential and performance of trainees. It helps considerably in developing many aspects of a manager's role.	The main difficulty is in assessing the probable results of the decisions made. Sometimes a computer is used for this purpose. The trainees may reject the whole of the learning if they feel the assessment of the probable outcome of their decisions is unrealistic. There is also a risk that the trainees may not take the training situation seriously.
Group dynamics	Trainees are put into situations in which: 1 the behaviour of each individual in the group is subject to examination and comment by the other trainees, 2 the behaviour of the group (or groups) as a whole is examined. (The trainer is a psychologist, sociologist or a person who has himself received special training.)	A vivid way for the trainee to learn the effect of his behaviour on other people and the effect of their behaviour upon him. It increases knowledge of how and why people at work behave as they do. It increases skill at working with other people and of getting work done through other people. A valuable way of learning the skill of communication.	Difficulties can arise if what the trainee learns about himself is distasteful to him. Trainees may 'opt out' if they feel put off by the searching examination of motives. It is important that problems arising within the group are resolved before the group breaks up.

Fig 9.8 Continued

The object of the training programme is to achieve 9/9 managers, and to achieve production through mature interpersonal relationships which are integrated with the purposes of the organization.

1–9 = Thoughtful attention to needs of people for satisfying relationships leads to a comfortable friendly organization atmosphere and work tempo.

9–1 = Efficiency in operation results from arranging conditions of work in such a way that human elements interfere to a minimum degree.

1–1 = Exertion of minimum effort to get work done is appropriate to sustain organizational membership.

5–5 = Adequate organizational performance is possible through balancing the necessity to get out work while maintaining morale of people at a satisfactory level.

9–9 = Work accomplishment is from committed people; interdependence is through a 'common stake' in organizational purpose and leads to relationships of trust and respect.

The 3–D organizational effectiveness programme

This training programme, advocated by W J Reddin, is based on his grid model of managerial behaviour which extends Blake's grid and adds a third dimension 'effectiveness' to 'tasks orientation' and 'relationships orientation'.

Again a test is completed to show each manager his own style. This is a flexible training programme which consists of nine stages and can be tailored to meet the needs of individual companies.

A final look at research on the nature of the relationship between management and supervisory style and the performance and satisfaction of co-operating individuals, must include the work of R. Likert, *The Human Organization* (1967, McGraw-Hill).

He put forward four recognizable systems of management:

System 1: Exploitative – authoritative.
This is a bureaucratic, hierarchical structure with rigid authoritarian control.
System 2: Benevolent – authoritative; results are achieved by a system of rewards plus some delegation.
System 3: Consultative – achieving a measure of employee involvement while reserving policy making for the top.
System 4: Participative – group; communications move freely up and down, management provides adequate rewards and full use is made of group involvement to set high performance goals.

The ideal – System 4 – he considers is more beneficial. The organization has mutual trust and supportive relationships between employees and managers. He claims that managements tending to System 4 have higher output and better industrial relations.

The approaches to management of McGregor, Blake and Likert appear similar. The needs and talents of workers and managers can be satisfied and utilized more effectively if the environment is suitable. Each one classifies a style of management, Blake, 9/9; Likert, System 4; McGregor, Theory Y. To the extent the managers do not reach these ideal positions, training is needed to change attitudes and behaviour towards them.

Evaluation of training

All control processes involve evaluation and this is the same in training. Feedback is required to assess the value of training, and the *more precisely standards of training are set, the more easy it is to evaluate.*

A well-known definition of evaluation by Hamblin (1974) is: 'Any attempt to obtain information (feedback) on the effects of a training programme, and to assess the value of the training in the light of that information.' Hamblin provides a detailed structure for the evaluation and control of training and describes five levels and strategies for obtaining evaluation:

Level 1 – reactions of *trainees* during training to the trainer, other trainees and external factors.
Level 2 – learning *attained* during the training period, assuming prerequisites such as basic aptitude and receptiveness on behalf of the trainee.
Level 3 – *job behaviour* in the work environment at the end of the training period.
Level 4 – *the overall effects* on the organization.
Level 5 – *ultimate values* such as survival, profit, social and political welfare of interested parties (in other words the impact on the goals of the organization).

The trainer should be able to test the training effectiveness or validate his claims that the training methods selected have brought about desired results. However, there must be a scientific approach to measurement to enable the costs incurred to be justified.

Job satisfaction

Research into job satisfaction usually involves dealing with matters of a subjective nature and this means results are difficult to evaluate. One element of importance is that workers in a successful undertaking which is publicly prominent derive satisfaction from their work. A worker's attitude to his work depends a lot on the informal social organization in the undertaking. The experiments of Elton Mayo were considered in Chapter 1 and those of Hertzberg in Chapter 5; research by Joan Woodward in her book *Industrial Organization: Theory and Practice*, points to several general conclusions about the effect of relations between workers and of different types of *work organization.*

She found that relations between workers on batch production work and flow production (motor vehicle industry) tend to be less good than those on unit (craftwork) or continuous process work (chemicals). On individual production work variety provides interest and workers have some control over quality. On continuous process work there tends to be a high ratio of managers to operatives who work in smaller groups and thus closer relations develop. In batch or flow production work, work groups may be large and difficult for supervisors to control closely; there is little opportunity to control quality and the worker is under continued pressure, as productivity usually depends upon speed of working.

It may also be true that *opportunities for promotion* may influence the degree of satisfaction a worker will have in his job. If educational attainments are going to be essential for promotion, opportunities for study may be essential to retain good worker relations.

Assessment centres

An assessment centre conducts a series of tests, exercises and interviews which are constructed and collated to enable an organization to formulate a comprehensive picture of the skills, abilities and characteristics of the candidate being assessed.

An assessment usually involves a group of assessors who evaluate a group of candidates over a period of a few days.

One type of centre is designed to test all, or some, of a set of predetermined factors, such as inter-personal skills, planning, organizing and communication skills. These are tested using exercises which are not job specific; but are applicable to various organizations. This type of centre's services can be purchased from organizations specializing in their design.

Another type of centre is tailor-made for an organization. Their work begins with a comprehensive job/personal specification analysis conducted for a vacant position. Exercises are subsequently designed which simulate the job; they are devised to examine candidates by the criteria established by the job analysis.

Assessment centres are one of the most accurate staff selection methods currently in use, and they have a high validity rating.

A survey of a number of large companies' attitudes and practices regarding their use of assessment centres showed that 37 per cent of respondent organizations used assessment centre exercises in 1989 compared with 7 per cent in 1973. ('Guidance and Assessment Review' by B Mabey.)

The original assessment centres were run by the armed forces and the method was later applied in an industrial setting. It was mainly used for assessing the potential of managers. Now they are used for diverse groups of people, from managers to supervisory and sales personnel. They are also used for staff development purposes where the assessor's role is more of a facilitator who assesses the performance of the candidate and discusses the results with the candidate with the aim of preparing a practical training and development plan.

Advantages and disadvantages of assessment centres

Advantages

- Data is comprehensive and candidates can demonstrate skills they may not usually display;
- individuals gain greater knowledge of their strengths and weaknesses which will help their career direction;
- assessors also benefit from the experience of assessing.

Disadvantages

- Centres may require great amounts of money and effort;
- management may not give their full commitment to centres;
- poorly qualified assessors can give inaccurate judgements;
- centres only concentrate on measuring behaviour that can be observed and evaluated.

PROMOTION AND TRANSFER

Promotion

A policy for promotion is needed and its contents may be:

- all promotions to be made, as far as possible, within the firm;
- the main basis of promotion to be merit and ability. Seniority (often the number of years' service) to be considered but not to form the sole reason for promotion;
- opportunities given to all employees to reach the highest grades;
- vacancies be advertised and be kept open to all employees;
- accurate personnel records must be kept and these must include grading and merit ratings and other relevant details.

Transfers

These occur from one department or job to another or both and may solve a number of problems. Clear records are essential to obtain knowledge of the new job's requirements and the qualities needed for it. The employee, or department head, may have requested the transfer. Care and tact are needed in these situations.

WAGE AND SALARY ADMINISTRATION

Remuneration policy and methods cannot be considered in isolation from the country's economic policies. Wages may account for up to 80 per cent of total costs in some industries.

The objects of a policy of remuneration are:

- to attract and retain sufficient staff of the required calibre to meet the organization's objectives;
- to provide staff with incentives for better work;
- to have a policy which is logical and consistent, easily understandable and flexible.

After objectives, policies and priorities have been determined, the methods of remuneration to be used to achieve them should be considered, i.e. job evaluation, merit rating, incentive schemes and fringe benefits.

Job evaluation

It is not easy to produce an acceptable system of wage structure, especially if inflation increases and social values change. The difficulty is in finding a base or pattern of stability for wage bargaining. A job evaluation plan may be agreed only to find that what was deemed a fair differential between grades is now no longer supported because social values have changed.

In the search to find a stable pattern, each yearly wage bargaining round has been associated with a 'normal' increase, which it is hoped will be sufficient until the next round of bargaining. Job evaluation systems also try to give a position of stability, but this can be affected by inflation.

Schemes to establish a systematic means of relating rates of pay to jobs are collectively known as *job evaluation*. This is intended to arrive at a rate for a job (usually through negotiation) irrespective of the attributes of individual workers who are employed on the job. The British Institute of Management defines job evaluation as 'the process of analysing and assessing the content of jobs, in order to place them in an acceptable rank order, which can then be used for a remuneration system'.

There is an increasing interest in job evaluation, because in addition to providing a measure of uniformity, a flexible pay structure can deal with changes in job content and complexity and the more there is company and plant bargaining, rather than national bargaining, the easier it is to incorporate job evaluation into agreements. The Equal Pay Act 1970 implies the need to use job evaluation to ensure that jobs are ranked in a fair and equal manner.

Although the scope of job evaluation is unlimited in principle, its application has been somewhat restricted to groups of relatively homogeneous jobs, e.g. manual or clerical.

A summary of the main points in the application of this technique will include:

1 Deciding *who* shall carry out the work.
2 *Training* the persons (usually a committee).
3 *Selecting key* jobs (benchmarks) to represent a range of levels and functions.
4 *Analysing* jobs, writing job descriptions and specifications for them and deciding on *job elements,* or factors, which provide main headings for job assessment.
5 Agreeing *importance* (or weight) of these factors and analysing all other jobs, then comparing them to produce a ranking order.
6 Noting *levels of payment,* nationally and locally, then deciding on a number of job grades and the rate of payment for each grade.
7 Agreeing structure, implementing and reviewing its application periodically.

A job *description* provides information on which each job can be rated or evaluated. The measures of value can then be translated into wages and salary rates. Evaluation gives one job a rating as compared with a rating for another job.

Workers' representatives frequently participate in job evaluation, which may be done by a committee representing management and workers. Once jobs have been described, one of the four main systems of job evaluation may be used.

Ranking systems
These assign measurable points values to jobs and establish a number of pay classes and determine the relative position of jobs. They often include a few broad qualities which are characteristic of all jobs to varying degrees, each job being treated as a whole and not broken down into factors. They are simple to operate and best suited to small organizations where the ranking committee will know all the jobs.

Job classification
For each main class of job, a specification is prepared, noting the work and responsibility that will be included. Salary ranges may be allocated to each class and sub-class. All jobs are fitted into these classes. This method also is suited to small units.

Points systems
A manual sets out the elements or factors upon which each job is to be rated and provides yardsticks by which each factor is to be valued. Job elements are described and *weighted,* and each job is given a total points value by adding up the factor points. The factors are usually:

- skill – comprising education, experience, initiative, dexterity and integrity;
- effort – physical, mental or visual demand;
- responsibility – for equipment or process, material or product, safety or the welfare of others;
- job conditions – working conditions, monotony and unavoidable hazards.

Against each of these factors will be a maximum points rating; each factor will be assessed for every individual and his points total noted. Then, depending upon the points number, a job classification will be allotted, e.g. A – up to 100 points; B – up to 150; C – up to 200. If for example a person had 140 points he would be in class B. A wage structure could then be determined from the above simple illustration by allowing a rate per hour for class A of £4; class B of £5; class C of £6.

Factor comparison
This is more involved and not easy to explain to employees, but resembles the points system as each job is analysed into factors considered common to all types of jobs. These factors are usually – mental and physical effort, skill, responsibility and working conditions. A survey is made of the wage structure, from which a number of *key jobs* are selected, representing various wage levels. An analysis is then made to determine the proportion of total wage paid for each factor. Scales are prepared for each factor, against which all the other jobs under review may be compared factor by factor; these jobs can then be placed in their relative positions of importance on the scales.

HAY-MSL guide chart method
This is derived from the previous basic methods and is based upon a points system where points are awarded to significant elements of a job. The importance of jobs relative to others is measured and this is determined mainly by

the *purpose* of the organization. Guide charts are produced which represent the structure of the organization and cover areas headed: problem-solving, accountability and know-how. *All* staff are included and jobs can be compared logically and effectively. Comparisons between salaries paid in other companies are included.

Know-how – is the amount of skill and knowledge and experience needed to do a job (including knowing how to work with people).
Problem-solving – the amount of discretion or judgement needed and the type and frequency of problems and the necessity for the holder to develop new ideas.
Accountability – assessment of the degree of impact the job has on the department or the company, the area affected by the job and whether it affected large or small amounts of money and the extent to which the job holders were responsible for large or small areas of work. Salary is paid according to performance (100 per cent is satisfactory).

Advantages of job evaluation

Job evaluation has the following advantages:

- it provides a systematic procedure, describing and placing a value on a job;
- job descriptions can be employed in recruitment and selection;
- people are paid for work performed, and the satisfaction derived can lead to higher morale and better co-operation;
- unions can play a part in deciding between levels of pay.

Disadvantages

The disadvantages are:

- no allowance is made for differences displayed in the performance of a job. (Merit awards can be used);
- pay rates are also affected by market conditions, i.e. supply of, and demand for, labour;
- assessment may be inaccurate and, if the number of grades is small, jobs of a different character may have to be put in the same grade.

The factors chosen by Barclays Bank International and the Banking, Insurance and Finance Union in evaluating secretarial jobs were – skills, supervision, contact and initiative and confidential information.

Merit rating

A person's ability can be assessed and a payment for merit may be given. It is a subjective assessment, usually made by department heads. They decide ratings by one of a number of systems. These could be alphabetical, i.e. A,B,C,D, or descriptive, e.g. very good, good, average, below average; or on a percentage rating. Some of the factors to consider are timekeeping, quantity and quality of work, initiative, co-operativeness, dependability. Points can again be awarded for each factor out of a maximum number. It is a system often applied to salaried staff.

Some qualities obviously are difficult to determine, but it may be better to use this method for promoting candidates rather than use it to select people at their first interviews.

Wages and incentives

In most incentive payment schemes, performance above a level taken as standard for job evaluation will receive a reward. The form of reward is usually cash. There are three main groups:

1 Merit rating.
2 Payment by results – the incentive here is linked purely with output, at a given level of quality.
3 Overall schemes, whereby the reward is more remote from the direct output of the individual or group, but is linked with the firm's output or profit or overall economy.

As many schemes are based upon subjective assessment by supervisors, they are opposed by trade unions as inequitable. About 35 per cent of industrial workers receive payment based on output. Schemes based on output are obviously inappropriate when the operator cannot control the level of output or where measurement is difficult. Such schemes may comprise payments which are:

- proportionate to output – i.e. straight piece work;
- proportionately less than output, e.g. Hasley, Rowan, Bedaux schemes, where workers 'share' the benefits of higher output with the employer;
- proportionately more than output, i.e. a high piece rate or accelerated bonus scheme, which is progressively proportionate – these can be used where the main consideration is maximum utilization of expensive capital equipment;
- variable in relation to output, e.g. Taylor, Merrick, Gantt, Emerson schemes, where reward has a different ratio at different levels of output.

High day or measured day rate

A number of progressive firms have been abandoning piece-work systems as no longer appropriate to their circumstances and have introduced such systems as measured day work, under which an employee is paid a time rate, plus a bonus, which is conditional on his maintaining a predetermined level of output. The standard required is high and if the level of performance is not maintained, a lower payment is made or transfer, training, or dismissal ensues. There is also a *contractual* measured day rate, where the employee is allowed to determine his own rate of working and must maintain it consistently. Such systems have advantages in the control of production as output is predictable, but must be used in appropriate circumstances, i.e. they would not be used if there were much slack time.

Overall, or collective bonus schemes

These have arrangements whereby the employee receives a bonus or periodic payment, e.g. weekly or annually, based upon a *number* of factors, such as reduction in labour costs, or total costs per unit or increase in total profit, or output. They are said to be economical to install and operate and encourage co-operation and improve the employee's interest in the business. They are of course very remote from the actual work and the bonus may be too small a part of the total wage to be significant and the employee cannot calculate in advance what he is to receive.

Examples of these schemes are the *Scanlon plan,* which starts by fixing a *ratio* between total manpower costs and total sales value of goods produced. A reduction in this ratio, therefore, is a saving, and the amount of the saving is distributed. The *Rucker plan* is based upon a formula relating payroll costs to *sales value added* by the manufacturer. Both are common in the USA but are little practised in the UK.

Incentives for indirect workers

The following schemes are used to give indirect workers, i.e. non-production workers (supervisors and managers), some incentive. Payment may be by:

- bonus based on profits of the company, e.g. if a 12 per cent dividend is paid on shares, then the bonus is 12 per cent on salaries;
- issue of shares in the company or an option to subscribe in the future;
- bonus given on output of department for which responsible.

Fringe benefits

There are two main types of fringe benefit, direct and indirect. *Direct* benefits may comprise profit sharing, co-partnership, sick pay and pension schemes; payments are generally made in cash. *Indirect* benefits are aimed at improving morale and increasing the stability of employment. Examples are free luncheon vouchers, sports or welfare amenities, provision of car or a mileage allowance, telephone, purchases at a discount, education for children, canteen, social facilities. Today, the provision of fringe benefits is increasingly recognized as being part of total remuneration but this was not always the case. They were originally provided on ethical and moral grounds to assist needy employees.

The question often arises, whether to give cash or fringe benefits. Many executive fringe benefits are quite high and one reason is that a firm can give its employees more this way than a cash payment which cannot avoid being taxed.

Staff status

Most manual workers are not able to share fringe benefits as they are confined to staff (usually monthly-paid workers). There is now a tendency to provide staff status for manual workers. A major responsibility for raising the status and security of workers must rest with management. Any raising of standards costs money and must be paid for by higher productivity. The granting of staff status has been put into effect by a few progressive firms. Certain of the workers, who may be the longest serving, or at a certain level of responsibility, are rewarded by staff benefits, e.g. longer holidays, annual salary and special sick pay schemes. Salary can be difficult to determine especially if the worker was used to piece-work rates and overtime.

JOB RESTRUCTURING

Early management writers proclaimed the advantages of specialization, particularly increased productivity. Some writers (Karl Marx and Friedrich Engels in the 1850s) were not so happy with job specialization. They saw division of work as a source of alienation of the worker, which ' . . . enslaves him instead of being controlled by him'. Other writers have also noted that both the individual and society would be affected adversely by too many dull, repetitive jobs. So when assembly line work became widespread, these problems increased, and later writers reinforced the point that the more highly specialized the jobs, the more employees tend to lose their individualism and need for challenge and became dissatisfied and dependent (Argyris, Hertzberg and McGregor).

This reduction in interest and motivation could lead to absences and careless work and possibly deliberate attempts to stop production. If higher wages were demanded to compensate for their dissatisfaction, the benefits of specialization may not then be realized.

Research studies on the relationship between specialization and job satisfaction vary in their conclusions, although the balance of opinion seems to indicate that there is a relationship and increased specialization can lead to job dissatisfaction. Hulin and Blood in *Psychological Bulletin* (Vol 69, No 1, pp 41–53, USA) suggest that workers' backgrounds largely determine their attitude. Those who deem work important and meaningful and are aiming to progress may become more dissatisfied in jobs that are too specialized. Those employees who are alienated from work may prefer restricted jobs as they are easier and require little effort to perform.

Before looking at job restructuring, an examination of the concept of *job depth and scope* are helpful in considering the idea of specialization.

The *extent* to which an individual can control his own work is called *job depth*. If a job is closely supervised and every detail of work to be done is laid down, the job has *low* job depth. The freer a person is to do a job and set the pace, the *higher* the job depth.

Job *scope* refers to the variety of tasks required in a job. A job with a small number of operations (i.e. highly repetitive) has a *small scope*. So by looking at a job in terms of scope and depth one can see how specialized it is.

Two basic dimensions of job restructuring are enlargement and enrichment.

Enlargement of jobs

Jobs can be enlarged by the addition of one or more related tasks. This term is used to describe changes to increase the *variety* of tasks of persons, the aim being to help problems of fatigue, low morale and apathy which occur because of the need for specialization. Workers are given more varied tasks and given increased scope for initiative and skill. A person who produces a 'whole' unit should, in theory, increase output and lead to greater job satisfaction.

Advantages
- Reduction in operator fatigue and relief from boredom where work is specialized and repetitive.
- Operator can exercise more control over his working speed and use a wider range of skills.

Disadvantages
- Although personal satisfaction is increased it may not produce a more technically efficient product. Reductions in output and quality have been noted in a number of cases.
- More time and cost in training is involved.
- Some workers resist change and may not wish for enlargement of their jobs.
- The actual system of production may not leave much scope for enlargement of jobs.

Enrichment of jobs

Jobs may be enriched by increasing the motivational content through the addition of different types of task, or the provision of increased worker participation and involvement. An *individual's* job has greater responsibility (NB: An autonomous working group (*see* p 151) is concerned with extending the responsibility for the *group).*

The idea of job enrichment leads on from the theories of McGregor and Hertzberg, who emphasized that individuals were more motivated when they were given opportunities to exercise discretion and were given more responsibility. The theories noted that a person *seeks* responsibility and will exercise discretion and aims for achievement and self-development. If he is allowed to do this he will be better motivated. So if a job is *extended* to include other duties, possibly of a higher level with more responsibility, the job is *enriched.*

Jobs can be enriched by giving a person the whole job to complete and allowing him more freedom to set targets; or re-defining a job to allow a person or team to have authority and discretion for a unit of work.

Reasons for job enrichment being installed are varied. Workers today are better educated and higher paid. People must be used more efficiently and effectively, if not, absenteeism and a high labour turnover and poorer workmanship are the result.

Advantages
- More workers are able to do various jobs; this can overcome the problem of absenteeism.
- Teams can do their own checking and less supervisors are needed.
- Reduction in labour turnover and absenteeism may occur.

Disadvantages
- Possible high cost of redesigning plant or re-tooling.
- Unless all levels of workers and management are committed to change, it may not work. It takes a long time to change attitudes.
- It is easier to introduce only if there is an *end* product.
- Some people do not want more responsibility and this must not be considered a substitute for an appropriate pay scheme.

Some management writers are of the opinion that job enlargement or enrichment may not be desirable in all cases. Some employees who derive satisfaction from relating to their co-workers may not like changes which give them less time for social interaction.

The true effects of enlargement or enrichment, designed to improve job scope and depth respectively, may well depend upon the employee's personality, background and values.

Job enlargement and enrichment schemes may therefore *not* increase productivity, as this may already have reached a good level because of specialization, but *increases work satisfaction* and *reduces absenteeism* and turnover of staff.

TERMINATION OF CONTRACTS

Employment may be terminated in a number of ways. The employee may be given notice, may be sacked on the spot, or may be made redundant. The legal rules governing these different situations will now be examined. It is important to note that the *Employment Protection (Consolidation) Act 1978* provides that an employee continuously employed for between 4 weeks and 2 years is entitled to not less than 1 week's notice, with further entitlement of 1 week for each succeeding year's continuous employment up to 12 years. Thus an employee with 12 years' or more continuous employment is entitled to not less than 12 weeks' notice. Employees with more than 4 weeks' continuous employment must give not less than 1 week's notice. The phrase 'not less' is important; there is nothing to stop an individual employee's contract entitling him to more than these periods. It is, of course, possible for the employee to be given wages in lieu of notice. However, it is vital to grasp that, even though an employee is given the notice which he is entitled to, he may still claim for unfair dismissal (see below). These provisions only apply to employees who are employed for 20 hours a week or more or whose contract normally involves employment for 20 hours or more a week. However, in some situations employees who only work 12 hours or more a week are covered, and the Act should be consulted for full details.

Dismissal

A dismissed employee, provided he is not within the 'excluded classes' (see below) may bring a claim before an Industrial Tribunal that he was unfairly dismissed. The legal rules here are once again contained in the Act. The employee must first prove that he has actually been dismissed. This will not usually be difficult, but it should be noted that the term 'dismissed' here includes:

- where the employee was employed under a fixed term contract, e.g. for one year, which has now ended without being renewed on the same terms;
- where the employee himself terminates his contract in circumstances where he is entitled to do so because of the employer's conduct. (This is known as constructive dismissal.)

Once proved, it is for the employer to try to show that the dismissal was fair. It is this idea of fairness which lies at the heart of the unfair dismissal laws, and not the idea of whether the dismissal was in breach of contract. Accordingly, even though the employee was given the correct notice and thus his contract was not broken, he may still claim for unfair dismissal.

The employer, to show the dismissal was fair, must prove that the dismissal was justified under one of the five grounds set out in the Act. These are that the reason for dismissal:

1 Related to the employee's capabilities or qualifications for performing work of the kind he was employed to do.
2 Related to the employee's conduct.
3 Was that the employee was redundant.
4 Was that the employee could not continue to work in the position he held without breaking a legal duty or restriction.
5 Was for some other substantial reason.

Even though the employer proves one of these reasons, the dismissal will still be unfair if he did not act fairly in treating it as a reason for dismissing the employee. Thus the procedures adopted by employers are of vital importance. ACAS has issued guidelines under the title of 'Disciplinary practices and procedures in employment' which deal with, for instance, warnings to be given to employees, the need for an investigation and hearing before any actual dismissal, and the provision of a right of appeal. As these are guidelines only, a failure to observe them will not necessarily mean that the employee is held to have been unfairly dismissed. However, their importance in the human resource management field scarcely needs stressing.

One small but important point should be noted here. A dismissed employee is entitled to ask his employer to provide, within 14 days of request, a written statement of reasons for dismissal.

A claim for unfair dismissal can also be made in certain specialized situations, each of which can only receive a bare mention here. The situations are:

● that the employee has been unfairly selected for redundancy;
● that the employee was dismissed because he was a member of an independent trade union or was involved in its activities. If this is shown to be the principal reason for dismissal, the dismissal will be held to be unfair;
● that the employee was dismissed for pregnancy.

An employer may dismiss employees who are on strike provided that, in effect, he dismisses them all. If he dismisses some but takes others back, those dismissed may claim for unfair dismissal. Dismissal of an employee will be automatically fair if there was a practice, in accordance with a union membership agreement (closed-shop) requiring all employees to belong to a specified independent trade union and the employee has refused to join. However, if he had genuine religious reasons for so refusing, the dismissal will be unfair.

Remedies

The primary remedy is re-instatement, where the employee is given his old job back. Re-engagement may be ordered instead, where the employee is to be given a job which is comparable to his old one. Where neither of these remedies are ordered, the tribunal will award compensation. There are two elements in this; the basic award, payable in all cases irrespective of whether the employee has suffered financial loss, and the compensatory award, which is advised to the tribunal within three months of dismissal. The 'excluded classes' (referred to above) are employees with less than 52 weeks of continuous employment and those who have reached the age of 65 (men) or 60 (women) or, alternatively, have reached the normal retirement age. In addition, the 20 hours a week provisions apply here also.

Redundancy

This is defined by the Employment Protection Act as being where the employee is dismissed because:

(a) the employer has ceased to carry on the business;
(b) the employer has ceased to carry on the business in the place where the employee was employed;
(c) the requirements of the business for employees to carry out work of a particular kind have ceased or diminished, or are expected to.

Redundant employees are entitled to compensation under the statutory scheme. The purpose is two-fold: to compensate for loss of security and to encourage employees to accept redundancy without damaging industrial relations. The actual amount of compensation is based on age and length of service. The employer pays the compensation, but is entitled to a 40 per cent rebate from the Redundancy Fund.

Where the employee unreasonably rejects a suitable offer of alternative employment made by his employer then he will not be entitled to any compensation. Each case must be individually examined to see whether the employment offered was indeed suitable. Where the offer is acceptable, the employee is entitled to a trial period of at least 4 weeks. If he finds, during this time, that the job is unsuitable he will still be able to claim a redundancy payment.

An employer planning redundancies is required to consult the appropriate trade unions about their implementation, and to take note of and reply to any representations made by them. If an employer does not consult the unions concerned they can apply to an industrial tribunal for a protective award. This requires the employer to continue to pay the employees affected by the redundancies for a specified period.

An employer is also required to notify the Secretary of State for Employment of any redundancies being planned which would affect more than 10 workers over a period of one month.

Labour turnover

This refers to the measurement of the numbers of employees leaving a company. From records, the labour turnover can be calculated by dividing either the total *separations* or the total *replacements* by the average number on the working force, and expressing the results as a percentage.

This figure is an indicator of the stability or otherwise of the labour force. A high turnover figure is wasteful and varies with the type of industry, sex (i.e. more women than men leave work) and age, which is one of the main reasons for leaving. Examination of the figure may pinpoint vital information; for example, it may indicate poor selection techniques, poor placement or working conditions. A high turnover is costly. It involves extra costs of recruitment, engagement, training, and possibly more accidents and failure to meet orders on time.

Employee interviews

A good human resources policy implies a guarantee against unfair dismissal. The human resources officer may call employees for interview if they have been recommended to be dismissed and examine the facts. The trade union representative or shop steward should preferably be there also.

Those employees leaving for personal reasons should also be interviewed in an 'exit interview'. Detailed records of the reasons should be kept, although the *real* reason may not be made known. An analysis of the records may spotlight weaknesses in the firm's policy or organization. Records may analyse causes under:

- voluntary leaving – personal betterment, dissatisfaction with job, or pay conditions;
- management action – discipline, incompetence, redundancy;
- unavoidable – retirement, death, incapacity, marriage, leaving district, etc.

Morale or attitude surveys

These should be made regularly, e.g. at least annually, as the knowledge gained about any dissatisfaction enables early remedial action to be taken *before* employees decide to leave.

Some schemes provide measured reactions to supervision, communication, working conditions, pay, employee benefits, security status and recognition, administration, confidence in management and opportunity of development.

Answers to questions must be secret or they may be inaccurate. An example of a question is: 'The company as a place to work is – very poor, poor, fair, good, excellent.' There may also be open-ended questions, e.g. 'What do you like best about working for the company?' Questions, of course, must not be biased or misleading. Persons skilled in interviewing are needed and the services of the National Institute of Industrial Psychology may be utilized.

Legislation has greatly affected this area and dismissal is now more costly and more difficult for the employer. Termination of contracts has been restrained by public policy.

Redundancy causes problems to employees and the human resources department can help adjustment to the new conditions by instituting counselling services.

Services to assist the redeployment of workers can include, advice on their future direction, financial arrangements, self-marketing and job-search techniques. Positive steps must be taken to reduce the impact of redundancy and offset negative feelings which may be held against the company.

EMPLOYEE SERVICES

Many undertakings have paid more attention to the improvement of the environment in which workers work and live. These are usually entitled employee services, and a number of them will be briefly mentioned.

1 **Superannuation.** Many firms conduct pension schemes either as *separate trust funds,* where the firm's contribution (and the employee's contribution in a contributory scheme) are invested and the scheme controlled by trustees, or as *life office* schemes, where a contract is made with a life assurance office. A firm may contract out of the state graduated pension scheme if it has its own scheme which gives a pension at least equal to the maximum under the State scheme.
2 **Catering.** This can be a very important service and plays a part in securing suitable labour. Most canteens are subsidized by the company, but its cost is allowable for purposes of taxation. The human resources manager may have to decide whether the company shall use the services of outside caterers, or provide the service itself.
3 **Sickness and benefit schemes.** Employees absent from work for certain periods may still be paid their full wage, or a proportion of the wage.
4 **Other services.** These may include sports or recreational clubs, assistance with housing, special provision for transport, assistance with tutorial fees and textbooks for those studying for professional examinations.

HEALTH AND SAFETY AT WORK

The maintenance of safe working conditions and the prevention of accidents are most important. Accident prevention is the responsibility of management and this responsibility is often delegated to the human resources manager. In other organizations, it may be the responsibility of the works engineer or works manager. The *Health and Safety at Work Act* 1974 lays down broad duties, which are supplemented by more detailed regulations. Although the UK adopted the EC Directives on health and safety on 1 January 1993, the 1974 Act remains in force to supplement these.

The principal duty which the Act lays on employers is to ensure, so far as is reasonably practicable, the health, safety and welfare at work of all employees. A series of slightly more precise duties follow, dealing with, for instance, plant and systems of work, handling and storage of materials. In all cases, however, the duty is qualified by the phrase 'reasonably practicable'. Accordingly, it appears that the employer can balance risk of injury against the measures necessary for eliminating that risk and, if the risk is insignificant in relation to these measures, the employer may not be liable.

The Act aims to encourage employers and employees to play a positive role in promoting safety. A duty is thus laid on employees to take reasonable care for their own safety and that of others, there is provision for the appointment of safety representatives and safety committees from among employees, and the employer must issue a written statement of his safety policy. In furtherance of this 'positive safety' aim, the idea of criminal sanctions for breach of the Act is pushed into the background. Although such sanctions exist, safety inspectors, who have statutory powers, will generally first issue notices requiring, for instance, an improvement of some matter, before there is resort to a prosecution. The primary job of inspectors is thus to provide detailed advice and assistance, rather than to be law enforcers in the strict sense. Clearly, the role of the human resources officer in encouraging this 'positive safety' attitude is of crucial importance. The Act also established two bodies: the Health and Safety Commission, which has overall responsibility for safety and whose role is one of advice, education, and research, and the Health and Safety Executive, which is responsible for the actual operation of all safety law.

Finally, it should be noted that an employee injured at work has two other remedies open to him: he may sue his employer for negligence and he may claim industrial injury benefit.

Health and Safety Regulations, 1993

The council of Ministers agreed to proposals by the European Commission for a further group of Directives made under the Treaty of Rome. These were the *framework Directive* on health and safety, together with five other Directives. They deal with health and safety for *the workplace*; the use of work *equipment*; *personal protective* equipment; *manual handling* of loads; and *display screen* equipment. Each Directive was implemented from 1 January 1993. The regulations require the application of management principles to workplace health and safety in such a way as positively to manage risk and reduce it to acceptable levels.

Risk assessments

The key to setting standards of health and safety, and thus one of the fundamental duties required of employers, is to carry out an adequate *risk assessment*. A risk assessment involves *identifying hazards present in a workplace* (arising out of the work activity or factors such as the layout of premises or equipment), together with an estimate of the risk involved. A hazard is something with the potential to cause harm; risk is the measure of likelihood of that potential being realized. The purpose of the assessment is to:

- identify the relevent duties demanded by legislation, or standards appropriate to the work;
- ensure that policy and arrangements attain safe work systems.

It must also be *continuous* to take account of new or changed circumstances.

The *duty to undertake risk assessment* will apply to *every* employer and self-employed person, regardless of the number of people employed. For undertakings with five or more employees it will be mandatory for the significant findings of assessments to be recorded.

Regulation 4, dealing with health and safety arrangements, will require *every* employer, having regard to the nature and size of the undertaking, *effectively* to plan, organize, control, monitor and review the protective and preventive measures which the risk assessment identifies as being appropriate. As these are specific requirements they should be integrated into existing safety policies. This will provide evidence that these matters are being attended to, and satisfy the further requirement that such arrangements are to be recorded where five or more employees are involved.

Safety officer

If a person is appointed to this position he may be responsible to the human resources officer or other department head. He should have good experience of industry, and knowledge of engineering principles and the relevant law, and have a common sense approach to problems. Qualities required include efficiency, high morale, courage, so that he can be respected, and he should be able to mix well with other people. His duties will include:

- making routine, thorough inspections of plant and buildings, etc., preferably with the department manager concerned;
- seeing that all safeguards are in operation, that protective gear is being worn and fire escapes are clear;
- seeing newcomers are instructed in safety measures;
- keeping records of accidents and their causes and taking effective action where special trends appear;
- advising on safety implications of plant layout, working methods, etc.

Dangerous features should be pointed out and full use made of posters, films, demonstrations.

'Good housekeeping' is essential. A well laid-out plant, clearly marked, having floors free from oil and litter, is a necessity. Education in handling and transporting materials is essential.

Works safety committees

These may be formed and the terms of reference should be specific. It should be an advisory committee which meets regularly, e.g. at least monthly, to discuss action required about unsafe working conditions or methods. Members of the committee may comprise the works manager, human resources manager, safety officer, department and union representatives. Chairmanship could alternate between management and workers and arrangements for retirement of members periodically would possibly ensure a flow of new ideas.

Stress

Stress arises from an imbalance between the demands made upon individuals and their capacity to cope with such demands.

It is easier to define and protect the *physical* well-being of employees than their *mental* well-being. Health and Safety legislation and ergonomics all try and ensure work can be carried out for the duration of a person's career, without damage to health or efficiency.

The *mental* well-being of employees is more difficult to define or protect. The *total* response of the body to any stimulus can be described as stress. Some stress is always evident in life and can be beneficial, for example, prompting a person to devise creative solutions. Too much stress has a *negative* impact on an individual's performance and mitigates against achieving enterprise objectives.

The following health conditions can be caused or aggravated by stress: alcoholism, cancer, dermatitis, headaches, insomnia and ulcers. Stress may *arise* from job related or personal factors and can be psychological or physiological. *Job related factors* could include shift work, difficult jobs, too much travel or overtime, job insecurity and unsatisfactory rules and procedures. The consequences of these include: job dissatisfaction, accidents, high labour turnover and absenteeism. *Personal* factors that may produce stress include ageing, low self-esteem, impatience, fear of failure.

Factors contributing to work-induced stress include the temperament and constitution of an individual. Stress is not only prevalent in those higher up in the organizational ladder. Research by B C Fletcher has shown that the incidence of deaths from stress-related disease in *lower* income groups were quite high. Unemployed or redundant people are also prone to psychologically damaging effects.

Alleviation of stress can be achieved by:

- attempting to control the situation, for example by avoiding unrealistic deadlines;
- discussing problems with others;
- planning carefully the time available for doing jobs;
- obtaining sufficient exercise and relaxation.

A problem today which is increasing, is the need to balance lifestyle and career to accommodate the career of a partner. The number of working married women is increasing and although this brings financial benefits it also brings challenges. Some enlightened companies are changing their human resource management practices to accommodate such dual-career couples. Examples of such changes are:

- allowing employment of two members of the same family;
- expanding child care services;
- scheduling career changes and transfers in consideration of both partner's needs.

INDUSTRIAL RELATIONS

The field covered by industrial relations is very wide, so only a few important sections of this large topic will be briefly mentioned.

Some firms have a department of industrial relations quite separate from other aspects of human resource management and its main functions may consist of:

- prevention and settlement of trade disputes;
- helping to form and maintain machinery of joint consultation;
- keeping in close touch with the state of employer–employee relations;
- advising the firm or the government on industrial relations problems.

Disputes may be settled by negotiation, conciliation, arbitration, investigation and formal enquiry. Each trade or industry's union regulations must be known by the human resources officer.

Human resources managers need to have a thorough knowledge of procedures of consultation and negotiation and the function of consultative bodies. Loss of output through industrial dispute can be costly to an organization and the proportion of strikes which occur without union support should be reduced.

Whether or not the purpose of an organization is to make a profit, employers are continually under pressure to ensure that resources are fully utilized and labour costs are stabilized or reduced. Workpeople have different interests. Their main concern is to maintain and improve their standard of living. They seek improvements in wages and salaries, increased leisure, better working conditions, stability of employment, opportunities for advancement and satisfaction in their work. Although interests are not usually the same, especially when technological and industrial changes keep occurring constantly, there is one common point of interest between employers and employees, and that is to ensure continuity of production and hence employment – to keep the enterprise viable.

Trade unions

The main function of a *trade union is* to advance and protect the interests of its members. There are craft unions, industrial and general workers' unions, also those for non-manual and professional groups. Most of these are affiliated to the voluntary body called the *Trades Union Congress,* which has as its objects 'to promote the interests of all its affiliated organizations and generally to improve the social and economic conditions of the workers'. Broader issues of national policy affecting trade unions are also discussed with the Trades Union Congress and the government.

Shop stewards first came into existence as far back as 1896 when district committees of the Amalgamated Society of Engineers allowed them to be appointed. Their function was to recruit new members and see old members did not break the rules and remained members. It was not until about twenty years later that they were formally recognized by management in the engineering industry.

Management should regard the shop steward as a vital link in its chain of communication. A lot depends upon the support he receives from local and national officials. There is an increasing tendency for firms to provide *training* for shop stewards. The National Council of Labour Colleges and the Trades Union Council offer courses covering functions of trade unions, collective bargaining and negotiating procedures, incentive schemes, effective speaking and writing, etc. It is unfortunate though that after receiving this training, over half do not return to the shop floor; they enter further education or become human resources managers.

Their position today varies from union to union (and their role and effectiveness depend upon several factors: one important factor is their personal characteristics). They are elected by union members and their duties are:

- to inspect union cards to see contributions are paid up to date;
- to act as recruiting officers;
- to see that working agreements between management and union are carried out;
- to represent their fellow workers who have grievances. They are in effect part-time union officers, but they do not normally receive payment from their union and they usually are allowed to negotiate with management during working hours with no loss of pay.

To establish a good basic framework of industrial relations, it is important to lay down clearly the roles and tasks that must be performed by each person. A system of training for industrial relations must therefore look at specific areas of training for different groups, for example, first-line management and supervisors; middle-line managers and human resource specialists; and senior managers.

There is a greater need for specialist advice in human resource matters, because of:

- Government action on traditional collective bargaining positions – it takes an active interest in wage levels and virtually all aspects of labour relations.
- The traditional right of a manager to hire and fire and determine the rate for a job has been *altered*. Employers' decisions on matters affecting the workforce are largely subject to bargaining and agreement. Negotiations between managers and shop stewards deal with most matters at shop floor level. Where managers refuse to negotiate, direct action by the workforce is possible.

So, as pressure from the government and the employees is severely limiting the freedom of managers, it is essential for every organization to have a carefully prepared *employee relations policy*.

Legal rules on collective bargaining

Legal rules on collective bargaining are contained in the Employment Protection (Consolidation) Act 1978. The Advisory, Conciliation and Arbitration Service (ACAS) is a statutory body which offers industrial relations advice, provides a conciliation service and may arrange for arbitration. It can conduct enquiries into industrial matters and publish its findings. ACAS also publishes (subject to parliamentary approval) codes of practice on industrial relations which replace the previous Code of Industrial Relations Practice. ACAS may refer disputes to the Central Arbitration Committee (CAC) for arbitration if the parties concerned agree. The CAC has powers in connection with trade union recognition and disclosure of information, as explained below.

A certification officer is responsible for certifying the independence of trade unions.

An Employment Appeal Tribunal hears appeals from the decisions of industrial tribunals on points of law. It also hears appeals from the decisions of the certification officer.

Recognition of trade unions

The 1978 Act sets out procedures for examining questions of recognition of trade unions by employers. If an employer refuses to recognize a trade union which has a certificate of independence, the union can ask ACAS to examine the matter. ACAS will consult all interested parties, including, of course, the employer. It will try to settle the issue by conciliation, but if that fails it may make a recommendation for recognition. If the employer fails to comply with that recommendation, the union may complain to CAC, which can if necessary make an enforceable award of terms and conditions of employment for the employees concerned (See also the Trade Union Reform and Employment Rights Act 1993.)

Disclosure of information

Employers are required to disclose information to the representatives of recognized, independent trade unions which it would be good industrial relations practice to disclose. The information must be requested by the union for collective bargaining purposes. There are limits set to the information which must be disclosed. For example:

- information which would be against the interests of national security;
- which would cause substantial injury to an employer's undertaking;
- which had been communicated in confidence;
- which was about an individual;
- which was relevant to legal proceedings; or
- which it would be illegal to disclose.

If CAC upholds a complaint from a union that an employer has failed to disclose information which, in its opinion, should have been disclosed, it will make a declaration to that effect. If the employer continues to refuse to disclose the information CAC will be able, if necessary, to make an enforceable award of terms and conditions of employment for the employees concerned.

Terms and conditions of employment

Under the 1978 Act a trade union or an employers' association may make a claim to ACAS that an employer is observing terms and conditions of employment which are less favourable than the recognized negotiated terms and conditions for the trade or industry. If there are no such terms and conditions, a union or an employers' association may claim that an employer is observing terms and conditions of employment less favourable than the general level in the same trade or industry in the district. ACAS may settle the claim by conciliation, but if this fails the claim can be referred to CAC which may make an award. In practice, these types of claims are becoming increasingly important.

Maternity

An employee is entitled to maternity leave and to have her old job back when she returns. In addition, she is entitled to maternity pay for six weeks of absence. However, to claim these rights the employee must have completed two years' continuous employment at the eleventh week before the time of her expected confinement, which is when her entitlement to maternity leave and pay begins.

THE NATURE OF GOALS AND GOAL CONFLICT

Human activity systems are not easy to predict or 'model'. Human resources have an *individual* as well as a *corporate* existence, each person having certain goals and aspirations. Conflicting goals can cause problems. Some organizations have full commitment to their goal, for example, a voluntary organization. Their main problems would be to agree on the various ways of achieving the goal, and there could be some personality conflict. When we consider industrial and commercial organizations where persons are brought together for *more* than one reason, e.g. to earn a living, interest in the job itself, conflicts are more likely to arise. Not many may be interested in seeing that the goals of the organization are achieved; those that may be interested are possibly more likely to be in a higher position in the organization.

It is worthwhile considering briefly the nature of individual goals – these may regard the job as an instrument to achieve: good pay, status, good domestic and social life, promotion and job satisfaction.

Even these may conflict with each other; for example, moving to another area for promotion may conflict with the desire for a settled family life in a certain area.

Within every organization there are various sub-goals of the various groups, and management attempts to manipulate these sub-goals to ensure the survival of the organization is more readily achieved. This involves co-ordinating all demands, both from inside and outside the organization (e.g. shareholders and government).

People usually work in groups and behave in a certain way within that group (a normal or accepted way). The group norm must be accepted or the person will be rejected from the group. It may happen that there is conflict between group norms, individual goals and organizational goals.

Sources of conflict

Conflict can be said to occur either on a *horizontal axis,* that is, between individual managers or between workers. Or on a *vertical axis,* between workers and managers. Conflict can exist between people in the organization and those *outside* the organization. Many of these conflicts would relate to economic aspects of pay and prices, others relate to competition for sales and markets.

The main source of conflict to be discussed here is *internal* and can be summarized under the following headings.

Money

The ratio of profits to wages – a conflict between workers and managers. Or between workers themselves where a sum of money is to be shared.

Job

Rates of pay are different for each job and sometimes one group 'claims' a job, possibly to safeguard their future security, or loss of earnings, if the job is given to others. This 'right' to do the job can lead to disagreement between groups on 'demarcation lines' between jobs, and frequently occurs (e.g. should a metal worker or a wood-worker fit a wooden frame to an aluminium surround?).

Goals

Managers are concerned with efficiency and workers with security. Managers may want newer, more efficient machinery, this may displace workers as less are needed. Conflict may occur *between* marketing and production *managers* as their policies and interests often differ.

Environmental factors

Downward fluctuations in the market for a product are a threat to workers' security. Such problems may cause conflict even within a union, if the rank and file do not think their leaders are doing sufficient to secure their jobs.

Authority and power

Workers are pressing for more say in decisions which affect their lives. This is vertical conflict. In addition, subordinates may resent the fact that there is always a superior above them.

Nature of work itself

The socio-technical system organizes people in a particular way which often leads to a boring job, no control of the pace of work, no responsibility or group identity.

It was mentioned in the first paragraph that human activity systems were difficult to model. Some attempts have been made to produce a general theory of conflict. The rest of this section will look at some theories and suggest ways in which conflict may be prevented. More consideration of these ideas can be examined in the reading list at the end of the chapter.

Model A – Unitary. Views the industrial enterprise as a team moving towards a common objective. The emphasis usually tends to be on profit maximization for the joint benefit of management and workers. Any conflict is seen as a weakness in interpersonal relations or leadership style. A remedy, influenced by the work of Elton Mayo, was to encourage workers to identify their aims with those of the organization, and to improve communications and adopt a more appropriate style of leadership. This model views all behaviour which is against the common objective as *irrational*. This can lead to more authoritarian ideas, that to achieve unity, one must accept the 'rational' views of management.

The approach does not consider the possible strong conflicting ideas regarding varying interests, values and goals.

Model B – Pluralist. This recognizes that there are many sources of constraint and many interested groups (e.g. shareholders, employees). There is a *plurality* of interest groups, all with various loyalties and goals which have to be *managed*. This recognizes the fact that decisions are made with many competing claims by government, employers, laws, consumers, etc. The various pressure groups set off interacting tensions that have to be held in *equilibrium*. So, *accepting conflict* and channelling it through institutional mechanisms (e.g. collective bargaining) may help to stabilize or *balance* the various conflicts of interest. The organization adapts to pressures from within and without; conflict is not repressed, it is brought *within the system* and absorbed. Thus it is held that conflict can be controlled by evolving a set of rules and procedures, as in collective bargaining – an institutional mechanism to resolve conflict.

Model C – Class conflicts. This newer approach has not been too readily accepted by managers in industry. It strongly criticizes pluralism and disagrees that conflict can be institutionalized, as basic differences between conflicting parties are too fundamental to lend themselves to compromise. They do not regard that there is equal power representation of management and workers, and that as it is *management* that determines the terms in which any problem is defined, management, therefore, sets the boundaries of any discussion.

Current thoughts on conflict are that it is *inevitable* and sometimes necessary. The implications are that it is harmful (or dysfunctional) to individuals and the attainment of organizational goals; but it is recognized that by clarifying issues it can lead to a search for solutions and can help innovation and change in organizations. Conflict therefore must be *managed* and at times *stimulated* to bring problems to light and ensure a better, more effective solution is obtained.

Conflict stimulation methods

- Engaging an outside person to 'put things right'.
- Changing existing work groups so as to encourage a change to better working methods.
- Encourage competition by bonuses for hard work.

Methods of resolving conflict

Participative style of leadership

A less authoritarian style of leadership has been shown to reduce conflicts from the workers' resentment of the power of managers. Where managers are pleasant and co-operative and acknowledge feelings of others, conflict is reduced. (Theory Y approach, *see* p 200.) There is also the idea to institute structural changes to *reduce* the amount of supervision a worker is subjected to and give him greater control over his own job. There is, of course, no guarantee that all workers will have higher morale and productivity, and sometimes output may fall if workers do not think an increase in productivity is in their *interest* (the goals of management and worker often differ).

Job design

Some researchers stress that too much emphasis has been placed upon mechanical efficiency, division of labour and specialization (i.e. *technical* aspects), and this has led to higher labour turnover, strikes or poor work. The harmful *social* effects were ignored. So advocates of the *socio-technical* approach regard these two aspects as parts interlocking in the organization system, where a change in either can affect the whole system. (*See* E L Trist, *Organizational Choice* (1963, Tavistock).) Job enlargement and job enrichment are techniques advocated for redesigning jobs.

Communications

Any improvement here is said to be beneficial. There is, though, no guarantee that if communications are good the workers will act rationally and agree to the 'wisdom' of management – clarity cannot guarantee *acceptance.*

Collective bargaining

This is an important technique or mechanism for resolving goal conflicts and may be said to have these main features:

- it is a joint activity where each side recognizes the right of the other to be present on equal terms;
- the respective interests of those represented in collective bargaining should be identified so common interests can be noted and means found to reconcile areas of conflict;
- the result is the joint regulation of the work situation by establishing a framework of rules and practice to govern relationships between the management and workforce.

The first step towards effective collective bargaining is for employers to recognize trade unions, who both agree to negotiating procedures resulting in collective agreements, which may be for a company, a unit, or the industry as a whole. The policy of the government has been to encourage and support collective bargaining and most employers negotiate with unions to agree terms and conditions of employment for 'blue collar' and 'white collar' workers. Collective agreements between unions and employers cover many issues and may relate to a whole industry, a company, or a single unit. In some industries joint negotiating bodies have been set up with formal constitutions. Other industries have more informal meetings between employers and unions. It is important that these agreements should be continually reviewed as they may soon become out of date. The pluralist approach still seems dominant, in that there seems to be an acceptance of the inevitability of conflict in industry and the need to negotiate joint solutions. Management still consider only *they* should determine some issues (e.g. hire and use of labour). Issues submitted to collective bargaining by management usually cover wage rates, hours of work, holidays, etc. The strength of the two sides determines the result. Strength depends upon:

- quality of organization of unions and management;
- ratio of capital to labour; the smaller the proportion of the labour cost to total costs the more likely management may grant their demands;
- degree of skill; the more skilled workers, who can move readily to other jobs, are in a stronger bargaining position;
- state of the market for products; the more a firm approaches a monopolistic position the more easily it can pass costs on to consumers by higher prices and still retain a good share of the market, then the firm may more readily accede to union demands;
- state of demand for products; full order books enable more concessions to be made by management; low order books may even encourage management to force a strike, which will reduce labour costs.

One final point to note in this brief summary is that there is a complex mixture of factors within and without the organization which affects the bargaining relationship and that although there is an agreement to go through grievance or disputes procedures (in a constitutional way) the *majority* of strikes in the UK are *unconstitutional,* that is, in breach of procedure.

Joint consultation   Joint consultation is used both to mean the arrangements in an *industry* as a whole for consultation between trade unions and employers' representatives, and committees set up within an *individual* firm. The industry bodies are usually permanent and are known as joint industrial councils (or Whitley Councils) and may constitute the negotiating machinery for collective bargaining. Within the firm they are known as works councils or joint production committees.

It is desirable that these committees do not concern themselves with pay rates, etc. Joint consultation provides means of:

- regular two-way communication between management and employees;
- keeping employees advised of the firm's policies and plans;
- obtaining employees' suggestions and giving them a say in the provision of amenities;
- enabling them to air their grievances regarding discipline or work rules, etc.

Like any organization, objectives must first be known. Mutual respect and confidence are needed and there should be a democratically elected committee representing all ranks, but not necessarily one person from each department. Subjects to be discussed should be clearly stated. Examples are holidays, welfare, discipline, recruitment, training. There should also be good secretarial arrangements and a system for reporting back to employees.

Works councils, or joint production committees, pay more attention to production details, e.g. efficient use of safety precautions and supplies of materials, improvements in production and maximum use of machinery.

Committees act as a forum for *discussion,* where common problems are discussed and measures considered to improve productivity, it is not a bargaining forum. This shows the uncertainty of the situation, a pluralist and unitary approach can be seen to exist side by side. The question is, are there issues which can be put into compartments by saying – here are items of *common interest* to discuss and here are *items of conflict*? Or, should management accept that there can be conflict on *all* items, and increase the issues coming under consultation and negotiation?

Productivity bargaining

The real difference between conventional methods of negotiations over union claims and productivity agreements is that, when new proposals are agreed, there is sufficient control to see they are carried out. Management offers an inducement to workers in return for increased production, the removing of demarcation lines, reductions in manning, or in overtime.

The long-term objective is to create an atmosphere in which employees will be more willing to accept new working arrangements and be more ready to co-operate in raising productivity.

Informal bargaining

Informal bargaining usually takes place between shop stewards and foremen or first line management and can relate to issues such as overtime, speed and manning of machines. These unwritten agreements become a custom and may be regarded as a 'law'. So although the agreements satisfy people on the shop floor, this may conflict with the ideas of higher management. Shop stewards can obtain wider control through such agreements. Foremen agree, in order to ensure work flows smoothly through their section, although the agreement may conflict with *overall* company policy.

There therefore seems to be a case for management to consider widening the range of issues in which formal bargaining occurs (i.e. a pluralist approach). Management may lose control in the long term if it does not do this, as many inhibiting customs and practices could be cleared away under a comprehensive agreement negotiated with the unions. The comment is made by W W Daniels and N McIntosh in *The Right to Manage* (1972, MacDonald), that those in subordinate positions have shown an increasing demand to be able to influence their own lives and if these strong social values, formed *outside* the organization, cannot be accommodated *within,* management may lose effective control.

WORK ROLES

Managerial authority is more likely to be obeyed if its actions are considered legitimate; such legitimation may be accorded by reward systems which fit the motivations of the staff in an organization.

The various approaches to analysing management – Classical, Human relations, Systems – do not really give guidance on the problems of organizational stress and conflict.

The aim in an organization is to achieve stated objectives; individuals participating in the organization assume or are allocated roles and interact in terms of these roles. It is this *role structure* which is important in linking separate individuals and the achievement of organizational objectives.

A *role* may be considered to be a set of rights, duties, or responsibilities laid down to guide human effort in a particular manner. A job with a title such as 'manager', to which are attributed rights, duties and responsibilities, is performed by a person in a social role. He *occupies a position,* but he *performs a role* and his behaviour is determined by accepted standards of working.

The role played by an individual in a group is influenced by that individual's:

- normal behaviour shown in the group;
- ability and personality;
- position in the network of communications.

A person may assume different roles depending upon which group he is in at a particular time. For example, a manager in a bank may have other roles, such as parent and spouse.

Role theory is a framework which involves concepts relating to an individual's position or role between himself and the external, social environment.

When a position has rights or duties and responsibilities, it takes on a social significance and becomes a *social role.* The person occupying the position is at the focal or central point and has interactions which differ, depending upon the nature of different types of environment. He is the centre of each situation, and the group of persons around him is called his *role set,* e.g. he has role relationships with his peers (other managers), subordinates, trade unions, suppliers, customers, superiors (*see* under Human Resource Management – implications for training, e.g. role playing exercises).

Role expectations are the ways members of the group see the focal role, and how their expectations may be defined, as in occupations, e.g. bank manager.

An individual *occupies* a position, but *performs* a role and conventions associated with this role tend to define the behaviour expected. A bank manager, for example, may at work have very impersonal relationships with his staff, he assumes this 'style' of approach gives better results than informal relationships would. His relationships in his home environment may be quite different, as norms of expectations are different. Some organizations may expect an individual to move from subsidiary to subsidiary, or branch to branch (as in banking) in order to gain experience for possible advancement. This could lead to conflict between the two areas demanding his attention, i.e. his work and his home life. Here home and work roles could be in conflict.

A manager should try and make it clear what role he is adopting at any one time. This is somewhat easier, for example, for an army officer, who has a uniform to denote his rank or status (known as a 'role-sign').

Role ambiguity. Job descriptions tend to have less role ambiguity at lower levels in an organization. More senior levels do not really specify the true nature of the role. The clearer the role of a person to himself and others, the clearer will be relationships. Role ambiguity exists where there is uncertainty in the mind of a person (or of members of his role-set) regarding his role at a point in time. For example, should an organization holding a monopoly of a service, e.g. a railway, reduce the number of branch lines to reduce costs, even though this would cause hardship and concern to the general public? There are still uncertainties in role theory due to key terms not being very rigorously defined or indeed universally agreed. Some instances of role ambiguity could be termed equally well 'role conflicts' (*see* below).

A knowledge of two other aspects of role theory can be most useful particularly for the recruitment, training and development of individuals.

Role overload is where a person may have a number of roles he cannot handle. He has to deal with orders and expectations from many sources that cannot be dealt with within given time and quality limits. The problem is, what should be sacrificed, quality or time? (NB: *Work* overload can be defined as having too much to do in *one* role; role overload involves greater variety as well as greater quantity of work.)

A person's assessment of his personal capabilities, his aspirations and his place in society is his *self-concept,* and will affect the strength and will of each of his needs. His ideas will be the result mainly of his education, environment and the individuals he has contact with and uses as models.

Role underload is when a person's *ideas* of self-concept are not compatible with the *definition* of his role in a particular situation. A good example of this is the search for suitable graduates for industry. Keenness in the recruiting campaign can lead to statements being made suggesting that a position offered is of a high standing. This may give the new recruit a higher view of his self-concept than is merited. So if the actual job he is given is below the person's opinion of his capability, or capacity, he could be in a state of conflict over his idea of the role. His perception of his role (although incorrect) causes role underload. In the writer's experience such persons placed in certain jobs, auditing in particular, may, due to role underload, not do an adequate job, and it can cause inefficiency.

Role conflict

Role conflict may arise from:

- an individual occupying two positions in conflict at one time, e.g. a manager who is also a union member;
- a person subjected to two kinds of role-set expectations, e.g. the position of a foreman as a 'middle-man' between management demands and workers' interests;
- the requirements of a quality controller and a salesperson.

Role conflict will be experienced if a person is confronted by two or more incompatible demands, and it can lead to role stress.

Role stress occurs at all levels of management. It can be caused by role ambiguity, role conflict, role overload or underload. Some stress may be considered acceptable or necessary at times; it must be controlled. Stress and strain can produce symptoms which may affect an organization, e.g. low morale, bad communication, sensitivity to rumours.

Role theory can suggest alternative hypotheses and is an aid to understanding problems and organizational behaviour, and offers suggestions for improvements, particularly in the area of social relations at the workplace. Role theory enables one to look at possible stress situations and thus enables actions to be taken to stop strain becoming evident.

There are a lot of points here that management should note and try to act upon, e.g. clearer definition of roles and expectations, better communication, no overload or underload of roles, and a clearer knowledge of how roles form a basis of interaction between individuals and so reduce misunderstandings.

TRAINING AND ENTERPRISE COUNCILS

Training and Enterprise Councils (TEC) were set up in the early 1990s in England and Wales and Local Enterprise Companies in Scotland (LEC). In England and Wales 82 were set up as private businesses, limited by guarantee, with a Board of Directors drawn from eminent members of the local business and public service communities. Their main aim is to tailor training and enterprise provision to the specific needs of local communities.

They receive their finance from the Department of Employment. Their activities vary widely but the following areas of operation are fairly common:

- To encourage enterprise, particularly through the growth of small business and self-employment.
- To strengthen employer investment in skills.
- To raise educational and vocational attainments to meet national targets.
- To improve the quality and flexibility of education and training provision.

INVESTORS IN PEOPLE (IIP) – A NATIONAL STANDARD

An Investor in People employer is one who has recognized and demonstrated the need to develop human resources, by providing a framework within which development takes place. This framework enables increased employee performance, involvement and commitment, which can translate directly to improving quality, profitability and a reduction in costs.

The programme is related to achieving agreed goals and standards and is seen as an investment and not a cost.

Investors in People has been developed by senior business people on the Government National Training Task Force, which advises the Secretary of State for Employment on training and enterprise issues. This task force led the way to setting up Training and Enterprise Councils (TECs) which, among other training activities, assist organizations to achieve the standard.

Before looking in more detail at the IIP standard, it is useful to examine the links between British Quality Standard BS 5750, International Quality Standard ISO 9000 and Total Quality Management (see p 329). BS 5750 is a British Quality Standard and ISO 9000 is its European equivalent.

Comparison of Total Quality Management (TQM) and Investors in People (IIP)

British Quality Standard (BS 5750)/International Quality Standard (ISO 9000) set out the requirements for systems and their operation. Such systems may not cover the *whole* organization. Issues which are integral to IIP may not be covered, e.g. total commitment and the need for *continuous improvement.*

BS 5750/ISO 9000 accreditation could, though, provide evidence of having met a number of IIP assessment indicators.

An Investor in People will be a very substantial practitioner of TQM. This can be shown by examining the following essential principles of TQM which are all explicit in the national standards for IIP:

- clear vision for future;
- effective and continuous communication;
- system improvements;
- total staff commitment;
- assessment and release of the potential of employees;
- customer/client requirements identified consistently;
- monitoring and evaluation of outcomes.

Reference to the Management Charter Initiative was made on p 33. The key aspect of this is that management training and development is based upon national standards within the National Vocational Qualifications (NVQ) framework, which is linked to demonstrations of competence in the workplace. IIP is concerned with developing competent managers who can get the best out of people and enable them to gain national qualifications through the NVQ framework.

The approach of Management Charter Initiative (MCI) to the Accreditation of Prior Learning (APL) is called Crediting Competence. It is a process which enables practising managers to receive credit for competence they already possess. The aim of Crediting Competence is to classify and assess a manager's practical experience, focusing on proven competences and capabilities rather than the actual learning process.

Competence standards are based on what employers would recognize as good working practice which reflects the real world and actual jobs of work in it.

SUMMARY

Objective 1 *Explain how effective human resource management contributes to the accomplishment of enterprise objectives.*

Human resource management is the process by which employees are selected, developed and rewarded for achieving enterprise objectives.

Effective human resource management contributes to the accomplishment of enterprise objectives by:

- promoting the efficient utilization of the talents of employees;
- assuring an adequate supply of trained employees;
- increasing the satisfaction of employees;
- developing and sustaining an environment that makes enterprise membership personally and socially desirable.

Objective 2 *Describe the term manpower planning and list the main points to consider in instituting such a system in an enterprise.*
Manpower planning is part of corporate planning and seeks to maintain and improve an organization's ability to achieve corporate objectives by developing strategies which are designed to increase the present and future contribution of manpower.

The brief points to consider are:

- examine the existing situation to see if manning effectiveness can be improved;
- plan to assess and determine future objectives of the business;
- determine the method of organization needed and the posts needing to be filled;
- note the present staff, their potential and career requirements;
- identify requirements for manpower required.

Objective 3 *Outline the purposes that can be served by a good system of performance appraisal.*
A good appraisal system can serve the following purposes:

- it provides data for decisions on training and development, promotion and pay and is a convenient way of communicating these decisions;
- it helps to make decisions on discharge or retention and provides a mechanism for warning staff about unsatisfactory performance;
- it assists managers in counselling subordinates so they can achieve better performance and develop their potential for achievement;
- it motivates subordinates through recognition and support and helps managers diagnose staffing problems.

Objective 4 *Describe the sources of the various types of conflict and methods used to manage conflict.*
Conflict existing between groups in the same organization may be caused by their need to share scarce resources and work activities and by their differences in goals, values or perceptions. Other sources are differences between individual styles, ambiguities in the organization, and problems in communication. Line and staff structures may also produce conflict in an organization.

Methods used to manage conflict include conflict stimulation, reduction or resolution. These may include bringing in outsiders, encouraging competition, restructuring the organization and redistributing power among groups and individuals.

Objective 5 *Appreciate the importance of an effective system of management education and training and development and indicate how training can be effectively evaluated.*
Management education deals with the theoretical aspects of management, usually acquired through formal methods of study. Management training is concerned with the practical aspects of management and implies preparation for an occupation or for specific skills and is job-orientated. Management development is a broader concept and is more career-orientated than job-orientated, and stresses potential rather than present skill. It enhances latent abilities made evident through education and training.

Training can be evaluated more effectively if precise training standards are set. The five levels and strategies for achieving evaluation stated by Hamblin should be noted. There must be a scientific approach to measurement to enable the costs incurred to be justified.

REVIEW QUESTIONS

1 Outline a schedule of responsibility for a human resources manager of a medium-sized engineering company.

2 What factors should be included in a human resources policy?

3 What is involved in manpower planning?

4 What are the main sources of recruitment?

5 Outline the various stages in the procedure which might be followed by a large firm in selecting employees. Explain the reasons for each stage.

6 Name and describe briefly two recent pieces of legislation affecting the human resources function.

7 What matters do you suggest should be included in service agreements with executives?

8 Indicate what you think should be included in induction training.

9 What is meant by the term 'Management by Objectives'?

10 What points should be considered in developing a policy for promotion of personnel?

11 Describe two systems of job evaluation.

12 What is meant by merit rating?

13 Consider the types of wage incentive and suggest schemes for giving non-productive workers some incentive.

14 What is meant by the terms (a) staff status, (b) fringe benefits?

15 What is meant by industrial relations?

16 What is the place and function of shop stewards?

17 Distinguish between joint consultation and collective bargaining.

18 What are the advantages of good employee services to the employer and employee? Give illustrations of such services.

19 How may managers deal with the problems of redundant staff?

20 How can organizations avoid getting involved in 'training for training's sake'?

21 In what ways is manpower planning likely to be affected by a general economic recession?

22 How are promotion policies linked to manpower planning?

23 'The real validity of job evaluation is related directly to employee satisfaction.' Discuss.

24 What are the disadvantages of an informal appraisal system?

25 Briefly describe a system for basic industrial relations training.

26 Describe the main features of assessment centres.

27 What do you understand by accreditation of prior learning?

REVIEW PROBLEMS

1 You are required to prepare a report to the chairman of a holding company with five horizontally-linked subsidiary companies, in an industry of your selection, giving the draft of a practicable management development scheme for the group.

2 You are chief financial executive of a company with a total number of employees of about 5000. The works accountant at one of the two factories of the company is due to retire in six months' time. You are responsible for appointing a replacement, either by internal promotion or by external appointment. Outline the procedures you would follow until the actual offer of appointment is made to the successful candidate.

3 You are the recently appointed production manager of a new factory owned by a large public company. You are requested by the chairman of the company to prepare a report advising him of:

   (a) The main factors to be considered in the selection and training of production control staff.
   (b) The duties and responsibilities of the staff of the production section.

4 What are the essentials of a sound policy for the training of supervisors? How would a training scheme for senior management differ from that for supervisors?

5 You are required to draft an advertisement for insertion in a professional journal, for the appointment of a group human resources officer. In addition you should prepare, in summary form, a schedule of the responsibilities of this officer.

6 You are required to prepare a standard human resources practices manual for a large firm. Give the main headings for the sections of such a manual. Take any two headings and give a detailed breakdown for each. How would you obtain management and supervision acceptance of the manual? Show how any one of the recent pieces of legislation would affect your manual.

7 Construct an executive rating scale which will indicate your view of the qualities to be considered in appraising an individual. For each trait on your scale, describe the several levels in such a way as will clearly convey a rating.

ASSIGNMENTS

8 Outline a management development scheme for a medium-sized company stating:
(a) The purpose of such a scheme.
(b) The techniques to be employed.
(c) The method of introduction to the management of the business.

State your views on appraisal interviews. Under what conditions would you expect such interviews to be effective?

9 When administered wisely, the attitude survey can be a very useful method of unearthing communication problems at all levels of an organization and of appraising the success – or otherwise – of communication methods. List the uses of a good attitude survey and state the possible disadvantages which accrue from such an operation.

10 'The safety officer should be a man of qualities rather than a man of qualifications.' Discuss this statement and also outline the functions of an industrial safety officer.

BIBLIOGRAPHY

11 Within all kinds of organizations there is a definite move towards participation at all levels and this is shown both in current legislation and in the 'mood' of management and employees.
  As a manager:

(a) what practical action would you take to increase participation amongst your staff?
(b) what problems and difficulties would you have to be particularly aware of when doing this?

12 (a) By what means can the cost effectiveness of recruitment policies and procedure be assessed?
(b) Robert Blake and Jane Mouton published their book *The Managerial Grid* in 1964 in which they described various managerial styles in terms of 'concern for people' and 'concern for production'. Describe briefly the significant managerial styles which can be shown on the 'grid' and their implications for an organization.

13 Job enrichment is a new approach to the problem of motivation and is concerned with the arrangement of both task and responsibilities in order to maximize work output and job satisfaction. One of the most famous examples of this approach is that of the Volvo car plant in Sweden.
  If you were introducing a job enrichment programme in your department what are the major principles you would wish to consider?
  Answers should be illustrated by practical examples.

14 What is the role of the human resources officer in the company? Should he, in a dispute, act independently or as a representative of management?
  How may the overall performance of the human resources officer be judged?

15 (a) Discuss the proposition that 'money, like prestige, if sought directly is almost never gained. It must come as a by-product of some worthwhile objective which is sought and gained for its own sake.'

(b) How far can this view be reconciled with executive incentive schemes?

(c) How can a company ensure that its managers are properly rewarded?

16 It is currently fashionable to communicate new ideas by means of staff conferences and seminars. What considerations would you bear in mind if required to organize such an event in your workplace?

17 The consequences of a wrong choice of internal candidate for promotion are likely to be serious. What steps should the organization take to ensure as far as possible the success of its arrangements for the internal promotion of staff?

18 Redundancy of middle managers has recently attracted considerable attention.

(a) For what reasons are middle managers made redundant?

(b) Explain why, when middle managers become redundant, many are unable to obtain appointments on at least equivalent terms.

(c) State the factors important for a policy for management development of the staff remaining after redundancies have taken place.

19 It is sometimes considered easier to manage in an expanding company operating in a buoyant market within the industry, but rather more difficult when business is depressed. Why should this be so?

  When may it become necessary to dismiss senior members of staff? How should this be done?

20 In a company employing several hundred staff, salaries have been proposed by department heads subject to approval by top management. Union action now seems likely because of complaints of salary variations for jobs similar in content. What steps should be taken to overhaul the present system and establish an equitable basis for pay levels?

21 Management selection agencies represent one method of obtaining new senior staff.

(a) What services does such an agency provide?

(b) What other methods of recruiting staff may be used?

(c) What are the factors which should govern the choice of method?

22 On what basis should a firm institute a scheme for staff training and development? How may the relative success of such a scheme be judged?

23 Your company has decided to engage five graduates in their early twenties as a first step in a management development programme. These graduates will spend two years in various departments 'learning the ropes'.

  This plan has been greeted with little enthusiasm by established executives, and especially by those who fear their prospects of promotion will be severely restricted by the introduction of these trainees.

  You are required to examine the probable advantages of this scheme.

24 Your organization has taken over several small companies, and has decided to centralize the main administration departments in a group office. It is found that there are now many anomalies in the administration, wages and salaries structure and it is suggested that a new structure be introduced based on job evaluation and merit rating.

You are required to prepare a memorandum explaining the concept of job evaluation and merit rating and state how you think the staff and the company might benefit from the introduction of such a scheme.

25 The managing director of your company has asked about the application of 'management by objectives' (MBO) as a control measure.

Prepare a summary for him in itemized paragraphs under the following headings:

(a) (i) the theory of MBO;
    (ii) the initial procedures required to apply MBO;
(b)   how the management accountant can assist in its operations.

26 (a) What are the duties of a company safety officer?
    (b) How can the company safety officer contribute towards company operational efficiency and cost saving?

27 It is generally agreed that the human resources manager has a very important advisory role. In addition, he may have a monitoring or controlling type of role, and even an executive one. How far are these roles compatible with one another and with the optimum performance of the human resources management job?

28 Traditionally, your organization has been 'non-unionized' but you are becoming increasingly aware of pressure from the employees to gain union recognition. From your management viewpoint, what are likely to be the advantages and disadvantages of recognizing trade union representation?

29 What are the arguments for and against the extension of industrial democracy through the appointment of employee representatives to company boards?

30 It is increasingly held that status differences (in terms of working conditions, hours of work, payment systems, etc.) between different groups of employees are undesirable and should be removed. Indicate the arguments for and against such a change.

31 Discuss the possible meanings of the term 'participation' when used in an industrial/commercial context. How far do you believe that participation holds any promise of improving industrial relations?

32 'Irrespective of the form of ownership the interests of management and shopfloor are bound to be in conflict.' Discuss this view.

(*See* p 482 for further problems on Human Resource Management.)

1 Select two representatives from the class, one will act as union organizer, the other as the representative of management. The rest of the class are workers who will soon be voting to determine whether they want to be represented by a union.

Each representative will talk to the workers for 15–20 minutes to try and persuade them to join, or not to join, the union. As much information as possible should be obtained by the two representatives in preparing their arguments. The class will then vote, for or against the union, in a secret ballot, with an official 'teller' appointed.

2 Take an organization with which you are familiar which has experienced various kinds of conflicts. Consider the causes of the conflicts and the methods used to resolve them.

3 Select about 15 advertisments which are currently in use and point out their good and bad features. See if you can identify any common advertising themes in particular product areas.

Armstrong, M, *Handbook of Personnel Management Practice* (London, Kogan Page, 4th edition, 1993).

Beardwell, I and Holden, L, *Human Resource Management: A Contemporary Perspective* (London, Pitman Publishing, 1994).

Connock, S and Vision, H R, *Managing a Quality Workforce* (London, IPM, 1991).

Dale, M and Iles, P, *Assessing Management Skills* (London, Kogan Page, 1992).

Graham, H T and Bennett, R, *Human Resources Management* (London, Pitman Publishing, 7th edition, 1992).

Green, G D, *Industrial Relations* (London, Pitman Publishing, 4th edition, 1994).

Hunt, J W, *Managing People at Work* (London, IPM, 2nd edition, 1986).

McGregor, D, *The Human Side of Enterprise* (New York, McGraw-Hill, 2nd edition, 1985).

Muchinsky, P M, *Personnel Selection Methods: An International Review of Industrial and Organizational Psychology* (New York, John Wiley and Sons, 1986).

Torrington and Hall, *Personnel Management* (London, Prentice-Hall, 2nd edition, 1991).

Woodruffe, C, *Assessment Centres* (London, IPM, 1990).

Woodward, J, *Industrial Organization: Theory and Practice* (Oxford, Oxford University Press, 2nd edition, 1980).

CHAPTER 10

Administrative management

The responsibility for the work of the office varies between one company and another. The provision of clerical services demands a specialist, particularly as the pace of change of electronic equipment has been so great. An administrative manager must be aware of the costs and benefits of all aspects of new information technology in order to provide efficient administrative services.

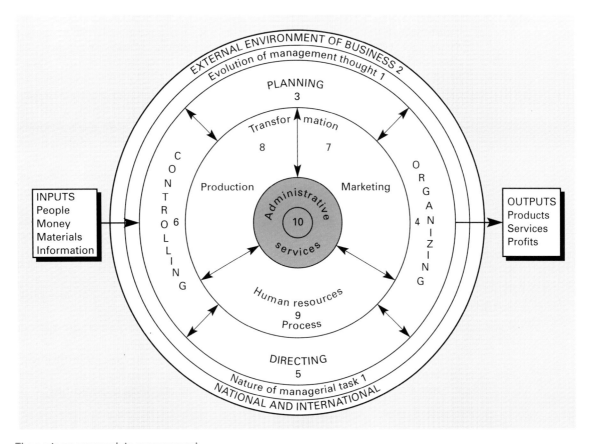

The systems approach to management

OBJECTIVES

Upon completing this chapter you should be able to:

- Understand the nature of administrative management and its role as a sub-system within the total environment of an enterprise;
- Appreciate that technological innovation will affect most aspects of office work and that managers should be aware of potential problems;
- Define the aim and scope of organization and methods in an office;
- Explain what is meant by electronic data interchange and discuss its potentially highly significant effect on office administrative functions.

The Institute of Administrative Management has defined office management as:

> that branch of management which is concerned with the services of obtaining, recording and analysing information, of planning, and of communicating, by means of which the management of a business safeguards its assets, promotes its affairs, and achieves its objectives.

The problems of the administrative manager are even greater today as new technology is increasing rapidly, bringing rapid change that involves people as well as working systems and newer machinery. These changes are well described by Clutterbuck and Hill in their book *The Re-making of Work* (Grant McIntyre, London, 1981). It covers the important areas of changing management styles, impact of technology, job sharing, flexi-time, etc., with examples from Europe, America and Japan, and examines the ways in which work will change, i.e. how our attitudes to work will change and how the traditional demarcation lines between full-time employment, part-time employment, unemployment and leisure will become increasingly blurred.

Technological change is affecting every industry and innovative ideas are needed for companies to compete effectively. Here the developments in communications and computers are linked very closely.

The word 'office' is not easy to define. It refers to work of a clerical nature which occurs to varying extents in every enterprise. It is convenient to refer to the office as a collection of departments carrying out clerical work.

An office can be said to comprise the following functions:

- receiving information, i.e. sorting, distributing, filing, entering up and posting;
- providing and arranging, i.e. rearranging information in a certain manner for management to act upon, also indexing and collating;
- communicating, i.e. typing, duplicating, photocopying, telephoning, teleprinting, mailing;
- control and protection of enterprise, inspecting, checking and auditing.

RESPONSIBILITY FOR OFFICE WORK

The person in charge may vary widely. He may be a secretary or accountant; some departmental heads may be in charge of their own clerical staffs.

There often is a central general office with one person in charge, who is responsible for the provision of clerical services throughout the enterprise. Such a person must be a specialist in this field as it calls for special skills and, in particular, a knowledge of alternative techniques by which results may be obtained. It also involves a knowledge of the economical use of office machines and the planning and co-ordinating of office procedures.

Such a person may be called the office manager and in a large enterprise his schedule of responsibilities may be as follows:

Schedule of responsibilities for office manager

Responsible to: Chief accountant.

Responsible for:

1 Advising and assisting departmental managers in the planning of clerical activities, including equipment, methods of work, supplies, personnel required and layout of office accommodation.
2 Scrutinizing all clerical procedures and the forms and stationery associated therewith, and making recommendations to the departmental managers concerned.
3 Maintaining the following general office services, including supervision of staff engaged therein:

- opening and distribution of inwards mail, collection and despatch of outwards mail;
- telephone, messenger and internal post services;
- central filing room;
- typing pool;
- duplicating section;
- stationery store.

4 Maintaining the Office Manual of Procedures and Forms and approving requisitions for office equipment and supplies for all departments, and establishing with the purchase manager a satisfactory procedure for their purchase.
5 Regularly reviewing office machinery and equipment with a view to its maintenance and replacement where necessary and reporting thereon to the chief accountant.
6 In association with departmental managers, establishing, in relation to clerical procedures, work schedules and output controls with a view to securing efficiency and economy in the use of clerical staff and the completion of routines to time.
7 Assisting the human resources manager in establishing satisfactory standards of welfare and grading arrangements for staff mentioned in item (1), informing him of expected vacancies in such staff and approving proposed appointments thereto.

Special responsibilities. Elimination of delays in clerical procedures in all departments, in association with managers thereof.

Limitations. No line authority over personnel other than those in item (1). No machinery or equipment costing over £2000 to be ordered without sanction of chief accountant.

PLANNING AND ORGANIZING THE OFFICE

Basic organization principles must be applied, bearing in mind that the position of the office in the hierarchy will vary with the type of enterprise. In small firms, responsibility for the position will form a part of the duties of another position, e.g. accountant. Where the volume of administration is great, e.g. banks and insurance companies, it may be a distinct section, possibly called office service department, under the direction of an administrative office manager.

Figure 10.1 shows such an organization.

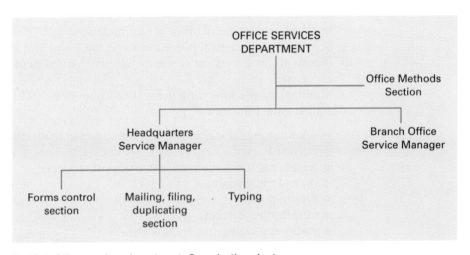

Fig 10.1 Office services department. Organization chart

Centralization and decentralization

As far as *office work* is concerned, *centralization* is desirable for the following reasons:

- there is economy of staff and machinery. Flexibility is improved as staff can more easily be moved to other work. Expensive machinery may be used economically;
- control is facilitated and standards of work can be made uniform;
- consultation and communication are easier and personal contact is possible;

- specialists can be employed. Where office work is confined to one building or location, it is possible to centralize the bulk of the clerical work. Where plant is in several locations more decentralization of office services may occur. In such a situation it is unlikely that accounting work will be decentralized as the more computers are used and the better the means of communication, the more accounting work can be centralized.

There are advantages of *decentralization of office work*:

- clerical work is better done near to the practical work to which it relates, since clerks are more likely to understand the implications of documents that they handle and are more likely to spot errors and obtain answers more easily;
- better service is given to department management.

Centralization of office services

Each of the main sections can be briefly considered:

1 **Typing/word processing.** The supervisor can ensure quality and uniformity of style. Work can be distributed evenly and experienced operators can be given more difficult work. Centralized dictation is possible which has the advantage that operators do not need to leave desks and transcription problems are avoided.

   This centralization is not too well liked by the operators, one of the main reasons being the lack of the human element. The 1993 EC Directive updates existing legislation regarding safety, health and welfare at work.

2 **Filing.** This again may be centralized or in departments.

   The main point to consider is – can a document be obtained in reasonable time? Where promptness is essential, e.g. for use on the telephone, department filing is needed.

3 **Duplicating and office printing.** Duplicating machines in departments are rarely fully used. Centralization can therefore make good use of expensive specialized equipment, which may be used and maintained by skilled operators. Small machines, e.g. photocopiers, may conveniently be used by departments.

Selection of office site

The main points to consider are:

- there must be space for employees and equipment and also for expansion in the future;
- the need to locate office services near to manufacturing or sales departments or to customers for convenience. Also proximity to banks and transport facilities;
- availability of labour and cost of premises (to rent or buy). A Location of Offices Bureau was set up in 1963 to provide information and help to firms that wish to leave the centre of a congested London. Outside London there were at the time lower building costs and cheaper rent, and it was consid-

ered healthier for staff. There is now a considerable amount of empty office space in London, and costs are therefore being reduced. On the other hand, premises away from town centres may suffer from communication problems, difficulty in obtaining specialist staff required and a possible loss of prestige.

Layout of office

After acquiring the building, the layout of departments must be studied. The following factors should be noted:

- large open spaces are more desirable than a series of small rooms;
- as much natural light should be used as possible;
- the chief executives may be given private rooms, situated near each other for convenience of consultation. This may not be so very important when closed-circuit television becomes more widespread;
- the flow of work should be facilitated by arranging departments in accordance with the normal work flow wherever possible;
- machines should be preferably kept out of general offices as their noise may distract.

The environment must be considered. There are statutory requirements laid down which, briefly, require the following minimum standards:

- temperature to be over 16°C (60.8°F) by one hour after the office opens;
- minimum of 400 cubic feet of space per worker;
- other rules include ventilation, lighting, washing, eating facilities, fencing of machinery, first aid and fire precautions.

Other important factors include the careful use of colour, which can influence morale and efficiency. Noise is always a problem, but acoustical cabinets enclosing machines, thick floor coverings and rubber-tipped chair legs and glass partitions help a great deal to absorb or mitigate noise.

Open offices

The traditional office building had a lot of wasted space. In open-plan offices a saving of space of about 33 per cent has been claimed, plus cheaper maintenance and cleaning because of no interior walls.

The main arguments in favour of open planning are increased flexibility of layout, economies of cost in building and running, and easier communication, administration and supervision.

A study was made by the Pilkington Research Unit into the design and performance of office buildings. The team consisted of an architect, psychologist, geographer and physicist. They investigated open-plan offices and some of their findings were:

- large offices have too many distractions;
- management became involved in routine matters;
- absence of 'status' symbols tended to lower morale of ambitious staff and the feeling emerged that they were likely to be forgotten in the mass of people around them;
- supervisors thought *esprit de corps* and discipline were adversely affected.

Another development, the *landscaped office* or, as it is known in the United Kingdom, *Panoramic Office Planning* (POP), differs from open-planning in a few ways. It is said to overcome the disadvantages of open-planning. This type of office, which is being used by a number of large firms, has a high standard of equipment and furnishings. Desks are placed in a rather random fashion and the use of acoustic screens, filing cabinets and plants breaks up the floor area. Status is served by allocating more space and better furnishings to supervisory staff. Noise and distraction are reduced greatly by furnishings and careful arranging of equipment.

Within each work area, an individual can have his own personal arrangement of screens, etc., and rest periods are not fixed, but the rest area at one end of the floor can be used whenever required. This rest area provides light refreshment and comfortable seating. These facilities have not been found to be abused.

ORGANIZATION AND METHODS (O AND M)

In many companies the office manager may not have the time to review specific clerical procedures in depth. This has led to the establishment of advisory services, with a full-time staff whose object is the analysis of administrative practices. The Civil Service a number of years ago set up departments known as 'Organization and Methods'. This term is now widespread, although the work of such departments may be done in sections called clerical work study or systems and procedures. There is as yet no accepted terminology in this field. The emphasis, in practice, is more on method than on organization.

O and M is a section of specialized staff which investigates systems in an office and tries to re-design and replace them with a more efficient or economical system.

There are advantages in such an appointment:

- such specialist staff can give undivided attention to the work whereas this is not easy for an office manager;
- the O and M team can be regarded as impartial, and can therefore view work objectively;
- they can obtain and apply specialized knowledge of systems and machines.

Qualities required in an O and M specialist are mainly an inquiring mind and the tenacity to keep a problem in mind until it is solved. He must be original in outlook and have tact and patience and be able to express himself clearly both orally and in writing. The other requirements can be learnt, and cover:

- background knowledge of company, its policy, products and services;
- knowledge of organizational structure;
- knowledge of office equipment in broad outline and knowledge of where to get more detailed information;
- basic office methods – he must know office practices for every section in which he is likely to be concerned;
- O and M techniques – the theory and practice of these techniques can be

taught. These include methods design and form design and will be mentioned later in more detail.

It is important to remember that O and M is purely an advisory section and ideally should report to the senior executive responsible for offices in an enterprise. Such a person may be a financial director, secretary, accountant or office manager.

The selection of suitable assignments is important. When the section begins work, it is preferable to give it assignments which are likely to produce profitable savings. Often the section must wait until it is called in by the management to deal with problems, but it can suggest to management areas in which it can be of assistance.

Costs of the O and M service should be kept and one method adopted is to charge the cost for the service to the department which has received benefit.

Members of the team may come from different backgrounds, e.g. accounting, engineering. Often each member specializes in one field, e.g. office machines. O and M departments have been set up for different reasons and vary widely in organization, so they have varying duties and responsibilities.

O and M may report to the accountant, especially if the section arose from internal audit. There may not, though, be objective application of O and M recommendations if they affect the chief accountant's area of work, so it is deemed preferable to make the section responsible to an independent executive, often the managing director.

Method of investigation

Where the department is called in to do a project:

1 The leader of the O and M team should talk over the job with the department head concerned and make a brief survey of the work involved, and then agree the aims and obtain 'terms of reference' for the assignment, to whom he/she is to report, and in what manner.
2 The O and M staff are allocated to parts of the job.
3 After the introduction of the O and M staff to departments and personnel involved, procedures are studied.
4 Reports are collated and the team prepare a revised procedure.
5 When the new procedure is ready, it is offered for criticism to colleagues and management and any revisions are then made.
6 The new system must be 'sold' to the department concerned. First the outline, then the details must be placed open for criticism and comment, i.e. by the staff, and often a specimen run-through of the system is a great help.
7 A detailed schedule of equipment and staff etc. is needed, and having been already prepared, the procedure is installed. It may be necessary to run the old and the new system together for a short while; this will enable staff to obtain experience and any problems can be sorted out.
8 A few months later, the procedure should be followed up to see if everything is performing correctly.

Ascertaining present procedure

The main methods used are:

Procedure narrative. This is a step by step statement of the procedure showing the person's name, type of action performed, e.g. posting, sorting, and a brief description of action taken, e.g. invoice checked.

Methods analysis. This is similar, but symbols are used to represent various types of operation, e.g. typing, sorting, transporting. These are noted in columns, so that by looking at these symbols a better picture of the operations can be seen, and unnecessary operations can be spotlighted.

Procedure or flow chart. This shows the movement of the forms and documents between members of staff and departments. Columns are drawn vertically representing departments in an office, documents are pictured by rectangles and their movements between departments indicated by horizontal arrows. This pictorial means of analysis can be used either on its own or in conjunction with procedure narrative or method analysis sheets.

String diagram. Desks and people are depicted on paper, and the flow of movement is noted by drawing lines, or by using string between pins. This method makes it easy to see if any doubling-back of documents, etc., occurs.

Specimen chart. A simple form of chart can be prepared by completing actual documents used in a procedure and pasting them on a large board in their order of preparation. Coloured tapes can be used to show movement and brief notes of operations may be made. Some standard symbols used in charting are shown in Fig 10.2.

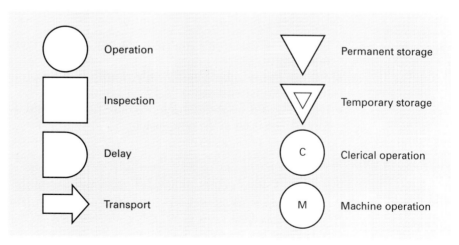

Fig 10.2 Standard charting symbols

Forms design and control

There is a mass of information in business and most of it can be recorded and communicated by putting it on paper. Most documents created for this purpose are forms, which are standard documents with descriptive matter and the use of them establishes a routine method of dealing with information.

Principles in form design

- The number of operations necessary in the use of the form should be reduced.
- The form must be easy to read and to use.
- The number of copies and the number of forms should be reduced. This can be done by designing forms to serve more than one purpose.
- The layout of the form must be such that it is related to other documents with which it will be used.
- Appearance must be attractive with entries easily made and instructions easily read. Colour should be used with care.
- The form must be large enough to contain all information required; any limits because of its use with machines must be noted, in addition to postal regulations and mailing and filing facilities.
- Instructions and identification. Titles should be concise, the form reference number and destination should be clearly visible.
- Paper and printing. The quality of the paper should be considered. This depends upon the use of the form. If it will be handled a lot, thick paper is needed. In addition, its use on duplicators may mean the use of special paper. Entries may be made by pen or machine, the paper surface must be suitable for these entries.
- Spaces for entries should be adequate and in the most natural order for use. Every fifth line may be thicker for guidance and columns for ticking or inserting notes allowed for.

Forms control

Forms control is vitally important. To initiate forms control, one person should be given the job to set up and maintain an efficient system of forms control. Steps in setting up such control may be as follows:

- inform staff that forms control is starting and that no new forms should be released;
- all new forms to be issued by the forms office which initially needs copies of every form in existence;
- forms should be standardized where possible and a register kept of all forms to be used in the new system.

Work measurement

It is not as simple to introduce work measurement in the office as it is in the factory. Some work is non-repetitive and an appropriate unit is not easy to establish. Standard rates of working are not easy to make as interruptions occur at varying intervals, e.g. phone calls. It may be possible to measure at least 50 per cent of the work in the office and the following methods are used:

Simple timing. This involves studying a number of average clerks doing repetitive work and setting a standard, e.g. 600 lines of typing per day.

Recording devices. These may be used on machines (e.g. tapometers) which register the number of key depressions or taps. Documents could be weighed. Audio-typists' work could be measured by the number of inches of dictated tape, or by pages typed.

Activity sampling. This consists of random observations taken periodically and is based upon the law of statistical regularity. It enables the time spent on various activities to be noted.

Predetermined motion time systems. Gilbreth's basic divisions of the fundamental motions were the forerunners of these systems.

In these methods, elements of an operation are described according to various physical and mental factors and, by analysing a job and dividing it into its basic motions, each motion receives a time value which is obtained from a table; when these are totalled, the *standard time* is obtained.

There are more than twelve methods available for determining standard time data, but the basic techniques are essentially the same. Two of these are Master Clerical Data and Methods Time Measurement.

Variable Factor Programming (VFP). This method uses a different approach. It was developed by the Wofac Corporation in America. The emphasis is on using measurement primarily as a psychological rather than a mechanical stimulus to greater productivity.

It can be applied to all forms of 'indirect' ancillary work, e.g. spares maintenance as well as the office. It is a technique for improving the work flow of indirect departments and eliminating idle time. It begins by measuring each activity the worker performs and setting a target time for each task. The total man hours needed and the manpower requirements can then be found. Work can then be programmed so that there is a smoother flow and idle time is at a minimum. Supervision is vitally important and there must be proper training for supervisors to implement the scheme, which comprises the following steps:

1 The work content is evaluated. Each member of the department lists the work performed by him. Data are then co-ordinated and definitions standardized.
2 Jobs are timed by workers and averaged over about four weeks. All breaks are noted, e.g. telephone calls, and reasonable target times are set.
3 Work is assigned in batches to control work flow and work not completed in the time fixed is investigated. Another method of control is for employees to record the time taken against the target time. Daily and weekly reports are sent to the supervisor.
4 *Variable manning tables* can be drawn up, based upon target time; these give the work load in man hours and from these the number of staff required can be estimated.

It is more suitable for repetitive work, but it has been applied to drawing offices and research laboratories with reasonable success. Projects, for example, can be noted and estimated times contained. There is a big problem in 'selling' the idea to workers and unions; if this can be done there can be large savings and greater job satisfaction.

Group Capacity Assessment (GCA). This has already been adopted by a number of firms in the United Kingdom. Its purpose, like VFP, is to analyse labour costs and reduce them where necessary. Its origin is again in America where the accounting consultants, Ernst and Young, perfected the idea of measuring *groups* rather than individuals.

In a cashier's or purchasing department, measurement of the work of an individual would produce a standard for him alone; such a standard would not be appropriate for others in the section because of the variety of jobs performed in it. But if the work of small groups is measured collectively, results can be collated for *each department.*

Analysts must be carefully trained, they are then divided into teams and given a department or group to assess.

Their work has two stages:

1 All tasks are defined and the number of times they are performed weekly determined. The rate of work on each element is then compared with that of a reasonably competent operator and a *standard time* is fixed for a group of people.
2 Man hours can then be calculated by multiplying the number of work units (of output) by the standard time for each type of task (i.e. each work unit). Over- or under-staffing is then apparent.

The advantages of this system are:

- manpower planning can be forecast more accurately;
- jobs can be more accurately evaluated and skills better utilized, e.g. skilled personnel may be doing simple clerical tasks;
- inefficiency is spotlighted, labour costs can be reduced, and staff morale can be improved.

OFFICE MACHINERY AND EQUIPMENT

Media of office communications

Office services comprise specialized activities, e.g. communication, filing, mailing and duplicating, which can be usually most effectively administered when centralized.

We will consider the essential features of each type of equipment and methods used, stressing advantages and disadvantages and other considerations to be noted when considering their purchase or use.

Selecting the means of office communication needs careful attention to the following factors:

- **speed and cost** – Will the extra cost for greater speed of delivery warrant the use of a particular medium? Does the frequency of using the medium influence the cost?
- **secrecy** – Is this essential?
- **responsibility** – Should responsibility for receipt be fixed by having it in written form with a copy retained?
- **error** – Does the possibility of error or misunderstanding make it necessary to have written rather than oral communications?

A simple start to the problem of effective communications is to decide first which communications must be in writing and which may be orally transmitted. The oral grouping is then divided into urgent and not so urgent; then those frequently used and those infrequently used. Then prepare a list of media of transmitting oral communications and study each method from the viewpoint of cost, speed and effectiveness.

The same process is followed with written communications.

Communications may be written and oral and transmitted both within and without an organization.

1. Written communication

Internal communications may be between offices or departments and of the nature of special and routine reports and data, etc. The volume of communications under each heading will determine which of the following methods are used:

- personal messenger – training and supervising may be costly;
- conveyor systems – used where volume of work is great and the following systems may be used:

  1 pneumatic tubes – container is sent to various centres by means of compressed air;
  2 conveyor belts – folders travel along motor-driven belts;
  3 vertical lift and chain wire conveyors;

- text produced by typewriter, word processor, teleprinter, electronic mail, telex, fax and radio-pager with LCD display.

We will now turn our attention to external written communications. Correspondence must conform to certain standards, these are easier to standardize if the work is centralized. *Centralized dictation* offers a simple way to increase office efficiency and has three main advantages:

- executive can dictate with minimum effort and delay;
- central pool means fewer typists than dictators;
- smoother work flow increases typing productivity.

The main systems of making written communications will be considered.

Dictating machines

Dictating systems may use a PAX network (private automatic exchange, i.e. the internal telephone system); the PABX network (private automatic branch exchange) or a separate wired system.

- PAX is generally the most economical, flexible and satisfactory when installed, as dictating points are readily available where an internal telephone exists and, by a push-button system, the dictator can have instantaneous communication.
- PABX dictation is not so satisfactory or so common as dictation may collide with external calls.
- Separately-wired systems entail higher installation costs but give excellent service, especially if the amount of dictation is great.

The audio-typing room may have recordings set out in a *single bank* of instruments, or in a *tandem* arrangement, where a typist has two machines. Transcription is made from one, while the other receives incoming material; this arrangement allows communication between dictator and typist.

The nature of the job will help to decide the best recording medium. It is usually *magnetic tape*.

Control facilities for these machines are basically similar. They are for starting, stopping, playback and correction. Most systems have provision for correction by the dictator by over-speaking and where provision is made for after-hours service this enables executives to dictate letters when working late. Other common features include intercom between dictator and transcriber, voice operated start/stop mechanism, visible and audible signals to handle urgent dictation, automatic indexing. A choice depends upon cost, suitability and balancing facilities offered.

Capital cost may be recouped in a year by the saving, on average, of a 40 per cent reduction in typing staff. Dictators must use the machines properly, otherwise there is delay and cost of alterations.

Facsimile reproduction and transmission

An exact duplicate of anything written, drawn or typed is transmitted between two distant points. A scanner passes over the surface, the light and dark areas are converted into corresponding impulses. At the receiving end a marking device governed by these impulses 'burns' a duplicate image on specially prepared paper.

Teleprinters and telex systems

A *teleprinter* is a machine fitted with a typewriter keyboard which is connected by telegraph wire to a similar machine. Messages typed at one machine are reproduced simultaneously on the other machine. Teleprinters are rented and are used *within* the individual firm and the rental varies with the distance between the machines. Once the rental is paid, calls may be made as often as required.

Telex is a kind of teleprinter connected to a public teleprinter system, where calls can be made to any other telex subscriber in the United Kingdom or overseas. A flat rental is paid plus a charge per call depending upon length and distance. Punched cards or paper tape can be transmitted by installing tape or card converters. There will be in the future a great increase in transmission speeds and a steady increase in the number of 'real-time' systems.

Real-time systems   These reduce the delays associated with entering data into the computer by connecting the communications channel directly (on-line) to the computer via control units. These real-time systems are able to process data at the instant they are transmitted from the remote point and send a reply in seconds. One example of this use is *airline booking systems*, where a booking clerk types a question on a console which is linked to a computer and receives a reply within seconds.

Routine paperwork can be cut immensely by such systems. In the field of insurance, a computer can assess risks, calculate premiums and print insurance certificates. Agents can type normal proposal forms on a combined policy schedule and certificate of insurance document. As the details are typed, they are transmitted simultaneously to a computer, which checks the proposal's acceptability, calculates a premium and transmits terms back to the agent's office, where they are automatically typed on the policy and certificate. Costs, though, are very high.

2. Oral communication

Telephone   Except for small offices, most systems require the use of a switchboard, so that several incoming and outgoing calls may be handled simultaneously. PAX and PABX have been mentioned. The main deciding factor as to which method is used will be the ratio of internal calls to external calls at different extensions. If all extensions need outgoing facilities frequently, PABX or PMBX (Private Manual Branch Exchange) may be used.

Answering machines are connected to the telephone and will answer the call and record any dictated message. These are recorded on magnetic tape and can be played back later by the person or persons interested.

Intercommunica-   These relieve the telephone switchboard. Some permit one-way, others two-
tion (intercom)   way, communications. There are two main types:
systems

1 Telephone type installations, independent of regular telephone service.
2 Electronic devices using principles of radio.

Telephone installations usually operate on a battery or transformer and calls can be sent by pressing a button to call in another office, where there is a similar machine which enables the conversation to be heard through a loudspeaker. Conversation may be two-way or one-way. They are direct and private and there are no operator delays. Conferences among any number of executives are possible without anyone leaving his desk.

Staff location or paging systems

- Loudspeakers; messages are relayed over all premises at once. This, though, may be distracting.
- Bells and buzzers.
- Radio paging. The executive carries a small radio connected with the closed circuit of the firm. A call transmitted on an executive's wavelength is made and a buzzer indicates the call; the executive may then go to a telephone or may be able to reply direct into a two-way radio. Alternatively, a message may be displayed.
- Mobile telephones.

Closed circuit television

Two-way sound can be added. This method is becoming cheaper; it eliminates the need to duplicate records and files, permits centralized record keeping, gives instantaneous transmission of recorded information, enabling it to be verified, identified or computed.

3. Telecommunications

The use of a telephone line to connect a remote terminal to a central computer has led to a number of important developments such as:

- a single high-powered computer serving an entire national or multinational company;
- a service bureau serving clients spread over a wide area;
- computerized airline reservation and other specialized systems.

In consequence, telephone lines are used to transmit data across countries and continents while space satellites are used to transmit data across oceans.

All terminals have the capacity to initiate the transmission of data to a central computer and to print or display data received from it. Many of the so-called 'intelligent' terminals, also have the capacity for some data processing. Some merely apply checks to data; others are capable of extensive data processing. Where there is a computer terminal, the opportunity exists to decide what processing is appropriate to the central, more powerful installation, with the high cost for computer time and transmission, and what is appropriate to the comparatively low-cost terminal.

Despite the option to use local computers, the volume of data transmission to central computers is increasing. It has been estimated that by 1995 the number of terminals, with a substantial proportion of them intelligent, was approaching $1q\text{-}\Sigma$ million in Europe alone; it will not be long before 100 000 million words, say the equivalent of a million novels, are transmitted in Europe every day.

Data can be transmitted by public telephone lines or by leased telephone lines. Leased lines have the advantage of being more reliable and less subject to data corruption; moreover, they are cheaper with sufficient volume, say of the order of six or more hours a day. However, the use of either kind of line requires the employment of sophisticated equipment, some of which is described below.

The change from electro-mechanical switchboards to electronic exchanges, coupled with the effect of the British Telecommunications Act 1981, markedly changed the whole area of telecommunications. Until the 1981 Act, British Telecom had a monopoly of the telephone network and of the supply of most types of equipment that could be connected to it. The Act allows other companies to compete with British Telecom. Users can *own* the equipment and not only *rent* it, as in the past. The private sector can now be licensed by the Secretary of State for Industry to provide independent telecommunication services in addition to equipment. An example is Mercury Communications. British Telecom can also license private sector organizations.

4. Other office services

Filing

Careful thought is needed in determining a system of filing. In all cases local conditions and problems must be examined to decide on the most appropriate system.

Questions to be considered are:

- How valuable is the record?
- How long does the record have to be kept?
- How quickly must a record be produced when required?
- Which departments may need to use the record?

The answers will help to determine the method of classifying files. Generally speaking, those with similar characteristics will be filed together.

The main methods of classification are alphabetical, numerical, geographical, subject, chronological, or combinations of these.

The essentials of a good filing system comprise:

- *economy* – in money cost, labour and overhead cost;
- *simplicity and accessibility* – simple to understand and operate and sited so that records are easily inserted or extracted;
- *compactness and safety* – it should take up minimum space and important documents given special protection;
- the system should be *capable of easy expansion* and records should be readily available;
- filing should be kept *up to date*, cross-references being used where necessary, and the most appropriate system of classification used.

Filing equipment

1 **Vertical** filing is the most common method used. Documents are filed behind each other, on edge; also they may be in pockets individually suspended. A file drawer when extended uses valuable space; to overcome this there are variations on this theme:

- *Open-shelf filing*, in which the folders are on shelves, visibility is unlimited, filing is quicker and more compact.
- *Roll-out filing*, in which drawers roll out sideways exposing all records in half the aisle required by vertical drawer files.

2 **Horizontal** filing is used for storing papers such as maps or drawings in a flat position, on top of each other.

3 **Lateral** filing consists of suspended files with the *end* of each file in view, which bears the index strip.

4 **Visible card** filing equipment is available in the form of trays that lie flat horizontally in a cabinet, on revolving racks, or in loose-leaf binders. Signalling devices may be effectively used on the edges of the cards which are visible at all times. Cards can be located and entries made quickly.

5 **Rotary card** filing equipment is a variation of the visible card equipment. The cards are attached to a belt or series of rings which surround the centre of a rotating wheel. Desks may be especially constructed to keep wheels in a vertical or horizontal position. Other systems are available and are based upon the principle that it is more efficient to have the work brought to the worker than to have the worker go to work.

Records retention

There should be a definite policy regarding retention of filed material, destruction or microfilming. Some material must be kept for the legal period of six years for simple contracts, twelve for contracts under seal, etc. Whatever method is adopted, it should be made clear to all and efficiently carried out.

Microphotography

Photographs may be taken of records and they can be reduced in size and stored in a very small area. Microfilming records may save filing cabinet space of up to 90 per cent. They are usually stored in one of two main forms; in very small 100-foot reels containing 600 frames, or in *aperture cards*. Aperture cards are thin, flexible manilla cards similar to punched cards. The film is processed and fixed on the card, which has reference data punched on it, which can then be sorted and processed by automatic machines. About 75,000 of these can be stored in a normal four-drawer filing cabinet. With a reader-printer enlarged copies of any document can be quickly reproduced from the reel of film, or shown on a screen. Retrieval speeds and methods are being constantly improved. It has been estimated that sufficient economies can be achieved in one year to repay the cost of an installation. Some firms buy only the reproduction equipment, and have the photographing and processing done by a service company.

Whatever system of filming is adopted, the records must be protected. Methods include fire-resisting safes and vaults, dispersal of essential records and duplication of vital documents.

Mailing

An important supplement to correspondence, transcription and records management is the efficient handling of mail, which comprises incoming, outgoing and inter-departmental mail. No matter what size of firm the job must be done efficiently and economically, making the best use of staff and space.

The *situation* of the post room is important. It should be as near as possible to the ground floor. The next item to consider is the number of temporary or permanent staff and the extent to which mechanization can be usefully employed. There are inevitably 'peaks and troughs' of workflow and this can be helped by mechanization. Procedures must be established for incoming and outgoing mail and full use should be made of available machines of which the following is a brief summary.

Before posting, letters must be folded, inserted in an envelope, sealed and the postage charge accounted for in one way or another.

1 **Folding, inserting and sealing machines.** These machines can produce a neat consistent fold or a number of folds. Some machines can fold the main enclosure, then insert a second enclosure inside the fold. The price of this model is of course rather high. Other machines slit, score or perforate if necessary. Inserting machines usually have attachments that seal also.

2 **Franking machines** make the laborious task of sticking stamps redundant. They operate quickly, obviate the need for storing and guarding stamps, tearing, moistening and sticking them. The machine is purchased from manufacturers who are licensed by the Post Office (PO). A lever on the machine can be set for the desired postage; before it can be used, payment for the required amount of stamps to be used must be made to the PO. When this number is reached, the machine locks. Dials record postage used and sometimes unused postage.

    The organization's trademark, or slogan or advertising message can also be imprinted beside the stamp impression. Franked mail now accounts for nearly one-third of the PO's postal revenue. One model feeds, seals, franks, counts and stacks letters at a rate well over 5000 an hour. Machines exist which do everything, i.e. collate, insert, seal, print advertisements, etc., meter the postage, count and stack at a rate of over 7000 per hour.

3 **Letter openers and scales** are useful. Some openers are automatic, opening several hundred letters in a few minutes, and they can also feed and stack. Scales for weighing letters are needed to assess correctly the postage for packets and parcels.

A high level of automation is now attainable in the mailroom. There are a wide range of small table top units on the market to automate the process of folding, inserting, collating and sealing. Most companies install their first paper handling equipment to dispatch invoices more quickly, to improve their flow of cash.

As there are many micros, minis and small business computers in use, an increasing number of companies are installing forms handling equipment, such as bursters and guillotines, to remove sprocket holes and convert continuous stationery into separate documents.

The power of the computer can be harnessed to pre-handle mailing material to qualify for reduced postal charges. For example, if the computer is programmed to produce mailing material in postal code areas, the Post Office will give a rebate on mailings of more than 4250 envelopes. Some companies have claimed savings of up to 30 per cent on postage bills.

Bar codes printed by the computer on selected documents enable great selectivity to be practised in mailings. The latest advance in automated in-line mailing systems is microprocessor control enabling up to 23 machine functions to be combined to create 10 different programs, thus giving great flexibility to change from one electronic mailing job to another.

5. Reproduction

Reproduction services in offices are increasingly important as conventional clerical help is costly, information is needed more quickly and technical improvements in duplicating and copying machines have made it cheap to obtain almost perfect reproductions.

In selecting the proper equipment from a very wide range, the suitability of the type of copy must be considered, plus cost, speed, ease of operation, servicing facilities and durability. Proper supervision is essential and this may mean centralization. A study of costs within the department should be made as compared with the costs of using outside agencies.

In some organizations a reproduction department is set up, use being made of outside printers or, in some cases, an organization will have its own printing department.

Reproduction services can be classed as duplicating, copying and imprinting.

6. Data Processing (DP)

A DP system involves the use of a computer and related equipment for analysing and recording many facts. Data are obtained from numerous sources and are processed quickly by being converted into a code consisting of electrical impulses. The code is based upon binary language, that is, a number system using two as its base instead of ten, as in the decimal system.

Input media are read into the control processing unit, treated mathematically, classified, sorted and stored. Data may be read into the processing unit by magnetic tape, paper tape, punched cards or cathode scanners. Output may take the form of magnetic or paper tape, punched cards or automatic printing on business forms and reports.

The computer is an integrated system of electronics which computes mathematical operations and retrieves information at speeds of around one millionth of a second or less.

Digital computers count numbers (e.g. trip mileage on a car).

Analogue computers are used mainly in scientific research and measure physical variables, e.g. voltage or speed (e.g. the speedometer of a car).

Business processing involves the digital computer. To be called a computer, equipment should:

- be automatic in action and have the power to obey stored instructions;
- be able to discriminate between different courses of action and operate at electronic speed.

Figure 10.3 shows the five components of a computer. These components are:

1 Input   This consists of data to be processed and the instructions to process the data. *Programmers* plan the logical arrangement, sequence, and correlation of data from various sources. The sequence of instruction to the computer is called the program.

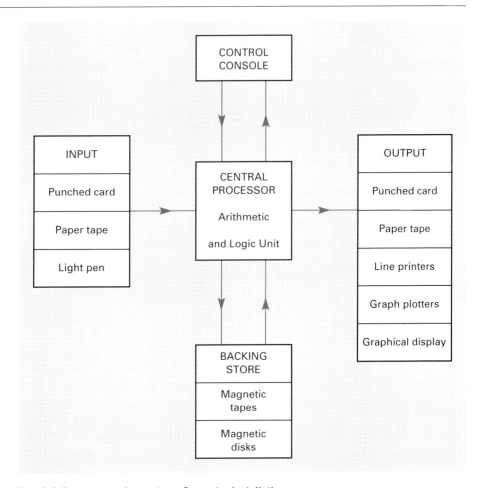

Fig 10.3 Data processing system. Computer installation

The following media may be used in preparing the input from the source of data: punched cards, punched tape, magnetic disks and drums, optical scanners, magnetic ink character readers, a console typewriter.

Some input media can be read directly into the control and the processing units, others may need to convert the data on punched cards or tape to magnetic tape; or, to adapt input media to the type of equipment used. If magnetic disks are used, *random access* is possible, i.e. the retrieval of data quickly from any portion of the disk. Punched cards and tapes are cheaper and adaptable, but are bulky, susceptible to damage and unable to hold large amounts of data, they are also slow in use. They are rarely used now.

2 Storage   This unit is often called the memory and retains input in coded form until called forward for processing or to be 'read out' . Data are stored *internally* by magnetic cores (hard disk), or *externally* in the form of floppy disks, punched cards, paper tape, magnetic drums or tape, until ready to be read into the computer.

3 Arithmetic unit (or processing unit)	Data are mathematically manipulated according to the program.
4 Output unit	This unit deals with results of the computing operations. The manner and position of printing are determined by the instructions. The results may be on a formal report or document or statement, or in a form for subsequent processing.

It may be useful to have results presented in the form of a graph or diagram. If the computer is connected to a *graphical display* unit, this unit then traces the image with a spot of light on the face of a cathode-ray tube. It can also be used as a combined input system in conjunction with a device known as a *light pen*. An engineering drawing can be displayed on the television screen and by using the light pen the designer can make amendments or additions on the screen. The computer will then execute alterations. Another feature is a *graphical output* which can be obtained when pen and paper move to trace out a diagram or graph.

On-line output means that the printing devices are operated *directly* from the computer and results are immediately available.

Off-line output refers to the results punched into cards or paper or magnetic tape. These are then placed in printing machines which are *separate* from the computer.

As printing is usually done mechanically, speeds are far slower than the electronic speeds of the computer, so storage devices are needed to accumulate data until the output unit can deal with them.

5 Control unit	A control unit interprets instructions recorded on input media, directs the various processing operations and checks to see instructions are correctly carried out. This unit directs the receipt of information in the storage unit, stores the intermediate results, and releases the information when needed in the arithmetic operations.
Some other terms used	Data. Basic facts about business activities, e.g. material used on a job, hours worked by staff.

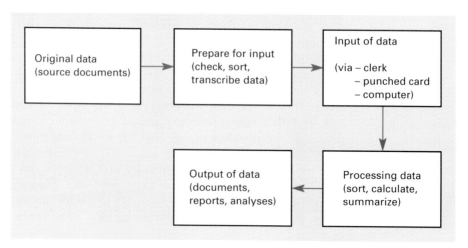

Fig 10.4 **Stages of processing data**

Data processing . Collecting all items of source data and converting them into information for processing, by manual, mechanical or electronic methods (Fig 10.4).

A direct data entry system is a visual display unit plus keyboard. Data are keyed in by the operator and shown on the screen and entered in the computer for processing. Another method is to key in data and print a record of transactions (e.g. in banks and building societies).

A point of sale terminal is an electronic cash register linked to a computer. These are becoming very common and can, for example, immediately check the availability of stock, current prices, or the credit position of a customer.

Data transmission is a term used to denote transmission by telecommunication systems linking a terminal with a central computer.

Real-time processing involves entering data in a computer and this is processed immediately, files are updated, giving current position (as in airline booking systems).

Microcomputer. This is basically a small computer which is smaller than a minicomputer. The popular PC (personal computer) is a microcomputer. In many cases, configurations vary so much that the same terms could be used. Once improvements in telecommunications occurred, the commercial use of minis and micros expanded greatly. They can be installed at a number of different sites; this aids decentralization.

A microprocessor forms part of a microcomputer and consists of an arithmetic unit, control unit and memory. Basically it is the same as the Central Processing Unit (CPU) of a large computer. The size is very small due to the circuits being stored on a small silicon chip.

The simplest form of minicomputer is a microprocessor, with a keyboard for input, display screen for output. Other peripheral equipment can be added, e.g. magnetic tape cassettes and floppy disk drives and character or line printers.

Modem. Device connecting the computer to a telephone line along which data may be sent to another distant computer terminal or one not part of the same network system.

Software is a term used to describe all programs supplied by manufacturers or specialists for use in a computer.

Hardware refers to basic machines in a computer system consisting of input and output devices, central processing unit and other storage devices.

Time-sharing. By using a terminal and sharing expensive computer time, a number of persons can use a computer simultaneously, thus reducing costs.

Procedure to determine whether to install a machine

The procedure to determine whether to install a machine may vary a little in detail depending upon the type of machine, but the main points are relevant to all machines.

1 An initial survey can be carried out by the staff of the organization or by a machine company. Usually a special *steering committee* is formed and they are asked to make recommendations on the feasibility of using new equipment.

2 Once a broad decision has been taken to proceed, a special *study group* can be formed, using existing personnel who may be relieved of normal duties, to make a full, detailed investigation of all sections of the firm and all types of available equipment.

3 A *complete examination of existing systems* and methods is required and progress periodically reported to the steering committee. This report will include detailed costs of equipment, accommodation, staff required, operating and running, ease of operation and flexibility of equipment, and potential savings, e.g. where a computer replaces keyboard machines. Other items include experience of manufacturer and servicing arrangements.

4 The *final report* and recommendations will be made to the steering committee for consideration, which will have to bear in mind the future overall policy and objectives of the organization before recommending a course of action to the board. Such a report may include – advantages to be gained, the best type of equipment to be installed, whether to buy or rent, estimate of total cost, depreciation and rental charges, site of installation and staffing, and the position in the organization of the new section.

This section may be placed under the control of an existing department, e.g. accountancy, or it may act as an independent service bureau to the rest of the organization, under its own manager. The installation of a computer can have a major effect on the company using it. An integrated management information system is needed and organizational structure must be reappraised.

Databases

Data can be stored easily in a computer. Master data files (databases) can be shared by a number of programs and systems. A large permanent mass store is required and must be permanently on-line, and organized in such a way that access can be made quickly. Databases are commonly stored on a mainframe 'host' computer, but are compiled for specialist third party suppliers such as Dunn and Bradstreet. The end-user pays the 'host' for the amount of time he has been connected to the mainframe, who then passes royalties on to the supplier. Examples of on-line databases are Data Star and Eurolex.

These 'storehouses of facts' can be accessed by computers coupled to an ordinary telephone line. There are many kinds of databases covering most areas of human knowledge. An office manager may wish to use, for example:

- business databases – giving exchange rates, commodities, etc.;
- stock market databases – giving details of companies;
- lexis database – covering all the latest court decisions.

The desk-top personal computer's great increase in power and adaptability coupled with improved communications software and standardization of telecommunication links, has made end-users aware of databases and encouraged organizations to set up many varying types. For instance, market research can be made very efficient and economical as data can be 'down loaded' on to a personal computer and used by staff in varying locations.

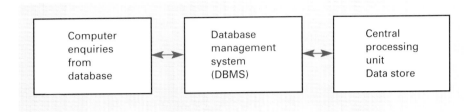

A database management system can organize, process and present selected data elements from the database, which can be held either within an organization (internal database) or externally, as in the above illustration. An example will show the benefits of the system. Assume a request is made to a large multinational company from a customer for an engineer familiar with a special type of engine. The engine was last made by the company eight years ago. The person sent to the customer abroad must speak German and be willing to go abroad. A properly set up database showing personnel records in detail would show date of employment, educational background, work experience and language ability. By using an on-line terminal, personnel records can be searched and names of suitable employees obtained to fill the overseas assignment.

Office information system

This is part of the total information system. Procedures and rules are set out for many activities in the office environment, other activities are dealt with by staff on a more personal, varied and informal basis.

Information about an organization can be kept very conveniently in computer systems which can give access to data immediately. Some organizations are now using modern technological developments, others are many years away from considering their use.

The main aims of these developments are to:

- provide information that *could not* be obtained before;
- provide accurate data, *when* it is required;
- help to do jobs more *efficiently*;
- allow a *wider range* of tasks to be performed;
- present data in a more understandable way (e.g. graphics/colour).

Advantages of office automation

- *Reduction in costs* of staff and equipment.
- *Greater* volume of total work completed.
- *Increase in availability* and accuracy of information.
- *Updating* of data is quicker.
- *Communication* between persons far apart is more efficient.
- *Access* to data available from many locations, e.g. home and office.
- More *time* available for main area of work of individual (less time on communicating, filing, retrieving).

As many of the above advantages cannot be so easily quantified, this may mean a slower interest in their development.

In commerce today, office practices are being made more cost-effective by microelectronics. This includes modifications to existing machines, e.g. photocopiers, calculators, accounting systems, to increase office productivity. Word processing, for example, has increased typing output by up to 300 per cent and at the same time has improved the typist's job satisfaction and working conditions. The trend is towards an integrated 'office or management information system', where the generation of documents, their editing, finalizing, copying and distribution, are all part of one system, with microprocessors assisting and integrating at each stage.

The sophistication of microelectronic components makes an overall 'systems' approach essential.

Word processor

Word processors consist of four main units: a microprocessor-based console, the nerve centre of the system; so called 'floppy disks', which hold the control program and store the data being processed (e.g. the text typed in); a visual display unit (VDU) and an input keyboard (as each character is typed on the keyboard, it comes up on the VDU); and a high-speed (45 characters per second) printer, e.g. a 'daisy-wheel' printer.

Once the operator has typed in a text, it can be easily and quickly amended or deleted, or inserted into any desired position on the VDU page, before being printed or stored as hard copy. Stored data can be read, printed out, edited, updated or sorted out in a particular way at any time; paragraphs can be repositioned in any order; letters can be written automatically according to pre-programmed instructions or duplicated extremely rapidly. Using a matching process, the operator can gain immediate access to any point in a particular document, and can instruct the processor to change any given sequence of text wherever it meets it in the document. A text can be automatically marked to indicate where deletions or additions have been made, or labelled with any combination of tags; and every portion of it meeting given criteria can be selected for display. Commands can be 'stacked' if necessary, allowing the operator to carry on with other work while the processor obeys them. If needed a calculator facility can be easily added to the word-processor function.

In this type of application the 'flexibility' of the microprocessor approach is dominant. Not only does it enable word processing, text processing and calculating facilities to be combined relatively easily by means of appropriately designed software; it also allows these facilities to be tailored to suit particular needs, and the machine to be continuously 'improved' by development of new programs.

Word processors are used for:

- standard letters and documents with use of standard paragraphs with some variables;
- updating reports and manuals periodically;
- producing good quality, consistent work.

The word processor is being linked with other office equipment, e.g. telex and phototypesetters, and can prepare material, e.g. tape, for direct input to the telex system.

A new word processor connected to a high-speed laser printer can produce work at five or more pages a minute.

Telex

This old slow communication system ($5q$-Σ characters a second) is used by over one million installations in the world. It will still have an important part to play in the first few years of the electronic office, before replacement systems take over. Telex transmissions have been *internationally* agreed.

Messages can be prepared and checked before sending. The message is typed on screen (or on paper tape on older machines). When ready it is transmitted to a receiving terminal which answers back, confirms the receipt of the message. Messages can also be received by unattended terminals at any hour of the day. (NB: A copy is acceptable as a legal record of message sent.)

Fax

This system, quickly transmits images such as drawings, as well as text, via the telephone system. The original message is scanned and the images converted to an electrical signal, which is transmitted to locations where copies of the originals are reproduced. One main use is for sending graphic material, e.g. newspaper photographs. However, it is replacing telex to a large extent as a means of sending typed or handwritten messages nationally and internationally. New developments will reduce the total transmission time, e.g. the optical character reader/facsimile reader, laser printers, and image printers.

Prestel

Prestel is a service which allows access to information stored on computers spread over areas of the country. Access is by a TV set and telephone. The cost is: cost of phone call to computer centre, plus rate for service, plus charge per frame. The type of information held in the store includes news, sports, timetables, financial and career guides, entertainment and secretarial services.

Messages can be stored at a centre and an indicator will show on the receiving terminal that a message is waiting.

Microcomputers can be linked to Prestel services and cash flow calculations, for example, can be performed.

It is interesting to note that the system can have facilities for the ordering of goods (from mail order catalogues, for example). Payment for goods ordered this way, by credit card, has significant implications for managers.

Electronic mail

Electronic mail systems (E mail) have been used for a number of years by larger organizations who transmit within sections of their own organization, or to other organizations, using computer networks. The *addressing* of a message enables normal mail to be processed and delivered; there is no need for the sender to inform the recipient that the message is to be despatched. Electronic mail systems at present store and then deliver to electronic 'mail boxes' which enable the recipient to retrieve the message when convenient.

There are many problems in a world-wide text-communication service, which must be internationally agreed. This is an important area in which to observe developments.

Conferencing systems

Costs of personnel travelling to meetings is very high and other ways of systems *substituting for meetings* could save money. The biggest problem is the loss which may occur because of the lack of face-to-face contact. These methods may be effected in a number of ways:

- by numerous *telephone handsets*. This leaves no opportunity to exchange written communications of details during the conference, although offering some personal contact;
- *video-conferencing* – uses continuous television pictures and sound of participants and can also show documents (e.g. Confravision, run by British Telecom);
- conferences using a *computer system's* power of processing. Members have a terminal screen of text/data which can be amended and discussed.

Such methods are less personally satisfying and there is still the problem of getting people all together at the same time in order to participate. Other methods being used offer facilities for contributions by persons in their *own* time. Data can be entered in a computer file and retrieved at their convenience and at a predetermined time a 'conference' can then be held.

Other communication systems

Private Branch Exchange (PBX) systems can be used as a data terminal whereby data can be collected and enquiries made to a central computer. Handsets enable work stations to link with each other (for conferencing) or to central data processors and printing equipment. They could be linked to public and private telephone networks and recent developments enable these facilities to be extended. A program, for example, stored in a PBX could automatically re-direct calls, call back a number engaged, direct calls to selected numbers, or allow several people to take part in a conversation.

Viewdata systems are linked to a computer terminal and information can be displayed on a *modified television receiver,* in the same form as a conventional visual display unit. The text can be displayed in seven colours and facilities exist to construct simple diagrams and charts. Information is transmitted by:

- *television signals* and displayed as text (e.g. Ceefax); these are called *teletext;*
- using *telephone network* where digital signals are converted to audio-like signals and the audio signals need to be converted back to digital signals after transmission. These are called viewdata systems, e.g. Prestel;

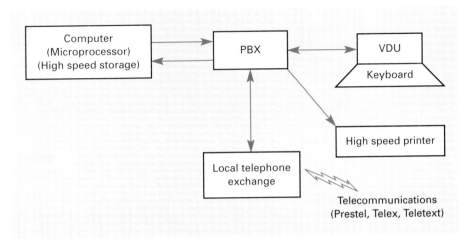

Fig 10.5 Control by PBX network

- retrieving from a *magnetic tape* cassette playback machine.

One terminal can be used to access either teletext or viewdata systems. In Fig 10.5 the PBX shown can transmit messages and enable work stations to have access to external facilities, e.g. data processing, computer printout and storage. Use of local networks and existing telephone networks is convenient and cheaper. Other variations are shown in the figure:

- Terminals using personal or mainframe computer and peripheral devices (shared-resource).
- Access to central processor via local British Telecom networks.

Figure 10.6 shows a single work station with small local storage facilities and a quality-printer. The better equipped stations will have links with phototypesetting, telex and character recognition equipment. Communication links to a central computer and other facilities could greatly enhance the system (see Fig 10.5).

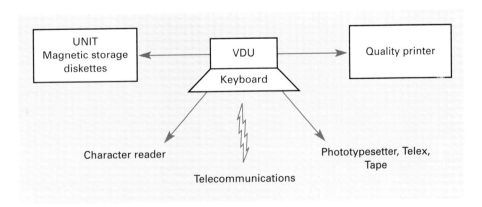

Fig 10.6 Single work station

Voice recognition systems may eventually replace the keyboard as the main human interface with the office. Existing voice recognition systems already allow for 1000 single phoneme commands.

Voice synthesis facilities at work position, as used in the Bank of America, enable a customer, via a touch-tone telephone, to key in a request for the cash balance position to date and a voice-synthesized answer is given. Man–machine 'interface' is an aim of current research.

Central facilities must be used for economic and convenience reasons; these include:

- high-speed printing for large volumes of data not economically handled on printers attached to a work station;
- central storage and retrieval facilities;
- central microfilm and microfiche preparation equipment;
- phototypesetting equipment.

Phototypesetting is often the next stage after word processing. Keyed images of the typefaces are on film on rotating disks or drums and the phototypesetter projects those images on to photosensitive paper, which is ready for printing. (Typesetting speeds are about 38 characters a second, and speeds are increasing rapidly by using electronic images.) Images are generated on a cathode-ray tube and transferred by optic fibre to paper or described by a laser. The next stage to speed up printing is to link up a word processor to a phototype-setter.

Minicomputer is the term used for a smaller version of a 'mainframe' larger machine, which can be installed easily in a normal office environment.

Videophone. A standard size push-button telephone has added to it a colour screen which can be raised to allow a person to be seen by means of a built in videocamera. Both parties have to raise their screen and press a video on/off button in order to see each other. Calls cost the same as conventional calls.

Video and audio signals are set down a standard telephone line simultaneously.

Some people doubt the benefit of a videophone. It has been estimated that about three-quarters of the impression made during a conversation is through body language and 15 per cent only through tone of voice. Facial expressions are most important.

A video-telephonic international network could provide for viewing new products, evaluating engineering designs and perhaps interviewing for jobs.

Compact Disk (Read Only Memory) CD-ROM. The same technology is used for compact discs as for sound. The optical disks are etched with *digital* data and read by lasers. The disks can store a large amount of data, e.g. *The Times* or *Financial Times* newspapers for a whole year can be stored on a single disk and selected items viewed and printed out if required from one disk.

The integrated office

The idea behind the 'integrated office' is that wherever possible there is not duplication of equipment and that different equipment is able to share the same information.

The integration of office equipment would give many benefits to businesses. With the advent of microcomputers many of the functions which in the past have been done by 'dedicated' machines limited to a single function can be performed by one machine. For example, one micro can do word processing, accounting, mailing, telex work, etc.

As a single stand-alone micro can only do one job at a time, it seemed beneficial if a number of micros could be *linked to central databases* to enable the same information to be shared by users simultaneously. *Multi-user systems* can be suitable for two to 32 terminals and consist of a number of 'dumb' terminals (which can only receive or input data) linked to a *central processor* for intelligence, programs and files. So one person could be doing word processing at the same time as another is doing accounting work.

The main problem is that the more terminals available the more the central processor is overstretched. Costs have now fallen to such an extent that separate terminals with their *own* processors can be linked to a central hard disk enabling them to share the same database and programs. Processors in this case are not shared, but distributed and thus response times are not affected much by the number of terminals. The method of *linking up* all the elements of this system is by a *local area network*. It is local as it refers to equipment in a single site or building.

Portable remote terminals are used as input devices; here data can be keyed into a portable terminal and sent over telephone lines (via an acoustic coupler) or entered directly from a terminal's disk into the main disk at a central base. This is being done by meter readers.

A term often used is 'distributed data processing'. This can have a number of meanings:

- *stand-alone* personal computers on every executive's desk;
- *a network of personal computers,* sharing resources (e.g. printers and disks) which can be linked to a more powerful central computer;
- *minicomputers networked* together with many terminals linked to each minicomputer;
- *mainframe computers* in control of hundreds of 'slave' terminals which are linked to them.

Problems of the electronic office

- **The cost of investment** in modern equipment may be high, but problems arise as *job content changes so more training* is needed for operators and management;
- **Lack of standardization** will slow development, e.g. telecommunications, data representation, keyboard display and printing;
- **Labour displacement** (redundancy or natural wastage). There will be changes in the structure of jobs and existing working relationships. Responsibilities will change, causing staff unrest and uncertainty just as happened with the first introduction of computers;
- **Ergonomic problems.** Operators of the equipment are more likely to make mistakes if they are not comfortable or are inconvenienced by badly

designed equipment or systems. Complaints made about mental and physical fatigue in using equipment may cover the following areas:

(a) *Visual display units and keyboards,* e.g. reflections, luminance, illegible documents.
(b) *Posture* – lack of movement, badly designed furniture.
(c) *Environment* – light, heat and noise.
(d) *Procedure design* – regular flow of work needed, adequate rest periods.

How problems
can be overcome

Most of these problems are not new and are dealt with elsewhere in the book, but are briefly mentioned here:

- changes are needed in *job content* (job design and possible regrading). Unions must be involved;
- key workers should be involved early and *retrained* if necessary;
- fewer staff being needed may affect *promotion* chances.

Selection and placement of office personnel must be more methodical than at present. Each person's skills, knowledge and experience should be examined together with work involved to increase *acceptance* of systems and increase *staff motivation* towards the changing office environment.

Jobs should be reviewed periodically to check to see that the organization's position relating to the following is up to date:

- job analysis, description and evaluation;
- career development schemes;
- equitable salary and wage schemes.

Feelings of insecurity will abound, so staff must be freed from such worries so that their support may be obtained. This may include a 'no redundancy' policy and a staff retraining scheme, explanation of need for changes in job content and possibly re-organization of office and responsibilities.

Electronic trading

The main motivation for investing in information technology during the 1980s was to reduce costs, improve productivity and become more competitive and efficient. During the 1990s there is a need to develop more interlinked processes, and share information both within the organization and among trading partners at home and abroad. The advent of global trading, just-in-time management and more collaborative business activities requires information to be shared between trading partners, nationally and internationally. In addition, the move to open systems and uniform standards for Electronic Data Interchange (EDI), Interpersonal Mail (IPM) and Electronic Funds Transfer at Point of Sale (EFTPOS) is causing changes in the way companies interact and exchange information with their partners, suppliers and customers worldwide.

The slowness in introducing electronic trading has been because of the lack of a reliable networking and communications infrastructure, and inadequate planning and control techniques.

Electronic trading, however, is firmly based in certain industries, particularly in the food retail markets in the United Kingdom. This is a highly competitive market where cost and efficiency gains are constantly being sought.

These have been achieved by *optical scanning*.

The use of optical scanning at the point of sale by leading supermarket chains has improved customer service by reducing queues and providing itemized bills. In addition, the sale of the item is recorded for stock control and the inventory has been reduced. This forces stockholding further up the supply chain, and stock replenishment cycles are faster.

Management in practice

Tesco is a large supermarket chain in the retail sector and has a distribution network which is the most up to date in Europe.

Investment in information and communication technology has been the key to continued success. Tesco was the first food retail chain to adopt ISDN – the Integrated Services Digital Network. Orders are now based upon actual and not estimated sales. The minimum time between a store requesting and receiving goods has been reduced from 72 hours to 24 hours. Tesco has a key objective and this is to ensure 100 per cent availability of goods on shelves.

The system in the 1980s was to have people counting goods on shelves using a manual accounting system. Then came the introduction of links made to stores and warehouses via a private data network. This was the interim stage.

In the 1990s a strategic decision was made to develop a sales-based ordering system that would enable sales data from bar-code scanners at checkout points to be analysed and translated into forecasts and orders from suppliers. The network had to be upgraded to do this.

Now a computer network links 390 Tesco stores direct to corporate data centres by transmitting data overnight using high capacity digital private circuits (these are called kilostream links).

Sales information from checkouts is passed nightly over the network so that orders can be generated to warehouses. Delivery vehicles can carry goods in three different temperature compartments, so that transport costs can be optimized. The advantages to Tesco are:

- reduced stock levels;
- a reduction in the risk of goods perishing on shelves;
- warehouse running costs were reduced.

Digital Image Processing (DIP)

Paper documents can now be converted into identical electronic documents, so that they can be stored, then retrieved quickly on demand. This has been made possible by advances in software and hardware design.

The system consists of a document scanner, a workstation with a high resolution screen, a laser printer, and an optical disk system for storage. Special software controls the process and handles the compression and decompression of the image. The arrival of the following technologies is very significant:

- The optical disk, which can store large amounts of data.
- The digital scanner for capturing and digitizing images.
- The high definition VDU.
- The laser printer to give a quality printout. Over 90 per cent of information is still stored on paper; 10 per cent is the maximum that is currently retained electronically.

Some advantages of DIP

- Saving of space. The contents of a large filing cabinet can be stored on a 5.25 inch optical disk.
- Fast retrieval speed, due to using a random access storage medium.
- Indexing is easier as the electronic image can be indexed and retrieved under a variety of headings.
- Access is available to people simultaneously, as compared with a paper file which is accessed by one person at a time.

Documents can now be viewed on any standard personal computer with a VGA (video graphics array) display. Optical disks can be either erasable or read only. Those read only (or WORM) disks are best where security is important, as the image cannot be altered.

Management in practice

> Optical imaging systems, known as computer scanners, are electronic photocopies which send the copied image to a computer screen, rather than on to a printed page. Insurance companies use scanners to scan claim forms, code them and make them available to insurance claims adjusters at the touch of a button.
>
> American Express, by providing a high quality image of each transaction on a customer's billing statement, was able to improve the quality and differentiation of its services while reducing billing costs by 25 per cent.

THE FUTURE OF THE OFFICE

Working from home (telecommuting)

The Henley Centre for Forecasting in the report 'Tomorrow's Workplace' (prepared for British Telecom, London, 1988) indicated that by 1995 the number of home-based workers would rise to over four million (between 15 and 20 per cent of the UK workforce). Most of the increase was expected to come from non-manufacturing activities and could include, for example, designers, accountants, computer programmers and architects.

Advantages **Employers:**

- Reduction in office costs, e.g. office space, furnishings and secretarial services.
- Greater productivity, because of less distractions (Henley Centre for Forecasting estimated that a home-worker's productivity increases by between 30 and 100 per cent).

Employees:

- Saving on travel and lunch expenses (an average person spends 14 hours travelling each week to and from the office).
- Less stress from travel.
- Greater flexibility to fit work around other home activities.

Disadvantages

- Isolation of people at home and need for interaction with colleagues;
- Lack of administrative support (need to develop keyboard skills).

It could be that the availability, portability and lower cost of communication systems and computers will threaten the traditions of a city-located office in the future.

Summary of position

Opportunities are here to reduce costs by introducing a minimum amount of new technology. This approach is cost saving, but may be too narrow. The present opportunities should be maximized by re-thinking the role of the 'office' to allow staff to concentrate on the *use* of information and *less* on the collection, updating, storing, retrieval and communication of data.

Staff are expensive – they should be used effectively and this can be done by embracing the new technology and investing in the office to obtain efficient output, just the same as investment is made in factories. Corporate strategy must encompass all functions, including the office. All members of a business organization will benefit from an efficient administrative system, whether they are an engineer or an accountant.

HUMAN ASPECTS OF COMPUTER USAGE

It is to be expected that any major technological innovation will have its effects upon the human way of life. While there are wider social aspects, business has its own problems arising from the effects upon individuals and on the organizational structure.

Managers at all levels have to understand what the computer can do for them and also what it cannot do. They must accept its inflexibilities and learn to determine their requirements well in advance. They must appreciate how to interpret the information provided to them and how to make correct decisions based on it. Attitudes and working methods must be adapted to enable the computer to take its proper place as an opportunity rather than a master or an enemy.

Those below management levels have also to adapt. For example, a number of branches might be provided with terminals linked with a central computer. Those working in the branches would transmit data and in return receive balances, totals, and other calculated results. If they are unable to accept these as correct and work to them without seeing the supporting details, the scheme will fail.

The solution to these human problems lies generally along three main paths:

1 **Guiding the period of transition.** As soon as there is an intention to change to computer methods, all levels of the staff who will be affected by the change, or who may think they will be affected, must be kept informed of the plans and of the company's intentions as to job opportunities, retraining and, if need be, redundancy. It is rarely too early to inform the staff even though the plans may still be tentative. Moreover, managers, supervisors and all other levels must continue to be informed at intervals. As plans develop, opportunities should be created to demonstrate plans and equipment.
2 **Integration and training.** Throughout the development period, training should take place at all levels and in all functions to bring about understanding and collaboration.
3 **Attention to output.** Particular regard must be given to producing the output to be used by people in a form that is acceptable to them. Experience shows that while planners and programmers can be relied upon to take care to ensure accurate input and processing they, and those who will use the output, often fail to give adequate attention to the form of the output until there are complaints about having to handle cumbersome and incomprehensible tabulations.

Ergonomic features of new technology

Ergonomics can be simply explained as the study of the efficiency of people at work. Now that the office is becoming more automated and integrated and more and more personal computers are being used, designers should look carefully at the way the computer presents itself to the user. A wider cross-section of persons have to come to terms with the machine. Managers, for example, learn keyboarding and how to access computers, etc. It needs, in effect, a serious look at the factors affecting the efficiency with which we use machinery. Suppliers are improving the ease of use of their products. It is important to reduce the numbers of items the user has to remember and do in order to make the system work properly (sometimes called user-friendly interface!).

SECURITY, DATA PROTECTION AND AUDIT

When an organization computerizes its procedures, it becomes dependent on a system to which it has committed vital business information. Disruption of the computer system could lead to losses from which the company may not recover.

In the USA *computer fraud* is said to be increasing at the rate of 500 per cent per annum. There are many other risks, e.g. software error, industrial action, system abuse, hardware failure, theft and vandalism, fire and flood, industrial espionage. Counter-measures are therefore needed to safeguard the business operation and in particular the computer installation.

In many parts of the world a person's privacy is considered a basic human right. However, information about individuals is stored for many organizations. Some data is held on computers, e.g. payroll, local authorities for council tax, social security, inland revenue and health authorities, car taxation, credit card agencies and electoral rolls. These are usually *separate databases*, but with telecommunication advances, they could be linked together. Illegal access to databases is more likely and a person's privacy could be said to be threatened. This privacy of personalized data held on computer databases is referred to as data protection.

In Sweden, anyone wishing to set up a name-linked computerized file must register with the Data Protection Agency. Their legislation covers three areas – accuracy of data, authorized usage, deletion from record after appropriate time has elapsed.

The Data Protection Act 1984

This Act marked a significant change in the legal responsibilities of data users holding or using personal information on computer systems. The Act created a new office – *The Data Protection Register* – where 'personal data users' and 'computer bureaux' have to register. The Act sets out, as required by European law, the general principles with which data users must comply when holding and using personal data.

'Data subjects' have legal rights, including access to their personal data. There is compensation available in cases where data is outdated or incorrect.

Main features of the Act

In a summary, the main features of the Act are as follows:

- Data must be *obtained and processed 'fairly and lawfully'*.
- Data must be held for one or more *specified lawful purposes*. The purposes for holding data have to be specified in the register.
- Personal data *must not be disclosed* or used for any purpose or purposes incompatible therewith.
- Personal data must be *'adequate, relevant and not excessive'* in relation to the purpose or purposes for which it is held.
- Personal data must *not be held longer than necessary* for the purposes registered.
- An *individual* is entitled to two main rights:

  1 To be *informed by the organization* holding the data whether or not it actually holds personal data on the individual and, if so, the individual is to have access to such data without undue expense or delay.

2 Where appropriate, the *data subject can demand* that information should be corrected or erased. The Court or the Data Register will consider claims of damage deemed to be suffered because of incorrect information.

If an individual asks an organization whether his or her personal data is held, the company must reply, provide a copy in writing and sufficient details to make such a reply intelligible (e.g. if it were in code).

● Companies using data, or providing data services must take *appropriate security measures* against unauthorized access to, alteration, disclosure or destruction of personal data – and against accidental loss.

There are some *exemptions* to registering. These refer to personal data held for:

● payroll and accounting purposes;
● crime, taxation, health and social work;
● judicial appointments and legal and professional privilege.

All organizations should be aware of the Act which required registration by over 1.3 million companies in the United Kingdom, according to the Institute of Chartered Accountants.

Security of information

A secure system

A secure system is one which follows laid-down security procedures with an alternative system to fall back on in an emergency and where the costs of failure are quantifiable and insured.

Security planning

This begins in the design stages of a computer system and requires constant reviewing and evaluating. Such a plan should cover:

● design of the system, its development and operation;
● physical and data security;
● communications;
● human resource and contingency planning;
● audit and insurance.

Computing staff

Computing staff are the key to all security measures and are the most vulnerable aspect of an installation. Qualifications and references of staff recruited should be verified. Most frauds require an operative in another organization or collusion with existing employees. Segregation of staff duties and accurate documentation of programs is essential.

Strict control of operations

The strict control of operations is vital, especially where satellite devices are connected to a central processor, allowing easy access to files. Where password systems are adopted, a log of procedure should be built into the software. Unauthorized users should be immediately locked out of the machine. Mathematical locks can be used on larger systems. Overtime can lead to inadequate supervision.

Records Records of old manual systems should be retained for a few years when a new system is being tried out, in case files and software are destroyed. The location of the central processor should be in an area of difficult access with suitable locking or card identifying systems employed. Master software tapes and disks with security copies of daily business transactions should be safely stored away.

Outside suppliers If outside software houses write systems programs, these should be screened. A back-up system with owners of a similar computer should be arranged.

Insurance Cover should be adequate, and cover the cost of hardware, software, costs of re-creating data and consequential loss.

The auditor The role of the auditor in designing secure systems is often ignored. The auditor is often dependent on data processing staff in order to run program checks on the computer. The company's auditors should be capable of running their own programs to monitor the installation without the need of assistance from staff they are monitoring. They should be involved in the design and implementation of control standards and program checks, including clerical controls. All packages purchased should be checked to ensure adequate audit trails and that no unauthorized persons can have access to protected information areas.

New technology brings new opportunities for crime, which ranges from computer theft, desk-top forgery, voice and electronic mail terrorism, to graffiti sent by facsimile transmission and electronic data interchange fraud, including 'hacking' and destruction of data by introducing computer viruses. Desk-top publishing software combined with the latest colour laser printers and photocopiers are increasingly being used by forgers. Many business documents, including cheques, can be forged. The extent of the forgery is only limited by the quality of the paper. Various measures are taken by organizations in an attempt to combat forgery. Another big security issue involves the use of networking computers, especially as they allow information to be transferred between databases from many locations worldwide. A crime can be committed at a distance from where the criminal actually is. Passwords by themselves are not adequate security. Computer software anti-virus programs will scan disks for known viruses, which destroy computer data. Use of disks not originated on the network should be avoided unless they have been throughly checked.

The latest security procedures incorporate IDES (Intruder Detection using Expert Systems) which have profiles of how employees of a company typically use a system. The computer can then inform the security division of a company if it identifies any significant deviation. It also monitors the system for failed log-in attempts and the amount of processing time being used and compares this with the historical averages.

MANAGEMENT SERVICES

A British Institute of Management study group in 1963 described management services as a 'generic term used to describe a number of specialist activities and services provided centrally especially in large companies or groups of companies. It is generally agreed that these centralized management services should be essentially of an advisory nature in effect, an internal consultancy service to general, divisional and departmental managers as well as to the board of directors'.

This definition can be amended with the experience obtained in the years since 1963. A variety of skills is needed which may need to alter as problems change. It is really a methodology for approaching management problems through analysis based upon modern management techniques.

The current changes in the external environment have been particularly great and this has been reflected in the internal results of companies. The role of management services is very important in seeking out new ideas and introducing relevant new techniques to implement changes smoothly within the company.

In his book *Future Shock* (1970, Random House), Alvin Toffler pointed out the great rate of change in the gross national product of countries. Countries that had high per capita growth rates, e.g. United Kingdom and United States of America, would find a marked fall in the future.

The directors should, as we have seen, try to foresee possible change and plan accordingly.

It is important that the board of directors use management services effectively. Whether this involves corporate financial models, design of management information systems, *information* is needed, not just *data* from the computer. Information must be related to a manager who is committed, e.g. to be responsible for a profit target. Computers issue vast amounts of *data*, but it is management's responsibility to check the relevance of the data and arrange for the production of *useful information*.

The place of management services in a company

There will not be a complete agreement with the following list of skills required in a management services team, but it is a guide:

- management accounting – standards, investment appraisal, information systems, costing, pricing systems;
- productivity services – value analysis, work study, job evaluation, engineering;
- computer systems – analysis and design of commercial systems;
- management science – operational research, financial modelling.

Other related skills may be considered as part of management services, and advice in these areas is obviously important, e.g. manpower planning, industrial relations, and market research.

The management services section may report to a related function, e.g. finance, or related operation, e.g. communications.

The section is usually centralized at first, responsible to a director, and it is advisable for it to be represented on the board of directors. The leader should have comparable status with senior executives, e.g. other functional heads.

The business of management is becoming more complex as there is an increasing rate of change in technological and social areas. Management services has emerged as an aid to management and has in the past been identified with the operation of computer systems, usually on a basis of centralization. Now that computers are more dispersed by terminal systems and management services staff have been decentralized, central management services groups can act more effectively and more objectively.

There is one problem where companies are formed into divisions, where line managers have a profit responsibility and where high costs of a centralized management service are charged to them. If overheads are to be kept low, then there is a direct incentive *not* to call in management services to assist. Thus short-term actions may be to the detriment of the future as valuable assistance is not available, and the trading divisions are encouraged to use their own less highly qualified staff.

Suggested responsibilities of a typical management services department	1 To assist operating divisions through the development and application of management services skills.

1 To assist operating divisions through the development and application of management services skills.
2 To give information and advice on relevance of management techniques and be involved with project work in divisions.
3 To give proper training, to develop and to deploy effectively management services staff.
4 To advise the board of directors on matters affecting company success.
5 To introduce and develop group standards (e.g. in accounting, productivity services and computers).
6 To develop contacts with educational organizations.

It is generally best for the computer department to be treated as a service to the organization as a whole and ideally it should form part of a management services department, which may compromise operational research, organization and methods and work study. The manager of this department should report direct to a director of the company.

Figure 10.7 shows a typical organization chart for a large establishment; in smaller concerns some functions will be combined.

The data processing (DP) manager

The DP manager is head of the computer department and requires a good technical knowledge as well as practical experience of data processing. He must have imagination and creative ability, clear and logical thought, ability to communicate with clarity and be diplomatic. He plans, co-ordinates and controls all activities relating to data processing and automation of office work; these activities comprise systems analysis, programming of computers and the operational control of the DP centre.

A systems analyst

A systems analyst is responsible for detailed design of systems. He should possess a good balance of commercial and data processing knowledge and be fully aware of the company's organization and procedures. He must be able to understand complex and possibly ill-defined problems, and be able to devise and select the most practical solutions. Ability to mix, communicate and be tactful is essential.

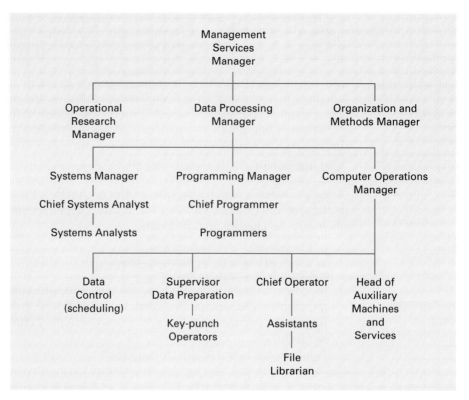

Fig 10.7 Management services section

A programmer

A programmer is responsible for writing, in machine language, the detailed programs of the system devised by the analyst. He must be logical, meticulous, tenacious, patient, and able to work as a member of a team.

The operations manager

The operations manager plans, co-ordinates and controls the operational activities of the computer, the auxiliary machines and services for the receipt, codification and inputting of primary data and the distribution of the results to the sections concerned.

As far as qualifications for programmers are concerned, a certain type of mind is required. Proven logical or mathematical ability is good evidence, so is skill at crosswords, chess or bridge. Tests give a reasonably reliable measure of aptitude, but should form only *part* of the selection procedure.

Installation of a mechanized system

The procedure for installing a mechanized system involves the following steps:

1 Plan the system, defining machines specifications, forms design, write programs, etc.
2 Train staff – special courses may be needed; this may in some cases precede the planning stage.

3 Physical take over of machines, testing and parallel running to establish the reliability that may be needed.
4 Final transfer to new system and *periodic review* of progress.

Organization of machine room

In this brief section, the organization of the machine room is considered. This includes physical conditions, flow of work, supervision and control and breakdown arrangements. The following points must be considered:

- there must be sufficient space to allow for expansion and access to the machines;
- heating, ventilation and humidity are important, and air conditioning may be needed to ensure that a suitable atmosphere is maintained;
- lighting must be adequate and sound-proofing essential;
- power, of sufficient capacity, must be available and many power points are needed. There may need to be a special alternative arrangement in the event of a power failure;
- machines may be laid out on a 'product' or 'process' basis. (*See* Chapter 8);
- the flow of work must be regular to obviate peak periods. Shift-working may be necessary, especially where a computer is installed;
- efficient records are needed for effective control, e.g. time sheets, progress charts, machine breakdown records;
- breakdown arrangements may include plans to rearrange work flow and obtain use of equipment of another company, or make use of agency services.

Use of computer service bureau

When a company grows in size and the data processing side needs to be modernized, management can:

- employ more staff and use existing manual system;
- buy a visible record computer;
- buy a small computer;
- use a computer bureau.

One of the most common reasons for not using a bureau is lack of knowledge of their services.

An organization with a low work volume, which is not large enough to justify purchasing its own machine, could use a bureau. Even if a company has its own computer, it may have periodic problems with large quantities of data at peak periods; again, a bureau could be useful at these times.

A bureau can offer:

- skill from specialization of staff in data processing;
- technical economies of scale;
- accountability; the true costs of data processing are known.

The first stage is to decide exactly what requires to be done at the bureau, whose services vary with size. These services may include the use of the bureau's own computer, systems analysis, writing programs, training company's staff, collecting, processing and distributing data.

Certain bureaux offer contract terms allowing computer time exclusively to a company each week.

When the company decides on the services it requires, the bureau conducts a survey to assess the situation and to enable a quotation to be given. Other bureaux offer package programs to companies with similar problems. Companies must adapt their own system to the prepared program, which is cheaper to use. Examples of these are programs for sales analysis, payroll and market research.

Good liaison is essential between bureau and client and this can be achieved by appointing a senior member of the company's staff to do the job.

ELECTRONIC DATA INTERCHANGE (EDI)

This will become an essential part of trading in the future. It is a form of computer-to-computer data interchange. In effect it is another type of electronic mail. The essential aspect of EDI is that the transfer of data between computers is *structured*. Data is encoded and decoded by specific recognized formats. The electronic transfer of a purchase order, for example, can be made between the computers of two different organizations.

The problem of making different types of computers 'converse' with one another is overcome by using a suitable *interface*. An interface is the hardware and software needed between processors and peripheral devices, to overcome the differences in their operating characteristics, e.g. speeds and codes.

Sometimes a third party provides a 'clearing house' to link different computer systems, e.g. Istel. Such a company provides the conversion facilities to enable different types of computer to communicate with one another and may be a more economic way of working, rather than a company providing its own dedicated centres.

Advantages of EDI

- **Competitive advantage** – increase in sales and market share.
- **Cost reductions** – reduction of data keying costs and errors, plus a saving in inventory costs and a reduction in paperwork.
- **Service to customers** – increase in customer satisfaction.

Problems of implementation

- Difficulty of managing and co-ordinating the EDI project.
- High costs need to be justified.
- Difficulty in agreeing EDI standards and message formats.
- Persuading (external) trading partners to agree to EDI.
- Organizing the necessary hardware and software.

- Overcoming the traditional preference for paper as the means of communicating.

Electronic Data Interchange (EDI) allows the computer systems of retailers and suppliers to communicate with the minimum of human intervention. A purchase of goods can feed its way back to the manufacturer's production scheduling system automatically. The sale at a store of a washing machine will automatically actuate an order to the production line for another machine to be sent.

EDI in principle works in a similar way to ordinary postal services. Orders are sent, received, recorded and acknowledged, then goods are dispatched with an invoice.

The difference is that with EDI the documents involved are exchanged electronically instead of on pieces of paper through a postal box. The benefits are speed and accuracy (if the original information is entered properly, there is no room for human error). Some estimates of cost savings have been made for changing to EDI and these can amount to 75 per cent saving on the equivalent paper cost. In addition, cash flow can be improved because invoices are sent out accurately and on time. Automatic acknowledgement is made so that there should no longer be the problem of invoices that in the past were lost or mislaid.

Agreement on European EDI standards should be a great boost to the growth of the system. In addition, when whole industries move towards paper-less trading and cross industry boundaries, and payments are made electronically, the real benefits of EDI will emerge.

In the banking and insurance industries, in particular, large numbers of paper-based transactions are handled by EDI and have produced cost and efficiency gains. The postal services and other government agencies are moving to electronic trading to give a wider range of cost-effective services.

From an oranization's point of view the improvement in communications can allow a move to flatter and leaner corporate structures which allow responsibility and accountability to be devolved further down the organization.

Management in practice

The ICL Company uses electronic trading extensively. It has around 30 000 users. Most of ICL's purchasing and ordering facilities are dealt with electronically and the point has been reached where suppliers need to agree to internetwork through EDI if they wish to achieve easier trading with the company.

SUMMARY

Objective 1 *Understand the nature of administrative management and its role as a sub-system within the total environment of an enterprise.*

An office (or administrative sub-system) can be said to compromise the following activities:

- receiving information;
- processing and arranging it in a certain manner;

- communicating;
- controlling and protection of enterprise assets.

The office sub-system is shown in this book as the central figure of a complete system. This will not be the case in organizations which do not have a centralized administrative function. There will be internal and external influences on the office sub-system; in particular the Health and Safety Acts and the Data Protection Act have had a significant effect on aspects of the work in the office.

Objective 2 *Appreciate that technological innovation will affect most aspects of office work and that managers should be aware of potential problems.*
Office managers should understand what machines can and cannot do for them. They need to learn to determine their requirements well in advance and appreciate how to interpret the information produced. The organization's working methods and staff are an expensive item, and technology may allow saving in the collection, updating, storage, retrieval and communication of data.

Problems include high cost of equipment, possible changes in job content, lack of standardization in equipment, and factors affecting the efficiency of staff in using new technology (ergonomics).

Objective 3 *Define the aim and scope of organization and methods in an office.*
The aim of the organization and methods is the improvement in effectiveness of clerical and other work through redesigning working methods, organization, conditions and the environment. This may include assistance from mechanization and computer technology. Organization and methods has an advisory role and usually carries few executive powers.

The methods used consist of questioning the need for procedures relating to a given activity and if the activity can be justified, of examining the effectiveness of the individual operations involved. The scope of organization and methods is limited to the extent and methodology of working.

Objective 4 *Explain what is meant by Electronic Data Interchange and discuss its potentially highly significant effect on office administrative functions.*
Electronic Data Interchange is the structured transfer of data between computers. It is a form of electronic mail whereby computers 'converse' with each other and enables documents to be automatically transferred from one company to another. There are substantial reductions in costs of data entry, errors are fewer, inventory costs are lower and paperwork is reduced substantially.

Once the high costs of setting up the system are overcome, common standards are set, and the traditional preference for paper is reduced, significant changes in a range of office systems will be effected.

REVIEW QUESTIONS

1 Draw up a schedule of responsibility for an office manager.

2 Discuss the centralization of distinct office services, such as (a) typing, (b) filing, (c) duplicating.

3 What advantages are claimed for open offices?

4 What do you understand by the organization and methods function? To whom should O and M be responsible?

5 Mention the various means for controlling the quality and accuracy of office work.

6 To what extent can work study be applied to the office, and with what objects?

7 What points must be attended to in selecting the media for office communications?

8 What forms of external communication are available?

9 What are the types of machines used for internal communication in an office?

10 What are the essentials of a good filing system?

11 Describe the various types of filing equipment available.

12 What machines may be used in the mailing section of an office to ensure speedy and efficient working?

13 Describe the three main duplicating processes.

14 List the salient features of the following methods of copying: thermal, electrostatic.

15 Explain the main features of an addressing machine and suggest a few of its applications.

16 Comment upon any new development in accounting machines.

17 Explain what you understand by the term database.

18 Distinguish between integrated data processing and electronic data processing.

19 Of what basic units is a digital computer composed? How can information be fed into a computer and in what forms may the results be provided?

20 What do you understand by the term 'management services'?

21 Draw an organization chart for a department concerned with management services.

22 What points should be considered in the organization of a machine room?

23 Outline the work of a computer service bureau.

24 What are the main problems of the 'electronic office'?

25 What do you understand by the term Electronic Data Interchange (EDI)?

26 Integrated Systems Digital Network (ISDN) allows all kinds of information to travel along the telephone network. Give two examples of the use of this for business.

27 Give three advantages of electronic mail over the ordinary post. Try to think of two disadvantages.

28 Explain why personal computers have had their greatest impact on the world of the office.

1 Discuss the stages in an O and M assignment. Explain how the investigation is carried out and the methods used for analysis and presentation of information.

2 The commercial director of your organization is attempting to make the paper work within the organization more efficient and effective. You are asked to advise on the re-designing of the forms used within the organization. Outline the points, in a report, to which you would give particular attention in form designing.

3 'As an office increases in size, it becomes more and more necessary to organize it according to some logical plan.' Comment on this statement and describe the steps you would take in re-planning an office organization.

4 In an organization where the volume of work has increased considerably, it is intended to introduce dictating machines and establish a central typing bureau. Senior executives only will retain personal secretaries.

(a) Describe the organization required to make the system efficient, paying particular attention to matters such as:
(i) giving priority to urgent matters,
(ii) making additions or alterations to recordings.
(b) List briefly the advantages that should accrue and the problems which might arise.

5 Outline the investigations which a company should require to be undertaken before a decision is made whether to purchase a computer for commercial work within the company.

6 The average earnings of a skilled craftsman are today likely to be significantly higher than those of a clerk in the same organization.

What problems may this situation impose on the office manager?
What effect may it have on staff attitudes to union membership?
What action should management take?

7 Your company has 500 employees, some of whom are paid by way of a bonus scheme. The present manual system used for payroll preparation runs late because of undue clerical work and the payroll analysis is inadequate.

What are the suitable alternatives to improve the situation and what factors would be taken into account in making your selection?

8 As newly appointed office manager, you soon come to realize that (a) many of your older men clerks are working excessive overtime, and (b) there is a high rate of turnover of more junior staff. Of what problems are these likely to be symptomatic? How may the situation be improved?

9 Your company has found the recruitment and retention of clerical and secretarial staff an almost insoluble problem.

You are asked to comment on this problem and suggest possible remedies.

10 Describe briefly the types of procedure chart used in O and M. What are their advantages and disadvantages in contrast with narrative descriptions? Draw a procedure chart for the receipt and payment of goods in sufficient detail to illustrate your answer.

11 (a) Set out the general principles which should be followed when designing forms for use within your organization; and
   (b) prepare a specimen form suitable for either:
      (i) Annual Staff Assessment, or
      (ii) Staff Holiday and Sickness Record,
      which demonstrates the principles you have outlined in (a) above.

12 The office environment can have a crucial influence on the effectiveness of work in the office.
   Discuss how and why.

13 The office supervisor has to achieve the optimum effectiveness of the staff under his control. This is a task crucial to the effectiveness of the organization as a whole as well as being very complex. Both psychological and sociological factors come into the process.
   Discuss ways in which the office supervisor should go about achieving this optimum effectiveness.

ASSIGNMENTS

1 Working on your own, record the various ways the latest microtechnology advances can aid managerial decision making. Compare your answers with other members of your group.

2 Your tutor intends to computerize the records of your assignment and examination grades. Advise on the procedures that should be adopted to conform with the requirements of the Data Protection Act.

BIBLIOGRAPHY

Anderson, R, *Data Processing*, 7th edition (London, M+E Handbboks, Pitman Publishing, 1990).
Haddow, M, *Administrative Management Case Studies* (London, Pitman Publishing, 1992).
Institute of Administrative Management, *Administration in the Office*, 1993 (One of series of booklets for course modules).
Langley, G, *Telecommunications Primer* (London, Pitman Publishing, 1990).
Shaw, J, *Business Administration* (London, Pitman Publishing, 1991).

1 'Every managerial act rests on assumptions, generalizations, and hypotheses – that is to say on theory' (Douglas McGregor). Examine this statement in relation to:

(a) The exercise of authority.
(b) Effective leadership of staff.
(c) Team work in management groups.

2 'Every manager is concerned with the quality of discipline and morale that characterizes his subordinates, for these factors have an important bearing upon the productivity of his department.' Discuss this statement showing any evidence you have of the relationship between discipline and morale on the one hand and productivity on the other.

3 In considering a large company in the consumer durable product field with highly developed modern marketing techniques, give your understanding of product planning, describing the various phases involved. Write a position description for a product planning and development manager in this company. What errors would you seek to avoid in test-marketing your new products?

4 Illustrate with a diagram your concept of the planning-control feedback cycle in business from policy planning to performance and results. What do you understand by control? Give examples of the forms of control operating in various parts of a business.

5 Many businesses are now engaging in long-range planning of their production and marketing effort. Why have they become conscious of the need for long-range planning? What benefits can be anticipated for such planning? In the planning process definite goals must be set in five fields. What are these fields?

6 Show why *innovation* – the creation and application of new ideas – is fundamental to the progress of a business in all its activities. What are the blocks to effective innovation? In what ways would you set out to remove these blocks and to induce an atmosphere favourable to new ideas? Outline a method of training management in creative thinking in relation to the business.

7 Packaging is an important factor in business, especially where the product is distributed through retailers to the public. What purposes are served by packaging a product? What factors should be considered in designing the container? What organization procedure would you advocate to ensure that all aspects of the packaging problem are considered and co-ordinated?

8 As secretary of an engineering company employing 9000 people, outline the mandate, or schedule of responsibilities for the manager, responsible to you, of a proposed electronic data processing department.

9 Outline a comprehensive training scheme to produce skilled employees in a large factory. The scheme should also provide for further training for senior technical posts, supervision and management.

10 What is a learning curve?

How can the benefits obtainable from the learning process be hastened?

Consider how management would use learning curves when fixing selling prices.

11 The works manager wants to engage a young, technically competent skilled crafts-man whom he believes to be a potential supervisor but is concerned about two much older men who have been in the section for many years and are reasonably able but appear to have reached the limit of their development.

Describe the problems that could arise and the solution thereto.

12 Indicate the benefits likely to arise from the operation of a company suggestion scheme. What features would you build into a suggestion scheme to avoid prob-lems and ensure the success of the scheme? How would you organize the valua-tion of suggestions?

13 What are the factors which cause clerical work to be more difficult to measure pre-cisely than production work?

What are the short-term and long-term objectives which should be determined by management regarding the purpose of clerical work measurement before its introduction in an organization?

14 The XYZ Co. has used the services of a computer bureau for the past two years, but as its requirements for computer usage are increasing, a feasibility study is to be carried out to determine whether or not a small 'in-house' computer should be purchased. Before the study is undertaken, you are required as chief accountant to prepare a report for the company chairman, comparing the advantages and disad-vantages of using a bureau with those of owning a small computer. In your com-parison you should refer to developments in the computer field expected within the next five years. A comparison of running costs will be considered by the feasibility study and should not be included in the report to the chairman.

Note: You are not required to report on how to conduct the feasibility study.

Candidates should tackle their 'best' questions first and leave the others until later rather than feel under any obligation to adhere to the numerical order specified in the question paper.

It is vital to allocate sufficient time for all questions: rare is the entrant who can accumulate a pass mark from the totals for, say, three questions out of the five requested.

There is no rule which restricts the length of answers (other than the need to write on all five questions adequately), and the deliberate compression of material merely makes the candidate's work look unappealing.

Those entrants who really wish to guarantee a pass for themselves must make an effort to familiarize themselves with management problems and the operation of policies within their own organizations, so that they can quote specific illustrations in their answers. For the particular benefit of overseas candidates, it is preferable to become acquainted with local law and practice, as opposed to United Kingdom procedures.

Candidates must pay more attention to the effectiveness with which they express themselves. A competent administrator must be able to communicate in writing through letters, reports, memoranda, etc. His credibility, and thus his ability to get things done, is substantially undermined if he appears not to be able to spell simple words, or if he cannot correctly distinguish between Elton Mayo, Maslow, the Hawthorne Experiments, Hertzberg, and so forth. Spelling mistakes are especially unforgivable when the words appear in the examination paper itself.

Candidates should write coherent answers in a logical and convincing form, with checklist points numbered in sequence, liberal use of underlined headings so that scripts are easier and more pleasant to read, and references to some up-to-date and well-informed sources in the literature.

It cannot be stressed too strongly that the citation of actual examples is one of the best ways in which the more meritorious candidates demonstrate their excellence. This approach, moreover, need not be confined to those students preparing for examinations who are engaged in full-time employment; for others, e.g. those on full-time courses, the remedy is to keep a file of cuttings of relevant material from *The Times*, especially the business news section, every day, the management page from the *Financial Times*, the *Sunday Times* business news, etc., or the equivalent publications for overseas candidates. In this way even a student totally lacking in first-hand commercial experience can keep himself abreast of policy developments in whole industries or particular companies.

Candidates must answer the question asked, and not some other question derived from their own imaginings. If they see some key phrase, like 'manpower planning' or 'safety policy', they should not expect to earn high marks for simply writing down all they know about the subject in question. Where students are being evaluated, it is not only on their knowledge, but also on their ability to organize and marshal their thoughts, and even on their capacity for thinking spontaneously and creatively about the implications of some issue.

GLOSSARY OF MANAGEMENT TERMS

The purpose of the glossary is to present definitions of some of the terms that are often used in the very wide range of subject areas covered in the book. Mutual understanding of words used forms the basis of communication of facts and ideas.

ACAS. Advisory, Conciliation and Arbitration Service. It was set up by the Employment Protection Act 1975, with the aim of promoting the improvement of industrial relations and to encourage collective bargaining.

Accountability. A concept whereby persons are held responsible for their own performance, and the performance of their subordinates. A person must account for and justify his actions to others.

Accreditation. The formal recognition that individuals have particular experience and/or have shown evidence of specified capabilities. Also, the formal recognition that organizations/institutions uphold specific standards, for example academic standards in an educational establishment. The term is also used to refer to the activities of the National Council for Vocational Qualifications in accepting awards as meeting the criteria specified for National vocational Qualifications.

Accreditation of Prior Learning (APL). A system of work-based management development created to meet the needs of managers with years of experience but no formal qualifications to show their competence. The system assesses a manager's current competence against national standards.

Acid test. A measure of financial solvency of a business. It is also called 'liquidity ratio' and compares assets, which can easily be converted into cash, with the amounts that must be paid in the current period. An acceptable ratio is 1:1.

Activity sampling. A technique whereby work activities are sampled rather than being observed continually. Random samples of activities are taken to ensure there is no bias.

Added value. A method used to replace profit-sharing plans. It is the balance of the company income after deducting costs of material and services. It is a measure of productivity expressed in financial terms.

Applications software. A program designed to do cetain types of work, for example payroll or word processing.

Appraisal. A process of reviewing and judging the value or worth of someone in his job and assessing his potential for future promotion.

Arbitration. This is a device for settling disputes, where parties do not agree. All parties agree to accept the decision of the arbitrator.

Assessment. The process of making a judgement, against evidence of an individual's competence.

Assessment centres. An assessment centre is a collection of tests, exercises and interviews constructed to enable a company to formulate a total picture of the skills, abilities and characteristics of candidates. They were originally designed for selection purposes and for aiding promotion decisions. They are now also used for early identification of employees' potential, diagnoses of training and development needs, organizational planning and the development of skills needed in the future. There is, however, no typical assessment centre.

Asset. Resources of a business that can be given a value in terms of money. Accounting assets can be classified according to their *use*, as fixed, e.g. land and buildings, or current, e.g. stocks. They can also be tangible or intangible, if they are classified as to *form*.

Authority. The right to influence individuals or groups. Superiors can give instructions to subordinates to perform activities within defined objectives.

Awards. A general term for qualifications issued by examining or validating bodies (for example, certificates, diplomas, licentiateships).

Balance sheet. A summary of the financial position of a firm at a point in time, showing the assets, balanced by the total of liabilities of the firm and the value of the *owners' equity*.

Bar chart. A diagram presenting control information to management. It shows the expected duration and timing of tasks by rectangles (bars) drawn along a scale which represents time. An example is the Gantt chart.

Bar code. A product identification code made up of thick and thin bars. This fast efficient system of capturing data is popular in libraries and supermarkets. The European Article system uses a 13 digit code number for products.

Behavioural science. The study of the individual and the group in a working environment. It includes a study of psychology, sociology and economics. Studies include motivation, structure of organizations, decision making and organizational change and development.

Benchmarking. The technique by which companies can compare their own performance in key areas against results achieved by the world's best companies.

Benefits. Items received in addition to earnings. Often termed 'fringe benefits' – including pensions, company cars, sickness benefits etc.

Black box. This is a concept that allows the operation of a system to be understood in broad terms, without the need to be involved with detail. The term is often used relating to the internal working of a computer which is the 'black box'. All one needs to know is the input and output, without needing to know how the computer works.

Blue chip. The term used to describe a well-known company with a world-wide reputation for profitable trading and good management, thus commanding a high level of confidence in stock market investors. The ordinary shares of such a company are also blue chip. (High value chips used in gambling are blue!)

Bonus. A payment made in addition to basic pay. It is usually related to the value, quality or quantity of work done. It is also used to describe any form of incentive payment.

Brainstorming. A technique for encouraging creative thinking. A small group of people are presented with a problem for a few minutes. They formulate various alternative statements and state their ideas rapidly to the group. Many ideas are encouraged and no criticism is allowed. Group members should build on ideas presented and useful ideas can emerge.

Break-even chart. Two curves are plotted on this chart. The sales *revenues* from producing different quantities of a product and the fixed and variable costs of producing these quantities. The curves intersect at the break-even point – where sales income equates to total cost.

Budget. This can be (a) a plan expressed in financial terms, summarizing planned financial receipts and expenditures over a period of time or (b) a list of authorized expenditures.

Budgetary control. This is control based on the use of budgets and comparison of actual with budgeted performance, either to secure by individual action the objective of a policy or provide a basis for its revision. It is a means of clearly identifying responsibility and accountability of executives.

Business game. This is a training or educational activity that *simulates* business operations for the purpose of evaluating results. The trainee is presented with the result of his decisions immediately after he has taken them. Groups of trainees may compete with one another and results may be speedily produced by a computer at suitable stages in the competition.

Capital. Money invested in *assets* in order to earn *income*, which is not intended to be reduced.

Capital expenditure. Expenditure on *fixed assets*, i.e. goods that have a long, useful life, e.g. machinery, equipment.

Cash flow. The flow of cash into and out of a business. The pattern of cash receipts and payments over a period.

CD-ROM, Compact disk ROM *(read only memory)*. Optical disks are etched with digital data and read by lasers. It has large storage capacity and can perform a detailed search in seconds.

Chain of command. The formal relationships between superior and subordinate. The chief executive's instructions are passed to each lower organizational level and information is passed back from the lower levels through the chain to the higher levels. (Also known as line of command.)

Change agent. Usually an outside consultant who has training in behavioural science acts as a catalyst by bringing changes about in an organization by means of an organizational development programme.

Closed shop. An agreement between employer and union that every employee shall become a member of a union. Non-compliance by the employee can lead to dismissal.

Collective bargaining. A process whereby terms and conditions of employment are negotiated by employees' representatives who may conduct negotiations with a single employer or a representative of a number of employers.

Competence. The ability to perform a particular activity to a prescribed standard. The ability to perform in the workplace to the standard required in employment.

Computer Aided Design (CAD). The use of a computer or graphics terminal to assist a designer. Drawings can be created in colour or black and white in two or three dimensions. Images can be viewed from different perspectives so a designer can evaluate a design before accepting it.

Computer Aided Manufacture (CAM). The use of computers to control machinery in manufacturing. For example, the use of computer controlled robots for welding and trolleys for transporting.

Conciliation. A third party tries to obtain agreement between the parties in a dispute. He attempts to find common ground between them which may lead to a settlement by *agreement*.

Contingency theory. A theory that suggests that optimal solutions to organizational problems are derived from matching the *internal* organizational structures and processes to their *external* environment.

Corporate planning. The activity of studying planning changes in the corporate strategy of an organization, over a future period. Objectives are defined and short- and long-term plans are made to achieve these objectives. (Also called strategic planning.)

Cost accounting. The application of methods and techniques to systematically record costs incurred by a firm or by activities, processes or departments and the analysis of variances to form a basis for control. Methods include: job, process, batch, contract and operation costing. Techniques include standard and uniform costing.

Credit accumulation and transfer system (CATS). A system in which students with previous study or experience which may count for credit towards a degree or post-graduate qualification can have these assessed.

Critical path analysis. A technique for planning and controlling large complex projects which consist of many interrelated activities and events. The critical path is a route through a network of events which will increase the duration time of a project if any of the activities on the path are delayed.

Current assets. Something owned by a firm which is intended for resale or conversion in a different form during business operations, within a short period of time (usually a trading period). Current assets include cash debtors, stocks and work in progress.

Current liabilities. Amounts owed by a firm in the near future (usually a year or a trading period). These could be, for example, amounts owing to creditors, bank loans or proposed dividends.

Cybernetics. The scientific study of communication and control in man and machine systems. Computers are given memories and facilities to sense events in the environment and respond in a suitable manner by comparing items sensed with a standard and then corrective action is automatically effected (e.g. the action of a thermostat).

Database. An information file centrally recorded containing a significant collection of data. Retrieval can be quickly obtained by computer and the data can be part of a database management system, serving the needs of major areas or all areas of a business.

Data processing. Systematic operation on data to produce new data, revise data or extract information. (This can be by recording, arranging, filing, processing or disseminating information.)

DATEL. A telecommunications system which allows a computer to communicate with other computers a long distance away. British Telecom offer the service and uses the telephone network, including satellite linking to transmit digital signals.

Decision theory. A part of mathematics that deals with ways of analysing alternative courses of action and providing methods for making optimum decisions.

Decision tree. This is a diagram of a sequence of decisions, each involving a choice between a known number of alternatives. These are decision branches, and depend upon the results of previous decisions.

Delegation. The process of assigning duties to subordinates who are allowed to act within the authority granted to them. The person assigning *retains* responsibility for that person's exercise of authority.

Discounted cash flow. A technique used to calculate the *present* value of a sequence of *future* cash flows, in order to determine the most profitable investment from several alternatives.

Discrimination. Usually refers to employment situations where there may be unfair treatment of an individual or group on grounds of sex, marital status, race or membership and activities of a trade union. Various laws have been passed for the protection of such individuals.

Dismissal. Action by an employer to end an employee's contract of employment.

Dividend. A distribution of profits paid to the proprietors (or shareholders) of a company based on the number of shares held and the rate of dividend per share declared.

Economic order quantity. The quantity of goods which minimizes the total of storage costs and ordering costs. A formula is used to find the optimum ordering quantity, which gives the lowest ordering costs (by buying large amounts) and lowest storage costs (by keeping goods for a short period).

Electronic Funds Transfer (EFT). The transfer of money between banks by computer. This relies on a large communications network with packet-switching computers passing on the electronic messages.

Endorsement. The term used by MCI to describe their recognition of programmes where methods used to assess competence, and the assessment, is in keeping with the National Standards.

Environmental impact study. Analysis of the impact of a proposed plant location on the quality of life in an area.

Ergonomics. A branch of study which ensures that working environments, operations and equipment are suitable for human capacities and limitations (sometimes called human engineering).

Expediting. A term used in place of 'progressing' which refers to an activity which seeks to ensure that production orders, jobs or processes achieve the right quantity at the right time. The aim is to eliminate delays in passing goods to customers.

Exponential smoothing. A forecasting technique providing for the correction of previous forecasting errors. The method predicts the *next* observations in a time series from the knowledge of previous observations. A *weighted arithmetic mean* is taken from previous observations and greater weights are assigned to most recent observations. A smoothing constant is applied to the error and this varies between 0 and 1.

External assessment. Assessment of candidates on behalf of an awarding body by an agent who is external to the institution where the candidates studied and/or are employed.

Factor comparison method. A method of job evaluation which analyses and compares specific factors, in order to determine the relative worth of each job. Factors could be skill, effort, physical requirements and working conditions. Marks are allocated for each factor and the total numerical value for each job is calculated.

Feedback. This is part of the output of a system, which communicates information about deviations from desired performance, action being effected to counteract them.

Fibre optics. Fine strands of glass are used to carry light-wave signals. Fibre optic technology is used in short-distance communications and provides a better service than the usual metal cable link.

Financial ratios. A ratio of two quantities that have been measured in monetary terms and used to analyse the financial position of a firm.

Fixed assets. Assets which are not current assets and not consumed during the course of business but are used to provide goods and services (over a period of a year or more), e.g. property, plant and equipment.

Flexible budget. A budget for which costs are estimated at various levels of activity.

Flexitime. Flexible working hours. A system allowing employees to choose times to start and finish work. They usually must attend between the 'core hours' 1000 hours and 1600 hours and attend for a minimum number of hours monthly.

Free enterprise. A system allowing the production of goods and services by individuals only for profit. Individual producers act according to their own judgment and not to any government direction.

Free trade. A process whereby international trade is conducted with no import or export quotas or tariffs being involved.

Frequency distribution. A mathematical function that indicates the probability distribution of a random variable. It enables variances and standard deviations to be computed.

Gearing. The term refers to the use of *debt* capital by a firm and is the relationship between fixed-interest capital (i.e. preference shares with a prior charge) and equity share capital (i.e. ordinary shares). If fixed-interest capital is a higher proportion than equity capital, it is said to be *high* geared. Preference shareholders thus have first claim on profits, leaving less for ordinary shareholders. When the reverse applies, it is *low* geared.

Generic skill. A skill expressed as fundamental to a whole range of competences.

Grapevine. A term used to refer to the informal, unofficial channel of communication in an organization.

Group dynamics. The study of groups of people to assess their behaviour and their interaction with individuals, other members of the group and other groups.

Group capacity assessment. A technique of work measurement and control applied to clerical and administrative areas of a business. Group work standards are set and this enables management to monitor the performance of sections.

Head hunting. A practice of recruitment agencies who search out and approach key personnel in companies and try and induce them to leave for another company by offering higher salaries and other benefits.

Hierarchy of needs. Abraham Maslow, an American psychologist, proposed that needs which dominate human behaviour can be grouped into five categories which fall into a 'hierarchy': where needs of lower classes must be satisfied before the need for higher classes becomes apparent.

Holding company. This is a company which owns all the shares or a majority of them in several companies, holding financial control over them. It is another name for a parent company.

Homeostasis. The process of maintaining the stability of a system automatically, countering external efforts to change the system.

Human asset accounting. Attempts to measure the value to a firm of its employees in monetary terms (also called human resources accounting).

Human relations. An approach to the theory of management emphasizing the need of the individual worker for satisfactory relationships with his work group.

Hygiene factor. An element of a job that can contribute to the dissatisfaction but not the satisfaction of the job holder (e.g. wages, status, security). To be distinguished from *motivators* (e.g. recognition etc.). Lack of attention to hygiene factors can lead to dissatisfaction with the job (based on the theory of F Hertzberg).

Incentives. Payments made to employees in addition to basic pay as an encouragement to increase the quality or quantity of output.

Index number. A number which shows the degree to which the quantities in a time series vary. It can show the relative changes in values (costs, prices, productivity). A base year is selected and given a value of 100. Subsequent variations are expressed as a percentage variation from the base, giving changes in the index number.

Induction. The process whereby a new employee is introduced into his job so he integrates quickly and smoothly.

Industrial relations. Relations between trade unions and employers, or between an employer and unions representing employees. Also the relations between management, government and employees in an industrial environment.

Industrial tribunals. Representatives from lawyers, employers and employees form a panel that has jurisdiction over a variety of disputes between employers and employees. Usually a legally qualified member and two lay persons pronounce on cases brought to them.

Ink jet printer. A high quality character printer that projects ink droplets on to paper. It uses static electricity to direct the ink to the correct place on the paper as the print head moves quietly across the line. They are fast and have low running costs.

Integrated Services Digital Network (ISDN). A single digital communications network for voice, television, computer, fax and other signals.

Interfirm comparison. The performance of different firms in an industry can be compared by using selected ratios. They can be used to compare different firms' achievements. Interfirm comparison can be assisted by the Centre for Interfirm Comparison.

Investment appraisal. A number of techniques for assessing investment in projects for new plant and buildings. Projects appraised are examined to see if the return on the investment is satisfactory as compared with alternative projects.

Job analysis. The process of examining a job in order to prepare a *job description* and/or job specification.

Job classification. A method of grading jobs based on skills, training, qualifications and level of responsibility needed to perform a task (also called job grading).

Job description. The detailed outline of a job, giving the purpose, scope, organizational relationships, tasks and responsibilities which constitute a particular job. The description is a product of *job analysis.*

Job design. The process of deciding on the tasks and responsibilities to be included in a job and deciding on the methods to be used to carry out the tasks specified.

Job enlargement. A method of *job design,* which involves changing the content of a job in order to build in additional tasks of a similar nature which do not require any increase in levels of responsibility. This is often known as horizontal job enlargement. The idea is to make the job more varied and interesting.

Job enrichment. A method of job design that involves changing the content of a job, in order to build in additional tasks which provide *greater* responsibility, challenge and opportunity for personal achievement and growth. Often referred to as *vertical* job enlargement, and used when additional remuneration has reached a disincentive level.

Job evaluation. A technique for establishing the relative worth of a number of jobs in an organization by considering their complexity, the amount of training or experience required and other aspects. The technique forms the basis for establishing pay differentials.

Job rotation. The process of transferring an employee from one job to another at a similar level in an organization so as to give him wider experience.

Job specification. A description of the personal characteristics required for performing a job, e.g. skill, experience, special aptitudes, and summarizes the working conditions. The specification could include limitations to authority, special relationships etc.

Joint consultation. Discussion between representatives of employees and management on matters of common interest, the aim being to resolve any matters of mutual concern. Committee decisions are advisory and some matters, such as pay and conditions, are excluded from consultation.

Just-in-Time (JIT). This refers to an inventory control system that is designed to minimize inventory in production operations. It seeks to eliminate waste by supplying required parts to the production line at the 'last minute'.

Key results analysis. Activity of *identifying* areas of a manager's job that are vital to the success of the job in the organization and *quantifying* the results that a manager must achieve in each area (the term is used in management by objectives).

Labour turnover. The rate at which employees leave an organization. Usually measured as a ratio:

$$\frac{\text{Number of employees left during year}}{\text{Average number employed during year}} \times 100$$

Laser printer. A high resolution printer for computer output. The printer uses a laser beam to charge a photostatic drum which transfers the image on to paper using a standard xerographic process.

Lead body. The Employment Department vests responsibility for the development, implementation and maintenance of occupational standards and nationally recognized vocational qualifications in representative and competent bodies known as 'lead bodies'.

Lead time. The time that elapses between placing an order for goods and the time they are received. Stock items should be held in sufficient quantities to satisfy requirements during the whole of the lead time.

Leaseback. A method of obtaining funds to finance business activities when a company owns buildings. These are then sold to a finance company and the company then leases the buildings back from the purchaser and so retains the use of them.

Limited liability. A possible liability that is limited in extent to a definite amount, particularly the liability that a member of a limited company could have for paying the debts of the company.

Line and staff. A structure in an organization that consists of line executive and staff advisory functions.

Liquid assets. An asset that either is cash or can be turned into a specific amount of cash quickly (e.g. debtors, Treasury bills).

Local Area Network (LAN). Computers linked by cable within a relatively close distance from one another. All computers can be linked in a building to a host computer system which stores all company files.

Longe-range planning. The process of preparing plans that cover long periods (over five years). Similar to corporate planning.

Loss leader. Goods sold by a retailer at a loss to encourage people to enter the shop and buy other items, which hopefully make a large profit.

Management Charter Initiative. This seeks to improve the development and competence of managers at work and is based upon their performance in the workplace. It has the backing of the British government, the Confederation of British Industry (CBI) and many employers.

Management competence. The ability to perform management functions to agreed standards of performance.

Management development. A process within an organization aimed at securing and improving the human resources so as to meet present and future needs. It includes performance appraisal and training, the acquisition of skills and improvements in attitude and personality.

Management style. The way in which a manager characteristically conducts his dealings with his subordinates.

Management by objectives (MBO). A procedure for planning the work of managers in an organization, whereby a manager and his superior analyses tasks to be accomplished by the manager, and set out with specific targets and time limits. The aim is to integrate the objectives of the organization with those of individuals.

Managerial grid. A grid designed by Blake and Mouton which classifies managerial style as a position on scales of 9 points, showing concern for people on the y axis and concern for production on the x axis. The preferred style is said to be 9:9 – this refers to a style with high concern for both people and production.

Manpower planning. A technique to estimate the number and type of employees required in an organization to meet present and future needs and making plans to meet requirements.

Market research. A systematic searching and analysing of information concerned with actual or potential markets for products.

Marketing mix. A combination of marketing methods used by a firm to market its products. The main variables are price, place, product and promotion.

Mentor. Formal pairing of one employee with another, who provides personalized guidance and support. (Generally managers from a different function or department.)

Merit rating. A technique for assessing an employee's performance and personal qualities. It is usually applied to administrative staff assessment.

Method study. An aspect of work study. A study of jobs to ensure they are performed in the best possible way. Normally it precedes work measurement.

Monopoly. The domination of a market by a single seller, who has control over supply and price.

Motivation. The keenness of a person to exert effort in order to achieve a desired outcome or goal which satisfies an individual need. It is the study of motivating people to behave in a particular way (motivation theory).

Multinational company. A company with manufacturing or trading facilities in countries overseas.

Nationalization. The public ownership of large businesses of national importance, enabling the government to plan and control their activities.

Negotiations. A term used to describe the bargaining between employers and trade union representatives, with the object of obtaining mutual agreement to improved terms and conditions of employment.

Network analysis. A technique for planning and controlling a complex project using a network diagram. Activities and events are recorded on a network analysis chart. Two common examples are the critical path method, and programme evaluation and review technique.

Nominal value. A value assigned to shares for the purposes of description or identification or as a basis for calculation.

Operational Research (OR). The process or activity of applying scientific (particularly mathematical) methods to the solution of problems involving the operations of a system. The aim is to give those in control of the system an optimum plan for its operation.

Organization and Methods (O and M). A term used for techniques used in method study and work measurement when applied to improving clerical performance in the office. It includes ways of arranging flows of work, methods of performing tasks and the design and use of data processing equipment.

Organizational development. The activity of improving the ability of an organization to achieve its goals by the more effective use of people.

Overtrading. A term used to define the financial position of a company when the incoming cash flow is not adequate to service the outward cash flow requirements. A company's scale of operations are expanding at a faster rate than can be supported by financial resources.

Payment by Results (PBR). A system of payment, whereby employee's earnings are related to the work done and other factors which are within the control of the employee. Employees are rewarded for extra effort, so that they also share in the benefits of higher productivity.

Performance appraisal. Assessment of how well an employee does his job; often carried out as part of the formal procedure of an organization in which regular assessments are made and results recorded, and action taken to improve performance.

Performance criteria. Statements describing appropriate actions by candidates in relation to each element of competence, used by assessors when assessing the extent of a candidate's competence.

Perpetual inventory. The continuous recording of stock movements enabling the stock position to be available at any time.

Picketing. The activity of trade union members in dispute with their employers, who try to peacefully persuade other workers not to enter or leave the premises for work.

Portfolio. A collection of work presented as evidence of achievement. It may include any materials which are relevant and portable, for example, written work, photographs, drawings, audio-cassettes and video-cassettes.

Preference shareholders. A class of shareholders which has prior right to the payment of a fixed dividend in preference to ordinary shareholders.

Prestel. A viewdata system. A computerized information system providing business and general information obtainable by a television set connected to a telephone line.

Probability. The likelihood or relevant frequency of occurrence of something – usually expressed as a number between 0 and 1.

Profit and loss account (or income statement). A statement of the revenues and expenses of a firm over a period of time.

Quality control. The activity, process or study of ensuring that the output of production processes conforms with an agreed standard.

Queuing theory. Part of mathematics that analyses business operations in which queues are involved, and the prediction of their size. The aim is to optimize service time, waiting or queuing time and the cost of resources.

Quorum. The minimum number of persons required to be in attendance at a meeting in order to transact business.

Redundancy. The loss of a job on the grounds that it is no longer required or available at a place of employment.

Reliability. The consistency or stability of measurement over time.

Reorder level. The quantity of a stock item which indicates that an order for replenishment is required to be placed.

Return on capital. This is used to indicate the results achieved by a business and the ratio is calculated by dividing the profit (before taxation) by the capital employed, and expressed as a percentage. Capital employed is usually determined by adding share capital and reserves.

Role playing. A training technique in which a trainee is asked to assume a specified role and act out a situation which involves that role.

Sales promotion. Arrangements by which firms attempt to draw the attention of buyers to one or more of their products. They are supplementary to normal advertising and include reduction in selling prices for a limited period, consumer contests, premium offers, etc.

Seven-point plan. A guide to the selection of candidates at interview. They are assessed under seven headings: physical make-up, attainments, general intelligence, interests, special aptitudes, disposition and domestic/family circumstances.

Shop steward. A member of a union elected by his colleagues to represent them to management in their place of work. Usually an unpaid, part-time official of a union.

Span of control. The number of individuals reporting to any one supervisor or manager. It is the number of subordinates to whom a manager delegates his authority.

Standard. The agreed and recognized levels of competence, to be achieved through training or required to perform a job or range of jobs.

Supervisor. A person who directly supervises the work of others (e.g. a foreman). The role is that of a manager who ensures that tasks specified are performed correctly and efficiently.

Synergy. A concept which suggests that the investment of additional resources produces a return which is proportionately greater than the sum of the resources invested (often known as the $2 + 2 = 5$ effect).

T group. A training group. This refers to training in interpersonal behaviour skills or sensitivity training. A group of persons meet in an unstructured situation and discuss the interplay of relationships between members of the group.

Takeover bid. An offer made by one person or company (the offeror) to buy from the existing shareholders so as to gain control of the offeree.

Telecommuting. This refers to situations where people do not commute from home to work, but whose work commutes to them through the medium of a computer terminal in their homes.

Teletext. Textual information displayed on a screen, broadcasted by a television company. It includes Ceefax (BBC) and Oracle (IBA).

Total Quality Management (TQM). This is a cost effective system for integrating the continuous quality improvement efforts of people at all levels in an organization to deliver products and services which ensure customer satisfaction.

Trade union. An association of employees with the objectives of regulating wages and conditions of work for its members by negotiation with employers.

Trades Union Congress (TUC). An association of UK trade unions to improve the social and economic conditions of working people. It is the national body for the co-ordination of trade union activities in the UK. It is advisory only and has no power over individual unions.

Training needs analysis. A logical approach to the assessment of the training and development needs of groups of employees. The needs of the job and the needs of the individuals are clarified in terms of the training that is required.

Transferable skills or abilities. Skills or abilities which can be applied in a variety of contexts. Core skills, general ablities, generic skills and process skills are proposed as being transferable, in contrast to specific skills and product skills which are defined as being non-transferable.

Unfair dismissal. Dismissal from employment that is deemed to be unfair by an industrial tribunal in accordance with the Employment Protection Consolidation Act 1978 (Section 54).

Value analysis. An activity which considers the function and costs of all the parts of the design of one of a firm's products, to see whether any changes in materials, design or manufacturing methods will increase the value of the product to the firm. This could be a reduction in cost in addition to improvement of the product leading to increased sales (sometimes known as value engineering).

Variable costs. Costs directly associated with a product. They vary in total in direct proportion to the level of activity, but remain constant per unit produced.

Venture capital. These are funds provided to a firm by outsiders on the basis that the providers will obtain a share in its profits. The term is often used for capital provided by specialist investment companies for the creation of new businesses.

Video conferencing. A method of providing audio and visual communication between remote sites in order to conduct a conference.

Videotex. The international name for systems that can display text on a screen or television set. Information may be broadcast like the teletext services Ceefax and Oracle, or it may be transmitted via the telephone network like Prestel, which is a Viewdata Service.

Viewdata. An information system accessed via the telephone network providing two-way communication. Prestel is the UK national viewdata service, which is supplied to a subscriber through a telephone socket. Teleshopping and home banking are two services obtainable.

Work measurement. A technique used in work study to establish the time for a qualified worker to carry out an agreed job at an agreed level of performance. (Called 'time study' in the USA.)

Work study. An activity which includes method study and work measurement and involves examining work with a view to making improvements in economy and efficiency. (Usually called motion and time study in the USA.)

Worker director. An employee of a company who is elected to serve as a member of a board of directors, to represent the interests of the employees of the company.

Working capital. The difference between the value of current assets and current liabilities. (Also called net current assets.)

WORM (Write Once Read Many times memory). A term given to types of media that do not allow overwriting; for example, optical disks and PROM chips.

INDEX

accountability, 26, 177
accounting, 160, 227–44
activities, 27, 38–41
administration
  definition and development, 5, 10–25
  production, 331–8
administrative management, 433–81
advertising, 285–93, 369, 372
APL (Accreditation of Prior Learning), 387–9, 425
appraisal, 373, 380, 381, 382, 383–4
assessment centres, 396–7
assets, 49, 52–4
attitudes, 65–6, 378
  changes and development, 10–11
  of management to labour, 68
  studies and surveys, 15–17, 70, 408
audits, 63, 69, 209, 226–7, 264, 345, 471
authority, 15, 26–8, 105, 137–8, 148, 154–7, 177, 417
  and decentralization, 159–60
  and delegation, 26, 157–9
  and leadership, 190–1
  and responsibility, 154–5
  line, 156
automation, 346–50
autonomy, 31, 151

bargaining, 421
  collective, 414–15, 419–20
behavioural science, 15–17, 22, 64, 170, 241
benefits, 401–2
bonus schemes, 401–2
Boston Portfolio Matrix, 292–3
British Standard (BS 5750), 329–30, 352, 425
budgets, 101, 124, 217–22, 319–20, 365–6
bureaucracy, 15, 135–6, 167

CAC (Central Arbitration Committee), 415
CAD (computer aided design), 352
CAM (computer aided manufacture), 353
capital, 47, 48–50, 54–6
  overseas, 73
  expenditure, planning, 236–8
  subscribers of, 68

centralization/decentralization, 14, 24, 30–1, 73, 159–60
  office work, 436–7
chairman, 185–6
change, 20, 166–7, 168–9, 434
  agent of, 170–3
CIC (Centre for Inter–firm Comparison), 224–5
CIM (computer integrated manufacture), 353
co-operative societies, 41
co-ordination, 24, 25
  and leadership, 197–9
collective bargaining, 414–15, 419–20
command, 24, 184–5
committees, 147–8, 227, 411, 421
communication, 204–9
  channels and equipment, 206, 444–66
  problems, 206
companies, types of, 39–41
comparative management, 77–8
competition, 248
computer
  aided design (CAD), 352
  aided manufacture (CAM), 353
  integrated manufacture (CIM), 353
  service bureaux, 475–6
computers, 294, 343–4, 350, 452–68
  databases and data processing, 452–7, 465–6
  human aspects of computer usage, 467–8
  security and data protection, 468–71
conciliation and arbitration services, 414–15
conferencing systems, 460–2
conflict, 28, 167–8, 416–21, 422, 423–4
consultants, selection or appointment, 368
consumers, 42, 68, 275–8
contingency approach, 17, 22–3, 174, 193–4
control, 24–5, 27, 37, 214–57
  capital, 56
  materials and stores, 335–8
  production, 333–4
  span of, 138, 142–4, 177
  see also quality
corporate planning, 101–5, 366
costs, 42, 299–301, 354

costs
  distribution, 282
  of PERT, 254
  ratios, 223
  standard, 220
CPM (critical path method), 250, 251, 254
creativity, 174
crediting competence, 425

data protection, 468–70
debentures, 49
decision making, 27–8, 111–23
delegation, 26, 28, 138, 157–9, 176
departmentation, 139–41
design
  and development, 320–3
  organization, 161–6
dictaphone systems, 446
DIP (digital image processing), 465–6
directors, 185–91
  and junior board, 385
discipline, 14, 204
dismissal of employees, 405–6
distribution, 278–83

economic systems and theory, 44–5
EDI (electronic data interchange), 476–7
electronic
  mail (email), 459–60
  office, 463–4
  trading, 464–5
Emerson, H, 13
employees, 43, 229
  dismissal, 405–6
  redundancy, 407
  services, 409
employment
  contracts and terms, 374, 375, 405–9, 416
  inventories, 367
  termination of, 405–9
energy, management of, 345
entrepreneurship/intrapreneurship, 29–30, 31
environment
  external, 58–67, 174
  office, 438
equal opportunities, 374–6
equipment, 141, 444–66

ergonomics, 333, 468
ethics, 70–1
European Community (EC), 40, 62, 74–5, 166, 188, 240, 275
European Union (EU) (*see* European Community)
expediting, 335
exporting, 55, 75–7, 304–6

factories, 11, 315–17
feedback, 18
filing systems, 449–50
finance, sources and institutions, 47, 48, 50–4
flexible manufacturing systems (FMS), 353–4
flexibility, 26–8
forecasting, 25, 87–91, 366–7
formal/informal approaches, 6, 15, 134–5
functional organization and management, 139–40, 146

game theory, 248
Gantt, H L, 13
GCA (Group Capacity Assessment), 444
Gilbreth, F, 13
goals, 20, 26
    and corporate strategy and planning, 99
    and goal conflict, 416–21
government
    departments and agencies, 41
    influence, 43, 64, 66–7
groups, 150–2, 417
growth rates, 105

health, 372, 374
    and safety at work, 409–12
human
    asset accounting, 242–4
    relations movement, 15–17
    resource management (HRM), 359–432

IIP (Investors in People), 424, 425
incentives, 401–2
induction, 376
industrial relations, 413–16
    see also conflict; trade unions
inflation, 51
information systems, 457–8
insurance, 54, 471
interdisciplinary approach, 10, 15
international
    management, 56–63

marketing, 302–6
interviews, 118, 373, 408
investment, 43
Investors in People (IIP), 424, 425

Japan, 56–7, 77, 78, 127, 327, 352
JIT (Just-in-Time), 351–2
jobs
    design/description, 370–1, 419
    evaluation, 398–400
    restructuring, 403–5
    rotation, 370, 384
    satisfaction, 395–6, 403
joint consultation, 420–1

labour, turnover, 407–8
leadership, 25, 27, 190–7, 382
    and conflict, 419
legislation
    collective bargaining, 414–15
    company classification, 39–41
    data protection, 469–70
    health and safety at work, 409–10
    human resource management, 361, 372, 374–6, 398, 405, 407
    marketing policies, 276–8
linear programming, 249–50
local authorities, 41, 47, 53
location, 46–7
logistics, 282–3

mailing equipment, 450–1
maintenance, 342–3
management
    definition and development, 5–25
    services, 471–6
    training, 377, 381–94
Management by objectives (MBO), 107–11, 383
Management Charter Initiative (MCI), 389, 425
management science school, 17, 64
managerial grid, 390, 394
managers, 15, 26–9
    data processing, 473
    human resources, 25, 360, 362–3
    marketing, 263, 269
    office, 435–6
    operations, 474
managing director, 186
manpower planning, 361, 364–72
manuals, organization, 164
market research, 283–5
marketing, 261–311
markets, 44–5
materials, 10
    handling, 345–6

materials requirements planning (MRP), 350–1
maternity leave, 416
mathematics, 16, 103
MBO (management by objectives), 107–11, 383
MCI (Management Charter Initiative), 389, 425
mechanization, 346–50, 474–5
merchandising, 294
merit rating, 400, 401
morale, 203
motivation, 16, 27, 79, 133, 199–203, 241–2
MPR II (manufacturing resource planning), 350–1
MPR (materials requirements planning), 350–1
multinational companies, 66, 71–3

nationalization, 73
networks, 250–4
NQV (National Vocational Qualifications), 425

O and M (organization and methods), 439–44
objectives, 100
    forecasting, theoretical requirements, 367
    management by (MBO), 107–11, 383
    marketing, 263–6
    and planning, 91–5
office
    defining, 434
    equipment, 444–66
    integrated, 458, 462–3
    planning and organizing, 436–9
operational research (OR), 244–6
organizing, 24, 25, 27, 37, 132–82
    marketing, 269–70
    offices, 436–9

packaging, 293–4
pensions, 52, 54
personal assistants, 385
PERT (programming evaluation and review technique), 250, 251, 253–4
planning, 24, 25, 27, 37
    and controlling, 215, 226
    and corporate strategy, 86–131
    manpower, 361, 364–72
    marketing, 264–5
    and office organization, 436–9
    pre-production, 338
    production, 334–5
    profit, 108, 109, 125

PMTS (predetermined motion time systems), 333
policies, 95–7
  human resources, 363–4
  marketing, 263–4
POP (panoramic office planning), 439
power, 155
PPBS (planning, programming and budgeting systems), 221–2
prices, 44–5, 73, 287
  pricing theory, 299–302
  resale price maintenance, 274–5
private sector, 38
process engineering, 331–3
production
  new developments in, 350–4
  and operations management, 312–58
  policy and methods, 44
productivity 395–6, 421
products, 315
  analysis of product range, 291–3
  branding, 288
  life-cycles, 266, 290–1
profit and loss, 67
  and sources of finance, 50–4
profit sharing, 40
projects and assignments, 148–9, 385
promotion, staff, 397
public relations (PR), 265, 290
public sector, 39, 41, 54
publicity, 285–93
purchasing, 338–42

quality, 315, 325–30
queues, 249
quotas, 296

RAMPS (resource allocation and multi-project scheduling), 254
ratio analysis, 222–4
records, 364, 367, 471
recruitment, 365, 367–72

redundancy, 407
remuneration, 14, 397
  of sales representatives, 296
research, 57, 317–20
  Ashridge Management Research Group, 32–3
  market, 283–5
resources, RAMPS (resource allocation and multi-project scheduling), 254
responsibilities, 26
  and authority, 154–5
  schedules of, 164–6
risks, 48, 56, 105–6, 410–11
robots, 354
roles, 421–4

safety, 9, 409–12
sales, 44
  forecasting, 88–9
  management, 294–8
  organization of sales office, 297–8
  promotion, 287–8
sampling, 118–19
scalar principle, 14, 177
security, 468–71
segmentation, 266–9
selection of staff, 372–3
sensitivity, 105–6
sequencing, 248
shareholders, 66
simulation, 246–8
skills, 378, 389
specialization, 325, 403
staff, 25, 295
  manpower planning, 361, 364–72
stakeholders, 59, 66, 91–2
standardization, 323–5
standards, 216
statistics, 114–23
stock, 248–9, 336–8, 343
stocks and shares, 40, 47–50
strategy, 86–131

stress, 412, 422
sub-contracting, 341–2
supervision, 26
surveys, 11, 117, 408
synectics, 174
systems analysts, 473
systems approach, 18–22, 23, 196–7
  'black box' concept, 67

Taylor, F W, 12–13
team spirit, 16–17, 203
telecommunications, 447, 448–9
telecommuting, 466–7
time management, 30–1, 332–3
TQM (Total Quality Management) system, 330–1, 425
trade unions, 413–14, 415, 419–20
trading outlets, 270–3
training, 376–95
Training and Enterprise Councils (TECs), 424
transport, 280–3

unity, 14
USA, 60, 77, 127

value engineering (VE)/value analysis, 330–1
values, 28, 60–1, 99–100
VFP (variable factor programming), 443–4

wages, 397–402
warehouses, 279–80, 283, 347–50
Weber, Max, 15, 135–6
women in management, 28–9
work
  measurement, 442–4
  nature and study of, 331–3
  roles, 421–4
works councils, 420–1